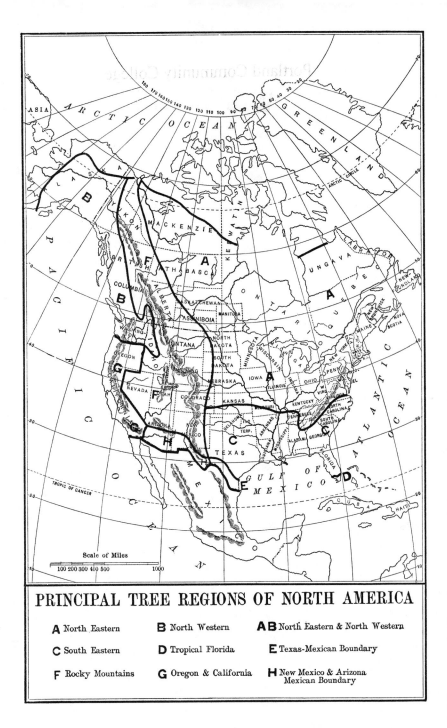

PRINCIPAL TREE REGIONS OF NORTH AMERICA

A North Eastern   **B** North Western   **AB** North Eastern & North Western

C South Eastern   **D** Tropical Florida   **E** Texas-Mexican Boundary

F Rocky Mountains   **G** Oregon & California   **H** New Mexico & Arizona Mexican Boundary

MANUAL OF THE TREES
OF NORTH AMERICA

(EXCLUSIVE OF MEXICO)

By

CHARLES
SPRAGUE SARGENT

Onetime Director of the Arnold Arboretum of Harvard University

With seven hundred and eighty-three illustrations by

CHARLES EDWARD FAXON
and
MARY W. GILL

Second Corrected Edition

In Two Volumes

VOL.
1

DOVER PUBLICATIONS, INC.
NEW YORK

Published in Canada by General Publishing Company, Ltd., 30 Lesmill Road, Don Mills, Toronto, Ontario.
Published in the United Kingdom by Constable and Company, Ltd., 10 Orange Street, London WC 2.

This Dover edition, first published in 1961, is an unabridged and unaltered republication of the second (1922) edition of the work originally published by Houghton Mifflin Company in 1905. The work previously appeared in one volume, but this Dover edition is published in two volumes.

The Table of Changes in Nomenclature beginning on page 899 was specially prepared for this Dover edition by E. S. Harrar, Dean of the School of Forestry, Duke University.

Standard Book Number: 486-20277-1

Manufactured in the United States of America
Dover Publications, Inc.
180 Varick Street
New York, N. Y. 10014

TO

M. R. S.

THE WISE AND KIND FRIEND OF THIRTY YEARS

THIS BOOK IS DEDICATED

WITH GRATITUDE AND AFFECTION

This Dover Edition is dedicated

to the memory of

CHARLES SPRAGUE SARGENT

1841-1927

for his contribution to

American arboriculture and forestry

PREFACE TO THE SECOND EDITION

THE studies of the trees of North America (exclusive of Mexico) which have been carried on by the agents and correspondents of the Arboretum in the sixteen years since the publication of the *Manual of the Trees of North America* have increased the knowledge of the subject and made necessary a new edition of this *Manual*. The explorations of these sixteen years have added eighty-nine species of trees and many recently distinguished varieties of formerly imperfectly understood species to the silva of the United States, and made available much additional information in regard to the geographical distribution of American trees. Further studies have made the reduction of seven species of the first edition to varieties of other species seem desirable; and two species, *Amelanchier obovalis* and *Cercocarpus parvifolius*, which were formerly considered trees, but are more properly shrubs, are omitted. The genus Anamomis is now united with Eugenia; and the Arizona *Pinus strobiformis* Sarg. (not Engelm.) is now referred to *Pinus flexilis* James.

Representatives of four Families and sixteen Genera which did not appear in the first edition are described in the new edition in which will be found an account of seven hundred and seventeen species of trees in one hundred and eighty-five genera, illustrated by seven hundred and eighty-three figures, or one hundred and forty-one figures in addition to those which appeared in the first edition.

An International Congress of Botanists which assembled in Vienna in 1905, and again in Brussels in 1910, adopted rules of nomenclature which the world, with a few American exceptions, has now generally adopted. The names used in this new *Manual* are based on the rules of this International Congress. These are the names used by the largest number of the students of plants, and it is unfortunate that the confusion in the names of American trees must continue as long as the Department of Agriculture, including the Forest Service of the United States, uses another and now generally unrecognized system.

The new illustrations in this edition are partly from drawings made by Charles Edward Faxon, who died before his work was finished; it was continued by the skillful pencil of Mary W. Gill, of Washington, to whom I am grateful for her intelligent coöperation.

It is impossible to name here all the men and women who have in the last sixteen years contributed to this account of American trees, and I will now only mention Mr. T. G. Harbison and Mr. E. J. Palmer, who as agents of the Arboretum have studied for years the trees of the Southeastern States and of the Missouri-Texas region, Professor R. S. Cocks, of Tulane University, who has explored carefully and critically the forests of Louisiana, and Miss Alice Eastwood, head of the Botanical Department of the California Academy of Sciences, who has made special journeys in Alaska and New Mexico in the interest of this *Manual*. Mr. Alfred Rehder, Curator of the Herbarium of the Arboretum, has added to the knowledge of our trees in several Southern journeys; and to him I am specially indebted for assistance and advice in the preparation of the keys to the different groups of plants found in this volume.

This new edition of the *Manual* contains the results of forty-four years of my continuous study of the trees of North America carried on in every part of the United States and in many foreign countries. If these studies in any way serve to increase the knowledge and the love of trees I shall feel that these years have not been misspent.

C. S. SARGENT.

ARNOLD ARBORETUM
September, 1921

PREFACE

In this volume I have tried to bring into convenient form for the use of students the information concerning the trees of North America which has been gathered at the Arnold Arboretum during the last thirty years and has been largely elaborated in my *Silva of North America*.

The indigenous trees of no other region of equal extent are, perhaps, so well known as those that grow naturally in North America. There is, however, still much to be learned about them. In the southern states, one of the most remarkable extratropical regions in the world in the richness of its arborescent flora, several species are still imperfectly known, while it is not improbable that a few may have escaped entirely the notice of botanists; and in the northern states are several forms of Cratægus which, in the absence of sufficient information, it has been found impracticable to include in this volume. Little is known as yet of the silvicultural value and requirements of North American trees, or of the diseases that affect them; and one of the objects of this volume is to stimulate further investigation of their characters and needs.

The arrangement of families and genera adopted in this volume is that of Engler & Prantl's *Die Natürlichen Pflanzenfamilien*, in which the procession is from a simpler to a more complex structure. The nomenclature is that of *The Silva of North America*. Descriptions of a few species of Cratægus are now first published, and investigations made since the publication of the last volume of *The Silva of North America*, in December, 1902, have necessitated the introduction of a few additional trees described by other authors, and occasional changes of names.

An analytical key to the families, based on the arrangement and character of the leaves, will lead the reader first to the family to which any tree belongs; a conspectus of the genera, embodying the important and easily discovered contrasting characters of each genus and following the description of each family represented by more than one genus, will lead him to the genus he is trying to determine; and a similar conspectus of the species, following the description of the genus, will finally bring him to the species for which he is looking. Further to facilitate the determination, one or more letters, attached to the name of the species in the conspectus following the description of the genus, indicate in which of the eight regions into which the country is divided according to the prevailing character of the arborescent vegetation that species grows (see map forming frontispiece of the volume). For example, the northeastern part of the country, including the high Appalachian Mountains in the southern states which have chiefly a northern flora, is represented by (A), and a person wishing to learn the name of a Pine-tree or of an Oak in that region need occupy himself only with those species which in the conspectus of the genus Quercus or Pinus are followed by the letter (A), while a person wishing to determine an Oak or a Pine-tree in Oregon or California may pass over all species which are not followed by (G), the letter which represents the Pacific coast region south of the state of Washington.

The sign of degrees (°) is used in this work to represent feet, and the sign of minutes (′) inches.

The illustrations which accompany each species and important variety are one half the size of nature, except in the case of a few of the large Pine cones, the flowers of some of the

Magnolias, and the leaves and flower-clusters of the Palms.   These are represented as less than half the size of nature in order to make the illustrations of uniform size.   These illustrations are from drawings by Mr. Faxon, in which he has shown his usual skill and experience as a botanical draftsman in bringing out the most important characters of each species, and in them will be found the chief value of this Manual.   For aid in its preparation I am indebted to him and to my other associates, Mr. Alfred Rehder and Mr. George R. Shaw, who have helped me in compiling the most difficult of the keys.

C. S. SARGENT.

ARNOLD ARBORETUM, JAMAICA PLAIN, MASS.
        January, 1905.

TABLE OF CONTENTS
Volume One

SYNOPSIS

OF THE FAMILIES OF PLANTS DESCRIBED IN THIS BOOK

Class I. GYMNOSPERMÆ.

Resinous trees; stems formed of bark, wood, or pith, and increasing in diameter by the annual addition of a layer of wood inside the bark; flowers unisexual; stamens numerous; ovules and seeds 2 or many, borne on the face of a scale, not inclosed in an ovary; embryo with 2 or more cotyledons; leaves straight-veined, without stipules.

I. **Pinaceæ** (p. 1). Flowers usually monœcious; ovules 2 or several; fruit a woody cone (*in Juniperus berry-like*); cotyledons 2 or many; leaves needle-shaped, linear or scale-like, persistent (*deciduous in Larix and Taxodium*).

II. **Taxaceæ** (p. 90). Flowers diœcious, axillary, solitary; ovules 1; fruit surrounded by or inclosed in the enlarged fleshy aril-like disk of the flower; cotyledons 2; leaves linear, alternate, persistent.

Class II. ANGIOSPERMÆ.

Carpels or pistils consisting of a closed cavity containing the ovules and becoming the fruit.

Division I. MONOCOTYLEDONES.

Stems with woody fibres distributed irregularly through them, but without pith or annual layers of growth; parts of the flower in 3's; ovary superior, 3-celled; embryo with a single cotyledon; leaves parallel-veined, persistent, without stipules.

III. **Palmæ** (p. 96). Ovule solitary; fruit baccate or drupaceous, 1 or rarely 2 or 3-seeded; leaves alternate, pinnate, flabellate or orbicular, persistent.

IV. **Liliaceæ** (p. 110). Ovules numerous in each cell; fruit 3-celled, capsular or baccate; leaves linear-lanceolate.

Division II. DICOTYLEDONES.

Stems formed of bark, wood, and pith, and increasing by the addition of an annual layer of wood inside the bark; parts of the flower mostly in 4's or 5's; embryo with a pair of opposite cotyledons; leaves netted-veined.

SUBDIVISION 1. APETALÆ. Flowers without a corolla and sometimes without a calyx.

Section 1. Flowers in unisexual aments (*female flowers of Juglans and Quercus solitary or in spikes*); ovary inferior (*superior in Leitneriaceæ*) when a calyx is present.

V. **Salicaceæ** (p. 119). Flowers diœcious, without a calyx. Fruit a 2–4-valved capsule. Leaves simple, alternate, with stipules, deciduous.

VI. **Myricaceæ** (p. 163). Flowers monœcious or diœcious; fruit a dry drupe, covered with waxy exudations; leaves simple, alternate, resinous-punctate, persistent.

VII. **Leitneriaceæ** (p. 167). Flowers diœcious, the staminate without a calyx; ovary superior; fruit a compressed oblong drupe; leaves alternate, simple, without stipules, deciduous.

VIII. **Juglandaceæ** (p. 168). Flowers monœcious; fruit a nut inclosed in an indehiscent (Juglans) or 4-valved (Carya) fleshy or woody shell; leaves alternate, unequally pinnate without stipules, deciduous.

IX. **Betulaceæ** (p. 200).   Flowers monœcious; fruit a nut at the base of an open leaf-like involucre (Carpinus), in a sack-like involucre (Ostrya), in the axil of a scale of an ament (Betula), or of a woody strobile (Alnus); leaves alternate, simple, with stipules, deciduous.

X. **Fagaceæ** (p. 227).   Flowers monœcious; fruit a nut more or less inclosed in a woody often spiny involucre; leaves alternate, simple, with stipules, deciduous (*in some species of Quercus and in Castanopsis and Lithocarpus persistent*).

Section 2.   Flowers unisexual (*perfect in Ulmus*); calyx regular, the stamens as many as its lobes and opposite them; ovary superior, 1-celled; seed 1.

XI. **Ulmaceæ** (p. 308).   Fruit a compressed winged samara (Ulmus), a drupe (Celtis and Trema), or nut-like (Planera), leaves simple, alternate, with stipules, deciduous (*persistent in Trema*).

XII. **Moraceæ** (p. 328).   Flowers in ament-like spikes or heads; fruit drupaceous, inclosed in the thickened calyx and united into a compound fruit, oblong and succulent (Morus), large, dry and globose (Toxylon), or immersed in the fleshy receptacle of the flower (Ficus); leaves simple, alternate, with stipules, deciduous (*persistent in Ficus*).

Section 3.   Flowers usually perfect; ovary superior or partly inferior, 1–4-celled, leaves simple, persistent in the North American species.

XIII. **Olacaceæ** (p. 336).   Calyx and corolla 4–6-lobed; ovary 1–4-celled; fruit a drupe more or less inclosed in the enlarged disk of the flower; leaves alternate or fascicled, without stipules.

XIV. **Polygonaceæ** (p. 338).   Calyx 5-lobed; ovary 1-celled; fruit a nutlet inclosed in the thickened calyx; leaves alternate, their stipules sheathing the stems.

XV. **Nyctaginaceæ** (p. 340).   Calyx 5-lobed; ovary 1-celled; fruit a nutlet inclosed in the thickened calyx; leaves alternate or opposite, without stipules.

SUBDIVISION 2.   PETALATÆ.   Flowers with both calyx and corolla (*without a corolla in Lauraceæ, in Liquidambar in Hamamelidaceæ, in Cercocarpus in Rosaceæ, in Euphorbiaceæ, in some species of Acer, in Reynosia, Condalia, and Krugiodendron in Rhamnaceæ, in Fremontia in Sterculiaceæ, in Chytraculia in Myrtaceæ, in Conocarpus in Combretaceæ and in some species of Fraxinus in Oleaceæ*).

Section 1.   POLYPETALÆ.   Corolla of separate petals.

A.   Ovary superior (*partly inferior in Hamamelidaceæ; inferior in Malus, Sorbus, Heteromeles, Cratægus, and Amelanchier in Rosaceæ*).

XVI. **Magnoliaceæ** (p. 342).   Flowers perfect; sepals and petals in 3 or 4 rows of 3 each; fruit cone-like, composed of numerous cohering carpels; leaves simple, alternate, their stipules inclosing the leaf-buds, deciduous or rarely persistent.

XVII. **Annonaceæ** (p. 353).   Flowers perfect; sepals 3; petals 6 in 2 series; fruit a pulpy berry developed from 1 or from the union of several carpels; leaves simple, alternate, without stipules, deciduous or persistent.

XVIII. **Lauraceæ** (p. 356).   Flowers perfect or unisexual; corolla 0; fruit a 1-seeded drupe or berry; leaves simple, alternate, punctate, without stipules, persistent (*deciduous in Sassafras*).

XIX. **Capparidaceæ** (p. 365).   Flowers perfect; sepals and petals 4; fruit baccate, elongated, dehiscent; leaves alternate, simple, without stipules, persistent.

XX. **Hamamelidaceæ** (p. 366).   Flowers perfect or unisexual; sepals and petals 5 (*corolla 0 in Liquidambar*); ovary partly inferior; fruit a 2-celled woody capsule opening at the summit; leaves simple, alternate, with stipules, deciduous.

XXI. **Platanaceæ** (p. 371).   Flowers monœcious, in dense unisexual capitate heads; fruit an akene; leaves simple, alternate, with stipules, deciduous.

XXII. **Rosaceæ** (p. 376).   Flowers perfect; sepals and petals 5 (petals 0 in Cercocarpus); ovary inferior in Malus, Sorbus, Heteromeles, Cratægus, and Amelanchier; fruit a drupe (Prunus and Chrysobalanus), a capsule (Vauquelinia and Lyonothamnus), an akene (Cowania and Cercocarpus), or a pome (Malus, Sorbus, Heteromeles, Cratægus, and Amelanchier); leaves simple or pinnately compound, alternate (*opposite in Lyonothamnus*), with stipules, deciduous or persistent.

XXIII. **Leguminosæ** (p. 585).   Flowers perfect, regular or irregular; fruit a legume; leaves compound, or simple (Dalea), alternate, with stipules, deciduous or persistent.

XXIV. **Zygophyllaceæ** (p. 630). Flowers perfect; calyx 5-lobed; petals 5; fruit capsular, becoming fleshy; leaves opposite, pinnate, with stipules, persistent.

XXV. **Malpighiaceæ** (p. 631). Flowers usually perfect rarely dimorphous; calyx 5-lobed: petals 5, unguiculate; fruit a drupe or samara; leaves opposite, simple, entire, persistent; often with stipules.

XXVI. **Rutaceæ** (p. 633). Flowers unisexual or perfect; fruit a capsule (Xanthoxylum), a samara (Ptelea), of indehiscent winged 1-seeded carpels (Helietta), or a drupe (Amyris); leaves alternate or opposite, compound, glandular-punctate, without stipules, persistent or rarely deciduous (*0 in Canotia*).

XXVII. **Simaroubaceæ** (p. 641). Flowers dioecious, calyx 5-lobed; petals 5; fruit drupaceous (Simarouba), baccate (Picramnia), a samara (Alvaradoa); leaves alternate, equally pinnate, without stipules, persistent.

XXVIII. **Burseraceæ** (p. 645). Flowers perfect; calyx 4 or 5-parted; petals 5; fruit a drupe; leaves alternate, compound, without stipules, deciduous.

XXIX. **Meliaceæ** (p. 648). Flowers perfect; calyx 5-lobed; petals 5; fruit a 5-celled dehiscent capsule; leaves alternate, equally pinnate, without stipules, persistent.

XXX. **Euphorbiaceæ** (p. 649). Flowers perfect; calyx 4–6-parted (Drypetes), 3-lobed (Hippomane), or 0 (Gymnanthes); petals 0; fruit a drupe (Drypetes and Hippomane), or a 3-lobed capsule (Gymnanthes).

XXXI. **Anacardiaceæ** (p. 655). Flowers usually unisexual, dioecious or polygamo-dioecious (*Pistacia without a calyx, and without a corolla in the North American species*); fruit a dry drupe; leaves simple or compound, alternate, without stipules, deciduous (*persistent in Pistacia and in one species of Rhus*).

XXXII. **Cyrillaceæ** (p. 665). Flowers perfect; calyx 5–8-lobed; petals 5–8; fruit an indehiscent capsule; leaves alternate, without stipules, persistent (*more or less deciduous in Cyrilla*).

XXXIII. **Aquifoliaceæ** (p. 668). Flowers polygamo-dioecious; calyx 4 or 5-lobed; petals 5; fruit a drupe, with 4–8 1-seeded nutlets; leaves alternate, simple, with stipules, persistent or deciduous.

XXXIV. **Celastraceæ** (p. 674). Flowers perfect, polygamous or dioecious; calyx 4 or 5-lobed; petals 4 or 5; fruit a drupe, or a capsule (Evonymus); leaves simple, opposite or alternate, with or without stipules, persistent (*deciduous in Evonymus*).

XXXV. **Aceraceæ** (p. 681). Flowers dioecious or monoeciously polygamous; calyx usually 5-parted; petals usually 5, or 0; fruit of 2 long-winged samara joined at the base; leaves opposite, simple or rarely pinnate, without or rarely with stipules, deciduous.

XXXVI. **Hippocastanaceæ** (p. 702). Flowers perfect, irregular; calyx 5-lobed; petals 4 or 5, unequal; fruit a 3-celled 3-valved capsule; leaves opposite, digitately compound, long-petiolate, without stipules, deciduous.

XXXVII. **Sapindaceæ** (p. 711). Flowers polygamous; calyx 4 or 5-lobed; corolla of 4 or 5 petals; fruit a berry (Sapindus and Exothea), a drupe (Hypelate), or a 3-valved capsule (Ungnadia); leaves alternate, compound, without stipules, persistent, or deciduous (Ungnadia).

XXXVIII. **Rhamnaceæ** (p. 718). Flowers usually perfect; calyx 4 or 5-lobed; petals 4 or 5 (*0 in Reynosia, Condalia, and Krugiodendron*); fruit drupaceous; leaves simple, alternate (*mostly opposite in Reynosia and Krugiodendron*), with stipules, persistent (*deciduous in some species of Rhamnus*).

XXXIX. **Tiliaceæ** (p. 732). Flowers perfect; sepals and petals 5; fruit a nut-like berry; leaves simple, alternate, mostly oblique at base, with stipules, deciduous.

XL. **Sterculiaceæ** (p. 749). Flowers perfect; calyx 5-lobed; petals 0; fruit a 4 or 5-valved dehiscent capsule; leaves simple, alternate, with stipules, persistent.

XLI. **Theaceæ** (p. 750). Flowers perfect; sepals and petals 5; fruit a 5-celled woody dehiscent capsule, loculicidally dehiscent; leaves simple, alternate, without stipules, persistent or deciduous.

XLII. **Canellaceæ** (p. 753). Flowers perfect; sepals 3; petals 5; filaments united into a tube; fruit a berry; leaves simple, alternate, without stipules, persistent.

XLIII. **Kœberliniaceæ** (p. 754). Flowers perfect; sepals and petals 4, minute; leaves bract-like, alternate, without stipules, caducous.

XLIV. **Caricaceæ** (p. 755). Flowers unisexual or perfect; calyx 5-lobed; petals 5; fruit baccate; leaves palmately lobed or digitate, alternate, without stipules, persistent.

B. Ovary inferior (*partly inferior in Rhizophora*).

XLV. **Cactaceæ** (p. 757). Flowers perfect; petals and sepals numerous; fruit a berry; leaves usually wanting.

XLVI. **Rhizophoraceæ** (p. 763). Flowers perfect; calyx 4-parted; petals 4; ovary partly inferior; fruit a 1-celled 1-seeded berry perforated at apex by the germinating embryo; leaves simple, opposite, entire, with stipules, persistent.

XLVII. **Combretaceæ** (p. 764). Flowers perfect or polygamous; calyx 5-lobed; petals 5 (*0 in Conocarpus*); fruit drupaceous; leaves simple, alternate or opposite, without stipules, persistent.

XLVIII. **Myrtaceæ** (p. 768). Flowers perfect; calyx usually 4-lobed, or reduced to a single body forming a deciduous lid to the flower (Chytraculia); petals usually 4 (*0 in Chytraculia*); fruit a berry; leaves simple, opposite, pellucid-punctate, without stipules, persistent.

XLIX. **Melastomaceæ** (p. 776). Flowers perfect; calyx and corolla 4 or 5-lobed; stamens as many or twice as many as the lobes of the corolla; fruit capsular or baccate, inclosed in the tube of the calyx; leaves opposite, rarely verticillate, 3–9-nerved, without stipules.

L. **Araliaceæ** (p. 777). Flowers perfect or polygamous; sepals and petals usually 5; fruit a drupe; leaves twice pinnate, alternate, with stipules, deciduous.

LI. **Nyssaceæ** (p. 779). Flowers diœcious, polygamous, diœcious or perfect; calyx 5-toothed or lobed; petals 5 or more, imbricate in the bud, or 0; stamens as many or twice as many as the petals; fruit drupaceous (Nyssa), usually 1-celled and 1-seeded; leaves alternate, deciduous, without stipules.

LII. **Cornaceæ** (p. 784). Flowers perfect or polygamo-diœcious; calyx 4 or 5-toothed; petals 4 or 5; fruit a fleshy drupe; leaves simple, opposite (*alternate in one species of Cornus*), without stipules, deciduous.

Section 2. GAMOPETALÆ. Corolla of united petals (*divided in Elliottia in Ericaceæ, 0 in some species of Fraxinus in Oleaceæ*).

A. OVARY SUPERIOR (*inferior in Vaccinium in Ericaceæ, partly inferior in Symplocaceæ and Styracaceæ*).

LIII. **Ericaceæ** (p. 790). Flowers perfect; calyx and corolla 5-lobed (*in Elliottia corolla of 4 petals*); (*ovary inferior in Vaccinium*); fruit capsular, drupaceous or baccate; leaves simple, alternate, without stipules, persistent (*deciduous in Elliottia and Oxydendrum*).

LIV. **Theophrastaceæ** (p. 804). Flowers perfect, with staminodia; sepals and petals 5; stamens 5; fruit a berry; leaves simple, opposite or alternate, entire, without stipules.

LV. **Myrsinaceæ** (p. 805). Flowers perfect; calyx and corolla 5-lobed; stamens 5; fruit a drupe; leaves simple, alternate, entire, without stipules, persistent.

LVI. **Sapotaceæ** (p. 808). Flowers perfect; calyx 5-lobed; corolla 5-lobed (*6-lobed in Mimusops*), often with as many or twice as many internal appendages borne on its throat; fruit a berry; leaves simple, alternate, without stipules, persistent (*deciduous in some species of Bumelia*).

LVII. **Ebenaceæ** (p. 820). Flowers perfect, diœcious, or polygamous; calyx and corolla 4-lobed; fruit a 1 or several-seeded berry; leaves simple, alternate, entire, without stipules, deciduous.

LVIII. **Styracaceæ** (p. 824). Flowers perfect; calyx 4 or 5-toothed; corolla 4 or 5-lobed or divided nearly to the base, or rarely 6 or 7-lobed; ovary superior or partly superior; fruit a drupe; leaves simple, alternate, without stipules, deciduous; pubescence mostly scurfy or stellate.

LIX. **Symplocaceæ** (p. 830). Flowers perfect; calyx and corolla 5-lobed; ovary inferior or partly inferior; fruit a drupe; leaves simple, alternate, without stipules, deciduous; pubescence simple.

LX. **Oleaceæ** (p. 832). Flowers perfect or polygamo-diœcious; calyx 4-lobed (*0 in some species of Fraxinus*); corolla 2–6-parted (*0 in some species of Fraxinus*); fruit a winged samara (Fraxinus) or a fleshy drupe (Forestiera, Chionanthus and Osmanthus); leaves pinnate (Fraxinus) or simple, opposite, without stipules, deciduous (*persistent in Osmanthus*).

LXI. **Borraginaceæ** (p. 858). Flowers perfect or polygamous; calyx and corolla 5-lobed; fruit a drupe; leaves simple, alternate, scabrous-pubescent, without stipules, persistent or tardily deciduous.

LXII. **Verbenaceæ** (p. 864). Flowers perfect; calyx 5-lobed; corolla 4 or 5-lobed; fruit a drupe or a 1-seeded capsule; leaves simple, opposite, without stipules, persistent.

LXIII. **Solanaceæ** (p. 867).   Flowers perfect; calyx campanulate, usually 5-lobed; corolla usually 5-lobed; fruit baccate, surrounded at base by the enlarged calyx; leaves alternate, rarely opposite, without stipules.

LXIV. **Bignoniaceæ** (p. 868).   Flowers perfect; calyx bilabiate; corolla bilabiate, 5-lobed; fruit a woody capsule (Catalpa and Chilopsis) or a berry (Enallagma); leaves simple, opposite (*sometimes alternate in Chilopsis*), without stipules, deciduous (*persistent in Enallagma*).

B. Ovary inferior (*partly superior in Sambucus in Caprifoliaceæ*).

LXV. **Rubiaceæ** (p. 875).   Flowers perfect; calyx and corolla 4 or 5-lobed; fruit a capsule (Exostema and Pinckneya), a drupe (Guettarda), or nut-like (Cephalanthus); leaves simple opposite, or in verticils of 3 (Cephalanthus), with stipules, persistent (*deciduous in Pinckneya and Cephalanthus*).

LXVI. **Caprifoliaceæ** (p. 882).   Flowers perfect; calyx and corolla 5-lobed; fruit a drupe; leaves unequally pinnate (Sambucus) or simple (Viburnum), opposite, without stipules, deciduous in North American species.

ANALYTICAL KEY

TO THE GENERA OF PLANTS INCLUDED IN THIS BOOK, BASED CHIEFLY ON THE CHARACTER OF THE LEAVES

I. Leaves parallel-veined, alternate, persistent, clustered at the end of the stem or branches. Monocotyledones.

Stem simple; leaves stalked.

Leaves fan-shaped.

Leaf stalks unarmed.

Rachis short; leaves usually silvery white below.

Leaves 2°–4° in diameter (*green below in No. 2*), their segments undivided at apex. **Thrinax** (p. 96).

Leaves 18′–24′ in diameter, their segments divided at apex.

Coccothrinax (p. 100).

Rachis elongated; leaves green below, their segments divided at apex.

Sabal (p. 101).

Leaf stalks armed with marginal teeth or spines.

Leaf stalks furnished irregularly with broad thin large and small, straight or hooked spines confluent into a thin bright orange-colored cartilaginous margin; leaves longer than wide, divided nearly to the middle into segments parted at apex and separating on the margins into thin fibres. **Washingtonia** (p. 104).

Leaf stalks furnished with stout or slender flattened teeth; leaves suborbicular, divided to the middle or nearly to the base into segments parted at apex; segments of the blade not separating on the margin into thin fibres.

Accelorraphe (p. 105).

Leaves pinnate.

Leaves 10°–12° in length, their pinnæ 2½°–3° long and often 1½° wide, deep green.

Roystonea (p. 107).

Leaves 5°–6° long, their pinnæ 18′ long and 1′ wide, dark yellow-green above, pale and glaucous below. **Pseudophœnix** (p. 109).

Stem simple or branched; leaves sessile, lanceolate, long- and usually sharp-pointed at apex. **Yucca** (p. 110).

II. Leaves 1-nerved, needle-shaped, linear or scale-like, persistent (deciduous in Larix and Taxodium). Gymnospermæ.

1. LEAVES PERSISTENT.

a Leaves fascicled, needle-shaped, in 1–5-leafed clusters enclosed at base in a membranaceous sheath. **Pinus** (p. 2).

aa Leaves scattered, usually linear.

b Leaves linear, often obtuse or emarginate.

Base of the leaves persistent on the branches.

Leaves sessile, 4-sided, or flattened and stomatiferous above. **Picea** (p. 34).

Leaves stalked, flattened and stomatiferous below, or angular, often appearing 2-ranked. **Tsuga** (p. 42).

Base of the leaves not persistent on the branches; leaves often appearing 2-ranked.

Leaves stalked, flattened, stomatiferous below; winter-buds pointed, not resinous. **Pseudotsuga** (p. 47).

Leaves sessile, flattened and often grooved on the upper side, or quadrangular, rarely stomatiferous above, on upper fertile branches often crowded; winter-buds obtuse, resinous (*except in No. 9*). **Abies** (p. 50).

bb Leaves linear-lanceolate, rigid, acuminate, spirally disposed, appearing 2-ranked by a twist in the petiole.

Leaves abruptly contracted at base, long-pointed, with pale bands of stomata on the lower surface on each side of the midveins; fruit drupelike.
Torreya (p. 91).
Leaves gradually narrowed at base, short-pointed, paler, and without distinct bands of stomata on the lower surface; fruit berry-like. **Taxus** (p. 93).
bbb Leaves ovate-lanceolate and scale-like, spreading in 2 ranks or linear on the same tree, acute, compressed, keeled on the back and closely appressed or spreading at apex. **Sequoia** (p. 61).
aaa Leaves opposite or whorled, usually scale-like.
Internodes distinctly longer than broad; branchlets flattened, of nearly equal color on both sides; leaves eglandular. **Libocedrus** (p. 65).
Internodes about as long as broad, often pale below, usually glandular.
Branchlets flattened.
Branchlets in one plane, much flattened, $\frac{1}{12}'-\frac{1}{9}'$ broad. **Thuja** (p. 67).
Branchlets slightly flattened, $\frac{1}{24}'-\frac{1}{18}'$ broad. **Chamæcyparis** (p. 75).
Branchlets terete or 4-angled.
Branchlets more or less in one plane; fruit a cone. **Cupressus** (p. 69).
Branchlets not in one plane; fruit a berry (*leaves needle-shaped, in whorls of 3 in No. 1*). **Juniperus** (p. 78).

2. LEAVES DECIDUOUS.

Leaves in many-leafed clusters on short lateral spurs. **Larix** (p. 31).
Leaves spreading in 2 ranks. **Taxodium** (p. 63).

III. Leaves netted-veined, rarely scale-like or wanting. Dicotyledones.

A. LEAVES OPPOSITE. (B, see p. xix).

1. LEAVES SIMPLE. (2, see p. xviii).

* Leaves persistent.

a Leaves with stipules.
b Leaves entire or occasionally slightly crenate or serrate.
c Leaves emarginate at apex, very short-stalked, $1\frac{1}{2}'-2'$ long.
Leaves obovate, gradually narrowed into the petiole. **Gyminda** (p. 678).
Leaves oval to oblong, rounded or broad-cuneate (*rarely alternate*).
Branchlets densely velutinous. **Krugiodendron** (p. 721).
Branchlets slightly puberulous at first, soon glabrous.
Reynosia (p. 720).
cc Leaves not emarginate at apex.
Leaves obtuse, rarely acutish or abruptly short-pointed.
Leaves elliptic, $3\frac{1}{2}'-5'$ long. **Rhizophora** (p. 763).
Leaves obovate, usually rounded at apex, $\frac{3}{4}'-2'$ long.
Byrsonima (p. 632).
Leaves acute to acuminate.
Leaves oblong-ovate to lanceolate; branchlets glabrous.
Exostema (p. 877).
Leaves broad-elliptic to oblong-elliptic; branchlets villose.
Guettarda (p. 879).
bb Leaves serrate (*often pinnate*). **Lyonothamnus** (p. 378).
a1 Leaves without stipules.
Petioles biglandular; leaves obtuse or emarginate, $1\frac{1}{2}'-2\frac{1}{2}'$ long.
Laguncularia (p. 767).
Petioles without glands.
Leaves furnished below with small dark glands, slightly aromatic; petioles short.
Leaves oblong to oblong-ovate and acuminate or elliptic and bluntly short-pointed. **Calyptranthes** (p. 769).
Leaves ovate, obovate or elliptic. **Eugenia** (p. 770).
Leaves without glands.

Leaves green and glabrous below.
Leaves obtuse or emarginate at apex (*rarely alternate*), 1′–1½′ long.
Torrubia (p. 341).
Leaves acute, acuminate, or sometimes rounded or emarginate, 3′–5′ long.
Leaves distinctly veined. **Citharexylon** (p. 864).
Leaves obscurely veined. **Osmanthus** (p. 856).
Leaves hoary tomentulose or scurfy below.
Leaves strongly 3-nerved, acuminate, densely scurfy below.
Tetrazygia (p. 776).
Leaves penniveined, rounded or acute at apex, hoary tomentulose below.
Avicennia (p. 865).

** Leaves deciduous.

a Leaves without lobes.
  b Leaves serrate.
    Winter-buds with several opposite outer scales.
      Leaves puberulous below, closely and finely serrate; axillary buds solitary.
      Evonymus (p. 675).
      Leaves glabrous below, remotely crenate-serrulate; axillary buds several, superposed. **Forestiera** (p. 853).
    Winter-buds enclosed in 2 large opposite scales. **Viburnum** (p. 886).
  bb Leaves entire.
    c Leaves without stipules.
      Leaves suborbicular or elliptic to oblong.
        Leaves rounded or acutish at apex, 1′–2′ long, occasionally 3-foliolate, glabrous; branchlets quadrangular. **Fraxinus anomala** (p. 837).
        Leaves acuminate or acute at apex, 3′–4′ long.
          Leaf-scars connected by a transverse line, with 3 bundle-traces; branchlets slender, appressed-pubescent. **Cornus** (p. 785).
          Leaf-scars not connected, with 1 bundle-trace; branchlets stout, villose, puberulous or glabrous. **Chionanthus** (p. 855).
      Leaves broad-ovate, cordate, acuminate, 5′–12′ long, on long petioles.
      Catalpa (p. 870).
      Leaves linear to linear-lanceolate, short-stalked or sessile (*sometimes alternate*). **Chilopsis** (p. 869).
    cc Leaves with persistent stipules, entire.
      Leaves oval or ovate; winter-buds resinous, the terminal up to ½′ in length.
      Pinckneya (p. 876).
      Leaves ovate to lanceolate; winter-buds minute. **Cephalanthus** (p. 878).
aa Leaves palmately lobed. **Acer** (p. 681).

2. Leaves Compound.

a Leaves persistent, with stipules.
    Leaves equally pinnate; leaflets entire. **Guaiacum** (p. 630).
    Leaves unequally pinnately parted into 3–8 linear-lanceolate segments (*sometimes entire*). **Lyonothamnus** (p. 378).
    Leaves trifoliate.
      Leaflets stalked. **Amyris** (p. 640).
      Leaflets sessile. **Helietta** (p. 637).
aa Leaves deciduous.
    Leaves unequally pinnate or trifoliate.
      Leaflets crenate-serrate or entire, the veins arching within the margins; stipules wanting; winter-buds with several opposite scales. **Fraxinus** (p. 833).
      Leaflets sharply or incisely serrate, the primary veins extending to the teeth.
        Leaflets 3–7, incisely serrate; stipules present; winter-buds with 1 pair of obtuse outer scales. **Acer Negundo** (p. 699).
        Leaflets 5–9, sharply serrate; stipules present; winter-buds with many opposite acute scales; pith thick. **Sambucus** (p. 882).
    Leaves digitate, with 5–7, sharply serrate leaflets; terminal buds large.
    Æsculus (p. 702).

B. LEAVES ALTERNATE.

1. LEAVES SIMPLE. (2, see p. xxiv).

* Leaves persistent. (** see p. xxii).

a Leaves deeply 3–5-lobed, $\frac{1}{3}'-\frac{1}{2}'$ long, with linear lobes, hoary tomentose below.
         Cowania (p. 549).

aa Leaves palmately lobed.
     Leaves stellate-pubescent, about $1\frac{1}{2}'$ in diameter, with stipules.
         Fremontia (p. 749).
     Leaves glabrous, 1°–2° in diameter, without stipules.   **Carica** (p. 755).

aaa Leaves not lobed or pinnately lobed.
     b Branches spinescent.
         Leaves clustered at the end of the branches, at least 2′–3′ long.
             Bucida (p. 765).
         Leaves fascicled on lateral branchlets, obtuse or emarginate, pale and glabrous
            beneath.   **Bumelia angustifolia** (p. 816).
         Leaves scattered.
            Leaves generally obovate, mucronate, not more than $\frac{1}{2}'-1'$ long, glabrous and
                 green or brownish tomentulose beneath.   **Condalia** (p. 719).
            Leaves elliptic-ovate to oblong, obtuse or emarginate, glabrous, 1–2 cm. long.
                 Ximenia (p. 337).

     bb Branches not spinescent.
         c Leaves serrate, or lobed (*in some species of Quercus*). (*cc*, see p. xx).
            d Juice watery. (*dd*, see p. xx).
                e Stipules present. (*ee*, see p. xxi).
                   f Primary veins extending straight to the teeth.
                       Leaves and branchlets glabrous or pubescent to tomentose with
                       fascicled hairs.
                           Leaves fulvous-tomentose beneath, repand-dentate, 3′–5′
                             long.   **Lithocarpus** (p. 236).
                           Leaves glabrous or grayish to whitish tomentose beneath,
                             entire, lobed or dentate.   **Quercus sp. 21–34** (p. 268).
                       Leaves and branchlets coated with simpled silky or woolly
                       hairs at least while young. not more than $2\frac{1}{2}'$ long.
                           Cercocarpus (p. 550).
                ff Primary veins arching and united within the margin.
                   Leaves 3-nerved from the base.   **Ceanothus** (p. 726).
                   Leaves not 3-nerved.
                   Leaves acute.
                     Leaves sinuately dentate, with few spiny teeth (*rarely en-*
                       tire), glabrous.   **Ilex opaca** (p. 669).
                     Leaves serrate.
                       Leaves tomentose below; branchlets tomentose.
                         Leaves narrow-lanceolate, glabrous and smooth above.
                           Vauquelinia (p. 377).
                         Leaves ovate, cordate, scabrate above. **Trema** (p. 327).
                       Leaves glabrous below.   **Heteromeles** (p. 392).
                   Leaves entire, very rarely toothed.
                     Leaves elliptic, glabrous.   **Prunus caroliniana** (p. 579).
                     Leaves oblanceolate, pubescent beneath when young.
                       Ilex Cassine (p. 670).
                 Leaves obtuse, sometimes mucronate.
                   Leaves spinose-serrate, glabrous.
                     Leaves broad-ovate to suborbicular or elliptic; branch-
                     lets dark red-brown, spinescent.
                       Rhamnus crocea (p. 723).
                   Leaves ovate to ovate-lanceolate; branchlets yellow or
                   orange-colored, not spinescent.
                     Prunus ilicifolia (p. 581).
               Leaves crenate (*often entire*), oval to oblong.
                 Ilex vomitoria (p. 671).

 ee Stipules wanting.

  Leaves resinous-dotted, aromatic, $1\frac{1}{2}'$–$4'$ long. **Myrica** (p. 163).

  Leaves not resinous-dotted, crenately serrate, $4'$–$6'$ long.

   Leaves dark green, glabrous below. **Gordonia Lasianthus** (p. 751).

   Leaves yellowish green, pubescent below, sometimes nearly entire.

    Symplocos (p. 831).

 dd Juice milky.

  Petioles $2\frac{1}{2}'$–$4'$ long; leaves broad-ovate. **Hippomane** (p. 652).

  Petioles about $\frac{1}{4}'$ long; leaves elliptic to oblong-lanceolate.

   Gymnanthes (p. 654).

cc Leaves entire (*rarely sparingly toothed on vigorous branchlets*).

 d Stipules present.

  e Stipules connate, at least at first.

   Stipules persistent, forming a sheath surrounding the branch above
    the node; leaves obtuse. **Coccolobis** (p. 338).

   Stipules deciduous, enveloping the unfolded leaf.

    Leaves ferrugineous-tomentose beneath.

     Magnolia grandiflora (p. 345).

    Leaves glabrous beneath, with milky juice. **Ficus** (p. 333).

  ee Stipules free.

   f Juice milky; leaves oval to oblong, $3'$–$5'$ long. **Drypetes** (p. 650).

   ff Juice watery.

    g Leaves obtuse or emarginate at apex.

     Leaves with ferrugineous scales beneath, their petioles
      slender. **Capparis** (p. 365).

     Leaves without ferrugineous scales.

      Leaves soft-pubescent on both sides.

       Colubrina cubensis (p. 730).

      Leaves glabrous at least at maturity.

       Leaves rarely $2'$–$3'$ long, standing on the branch at
        acute angles. **Chrysobalanus** (p. 583).

       Leaves rarely more than $1'$ long, spreading (sometimes
        3-nerved). **Ceanothus spinosus** (p. 728).

    gg Leaves acute or acutish.

     Petioles with 2 glands. **Conocarpus** (p. 766).

     Petioles without glands.

      Leaves and branchlets more or less pubescent, at least
      while young.

       Leaves fascicled except on vigorous branchlets.

        Cercocarpus (p. 550).

       Leaves not fascicled.

        Winter-buds minute, with few pointed scales.

         Leaves rounded or nearly rounded at base.

          Colubrina sp. 1, 3 (p. 729).

         Leaves broad-cuneate at base.

          Ilex Cassine (p. 670).

        Winter-buds conspicuous, with numerous scales.

         Leaves usually lanceolate, entire, covered below
          with yellow scales. **Castanopsis** (p. 234).

         Leaves oblong or oblong-obovate, repand-dentate,
          fibrous tomentose below. **Lithocarpus** (p. 236).

      Leaves and branchlets glabrous.

       Leaf-scar with 1 bundle-trace. **Ilex Krugiana** (p. 672).

       Leaf-scar with 3 bundle-traces. Cherry Laurels.

        Prunus sp. 19–22 (p. 579).

 dd Stipules wanting.

  e Leaves aromatic when bruised.

   Leaves resinous-dotted. **Myrica** (p. 163).

   Leaves not resinous-dotted.

    Leaves obtuse, obovate, glabrous. **Canella** (p. 753).

    Leaves acute.

Leaves mostly rounded at the narrowed base, ovate to oblong, acute, glabrous.   **Annona** (p. 354).
Leaves more or less cuneate at base, elliptic to lanceolate, usually acuminate.
 Leaves abruptly long-acuminate, glabrous, the margin undulate; branchlets red-brown.   **Misanteca** (p. 364).
 Leaves gradually acuminate or nearly acute.
  Leaves strongly reticulate beneath.
   Branchlets glabrous, light grayish brown; leaves glabrous, light green beneath.   **Ocotea** (p. 359).
   Branchlets pubescent while young, greenish or yellowish; leaves pale beneath, pubescent while young.
      Umbellularia (p. 360).
  Leaves not or slightly reticulate, glaucous, glabrous or pubescent beneath.   **Persea** (p. 356).
ee Leaves not aromatic.
 f Leaves acute or acutish.
  Leaves obovate, gradually narrowed into short petioles.
   Leaves 2′–2½′ long.   **Schæfferia** (p. 679).
   Leaves at least 6′–8′ long.   **Enallagma** (p. 873).
  Leaves elliptic to oblong or ovate.
   Leaves rough or pubescent above, pubescent below, subcordate to cuneate at base.
    Leaves stellate-pubescent.   **Solanum** (p. 867).
    Leaves scabrous above.
     Petiole ⅛′–¼′ long; leaves oval or oblong, 1¼′–4′ long.
       Ehretia (p. 862).
     Petiole 1′–1½′ long; leaves ovate to oblong-ovate, 3′–7′ long.   **Cordia** (p. 858).
   Leaves smooth above.
    Winter-buds scaly.
     Leaves covered below with ferrugineous or pale scales, 1′–3′ long.   **Lyonia** (p. 797).
     Leaves glabrous or nearly so below.
      Leaves ovate-lanceolate or obovate-lanceolate, 4′–12′ long, usually clustered at end of branchlet, veinlets below obscure.   **Rhododendron** (p. 792).
      Leaves elliptic or oval to oblong or lanceolate.
       Leaves light yellowish green below and without distinctly visible veins or veinlets, entire, 3′–4′ long.
        Kalmia (p. 794).
       Leaves pale below and more or less distinctly reticulate, occasionally serrate or denticulate, 1′–5′ long; bark of branches red.   **Arbutus** (p. 799).
    Winter-buds naked.
     Leaves pubescent below when unfolding.
      Mature leaves nearly glabrous below.
       Leaves oblong-lanceolate to narrow-obovate.
        Dipholis (p. 810).
       Leaves oval.   **Sideroxylum** (p. 809).
      Mature leaves covered below with brilliant copper-colored pubescence.
     Leaves glabrous below.   **Chrysophyllum** (p. 817).
      Leaves marked by minute black dots, ovate to oblong-lanceolate.   **Ardisia** (p. 806).
      • Leaves lepidote, oblong-obovate.   **Rapanea** (p. 807).
ff Leaves obtuse or emarginate at apex.
 g Leaves rounded or cordate at base, emarginate, their petioles slender.
  Leaves reniform to broad-ovate, cordate; juice watery.
      Cercis (p. 603).

Leaves elliptic to oblong, rounded at base; juice milky or viscid.

Leaves emarginate; petioles slender, rufous-tomentulose. **Mimusops** (p. 819).

Leaves obtuse at apex; petioles stout, grayish-tomentulose or glabrous. **Rhus integrifolia** (p. 664).

gg Leaves cuneate at base.

Petioles slender, ½′ long. **Beureria** (p. 861).

Petioles short and stout.

Leaves coriaceous, with thick revolute margins (*sometimes opposite*). **Jacquinia** (p. 804).

Leaves subcoriaceous, slightly revolute.

Leaves reticulate-veined beneath.

Leaves oval to obovate or oblong-oval, more or less pubescent while young. **Vaccinium** (p. 802).

Leaves oblong to oblong-obovate, glabrous. **Cyrilla** (p. 666).

Leaves obscurely veined beneath, glabrous.

Leaves oblong-lanceolate, narrowed toward the emarginate apex, decurrent nearly to base of petiole. **Cliftonia** (p. 667).

Leaves rounded at apex, distinctly petioled. **Maytenus** (p. 676).

**Leaves deciduous.

† Leaves conspicuous. (††, see p. xxiv).

a Leaves entire, sometimes 3 or 4-lobed. (*aa*, see p. xxiii).

b Stipules present.

Juice milky. **Maclura** (p. 331).

Juice watery.

Stipules connate, enveloping the young leaves, their scars encircling the branchlet.

Leaves acute or acuminate, entire; winter-buds pointed, nearly terete. **Magnolia** (p. 342).

Leaves truncate, sinuately 4-lobed; winter-buds obtuse, compressed. **Liriodendron** (p. 351).

Stipules distinct.

Branches spinescent; leaves glandular, caducous (*crenately serrate on vigorous shoots*). **Dalea** (p. 621).

Branches not spinescent; leaves without glands.

Winter-buds with a single pair of connate scales. **Salix** (p. 138).

Winter-buds with several pairs of imbricate scales.

Branchlets without a terminal bud; leaves 3-nerved. **Celtis** (p. 318).

Branchlets with a terminal bud, leaves penniveined. **Quercus sp.** 17–20 (p. 262).

bb Stipules wanting.

c Branchlets bright green and lustrous for the first 2 or 3 years; leaves sometimes 3-lobed, aromatic. **Sassafras** (p. 362).

cc Branchlets brown or gray.

d Leaves acute or acuminate.

Leaves 10′–12′ long, obovate-oblong, acuminate, glabrous, emitting a disagreeable odor. **Asimina** (p. 353).

Leaves smaller.

Petioles very slender, 1′–2′ long; leaves elliptic, acuminate. **Cornus alternifolia** (p. 789).

Petioles short.

Branchlets with a terminal bud.

Leaf-scars about as long as broad; branchlets without lenticels, light reddish brown. **Elliottia** (p. 791).

Leaf-scars crescent-shaped, broader than long, with 3 distinct bundle-traces.

Leaves pubescent on both sides, rugulose above; petioles 1'–2' long, like the young branchlet densely pubescent.
                                        Leitneria (p. 167).
Leaves glabrous and smooth above, glabrous or pubescent below; petioles and branchlets usually glabrous or nearly so at maturity.   **Nyssa** (p. 779).
Branchlets without a terminal bud.
Pubescence consisting of simple hairs or wanting.
Leaves 4'–6' long, pubescent beneath while young; branchlet light brown or gray.   **Diospyros virginiana** (p. 821).
Leaves 1½'–3' long, glabrous; branches light yellowish gray.
                                        Schœpfia (p. 336)
Pubescence stellate; leaves obovate or elliptic, 2½'–5' long, pubescent below.   **Styrax** (p. 829).
dd Leaves obtuse or acute.
Branchlets not spinescent.
Leaves glabrous at maturity, their petioles slender. **Cotinus** (p. 657).
Leaves pubescent below at maturity; their petioles short and thick.
                                        Diospyros texana (p. 823).
Branchlets spinescent; leaves often fascicled on lateral branchlets.
                                        Bumelia (p. 812).
aa Leaves serrate or pinnately lobed.
  b Stipules present. (*bb*, see p. xxiv).
    c Winter-buds naked.
Leaves oblique at base, the upper side rounded or subcordate, obovate, coarsely toothed.   **Hamamelis** (p. 368).
Leaves equal at base, cuneate, finely serrate or crenate.
                                        Rhamnus sp. 2, 3 (p. 724, 725).
    cc Winter-buds with a single pair of connate scales.
Primary veins arching and uniting within the margins; leaves simply serrate or crenate, sometimes entire.   **Salix** (p. 138).
Primary veins extending to the teeth, leaves doubly serrate, often slightly lobed.   **Alnus** (p. 220).
    ccc Winter-buds with several pairs of imbricate scales.
      d Terminal buds wanting; branchlets prolonged by an upper axillary bud.
Juice milky; leaves usually ovate, often lobed.   **Morus** (p. 328).
Juice watery; leaves not lobed.
Leaves distinctly oblique at base.
Leaves with numerous prominent lateral veins.
Leaves generally broad-ovate, simply serrate, stellate-pubescent at least while young, rarely glabrous.   **Tilia** (p. 732).
Leaves never broad-ovate, usually doubly serrate, more or less pubescent with simple hairs, at least while young.
Winter-buds ovoid, usually acute, ⅓ to nearly as long as petioles; leaves 1'–7' long, doubly serrate.   **Ulmus** (p. 309).
Winter-buds subglobose, minute; leaves 2'–2½' long, crenate-serrate.   **Planera** (p. 316).
Leaves 3 or 4-nerved from the base.   **Celtis** (p. 318).
Leaves slightly or not at all oblique at base.
Leaves 3-nerved from the base, glandular-crenate or glandular-serrate.   **Ceanothus** (p. 726).
Leaves not or obscurely 3-nerved at base, usually doubly serrate.
Leaves blue-green; petioles ¼'–½' long; bark smooth, gray-brown.
                                        Carpinus (p. 201).
Leaves yellow-green.
Bark rough, furrowed; petioles ⅛'–¼' long; leaves not resinous-glandular.   **Ostrya** (p. 202).
Bark flaky or cherry-tree like; petioles ¼'–1' long; leaves often resinous-glandular while young.   **Betula** (p. 205).
dd Terminal buds present.
Primary veins arching and uniting within the margin (*extending to the margin in the lobed leaves of Malus*).

Winter-buds resinous; leaves crenate, usually truncate at base; petioles slender.   **Populus** (p. 119).
Winter-buds not resinous.
Leaf-scars with 3 bundle-traces.
Leaves involute in bud, often lobed on vigorous shoots; winterbuds obtuse, short, pubescent.   **Malus** (p. 379).
Leaves conduplicate (*or in some species of Prunus convolute*), never lobed; winter-buds acute.
Winter-buds elongated; branches never spinescent.
Amelanchier (p. 393).
Winter-buds not elongated, ovoid; branches sometimes spinescent.   **Prunus** (p. 555).
Leaf-scars with 1 bundle-trace; leaves simply serrate.
Ilex sp. 5–6 (p. 673).
Primary veins extending to the teeth or to the lobes.
Leaves lobed.   **Quercus sp.** 1–16, 35–50 (pp. 241, 283).
Leaves serrate-toothed.
Winter-buds with numerous scales.
Leaves lustrous beneath, remotely serrate or denticulate; winterbuds elongated, acuminate.   **Fagus** (p. 228).
Leaves pale beneath, coarsely dentate or serrate; winter-buds acute. Chestnut Oaks.   **Quercus sp.** 51–54 (p. 303).
Winter-buds with 2 pairs of scales.   **Castanea** (p. 230).
Leaves doubly or simply serrate, or lobed, with serrate lobes; branches often furnished with spines.
Leaves involute in the bud; branchlets often ending in blunt spines.
Malus (p. 379).
Leaves conduplicate in the bud; branches usually armed with sharppointed single or branched axillary spines. **Cratægus** (p. 397).
bb Stipules wanting.
    c Leaves not lobed.
Leaves subcoriaceous, oblong, sometimes nearly entire, glabrous.
Symplocos (p. 831).

Leaves thin.
Leaves oblong-obovate, acute, pubescent beneath.
Gordonia alatamaha (p. 752).
Leaves oblong or lanceolate, acuminate, glabrous or puberulous while young, turning scarlet in the autumn.   **Oxydendrum** (p. 796).
Leaves ovate to elliptic, stellate-pubescent or glabrous, turning yellow in the autumn.   **Halesia** (p. 824).
    cc Leaves palmately lobed.
Stipules large, foliaceous, united; branchlets without a terminal bud.
Platanus (p. 371).
Stipules small, free, caducous; branchlets with a terminal bud.
Liquidambar (p. 367).

    †† Leaves inconspicuous or wanting; branches spiny or prickly.

Branches or stems succulent, armed with numerous prickles.
Branches and stems columnar, ribbed, continuous; leaves 0.   **Cereus** (p. 757).
Branches jointed, tuberculate; leaves scale-like.   **Opuntia** (p. 759).
Branches rigid, spinescent.
Leaves minute, narrow-obovate.
Branchlets bright green.   **Kœberlinia** (p. 754).
Branchlets red-brown.   **Dalea** (p. 621).
Leaves scale-like, caducous.   **Canotia** (p. 677).

2. LEAVES COMPOUND.

* Leaves 3-foliolate, without stipules.

Leaves persistent; leaflets obovate, entire, sessile.   **Hypelate** (p. 716).
Leaves deciduous.

Leaflets deltoid to hastate, entire, rounded at apex; branches prickly.

Erythrina (p. 627).

Leaflets ovate to oblong, acuminate, strongly scented and bitter; branches unarmed.

Ptelea (p. 639).

** Leaves twice pinnate; stipules present.

a Leaves unequally twice pinnate, 2°–4° long, deciduous; leaflets serrate, 2′–3′ in length; branches and stem armed with scattered prickles.   **Aralia** (p. 778).

aa Leaves equally twice pinnate, usually smaller; branches unarmed or armed with stipular or axillary spines (in *Parkinsonia* often apparently simply pinnate).

  b Leaflets crenate; leaves simply or twice-pinnate on the same plant, deciduous, usually armed with simple or branched axillary spines.   **Gleditsia** (p. 607).

  bb Leaflets entire.

Leaflets 2–2½′ long; leaves deciduous; branchlets stout, unarmed.

Gymnocladus (p. 605).

Leaflets smaller; leaves usually persistent; branchlets slender.

Branches armed with prickles or spines.

Leaves with 2 or rarely 4 pinnæ.

Branches armed with axillary spines or spiny rachises.

Pinnæ with 4–8 leaflets; branches with short axillary spines.

Cercidium (p. 613).

Pinnæ with 8–60 leaflets; branches armed with spiny rachises or rigid branchlets terminating in stout spines.   **Parkinsonia** (p. 611).

Branches armed with stipular prickles; leaves persistent.

Pinnæ with many oblong to linear leaflets.   **Prosopis** (p. 599).

Pinnæ with 1 pair of orbicular to broad-oblong leaflets.

Pithecolobium unguis-cati (p. 586).

Leaves with 6, or more, rarely 4, pinnæ.

Prickles usually spreading, often recurved.   **Acacia** (p. 591).

Prickles usually more or less ascending, straight. **Pithecolobium** (p. 586).

Branches unarmed.

Branchlets and petioles glabrous; leaves with 2–5 pair of pinnæ, each with 40–80 leaflets.   **Lysiloma** (p. 589).

Branchlets and petioles pubescent while young; leaves with 5–17 pair of many-foliolate pinnæ, or pinnæ 2–4 and each with 8–16 leaflets.

Leucæna (p. 596).

*** Leaves simply pinnate.

a Leaves equally pinnate.

Stipules wanting.

Leaflets 2–4, generally oblong-obovate.   **Exothea** (p. 714).

Leaflets 6–12.

Leaflets obtuse, usually oblong-obovate.

Leaflets 8–12, 2′–3′ long, pale below; leaves occasionally opposite.

Simarouba (p. 642).

Leaflets 6–8, 1′–1½′ long, green below.   **Xanthoxylum coriaceum** (p. 637).

Leaflets 6–8, acuminate.   **Swietenia** (p. 648).

Stipules present.

Branches armed with infra-stipular spines in pairs; leaflets 10–15, usually oblong-obovate, ½′–¾′ long, persistent.   **Olneya** (p. 626).

Branches unarmed; leaflets 20–46, ovals ½′–⅔′ long.   **Eysenhardtia** (p. 620).

aa Leaves unequally pinnate.

  b Stipules present.

Leaflets sharply serrate; leaves deciduous; winter-buds resinous.

Sorbus (p. 390).

Leaflets entire or crenately serrate.

Leaves deciduous.

Leaflets 7–11, 3′–4½′ long; branches unarmed.

Leaflets usually alternate, thin and glabrous at maturity.

Cladrastis (p. 618).

Leaflets opposite, coriaceous, pubescent beneath at least along the veins.
Ichthyomethia (p. 628).
Leaflets 9–21, 1–2 cm. long.
Branches usually with stipular prickles, sometimes viscid.
Robinia (p. 622).
Branches unarmed, not viscid; leaflets 13–19, elliptic.
Sophora affinis (p. 617).
Leaves persistent.
Leaflets 7–9, oblong-elliptic, 1′–2½′ long; branches unarmed.
Sophora secundiflora (p. 616).
Leaflets 10–15; branches prickly.   **Olneya** (p. 626).
bb Stipules wanting.
    d Leaves persistent.
Leaflets long-stalked (*sometimes nearly sessile in Xanthoxylum flavum*).
Leaflets oblong-ovate, cuneate at base.
Leaflets acuminate, glabrous.   **Picramnia** (p. 643).
Leaflets obtuse, tomentose when unfolding.
Xanthoxylum flavum (p. 636).
Leaflets broad-ovate, usually rounded or subcordate at base.
Metopium (p. 658).
Leaflets sessile or nearly so.
Petiole and rachis winged.
Leaflets crenate, obovate, about ½′ long; branches prickly.
Xanthoxylum Fagara (p. 634).
Leaflets entire.
Leaflets oblong, usually acute, 3′–4′ long.
Sapindus saponaria (p. 712).
Leaflets spathulate, rounded at apex, not more than ¾′ long.
Pistacia (p. 656).
Petiole and rachis not winged.
Leaflets 7–19, acuminate, 2′–5′ long.   **Sapindus marginatus** (p. 713).
Leaflets 21–41, obtuse, ½′–¾′ long.   **Alvaradoa** (p. 644).
dd Leaves deciduous.
Leaflets long-stalked, 3–7, entire, acute.   **Bursera** (p. 645).
Leaflets sessile or nearly so.
Branches prickly; leaflets crenate. **Xanthoxylum clava-Herculis** (p. 635).
Branches unarmed.
Juice milky or viscid; leaflets serrate or entire; rachis sometimes
winged.   **Rhus species** 1–3 (p. 660).
Juice watery.
Rachis without wings.
Leaflets entire, acuminate, 7–9.   **Sapindus Drummondii** (p. 714).
Leaflets serrate or crenate.
Winter-buds large; leaflets 5–23, aromatic.
Winter-buds naked.   **Juglans** (p. 169).
Winter-buds covered with scales.   **Carya** (p. 176).
Winter-buds minute, globose, scaly; leaflets 5–7, ovate, not
aromatic.   **Ungnadia** (p. 717).
Rachis winged; leaflets 10–20, entire, rounded at apex, not more than
½′ long.   **Bursera microphylla** (p. 647).

TREES OF NORTH AMERICA

TREES OF NORTH AMERICA

(Exclusive of Mexico)

Class 1. GYMNOSPERMÆ.

Ovules and seeds borne on the face of a scale, not inclosed in an ovary; resinous trees, with stems increasing in diameter by the annual addition of a layer of wood inside the bark.

I. PINACEÆ.

Trees, with narrow or scale-like generally persistent clustered or alternate leaves and usually scaly buds. Flowers appearing in early spring, mostly surrounded at the base by an involucre of the more or less enlarged scales of the buds, unisexual, monœcious (*diœcious in Juniperus*), the male consisting of numerous 2-celled anthers, the female of scales bearing on their inner face 2 or several ovules, and becoming at maturity a woody cone or rarely a berry. Seeds with or without wings; seed-coat of 2 layers; embryo axile in copious albumen; cotyledons 2 or several. Of the twenty-nine genera scattered over the surface of the globe, but most abundant in northern temperate regions, thirteen occur in North America.

CONSPECTUS OF THE NORTH AMERICAN GENERA.

Scales of the female flowers numerous; spirally arranged in the axils of persistent bracts; ovules 2, inverted; seeds borne directly on the scales, attached at the base in shallow depressions on the inner side of the scales, falling from them at maturity and usually carrying away a scarious terminal wing; leaves fascicled or scattered (*deciduous in Larix*). ABIETINEÆ.

Fruit maturing in two or rarely in three seasons; leaves fascicled, needle-shaped in axillary 1–5-leaved clusters, inclosed at the base in a membranaceous sheath; cone-scales thick and woody, much longer than their bracts.   1. **Pinus**

Fruit maturing in one season.

Leaves in many-leaved clusters on short spur-like branchlets, deciduous; cone-scales thin, usually shorter than their bracts.   2. **Larix.**

Leaves scattered, linear.

Cones pendulous, the scales persistent on the axis.

Branchlets roughened by the persistent leaf-bases; leaves deciduous in drying; bracts shorter than the cone-scales.

Leaves sessile, 4-sided, or flattened and stomatiferous above.   3. **Picea.**

Leaves stalked, flattened and stomatiferous below, or angular.   4. **Tsuga.**

Branchlets not roughened by leaf-bases; leaves stalked, flattened; not deciduous in drying; bracts of the cone 2-lobed, aristate, longer than the scales.   5. **Pseudotsuga.**

Cones erect, their scales deciduous from the axis, longer or shorter than the bracts; leaves sessile, flat or 4-sided.   6. **Abies.**

Scales of the female flowers without bracts; ovules and seeds borne on the face of minute scales adnate to the base of the flower-scales, enlarging and forming the scales of the cone. Seeds with a narrow marginal wing (*wingless in Juniperas*).

Scales of the female flowers numerous, spirally arranged, forming a woody cone; ovules erect, 2 or many under each scale; leaves linear, alternate, often of 2 forms (*deciduous in Taxodium*). TAXODIÆ.

Ovules and seeds numerous under each scale.   7. Sequoia.

Ovules and seeds 2 under each scale; leaves mostly spreading in 2 ranks.   8. Taxodium,

Scales of the female flower few, decussate, forming a small cone, or rarely a berry; ovules 2 or many under each scale; leaves decussate or in 3 ranks, often of 2 forms, usually scale-like, mostly adnate to the branch, the earliest free and subulate. CUPRESSINEÆ.

Fruit a cone; leaves scale-like.

Cones oblong, their scales oblong, imbricated or valvate; seeds 2 under each scale, maturing the first year.

Scales of the cone 6, the middle ones only fertile; seeds unequally 2-winged.

9. Libocedrus.

Scales of the cone 8–12; seeds equally 2-winged.   10. Thuja.

Cones subglobose, the scales peltate, maturing in one or two years; seeds few or many under each scale.

Fruit maturing in two seasons; seeds many under each scale; branchlets terete or 4-winged.   11. Cupressus.

Fruit maturing in one season; seeds 2 under each scale; branchlets flattened.

12. Chamæcyparis.

Fruit a berry formed by the coalition of the scales of the flower; ovules in pairs or solitary; flowers diœcious; leaves decussate or in 3's, subulate or scale-like, often of 2 forms.   13. Juniperus.

1. PINUS Duham. Pine.

Trees or rarely shrubs, with deeply furrowed and sometimes laminate or with thin and scaly bark, hard or often soft heartwood often conspicuously marked by dark bands of summer cells impregnated with resin, pale nearly white sapwood, and large branch-buds formed during summer and composed of minute buds in the axils of bud-scales, becoming the bracts of the spring shoot. Leaves needle-shaped, clustered, the clusters borne on deciduous spurs in the axils of scale-like primary leaves, inclosed in the bud by numerous scales lengthening and forming a more or less persistent sheath at the base of each cluster. Male flowers clustered at the base of leafy growing shoots of the year, each flower surrounded at the base by an involucre of 3–6 scalelike bracts, composed of numerous sessile anthers, imbricated in many ranks and surmounted by crest-like nearly orbicular connectives; the female subterminal or lateral, their scales in the axils of non-accrescent bracts. Fruit a woody cone maturing at the end of the second or rarely of the third season, composed of the hardened and woody scales of the flower more or less thickened on the exposed surface (the *apophysis*), with the ends of the growth of the previous year appearing as terminal or dorsal brown protuberances or scars (the *umbo*). Seeds usually obovoid, shorter or longer than their wings or rarely wingless; outer seed-coat crustaceous or thick, hard, and bony, the inner membranaceous; cotyledons 3–18, usually much shorter than the inferior radicle.

Pinus is widely distributed through the northern hemisphere from the Arctic Circle to the West Indies, the mountains of Central America, the Canary Islands, northern Africa, the Philippine Islands, and Sumatra. About sixty-six species are recognized. Of exotic species the so-called Scotch Pine, *Pinus sylvestris* L., of Europe and Asia, the Swiss Stone Pine, *Pinus cembra* L., and the Austrian Pine and other forms of *Pinus nigra* Arnold, from central and southern Europe, are often planted in the northeastern states, and *Pinus Pinaster* Ait., of the coast region of western France and the Mediterranean Basin is successfully cultivated in central and southern California. *Pinus* is the classical name of the Pine-tree.

The North American species can be conveniently grouped in two sections, Soft Pines and Pitch Pines.

SOFT PINES.

Wood soft, close-grained, light-colored, the sapwood thin and nearly white; sheaths of the leaf-clusters deciduous; leaves with one fibro-vascular bundle.

Leaves in 5-leaved clusters.

Cones long-stalked, elongated, cylindric bright green at maturity, becoming light yellow brown, their scales thin, with terminal unarmed umbos; seeds shorter than their wings. WHITE PINES.

Leaves without conspicuous white lines on the back.

Leaves slender, flexible; cones 4'-8' long.   **1. P. Strobus (A)·**

Leaves stout, more rigid; cones 5'-11' long.   **2. P. monticola (B, G).**

Leaves with conspicuous white lines on the back; cones 12'-18' long.

    3. P. Lambertiana (G).

Cones short-stalked, green or purple at maturity, their scales thick.

Cones cylindric or subglobose, their scales with terminal umbos; leaves 2' long or less. STONE PINES.

Cones 3'-10' long, their scales opening at maturity; seeds with wings.

    4. P. flexilis (F, H).

Cones $\frac{1}{2}$'-3' long, their scales remaining closed at maturity; seeds wingless.

    5. P. albicaulis (B, F, G).

Cones ovoid-oblong, their scales with dorsal umbos armed with slender prickles; seeds shorter than their wings; leaves in crowded clusters, incurved, less than 2' long. FOXTAIL PINES.

Cones armed with minute incurved prickles.   **6. P. Balfouriana (G).**

Cones armed with long slender prickles.   **7. P. aristata (F, G).**

Leaves in 1-4-leaved clusters; cones globose, green at maturity, becoming light brown, their scales few, concave, much thickened, only the middle scales seed-bearing; seeds large and edible, their wings rudimentary; leaves 2' or less, often incurved. NUT PINES.   **8. P. cembroidés (C, F, G, H).**

1. Pinus Strobus L. White Pine.

Leaves soft bluish green, whitened on the ventral side by 3-5 bands of stomata, 3'-5' long, mostly turning yellow and falling in September in their second season, or persistent until the following June. **Flowers:** male yellow; female bright pink, with purple scale margins. **Fruit** fully grown in July of the second season, 4'-8' long, opening and discharging its seeds in September; **seeds** narrowed at the ends, $\frac{1}{4}$' long, red-brown mottled with black, about one fourth as long as their wings.

A tree, while young with slender horizontal or slightly ascending branches in regular whorls usually of 5 branches; at maturity often 100°, occasionally 220° high, with a tall straight stem 3°-4° or rarely 6° in diameter, when crowded in the forest with short branches forming a narrow head, or rising above its forest companions with long lateral branches sweeping upward in graceful curves, the upper branches ascending and forming a broad open irregular head, and slender branchlets coated at first with rusty tomentum, soon glabrous, and orange-brown in their first winter. **Bark** on young stems and branches thin, smooth, green tinged with red, lustrous during the summer, becoming 1'-2' thick on old trunks and deeply divided by shallow fissures into broad connected ridges covered with small closely appressed purplish scales. **Wood** light, not strong, straight-grained, easily worked, light brown often slightly tinged with red; largely manufactured into lumber, shingles, and laths, used in construction, for cabinet-making, the interior finish of buildings, woodenware, matches, and the masts of vessels.

Distribution. Newfoundland to Manitoba, southward through the northern states to Pennsylvania, northern and eastern (Belmont County) Ohio, central Indiana, valley of the Rocky River near Oregon, Ogie County, Illinois, and central and southeastern Iowa, and along the Appalachian Mountains to eastern Kentucky and Tennessee and northern

Georgia; forming nearly pure forests on sandy drift soils, or more often in small groves scattered in forests of deciduous-leaved trees on fertile well-drained soil, also on the banks of streams, or on river flats, or rarely in swamps.

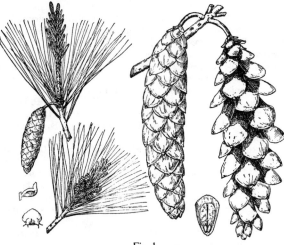

Fig. 1

Largely planted as an ornament of parks and gardens in the eastern states, and in many European countries, where it grows with vigor and rapidity; occasionally used in forest planting in the United States.

2. Pinus monticola D. Don. White Pine.

Leaves blue-green, glaucous, whitened by 2–6 rows of ventral and often by dorsal stomata, mostly persistent 3 or 4 years. **Flowers:** male yellow; female pale purple. **Fruit**

Fig. 2

5′–11′ long, shedding its seeds late in the summer or in early autumn; **seeds** narrowed at the ends, ⅓′ long, pale red-brown mottled with black, about one third as long as their wings.

A tree, often 100° or occasionally 150° high, with a trunk frequently 4°–5° or rarely 7°–8° in diameter, slender spreading slightly pendulous branches clothing young stems to the ground and in old age forming a narrow open often unsymmetrical pyramidal head, and stout tough branchlets clothed at first with rusty pubescence, dark orange-brown and puberulous in their first and dark red-purple and glabrous in their second season. **Bark** of young stems and branches thin, smooth, light gray, becoming on old trees $\frac{3}{4}$'–1$\frac{1}{2}$' thick and divided into small nearly square plates by deep longitudinal and cross fissures, and covered by small closely appressed purple scales. **Wood** light, soft, not strong, close, straight-grained, light brown or red; sometimes manufactured into lumber, used in construction and the interior finish of buildings.

Distribution. Scattered through mountain forests from the basin of the Columbia River in British Columbia to Vancouver Island; on the mountains of northern Washington to the western slopes of the Rocky Mountains of northern Montana; on the coast ranges of Washington and Oregon; and on the Cascade and Sierra Nevada ranges southward to the Kern River valley, California; most abundant and of its greatest value in northern Idaho on the bottom-lands of streams tributary to Lake Pend Oreille; reaching the sea-level on the southern shores of the Straits of Fuca and elevations of 10,000° on the California Sierras.

Often planted as an ornamental tree in Europe, and occasionally in the eastern United States where it grows more vigorously than any other Pine-tree of western America.

3. Pinus Lambertiana Dougl. Sugar Pine.

Leaves stout, rigid, 3$\frac{1}{2}$'–4' long, marked on the two faces by 2–6 rows of stomata; deciduous during their second and third years. **Flowers:** male light yellow; female pale green. **Fruit** fully grown in August and opening in October, 11'–18' or rarely 21' long; **seeds** $\frac{1}{2}$'–$\frac{5}{8}$' long, dark chestnut-brown or nearly black, and half the length of their firm dark brown obtuse wings broadest below the middle and $\frac{1}{2}$' wide.

A tree, in early life with remote regular whorls of slender branches often clothing the stem to the ground and forming an open narrow pyramid; at maturity 200°–220° high,

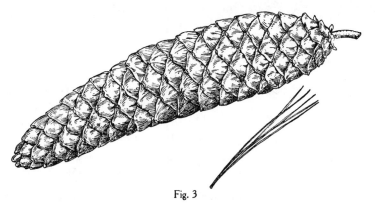

Fig. 3

with a trunk 6°–8° or occasionally 12° in diameter, a flat-topped crown frequently 60° or 70° across of comparatively slender branches sweeping outward and downward in graceful curves, and stout branchlets coated at first with pale or rufous pubescence, dark orange-brown during their first winter, becoming dark purple-brown. **Bark** on young stems and branches thin, smooth, dark green, becoming on old trunks 2'–3' thick and deeply and irregularly divided into long thick plate-like ridges covered with large loose rich purple-brown or cinnamon-red scales. **Wood** light, soft, straight-grained, light red-brown;

largely manufactured into lumber and used for the interior finish of buildings, woodwork, and shingles. A sweet sugar-like substance exudes from wounds made in the heartwood.

Distribution. Mountain slopes and the sides of ravines and cañons; western Oregon from the valley of the north branch of the Santiam River southward on the Cascade and coast ranges; California along the northern and coast ranges to Sonoma County; along the western slopes of the Sierra Nevada, where it grows to its greatest size at elevations between 3000° and 7000°; reappearing on the Santa Lucia Mountains of the coast ranges; and on the high mountains in the southwestern part of the state from Santa Barbara County southward usually at elevations of 5000°–7000° above the sea; and on the San Pedro Mártir Mountains in Lower California.

Occasionally planted as an ornamental tree in western Europe and in the eastern states, the Sugar Pine has grown slowly in cultivation and shows little promise of attaining the large size and great beauty which distinguish it in its native forests.

4. Pinus flexilis James. Rocky Mountain White Pine.

Pinus strobiformis Sarg., not Engelm.

Leaves stout, rigid, dark green, marked on all sides by 1–4 rows of stomata, $1\frac{1}{2}'$–3′ long, deciduous in their fifth and sixth years. **Flowers:** male reddish; female clustered, bright red-purple. **Fruit** subcylindric, horizontal or slightly declining, green or rarely purple at maturity, 3′–10′ long, with narrow and more or less reflexed scales opening at maturity; **seeds** compressed, $\frac{1}{3}'$–$\frac{1}{2}'$ long, dark red-brown mottled with black, with a thick shell pro-

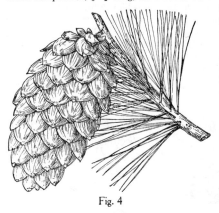

duced into a narrow margin, their wings about $\frac{1}{12}'$ wide, generally persistent on the scale after the seed falls.

A tree, usually 40°–50°, occasionally 80° high, with a short trunk 2°–5° in diameter, stout long-persistent branches ultimately forming a low wide round-topped head, and stout branchlets orange-green and covered at first with soft fine pubescence, usually soon glabrous and darker colored; at high elevations often a low spreading shrub. **Bark** of young stems and branches thin, smooth, light gray or silvery white, becoming on old trunks 1′–2′ thick, dark brown or nearly black, and divided by deep fissures into broad ridges broken into nearly square plates covered by small closely appressed scales. **Wood** light,

Fig. 4

soft, close-grained, pale clear yellow, turning red with exposure; occasionally manufactured into lumber.

Distribution. Eastern slope of the Rocky Mountains from Alberta to western Texas and westward on mountain ranges at elevations of 5000° to 12,000° to Montana, and southern California, reaching the western slopes of the Sierra Nevada at the head of King's River near the summit of San Gorgonio Mountain and in Snow Cañon, San Bernardino Range; usually scattered singly or in small groves; forming open forests on the eastern foothills of the Rocky Mountains of Montana and on the ranges of central Nevada; attaining its largest size on those of northern New Mexico and Arizona.

5. Pinus albicaulis Engelm. White Pine.

Leaves stout, rigid, slightly incurved, dark green, marked by 1–3 rows of dorsal stomata, clustered at the ends of the branches, $1\frac{1}{2}'$–$2\frac{1}{2}'$ long, persistent for from five to eight years. **Flowers** opening in July, scarlet. **Fruit** ripening in August, oval or subglobose, horizontal, sessile, dark purple, $1\frac{1}{2}'$–$3'$ long, with scales thickened, acute, often armed with stout pointed umbos, remaining closed at maturity; seeds wingless, acute, subcylindric or flattened on one side, $\frac{1}{3}'$–$\frac{1}{2}'$ long, $\frac{1}{4}'$ thick, with a thick dark chestnut-brown hard shell.

A tree, usually $20°$–$30°$ or rarely $60°$ high, generally with a short trunk $2°$–$4°$ in diameter, stout very flexible branches, finally often standing nearly erect and forming an open very irregular broad head, and stout dark red-brown or orange-colored branchlets puberulous for two years or sometimes glabrous; at high elevations often a low shrub, with wide-spreading nearly prostrate stems. **Bark** thin, except near the base of old trunks and broken by narrow fissures into thin narrow brown or creamy white plate-like scales. **Wood** light, soft, close-grained, brittle, light brown. The large sweet seeds are gathered and eaten by Indians.

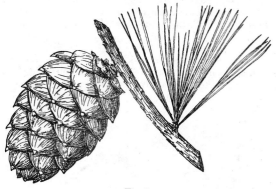

Fig. 5

Distribution. Alpine slopes and exposed ridges between $5000°$ and $12,000°$ elevation, forming the timber-line on many mountain ranges from latitude $53°$ north in the Rocky Mountains and British Columbia, southward to the Wind River and Salt River Ranges, Wyoming, the mountains of eastern Washington and Oregon, the Cascade Range, the mountains of northern California and the Sierra Nevada to Mt. Whitney.

6. Pinus Balfouriana Balf. Foxtail Pine.

Leaves stout, rigid, dark green and lustrous on the back, pale and marked on the ventral faces by numerous rows of stomata, $1'$–$1\frac{1}{2}'$ long, persistent for ten or twelve years. **Flowers:** male dark orange-red; female dark purple. **Fruit** $3\frac{1}{2}'$–$5'$ long, with scales armed with minute incurved prickles, dark purple, turning after opening dark red or mahogany color; seeds full and rounded at the apex, compressed at the base, pale, conspicuously mottled with dark purple, $\frac{1}{3}'$ long, their wings narrowed and oblique at the apex, about $1'$ long and $\frac{1}{4}'$ wide.

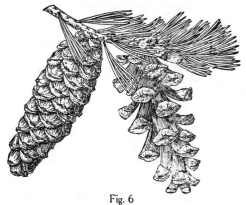

Fig. 6

A tree, usually $30°$–$40°$ or rarely $90°$ high, with a trunk generally $1°$–$2°$ or rarely $5°$ in diameter, short stout branches forming an open irregular pyramidal picturesque head, and long rigid more or less spreading puberulous, soon glabrous, dark orange-brown ultimately dark gray-brown or nearly black branchlets, clothed only at the extremities with the long dense brush-like masses of foliage. **Bark** thin, smooth, and milky white on the stems and branches of young trees, becoming on old trees sometimes $\frac{3}{4}'$ thick, dark red-brown, deeply divided into broad flat ridges, broken into nearly square plates separating on the surface into small closely appressed scales. **Wood** light, soft and brittle, pale reddish brown.

Distribution. California, on rocky slopes and ridges, forming scattered groves on Scott Mountain, Siskiyou County, at elevations of 5000°–6000°; on the mountains at the head of the Sacramento River; on Mt. Yolo Bally in the northern Coast Range, and on the southern Sierra Nevada up to elevations of 11,500°, growing here to its largest size and forming an extensive open forest on the Whitney Plateau east of the cañon of Kern River, and at the highest elevations often a low shrub, with wide-spreading prostrate stems.

7. Pinus aristata Engelm. Foxtail Pine. Hickory Pine.

Leaves stout or slender, dark green, lustrous on the back, marked by numerous rows of stomata on the ventral faces, $1'-1\frac{1}{2}'$ long, often deciduous at the end of ten or twelve years or persistent four or five years longer. **Flowers** male dark orange-red; female dark

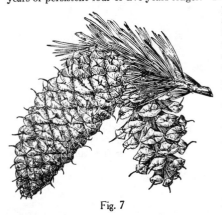

purple. **Fruit** $3'-3\frac{1}{2}'$ long, with scales armed with slender incurved brittle prickles nearly $\frac{1}{4}'$ long, dark purple-brown on the exposed parts, the remainder dull red, opening and scattering their seeds about the 1st of October; **seeds** nearly oval, compressed, light brown mottled with black, $\frac{1}{4}'$ long, their wings broadest at the middle, about $\frac{1}{3}'$ long and $\frac{1}{4}'$ wide.

A bushy tree, occasionally 40°–50° high, with a short trunk 2°–3° in diameter, short stout branches in regular whorls while young, in old age growing very irregularly, the upper erect and much longer than the usually pendulous lower branches, and stout light orange-colored, glabrous, or at first puberulous, ultimately dark gray-brown or nearly black

Fig. 7

branchlets clothed at the ends with long compact brush-like tufts of foliage. **Bark** thin, smooth, milky white on the stems and branches of young trees, becoming on old trees $\frac{1}{2}'-\frac{3}{4}'$ thick, red-brown, and irregularly divided into flat connected ridges separating on the surface into small closely appressed scales. **Wood** light, soft, not strong, light red; occasionally used for the timbers of mines and for fuel.

Distribution. Rocky or gravelly slopes at the upper limit of tree growth and rarely below 8,000° above the sea from the outer range of the Rocky Mountains of Colorado to those of southern Utah, central and southern Nevada, southeastern California, and the San Francisco peaks of northern Arizona.

8. Pinus cembroides Zucc. Nut Pine. Piñon.

Leaves in 2 or 3-leaved clusters, slender, much incurved, dark green, sometimes marked by rows of stomata on the 3 faces, $1'-2'$ long, deciduous irregularly during their third and fourth years. **Flowers:** male in short crowded clusters, yellow; female dark red. **Fruit** subglobose, $1'-2'$ broad; **seeds** subcylindric or obscurely triangular, more or less compressed at the pointed apex, full and rounded at base, nearly black on the lower side and dark chestnut-brown on the upper, $\frac{1}{2}'-\frac{3}{4}'$ long, the margin of their outer coat adnate to the cone-scale.

A bushy tree, with a short trunk rarely more than a foot in diameter and a broad round-topped head, usually 15°–20° high, stout spreading branches, and slender dark orange-colored branchlets covered at first with matted pale deciduous hairs, dark brown and sometimes nearly black at the end of five or six years; in sheltered cañons on the mountains of Arizona and in Lower California occasionally 50° or 60° tall. **Bark** about $\frac{1}{2}'$ thick, irregularly divided by remote shallow fissures and separated on the surface into numerous large thin light red-brown scales. **Wood** light, soft, close-grained, pale clear yellow. The large oily seeds are an important article of food in northern Mexico, and are sold in large quantities in Mexican towns.

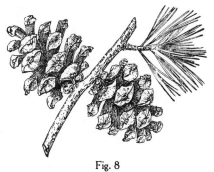

Distribution. Mountain ranges of central and southern Arizona, usually only above elevations of 6500°, often covering their upper slopes with open forests; in an isolated station on the Edwards Plateau on uplands and in cañons at the headwaters of the Frio and Nueces Rivers, Edwards and Kerr Counties, Texas; on the Sierra de Laguna, Lower California, and on many of the mountain ranges of northern Mexico; passing into the following varieties differing only in the number of the leaves in the leaf-clusters, and in their thickness.

Fig. 8

Pinus cembroides var. Parryana Voss. Nut Pine. Piñon.

Pinus quadrifolia Sudw.

Leaves in 1–5 usually 4-leaved clusters, stout, incurved, pale glaucous green, marked on the three surfaces by numerous rows of stomata, $1\frac{1}{4}'$–$1\frac{1}{2}'$ long, irregularly deciduous, mostly falling in their third year.

A tree, 30°–40° high, with a short trunk occasionally 18' in diameter, and thick spreading branches forming a compact regular pyramidal or in old age a low round-topped irregular head, and stout branchlets coated at first with soft pubescence, and light orange-brown. **Bark** $\frac{1}{2}'$–$\frac{3}{4}'$ thick, dark brown tinged with red, and divided by shallow fissures into broad flat connected ridges covered by thick closely appressed plate-like scales. **Wood** light, soft, close-grained, pale brown or yellow. The seeds form an important article of food for the Indians of Lower California.

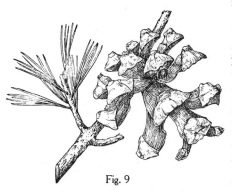

Fig. 9

Distribution. Arid mesas and low mountain slopes of Lower California southward to the foothills of the San Pedro Mártir Mountains, extending northward across the boundary of California to the desert slopes of the Santa Rosa Mountains, Riverside County, where it is common at elevations of 5000° above the sea-level.

Pinus cembroides var. edulis Voss. Nut Pine. Piñon.

Pinus edulis Engelm.

Leaves in 2 or rarely in 3-leaved clusters, stout, semiterete or triangular, rigid, incurved, dark-green, marked by numerous rows of stomata, $\frac{3}{4}'$–$1\frac{1}{2}'$ long, deciduous during the third or not until the fourth or fifth year, dropping irregularly and sometimes persistent for eight or nine years.

A tree often 40°–50° high with a tall trunk occasionally 2° in diameter and short erect branches forming a narrow head, or frequently with a short divided trunk and a low round-topped head of spreading branches, and thick branchlets orange color during their

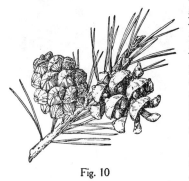

first and second years, finally becoming light gray or dark brown sometimes tinged with red. **Bark** $\frac{1}{2}'-\frac{3}{4}'$ thick and irregularly divided into connected ridges covered by small closely appressed light brown scales tinged with red or orange color. **Wood** light, soft, not strong, brittle, pale brown; largely employed for fuel and fencing, and as charcoal used in smelting; in western Texas occasionally sawed into lumber. The seeds form an important article of food among Indians and Mexicans, and are sold in the markets of Colorado and New Mexico.

Distribution. Eastern foothills of the outer ranges of the Rocky Mountains, from northern Colorado (Owl Cañon, Larimer County); to the extreme western part of Oklahoma (near Kenton, Cimmaron County, *G. W. Stevens*) and to western Texas, westward to eastern Utah, southwestern Wyoming, and to northern and central Arizona; over the mountains of northern Mexico, and on the San Pedro Mártir Mountains, Lower California; often forming extensive open forests at the eastern base of the Rocky Mountains, on the Colorado plateau, and on many mountain ranges of northern and central Arizona up to elevations of 7000° above the sea.

Fig. 10

Pinus cembroides var. monophylla Voss.   Nut Pine.   Piñon.

Pinus monophylla Torr.

Leaves in 1 or 2-leaved clusters, rigid, incurved, pale glaucous green, marked by 18–20 rows of stomata, usually about $1\frac{1}{2}'$ long, sometimes deciduous during their fourth and fifth seasons, but frequently persistent until their twelfth year.

A tree usually 15°–20°, occasionally 40°–50° high, with a short trunk rarely more than a foot in diameter and often divided near the ground into several spreading stems, short thick branches forming while the tree is young a broad rather compact pyramid, and in old age often pendulous and forming a low round-topped often picturesque head, and stout light orange-colored ultimately dark brown branchlets. **Bark** about $\frac{3}{4}'$ thick and divided by deep irregular fissures into narrow connected flat ridges broken on the surface into thin closely appressed light or dark brown scales tinged with red or orange color. **Wood** light, soft, weak, and brittle; largely used for fuel, and charcoal used in smelting. The seeds supply an important article of food to the Indians of Nevada and California.

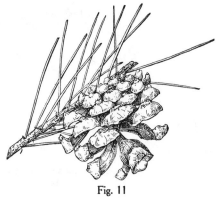

Fig. 11

Distribution. Dry gravelly slopes and mesas from the western base of the Wasatch Mountains of Utah, westward over the mountain ranges of Nevada to the eastern slopes of the southern Sierra Nevada, and to their western slope at the head-waters of the Tuolumne, Kings and Kern Rivers, and southward to northern Arizona and to the mountains of southern California where it is common on the San Bernadino and San Jacinto Mountains between altitudes of 3500° and 7000°, and on the Sierra del Pinal, Lower California; often forming extensive open forests at elevations between 5000° and 7000°.

PITCH PINES.

Wood usually heavy, coarse-grained, generally dark-colored, with pale often thick sapwood; cones green at maturity (*sometimes purple in* 10 *and* 21) becoming various shades of brown; cone-scales more or less thickened, mostly armed; seeds shorter than their wings (*except in* 17 *and* 28); leaves with 2 fibro-vascular bundles.

Sheaths of the leaf-clusters deciduous; cones $\frac{1}{2}'$–$2'$ long, maturing in the third year, leaves in 3-leaved clusters, slender, $2\frac{1}{2}'$–$4'$ long.   9. **P. leiophylla** (H).
Sheaths of the leaf-clusters persistent.
   Leaves in 3-leaved clusters (3 and 5-leaved in 10, 3–2 leaved in 12).
      Cones subterminal, usually deciduous above the basal scales persistent on the branch.
         Buds brown; leaves in 2–5-leaved clusters.   10. **P. ponderosa** (B,F,G,H).
         Buds white.   11. **P. palustris** (C).
      Cones lateral.
         Cones symmetrical, their outer scales not excessively developed.
            Leaves in 2 and 3-leaved clusters, $8'$–$12'$ long; cones short-stalked.
                                12. **P. caribaea** (C).
            Leaves in 3-leaved clusters; cones sessile.
               Cones oblong-conic, prickles stout; leaves $6'$–$9'$ long.   13. **P. taeda** (A, C).
               Cones ovoid, prickles slender; leaves $3'$–$5'$ long.   14. **P. rigida** (A, C).
         Cones unsymmetrical by the excessive development of the scales on the outer side.
            Cones $5'$–$6'$ long, their scales not prolonged into stout, straight or curved spines.
               Prickles of the cone-scales minute.   15. **P. radiata** (G).
               Prickles of the cone-scales stout.   16. **P. attenuata** (G).
            Cones $6'$–$14'$ long, their scales prolonged into stout, straight or curved spines; leaves long and stout.
            Cones oblong-ovoid; seeds longer than their wings.   17. **P. Sabiniana** (G).
            Cones oblong-conic; seeds shorter than their wings.   18. **P. Coulteri** (G).
   Leaves in 2-leaved clusters (2 and 3-leaved in 23).
      Cones subterminal.
         Cones symmetrical, $2'$–$2\frac{1}{2}'$ long, their scales unarmed; leaves $5'$–$6'$ long.
                                19. **P. resinosa** (A).
        Cones unsymmetrical by the greater development of the scales on the outer side, armed with slender prickles; leaves $1'$–$4'$ long.   20. **P. contorta** (B, F, G).
      Cones lateral.
         Cones about $2'$ long.
            Cone-scales very unevenly developed and mostly unarmed; cones incurved; leaves less than $2'$ long.   21. **P. Banksiana** (A).
            Cone-scales evenly developed, armed with weak or deciduous prickles; leaves up to $4'$ in length.
               Bark of the branches and upper trunk smooth.   22. **P. glabra** (C).
               Bark of the branches and upper trunk roughened.   23. **P. echinata** (A, C).
        Cones about $3'$ long, armed with persistent spines.
           Cone-scales armed with slender or stout prickles.
               Cone-scales evenly developed, their prickles slender, acuminate, from a broad base; leaves $3'$ long or less.
                   Cones opening at maturity.   24. **P. virginiana** (A, C).
                   Cones often remaining closed for many years.   25. **P. clausa** (C).
               Cone-scales unevenly developed and armed with stout prickles; cones $2'$–$3\frac{1}{2}'$ long, remaining closed; leaves $4'$–$6'$ long.   26. **P. muricata**.

Cone-scales armed with very stout hooked spines; cones $2\frac{1}{2}'$–$3'$ long; opening in the autumn or remaining closed for two or three years; leaves $2'$ long or less.

27. **P. pungens.**

Leaves in 5-leaved clusters; cones $4'$–$6'$ long, unsymmetrical, their scales thick; seeds longer than their wings; leaves stout, $9'$–$13'$ long.   28. **P. Torreyana** (G).

9. Pinus leiophylla Schlecht. and Cham. Yellow Pine.

Pinus chihuahuana Engelm.

Leaves slender, pale glaucous green, marked by 6–8 rows of conspicuous stomata on each of the 3 sides, $2\frac{1}{2}'$–$4'$ long, irregularly deciduous from their fourth season, their sheaths deciduous. **Flowers:** male yellow; female yellow-green. **Fruit** ovoid, horizon-

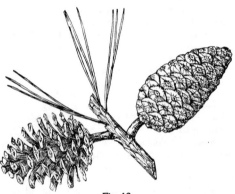

Fig. 12

tal or slightly declining, long-stalked, $1\frac{1}{2}'$–$2'$ long, becoming light chestnut-brown and lustrous, maturing at the end of the third season, with scales only slightly thickened, their ultimately pale umbos armed with recurved deciduous prickles; **seeds** oval, rounded above and pointed below, about $\frac{1}{8}'$ long, with a thin dark brown shell, their wings $\frac{1}{2}'$ long and broadest near the middle.

A tree, rarely more than 40°–50° high, with a tall trunk sometimes 2° in diameter, stout slightly ascending branches forming a narrow open pyramidal or round-topped head of thin pale foliage, and slender bright orange-brown branchlets, soon becoming dull red-brown. **Bark** of old trunks $\frac{3}{4}'$–$1\frac{1}{2}'$ thick, dark reddish brown or sometimes nearly black, and deeply divided into broad flat ridges covered with thin closely appressed scales. **Wood** light, soft, not strong but durable, light orange color, with thick much lighter colored sapwood. Often forming coppice by the growth of shoots from the stump of cut trees.

Distribution. Mountain ranges of southern New Mexico and Arizona, usually at elevations between 6000° and 7000°; not common; more abundant on the Sierra Madre of northern Mexico and on several of the short ranges of Chihuahua and Sonora, and of a larger size in Mexico than in the United States.

10. Pinus ponderosa Laws. Yellow Pine. Bull Pine.

Leaves tufted at the ends of naked branches, in 2 or in 2 and 3-leaved clusters, stout, dark yellow-green, marked by numerous rows of stomata on the 3 faces, $5'$–$11'$ long, mostly deciduous during their third season. **Flowers:** male yellow; female clustered or in pairs, dark red. **Fruit** ellipsoidal, horizontal or slightly declining, nearly sessile or short-stalked, $3'$–$6'$ long, often clustered, bright green or purple when fully grown, becoming light reddish brown, with narrow scales much thickened at the apex and armed with slender prickles, mostly falling soon after opening and discharging their seeds, generally leaving the lower scales attached to the peduncle; **seeds** ovoid, acute, compressed at the apex, full and rounded below, $\frac{1}{4}'$ long, with a thin dark purple often mottled shell, their wings usually broadest below the middle, gradually narrowed at the oblique apex, $1'$–$1\frac{1}{4}'$ long, about $1'$ wide.

A tree, sometimes 150°–230° high, with a massive stem 5°–8° in diameter, short thick many-forked often pendulous branches generally turned upward at the ends and forming

a regular spire-like head, or in arid regions a broader often round-topped head surmount-
ing a short trunk, and
stout orange-colored
branchlets frequently
becoming nearly black
at the end of two or
three years. **Bark** for
80–100 years broken
into rounded ridges
covered with small
closely appressed
scales, dark brown,
nearly black or light
cinnamon-red, on older
trees becoming 2′–4′
thick and deeply and
irregularly divided in-
to plates sometimes
4°–5° long and 12′–18′

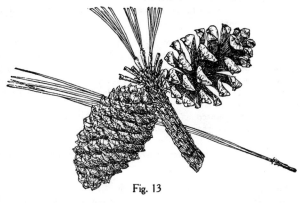

Fig. 13

wide, and separating into thick bright cinnamon-red scales. **Wood** hard, strong, comparatively fine-grained, light red, with nearly white sapwood sometimes composed of
more than 200 layers of annual growth; largely manufactured into lumber used for all
sorts of construction, for railway-ties, fencing, and fuel.

Distribution. Mountain slopes, dry valleys, and high mesas from northwestern Nebraska and western Texas to the shores of the Pacific Ocean, and from southern British
Columbia to Lower California and northern Mexico; extremely variable in different parts
of the country in size, in the length and thickness of the leaves, size of the cones, and in the
color of the bark. The form of the Rocky Mountains (var. *scopulorum*, Engelm.), ranging
from Nebraska to Texas, and over the mountain ranges of Wyoming, eastern Montana
and Colorado, and to northern New Mexico and Arizona, where it forms on the Colorado
plateau with the species the most extensive Pine forests of the continent, has nearly black
furrowed bark, rigid leaves in clusters of 2 or 3 and 3′–6′ long, and smaller cones, with thin
scales armed with slender prickles hooked backward. More distinct is

Pinus ponderosa var. Jeffreyi Vasey.

This tree forms great forests about the sources of the Pitt River in northern California,

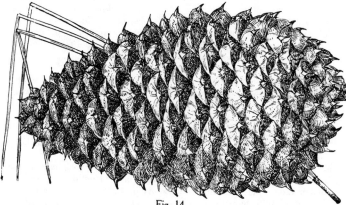

Fig. 14

along the eastern slopes of the central and southern Sierra Nevada, growing often on the most exposed and driest ridges, and in southern California on the San Bernardino and San Jacinto ranges up to elevations of 7000° above the sea, on the Cuyamaca Mountains, and in Lower California on the Sierra del Pinal and the San Pedro Mártir Mountains.

A tree, 100° to nearly 200° high, with a tall massive trunk 4°–6° in diameter, covered with bright cinnamon-red bark deeply divided into large irregular plates, stiffer and more elastic leaves 4′–9′ long and persistent on the glaucous stouter branchlets for six to nine years, yellow-green staminate flowers, short-stalked usually purple cones 5′–15′ long, their scales armed with stouter or slender prickles usually hooked backward, and seeds often nearly ½′ long with larger wings.

Occasionally planted as an ornamental tree in eastern Europe, especially the variety *Jeffreyi*, which is occasionally successfully cultivated in the eastern states.

Pinus ponderosa var. arizonica Shaw.   Yellow Pine.

Pinus arizonica Engelm.

Leaves tufted at the ends of the branches, in 3–5-leaved clusters, stout, rigid, dark green, stomatiferous on their 3 faces, 5′–7′ long, deciduous during their third season.   **Fruit** ovoid, horizontal, 2′–2½′ long, becoming light red-brown, with thin scales much thickened at the

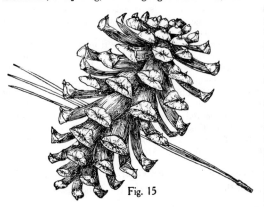

apex and armed with slender recurved spines; **seeds** full and rounded below, slightly compressed towards the apex, ⅛′ long, with a thick shell, their wings broadest above the middle, about ⅓′ long and ¼′ wide.

A tree, 80°–100° high, with a tall straight massive trunk 3°–4° in diameter, thick spreading branches forming a regular open round-topped or narrow pyramidal head, and stout branchlets orange-brown and pruinose when they first appear, becoming dark gray-brown.
Bark on young trunks dark brown or almost black and

Fig. 15

deeply furrowed, becoming on old trees 1½′–2′ thick and divided into large unequally shaped plates separating on the surface into thin closely appressed light cinnamon-red scales.   **Wood** light, soft, not strong, rather brittle, light red or often yellow, with thick lighter yellow or white sapwood; in Arizona occasionally manufactured into coarse lumber.

Distribution.   High cool slopes on the sides of cañons of the mountain ranges of southern Arizona at elevations between 6000° and 8000°, sometimes forming nearly pure forests; more abundant and of its largest size on the mountains of Sonora and Chihuahua.

11. Pinus palustris Mill.   Long-leaved Pine.   Southern Pine.

Leaves in crowded clusters, forming dense tufts at the ends of the branches, slender, flexible, pendulous, dark green, 8′–18′ long, deciduous at the end of their second year.
Flowers in very early spring before the appearance of the new leaves, male in short dense clusters, dark rose-purple; female just below the apex of the lengthening shoot in pairs or in clusters of 3 or 4, dark purple.   **Fruit** cylindric-ovoid, slightly curved, nearly sessile, horizontal or pendant, 6′–10′ long, with thin flat scales rounded at apex and armed with small

reflexed prickles, becoming dull brown; in falling leaving a few of the basal scales attached to the stem; **seeds** almost triangular, full and rounded on the sides, prominently ridged, about $\frac{1}{2}'$ long, with a thin pale shell marked with dark blotches on the upper side, and wings widest near the middle, gradually narrowed to a very oblique apex, about $1\frac{3}{4}'$ long and $\frac{7}{16}'$ wide.

A tree, 100°–120° high, with a tall straight slightly tapering trunk usually 2°–2$\frac{1}{2}$° or occasionally 3° in diameter, stout slightly branched gnarled and twisted limbs covered with thin dark scaly bark and forming an open elongated and usually very irregular head one third to one half the length of the tree, thick orange-brown branchlets, and acute winter-buds covered by elongated silvery white lustrous scales divided into long spreading filaments forming a cobweb-like network over the bud. **Bark** of the trunk $\frac{1}{6}'$–$\frac{1}{2}'$ thick, light orange-brown, separating on the surface into large closely appressed papery scales.

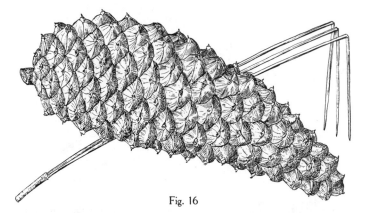

Fig. 16

Wood heavy, exceedingly hard, strong, tough, coarse-grained, durable, light red to orange color, with very thin nearly white sapwood; largely used as "southern pine" or "Georgia pine" for masts and spars, bridges, viaducts, railway-ties, fencing, flooring, the interior finish of buildings, the construction of railway-cars, and for fuel and charcoal. A large part of the naval stores of the world is produced from this tree, which is exceedingly rich in resinous secretions.

Distribution. Generally confined to a belt of late tertiary sands and gravels stretching along the coast of the Atlantic and Gulf states and rarely more than 125 miles inland, from southeastern Virginia to the shores of Indian River and the valley of the Caloosahatchee River, Florida, and along the Gulf coast to the uplands east of the Mississippi River, extending northward in Alabama to the southern foothills of the Appalachian Mountains and to central and western Mississippi (Hinds and Adams Counties) ranging inland in Georgia to the neighborhood of Cartersville and Rome, and ascending to altitudes of 1900 feet on the Blue Ridge in Alabama; and west of the Mississippi River to the valley of the Trinity River, Texas, and through eastern Texas and western Louisiana nearly to the northern borders of this state.

12. Pinus caribæa Morelet. Slash Pine. Swamp Pine.

Pinus Elliottii Engelm. *Pinus heterophylla* Sudw.

Leaves stout, in crowded 2 and 3-leaved clusters, dark green and lustrous, marked by numerous bands of stomata on each face, 8′–12′ long, deciduous at the end of their second season. **Flowers** in January and February before the appearance of the new leaves, male in short crowded clusters, dark purple; female lateral on long peduncles, pink. **Fruit** ovoid or ovoid-conic, reflexed during its first year, pendant, 2'–6' long, with thin flexible flat scales armed with minute incurved or recurved prickles, becoming dark rich lustrous brown; seeds almost triangular, full and rounded on the sides, $1\frac{1}{8}'$–$1\frac{1}{4}'$ long, with a thin brittle dark gray shell mottled with black, and dark brown wings $\frac{3}{4}'$–1' long, $\frac{1}{4}'$ wide, their thickened bases encircling the seeds and often covering a large part of their lower surface.

A tree, often 100° high, with a tall tapering trunk $2\frac{1}{2}°$–3° in diameter, heavy horizontal branches forming a handsome round-topped head, and stout orange-colored ultimately dark branchlets. **Bark** $\frac{3}{4}'$–$1\frac{1}{2}'$ thick, and separating freely on the surface into large thin scales. **Wood** heavy, exceedingly hard, very strong, durable, coarse-grained, rich dark orange color, with thick nearly white sapwood; manufactured into lumber and used for construction and railway-ties. Naval stores are largely produced from this tree.

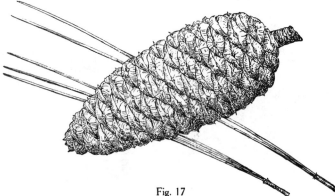

Fig. 17

Distribution. Coast region of South Carolina southward over the coast plain to the keys of southern Florida and along the Gulf coast to eastern Louisiana (Saint Tammany, Washington, southern Tangipahoa and eastern Livingston Parishes); common on the Bahamas, on the Isle of Pines, and on the lowlands of Honduras and eastern Guatemala; in the coast region of the southern states gradually replacing the Long-leaved Pine, *Pinus palustris*, Mill.

13. Pinus tæda L. Loblolly Pine. Old Field Pine.

Leaves slender, stiff, slightly twisted, pale green and somewhat glaucous, 6'–9' long, marked by 10–12 rows of large stomata on each face, deciduous during their third year. **Flowers** opening from the middle of March to the first of May; male crowded in short spikes, yellow; female lateral below the apex of the growing shoot, solitary or clustered, short-stalked, yellow. **Fruit** oblong-conic to ovoid-cylindric, nearly sessile, 2'–6' long, becoming light reddish brown, with thin scales rounded at the apex and armed with short stout straight or reflexed prickles, opening irregularly and discharging their seeds during the autumn and winter, and usually persistent on the branches for another year; **seeds** rhomboidal, full and rounded, $\frac{1}{4}'$ long, with a thin dark brown rough shell blotched with black, and produced into broad thin lateral margins, encircled to the base by the narrow border of their thin pale brown lustrous wing broadest above the middle, 1' long, about $\frac{1}{4}'$ wide.

A tree, generally 80°–100° high, with a tall straight trunk usually about 2° but occasionally 5° in diameter, short thick much divided branches, the lower spreading, the upper ascending and forming a compact round-topped head, and comparatively slender glabrous branchlets brown tinged with yellow during their first season and gradually growing darker in their second year. **Bark of the trunk** $\frac{3}{4}$–$1\frac{1}{2}'$ thick, bright red-brown, and irregularly divided by shallow fissures into broad flat ridges covered with large thin closely appressed scales. **Wood** weak, brittle, coarse-grained, not durable, light brown, with orange-colored or often nearly white sapwood, often composing nearly half the trunk; largely manufactured into lumber, used for construction and the interior finish of buildings.

Distribution. Cape May, New Jersey through southern Delaware and eastern Maryland and southward to near Palatka, Putnam County, in eastern Florida, and in western Florida to the neighborhood of San Antonio, Pasco Coun-

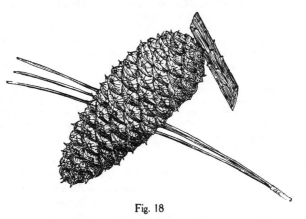

Fig. 18

ty, westward to middle North Carolina and through South Carolina and Georgia and the eastern Gulf states to the Mississippi River, extending into southern Tennessee and northeastern Mississippi; in Georgia and Alabama sometimes ascending to altitudes of 1500 feet; west of the Mississippi River from southern Arkansas and the southwestern part of Oklahoma through western Louisiana to the shores of the Gulf of Mexico, and through eastern Texas to the valley of the Colorado River; on the Atlantic coast often springing up on lands exhausted by agriculture; west of the Mississippi River one of the most important timber-trees, frequently growing in nearly pure forests on rolling uplands.

14. Pinus rigida Mill. Pitch Pine.

Leaves stout, rigid, dark yellow-green, marked on the 3 faces by many rows of stomata, $3'$–$5'$ long, standing stiffly and at right angles with the branch, deciduous during their

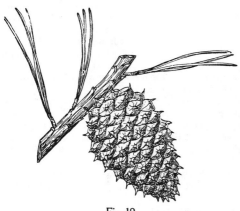

Fig. 19

second year. **Flowers:** male in short crowded spikes, yellow or rarely purple; female often clustered and raised on short stout stems, light green more or less tinged with rose color. **Fruit** ovoid, acute at apex, nearly sessile, often clustered, $1'$–$3\frac{1}{2}'$ long, becoming light brown, with thin flat scales armed with recurved rigid prickles, often remaining on the branches for ten or twelve years; **seeds** nearly triangular, full and rounded on the sides, $\frac{1}{4}'$ long, with a thin dark brown mottled roughened shell and wings broadest below the middle, gradually narrowed to the very oblique apex, $\frac{3}{4}'$ long, $\frac{1}{3}'$ wide.

A tree, $50°$–$60°$ or rarely $100°$ high, with a short trunk occasionally 3° in diameter, thick contorted often pendulous branches covered with thick much roughened bark, forming a round-topped thick head, often irregular and picturesque, and stout bright green branchlets becoming dull orange color during their first winter and dark gray-brown at the end of four or five years; often fruitful when only a few feet high. **Bark** of young stems thin and broken into plate-like dark red-brown scales, becoming on old trunks $\frac{3}{4}'$–$1\frac{1}{2}'$ thick, deeply and irregularly fissured, and divided into broad flat connected ridges separating on the surface into thick dark red-brown scales often tinged with purple. **Wood** light, soft, not strong, brittle, coarse-grained, very durable, light brown or red, with thick yellow or often white sap-wood; largely used for fuel and in the manufacture of charcoal; occasionally sawed into lumber.

Distribution. Sandy plains and dry gravelly uplands, or less frequently in cold deep swamps; island of Mt. Desert, Maine, to the northern shores of Lake Ontario, and southward to southern Delaware and southern Ohio (Scioto County) and along the Appalachian Mountains to northern Georgia and to their western foothills in West Virginia, Kentucky, and Tennessee; very abundant in the coast region south of Massachusetts; sometimes forming pure forests in New Jersey and Pennsylvania.

Pinus rigida var. serotina Loud.   Pond Pine.   Marsh Pine.

Pinus serotina Michx.

Leaves in clusters of 3 or occasionally of 4, slender, flexuose, dark yellow-green, 6'–8' long, marked by numerous rows of stomata on the 3 faces, deciduous during their third and

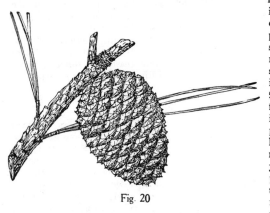

fourth years. **Flowers:** male in crowded spikes, dark orange color; female clustered or in pairs on stout stems. **Fruit** subglobose to ovoid, full and rounded or pointed at apex, subsessile or short-stalked, horizontal or slightly declining, 2–2$\frac{1}{2}'$ long, with thin nearly flat scales armed with slender incurved mostly deciduous prickles, becoming light yellow-brown at maturity, often remaining closed for one or two years and after opening long-persistent on the branches; **seeds** nearly triangular, often ridged below, full and rounded at the sides, $\frac{1}{8}'$ long, with a

Fig. 20

thin nearly black roughened shell produced into a wide border, the wings broadest at the middle, gradually narrowed at the ends, $\frac{3}{4}'$ long, $\frac{1}{4}'$ wide.

A tree, usually 40°–50° or occasionally 70°–80' high, with a short trunk sometimes 3° but generally not more than 2° in diameter, stout often contorted branches more or less pendulous at the extremities, forming an open round-topped head, and slender branchlets dark green when they first appear, becoming dark orange color during their first winter and dark brown or often nearly black at the end of four or five years. **Bark** of the trunk $\frac{1}{2}'$–$\frac{3}{4}'$ thick, dark red-brown and irregularly divided by narrow shallow fissures into small plates separating on the surface into thin closely appressed scales. **Wood** very resinous, heavy, soft, brittle, coarse-grained, dark orange color, with thick pale yellow sapwood; occasionally manufactured into lumber.

Distribution. Low wet flats or sandy or peaty swamps; near Cape May, New Jersey, and southeastern Virginia southward near the coast to northern Florida (near Kissimmee, Osceola County) and central Alabama.

15. Pinus radiata D. Don. Monterey Pine.

Leaves in 3, rarely in 2-leaved clusters, slender, bright rich green, 4'–6' long, mostly deciduous during their third season. **Flowers:** male in dense spikes, yellow; female clustered, dark purple. **Fruit** ovoid, pointed at apex, very oblique at base, short-stalked, reflexed, 3'–7' long, becoming deep chestnut-brown and lustrous, with scales much thickened and mammillate toward the base on the outer side of the cone, thinner on the inner side and at its apex, and armed with minute thickened incurved or straight prickles, long-persistent and often remaining closed on the branches for many years; **seeds** ellipsoidal, compressed, ¼' long, with a thin brittle rough nearly black shell, their wings light brown, longitudinally striped, broadest above the middle, gradually narrowed and oblique at apex, 1' long, ¼' wide.

A tree, usually 40°–60° rarely 100°–115° high, with a tall trunk usually 1°–2° but occasionally 4½° in diameter, spreading branches forming a regular narrow open round-topped head, and slender branchlets light or dark orange color, at first often covered with a glaucous bloom, ultimately dark red-brown. **Bark** of the trunk 1½'–2' thick, dark red-brown, and deeply divided into broad flat ridges broken on the surface into thick appressed plate-like scales. **Wood** light, soft, not strong, brittle, close-grained; occasionally used as fuel.

Distribution. In a narrow belt a few miles wide on the California coast from Pescadero to the shores of San Simeon Bay; in San Luis Obispo County near the village of Cambria; on

Fig. 21

the islands of Santa Rosa and Santa Cruz of the Santa Barbara group; and on Guadaloupe Island off the coast of Lower California; most abundant and of its largest size on Point Pinos south of the Bay of Monterey, California.

Largely planted for the decoration of parks in western and southern Europe, occasionally planted in the southeastern states and in Mexico, Australia, New Zealand, and other regions with temperate climates, and more generally in the coast region of the Pacific states from Vancouver Island southward than any other Pine-tree.

16. Pinus attenuata Lemm. Knob-cone Pine.

Leaves slender, firm and rigid, pale yellow or bluish green, marked by numerous rows of stomata on their 3 faces, 3'–7', usually 4'–5' long. **Flowers:** male orange-brown; female fascicled, often with several fascicles on the shoot of the year. **Fruit** elongated, conic, pointed, very oblique at base by the greater development of the scales on the outer side, whorled, short-stalked, strongly reflexed and incurved, 3'–6' long, becoming light yellow-brown, with thin flat scales rounded at apex, those on the outer side being enlarged into prominent transversely flattened knobs armed with thick flattened incurved spines, those on the inner side of the cone slightly thickened and armed with minute recurved prickles, persistent on the stems and branches for thirty or forty years, sometimes becoming completely imbedded in the bark of old trunks, and usually not opening until the death of the tree; **seeds** ellipsoidal, compressed, acute at apex, ¼' long, with a thin oblique shell, their wings broadest at the middle, gradually narrowed to the ends, 1¼' long, ⅓' wide.

A tree, usually about 20° high, with a trunk a foot in diameter, and often fruitful when only 4° or 5° tall; occasionally growing to the height of 80°–100°, with a trunk 2½° thick, and frequently divided above the middle into two ascending stems, slender branches ar-

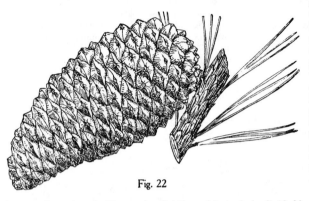

ranged in regular whorls while the tree is young, and in old age forming a narrow round-topped strag- gling head of sparse thin foliage, and slender dark orange- brown branchlets growing darker dur- ing their second sea- son. **Bark** of young stems and branches thin, smooth, pale brown, becoming at the base of old trunks ¼′–½′ thick and dark

Fig. 22

brown often tinged with purple, slightly and irregularly divided by shallow fissures and broken into large loose scales. **Wood** light, soft, not strong, brittle, coarse-grained, light brown, with thick sapwood sometimes slightly tinged with red.

Distribution. Dry mountain slopes from the valley of the Mackenzie River in Oregon over the mountains of southwestern Oregon, where it is most abundant and grows to its largest size, often forming pure forests over large areas, southward along the western slopes of the Cascade Mountains; in California on the northern cross ranges, the coast ranges from Trinity to Sonoma Counties, the western slopes of the Sierra Nevada to Mariposa County, and over the southern coast ranges from Santa Cruz to the dry arid southern slopes of the San Bernardino Mountains, where it forms a belt between City and East Twin Creeks at an altitude of 3500° above the sea.

17. Pinus Sabiniana Dougl. Digger Pine. Bull Pine.

Leaves stout, flexible, pendant, pale blue-green, marked on each face with numerous

rows of pale stomata, 8′–12′ long, deciduous usually in their third and fourth years. **Flow- ers:** male yellow; fe- male on stout pedun- cles, dark purple. **Fruit** oblong-ovoid, full and rounded at base, point- ed, becoming light red- dish brown, 6′–10′ long, long-stalked, pendu- lous, the scales nar- rowed into a stout in- curved sharp hook, strongly reflexed to- ward the base of the cone and armed with spur-like incurved

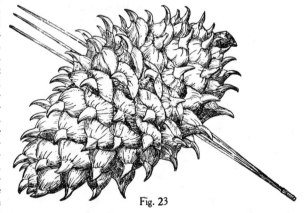

Fig. 23

spines; **seeds** full and rounded below, somewhat compressed toward the apex, ¾′ long, ⅓′ wide, dark brown or nearly black, with a thick hard shell, encircled by their wings much thickened on the inner rim, obliquely rounded at the broad apex and about ½ length of nuts.

A tree, usually 40°–50° but occasionally 80° high, with a trunk 3°–4° in diameter, divided generally 15°–20° above the ground into 3 or 4 thick secondary stems, clothed with short crooked branches pendant below and ascending toward the summit of the tree, and forming an open round-topped head remarkable for the sparseness of its foliage, and stout pale glaucous branchlets, becoming dark brown or nearly black during their second season. **Bark** of the·trunk 1½′–2′ thick, dark brown slightly tinged with red or nearly black and deeply and irregularly divided into thick connected ridges covered with small closely appressed scales. **Wood** light, soft, not strong, close-grained, brittle, light brown or red with thick nearly white sapwood. Abietine, a nearly colorless aromatic liquid with the odor of oil of oranges, is obtained by distilling the resinous juices. The large sweet slightly resinous seeds formed an important article of food for the Indians of California.

Distribution. Scattered singly or in small groups over the dry foothills of western California, ranging from 500° up to 4000° above the sea-level and from the southern slopes of the northern cross ranges to the Tehachapi Mountains and the Sierra de la Liebre; most abundant and attaining its largest size on the eastern foothills of the Sierra Nevada near the centre of the state at elevations of about 2000°; here often the most conspicuous feature of the vegetation.

18. Pinus Coulteri D. Don. Pitch Pine.

Leaves tufted at the ends of the branches, stout, rigid, dark blue-green, marked by numerous bands of stomata on the 3 faces, 6′–12′ long, deciduous during their third and

Fig. 24

fourth seasons. **Flowers:** male yellow; female dark reddish brown. **Fruit** oblong-conic, short-stalked and pendant, 10′–14′ long, becoming light yellow-brown, with thick broad scales terminating in a broad, flat, incurved, hooked claw ½′–1½′ long, gradually opening in the autumn and often persistent on the branches for several years; seeds ellipsoidal, compressed, ½′ long, ¼′–⅓′ wide, dark chestnut-brown, with a thick shell, inclosed by their wings, broadest above the middle, oblique at apex, nearly 1′ longer than the seed, about ⅝′ wide.

A tree, 40°–90° high, with a trunk 1°–2½° in diameter, thick branches covered with dark scaly bark, long and mostly pendulous below, short and ascending above, and forming a loose unsymmetrical often picturesque head, and very stout branchlets dark orange-brown at first, becoming sometimes nearly black at the end of three or four years. **Bark** of the

trunk 1½'–2' thick, dark brown or nearly black and deeply divided into broad rounded connected ridges covered with thin closely appressed scales. **Wood** light, soft, not strong, brittle, coarse-grained, light red, with thick nearly white sapwood; occasionally used for fuel. The seeds were formerly gathered in large quantities and eaten by the Indians of southern California.

Distribution. Scattered singly or in small groves through coniferous forests on the dry slopes and ridges of the coast ranges of California at elevations of 3000°–6000° above the sea, from Mount Diablo and the Santa Lucia Mountains to the San Bernardino and Cuyamaca Mountains; and on the Sierra del Pinal, Lower California; most abundant on the San Bernardino and San Jacinto ranges at elevations of about 5000°.

19. Pinus resinosa Ait. Red Pine. Norway Pine.

Leaves slender, soft and flexible, dark green and lustrous, 5'–6' long, obscurely marked on the ventral faces by bands of minute stomata, deciduous during their fourth and fifth seasons. **Flowers:** male in dense spikes, dark purple; female terminal, short-stalked, scarlet. **Fruit** ovoid-conic, subsessile, 2'–2¼' long, with thin slightly concave scales, un-

Fig. 25

armed, becoming light chestnut-brown and lustrous at maturity; shedding their seeds early in the autumn and mostly persistent on the branches until the following summer; **seeds** oval, compressed, ⅛' long, with a thin dark chestnut-brown more or less mottled shell and wings broadest below the middle, oblique at apex, ¾' long, ¼–⅓' broad.

A tree, usually 70°–80° or occasionally 120° high, with a tall straight trunk 2°–3° or rarely 5° in diameter, thick spreading more or less pendulous branches clothing the young stems to the ground and forming a broad irregular pyramid, and in old age an open round-topped picturesque head, and stout branchlets at first orange color, finally becoming light reddish brown. **Bark** of the trunk ¾'–1¼' thick and slightly divided by shallow fissures into broad flat ridges covered by thin loose light red-brown scales. **Wood** light, hard, very close-grained, pale red, with thin yellow often nearly white sapwood; largely used in the construction of bridges and buildings, for piles, masts, and spars. The bark is occasionally used for tanning leather.

Distribution. Light sandy loam or dry rocky ridges, usually forming groves rarely more than a few hundred acres in extent and scattered through forests of other Pines and deciduous-leaved trees; occasionally on sandy flats forming pure forests; Nova Scotia to Lake St. John, westward through Quebec and central Ontario to the valley of the Winnipeg River, and southward to eastern Massachusetts, the mountains of northern Pennsylvania, and to central and southwestern (Port Huron) Michigan, Wisconsin, and Minnesota, most abundant, and growing to its largest size in the northern parts of these states; rare and local in eastern Massachusetts and southward.

Often planted for the decoration of parks, and the most desirable as an ornamental tree of the Pitch Pines which flourish in the northern states.

20. Pinus contorta Loud. Scrub Pine.

Leaves dark green, slender, $1'-1\frac{1}{2}'$ long, marked by 6–10 rows of stomata on each face, mostly persistent 4–6 years. **Flowers** orange-red: male in short crowded spikes; female clustered or in pairs on stout stalks. **Fruit** ovoid to subcylindric, usually very oblique at base, horizontal or declining, often clustered, $\frac{3}{4}'-2'$ long, with thin slightly concave scales armed with long slender more or less recurved often deciduous prickles, and toward the base of the cone especially on the upper side developed into thick mammillate knobs, becoming light yellow-brown and lustrous, sometimes opening and losing their seeds as soon as ripe, or remaining closed on the branches and preserving the vitality of their seeds for many years; **seeds** oblique at apex, acute below, about $\frac{1}{8}'$ long, with a thin brittle dark red-brown shell mottled with black and wings widest above the base, gradually tapering toward the oblique apex, $\frac{1}{2}'$ long.

A tree, sometimes fertile when only a few inches high, usually 15°–20° or occasionally 30° tall, with a short trunk rarely more than 18′ in diameter, comparatively thick branches forming a round-topped compact and symmetrical or an open picturesque head, and stout branchlets light orange color when they first appear, finally becoming dark red-brown or occasionally almost black. **Bark** of the trunk $\frac{3}{4}'-1'$ thick, deeply and irregularly divided by vertical and cross fissures into small oblong plates covered with closely appressed dark red-brown scales tinged with purple or orange color. **Wood**

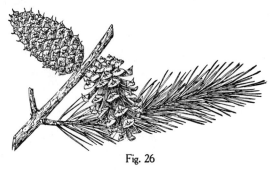

Fig. 26

light, hard, strong although brittle, coarse-grained, light brown tinged with red, with thick nearly white sapwood; occasionally used for fuel.

Distribution. Coast of Alaska, usually in sphagnum-covered bogs southward in the immediate neighborhood of the coast to the valley of the Albion River, Mendocino County, California; south of the northern boundary of the United States generally inhabiting sand dunes and barrens or occasionally near the shores of Puget Sound the margins of tide pools and deep wet swamps; spreading inland and ascending the coast ranges and western slopes of the Cascade Mountains, where it is not common and where it gradually changes its habit and appearance, the thick deeply furrowed bark of the coast form being found only near the ground, while the bark higher on the stems is thin, light-colored, and inclined to separate into scales, and the leaves are often longer and broader. This is

Pinus contorta var. latifolia S. Wats. Lodge-pole Pine.
Pinus contorta var. *Murrayana* Engelm.

Leaves yellow-green, usually about 2′ long, although varying from 1′–3′ in length and from $\frac{1}{16}'$ to nearly $\frac{1}{8}'$ in width. **Fruit** occasionally opening as soon as ripe but usually remaining closed and preserving the vitality of the seeds sometimes for twenty years.

A tree, usually 70°–80° but often 150° high, with a trunk generally 2°–3° but occasionally 5°–6° in diameter, slender much-forked branches frequently persistent nearly to the base of the stem, light orange-colored during their early years, somewhat pendulous below, ascending near the top of the tree, and forming a narrow pyramidal spire-topped head.

Bark of the trunk rarely more than $\frac{1}{4}'$ thick, close and firm, light orange-brown and covered by small thin loosely appressed scales. **Wood** light, soft, not strong, close, straight-grained and easily worked, not durable, light yellow or nearly white, with thin lighter colored sap-

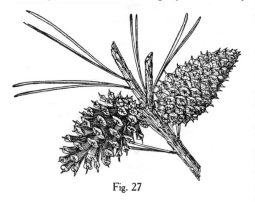

Fig. 27

wood; occasionally manufactured into lumber; also used for railway-ties, mine-timbers, and for fuel.

Distribution. Common on the Yukon hills in the valley of the Yukon River; on the interior plateau of northern British Columbia and eastward to the eastern foot-hills of the Rocky Mountains, covering with dense forests great areas in the basin of the Columbia River; forming forests on both slopes of the Rocky Mountains of Montana; on the Yellowstone plateau at elevations of 7000°–8000°; common on the mountains of Wyoming, and extending southward

to southern Colorado; the most abundant coniferous tree of the northern Rocky Mountain region; common on the ranges of eastern Washington and Oregon, on the mountains of northern California, and southward along the Sierra Nevada, where it attains its greatest size and beauty in alpine forests at elevations between 8000° and 9500°; in southern California the principal tree at elevations between 7000° and 10,000° on the high peaks of the San Bernardino and San Jacinto Mountains; on the upper slopes of the San Pedro Mártir Mountains, Lower California.

21. Pinus Banksiana Lamb. Gray Pine. Jack Pine.
Pinus divaricata Du Mont de Cours.

Leaves in remote clusters, stout, flat or slightly concave on the inner face, at first light yellow-green, soon becoming dark green, $\frac{3}{4}'$–$1\frac{1}{4}'$ long, gradually and irregularly deciduous in their second or third year. **Flowers:** male in short crowded clusters, yellow; female

Fig. 28

clustered, dark purple, often with 2 clusters produced on the same shoot. **Fruit** oblong-conic, acute, oblique at base, sessile, usually erect and strongly incurved, $1\frac{1}{2}'$–$2'$ long, dull purple or green when fully grown, becoming light yellow and lustrous, with thin stiff scales often irregularly developed, and armed with minute incurved often deciduous prickles; **seeds** nearly triangular, full and rounded on the sides, $\frac{1}{12}'$ long, with an almost black roughened shell and wings broadest at the middle, full and rounded at apex, $\frac{1}{2}'$ long, $\frac{1}{4}'$ wide.

A tree, frequently 70° high, with a straight trunk sometimes free of branches for 20°–30° and rarely exceeding 2° in diameter, long spreading branches forming an open symmetrical head, and slender tough flexible pale yellow-green branchlets turning dark purple during their first winter and darker the following year; often not more than 20°–30° tall, with a stem 10′–12′ in diameter; generally fruiting when only a few years old; sometimes shrubby with several low slender stems. **Bark** of the trunk thin, dark brown slightly tinged with red, very irregularly divided into narrow rounded connected ridges separating on the surface into small thick closely appressed scales. **Wood** light, soft, not strong, close-grained, clear pale brown or rarely orange color, with thick nearly white sapwood; used for fuel and occasionally for railway-ties and posts; occasionally manufactured into lumber.

Distribution. From Nova Scotia to the valley of the Athabasca River and down the Mackenzie to about latitude 65° north, ranging southward to the coast of Maine, northern New Hampshire and Vermont, the Island of Nantucket (Wauwinet, *J. W. Harshberger*), northern New York, the shores of Saginaw Bay, Michigan, the southern shores of Lake Michigan in Illinois, the valley of the Wisconsin River, Wisconsin, and central and southeastern Minnesota (with isolated groves in Root River valley, near Rushford, Fillmore County); abundant in central Michigan, covering tracts of barren lands; common and of large size in the region north of Lake Superior; most abundant and of its greatest size west of Lake Winnipeg and north of the Saskatchewan, here often spreading over great areas of sandy sterile soil.

22. Pinus glabra Walt. Spruce Pine. Cedar Pine.

Leaves soft, slender, dark green, $1\frac{1}{2}'$–3′ long, marked by numerous rows of stomata, deciduous at the end of their second and in the spring of their third year. **Flowers:** male in short crowded clusters, yellow; female raised on slender slightly ascending peduncles. **Fruit** single or in clusters of 2 or 3, reflexed on short stout stalks, subglobose to oblong-ovoid, $\frac{1}{2}'$–2′ long, becoming reddish brown and rather lustrous, with thin slightly concave scales armed with minute straight or incurved usually deciduous prickles; **seeds** nearly triangular, full and rounded on the sides, $\frac{1}{8}'$ long, with a thin dark gray shell mottled with black and wings broadest below the middle, $\frac{5}{8}'$ long, $\frac{1}{4}'$ wide.

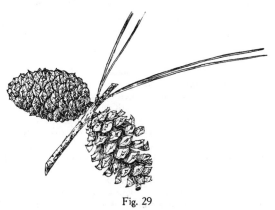

Fig. 29

A tree, usually 80°–100° or occasionally 120° high, with a trunk 2°–2$\frac{1}{2}$° or rarely 3$\frac{1}{2}$° in diameter, comparatively small horizontal branches, and slender flexible branchlets at first light red more or less tinged with purple, ultimately dark reddish brown. **Bark** of young trees and upper trunks smooth pale gray becoming on old stems $\frac{1}{2}'$–$\frac{3}{4}'$ thick, slightly and irregularly divided by shallow fissures into flat connected ridges. **Wood** light, soft, not strong, brittle, close-grained, light brown, with thick nearly white sapwood; occasionally used for fuel and rarely manufactured into lumber.

Distribution. Valley of the lower Santee River, South Carolina to middle and north-western Florida; banks of the Alabama River, Dallas County, Alabama; east central Mississippi, and sandy banks of streams in southeastern Louisiana; usually growing singly or in small groves; attaining its largest size and often occupying areas of considerable extent in northwestern Florida.

23. Pinus echinata Mill. Yellow Pine. Short-leaved Pine.

Leaves in clusters of 2 and of 3, slender, flexible, dark blue-green, 3'–5' long, beginning to fall at the end of their second season and dropping irregularly until their fifth year. **Flowers:** male in short crowded clusters, pale purple; female in clusters of 2 or 3 on stout ascending stems, pale rose color. **Fruit** ovoid to oblong-conic, subsessile and nearly horizontal or short-stalked and pendant, generally clustered, $1\frac{1}{2}'$–$2\frac{1}{2}'$ long, becoming dull brown, with thin scales nearly flat below and rounded at the apex, armed with short straight or somewhat recurved frequently deciduous prickles; **seeds** nearly triangular, full and rounded on the sides, about $\frac{3}{16}'$ long, with a thin pale brown hard shell conspicuously mottled with black, their wings broadest near the middle, $\frac{1}{2}'$ long, $\frac{1}{8}'$ wide.

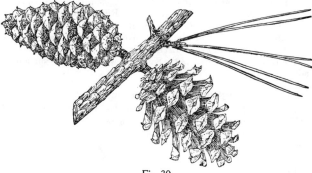

Fig. 30

A tree, usually 80°–100° occasionally 120° high, with a tall slightly tapering trunk 3°–4° in diameter, a short pyramidal truncate head of comparatively slender branches, and stout brittle pale green or violet-colored branchlets covered at first with a glaucous bloom, becoming dark red-brown tinged with purple before the end of the first season, their bark beginning in the third year to separate into large scales. **Bark** of the trunk $\frac{3}{4}'$–1' thick and broken into large irregularly shaped plates covered with small closely appressed light cinnamon-red scales. **Wood** very variable in quality, and in the thickness of the nearly white sapwood, heavy, hard, strong and usually coarse-grained, orange-colored or yellow-brown; largely manufactured into lumber.

Distribution. Long Island (near Northport), and Staten Island, New York, and southern Pennsylvania to northern Florida, and westward through the Gulf states to eastern Texas, through Arkansas to southwestern Oklahoma (near Page, Leflore County, *G. W. Stevens*) and to southern Missouri and southwestern Illinois and to eastern Tennessee and western West Virginia; most abundant and of its largest size west of the Mississippi River.

24. Pinus virginiana Mill. Jersey Pine. Scrub Pine.

Leaves in remote clusters, stout, gray-green, $1\frac{1}{2}'$–3' long, marked by many rows of minute stomata, gradually and irregularly deciduous during their third and fourth years. **Flowers:** male in crowded clusters, orange-brown; female on opposite spreading peduncles near the middle of the shoots of the year, generally a little below and alternate with 1 or 2 lateral branchlets, pale green, 2′–3′ long, the scale-tips tinged with rose color. **Fruit** ovoid-conic, often reflexed, dark red-brown and lustrous, with thin nearly flat scales, and stout or slender persistent prickles, opening in the autumn and slowly shedding their seeds, turning dark reddish brown and remaining on the branches for three or four years; **seeds** nearly oval, full and rounded, ¼′ long, with a thin pale brown rough shell, their wings broadest at the middle, ⅓′ long, about ⅛′ wide.

A tree, usually 30°–40° high, with a short trunk rarely more than 18′ in diameter, long horizontal or pendulous branches in remote whorls forming a broad open often flat-topped pyramid, and slender tough flexible branchlets at first pale green or green tinged with purple and covered with a glaucous bloom, becoming purple and later light gray-brown; toward the western limits of its range a tree frequently 100° tall, with a trunk 2½°–3° in

Fig. 31

diameter. **Bark** of the trunk ¼′–½′ thick, broken by shallow fissures into flat plate-like scales separating on the surface into thin closely appressed dark brown scales tinged with red. **Wood** light, soft, not strong, brittle, coarse-grained, durable in contact with the soil, light orange color, with thick nearly white sapwood; often used for fuel and occasionally manufactured into lumber.

Distribution. Middle and southern New Jersey west of the pine barren region; Plymouth, Luzerne County, and central, southern and western Pennsylvania to Columbia County, Georgia, Dallas County, Alabama (near Selma, *T. G. Harbison*), and to the hills of northeastern Mississippi (Bear Creek near its junction with the Tennessee River, *E. N. Lowe*), through eastern and middle Tennessee to western Kentucky and to southeastern and southern (Scioto County) Ohio, and southern Indiana; usually small in the Atlantic states and only on light sandy soil, spreading rapidly over exhausted fields; of its largest size west of the Alleghany Mountains on the low hills of southern Indiana.

25. Pinus clausa Sarg. Sand Pine. Spruce Pine.

Leaves slender, flexible, dark green, 2′–3½′ long, marked by 10–20 rows of stomata, deciduous during their third and fourth years. **Flowers:** male in short crowded spikes, dark orange color; female lateral on stout peduncles. **Fruit** elongated ovoid-conic, often oblique at base, usually clustered and reflexed, 2′–3½′ long, nearly sessile or short-stalked, with convex scales armed with short stout straight or recurved prickles, becoming dark yellow-brown in autumn; some of the cones opening at once, others remaining closed for three or four years before liberating their seeds, ultimately turning to an ashy gray color; others still unopened becoming enveloped in the growing tissues of the stem and branches and finally entirely covered by them; **seeds** nearly triangular, compressed, ¼′ long, with a black slightly roughened shell, their wings widest near or below the middle, $\frac{3}{4}'$ long, about $\frac{1}{4}'$ wide.

A tree, usually 15°–20° high, with a stem rarely a foot in diameter, generally clothed to the ground with wide-spreading branches forming a bushy flat-topped head, and slender

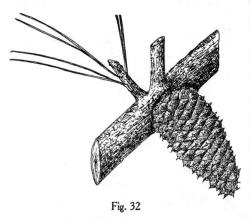

tough flexible branchlets, pale yellow-green when they first appear, becoming light orange-brown and ultimately ashy gray; occasionally growing to the height of 70°–80° with a trunk 2° in diameter. **Bark** on the lower part of the trunk $\frac{1}{3}'-\frac{1}{2}'$ thick, deeply divided by narrow fissures into irregularly shaped generally oblong plates separating on the surface into thin closely appressed bright red-brown scales; on the upper part of the trunk and on the branches thin, smooth, ashy gray. **Wood** light, soft, not strong, brittle, light orange color or yellow, with thick nearly white sapwood; occasionally used for the masts of small vessels.

Fig. 32

Distribution. Coast of the Gulf of Mexico from southern Alabama to Peace River, western Florida; eastern Florida from the neighborhood of St. Augustine to New River, Dade County, covering sandy wind-swept plains near the coast; growing to its largest size and most abundant in the interior of the peninsula (Lake and Orange Counties).

26. Pinus muricata D. Don.   Prickle-cone Pine.

Leaves in crowded clusters, thick, rigid, dark yellow-green, 4′–6′ long, beginning to fall in their second year. **Flowers:** male in elongated spikes, orange-colored; female short-

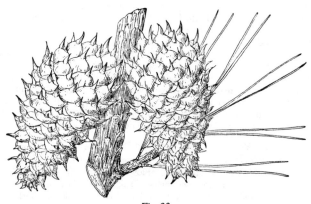

Fig. 33

stalked, whorled, 2 whorls often being produced on the shoot of the year. **Fruit** ovoid, oblique at base, sessile, in clusters of 3–5 or sometimes of 7, 2′–3½′ but usually about 3′ long, becoming light chestnut-brown and lustrous, with scales much thickened on the outside of the cone, those toward its base produced into stout incurved knobs sometimes armed with stout flattened spur-like often incurved spines, and on the inside of the cone slightly flattened and armed with stout or slender straight prickles; often remaining closed for several years and usually persistent on the stem and branches during the entire life of the tree without becoming imbedded, in the wood; seeds nearly triangular, $\frac{1}{4}'$ long, with a thin nearly black roughened shell, their wings broadest above the middle, oblique at apex, nearly 1' long, $\frac{1}{8}'$ wide.

A tree, usually 40°–50° but occasionally 90° high, with a trunk 2°–3° in diameter, thick spreading branches covered with dark scaly bark, in youth forming a regular pyramid, and at maturity a handsome compact round-topped head of dense tufted foliage, and stout branchlets dark orange-green at first, turning orange-brown more or less tinged with purple. Bark of the lower part of the trunk often 4'–6' thick and deeply divided into long narrow rounded ridges roughened by closely appressed dark purplish brown scales. Wood light, very strong, hard, rather coarse-grained, light brown, with thick nearly white sapwood; occasionally manufactured into lumber.

Distribution. California coast region from Mendocino County southward, usually in widely separated localities to Point Reyes Peninsula, north of the Bay of San Francisco, and from Monterey to Coon Creek, San Luis Obispo County; in Lower California on Cedros Island and on the west coast between Ensenada and San Quentin; of its largest size and the common Pine-tree on the coast of Mendocino County.

27. Pinus pungens Lamb. Table Mountain Pine. Hickory Pine.

Leaves in crowded clusters, rigid, usually twisted, dark blue-green, $1\frac{1}{4}'$–$2\frac{1}{2}'$ long, deciduous during their second and third years. **Flowers:** male in elongated loose spikes, yellow; female clustered, long-stalked. **Fruit** ovoid-conic, oblique at base by the greater development of the scales on the outer than on the inner side, sessile, reflexed, in clusters usually of 3 or 4, or rarely of 7 or 8, 2'–$3\frac{1}{2}'$ long, becoming light brown and lustrous, with thin tough scales armed with stout hooked curved spines produced from much thickened mammillate knobs, opening as soon as ripe and gradually shedding their seeds, or often remaining closed for two or three years longer, and fre-

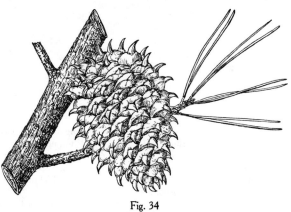

Fig. 34

quently persistent on the branches for eighteen or twenty years; seeds almost triangular, full and rounded on the sides, nearly $\frac{1}{4}'$ long, with a thin conspicuously roughened light brown shell, their wings widest below the middle, gradually narrowed to the ends, 1' long, $\frac{1}{4}'$ wide.

A tree, when crowded in the forest occasionally 60° high, with a trunk 2°–3° in diameter, and a few short branches near the summit forming a narrow round-topped head; in open ground usually 20°–30° tall, and often fertile when only a few feet high, with a short thick trunk frequently clothed to the ground, and long horizontal branches, the lower pendulous toward the extremities, the upper sweeping in graceful upward curves and forming a flat-topped often irregular head, and stout branchlets, light orange color when they first appear, soon growing darker and ultimately dark brown. **Bark** on the lower part of the trunk $\frac{3}{4}'$–1' thick and broken into irregularly shaped plates separating on the surface into thin loose dark brown scales tinged with red, higher on the stem, and on the branches dark brown and broken into thin loose scales. **Wood** light, soft, not strong, brittle, very coarse-grained, pale brown, with thick nearly white sapwood; somewhat used for fuel, and in Pennsylvania manufactured into charcoal.

Distribution. Dry gravelly slopes and ridges of the Appalachian Mountains from southern Pennsylvania to North Carolina, eastern Tennessee and northern Georgia, sometimes ascending to elevations of 4000°, with isolated outlying stations in eastern Pennsylvania, western New Jersey, Maryland, the District of Columbia and Virginia; often forming toward the southern limits of its range pure forests of considerable extent.

28. Pinus Torreyana Carr.   Torrey Pine.

Leaves forming great tufts at the ends of the branches, stout, dark green, conspicuously marked on the 3 faces by numerous rows of stomata, 8'–13' long. **Flowers** from January to March; male yellow, in short dense heads; female subterminal on long stout peduncles.

Fig. 35

Fruit broad-ovoid, spreading or reflexed on long stalks, 4'–6' in length, becoming deep chestnut-brown, with thick scales armed with minute spines; mostly deciduous in their fourth year and in falling leaving a few of the barren scales on the stalk attached to the branch; **seeds** oval, more or less angled, $\frac{3}{4}'$–1' long, dull brown and mottled on the lower side, light yellow-brown on the upper side, with a thick hard shell, nearly surrounded by their dark brown wings often nearly $\frac{1}{2}'$ long.

A tree, usually 30°–40° high, with a short trunk about 1° in diameter, or occasionally 50°–60° tall, with a long straight slightly tapering stem $2\frac{1}{2}$° in diameter, stout spreading and often ascending branches, and very stout branchlets bright green in their first season, becoming light purple and covered with a metallic bloom the following year, ultimately nearly black. **Bark** $\frac{3}{4}'$–1' thick, deeply and irregularly divided into broad flat ridges covered by large thin closely appressed light red-brown scales. **Wood** light, soft, not strong, coarse-grained, light yellow, with thick yellow or nearly white sapwood; occasionally used for fuel. The large edible seeds are gathered in large quantities and are eaten raw or roasted.

Distribution. Only in a narrow belt a few miles long on the coast near the mouth of the Soledad River just north of San Diego and on the island of Santa Rosa, California; the least widely distributed Pine-tree of the United States.

Now planted in the parks of San Diego, California, and in New Zealand, growing rapidly in cultivation, and promising to attain a much larger size than on its native cliffs.

2. LARIX Adans. Larch.

Tall pyramidal trees, with thick sometimes furrowed scaly bark, heavy heartwood, thin pale sapwood, slender remote horizontal often pendulous branches, elongated leading branchlets, short thick spur-like lateral branchlets, and small subglobose buds, their inner scales accrescent and marking the lateral branchlets with prominent ring-like scars. Leaves awl-shaped, triangular and rounded above, or rarely 4-angled, spirally disposed and remote on leading shoots, on lateral branchlets in crowded fascicles, each leaf in the axil of a deciduous bud-scale, deciduous. Flowers solitary, terminal, the staminate globose, oval or oblong, sessile or stalked, on leafless branches, yellow, composed of numerous spirally arranged anthers with connectives produced above them into short points, the pistillate appearing with the leaves, short-oblong to oblong, composed of few or many green nearly orbicular stalked scales in the axes of much longer mucronate usually scarlet bracts. Fruit a woody ovoid-oblong conic or subglobose short-stalked cone composed of slightly thickened suborbicular or oblong-obovate concave scales, shorter or longer than their bracts, gradually decreasing from the centre to the ends of the cone, the small scales usually sterile. Seeds nearly triangular, rounded on the sides, shorter than their wings; the outer seed-coat crustaceous, light brown, the inner membranaceous, pale chestnut-brown and lustrous; cotyledons usually 6, much shorter than the inferior radicle.

Larix is widely distributed over the northern and mountainous region of the northern hemisphere from the Arctic Circle to the mountains of West Virginia and Oregon in the New World, and to central Europe, the Himalayas, Siberia, Korea western China, and Japan in the Old World. Ten species are recognized. Of the exotic species the European *Larix decidua*, Mill., has been much planted for timber and ornament in the northeastern states, where the Japanese *Larix Kæmpferi*, Sarg., also flourishes.

Larix is the classical name of the Larch-tree.

CONSPECTUS OF THE NORTH AMERICAN SPECIES.

Cones small, subglobose; their scales few, longer than the bracts, leaves triangular.
1. L. laricina (A, B, F).

Cones elongated; their scales numerous, shorter than the bracts.

Young branchlets pubescent, soon becoming glabrous; leaves triangular.
2. L. occidentalis (B, G).

Young branchlets tomentose; leaves 4-angled.   3. L. Lyallii (B, F).

1. Larix laricina K. Koch. Tamarack. Larch.
Larix americana Michx.

Leaves linear, triangular, rounded above, prominently keeled on the lower surface, $\frac{3}{4}$–$1\frac{1}{4}'$ long, bright green, conspicuously stomatiferous when they first appear; turning yellow and falling in September or October. **Flowers:** male subglobose and sessile; female oblong, with light-colored bracts produced into elongated green tips, and nearly orbicular rose-red scales. **Fruit** on stout incurved stems, subglobose, rather obtuse, $\frac{1}{2}$–$\frac{3}{4}'$ long, composed of about 20 scales slightly erose on their nearly entire margins, rather longer than broad and twice as long as their bracts, bright chestnut-brown at maturity; usually falling during their second year; **seeds** $\frac{1}{8}'$ long, about one third as long as their light chestnut-brown wings broadest near the middle and obliquely rounded at apex.

A tree, 50°–60° high, with a trunk 18′–20′ in diameter, small horizontal branches forming during the early life of the tree a narrow regular pyramidal head always characteristic of this tree when crowded in the forest, or with abundant space sweeping out in graceful curves, often becoming contorted and pendulous and forming a broad open frequently picturesque head, and slender leading branchlets often covered at first with a glaucous bloom, becoming light orange-brown during their first winter and conspicuous from the small globose dark red lustrous buds. **Bark** $\frac{1}{2}'-\frac{3}{4}'$ thick, separating into thin closely appressed rather bright reddish brown scales. **Wood** heavy, hard, very strong, rather coarse-grained, very durable, light brown; largely used for the upper knees of small vessels, fence-posts, telegraph-poles, and railway-ties.

Distribution. At the north often on well-drained uplands, southward in cold deep swamps which it often clothes with forests of closely crowded trees, from Labrador to the Arctic Circle, ranging west of the Rocky Mountains to latitude 65° 35′ north, and south-

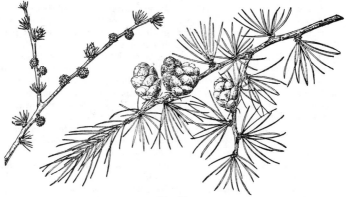

Fig. 36

ward through Canada and the northern states to northern and eastern Pennsylvania, Garrett County, Maryland (Oakland to Thayerville), and Preston County, West Virginia (Cranesville Swamp), northern Indiana and Illinois, and northeastern Minnesota; along the eastern foothills of the Rocky Mountains to about latitude 53° and between the Yukon River and Cook Inlet, Alaska (*Larix alaskensis* Wight.); very abundant in the interior of Labrador, where it is the largest tree; common along the margins of the barren lands stretching beyond the sub-Arctic forest to the shores of the Arctic Sea; attaining its largest size north of Lake Winnipeg on low benches which it occasionally covers with open forests; on the eastern slopes of the northern Rocky Mountains usually at elevation from 600°–1700° above the sea; rare and local toward the southern limits of its range.

Occasionally planted as an ornamental tree in the northeastern states, growing rapidly and attaining in cultivation a large size and picturesque habit.

2. Larix occidentalis Nutt. Tamarack.

Leaves triangular, rounded on the back, conspicuously keeled below, rigid, sharp-pointed, $1'-1\frac{3}{4}'$ long, about $\frac{1}{32}'$ wide, light pale green, turning pale yellow early in the autumn. **Flowers:** male short-oblong; female oblong, nearly sessile, with orbicular scales and bracts produced into elongated tips. **Fruit** oblong, short-stalked, $1'-1\frac{1}{2}'$ long, with numerous thin stiff scales nearly entire and sometimes a little reflexed on their margins, much shorter than their bracts, more or less thickly coated on the lower surface below the middle with hoary tomentum, and standing after the escape of the seeds at right angles to the axis of the cone, or often becoming reflexed; **seeds** nearly $\frac{1}{4}'$ long, with a pale brown shell, one half to two thirds as long as the thin fragile pale wings broadest near the middle and obliquely rounded at apex.

A tree, sometimes 180° high, with a tall tapering naked trunk 6°–8° in diameter, or on dry soil and exposed mountain slopes usually not more than 100° tall, with a short narrow pyramidal head of small branches clothed with scanty foliage, or occasionally with a larger crown of elongated drooping branches, stout branchlets covered when they first appear with soft pale pubescence, usually soon glabrous, bright orange-brown in their first year, ultimately becoming dark gray-brown, and dark chestnut-brown winter-buds about ⅛′ in diameter. **Bark** of young stems thin, dark-colored and scaly, becoming near the base of old trunks 5′ or 6′ thick and broken into irregularly shaped oblong plates often 2° long and covered with thin closely appressed light cinnamon-red scales. **Wood** very heavy, exceedingly hard and strong, close-grained, very durable in contact with the soil, bright

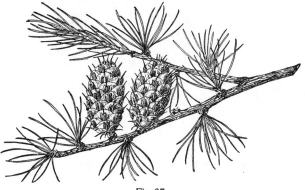

Fig. 37

light red, with thin nearly white sapwood; largely used for railway-ties and fence-posts, and manufactured into lumber used in cabinet-making and the interior finish of buildings.

Distribution. Moist bottom-lands and on high benches and dry mountain sides generally at elevations between 2000° and 7000° above sea-level, usually singly or in small groves, through the basin of the upper Columbia River from southern British Columbia to the western slopes of the continental divide of northern Montana, and to the eastern slopes of the Cascade Mountains of Washington and northern Oregon; most abundant and of its largest size on the bottom-lands of streams flowing into Flat Head Lake in northern Montana, and in northern Idaho.

Occasionally planted in the eastern states and in Europe, but in cultivation showing little promise of attaining a large size or becoming a valuable ornamental or timber-tree.

3. Larix Lyallii Parl. Tamarack.

Leaves 4-angled, rigid, short-pointed, pale blue-green, 1′–1½′ long. **Flowers:** male short-oblong; female ovoid-oblong, with dark red or occasionally pale yellow-green scales and dark purple bracts abruptly contracted into elongated slender tips. **Fruit** ovoid, rather acute, 1½′–2′ long, subsessile or raised on a slender stalk coated with hoary tomentum, with dark reddish purple or rarely green erose scales, fringed and covered on their lower surface with matted hairs at maturity spreading nearly at right angles and finally much reflexed, much shorter than their dark purple very conspicuous long-tipped bracts; **seeds** full and rounded on the sides, ⅛′ long and about half as long as their light red lustrous wings broadest near the base with nearly parallel sides.

A tree, usually 25°–50° high, with a trunk generally 18′–20′ but rarely 3°–4° in diameter, and remote elongated exceedingly tough persistent branches sometimes pendulous, developing very irregularly and often abruptly ascending at the extremities, stout branchlets coated with hoary tomentum usually persistent until after their second winter, ultimately becoming nearly black, and prominent winter-buds with conspicuous long white matted hairs fringing the margins of their scales and often almost entirely covering the bud. **Bark** of young trees and of the branches thin, rather lustrous, smooth, and pale gray tinged with yellow, becoming loose and scaly on larger stems and on the large branches of

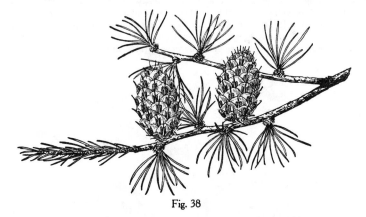

Fig. 38

old trees, and on fully grown trunks $\frac{1}{2}'-\frac{3}{4}'$ thick and slightly divided by shallow fissures into irregularly shaped plates covered by thin dark-red brown loosely attached scales. **Wood** heavy, hard, coarse-grained, light reddish brown.

Distribution. Near the timber-line on mountain slopes at elevations of 4000°–8000°, from southern Alberta on the eastern slope of the Rocky Mountains and from the interior of southern British Columbia, southward along the eastern slopes of the Cascade Mountains of northern Washington to Mt. Stewart at the head of the north fork of the Yakima River, and along the continental divide to the middle fork of Sun River, Montana, forming here a forest of considerable size at elevations of 7000°–8000°, and on the Bitter Root Mountains to the headwaters of the south fork of the Clearwater River, Idaho.

3. PICEA Dietr. Spruce.

Pyramidal trees, with tall tapering trunks often stoutly buttressed at the base, thin scaly bark, soft pale wood containing numerous resin-canals, slender whorled twice or thrice ramified branches, their ultimate divisions stout, glabrous or pubescent, and leaf-buds usually in 3's, the 2 lateral in the axils of upper leaves. Leaves linear, spirally disposed, extending out from the branch on all sides or occasionally appearing 2-ranked by the twisting of those on its lower side, mostly pointing to the end of the branch, entire, articulate on prominent persistent rhomboid ultimately woody bases, keeled above and below, 4-sided and stomatiferous on the 4 sides, or flattened and stomatiferous on the upper and occasionally on the lower side, persistent from seven to ten years, deciduous in drying. Flowers terminal or in the axils of upper leaves, the male usually long-stalked, composed of numerous spirally arranged anthers with connectives produced into broad nearly circular toothed crests, the female oblong, oval or cylindric, with rounded or pointed scales, each in the axis of an accrescent bract shorter than the scale at maturity. Fruit an ovoid or oblong, cylindric pendant cone, crowded on the upper branches or in some species scattered over the upper half of the tree. Seeds ovoid or oblong, usually acute at base, much shorter than their wings; outer seed-coat crustaceous, light or dark brown, the inner membranaceous, pale chestnut-brown; cotyledons 4–15.

Picea is widely distributed through the colder and temperate regions of the northern hemisphere, some species forming great forests on plains and high mountain slopes. Thirty-seven species are now recognized, ranging from the Arctic Circle to the slopes of the southern Appalachian Mountains and to those of northern New Mexico and Arizona in the New World, and to central and southeastern Europe, the Caucasus, the Himalayas, western China, Formosa and Japan. Of exotic species the so-called Norway Spruce, *Picea Abies* Karst., one of the most valuable timber-trees of Europe, has been largely planted for ornament and shelter in the eastern states, where the Caucasian *Picea orientalis* Carr., and some of the Japanese species also flourish.

Picea was probably the classical name of the Spruce-tree.

CONSPECTUS OF THE NORTH AMERICAN SPECIES.

Leaves 4-sided, with stomata on the 4 sides.
  Cone-scales rounded at apex.
    Cone-scales stiff and rigid at maturity; branchlets pubescent.
      Cones ovoid on strongly incurved stalks, persistent for many years, their scales erose or dentate; leaves blue-green.   **1. P. mariana** (A, B, F).
      Cones ovoid-oblong, early deciduous, their scales entire or denticulate; leaves dark yellow-green.   **2. P. rubra** (A).
    Cone-scales soft and flexible at maturity; branchlets glabrous; cones oblong-cylindric, slender, their scales entire; leaves blue-green.   **3. P. glauca** (A, B, F).
  Cone-scales truncate or acute at apex, oblong or rhombic; leaves blue-green.
    Cones oblong-cylindric or ellipsoidal; branchlets pubescent; leaves soft and flexible.   **4. P. Engelmannii** (F, B, G).
    Cones oblong-cylindric; branchlets glabrous; leaves rigid, spinescent.   **5. P. pungens** (F).
Leaves flattened, usually with stomata only on the upper surface; cone-scales rounded.
  Cone-scales ovate, entire; branchlets pubescent; cones ellipsoidal, leaves obtuse.   **6. P. Breweriana** (G).
  Cone-scales elliptic, denticulate above the middle; branchlets glabrous; cones oblong-cylindric, leaves acute or acuminate, with stomata occasionally on the lower surface.   **7. P. sitchensis** (B, G).

1. Picea mariana B. S. P.   Black Spruce.

Leaves slightly incurved above the middle, abruptly contracted at apex into short callous tips, pale blue-green and glaucous at maturity, $\frac{1}{4}'-\frac{3}{4}'$ long, hoary on the upper surface from the broad bands of stomata, and lustrous and slightly stomatiferous on the lower surface. **Flowers:** male subglobose, with dark red anthers; female oblong-cylindric, with obovate purple scales rounded above, and oblong purple glaucous bracts rounded and denticulate at apex. **Fruit** ovoid, pointed, gradually narrowed at the base into short strongly incurved stalks, $\frac{1}{2}'-1\frac{1}{2}'$ long, with rigid puberulous scales rounded or rarely somewhat pointed at apex and more or less erose on the notched pale margins, turning as they ripen dull gray-brown and becoming as the scales gradually open and slowly discharge their seeds almost globose; sometimes remaining on the branches for twenty or thirty years, the oldest close to the base of the branches near the trunk; **seeds** oblong, narrowed to the acute base, about $\frac{1}{8}'$ long, very dark brown, with delicate pale brown wings broadest above the middle, very oblique at the apex, about $\frac{1}{2}'$ long, $\frac{1}{8}'$ wide.

A tree, usually $20°-30°$ and occasionally $100°$ high, with a trunk $6'-12'$ and rarely $3°$ in diameter, and comparatively short branches generally pendulous with upward curves, forming an open irregular crown, light green branchlets coated with pale pubescence, soon beginning to grow darker, and during their first winter light cinnamon-brown and covered with short rusty pubescence, their thin brown bark gradually becoming glabrous and beginning to break into small thin scales during their second year; at the extreme **north** sometimes cone-bearing when only 2°-3° high. **Winter-buds** ovoid, acute, light reddish brown, puberulous, about ⅛′ long. **Bark** ¼′-½′ thick and broken on the surface into thin rather closely appressed gray-brown scales. **Wood** light, soft, not strong, pale yellow-white, with thin sapwood; probably rarely used outside of Manitoba and Saskatchewan, except in the manufacture of paper pulp. Spruce-gum, the resinous exudations of the Spruce-trees of northeastern America, is gathered in considerable quantities principally in northern New England and Canada, and is used as a masticatory. Spruce-beer is made by boiling the branches of the Black and Red Spruces

Fig. 39

Distribution. At the north on well-drained bottom-lands and the slopes of barren stony hills, and southward in sphagnum-covered bogs, swamps, and on their borders, from Labrador to the valley of the Mackenzie River in about latitude 65° north, and, crossing the Rocky Mountains, through the interior of Alaska to the valley of White River; southward through Newfoundland, the maritime provinces, eastern Canada and the northeastern United States to central Pennsylvania, and along the Alleghany Mountains to northern Virginia; and from the eastern foothills of the Rocky Mountains in Alberta, through northern Saskatchewan and northern Manitoba, and south to northeastern and northern Minnesota, and central Wisconsin and Michigan; very abundant at the far north and the largest coniferous tree of Saskatchewan and northern Manitoba, covering here large areas and growing to its largest size; common in Newfoundland and all the provinces of eastern Canada except southern Ontario; in the United States less abundant, of small size, and usually only in cold sphagnum swamps (var. *brevifolia* Rehd.)

Occasionally planted as an ornamental tree, the Black Spruce is short-lived in cultivation and one of the least desirable of all Spruce-trees for the decoration of parks and gardens.

2. Picea rubra Link.   Red Spruce.

Picea rubens Sarg.

Leaves more or less incurved above the middle, acute or rounded and furnished at the apex with short callous points, dark green often slightly tinged with yellow, very lustrous, marked on the upper surface by 4 rows and on the lower less conspicuously by 2 rows of stomata on each side of the prominent midrib, ½′-⅝′ long, nearly ₁/₁₆′ wide. **Flowers:** male oval, almost sessile, bright red; female oblong-cylindric, with thin rounded scales reflexed and slightly erose on their margins, and obovate bracts rounded and laciniate above. **Fruit** on very short straight or incurved stalks, ovoid-oblong, gradually narrowed from near the middle to the acute apex, 1¼′-2′ long, with rigid puberulous scales entire or slightly toothed at the apex; bright green or green somewhat tinged with purple when fully grown, becoming light reddish brown and lustrous at maturity, beginning to fall as soon as the scales open in the autumn or early winter, and generally disappearing from the branches the following summer; **seeds** dark brown, about $\frac{1}{8}'$ long, with short broad wings full and rounded above the middle.

A tree, usually 70°–80° and occasionally 100° high, with a trunk 2°–3° in diameter, branches long-persistent on the stem and clothing it to the ground, forming a narrow rather conical head, or soon disappearing below from trees crowded in the forest, stout pubescent light green branchlets, becoming bright reddish brown or orange-brown during their first winter, gla-brous the following year, and covered in their third or fourth year with scaly bark. **Winter-buds** ovoid, acute, $\frac{1}{4}'-\frac{1}{3}'$ long, with light reddish brown scales. **Bark** $\frac{1}{4}'-\frac{1}{2}'$ thick, and broken into thin closely appressed irregularly shaped red-brown scales. **Wood** light, soft, close-grained, not strong, pale slightly tinged with red, with paler sapwood usually about

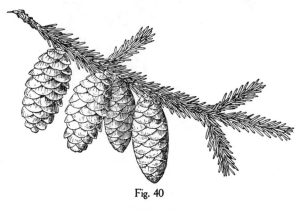

Fig. 40

2′ thick; largely manufactured into lumber in the northeastern states, Pennsylvania, and Virginia, and used for the flooring and construction of houses, for the sounding-boards of musical instruments, and in the manufacture of paper-pulp.

Distribution. Well-drained uplands and mountain slopes, often forming a large part of extensive forests, from Prince Edward Island and the valley of the St. Lawrence southward to the coast of Massachusetts, along the interior hilly part of New England, New York, and northern Pennsylvania and on the slopes of the Alleghany Mountains at elevations above 2500 feet from West Virginia to North Carolina and Tennessee.

Occasionally planted in the eastern states and in Europe as an ornamental tree, but growing in cultivation more slowly than any other Spruce-tree.

3. Picea glauca Voss. White Spruce.

Picea canadensis B. S. P.

Leaves crowded on the upper side of the branches by the twisting of those on the lower side, incurved, acute or acuminate with rigid callous tips, pale blue and hoary when they first appear, becoming dark blue-green or pale blue, marked on each of the 4 sides by 3 or 4 rows of stomata, $\frac{1}{3}'-\frac{3}{4}'$ long. **Flowers:** male pale red, soon appearing yellow from the thick covering of pollen; female oblong-cylindric, with round nearly entire pale red or yellow-green scales, broader than long, and nearly orbicular denticulate bracts. **Fruit** nearly sessile or borne on short thin straight stems, oblong-cylindric, slender, slightly narrowed to the ends, rather obtuse at apex, usually about 2′ long, pale green sometimes tinged with red when fully grown, becoming at maturity pale brown and lus-trous, with nearly orbicular scales, rounded, truncate, and slightly emarginate, or rarely narrowed at apex, and very thin, flexible and elastic at maturity, usually deciduous in the autumn or during the following winter; **seeds** about $\frac{1}{8}'$ long, pale brown, with narrow wings gradually widened from the base to above the middle and very oblique at the apex.

A tree, with disagreeable smelling foliage, rarely more than 60°–70° tall, with a trunk not more than 2° in diameter, long comparatively thick branches densely clothed with stout rigid laterals sweeping out in graceful upward curves, and forming a broad-based rather open pyramid often obtuse at the apex, stout glabrous branchlets orange-brown during their first autumn and winter, gradually growing darker grayish brown. **Winter-buds** broadly ovoid, obtuse, covered by light chestnut-brown scales with thin often reflexed ciliate margins. **Bark** $\frac{1}{4}'-\frac{1}{2}'$ thick, separating irregularly into thin plate-like light gray scales more or less tinged with brown. **Wood** light, soft, not strong, straight-grained light yellow,

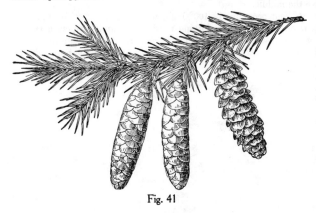

Fig. 41

with hardly distinguishable sapwood; manufactured into lumber in the eastern provinces of Canada and in Alaska, and used in construction, for the interior finish of buildings, and for paper-pulp.

Distribution. Banks and borders of streams and lakes, ocean cliffs, and in the north the rocky slopes of low hills, from Labrador along the northern frontier of the forest nearly to the shores of the Arctic Sea, reaching Behring Strait in 66° 44′ north latitude, and southward down the Atlantic coast to southern Maine, northern New Hampshire, Vermont, and New York, shores of Saginaw Bay, Michigan, northern Wisconsin and Minnesota, and through the interior of Alaska.

The variety (var. *albertiana* Sarg.) of the Gaspé Peninsula and the valleys of the Black Hills of South Dakota and of the Rocky Mountains of northern Wyoming, Montana, Alberta and northward, is a tree with a narrow pyramidal head, sometimes 150° high, with a trunk 3° to 4° in diameter, and shorter and rather broader cones than those of the typical White Spruce of the east, although not shorter or as short as the cones of that tree in the extreme north.

Often planted in Canada, northern New England, and northern Europe as an ornamental tree; in southern New England and southward suffering from heat and dryness.

4. Picea Engelmannii Engelm. White Spruce. Engelmann Spruce.

Leaves soft and flexible, with acute callous tips, slender, nearly straight or slightly incurved on vigorous sterile branches, stouter, shorter, and more incurved on fertile branches, $1'-1\frac{1}{8}'$ long, marked on each face by 3–5 rows of stomata, covered at first with a glaucous bloom, soon becoming dark blue-green or pale steel-blue. **Flowers:** male dark purple; female bright scarlet, with pointed or rounded and more or less divided scales, and oblong bracts rounded or acute or acuminate and denticulate at apex or obovate-oblong and abruptly acuminate. **Fruit** oblong-cylindric to ellipsoidal, gradually narrowed to the ends, usually about 2′ long, sessile or very short-stalked, produced in great numbers on the upper branches, horizontal and ultimately pendulous, light green somewhat tinged with scarlet when fully grown, becoming light chestnut-brown and lustrous, with thin flexible slightly concave scales, generally erose-dentate or rarely almost entire on the margins, usually broadest at the middle, wedge-shaped below, and gradually contracted above into a truncate or acute apex, or occasionally obovate and rounded above; mostly deciduous in the autumn or early in their first winter soon after the escape of the seeds; **seeds** obtuse at the base, nearly black, about ⅛′ long and much shorter than their broad very oblique wings.

A tree, with disagreeable smelling foliage sometimes 120° high, with a trunk 3° in diameter, spreading branches produced in regular whorls and forming a narrow compact pyramidal head, gracefully hanging short lateral branches, and comparatively slender branchlets pubescent for three or four years, light or dark orange-brown or gray tinged with brown during their first winter, their bark beginning to separate into small flaky scales in their fourth or fifth year; at its highest altitudes low and stunted with elongated branches pressed close to the ground. **Winter-buds** conic or slightly obtuse, with pale chestnut-brown scales scarious and often free and slightly reflexed on the margins. **Bark** ¼′–½′ thick, light cinnamon-red, and broken into large thin loose scales. **Wood** light, soft, not strong, close-grained, pale yellow tinged with red, with thick hardly distinguishable sapwood; largely manufactured into lumber used in the construction of buildings; also employed for fuel and charcoal. The bark is sometimes employed in tanning leather.

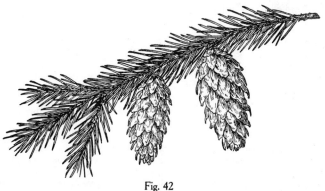

Fig. 42

Distribution. High mountain slopes, often forming great forests from the mountains of Alberta, British Columbia and Alaska, southward over the interior mountain systems of the continent to southern New Mexico (the Sacramento Mountains) and northern Arizona, from elevations of 5000° at the north up to 11,500° and occasionally to 12,000° at the south, and westward through Montana and Idaho to the eastern slopes of the Cascade Mountains of Washington and Oregon; attaining its greatest size and beauty north of the northern boundary of the United States.

Occasionally planted as an ornamental tree in the New England states and northern Europe, where it grows vigorously and promises to attain a large size; usually injured in western Europe by spring frosts.

5. Picea pungens Engelm. Blue Spruce. Colorado Spruce.

Picea Parryana Sarg.

Leaves strongly incurved, especially those on the upper side of the branches, stout, rigid, acuminate and tipped with long callous sharp points, 1′–1⅛′ long on sterile branches, often not more than half as long on the fertile branches of old trees, marked on each side by 4–7 rows of stomata, dull bluish green on some individuals and light or dark steel-blue or silvery white on others, the blue colors gradually changing to dull blue-green at the end of three or four years. **Flowers:** male yellow tinged with red; female with broad oblong or slightly obovate pale green scales truncate or slightly emarginate at the denticulate apex, and acute bracts. **Fruit** produced on the upper third of the tree, sessile or short-stalked, oblong-cylindric, slightly narrowed at the ends, usually about 3' long, green more or less tinged with red when fully grown at midsummer, becoming pale chestnut-brown and lustrous, with flat tough rhombic scales flexuose on the margins, and acute, rounded or truncate at the elongated erose apex; seeds $\frac{1}{8}'$ long or about half the length of their wings, gradually widening to above the middle and full and rounded at apex.

A tree, usually 80°–100° or occasionally 150° high, with a trunk rarely 3° in diameter and occasionally divided into 3 or 4 stout secondary stems, rigid horizontal branches disposed on young trees in remote whorls and decreasing regularly in length from below upward, the short stout stiff branchlets pointing forward and making flat-topped masses of foliage; branches on old trees short and remote, with stout lateral branches forming a thin ragged pyramidal crown; branchlets stout, rigid, glabrous, pale glaucous green, becoming bright orange-brown during the first winter and ultimately light grayish brown. **Winter-buds** stout, obtuse or rarely acute, $\frac{1}{4}'-\frac{1}{2}'$ long, with

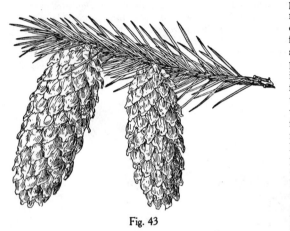

Fig. 43

thin pale chestnut-brown scales usually reflexed on the margins. **Bark** of young trees gray or gray tinged with cinnamon-red and broken into small oblong plate-like scales, becoming on the lower part of old trunks $\frac{3}{4}'-1\frac{1}{2}'$ thick and deeply divided into broad rounded ridges covered with small closely appressed pale gray or occasionally bright cinnamon-red scales. **Wood** light, soft, close-grained, weak, pale brown or often nearly white, with hardly distinguishable sapwood.

Distribution. Banks of streams or on the first benches above them singly or in small groves at elevations between 6500° and 11,000° above the sea; Colorado and eastern Utah northward to the northern end of the Medicine Bow Mountains and on the Laramie Range in southern and on the Shoshone and Teton Mountains in northwestern Wyoming, and southward into northern New Mexico (Sierra Blanca, alt. 8000°–11,000°, Sacramento Mountains, Pecos River National Forest).

Often planted as an ornamental tree in the eastern and northern states and in western and northern Europe, especially individuals with blue foliage; very beautiful in early life but in cultivation soon becoming unsightly from the loss of the lower branches.

6. Picea Breweriana S. Wats. Weeping Spruce.

Leaves abruptly narrowed and obtuse at apex, straight or slightly incurved, rounded and obscurely ridged and dark green and lustrous on the lower surface, flattened and conspicuously marked on the upper surface by 4 or 5 rows of stomata on each side of the prominent midrib, $\frac{3}{4}'-1\frac{1}{8}'$ long, $\frac{1}{16}'-\frac{1}{10}'$ wide. **Flowers:** male dark purple; female oblong-cylindric, with obovate scales rounded above and reflexed on the entire margins, and oblong bracts laciniately divided at their rounded or acute apex. **Fruit** ellipsoidal, gradually narrowed from the middle to the ends, acute at apex, rather oblique at base, suspended on straight slender stalks, deep rich purple or green more or less tinged with purple when fully grown, becoming light orange-brown, 2'–4' long, with thin broadly ovate flat scales longer than broad, rounded at apex, opening late in the autumn after the escape of the seeds, often becoming strongly reflexed and very flexible; usually remaining on the branches until their second winter; **seeds** acute at base, full and rounded on the sides, $\frac{1}{8}'$ long, dark brown, and about one quarter the length of their wings broadest toward the full and rounded apex.

A tree, usually 80°–100° high, with a trunk 2°–3° in diameter above the swelling of its enlarged and gradually tapering base, and furnished to the ground with crowded branches, those at the top of the tree short and slightly ascending, with comparatively short pendulous lateral branches, those lower on the tree horizontal or pendulous and clothed with slender flexible whip-like laterals often 7°–8° long and not more than $\frac{1}{4}'$ thick and furnished with numerous long thin lateral branchlets, their ultimate divisions slender, coated with fine pubescence persistent until their third season, bright red-brown during their first winter, gradually growing dark gray-brown. **Winter-buds** conic, light chestnut-brown, $\frac{1}{4}'$

Fig. 44

long and $\frac{1}{8}'$ thick. **Bark** $\frac{1}{2}'-\frac{3}{4}'$ thick, broken into long thin closely appressed scales dull red-brown on the surface. **Wood** heavy, soft, close-grained, light brown or nearly white, with thick hardly distinguishable sapwood.

Distribution. Dry mountain ridges and peaks near the timber-line on both slopes of the Siskiyou Mountains on the boundary between California and Oregon, forming small groves at elevations of about 7000° above the sea; on a high peak west of Marble Mountain in Siskiyou County, California; on the coast ranges of southwestern Oregon at elevations of 4000°–5000°.

7. Picea sitchensis Carr. Tideland Spruce. Sitka Spruce.

Leaves standing out from all sides of the branches and often nearly at right angles to them, frequently bringing their white upper surface to view by a twist at their base, straight or slightly incurved, acute or acuminate with long callous tips, slightly rounded, green, lustrous, and occasionally marked on the lower surface with 2 or 3 rows of small conspicuous stomata on each side of the prominent midrib, flattened, obscurely ridged and almost covered with broad silvery white bands of numerous rows of stomata on the upper surface, $\frac{1}{2}'-1\frac{1}{8}'$ long and $\frac{1}{16}'-\frac{1}{12}'$ wide, mostly persistent 9–11 years. **Flowers:** male at the ends of the pendant lateral branchlets, dark red; female on rigid terminal shoots of the branches of the upper half of the tree, with nearly orbicular denticulate scales, often slightly truncate above and completely hidden by their elongated acuminate bracts. **Fruit** oblong-cylindric, short-stalked, yellow-green often tinged with dark red when fully grown, becoming lustrous and pale yellow or reddish brown, $2\frac{1}{2}'-4'$ long, with thin stiff elliptic scales rounded toward the apex, denticulate above the middle, and nearly twice as long as their lanceolate denticulate bracts; deciduous mostly during their first autumn and winter; **seeds** full and rounded, acute at the base, pale reddish brown, about $\frac{1}{8}'$ long, with narrow oblong slightly oblique wings $\frac{1}{3}'$–$\frac{1}{2}'$ in length.

A tree, usually about 100° high, with a conspicuously tapering trunk often 3°–4° in diameter above its strongly buttressed and much-enlarged base, occasionally 200° tall, with a trunk 15°–16° in diameter, horizontal branches forming an open loose pyramid and on older trees clothed with slender pendant lateral branches frequently 2°–3° long, and stout rigid glabrous branchlets pale green at first, becoming dark or light orange-brown during their first autumn and winter and finally dark gray-brown; at the extreme northwestern limits of its range occasionally reduced to a low shrub. **Winter-buds** ovoid, acute or conical, $\frac{1}{4}'$–$\frac{1}{2}'$ long, with pale chestnut-brown acute scales, often tipped with

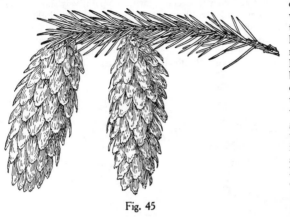

Fig. 45

short points and more or less reflexed above the middle. **Bark** $\frac{1}{4}'$–$\frac{1}{2}'$ thick and broken on the surface into large thin loosely attached dark red-brown or on young trees sometimes bright cinnamon-red scales. **Wood** light, soft, not strong, straight-grained, light brown tinged with red, with thick nearly white sapwood; largely manufactured into lumber used in the interior finish of buildings, for fencing, boat-building, aeroplanes, cooperage, wooden-ware, and packing-cases.

Distribution. Moist sandy, often swampy soil, or less frequently at the far north on wet rocky slopes, from the eastern end of Kadiak Island, southward through the coast region of Alaska, British Columbia, Washington, and Oregon to Mendocino County, California; in Washington, occasionally ranging inland to the upper valley of the Nesqually River.

Often planted in western and central Europe and occasionally in the middle Atlantic states as an ornamental tree.

4. TSUGA Carr. Hemlock.

Tall pyramidal trees, with deeply furrowed astringent bark bright cinnamon-red except on the surface, soft pale wood, nodding leading shoots, slender scattered horizontal often pendulous branches, the secondary branches three or four times irregularly pinnately ramified, with slender round glabrous or pubescent ultimate divisions, the whole forming graceful pendant masses of foliage, and minute winter-buds. Leaves flat or angular, obtuse and often emarginate or acute at apex, spirally disposed, usually appearing almost 2-ranked by the twisting of their petioles, those on the upper side of the branch then much shorter than the others, abruptly narrowed into short petioles jointed on ultimately woody persistent bases, with stomata on the lower surface; on one species not 2-ranked, and of nearly equal length, with stomata on both surfaces. Flowers solitary, the male in the axils of leaves of the previous year, globose, composed of numerous subglobose anthers, with connectives produced into short gland-like tips, the female terminal, erect, with nearly circular scales slightly longer or shorter than their membranaceous bracts. Fruit an ovoid-oblong, oval, or oblong-cylindric obtuse usually pendulous nearly sessile green or rarely purple cone becoming light or dark reddish brown, with concave suborbicular or ovate-oblong scales thin and entire on the margins, much longer than their minute bracts, persistent on the axis of the cone after the escape of the seeds. Seeds furnished with resin-vesicles, ovoid-oblong, compressed, nearly surrounded by their much longer obovate-oblong wings; outer seed-coat crustaceous, light brown, the inner membranaceous, pale chestnut-brown, and lustrous; cotyledons 3–6, much shorter than the inferior radicle.

Tsuga is confined to temperate North America, Japan, central and southwestern China, Formosa, and the Himalayas; nine species have been distinguished.

Tsuga is the Japanese name of the Hemlock-tree.

CONSPECTUS OF THE NORTH AMERICAN SPECIES.

Leaves flat, obtuse or emarginate at apex, with stomata only on the lower surface; cones ovoid, oblong or oblong-ovoid.
    Cones stalked.
        Cone-scales broad-obovate, about as wide as long, their bracts broad and truncate.
                    1. **T. canadensis** (A).
        Cone-scales narrow-oval, much longer than wide, their bracts obtusely pointed.
                    2. **T. caroliniana** (A).
    Cones sessile; cone-scales oval, often abruptly contracted near the middle, their bracts gradually narrowed to an obtuse point.
                    3. **T. heterophylla** (B, F, G).
Leaves convex or keeled above, bluntly pointed, with stomata on both surfaces; cones oblong-cylindric, their scales oblong-obovate, longer than broad, much longer than their acuminate short-pointed bracts.   4. **T. Mertensiana** (B, F, G).

1. Tsuga canadensis Carr. Hemlock.

Leaves, rounded and rarely emarginate at apex, dark yellow-green, lustrous and obscurely grooved especially toward the base on the upper surface, marked on the lower surface by 5 or 6 rows of stomata on each side of the low broad midrib, $\frac{1}{3}-\frac{2}{3}'$ long, about $\frac{1}{15}'$

Fig. 46

wide, deciduous in their third season from dark orange-colored persistent bases. **Flowers:** male light yellow; female pale green, with broad bracts coarsely laciniate on the margins and shorter than their scales. **Fruit** on slender puberulous stalks often $\frac{1}{4}'$ long, ovoid, acute, $\frac{1}{2}-\frac{3}{4}'$ long, with broad-obovate scales almost as wide as long, and broad truncate bracts slightly laciniate on the margins, opening and gradually losing their seeds during the winter and mostly persistent on the branches until the following spring; seeds $\frac{1}{16}'$ long, usually with 2 or 3 large oil-vesicles, nearly half as long as their wings broad at the base and gradually tapering to the rounded apex.

A tree, usually 60°–70°, and occasionally 100° high, with a trunk 2°–4° in diameter, gradually and conspicuously tapering toward the apex, long slender horizontal or pendulous branches, persistent until overshadowed by other trees, and forming a broad-based rather obtuse pyramid, and slender light yellow-brown pubescent branchlets, growing darker during their first winter and glabrous and dark red-brown tinged with purple in their third season. **Winter-buds** obtuse, light chestnut-brown, slightly puberulous, about $\frac{1}{16}'$ long. **Bark** $\frac{1}{2}'$–$\frac{3}{4}'$ thick, deeply divided into narrow rounded ridges covered with thick closely appressed scales varying from cinnamon-red to gray more or less tinged with purple. **Wood** light, soft, not strong, brittle, coarse-grained, difficult to work, liable to wind-shake and splinter, not durable when exposed to the air, light brown tinged with red, with thin somewhat darker sapwood; largely manufactured into coarse lumber employed for the outside finish of buildings. The astringent inner bark affords the largest part of the material used in the northeastern states and Canada in tanning leather. From the young branches oil of hemlock is distilled.

Distribution. Scattered through upland forests and often covering the northern slopes of rocky ridges and the steep rocky banks of narrow river-gorges from Nova Scotia to eastern Minnesota (Carleton County), and southward through the northern states to Newcastle County, Delaware, cliffs of Tuckahoe Creek, Queen Anne's County, Maryland, southern Michigan, southern Indiana (bank of Back Creek near Leesville, Laurence County), southwestern Wisconsin, and along the Appalachian Mountains to northern Georgia, and in northern Alabama; most abundant and frequently an important element of the forest in New England, northern New York, and western Pennsylvania; attaining its largest size near streams on the slopes of the high mountains of North Carolina and Tennessee.

Largely cultivated with numerous seminal varieties as an ornamental tree in the northern states, and in western and central Europe.

2. Tsuga caroliniana Engelm. Hemlock.

Leaves retuse or often emarginate at apex, dark green, lustrous and conspicuously grooved on the upper surface, marked on the lower surface by a band of 7 or 8 rows of

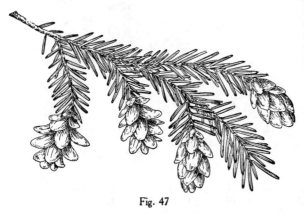

stomata on each side of the midrib, $\frac{1}{3}'$–$\frac{3}{4}'$ long, about $\frac{1}{12}'$ wide, deciduous from the orange-red bases during their fifth year. **Flowers:** male tinged with purple; female purple, with broadly ovate bracts, scarious and erose on the margins and about as long as their scales. **Fruit** on short stout stalks, oblong, $1'$–$1\frac{1}{2}'$ long, with narrow-oval scales gradually narrowed and rounded at apex, rather abruptly con-

Fig. 47

tracted at base into distinct stipes, thin, concave, puberulous on the outer surface, twice as long as their broad pale bracts, spreading nearly at right angles to the axis of the cone at maturity, their bracts rather longer than wide, wedge-shaped, pale, nearly truncate or slightly pointed at the broad apex; **seeds** $\frac{1}{8}'$ long, with numerous small oil-vesicles on the lower side, and one quarter as long as the pale lustrous wings broad or narrow at the base and narrowed to the rounded apex.

A tree, usually 40°–50°, or occasionally 70° high, with a trunk rarely exceeding 2° in diameter, short stout often pendulous branches forming a handsome compact pyramidal head, and slender light orange-brown pubescent branchlets, usually becoming glabrous and dull brown more or less tinged with orange during their third year. **Winter-buds** obtuse, dark chestnut-brown, pubescent, nearly $\frac{1}{8}'$ long. **Bark** of the trunk $\frac{3}{4}'$–$1\frac{1}{4}'$ thick, red-brown, and deeply divided into broad flat connected ridges covered with thin closely appressed plate-like scales. **Wood** light, soft, not strong, brittle, coarse-grained, pale brown tinged with red, with thin nearly white sapwood.

Distribution. Rocky banks of streams usually at elevations between 2500° and 4000° on the Blue Ridge from southwestern Virginia to northern Georgia, generally singly or in small scattered groves of a few individuals.

Occasionally planted as an ornamental tree in the northern states, and in western Europe.

3. Tsuga heterophylla Sarg. Hemlock.

Leaves rounded at apex, conspicuously grooved, dark green and very lustrous on the upper surface, marked below by broad white bands of 7–9 rows of stomata, abruptly contracted at the base into slender petioles, $\frac{1}{4}'$–$\frac{3}{4}'$ long and $\frac{1}{16}'$–$\frac{1}{12}'$ wide, mostly persistent

Fig. 48

4–7 years. **Flowers:** male yellow; female purple and puberulous, with broad bracts gradually narrowed to an obtuse point and shorter than their broadly ovate slightly scarious scales. **Fruit** oblong-ovoid, acute, sessile, $\frac{3}{4}'$–$1'$ long, with slightly puberulous oval scales, often abruptly narrowed near the middle, and dark purple puberulous bracts rounded and abruptly contracted at apex; **seeds** $\frac{1}{8}'$ long, furnished with occasional oil-vesicles, one third to one half as long as their narrow wings.

A tree, frequently 200° high, with a tall trunk 6°–10° in diameter, and short slender usually pendulous branches forming a narrow pyramidal head, and slender pale yellow-brown branchlets ultimately becoming dark reddish brown, coated at first with long pale hairs, and pubescent or puberulous for five or six years. **Winter-buds** ovoid, bright chestnut-brown, about $\frac{1}{16}'$ long. **Bark** on young trunks thin, dark orange-brown, and separated by shallow fissures into narrow flat plates broken into delicate scales, becoming on fully grown trees $1'$–$1\frac{1}{2}'$ thick and deeply divided into broad flat connected ridges covered with closely appressed brown scales more or less tinged with cinnamon-red. **Wood** light, hard and tough, pale brown tinged with yellow, with thin nearly white sapwood; stronger and more durable than the wood of the other American hemlocks; now largely manufactured into lumber used principally in the construction of buildings. The bark is used in large quantities in tanning leather; from the inner bark the Indians of Alaska obtain one of their principal articles of vegetable food.

Distribution. Southeastern Alaska, southward near the coast to southern Mendocino County, California, extending eastward over the mountains of southern British Columbia, northern Washington, Idaho and Montana, to the western slopes of the continental divide, and through Oregon to the western slopes of the Cascade Mountains, sometimes ascending in the interior to elevations of 6000° above the sea; most abundant and of its largest size on the coast of Washington and Oregon; often forming a large part of the forests of the northwest coast.

Frequently planted as an ornamental tree in temperate Europe.

4. Tsuga Mertensiana Sarg.   Mountain Hemlock.   Black Hemlock.

Leaves standing out from all sides of the branch, remote on leading shoots and crowded on short lateral branchlets, rounded and occasionally obscurely grooved or on young plants sometimes conspicuously grooved on the upper surface, rounded and slightly ribbed

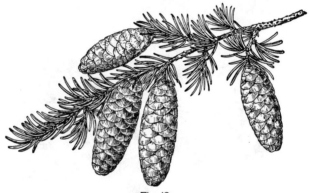

Fig. 49

on the lower surface, bluntly pointed, often more or less curved, stomatiferous above and below, with about 8 rows of stomata on each surface, light bluish green or on some individuals pale blue, $\frac{1}{2}'$–$1'$ long, about $\frac{1}{16}'$ wide, abruptly narrowed into nearly straight or slightly twisted petioles articulate on bases as long or rather longer than the petioles; irregularly deciduous during their third and fourth years. **Flowers:** male borne on slender pubescent drooping stems, violet-purple; female erect, with delicate lustrous dark purple or yellow-green bracts gradually narrowed above into slender often slightly reflexed tips and much longer than their scales. **Fruit** sessile, oblong-cylindric, narrowed toward the blunt apex and somewhat toward the base, erect until more than half grown, pendulous or rarely erect at maturity, $\frac{5}{8}'$–$3'$ long, with thin delicate oblong-obovate scales gradually contracted from above the middle to the wedge-shaped base, rounded at the slightly thickened more or less erose margins, puberulous on the outer surface, usually bright bluish purple or occasionally pale yellow-green, four or five times as long as their short-pointed dark purple or brown bracts; **seeds** light brown, $\frac{1}{8}'$ long, often marked on the surface next their scales with 1 or 2 large resin-vesicles, with wings nearly $\frac{1}{2}'$ long, broadest above the middle, gradually narrowed below, slightly or not at all oblique at the rounded apex.

A tree, usually 70°–100° but occasionally 150° high, with a slightly tapering trunk 4°–5° in diameter, gracefully pendant slender branches furnished with drooping frond-like lateral branches, their ultimate divisions erect and forming an open pyramid surmounted by the long drooping leading shoot, and thin flexible or sometimes stout rigid branchlets light reddish brown and covered for two or three years with short pale dense pubescence, becoming grayish brown and very scaly. **Winter-buds** acute, about $\frac{1}{8}'$ long, the scales of the outer ranks furnished on the back with conspicuous midribs produced into slender deciduous awl-like tips. **Bark** $1'–1\frac{1}{2}'$ thick, deeply divided into connected rounded ridges broken into thin closely appressed dark cinnamon scales shaded with blue or purple. **Wood** light, soft, not strong, close-grained, pale brown or red, with thin nearly white sap-wood; occasionally manufactured into lumber.

Distribution. Exposed ridges and slopes at high altitudes along the upper border of the forest from southeastern Alaska, southward over the mountain ranges of British Columbia to the Olympic Mountains of Washington, and eastward to the western slopes of the Selkirk Mountains in the interior of southern British Columbia, and along the Bitter Root Mountains to the headwaters of the Clearwater River, Idaho; along the Cascade Mountains of Washington and Oregon, on the mountain ranges of northern California, and along the high Sierra Nevada to the cañon of the south fork of King's River, California; in Alaska occasionally descending to the sea-level, and toward the southern limits of its range often ascending to elevations of 10,000°.

Often planted as an ornamental tree in western and central Europe, and rarely in the eastern United States.

5. PSEUDOTSUGA Carr.

Pyramidal trees, with thick deeply furrowed bark, hard strong wood, with spirally marked wood-cells, slender usually horizontal irregularly whorled branches clothed with slender spreading lateral branches forming broat flat-topped masses of foliage, ovoid acute leaf-buds, the lateral buds in the axils of upper leaves, their inner scales accrescent and marking the branchlets with ring-like scars. Leaves petiolate, linear, flat, rounded and obtuse or acuminate at apex, straight or incurved, grooved on the upper side, marked on the lower side by numerous rows of stomata on each side of the prominent midrib, spreading nearly at right angles with the branch. Flowers solitary, the male axillary, scattered along the branches, oblong-cylindric, with numerous globose anthers, their connectives terminating in short spurs, the female terminal or in the axils of upper leaves, composed of spirally arranged ovate rounded scales much shorter than their acutely 2-lobed bracts, with midribs produced into elongated slender tips. Fruit an ovoid-oblong acute pendulous cone maturing in one season, with rounded concave rigid scales persistent on the axis of the cone after the escape of the seeds, and becoming dark red-brown, much shorter than the 2-lobed bracts with midribs ending in rigid woody linear awns, those at the base of the cone without scales and becoming linear-lanceolate by the gradual suppression of their lobes. Seeds nearly triangular, full, rounded and dark-colored on the upper side and pale on the lower side, shorter than their oblong wings infolding the upper side of the seeds in a dark covering; outer seed-coat thick and crustaceous, the inner thin and membranaceous; cotyledons 6–12, much shorter than the inferior radicle.

Pseudotsuga is confined to western North America, southern Japan, southwestern China and Formosa Four species are recognized.

Pseudotsuga, a barbarous combination of a Greek with a Japanese word, indicates the relation of these trees with the Hemlocks.

CONSPECTUS OF THE NORTH AMERICAN SPECIES.

Leaves usually rounded and obtuse at apex, dark yellow-green or rarely blue-green; cones 2′–4½′ long, their bracts much exserted.   1. P. taxifolia (B, E, F, G, H).
Leaves acuminate at apex, bluish gray; cones 4′–6½′ long, their bracts slightly exserted.
                                                                    2. P. macrocarpa (G).

1. Pseudotsuga taxifolia Britt.   Douglas Spruce.   Red Fir.
Pseudotsuga mucronata Sudw.

Leaves straight or rarely slightly incurved, rounded and obtuse at apex, or acute on leading shoots, ¾′–1¼′ long, $\frac{1}{16}′-\frac{1}{12}′$ wide, dark yellow-green or rarely light or dark bluish green, occasionally persistent until their sixteenth year. **Flowers:** male orange-red; fe-

Fig. 50

male with slender elongated bracts deeply tinged with red. **Fruit** pendant on long stout stems, 4′–6½′ long, with thin slightly concave scales rounded and occasionally somewhat elongated at apex, usually rather longer than broad, when fully grown at midsummer slightly puberulous, dark blue-green below, purplish toward the apex, bright red on the closely appressed margins, and pale green bracts becoming slightly reflexed above the middle, ⅕′–¼′ wide, often extending ½′ beyond the scales; **seeds** light reddish brown and lustrous above, pale and marked below with large irregular white spots, ¼′ long, nearly ⅛′ wide, almost as long as their dark brown wings broadest just below the middle, oblique above and rounded at the apex.

A tree, often 200° high, with a trunk 3°–4° in diameter, frequently taller, with a trunk 10°–12° in diameter, but in the dry interior of the continent rarely more than 80°–100° high, with a trunk hardly exceeding 2°–3° in diameter, slender crowded branches densely clothed with long pendulous lateral branches, forming while the tree is young an open pyramid, soon deciduous from trees crowded in the forest, often leaving the trunk naked for two thirds of its length and surmounted by a comparatively small narrow head sometimes becoming flap-topped by the lengthening of the upper branches, and slender branchlets pubescent for three or four years, pale orange color and lustrous during their first season, becoming bright reddish brown and ultimately dark gray-brown. **Winter-buds** ovoid, acute, the terminal bud often ¼′ long and nearly twice as large as the lateral buds. **Bark** on young trees smooth, thin, rather lustrous, dark gray-brown, usually becoming on old trunks 10′–12′ thick, and divided into oblong plates broken into great broad rounded and irregularly connected ridges separating on the surface into small thick closely appressed dark red-brown scales. **Wood** light, red or yellow, with nearly white sapwood; very variable in density, quality, and in the thickness of the sapwood; largely manufactured into lumber in British Columbia, western Washington and Oregon, and used for all kinds of construction, fuel, railway-ties, and piles; known commercially as "Oregon pine." The bark is sometimes used in tanning leather.

Distribution. From about latitude 55° north in the Rocky Mountains and from the head of the Skeena River in the coast range, southward through all the Rocky Mountain system to the mountains of western Texas, southern New Mexico and Arizona, and of northern Mexico, and from the Big Horn and Laramie Ranges in Wyoming and from eastern base of the Rocky Mountains of Colorado to the Pacific coast, but absent from the arid mountains in the great basin between the Wahsatch and the Sierra Nevada ranges and from the mountains of southern California; most abundant and of its largest size near the sea-level in the coast region of southern British Columbia and of Washington and Oregon, and on the western foothills of the Cascade Mountains; ascending on the California Sierras to elevations of 5500°, and on the mountains of Colorado to between 6000° and 11,000°, above the sea.

Often planted for timber and ornament in temperate Europe, and for ornament in the eastern and northern states, where only the form from the interior of the continent flourishes. (*P. glauca Mayr.*)

2. Pseudotsuga macrocarpa Mayr. Hemlock.

Leaves acute or acuminate, terminating in slender rigid callous tips, apparently 2-ranked by the conspicuous twist of their petioles, incurved above the middle, $\frac{3}{4}'$–$1\frac{1}{4}'$ long, about $\frac{1}{16}'$ wide, dark bluish gray. **Flowers:** male pale yellow, inclosed for half their length

Fig. 51

in conspicuous involucres of the lustrous bud-scales; female with pale green bracts tinged with red. **Fruit** produced on the upper branches and occasionally on those down to the middle of the tree, short-stalked, with scales near the middle of the cone $1\frac{1}{2}'$–$2'$ across, stiff, thick, concave, rather broader than long, rounded above, abruptly wedge-shaped at the base, puberulous on the outer surface, often nearly as long as their comparatively short and narrow bracts with broad midribs produced into short flattened flexible tips; **seeds** full and rounded on both sides, rugose, dark chestnut-brown or nearly black and lustrous above, pale reddish brown below, $\frac{1}{2}'$ long, $\frac{3}{8}'$ wide, with a thick brittle outer coat, and wings broadest near the middle, about $\frac{1}{2}'$ long, nearly $\frac{1}{4}'$ wide, and rounded at the apex.

A tree, usually 40°–50° and rarely 90° high, with a trunk 3°–4° in diameter, remote elongated branches pendulous below, furnished with short stout pendant or often erect laterals forming an open broad-based symmetrical pyramidal head, slender branchlets dark reddish brown and pubescent during their first year, becoming glabrous and dark or light orange-brown and ultimately gray-brown. **Winter buds** ovoid, acute, usually not more than $\frac{1}{8}'$ long, often nearly as broad as long. **Bark** 3'-6' thick, dark reddish brown, deeply divided into broad rounded ridges covered with thick closely appressed scales. **Wood** heavy, hard, strong, close-grained, not durable; occasionally manufactured into lumber; largely used for fuel.

Distribution. Steep rocky mountain slopes in southern California at elevations of 3000°–5000° above the sea, often forming open groves of considerable extent, from the Santa Inez Mountains in Santa Barbara County to the Cuyamaca Mountains.

6. ABIES Link. Fir.

Tall pyramidal trees, with bark containing numerous resin-vesicles, smooth, pale, and thin on young trees, often thick and deeply furrowed in old age, pale and usually brittle wood, slender horizontal wide-spreading branches in regular remote 4 or 5-branched whorls, clothed with twice or thrice forked lateral branches forming flat-topped masses of foliage gradually narrowed from the base to the apex of the branch, the ultimate divisions stout, glabrous or pubescent, and small subglobose or ovoid winter branch-buds usually thickly covered with resin, or in one species large and acute, with thin loosely imbricated scales. Leaves linear, sessile, on young plants and on lower sterile branches flattened and mostly grooved on the upper side, or in one species 4-sided, rounded and usually emarginate at apex, appearing 2-ranked by a twist near their base or occasionally spreading from all sides of the branch, only rarely stomatiferous above, on upper fertile branches and leading shoots usually crowded, more or less erect, often incurved or falcate, thick, convex on the upper side, or quadrangular in some species and then obtuse, or acute at apex and frequently stomatiferous on all sides; persistent usually for eight or ten years, in falling leaving small circular scars. Flowers axillary, from buds formed the previous season on branchlets of the year, surrounded at the base by conspicuous involucres of enlarged bud-scales, the male very abundant on the lower side of branches above the middle of the tree, oval or oblong-cylindric with yellow or scarlet anthers surmounted by short knob-like projections, the female usually on the upper side only of the topmost branches, or in some species scattered also over the upper half of the tree, erect, globose, ovoid or oblong, their scales imbricated in many series, obovate, rounded above, cuneate below, much shorter than their acute or dilated mucronate bracts. Fruit an erect ovoid or oblong-cylindric cone, its scales closely imbricated, thin, incurved at the broad apex and generally narrowed below into long stipes, decreasing in size and sterile toward the ends of the cone, falling at maturity with their bracts and seeds from the stout tapering axis of the cone long-persistent on the branch. Seeds furnished with large conspicuous resin-vesicles, ovoid or oblong, acute at base, covered on the upper side and infolded below on the lower side by the base of their thin wing abruptly enlarged at the oblique apex; seed-coat thin, of 2 layers, the outer thick, coriaceous, the inner membranaceous; cotyledons 4–10, much shorter than the inferior radicle.

Abies is widely distributed in the New World from Labrador and the valley of the Athabasca River to the mountains of North Carolina, and from Alaska through the Pacific and Rocky Mountain regions to the highlands of Guatemala, and in the Old World from Siberia and the mountains of central Europe to southern Japan, central China, Formosa, the Himalayas, Asia Minor, and the highlands of northern Africa. Thirty-three species are now recognized. Several exotic species are cultivated in the northern and eastern states; of these the best known and most successful as ornamental trees are *Abies Nordmanniana*, Spach, of the Caucasus, *Abies cilicica* Carr., of Asia Minor, *Abies cephalonica* Loud., a native of Cephalonia, *Abies Veitchii* Lindl., and *Abies homolepis* S. & Z., of Japan, and *Abies pinsapo*, Boiss., of the Spanish Sierra Nevada.

Abies is the classical name of the Fir-tree.

CONSPECTUS OF THE NORTH AMERICAN SPECIES.

Winter-buds subglobose, with closely imbricated scales.

Leaves flat and grooved above, with stomata on the lower surface (in Nos. 3 and 5, also on the upper surface), rounded and often notched, or on fertile branches frequently acute at apex.

Leaves on sterile branches spreading, not crowded.

Cones purple.

Leaves dark green and lustrous above, pale below.

Bracts of the cone-scales much longer than their scales, reflexed.

1. **A. Fraseri** (A).

Bracts of the cone-scales shorter or rarely slightly longer than their scales.

2. **A. balsamea** (A).

Leaves pale blue-green, stomatose above.   3. **A. lasiocarpa** (B, F, G).

Cones green (green, yellow, and purple in No. 5).

Leaves dark green and lustrous above, pale below.   4. **A. grandis** (B, G).

Leaves pale blue or glaucous, often stomatose above on the upper surface.

5. **A. concolor** (F, G, H).

Leaves on sterile branches pointing forward, densely crowded, dark green and lustrous above, pale below.   6. **A. amabilis** (B, G).

Leaves often 4-sided, with stomata on all surfaces, blue-green, usually glaucous, bluntly pointed or acute, incurved and crowded on fertile branches; cones purple.

Leaves of sterile branches flattened and distinctly grooved above; bracts of the cone-scales rounded and fimbriate above, long-pointed, incurved, light green, much longer than and covering their scales.   7. **A. nobilis** (G).

Leaves of sterile branches 4-sided; bracts of the cone-scales acute or acuminate or rounded above, with slender tips shorter or longer than their scales.

8. **A. magnifica** (G).

Winter-buds acuminate, with loosely imbricated scales; bracts of the cone-scales produced into elongated ridged flat tips many times longer than the obtusely pointed scales; leaves acuminate, dark yellow-green above, white below, similar on sterile and fertile branches.   9. **A. venusta** (G).

1. Abies Fraseri Poir., Balsam Fir.   She Balsam.

Leaves obtusely short-pointed or occasionally slightly emarginate at apex, dark green and lustrous on the upper surface, marked on the lower surface by wide bands of 8-12

Fig. 52

rows of stomata, $\frac{1}{2}'$ to nearly $1'$ long, about $\frac{1}{16}'$ wide. **Flowers:** male yellow tinged with red; female with scales rounded above, much broader than long and shorter than their oblong pale yellow-green bracts rounded at the broad apex terminating in a slender elongated tip. **Fruit** oblong-ovoid or nearly oval, rounded at the somewhat narrowed apex, dark purple, puberulous, about $2\frac{1}{2}'$ long, with scales twice as wide as long, at maturity nearly half covered by their pale yellow-green reflexed bracts; **seeds** $\frac{1}{8}'$ long, with dark lustrous wings much expanded and very oblique at apex.

A tree, usually $30°-40°$ and rarely $70°$ high, with a trunk occasionally $2\frac{1}{2}°$ in diameter, and rather rigid branches forming an open symmetrical pyramid and often disappearing early from the lower part of the trunk, and stout branchlets pubescent for three or four years, pale yellow-brown during their first season, becoming dark reddish brown often tinged with purple, and obtuse orange-brown winter-buds. **Bark** $\frac{1}{4}'-\frac{1}{2}'$ thick, covered with thin closely appressed bright cinnamon-red scales, generally becoming gray on old trees. **Wood** light, soft, not strong, coarse-grained, pale brown, with nearly white sapwood; occasionally manufactured into lumber.

Distribution. Appalachian Mountains; Cheat Mountain, near Cheat Bridge, Randolph County, West Virginia, and from southwestern Virginia to western North Carolina and eastern Tennessee, often forming forests of considerable extent at elevations between $4000°$ and $6000°$ above the sea-level.

Occasionally planted in the parks and gardens of the northern states and of Europe, but short-lived in cultivation and of little value as an ornamental tree.

2. Abies balsamea Mill. Balsam Fir.

Leaves dark green and lustrous on the upper surface, silvery white on the lower surface, with bands of 4–8 rows of stomata, $\frac{1}{2}'$ long on cone-bearing branches to $1\frac{1}{4}'$ long on the sterile branches of young trees, straight, acute or acuminate, with short or elongated rigid

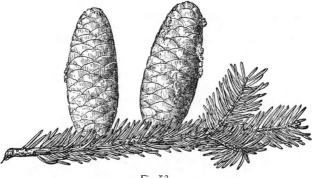

Fig. 53

callous tips, spreading at nearly right angles to the branch on young trees and sterile branches, on the upper branches of older trees often broadest above the middle, rounded or obtusely short-pointed at apex, occasionally emarginate on branches at the top of the tree. **Flowers:** male yellow, more or less deeply tinged with reddish purple; female with nearly orbicular purple scales much shorter than their oblong-obovate serrulate pale yellow-green bracts emarginate with a broad apex abruptly contracted into a long slender recurved tip. **Fruit** oblong-cylindric, gradually narrowed to the rounded apex, puberulous, dark rich purple, $2'-4'$ long, with scales usually longer than broad, generally almost twice as long; rarely not as long as their bracts, (var. *phanerolepis* Fern.); **seeds** about $\frac{1}{4}'$ long and rather shorter than their light brown wings.

A tree, 50°–60° high, with a trunk usually 12′–18′, or rarely 30′ in diameter, spreading branches forming a handsome symmetrical slender pyramid, the lower branches soon dying from trees crowded in the forest, and slender branchlets pale yellow-green and coated with fine pubescence at first, becoming light gray tinged with red, and often when four or five years old with purple. **Winter-buds** nearly globose, ⅛′–¼′ in diameter, with lustrous dark orange-green scales. **Bark** on old trees often ½′ thick, rich brown, much broken on the surface into small plates covered with scales. **Wood** light, soft, not strong, coarse-grained, perishable, pale brown streaked with yellow, with thick lighter colored sapwood; occasionally made into lumber principally used for packing-cases. From the bark of this tree oil of fir used in the arts and in medicine is obtained.

Distribution. From the interior of the Labrador peninsula westward to the shores of Lesser Slave Lake, southward through Newfoundland, the maritime provinces of Canada, Quebec and Ontario, northern New England, northern New York, northern Michigan to the shores of Saginaw Bay, and northern Minnesota and northeastern Iowa, and along the Appalachian Mountains from western Massachusetts and the Catskills of New York to the high mountains of southwestern Virginia; common and often forming a considerable part of the forest on low swampy ground; on well-drained hillsides sometimes singly in forests of spruce or forming small almost impenetrable thickets; in northern Wisconsin and vicinity occurs a form with longer and more crowded leaves and larger cones (var. *macrocarpa* Kent); near the timber-line on the mountains of New England and New York reduced to a low almost prostrate shrub.

Sometimes planted in the northern states in the neighborhood of farmhouses, but usually short-lived and of little value as an ornamental tree in cultivation; formerly but now rarely cultivated in European plantations; a dwarf form (var. *hudsonia* Sarg.) growing only a few inches high and spreading into broad nests is often cultivated.

3. Abies lasiocarpa Nutt. Balsam Fir.

Leaves marked on the upper surface but generally only above the middle with 4 or 5 rows of stomata on each side of the conspicuous midrib and on the lower surface by 2 broad bands each of 7 or 8 rows, crowded, nearly erect by the twist at their base, on lower branches 1′–1¾′ long, about 1/12′ wide, and rounded and occasionally emarginate at apex, on upper branches somewhat thickened, usually acute, generally not more than ½′ long, on leading shoots flattened, closely appressed, with long slender rigid points. **Flowers:** male dark indigo-blue, turning violet when nearly ready to open; female with dark violet-purple obovate scales much shorter than their strongly reflexed bracts contracted into slender tips. **Fruit** oblong-cylindric, rounded, truncate or depressed at the narrowed apex, dark purple, puberulous, 2½′–4′ long, with scales gradually narrowed from the broad rounded or nearly truncate apex to the base, usually longer than broad, about three times as long as their oblong-obovate red-brown bracts laciniately cut on the margins, rounded, emarginate and abruptly contracted at the apex into long slender tips; **seeds** ¼′ long, with dark lustrous wings covering nearly the entire surface of the scales.

A tree, usually 80°–100°, occasionally 175°, or southward rarely more than 50° high, with a trunk 2°–5° in diameter, short crowded tough branches, usually slightly pendulous near the base of the tree, generally clothing the trunks of the oldest trees nearly to their base and forming dense spire-like slender heads, and comparatively stout branchlets coated for three or four years with fine rufous pubescence, or rarely glabrous before the end of their first season, pale orange-brown, ultimately gray or silvery white. **Winter-buds** sub-globose, ⅛′–¼′ thick, covered with light orange-brown scales. **Bark** becoming on old trees ¾′–1½′ thick, divided by shallow fissures and roughened by thick closely appressed cinnamon-red scales; on the San Francisco Mountains, Arizona, thicker and spongy (var. *arizonica* Lem.). **Wood** light, soft, not strong, pale brown or nearly white, with light-colored sapwood; little used except for fuel.

Distribution. High mountain slopes and summits from about latitude 61° in Alaska, southward along the coast ranges to the Olympic Mountains of Washington, over all the high mountain ranges of British Columbia and Alberta, and southward along the Cascade Mountains of Washington and Oregon to the neighborhood of Crater Lake, over

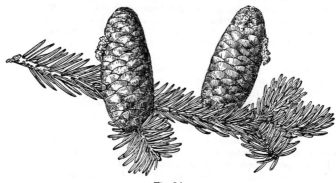

Fig. 54

the mountain ranges of eastern Washington and Oregon, and of Idaho, Wyoming, Colorado, and Utah to the San Francisco peaks of northern Arizona, and on the Sandia and Mogollon Mountains of New Mexico. This southern form is now often considered a species as *Abies arizonica* Merr.

Occasionally planted as an ornamental tree in the northern United States and in northern Europe, but of little value in cultivation.

4. Abies grandis Lindl.   White Fir.

Leaves thin and flexible, deeply grooved very dark green and lustrous on upper surface, silvery white on lower surface, with two broad bands of 7–10 rows of stomata, on sterile branches remote, rounded and conspicuously emarginate at apex, $1\frac{1}{2}'$–$2\frac{1}{4}'$ long, usu-

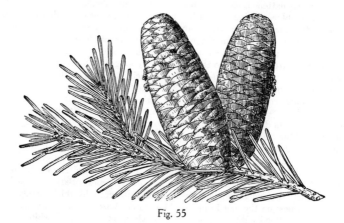

Fig. 55

ally about $\frac{1}{8}'$ wide, spreading in two ranks nearly at right angles to the branch, on cone-bearing branches more crowded, usually $1'$–$1\frac{1}{2}'$ long, less spreading or nearly erect, blunt-pointed or often notched at apex, on vigorous young trees $\frac{1}{2}'$–$\frac{3}{4}'$ long, acute or acuminate, usually persistent 4–10 years. **Flowers:** male pale yellow sometimes tinged with purple; female light yellow-green, with semiorbicular scales and short-oblong bracts emarginate and denticulate at the broad obcordate apex furnished with a short strongly reflexed tip. **Fruit** cylindric, slightly narrowed to the rounded and sometimes retuse apex, puberulous, bright green, 2′–4′ long, with scales usually about two thirds as long as wide, gradually or abruptly narrowed from their broad apex and three or four times as long as their short pale green bracts; **seeds** $\frac{3}{8}'$ in length, light brown, with pale lustrous wings $\frac{1}{2}'-\frac{5}{8}'$ long and nearly as broad as their abruptly widened rounded apex.

A tree, in the neighborhood of the coast 250°–300° high, with a slightly tapering trunk often 4° in diameter, long somewhat pendulous branches sweeping out in graceful curves, and comparatively slender pale yellow-green puberulous branchlets becoming light reddish brown or orange-brown and glabrous in their second season; on the mountains of the interior rarely more than 100° tall, with a trunk usually about 2° in diameter, often smaller and much stunted at high elevations. **Winter-buds** subglobose, $\frac{1}{8}'-\frac{1}{4}'$ thick. **Bark** becoming sometimes 2′ thick at the base of old trees and gray-brown or reddish brown and divided by shallow fissures into low flat ridges broken into oblong plates roughened by thick closely appressed scales. **Wood** light, soft, coarse-grained, not strong nor durable, light brown, with thin lighter colored sapwood; occasionally manufactured into lumber in western Washington and Oregon and used for the interior finish of buildings, packing-cases, and wooden-ware.

Distribution. Northern part of Vancouver Island southward in the neighborhood of the coast to northern Sonoma County, California, and along the mountains of northern Washington and Idaho to the western slopes of the continental divide in northern Montana, and to the mountains of eastern Oregon; near the coast scattered on moist ground through forests of other conifers; common in Washington and northern Oregon from the sea up to elevations of 4000°; in the interior on moist slopes in the neighborhood of streams from 2500° up to 7000° above the sea; in California rarely ranging more than ten miles inland or ascending to altitudes of more than 1500° above the sea.

Occasionally planted in the parks and gardens of temperate Europe, where it grows rapidly and promises to attain a large size; rarely planted in the United States.

5. Abies concolor Lindl. & Gord. White Fir.

Leaves crowded, spreading in 2 ranks and more or less erect from the strong twist at their base, pale blue or glaucous, becoming dull green at the end of two or three years, with 2 broad bands of stomata on the lower, and more or less stomatiferous on the upper surface, on lower branches flat, straight, rounded, acute or acuminate at apex, 2′–3′ long, about $\frac{1}{16}'$ wide, on fertile branches and on old trees frequently thick, keeled above, usually falcate, acute or rarely notched at apex, $\frac{3}{4}'-1\frac{1}{2}'$ long, often $\frac{1}{8}'$ wide. **Flowers:** male dark red or rose color; female with broad rounded scales, and oblong strongly reflexed obcordate bracts laciniate above the middle and abruptly contracted at apex into short points. **Fruit** oblong, slightly narrowed from near the middle to the ends, rounded or obtuse at apex, 3′–5′ long, puberulous, grayish green, dark purple or bright canary-yellow, with scales much broader than long, gradually and regularly narrowed from the rounded apex, rather more than twice as long as their emarginate or nearly truncate bracts broad at the apex and terminating in short slender tips; **seeds** $\frac{1}{3}'-\frac{1}{2}'$ long, acute at base, dark dull brown, with lustrous rose-colored wings widest near the middle and nearly truncate at apex.

A tree, on the California sierras 200°–250° high, with a trunk often 6° in diameter or in the interior of the continent rarely more than 125° tall, with a trunk seldom exceeding 3° in diameter, a narrow spire-like crown of short stout branches clothed with long lateral branches pointing forward and forming great frond-like masses of foliage, and glabrous lustrous comparatively stout branchlets dark orange color during their first season, becoming light grayish green or pale reddish brown, and ultimately gray or grayish brown. **Winter-buds** subglobose, $\frac{1}{8}'-\frac{1}{4}'$ thick. **Bark** becoming on old trunks sometimes 5′–6′ thick near the ground and deeply divided into broad rounded ridges broken on the surface into irregularly shaped plate-like scales. **Wood** very light, soft, coarse-grained and not strong nor durable, pale brown or sometimes nearly white; occasionally manufactured into lumber, in northern California used for packing-cases and butter-tubs.

Distribution. Rocky Mountains of southern Colorado, westward to the mountain ranges of California, extending northward into northern Oregon, and southward over

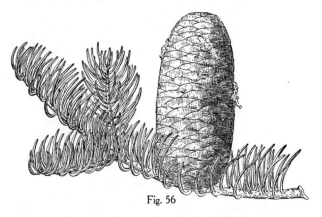

Fig. 56

the mountains of New Mexico and Arizona into northern Mexico and Lower California (Mt. San Pedro Mártir Mountains); the only Fir-tree in the arid regions of the Great Basin, of southern New Mexico and Arizona, and of the mountain forests of southern California.

Often planted as an ornamental tree in Europe (the California form usually as *A. Lowiana* Murr.) and in the eastern states where it grows more vigorously than other Fir-trees.

6. Abies amabilis Forbes. White Fir.

Leaves deeply grooved, very dark green and lustrous on the upper surface, silvery white on the lower, with broad bands of 6 or 8 rows of stomata between the prominent midribs and incurved margins, on sterile branches obtuse and rounded, or notched or occasionally acute at apex, $\frac{3}{4}'-1\frac{1}{4}'$ long, $\frac{1}{16}'-\frac{1}{12}'$ wide, often broadest above the middle, erect by a twist at their base, very crowded, those on the upper side of the branch much shorter than those on the lower and usually parallel with and closely appressed against it, on fertile branches acute or acuminate with callous tips, occasionally stomatiferous on the upper surface near the apex, $\frac{1}{2}'-\frac{3}{4}'$ long; on vigorous leading shoots acute, with long rigid points, closely appressed or recurved near the middle, about $\frac{3}{4}'$ long and nearly $\frac{1}{8}'$ wide. **Flowers:** male red; female with broad rounded scales and rhombic dark purple lustrous bracts erose above the middle and gradually contracted into broad points. **Fruit** oblong, slightly narrowed to the rounded and often retuse apex, deep rich purple, puberulous, $3\frac{1}{2}'-6'$ long, with scales $1'-1\frac{1}{8}'$ wide, nearly as long as broad, gradually narrowed from the rounded apex and rather more than twice as long as their reddish rhombic or oblong-obovate bracts terminating in long slender tips; **seeds** light yellow-brown, $\frac{1}{2}'$ long, with oblique pale brown lustrous wings about $\frac{3}{4}'$ long.

A tree, often 250° tall, or at high altitudes and in the north usually not more than 70°–80° tall, with a trunk 4°–6° in diameter, in thick forests often naked for 150°, but in open situations densely clothed to the ground with comparatively short branches sweeping down in graceful curves, and stout branchlets clothed for four or five years with soft fine pubescence, light orange-brown in their first season, becoming dark purple and ultimately reddish brown. **Winter-buds** nearly globose, $\frac{1}{8}'-\frac{1}{4}'$ thick, with closely imbricated lustrous purple scales. **Bark** on trees up to 150 years old thin, smooth, pale or silvery white, becoming near the ground on old trees $1\frac{1}{2}'-2\frac{1}{2}'$ thick, and irregularly divided into comparatively small plates covered with small closely appressed reddish brown or reddish gray scales. **Wood** light, hard, not strong, close-grained, pale brown, with nearly white sapwood; in Washington occasionally manufactured into lumber used in the interior finish of buildings.

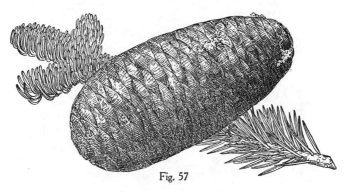

Fig. 57

Distribution. High mountain slopes and benches from southeastern Alaska (Boca de Quadra Inlet and Sandfly Bay), to Vancouver Island and southward along the coast ranges to Saddle Mountain near Astoria, Oregon, and on the Cascade Mountains to the slopes of Old Bailey Mountain, Oregon, ranging from the sea level at the north to elevations of from 3000°–6000° southward; attaining its largest size on the Olympic Mountains of Washington, where it is the most common Fir-tree.

Occasionally cultivated as an ornamental tree in the eastern states and in western Europe, but without developing the beauty which distinguishes this species in its native forests.

7. Abies nobilis Lindl. Red Fir.

Leaves marked on the upper surface with a deep sharply defined groove, rounded and obscurely ribbed on the lower surface, stomatiferous above and below, dark or light blue-green, often very glaucous during their first season, crowded in several rows, those on the lower side of the branch two-ranked by the twisting of their bases, the others crowded, strongly incurved, with the points erect or pointing away from the end of the branch, on young plants and on the lower sterile branches of old trees flat, rounded, usually slightly notched at apex, $1'-1\frac{1}{2}'$ long, about $\frac{1}{18}'$ wide, on fertile branches much thickened and almost equally 4-sided, acuminate, with long rigid callous tips, $\frac{1}{2}'-\frac{3}{4}'$ long, on leading shoots flat, gradually narrowed from the base, acuminate, with long rigid points, about $1'$ long. **Flowers:** male reddish purple; female often scattered over the upper part of the tree, with broad rounded scales much shorter than their nearly orbicular bracts erose on the margins and contracted above into slender elongated strongly reflexed tips. **Fruit** oblong-cylindric, slightly narrowed but full and rounded at apex, $4'-5'$ long, purple or olive-brown, pubescent, with scales about one third wider than long, gradually narrowed from the rounded apex to the base, or full at the sides, rounded and denticulate above the middle and sharply contracted and wedge-shaped below, nearly or entirely covered by their strongly reflexed pale green spatulate bracts full and rounded above, fimbriate on the margins, with broad midribs produced into short broad flattened points; **seeds** $\frac{1}{2}'$ long, pale reddish brown, about as long as their wings, gradually narrowed from below to the nearly truncate slightly rounded apex.

A tree, in old age with a comparatively broad somewhat rounded head, usually 150°–200° and occasionally 250° high, with a trunk 6°–8° in diameter, short rigid branches, short stout remote lateral branches standing out at right angles, and slender reddish brown branchlets puberulous for four or five years and generally pointing forward. **Winter-buds** ovoid-oblong, red-brown, about ⅛′ long. **Bark** becoming on old trunks 1′–2′ thick, bright red-brown, and deeply divided into broad flat ridges irregularly broken by cross fissures and

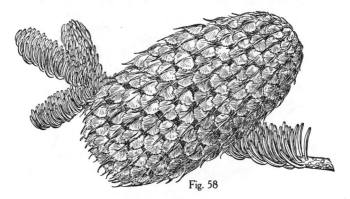

Fig. 58

covered with thick closely appressed scales. **Wood** light, hard, strong, rather close-grained, pale brown streaked with red, with darker colored sapwood; occasionally manufactured into lumber and used under the name of larch for the interior finish of buildings and for packing-cases.

Distribution. Slopes of Mt. Baker in northern Washington and southward to the valley of the Mackenzie River, Oregon, and the Siskiyou Mountains, California, at elevations of from 2000°–5000° above the sea; most abundant and often forming extensive forests on the Cascade Mountains of Washington; less abundant and of smaller size on the eastern and northern slopes of these mountains. In Oregon sometimes called Larch.

Often planted in western and central Europe as an ornamental tree, and in the eastern states hardy in sheltered positions as far north as Massachusetts.

8. Abies magnifica A. Murr. Red Fir.

Leaves almost equally 4-sided, ribbed above and below, with 6–8 rows of stomata on each of the 4 sides, pale and very glaucous during their first season, later becoming blue-green, persistent usually for about ten years; on young plants and lower branches oblanceolate, somewhat flattened, rounded, bluntly pointed, ¾′–1½′ long, ⅛′ wide, those on the lower side of the branch spreading in 2 nearly horizontal ranks by the twist at their base, on upper, especially on fertile branches, much thickened, with more prominent

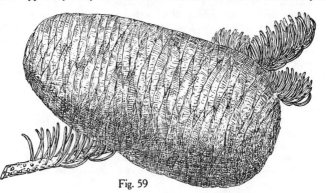

Fig. 59

midribs, acute, with short callous tips, $\frac{1}{3}'$ long on the upper side of the branch to $1\frac{1}{4}'$ long on the lower side, crowded, erect, strongly incurved, completely hiding the upper side of the branch, on leading shoots $\frac{3}{4}'$ long, erect and acuminate, with long rigid points pressed against the stem. **Flowers:** male dark reddish purple; female with rounded scales much shorter than their oblong pale green bracts terminating in elongated slender tips more or less tinged with red. **Fruit** oblong-cylindric, slightly narrowed to the rounded, truncate, or retuse apex, dark purplish brown, puberulous, from 6′–9′ long, with scales often $1\frac{1}{2}'$ wide and about two thirds as wide as long, gradually narrowed to the cordate base, somewhat longer or often two thirds as long as their spatulate acute or acuminate bracts slightly serrulate above the middle and often sharply contracted and then enlarged toward the base; **seeds** dark reddish brown, $\frac{3}{4}'$ long, about as wide as their lustrous rose-colored obovate cuneate wings nearly truncate and often $\frac{3}{4}'$ wide at apex.

A tree, in old age occasionally somewhat round-topped, frequently 200° high, with a trunk 8°–10° in diameter and often naked for half the height of the tree, comparatively short small branches, the upper somewhat ascending, the lower pendulous, and stout light yellow-green branchlets pointing forward, slightly puberulous during their first season, becoming light red-brown and lustrous and ultimately gray or silvery white. **Winter-buds** ovoid, acute, $\frac{1}{4}'–\frac{1}{3}'$ long, their bright chestnut-brown scales with prominent midribs produced into short tips. **Bark** becoming 4′–6′ thick near the ground, deeply divided into broad rounded ridges broken by cross fissures and covered by dark red-brown scales. **Wood** light, soft, not strong, comparatively durable, light red-brown, with thick somewhat darker sapwood; largely used for fuel, and in California occasionally manufactured into coarse lumber employed in the construction of cheap buildings and for packing-cases.

Distribution. Cascade Mountains of southern Oregon, southward over the mountain ranges of northern California (summits of the Trinity and Salmon Mountains and on the inner north coast ranges), and along the western slope of the Sierra Nevada to the divide between White and Kern Rivers; common in southern Oregon at elevations between 5000° and 7000° above the sea, forming sometimes nearly pure forests; very abundant on the Sierra Nevada, and the principal tree in the forest belt at elevations between 6000° and 9000°; ascending towards the southern extremity of its range to over 10,000°. Small stunted trees from the neighborhood of Meadow Lake, Sierra County, California, with yellowish cones have been described as var. *xanthocarpa* Lemm.

Often planted as an ornamental tree in western and central Europe, and sometimes hardy in the United States as far north as eastern Massachusetts.

A distinct form is

Abies magnifica var. shastensis Lemm. Red Fir.

On the mountains of southern Oregon and at high elevations on those of northern California, and on the southern Sierra Nevada, occurs this form distinguished only by the

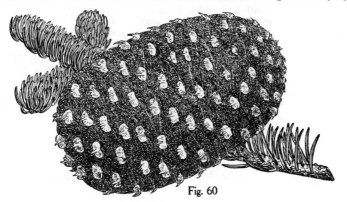

Fig. 60

longer rounded or obtusely pointed (not acute) bright yellow bracts which sometimes cover nearly half their scales.

9. Abies venusta K. Koch.   Silver Fir.

Abies bracteata D. Don.

Leaves thin, flat, rigid, linear or linear-lanceolate, gradually or abruptly narrowed toward the base, often falcate, especially on fertile branches, acuminate, with long slender callous tips, dark yellow-green, lustrous and slightly rounded on the upper surface marked below the middle with an obscure groove, silvery white or on old leaves pale on the lower surface, with bands of 8–10 rows of stomata between the broad midrib and the thickened strongly revolute margins, 2-ranked from the conspicuous twist near their base and spreading at nearly right angles to the branch, or pointing forward on upper fertile branches, $1\frac{1}{2}'-2\frac{1}{4}'$ long, on leading shoots standing out at almost right angles, rounded on the upper surface, more or less incurved above the middle, $1\frac{1}{2}'-1\frac{3}{4}'$ long, about $\frac{1}{8}'$ wide. **Flowers:** male produced in great numbers near the base of the branchlets on branches from the middle of the tree upward, pale yellow; female near the ends of the branchlets of the

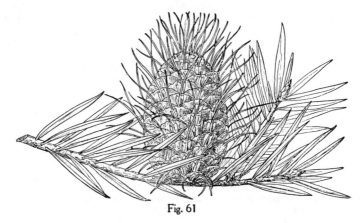

Fig. 61

upper branches only, with oblong scales rounded above and nearly as long as their cuneate obcordate yellow-green bracts ending in slender elongated awns. **Fruit** on stout peduncles sometimes $\frac{1}{2}'$ long, oval or subcylindric, full and rounded at apex, glabrous, pale purple-brown, $3'-4'$ long, with thin scales strongly incurved above, obtusely short-pointed at apex, obscurely denticulate on the thin margins, about one third longer than their oblong-obovate obcordate pale yellow-brown bracts terminating in flat rigid tips $1'-1\frac{3}{4}'$ long, above the middle of the cone pointing toward its apex and often closely appressed to its sides, below the middle spreading toward its base and frequently much recurved, firmly attached to the cone-scales and deciduous with them from the thick conical sharp-pointed axis of the cone; **seeds** dark red-brown, about $\frac{3}{8}'$ long, and nearly as long as their oblong-obovate pale reddish brown lustrous wings rounded at the apex.

A tree, $100°-150°$ high, with a trunk sometimes $3°$ in diameter, comparatively short slender usually pendulous branches furnished with long sinuous rather remote lateral branches sparsely clothed with foliage, forming a broad-based pyramid abruptly narrowed $15°-20°$ from the top of the tree into a thin spire-like head, and stout glabrous light reddish brown branchlets covered at first with a glaucous bloom. **Winter-buds** ovoid, acute, $\frac{3}{4}'-1'$ long, $\frac{1}{4}'-\frac{1}{3}'$ thick, with very thin, loosely imbricated, pale chestnut-brown, acute, boat-shaped scales. **Bark** becoming near the base of the tree $\frac{1}{2}'-\frac{3}{4}'$ thick, light reddish brown, slightly and irregularly fissured and broken into thick closely appressed scales. **Wood** heavy, not hard, coarse-grained, light brown tinged with yellow, with paler sapwood.

Distribution. In the moist bottoms of cañons and on dry rocky summits, usually at elevations of about 3000° above the sea on both slopes of the outer western ridge of the Santa Lucia Mountains, Monterey County, California.

Occasionally and successfully grown as an ornamental tree in the milder parts of Great Britain and in northern Italy; not hardy in the eastern United States.

7. SEQUOIA Endl.

Resinous aromatic trees, with tall massive lobed trunks, thick bark of 2 layers, the outer composed of fibrous scales, the inner thin, close and firm, soft, durable, straight-grained red heartwood, thin nearly white sapwood, short stout horizontal branches, terete lateral branchlets deciduous in the autumn, and scaly or naked buds. Leaves ovate-lanceolate or linear and spreading in 2 ranks especially on young trees and branches, or linear, acute, compressed, keeled on the back and closely appressed or spreading at apex, the two forms appearing sometimes on the same branch or on different branches of the same tree. Flowers minute, solitary, monœcious, appearing in early spring from buds formed the previous autumn, the male terminal in the axils of upper leaves, oblong or ovoid, surrounded by an involucre of numerous imbricated ovate, acute, and apiculate bracts, with numerous spirally disposed filaments dilated into ovoid acute subpeltate denticulate connectives bearing on their inner face 2–5 pendulous globose 2-valved anther-cells; the female terminal, ovoid or oblong, composed of numerous spirally imbricated ovate scales abruptly keeled on the back, the keels produced into short or elongated points closely adnate to the short ovule-bearing scales rounded above and bearing below their upper margin in 2 rows 5–7 ovules at first erect, becoming reversed. Fruit an ovoid or short-oblong pendulous cone maturing during the first or second season, persistent after the escape of the seeds, its scales formed by the enlargement of the united flower and ovuliferous scales, becoming woody, bearing large deciduous resin-glands, gradually enlarged upward and widening at the apex into a narrow thickened oblong disk transversely depressed through the middle and sometimes tipped with a small point. Seeds 5–7 under each scale, oblong-ovoid, compressed; seed-coat membranaceous, produced into broad thin lateral wings; cotyledons 4–6, longer than the inferior radicle.

Sequoia, widely scattered with several species over the northern hemisphere during the cretaceous and tertiary epochs, is now confined to the coast of Oregon and California and the mountains of California, where two species exist.

The name of the genus is formed from Sequoiah, the inventor of the Cherokee alphabet.

CONSPECTUS OF THE NORTH AMERICAN SPECIES.

Leaves mostly spreading in 2 ranks; cones maturing in one season; buds scaly.
1. S. sempervirens (G).

Leaves slightly spreading or appressed; cones maturing in their second season; buds naked.   **2. S. gigantea** (G).

1. Sequoia sempervirens Endl. Redwood.

Leaves of secondary branches and of lower branches of young trees lanceolate, more or less falcate, acute or acuminate and usually tipped with slender rigid points, slightly thickened on the revolute margins, decurrent at the base, spreading in 2 ranks by a half-turn at their base, ¼′–½′ long, about ⅛′ wide, obscurely keeled and marked above by 2 narrow bands of stomata, glaucous and stomatiferous below on each side of their conspicuous midrib, on leading shoots disposed in many ranks, more or less spreading or appressed, ovate or ovate-oblong, incurved at the rounded apiculate apex, thickened, rounded, and stomatiferous on the lower surface, concave, prominently keeled and covered with stomata on the upper surface, usually about $\frac{1}{4}'$ long; dying and turning reddish brown at least two years before falling. **Flowers** opening in December or January; male oblong, obtuse; female with about 20 broadly ovate acute scales tipped with elongated and incurved or short points. **Fruit** ripening in October, oblong, $\frac{3}{4}'-1'$ long, $\frac{1}{2}'$ broad, its scales gradually enlarged from slender stipes abruptly dilated above into disks penetrated by deep narrow grooves, and usually without tips; **seeds** about $\frac{1}{18}'$ long, light brown, with wings as broad as their body.

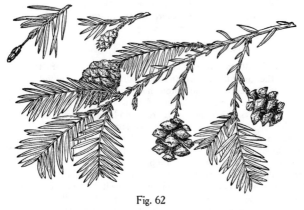

Fig. 62

A tree, from 200°–340° high, with a slightly tapering and irregularly lobed trunk usually free of branches for 75°–100°, usually 10°–15°, rarely 28° in diameter at the much buttressed base, slender branches, clothed with branchlets spreading in 2 ranks and forming while the tree is young an open narrow pyramid, on old trees becoming stout and horizontal, and forming a narrow rather compact and very irregular head remarkably small in proportion to the height and size of the trunk, and slender leading branchlets covered at the end of three or four years after the leaves fall with cinnamon-brown scaly bark ; when cut producing from the stump numerous vigorous long-lived shoots. **Buds** with numerous loosely imbricated ovate acute scales persistent on the base of the branchlet. **Bark** $6'-12'$ thick, divided into rounded ridges and separated on the surface into long narrow dark brown fibrous scales often broken transversely and in falling disclosing the bright cinnamon-red inner bark. **Wood** light, soft, not strong, close-grained, easily split and worked, very durable in contact with the soil, clear light red; largely manufactured into lumber and used for shingles, fence-posts, railway-ties, wine-butts, and in buildings.

Distribution. Valley of the Chetco River, Oregon, 8 miles north of the California state line, southward near the coast to Monterey County, California; rarely found more than twenty or thirty miles from the coast, or beyond the influence of the ocean fogs, or over 3000° above the sea-level; often forming in northern California pure forests occupying the sides of ravines and the banks of streams; southward growing usually in small groves scattered among other trees; most abundant and of its largest size north of Cape Mendocino.

Often cultivated as an ornamental tree in the temperate countries of Europe, and occasionally in the southeastern United States.

2. Sequoia gigantea Decne.   Big Tree.

Sequoia Wellingtonia Seem.

Leaves ovate and acuminate, or lanceolate, rounded and thickened on the lower surface, concave on the upper surface, marked by bands of stomata on both sides of the obscure midrib, rigid, sharp-pointed, decurrent below, spreading or closely appressed above the middle, $\frac{1}{8}'-\frac{1}{4}'$ or on leading shoots $\frac{1}{2}'$ long. **Flowers** opening in late winter and early spring; male in great profusion over the whole tree, oblong-ovoid, with ovate acute or acuminate connectives; female with 25–40 pale yellow scales slightly keeled on the back and gradually narrowed into long slender points. **Fruit** maturing in the second year, ovoid-oblong, $2'-3\frac{1}{2}'$ long, $1\frac{1}{2}'-2\frac{1}{4}'$ wide, dark reddish brown, the scales gradually thickened upward from the base to the slightly dilated apex, $\frac{3}{4}'-1\frac{1}{4}'$ long, and $\frac{1}{4}'-\frac{1}{2}'$ wide, deeply pitted in the middle, often furnished with an elongated reflexed tip and on the upper side near the base with two or three large deciduous resin-glands; **seeds** linear-lanceolate, compressed, $\frac{1}{8}'-\frac{1}{4}'$ long, light brown, surrounded by laterally united wings broader than the body of the seed, apiculate at the apex, often very unequal.

A tree, at maturity usually about 275° high, with a trunk 20° in diameter near the ground, occasionally becoming 320° tall, with a trunk 35° in diameter, much enlarged and buttressed

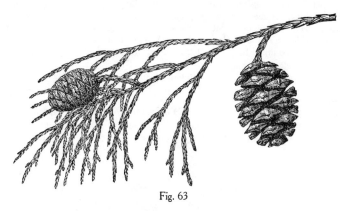

Fig. 63

at base, fluted with broad low rounded ridges, in old age naked often for 150° with short thick horizontal branches, slender leading branchlets becoming after the disappearance of the leaves reddish brown more or less tinged with purple and covered with thin close or slightly scaly bark and naked buds. **Bark** 1°–2° thick, divided into rounded lobes 4°–5° wide, corresponding to the lobes of the trunk, separating into loose light cinnamon-red fibrous scales, the outer scales slightly tinged with purple. **Wood** very light, soft, not strong, brittle and coarse-grained, turning dark on exposure; manufactured into lumber and used for fencing, in construction, and for shingles.

Distribution. Western slopes of the Sierra Nevada of California, in an interrupted belt at elevations of 5000°–8400° above the level of the sea, from the middle fork of the American River to the head of Deer Creek just south of latitude 36°; north of King's River in isolated groves, southward forming forests of considerable extent, and best developed on the north fork of the Tule River.

Universally cultivated as an ornamental tree in all the countries of western and southern Europe; and occasionally in the middle eastern United States.

8. TAXODIUM Rich. Bald Cypress.

Resinous trees, with furrowed scaly bark, light brown durable heartwood, thin white sapwood, erect ultimately spreading branches, deciduous usually 2-ranked lateral branchlets, scaly globose buds, and stout horizontal roots often producing erect woody projections (*knees*). Leaves spirally disposed, pale and marked with stomata below on both sides of the obscure midrib, dark green above, linear-lanceolate, spreading in 2 ranks, or scale-like and appressed on lateral branchlets, the two forms appearing on the same or on different branches of the same tree or on separate trees, deciduous. Flowers unisexual, from buds formed the previous year; male in the axils of scale-like bracts in long terminal drooping panicles, with 6–8 stamens opposite in 2 ranks, their filaments abruptly enlarged into broadly ovate peltate yellow connectives bearing on their inner face in 2 rows **4–9** 2-valved pendulous anther-cells; female scattered near the ends of the branches of the previous year, subglobose, composed of numerous ovate spirally arranged long-pointed scales, adnate below to the thickened fleshy ovuliferous scales bearing at their base 2 erect bottle-shaped ovules.   Fruit a globose or obovoid short-stalked woody cone maturing the first year and persistent after the escape of the seeds, formed from the enlargement and union of the flower and ovule-bearing scales abruptly dilated from slender stipes into irregularly 4-sided disks often mucronate at maturity, bearing on the inner face, especially on the stipes, large dark glands filled with blood-red fragrant liquid resin.   Seeds in pairs under each scale, attached laterally to the stipes, erect, unequally 3-angled; seed-coat light brown and lustrous, thick, coriaceous or corky, produced into 3 thick unequal lateral wings and below into a slender elongated point; cotyledons 4–9, shorter than the superior radicle.

Taxodium, widely distributed through North America and Europe in Miocene and Pliocene times, is now confined to the southern United States and Mexico.   Two species are distinguished.

The generic name, from τάξος and εἶδος, indicates a resemblance of the leaves to those of the Yew-tree.

1. Taxodium distichum Rich. Bald Cypress. Deciduous Cypress.

Leaves on distichously spreading branchlets, apiculate, $\frac{1}{2}'-\frac{3}{4}'$ long, about $\frac{1}{12}'$ wide, light bright yellow-green or occasionally silvery white below; or on the form with pendulous

Fig. 64

compressed branchlets long-pointed, keeled and stomatiferous below, concave above more or less spreading at the free apex, about $\frac{1}{2}'$ long; in the autumn turning with the branchlets dull orange-brown before falling. **Flowers:** panicles of staminate flowers $4'-5'$ long, $1\frac{1}{2}'-2'$ wide, with slender red-brown stems, obovoid flower-buds nearly $\frac{1}{8}'$ long, pale silvery-gray during winter and purple when the flowers expand in the spring. **Fruit** usually produced in pairs at the end of the branch or irregularly scattered along it for several inches, nearly globose or obovoid, rugose, about 1' in diameter, the scales generally destitute of tips; **seeds** with wings nearly $\frac{1}{4}'$ long, $\frac{1}{8}'$ wide.

A tree, with a tall lobed gradually tapering trunk, rarely 12° and generally 4°–5° in diameter above the abruptly enlarged strongly buttressed usually hollow base, occasionally 150° tall, in youth pyramidal, with slender branches often becoming elongated and slightly pendulous, in old age spreading out into a broad low rounded crown often 100° across, and slender branchlets light green when they first appear, light red-brown and rather lustrous during their first winter, becoming darker the following year, the lateral branchlets deciduous, 3′–4′ long, spreading at right angles to the branch, or in the form with acicular leaves pendulous or erect and often 6′ long. **Bark** 1′–2′ thick, light cinnamon-red and divided by shallow fissures into broad flat ridges separating on the surface into long thin closely appressed fibrous scales. **Wood** light, soft, not strong, very durable, easily worked, light or dark brown, sometimes nearly black; largely used for construction, railway-ties, posts, fences, and in cooperage.

Distribution. River swamps usually submerged during several months of the year, low wet banks of streams, and the wet depressions of Pine-barrens from southern New Jersey and southern Delaware southward generally near the coast to the Everglade Keys, southern Florida, and through the Gulf-coast region to the valley of Devil River, Texas, through Louisiana to southern Oklahoma, through southern and western Arkansas to southeastern Missouri, and through western and northern Mississippi to Tishomingo County, and in western Tennessee and Kentucky to southern Illinois and southwestern Indiana; most common and of its largest size in the south Atlantic and Gulf states, often covering with nearly pure forests great river swamps. From the coast of North Carolina to southern Florida, southern Alabama and eastern and western Louisiana the form with acicular leaves (*Taxodium distichum* var. *imbricarium*, Croom.) is not rare as a small tree in Pine-barren ponds and swamps.

Taxodium distichum var. *imbricarium* is now usually and rightly considered a distinct species for which the correct name is *Taxodium ascendens* Brong.; the extension of its range into western Louisiana is not supported by specimens.

Often cultivated as an ornamental tree in the northern United States, and in the countries of temperate Europe, especially the var. *imbricarium* (as *Glyptostrobus sinensis* Hort. not Endl.).

9 LIBOCEDRUS Endl.

Tall resinous aromatic trees, with scaly bark, spreading branches, flattened branchlets disposed in one horizontal plane and forming an open 2-ranked spray and often ultimately deciduous, straight-grained durable fragrant wood, and naked buds. Leaves scale-like, in 4 ranks, on leading shoots nearly equally decussate, closely compressed or spreading, dying and becoming woody before falling, on lateral flattened branchlets much compressed, conspicuously keeled, and nearly covering those of the other ranks; on seedling plants linear-lanceolate and spreading. Flowers monœcious, solitary, terminal, the two sexes on different branchlets; male oblong, with 12–16 decussate filaments dilated into broad connectives usually bearing 4 subglobose anther-cells; female oblong, subtended at base by several pairs of leaf-life scales slightly enlarged and persistent under the fruit, composed of 6 acuminate short-pointed scales, those of the upper and middle ranks much larger than those of the lower rank, ovate or oblong, fertile and bearing at the base of a minute accrescent ovuliferous scale 2 erect ovules. Fruit an oblong cone maturing in one season, with subcoriaceous scales marked at the apex by the free thickened mucronulate border of the enlarged flower-scales, those of the lowest pair ovate, thin, reflexed, much shorter than the oblong thicker scales of the second pair widely spreading at maturity; those of the third pair confluent into an erect partition. Seeds in pairs, erect on the base of the scale; seed-coat membranaceous, of 2 layers, produced into thin unequal lateral wings, one narrow, the other broad, oblique, nearly as long as the scale; cotyledons 2, about as long as the superior radicle.

Libocedrus is confined to western North America, western South America, where it is distributed from Chili to Patagonia, New Zealand, New Caledonia, New Guinea, Formosa, and southwestern China. Eight species are distinguished.

Libocedrus, from λιβάς and *Cedrus*, relates to the resinous character of these trees.

1. Libocedrus decurrens Torr. Incense Cedar.

Leaves oblong-obovate, decurrent and closely adnate on the branchlets except at the callous apex, ⅛′ long on the ultimate lateral branchlets to nearly ½′ long on leading shoots, those of the lateral ranks gradually narrowed and acuminate at apex, keeled and glandular on the back, and nearly covering the flattened obscurely glandular-pitted and abruptly pointed leaves of the inner ranks. **Flowers** appearing in January on the ends of short lateral branchlets of the previous year; male tingeing the tree with gold during the winter and early spring, ovate, nearly $\frac{1}{4}'$ long, with nearly orbicular or broadly ovate connectives, rounded, acute or acuminate at the apex and slightly erose on the margins; female subtended by 2–6 pairs of leaf-like scales, with ovate acute light yellow-green slightly spreading scales. **Fruit** ripening and discharging its seeds in the autumn, oblong, $\frac{3}{4}'$–$1'$ long, pendulous, light red-brown; **seeds** oblong-lanceolate, $\frac{1}{3}'$–$\frac{1}{2}'$ long, semiterete and marked below by a conspicuous pale basal hilum; inner layer of the seed-coat penetrated by elongated resin-chambers, filled with red liquid balsamic resin.

A tree, usually 80°–100° or rarely 150° high, with a tall straight slightly and irregularly lobed trunk tapering from a broad base, 3° or 4° or occasionally 6° or 7° in diameter,

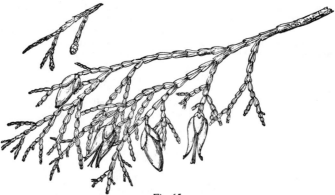

Fig. 65

slender branches erect at the top of the tree, below sweeping downward in bold curves, forming a narrow open feathery crown becoming in old age irregular in outline by the greater development of a few ultimately upright branches forming secondary stems, and stout branchlets somewhat flattened and light yellow-green at first, turning light red-brown during the summer and ultimately brown more or less tinged with purple, the lateral branchlets much flattened, 4'–6' long, and usually deciduous at the end of the second or third season. **Bark** $\frac{1}{2}'$–$1'$ thick, bright cinnamon-red, and broken into irregular ridges covered with closely appressed plate-like scales. **Wood** light, soft, close-grained very durable in contact with the soil, light reddish brown, with thin nearly white sapwood; often injured by dry rot but largely used for fencing, laths and shingles, the interior finish of buildings, for furniture, and in the construction of flumes.

Distribution. Singly or in small groves from the southeastern slope of Mt. Hood, Oregon, and southward along the Cascade Mountains; on the high mountains of northern California, on the western slopes of the Sierra Nevada, and in Alpine County on their eastern slope, on the Washoe Mountains, western Nevada, in the California coast ranges from the Santa Lucia Mountains, Monterey County to the high mountains in the southern part of the state; on the Sierra del Pimal and the San Pedro Mártir Mountains, Lower California; most abundant and of its largest size on the Sierra Nevada, of central California at elevations of 5000°–7000° above the sea.

Often cultivated as an ornamental tree in western and central Europe, where it grows rapidly and promises to attain a large size; occasionally planted in the New England and middle Atlantic states; hardy in the Arnold Arboretum.

10. THUJA L. Arbor-vitæ.

Resinous aromatic trees, with thin scaly bark, soft durable straight-grained heartwood, thin nearly white sapwood, slender spreading or erect branches, pyramidal heads, flattened lateral pendulous branchlets disposed in one horizontal plane, forming a flat frond-like spray and often finally deciduous, and naked buds. Leaves decussate, scale-like, acute, stomatiferous on the back, on leading shoots appressed or spreading, rounded or slightly keeled on the back, narrowed into long slender points, on lateral branchlets much compressed in the lateral ranks, prominently keeled and nearly covering those of the other ranks; on seedling plants linear-lanceolate, acuminate, spreading or reflexed. Flowers minute, monœcious, from buds formed the previous autumn, terminal, solitary, the two sexes usually on different branchlets; male ovoid, with 4–6 decussate filaments, enlarged into suborbicular peltate connectives bearing on their inner face 2–4 subglobose anther-cells; female oblong, with 8–12 oblong acute scales opposite in pairs, the ovuliferous scales at their base bearing usually 2 erect bottle-shaped ovules. Fruit an ovoid-oblong erect pale cinnamon-brown cone maturing in one season, its scales thin (thick in one species), leathery, oblong, acute, marked near the apex by the thickened free border of the enlarged flower-scales, those of the 2 or 3 middle ranks largest and fertile. Seeds usually 2, erect on the base of the scale, ovoid, acute, compressed, light chestnut-brown; seed-coat membranaceous, produced except in one species into broad lateral wings distinct at the apex; cotyledons 2, longer than the superior radicle.

Thuja is confined to northeastern and northwestern America, to Japan, Korea and northern China. Five species are recognized. Of the exotic species the Chinese *Thuja orientalis*, L., with many varieties produced by cultivation, is frequently planted in the United States, especially in the south and west, for the decoration of gardens, and is distinguished from the other species by the thick umbonate scales of the cone, only the 4 lower scales being fertile, and by the thick rounded dark red-purple seeds without wings.

Thuja is the classical name of some coniferous tree.

CONSPECTUS OF THE NORTH AMERICAN SPECIES.

Fruit with usually 4 fertile scales.	1. **T. occidentalis** (A).
Fruit with usually 6 fertile scales.	2. **T. plicata.** (B, F, G).

1. Thuja occidentalis L. White Cedar. Arbor-vitæ.

Leaves on leading shoots often nearly $\frac{1}{4}'$ long, long-pointed and usually conspicuously glandular, on lateral branchlets much flattened, rounded and apiculate at apex, without glands or obscurely glandular-pitted, about $\frac{1}{8}'$ long. **Flowers** opening in April and May, liver color. **Fruit** ripening and discharging its seeds in the early autumn, $\frac{1}{3}'-\frac{1}{2}'$ long; **seeds** $\frac{1}{8}'$ long, the thin wings as wide as the body.

A tree, 50°–60° high, with a short often lobed and buttressed trunk, occasionally 6° although usually not more than 2°–3° in diameter, often divided into 2 or 3 stout secondary stems, short horizontal branches soon turning upward and forming a narrow compact pyramidal head, light yellow-green branchlets paler on the lower surface than on the upper, changing with the death of the leaves during their second season to light cinnamon-red, growing darker the following year, gradually becoming terete and abruptly enlarged at the base and finally covered with smooth lustrous dark orange-brown bark, and marked by conspicuous scars left by the falling of the short pendulous lateral branchlets. **Bark** $\frac{1}{4}'-\frac{1}{3}'$ thick, light red-brown often tinged with orange color and broken by shallow fissures into narrow flat connected ridges separating into elongated more or less persistent scales. **Wood** light, soft, brittle, very coarse-grained, durable, fragrant, pale yellow-brown; largely used in Canada and the northern states for fence-posts, rails, railway-ties, and shingles. Fluid extracts and tinctures made from the young branchlets are sometimes used in medicine.

Distribution. Frequently forming nearly impenetrable forests on swampy ground or often occupying the rocky banks of streams, from Nova Scotia and New Brunswick, north-westward to the mouth of the Saskatchewan, and southward through eastern Canada to southern New Hampshire, central Massachusetts, New York, central Ohio, northern

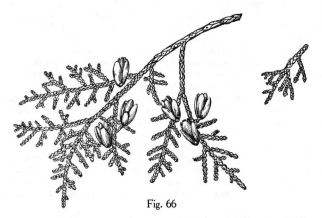

Fig. 66

Indiana and Illinois, and Minnesota; occasionally on the high mountains of Virginia, West Virginia, and northeastern Tennessee, and on the mountains of western Burke County, North Carolina, at an altitude of 3000 feet; very common at the north, less abundant and of smaller size southward.

Often cultivated, with many, often dwarf, forms produced in nurseries, as an ornamental tree and for hedges; and in Europe from the middle of the sixteenth century.

2. Thuja plicata D. Don.   Red Cedar.   Canoe Cedar.

Leaves on leading shoots ovate, long-pointed, often conspicuously glandular on the back, frequently $\frac{1}{4}'$ long, on lateral branchlets ovate, apiculate, without glands or obscurely glandular-pitted, usually not more than $\frac{1}{8}'$ long, mostly persistent 2–5 years. **Flowers** about $\frac{1}{12}'$ long, dark brown.

Fruit ripening early in the autumn, clustered near the ends of the branches, much reflexed, $\frac{1}{2}'$ long, with thin leathery scales, conspicuously marked near the apex by the free border of the flower-scale furnished with short stout erect or recurved dark mu-cros; **seeds** often 3 under each fertile scale, rather shorter than their usually slightly unequal wings about $\frac{1}{4}'$ long.

A tree, frequently 200° high, with a broad gradually tapering buttressed base some-times 15° in diameter at the

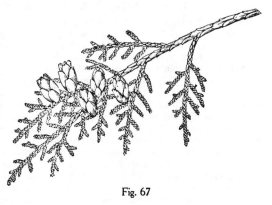

Fig. 67

ground and in old age often separating toward the summit into 2 or 3 erect divisions, short horizontal branches, usually pendulous at the ends, forming a dense narrow py-ramidal head, and slender much compressed branchlets often slightly zigzag, light bright yellow-green during their first year, then cinnamon-brown, and after the falling of the leaves, lustrous and dark reddish brown often tinged with purple, the lateral branchlets $5'$–$6'$ long, light green and lustrous on the upper surface, somewhat paler on the lower surface, turning yellow and falling generally at the end of their second season. **Bark** bright cinnamon-red, $\frac{1}{2}'$–$\frac{3}{4}'$ thick, irregularly divided by narrow shallow fissures into broad ridges rounded on the back and broken on the surface into long narrow rather loose plate-like scales. **Wood** light, soft, not strong, brittle, coarse-grained, easily split, dull brown tinged with red; largely used in Washington and Oregon for the interior finish of buildings, doors, sashes, fences, shingles, and in cabinet-making and cooperage. From this tree the Indians of the northwest coast split the planks used in the construction of their lodges, carved the totems which decorate their villages, and hollowed out their great war canoes, and from the fibres of the inner bark made ropes, blankets, and thatch for their cabins.

Distribution. Singly and in small groves on low moist bottom-lands or near the banks of mountain streams, from the sea-level to elevations of 6000° in the interior, from Baranoff Island, Alaska, southward along the coast ranges of British Columbia, western Washington, and Oregon, where it is the most abundant and grows to its largest size, and through the California-coast region to Mendocino County, ranging eastward along many of the interior ranges of British Columbia, northern Washington, Idaho, and Montana to the western slope of the continental divide.

Often cultivated as an ornamental tree in the parks and gardens of western and central Europe where it has grown rapidly and vigorously, and occasionally in the middle and north Atlantic states.

11. CUPRESSUS L. Cypress.

Resinous trees, with bark often separating into long shred-like scales, fragrant durable usually light brown heartwood, pale yellow sapwood, stout erect branches often becoming horizontal in old age, slender 4-angled branchlets, and naked buds. Leaves scale-like, ovate, acute, acuminate, or bluntly pointed at apex, with slender spreading or appressed tips, thickened, rounded, and often glandular on the back, opposite in pairs, becoming brown and woody before falling; on vigorous leading shoots and young plants needle-shaped or linear-lanceolate and spreading. Flowers minute, monœcious, terminal, yellow, the two sexes on separate branchlets; the male oblong, of numerous decussate stamens, with short filaments enlarged into broadly ovate connectives bearing 2–6 globose pendulous anther-cells; female oblong or subglocose, composed of 6–10 thick decussate scales bearing in several rows at the base of the ovuliferous scale numerous erect bottle-shaped ovules. Fruit an erect nearly globose cone maturing in the second year, composed of the much thickened ovule-bearing scales of the flower, abruptly dilated, clavate and flattened at the apex, bearing the remnants of the flower-scales developed into a short central more or less thickened mucro or boss; long-persistent on the branch after the escape of the seeds. Seeds numerous, in several rows, erect, thick, and acutely angled or compressed, with thin lateral wings; seed-coat of 2 layers, the outer thin and membranaceous, the inner thicker and crustaceous; cotyledons 3 or 4, longer than the superior radicle.

Cupressus with ten or twelve species is confined to Pacific North America and Mexico in the New World and to southeastern Europe, southwestern Asia, the Himalayas, and China in the Old World. Of the exotic species *Cupressus sempervirens* L., of southeastern Europe and southwestern Asia, and especially its pyramidal variety, are often planted for ornament in the south Atlantic and Pacific states.

Cupressus is the classical name of the Cypress-tree.

CONSPECTUS OF THE NORTH AMERICAN SPECIES

Leaves dark green.
  Leaves eglandular or obscurely glandular on the back.
    Leaves obtusely pointed; cones puberulous, $1'$–$1\frac{1}{2}'$ in diameter; seeds light chestnut-brown.   1. C. **macrocarpa** (G).

Leaves acutely pointed; cones $\frac{1}{2}'$–$\frac{3}{4}'$ in diameter; seeds dark brown or black.

2. C. Goveniana (G).

Leaves glandular-pitted on the back, acute.

Cones $\frac{2}{3}'$–1' in diameter; seeds brown, often glaucous.   3. C. Sargentii (G).

Cones $\frac{1}{2}'$–1' in diameter, often covered with a glaucous bloom; seeds dark chestnut-brown.   4. C. Macnabiana (G).

Leaves pale bluish green.

Leaves obtusely pointed, with small gland-pits; bark of the trunk smooth, lustrous, mahogany brown; branches bright red.   5. C. guadaloupensis (G).

Leaves acute, eglandular or occasionally obscurely glandular (in var. *glabra* conspicuously glandular); bark of the trunk dark brown, separating into long narrow persistent fibres; branchlets gray.   6. C. arizonica (H).

1. Cupressus macrocarpa Gord.   Monterey Cypress.

Leaves dark green, bluntly pointed, eglandular, and $\frac{1}{4}'$–$\frac{1}{2}'$ long; deciduous at the end of three or four years. **Flowers** opening late in February or early in March, yellow. **Fruit**

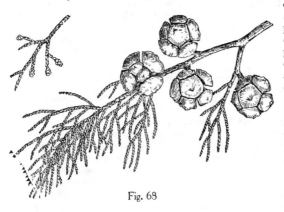

clustered on short stout stems subglobose, slightly puberulous, 1'–1$\frac{1}{2}'$ in diameter, composed of 4 or 6 pairs of scales, with broadly ovoid thickened or occasionally on the upper scales subconical bosses, the scales of the upper and lower pairs being smaller than the others and sterile; seeds about 20 under each fertile scale, angled, light chestnut-brown, about $\frac{1}{16}'$ long.

A tree, often 60°–70° high, with a short trunk 2°–3° or exceptionally 5°–6° in diameter, slender erect branches

Fig. 68

forming a narrow or broad bushy pyramidal head, becoming stout and spreading in old age into a broad flat-topped crown, and stout branchlets covered when the leaves fall at the end of three or four years with thin light or dark reddish brown bark separating into small papery scales. Bark $\frac{3}{4}'$–1' thick and irregularly divided into broad flat connected ridges separating freely into narrow elongated thick persistent scales, dark red-brown on young stems and upper branches, becoming at last almost white on old and exposed trunks. **Wood** heavy, hard and strong, very durable, close-grained.

Distribution. Coast of California south of the Bay of Monterey, occupying an area about two miles long and two hundred yards wide from Cypress Point to the shores of Carmel Bay, with a small grove on Point Lobos, the southern boundary of the bay.

Universally cultivated in the Pacific states from Vancouver Island to Lower California, and often used in hedges and for wind-breaks; occasionally planted in the southeastern states; much planted in western and southern Europe, temperate South America, and in Australia and New Zealand.

2. Cupressus Goveniana Gord.

Cupressus pygmœa Sarg.

Leaves acutely pointed, dark green. **Flowers:** male obscurely 4-angled, with broadly ovate peltate connectives: female with 6–10 ovate pointed scales. **Fruit** usually sessile, subglobose $\frac{1}{4}'-\frac{7}{8}'$ in diameter, its scales terminating in small bosses; **seeds** compressed, black, or dark brown, papillose, about $\frac{1}{8}'$ long.

A tree rarely 75° high, with a tall trunk up to 2°10′ in diameter, often not more than 25° high, more often a shrub with numerous stems 1°–15° tall, ascending branches, and comparatively stout bright reddish brown branchlets, becoming purple and ultimately dark reddish

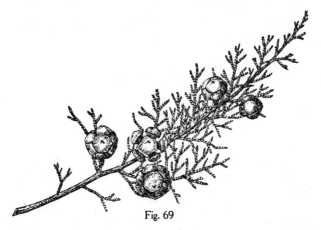

Fig. 69

brown ; often beginning to produce fertile cones when only 1° or 2° tall. **Bark** bright reddish brown, about $\frac{1}{4}'$ thick, and divided by shallow fissures into flat ridges separating on the surface into long thread-like scales. **Wood** soft, very coarse-grained, pale reddish brown.

Distribution. California : pine barrens on the western slope of Point Pinos Ridge two miles west of Monterey, and on alkaline soil in a narrow belt beginning about three quarters of a mile from the shore of Mendocino County and extending inland for three or four miles from Ten Mile Run on the north to the Navarro River on the south; arborescent and also of its smallest size only in this northern station.

3. Cupressus Sargentii Jeps. Sargent's Cypress.

Cupressus Goveniana Engelm. not Gord. (*Silva N. Am.* x. 107 t. 527)

Leaves obscurely glandular or without glands, dark green, pungently aromatic, $\frac{1}{16}'-\frac{1}{8}'$ long, turning bright red-brown in drying and falling at the end of three or four years ; on young plants $\frac{1}{8}'-\frac{1}{4}'$ long. **Flowers:** male with thin slightly erose connectives: female of 6 or 8 acute slightly spreading scales. Fruit often in crowded clusters, short-stalked, subglobose, $\frac{1}{2}'-1'$ in diameter, reddish brown or purple, lustrous, puberulous, its 6 or 8 scales with broadly

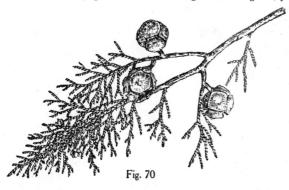

Fig. 70

ovoid generally rounded and flattened and rarely short-obconic bosses; **seeds** brown, lustrous, often glaucous, with an acute margin, $\frac{1}{6}'$ long, about 20 under each fertile scale.

A tree, shrub, or small bushy tree rarely more than 15° or 16° high, with a short trunk 2° in diameter, slender erect or spreading branches forming a handsome open head, and thin branchlets covered with close smooth bark, at first orange-colored, becoming bright reddish brown, and ultimately purple or dark brown. **Bark** $\frac{1}{4}'-\frac{1}{2}'$ thick, dark grayish brown, irregularly divided into narrow ridges covered with thin persistent oblong scales. **Wood** light, soft, not strong, light brown, with thick nearly white sapwood.

Distribution. California: dry mountain slopes usually between altitudes of 1300° and 2300° in few widely isolated stations, Red Mountain, Mendocino County, to Mt. Tamalpais, Marin County; Cedar Mountain, Alameda County; Santa Cruz Mountains, Santa Cruz County; Santa Lucia Mountains, Monterey County; often covering great areas on the hills of Marin County with dense thickets only a few feet high.

Occasionally cultivated as *C. Goveniana* in western and southern Europe as an ornamental tree.

4. Cupressus Macnabiana A. Murr. Cypress.

Cupressus Bakeri Jeps.

Cupressus nevadensis Abrams.

Leaves acute or rounded at apex, rounded and conspicuously glandular on the back, deep green, often slightly glaucous, usually not more than $\frac{1}{16}'$ long. **Flowers** in March and April, male nearly cylindric, obtuse, with broadly ovate rounded connectives: female subglobose, with broadly ovate scales short-pointed and rounded at apex. **Fruit** oblong, subsessile or raised on a slender stalk, $\frac{1}{2}'-1'$ long, dark reddish brown more or less covered with a glaucous bloom, slightly puberulous, especially along the margins of the 6 or rarely 8 scales, their prominent bosses thin and recurved on the lower scales, and much thickened, conical, and more or less incurved on the upper scales; **seeds** dark chestnut-brown, usually rather less than $\frac{1}{16}'$ long, with narrow wings.

A tree in Oregon occasionally 80° high with a tall trunk sometimes $3\frac{1}{2}°$ in diameter, southward rarely more than 30° high, with a short trunk 12'–15' in diameter, slender branches covered with close smooth compact bark, bright purple after the falling of the leaves, soon becoming dark brown; more often a shrub with numerous stems 6°–12° tall forming a broad open irregular head. **Bark** thin, dark reddish brown, broken into brown

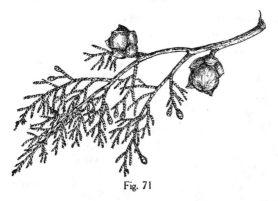

flat ridges, and separating on the surface into elongated thin slightly attached long-persistent scales. **Wood** light, soft, very close-grained.

Distribution. Rare and local, usually in small groves; dry ridges of Mount Steve and adjacent mountains up to altitudes of 5300°, Josephine County, southwestern Oregon; California; on lava beds, southeastern Siskiyou and southwestern Mono Counties (*C. Bakeri*); dry hills and low slopes, Mt.

Fig. 71

Ætna, in central Napa County; through Lake County to Red Mountain on the east side of Ukiah Valley, Mendocino County; in Trinity County between Shasta and Whiskeytown; and on the Sierra Nevada (Red Hill, Piute Mountains near Bodfish) Kern County, at an altitude of 5000° (*C. nevadensis*).

Occasionally cultivated in western and southern Europe as an ornamental tree.

5. Cupressus guadaloupensis S. Wats. Tecate Cypress.

Leaves acute, rounded and minutely glandular-pitted or eglandular on the back, light blue-green, about $\frac{1}{16}'$ long. **Fruit** on stout stems $\frac{1}{4}'-\frac{1}{3}'$ in length, subglobose to short-oblong, $\frac{3}{4}'-1\frac{1}{4}'$ in diameter, puberulous especially along the margins of the six or eight scales, with prominent flattened or conic acute often incurved bosses; **seeds** about 70 under each scale, short-oblong, nearly square, light chestnut-brown up to $\frac{1}{4}'$ in length, with a narrow wing.

A tree in California sometimes 20°–25° in height, with a short slender or on exposed mountain slopes a trunk occasionally 2° or 3° in diameter, few short spreading or as-

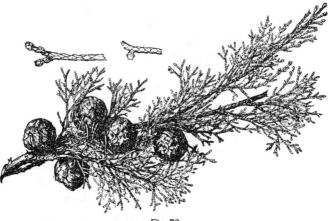

Fig. 72

cending branches forming an open head, and light red-brown lustrous branchlets becoming purplish. Bark smooth, lustrous, without resin or fibres, mahogany brown, the thin scales in falling leaving pale marks.

Distribution. San Diego County, California, rare and local; valley of the San Luis Rey River between Valley Centre and Pala; at altitudes between 1100° and 4000° in the gulches and on the summit of Mt. Tecate on the border between the United States and Lower California; on a mountain below Descanso and Pine Valley; in Cedar Cañon between El-nido and Dulzura; in Lower California on San Pedro Mártir Mountain and Guadaloupe Island. The insular form is a larger tree often with larger gland-pits on the leaves, and now often cultivated in California, western Europe, and in other countries with temperate climates.

6. Cupressus arizonica Greene. Cypress.

Leaves obtusely pointed, rounded, eglandular or rarely glandular-pitted on the back, pale green, $\frac{1}{16}'$ long, dying and turning red-brown in their second season, generally falling four years later. **Flowers:** male oblong, obtuse, their 6 or 8 stamens with broadly ovate acute yellow connectives slightly erose on the margins: female not seen. **Fruit** on stout pedicels $\frac{1}{4}'-\frac{1}{2}'$ in length, subglobose, rather longer than broad, wrinkled, dark red-brown and covered with a glaucous bloom, the six or eight scales with stout flattened incurved prominent bosses; **seeds** oblong to nearly triangular, dark red-brown, $\frac{1}{16}'-\frac{1}{8}'$ long with a thin narrow wing.

A conical tree 40°–70° high with a trunk 2°–4° in diameter, and stout spreading branches covered with bark separating into thin plates, leaving a smooth red surface, and branchlets dark gray after the leaves fall.   **Bark** on young trunks separating into large irregular curling thin scales, on old trees becoming dark red-brown and fibrous.

Distribution.   Mountains above Clifton, Greenlee County, eastern Arizona; on the

Fig. 73

San Francisco Mountains, Socorro County, and San Luis Mountains, Grant County, western New Mexico; and in Chihuahua.   Passing into

Cupressus arizonica var. bonita Lemm.

Cupressus glabra Sudw.

Differing from the type in the prominent oblong or circular glandular depressions on the backs of the leaves.

A tree 30°–70° high, with a trunk 18′–24′ or rarely 5° in diameter, erect branches forming a rather compact conical head.   **Bark** of the trunk and large branches thin, smooth, dark

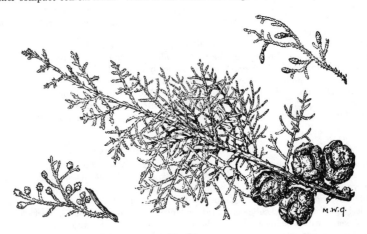

Fig. 74

reddish brown, separating into small curled scale-like plates, becoming on old trees dark gray and fibrous.   **Wood** heavy, hard, pale straw color with lighter-colored sapwood, durable in contact with the ground, somewhat used for fence-posts, corral-piles, mine-timbers and in log cabins.

Distribution. Gravelly slopes and moist gulches often in groups of considerable size at altitudes between 4000° and 7000°, Arizona; near Camp Verde, Tonto Basin; Natural Bridge, Payson, etc.; on the Chiracahua Mountains (*J. W. Toumey*, July, 1894); on the Santa Rita and Santa Catalina Mountains, and in Oak Creek Cañon twenty miles south of Flagstaff (*P. Lowell*, June, 1911).

Now often cultivated in western Europe as *C. arizonica*.

12. CHAMÆCYPARIS.

Tall resinous pyramidal trees, with thin scaly or deeply furrowed bark, nodding leading shoots, spreading branches, flattened, often deciduous or ultimately terete branchlets 2-ranked in one horizontal plane, pale fragrant durable heartwood, thin nearly white sap-wood, and naked buds. Leaves scale-like, ovate, acuminate, with slender spreading or appressed tips, opposite in pairs, becoming brown and woody before falling, on vigorous sterile branches and young plants needle-shaped or linear-lanceolate and spreading. Flowers minute, monœcious, terminal, the two sexes on separate branchlets; the male oblong, of numerous decussate stamens, with short filaments enlarged into ovate connectives decreasing in size from below upward and bearing usually 2 pendulous globose anther-cells; the female subglobose, composed of usually 6 decussate peltate scales bearing at the base of the ovuliferous scales 2–5 erect bottle-shaped ovules. Fruit an erect globose cone maturing at the end of the first season, surrounded at the base by the sterile lower scales of the flowers, and formed by the enlargement of the ovule-bearing scales, abruptly dilated, club-shaped and flattened at the apex, bearing the remnants of the flower-scales as short prominent points or knobs; persistent on the branches after the escape of the seeds. Seeds 1–5, erect on the slender stalk-like base of the scale, subcylindric and slightly compressed; seed-coat of 2 layers, the outer thin and membranaceous, the inner thicker and crustaceous, produced into broad lateral wings; cotyledons 2, longer than the superior radicle.

Chamæcyparis is confined to the Atlantic and Pacific coast regions of North America, and to Japan and Formosa. Six species are distinguished. Of exotic species the Japanese Retinosporas, *Chamæcyparis obtusa* Endl., and *Chamæcyparis pisifera* Endl., with their numerous abnormal forms are familiar garden plants in all temperate regions.

Chamæcyparis is from χαμαί, on the ground, and κυπάρισσος, cypress.

CONSPECTUS OF THE NORTH AMERICAN SPECIES.

Bark thin, divided into flat ridges;
    Branchlets slender, often compressed; leaves dull blue-green, usually conspicuously
        glandular.   **1. C. thyoides** (A, C).
    Branchlets stout, slightly flattened or terete; leaves dark blue-green, usually without
        glands.   **2. C. nootkatensis** (B, G).
Bark thick, divided into broad rounded ridges; branchlets slender, compressed; leaves
    bright green, conspicuously glandular.   **3. C. Lawsoniana** (G).

1. Chamæcyparis thyoides B. S. P. White Cedar.

Cupressus thyoides L.

Leaves closely appressed, or spreading at the apex especially on vigorous leading shoots, keeled and glandular or conspicuously glandular-punctate on the back, dark dull blue-green or pale below, at the north becoming russet-brown during the winter, $\frac{1}{16}'-\frac{1}{8}'$ long, dying during the second season and then persistent for many years. **Flowers:** male composed of 5 or 6 pairs of stamens, with ovate connectives rounded at apex, dark brown below the middle, nearly black toward the apex: female subglobose, with ovate acute spreading pale liver-colored scales and black ovules. **Fruit** $\frac{1}{4}'$ in diameter, sessile on a short leafy branch, light green, covered with a glaucous bloom when fully grown, later bluish purple and very glaucous, finally becoming dark red-brown, its scales terminating in ovate acute, often reflexed bosses; **seeds** 1 or 2 under each fertile scale, ovoid, acute, full and rounded at the base, slightly compressed, gray-brown, about $\frac{1}{8}'$ long, with wings as broad as the body of the seed and dark red-brown.

A tree, 70°–80° high, with a tall trunk usually about 2 and occasionally 3°–4° in diameter, or northward much smaller, slender horizontal branches forming a narrow spire-like head, and 2-ranked compressed branchlets disposed in an open fan-shaped more or less de-

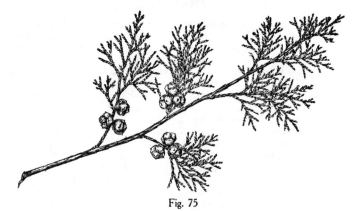

Fig. 75

ciduous spray, the persistent branchlets gradually becoming terete, light green tinged with red, light reddish brown during their first winter, and then dark brown, their thin close bark separating slightly at the end of three or four years into small papery scales. **Bark** $\frac{3}{4}'$–1' thick, light reddish brown, and divided irregularly into narrow flat connected ridges often spirally twisted round the stem, separating on the surface into elongated loose or closely appressed plate-like scales. **Wood** light, soft, not strong, close-grained, slightly fragrant, light brown tinged with red; largely used in boat-building and cooperage, for woodenware, shingles, the interior finish of houses, fence-posts, and railway-ties.

Distribution. Cold swamps usually immersed during several months of the year, often forming dense pure forests; near Concord, New Hampshire, southern Maine, southward near the coast to northern Florida, and westward to southeastern Mississippi; most abundant south of Massachusetts Bay; comparatively rare east of Boston and west of Mobile Bay.

Occasionally planted as an ornamental tree in the eastern states and in the countries of temperate Europe.

2. Chamæcyparis nootkatensis Sudw. Yellow Cypress. Sitka Cypress.

Cupressus nootkatensis Lamb.

Leaves rounded, eglandular or glandular-pitted on the back, dark blue-green, closely appressed, about $\frac{1}{8}'$ long, on vigorous leading branchlets somewhat spreading and often $\frac{1}{4}'$ long, with more elongated and sharper points, beginning to die at the end of their second year and usually falling during the third season. **Flowers:** male on lateral branchlets of the previous year, composed of 4 or 5 pairs of stamens, with ovate rounded slightly erose light yellow connectives: female clustered near the ends of upper branchlets, dark liver color, the fertile scales each bearing 2–4 ovules. **Fruit** ripening in September and October, nearly $\frac{1}{2}'$ in diameter, dark red-brown, with usually 4 or 6 scales tipped with prominent erect pointed bosses and frequently covered with conspicuous resin-glands; **seeds** 2–4 under each scale, ovoid, acute, slightly flattened, about $\frac{1}{4}'$ long, dark red-brown, with thin light red-brown wings often nearly twice as wide as the body of the seed.

A tree, frequently 120° high, with a tall trunk 5°–6° in diameter, horizontal branches forming a narrow pyramidal head, stout distichous somewhat flattened or terete light yellow branchlets often tinged with red at first, dark or often bright red-brown during their third

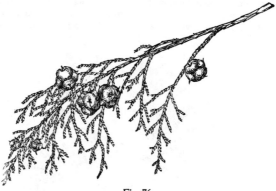

Fig. 76

season, ultimately paler and covered with close thin smooth bark. **Bark** $\frac{1}{2}'-\frac{3}{4}'$ thick, light gray tinged with brown, irregularly fissured, and separated on the surface into large thin loose scales. **Wood** hard, rather brittle, very close-grained, exceedingly durable, bright clear yellow, with very thin nearly white sapwood; fragrant with an agreeable resinous odor; used in boat and shipbuilding, the interior finish of houses, and the manufacture of furniture.

Distribution. Islands of Prince William Sound, Alaska, and southward over the coast mountains of Alaska and British Columbia, and along the Cascade Mountains of Washington and Oregon to the northeastern slopes of Mt. Jefferson, extending eastward to the headwaters of the Yakima River on the eastern slope of the range; on Whiskey Peak of the Siskiyou Mountains in the southeastern corner of Josephine County, Oregon and about two miles from the California line; most abundant and of its largest size near the coast of Alaska and northern British Columbia, ranging from the sea-level up to altitudes of 3000°; at high elevations on the Cascade Mountains sometimes a low shrub.

Occasionally cultivated, with its several abnormal forms, as an ornamental tree in the middle Atlantic states and in California, and commonly in the countries of western and central Europe.

3. Chamæcyparis Lawsoniana Parl.   Port Orford Cedar.   Lawson Cypress.

Cupressus Lawsoniana A. Murr.

Leaves bright green or pale below, conspicuously glandular on the back, usually not more than $\frac{1}{16}'$ long on lateral branchlets, on leading shoots often spreading at the apex, $\frac{1}{8}'$ to nearly $\frac{1}{4}'$ long, usually dying, turning bright red-brown and falling during their third year. **Flowers:** male with bright red connectives bearing usually 2 pollen-sacs: female with dark ovate acute spreading scales, each bearing 2–4 ovules. **Fruit** clustered on the upper lateral branchlets and produced in great profusion, ripening in September and October, about $\frac{1}{3}'$ in diameter, green and glaucous when full grown, red-brown and often covered with a bloom at maturity, its scales with thin broadly ovate acute reflexed bosses; **seeds** 2–4 under each fertile scale, ovoid, acute, slightly compressed, $\frac{1}{8}'$ long, light chestnut-brown, with broad thin wings.

A tree, often 200° high, with a tall trunk frequently 12° in diameter above its abruptly enlarged base, a spire-like head of small horizontal or pendulous branches clothed with remote flat spray frequently 6'–8' long. **Bark** often 10' thick at the base of old trees and 3'–4' thick on smaller stems, dark reddish brown, with 2 distinct layers, the inner $\frac{1}{8}'-\frac{1}{4}'$ thick, darker, more compact, and firmer than the outer, divided into great broad-based rounded ridges separated on the surface into small thick closely appressed scales. **Wood** light, hard, strong, very close-grained, abounding in fragrant resin, durable, easily worked,

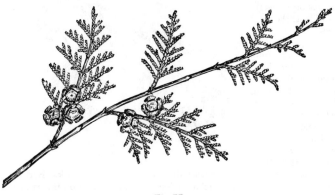

Fig. 77

light yellow, or almost white, with hardly distinguishable sapwood; largely manufactured into lumber used for the interior finish and flooring of buildings, railway-ties, fence-posts, and boat and shipbuilding, and on the Pacific coast almost exclusively for matches. The resin is a powerful diuretic.

Distribution. Usually scattered in small groves from the shores of Coos Bay, southwestern Oregon, south to the mouth of the Klamath River, California, ranging inland usually for about thirty miles; near Waldorf, in Josephine County, Oregon, on the slopes of the Siskiyou Mountains, and on the southern flanks of Mt. Shasta, California; most abundant north of Rogue River on the Oregon coast and attaining its largest size on the western slopes of the Coast Range foothills, forming between Point Gregory and the mouth of the Coquille River a nearly continuous forest belt twenty miles long.

Often cultivated with the innumerable forms originated in nurseries, in the middle Atlantic states and California, in all the temperate countries of Europe, and in New Zealand.

13. JUNIPERUS L. Juniper.

Pungent aromatic trees or shrubs, with usually thin shreddy bark, soft close-grained durable wood, slender branches, and scaly or naked buds. Leaves sessile, in whorls of 3, persistent for many years, convex on the lower side, concave and stomatiferous above, linear-subulate, sharp-pointed, without glands (*Oxycedrus*); or scale-like, ovate, opposite in pairs or ternate, closely imbricated, appressed and adnate to the branch, glandular or eglandular on the back, becoming brown and woody on the branch, but on young plants and vigorous shoots often free and awl-shaped (*Sabina*). Flowers minute, diœcious, axillary or terminal on short axillary branches from buds formed the previous autumn on branches of the year; the male solitary, oblong-ovoid, with numerous stamens decussate or in 3's, their filaments enlarged into ovate or peltate yellow scale-like connectives bearing near the base 2–6 globose pollen-sacs; the female ovoid, surrounded at the base by many minute scale-like bracts persistent and unchanged under the fruit, composed of 2–6 opposite or ternate pointed scales alternate with or bearing on their inner face at the base on a minute ovuliferous scale 1 or 2 ovules. Fruit a berry-like succulent fleshy blue, blue-black, or red strobile formed by the coalition of the flower-scales, inclosed in a membranaceous skin covered with a glaucous bloom, ripening during the first, second, or rarely during the third season, smooth or marked by the ends of the flower-scales, or by the pointed tips of the ovules, closed, or open at the top and exposing the apex of the seeds. Seeds 1–12, ovoid, acute or obtuse, terete or variously angled, often longitudinally grooved by depressions caused by the pressure of resin-cells in the flesh of the fruit, smooth or roughened and tuberculate, chestnut-brown, marked below by the large conspicuous usually 2-lobed hilum; seed-coat of 2 layers, the outer thick and bony, the inner thin, membranaceous or crustaceous; cotyledons 2, or 4–6, about as long as the superior radicle.

Juniperus is widely scattered over the northern hemisphere from the Arctic Circle to the highlands of Mexico, Lower California, and the West Indies in the New World, and to the Azores and Canary Islands, northern Africa, Abyssinia, the mountains of east tropical Africa, Sikkim, central China, Formosa, Japan and the Bonin Islands in the Old World. About thirty-five species are now distinguished. Of the exotic species cultivated in the United States the most common are European forms of *Juniperus communis* L. with fastigiate branches, and dwarf forms of the European *Juniperus Sabina* L., and of *Juniperus chinensis* L.

Juniperus is the classical name of the Juniper.

CONSPECTUS OF THE NORTH AMERICAN SPECIES.

Flowers axillary; stamens decussate; ovules 3, alternate with the scales of the flower, their tips persistent on the fruit; seeds usually 3; leaves ternate, linear-lanceolate, prickle-pointed, jointed at the base, eglandular, dark yellow-green, channeled, stomatose, and glaucous above; fruit maturing in the third year, subglobose, bright blue, covered with a glaucous bloom; buds scaly (*Oxycedrus*). **1. J. communis.**

Flowers terminal on short axiliary branchlets; stamens decussate or in 3's; ovules in the axils of small fleshy scales often enlarged and conspicuous on the fruit; seeds 1–12; leaves ternate or opposite, mostly scale-like, crowded, generally closely appressed, free and awl-shaped on vigorous shoots and young plants; buds naked (*Sabina.*)

Fruit red or reddish brown.

Bark of the trunk separating into long thin persistent scales; fruit maturing in one season.

Leaves closely appressed to the branchlet, obtusely pointed.

Leaves conspicuously glandular-pitted, ternate or opposite; fruit red, subglobose, $\frac{1}{4}'$ in diameter. **2. J. Pinchotii (C, H).**

Leaves eglandular or slightly glandular; fruit reddish brown.

Leaves ternate, rarely opposite; fruit short-oblong, $\frac{1}{4}'-\frac{1}{2}'$ in diameter. **3. J. californica (G).**

Leaves opposite, rarely ternate; fruit subglobose, $\frac{1}{8}'-\frac{1}{4}'$, in one form $\frac{3}{4}'$ in diameter. **4. J. utahensis (F, G).**

Leaves not closely appressed, spreading at the apex, long-pointed, glandular or eglandular; fruit subglobose, $\frac{1}{3}'-\frac{1}{2}'$ in diameter. **5. J. flaccida (L).**

Bark of the trunk divided into thick nearly square plates; leaves eglandular or occasionally glandular-pitted; fruit subglobose to short-oblong, $\frac{1}{2}'$ in diameter, ripening at the end of its second season. **6. C. pachyphlæa (H).**

Fruit blue or blue-black, with resinous juicy flesh, subglobose to short-oblong, $\frac{1}{12}'-\frac{1}{3}'$ in diameter; seeds, 1–4; cotyledons 2.

Leaves denticulately fringed, opposite or ternate; fruit maturing in one season.

Branchlets about $\frac{1}{12}'$ in diameter; leaves acute, conspicuously glandular; fruit short-oblong, $\frac{1}{4}'-\frac{1}{3}'$ in diameter; seeds 2 or 3. **7. J. occidéntalis (B. G).**

Branchlets not more than $\frac{1}{24}'$ in diameter; leaves usually ternate; fruit short-oblong.

Seeds 1 or rarely 2, pale chestnut-brown, obtuse, prominently ridged; leaves acute or acuminate, usually glandular. **8. J. monosperma (F).**

Seeds 1 or 2, dark chestnut-brown, acute, obscurely ridged; leaves obtusely
pointed, often eglandular.   9. J. **mexicana** (C).
Leaves naked on the margins, mostly opposite, glandular or eglandular; fruit subglobose.
Fruit ripening at the end of the first season.
Fruit $\frac{1}{4}'-\frac{1}{3}'$ in diameter; seeds 1 or 2, rarely 3 or 4; leaves acute or acuminate;
branches spreading or erect.   10. J. **virginiana** (A, C).
Fruit $\frac{1}{12}'-\frac{1}{6}'$ in diameter; seeds 1 or 2; leaves acute; branches usually pendulous.
11. J. **lucayana** (C).
Fruit ripening at the end of the second season, $\frac{1}{4}'-\frac{1}{3}'$ in diameter; seeds 1 or 2;
leaves acute or acuminate.   12. J. **scopulorum** (B, F).

1. Juniperus communis L.   Juniper.

Leaves spreading nearly at right angles to the branchlets, $\frac{1}{3}'-\frac{1}{2}'$ long, about $\frac{1}{32}'$ wide,
turning during winter a deep rich bronze color on the lower surface, persistent for many
years.   **Flowers:** male composed of 5 or 6 whorls each of 3 stamens, with broadly ovate acute
and short-pointed connectives, bearing at the very base 3 or 4 globose anther-cells; female

Fig. 78

surrounded by 5 or 6 whorls of ternate leaf-like scales, composed of 3 slightly spreading ovules
abruptly enlarged and open at the apex, with 3 minute obtuse fleshy scales below and alternate with them.   **Fruit** maturing in the third season, subglobose or short-oblong, about
$\frac{1}{4}'$ in diameter, with soft mealy resinous sweet flesh and 1–3 seeds; often persistent on the
branches one or two years after ripening; **seeds** ovoid, acute, irregularly angled or flattened,
deeply penetrated by numerous prominent thin-walled resin-glands, about $\frac{1}{8}'$ long, the
outer coat thick and bony, the inner membranaceous.
In America only occasionally tree-like and 10°–20° tall, with a short eccentric irregularly
lobed trunk rarely a foot in diameter, erect branches forming an irregular open head, slender branchlets, smooth, lustrous, and conspicuously 3-angled between the short nodes during their first and second years, light yellow tinged with red, gradually growing darker,
their dark red-brown bark separating in the third season into small thin scales, and ovoid
acute buds about $\frac{1}{8}'$ long and loosely covered with scale-like leaves; more often a shrub,
with many short slender stems prostrate at the base and turning upward and forming a
broad mass sometimes 20° across and 3° or 4° high (var. *depressa* Pursh.); at high elevations
and in the extreme north prostrate, with long decumbent stems and shorter and more
crowded leaves (var. *montana* Ait.) passing into the var. *Jackii* Rehdr. with long trailing
branches and broader incurved leaves.   **Bark** about $\frac{1}{16}'$ thick, dark reddish brown, sepa-

rating irregularly into many loose papery persistent scales. **Wood** hard, close-grained, very durable in contact with the soil, light brown, with pale sapwood. In northern Europe the sweet aromatic fruit of this tree is used in large quantities to impart its peculiar flavor to gin; occasionally employed in medicine.

Distribution. Occasionally arborescent in New England, eastern Pennsylvania, and on the high mountains of North Carolina; the var. *depressa*, common in poor rocky soil, Newfoundland to southern New England, and to the shores of the Great Lakes and north-westward; the var. *montana* from the coast of Greenland to northern New England, on the high Appalachian Mountains, North Carolina, and to northern Nebraska, along the Rocky Mountains from Alberta to western Texas, and on the Pacific coast from Alaska, southward along mountain ranges to the high Sierras of central California, extending eastward to the mountains of eastern Washington and Oregon, and on the high peaks of northern Arizona up to altitudes of 10,000°–11,500° (*P. Lowell*); the var. *Jackii* on the coast mountains from northern California to Vancouver Island; in the Old World widely distributed in many forms through all the northern hemisphere from arctic Asia and Europe to Japan, the Himalayas and the mountains of the Mediterranean Basin.

Often planted, especially in several of its pyramidal and dwarf forms, in the eastern United States and in the countries of western, central, and northern Europe.

2. Juniperus Pinchotii Sudw.

Leaves ternate, obtusely pointed, rounded and glandular-pitted on the back, $\frac{1}{16}'$ long, dark yellow-green, turning light red-brown before falling; on vigorous shoots and seedling

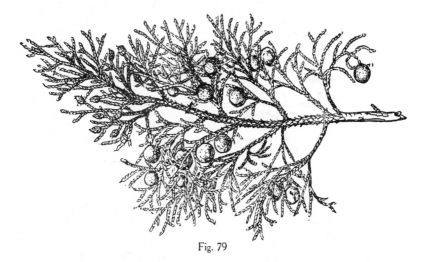

Fig. 79

plants linear-lanceolate, thin, acuminate, eglandular, $\frac{1}{4}'-\frac{1}{3}'$ in length. **Fruit** ripening in one season, subglobose, bright red, $\frac{1}{4}'$ in diameter, with a thin skin and thick dry mealy resinous flesh and 1 seed; **seed** ovoid, bluntly pointed, deeply grooved, irregularly marked by the usually two-lobed hilum, $\frac{1}{8}'-\frac{1}{4}'$ long and 2 cotyledons.

A tree rarely 20 feet high, with a trunk 1 foot in diameter, stout wide-spreading branches forming an open irregular head and thick branchlets covered with dark gray-brown scaly bark, their ultimate divisions about $\frac{1}{12}'$ in diameter; more often a shrub with several stems 1° to 12° tall. **Bark** thin, light brown, separating into long narrow persistent scales.

Distribution. Dry rocky slopes and the rocky sides of cañons, Panhandle of western

Texas (Armstrong, Potter and Hartley Counties), and in Hardaman, Garza, Tom Green, Kemble, Valverde and Menard Counties; on Comanche Peak near Granbury, Hood County, Texas; in central and on the mountains of southern Arizona.

3. Juniperus californica Carr.   Desert White Cedar.   Sweet-berried Cedar.

Leaves usually in 3's, closely appressed, thickened, slightly keeled and conspicuously glandular-pitted on the back, pointed at apex, cartilaginously fringed on the margins, light yellow-green, about $\frac{1}{8}'$ long, dying and turning brown on the branch at the end of two or three years; on vigorous shoots linear-lanceolate, rigid, sharp-pointed, $\frac{1}{4}'-\frac{1}{2}'$ long, whitish on the upper surface.

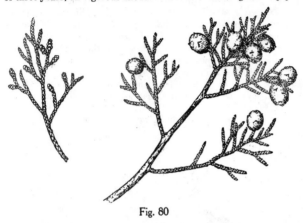

Fig. 80

Flowers from January to March; male of 18–20 stamens, disposed in 3's, with rhomboidal short-pointed connectives; scales of the female flower usually 6, ovate, acute, spreading, obliterated or minute on the fruit. **Fruit** short-oblong or ovoid, $\frac{1}{2}'-\frac{3}{4}'$ long, reddish brown, with a membranaceous loose skin covered with a thick glaucous bloom, thick fibrous dry sweet flesh, and 1 or 2 seeds; **seeds** ovoid, obtusely pointed, irregularly lobed and angled, and 4–6 cotyledons.

A conical tree, occasionally 40° high, with a straight, large-lobed unsymmetrical trunk 1°–2° in diameter; more often shrubby, with many stout irregular usually contorted stems forming a broad open head. **Bark** thin and divided into long loose plate-like scales ashy gray on the outer surface and persistent for many years. **Wood** soft, close-grained, durable in contact with the soil, light brown slightly tinged with red, with thin nearly white sapwood; used for fencing and fuel. The fruit is eaten by Indians fresh or ground into flour.

Distribution. Dry mountain slopes and hills at altitudes between 400° and 4000°, from Moraga Pass and Mt. Diabolo, Contra Costa County, California, southward on the coast ranges, spreading inland to their union with the Sierra Nevada, and northward at low altitudes along the western slopes of the Sierras to Kern and Mariposa Counties; on the desert slopes of the Tehachapi Mountains, the northern foothills of the San Bernardino Mountains, on the western slopes of the San Jacinto and Cayamaca Ranges, and southward in Lower California to Agua Dulce; arborescent and probably of its largest size on the Mohave Desert.

4. Juniperus utahensis Lemm.   Juniper.

Leaves opposite or in 3's, rounded, usually glandular, acute or often acuminate, light yellow-green, rather less than $\frac{1}{8}'$ long, persistent for many years. **Flowers:** male with 18–24 opposite or tenate stamens, their connectives rhomboidal; scales of the female flower acute, spreading, often in pairs. **Fruit** ripening during the autumn of the second season, subglobose or short-oblong, marked by the more or less prominent tips of the flower-scales, reddish brown, with a thick firm skin covered with a glaucous bloom and closely investing the thin dry sweet flesh, $\frac{1}{4}'-\frac{1}{3}'$ long, with 1 or rarely 2 seeds; **seeds** ovoid, acute, ob-tusely angled, marked to the middle by the hilum, with a hard bony shell, and 4–6 cotyle-dons.

A bushy tree, rarely exceeding 20° in height, with a short usually eccentric trunk some-times 2° in diameter, generally divided near the ground by irregular deep fissures into broad rounded ridges, many erect contorted branches forming a broad open head, slender light yellow-green branchlets covered after the falling of the leaves with thin light red-brown scaly bark; more often with numerous stems spreading from the ground and fre-quently not more than 8°–10° high. **Bark** about $\frac{1}{4}'$ thick, ashy gray or sometimes nearly

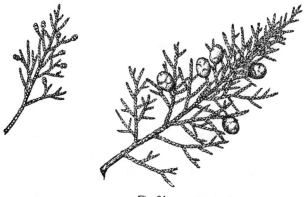

Fig. 81

white, and broken into long thin persistent scales. **Wood** light brown, slightly fragrant, with thick nearly white sapwood; largely used locally for fuel and fencing. The fruit is eaten by Indians fresh, or ground and baked into cakes.

Distribution. Southwestern Wyoming (*J. Knightii* A. Nels.), southwestern Idaho (Po-catello, Bannock County), western Colorado, eastern Utah, and western New Mexico to northern Arizona and southeastern California at altitudes from 5000° to 8000°; the most abundant and generally distributed tree of the Great Basin, forming in the valleys open forests of stunted trees and shrubs, and on arid slopes more numerous and of larger size in dense nearly pure forests.

A variety (var. *megalocarpa* Sarg.) occurs in eastern New Mexico and northern Arizona, with fruit sometimes $\frac{3}{4}'$ in diameter. A tree often 40° high with a single erect stem some-times 3° in diameter.

5. Juniperus flaccida Schlecht.   Juniper.

Leaves opposite, acuminate and long-pointed, spreading at the apex, glandular or eglandular on the back, light yellow-green, about $\frac{1}{8}'$ long, turning cinnamon-red and dy-ing on the branch; on vigorous young shoots ovate-lanceolate, sometimes $\frac{1}{2}'$ long, with elongated rigid callous tips. **Flowers:** male slender, composed of 16–20 stamens, with ovate pointed connectives prominently keeled on the back; female with acute or acumin-ate spreading scales. **Fruit** subglobose, dull red-brown, more or less covered with a glau-cous bloom, $\frac{1}{3}'-\frac{1}{2}'$ in diameter, with a close firm skin and thick resinous flesh; **seeds** 4–12, pointed at apex, slightly ridged, often abortive and distorted, $\frac{1}{8}'-\frac{1}{4}'$ long, with 2 cotyledons.

A tree, occasionally 30° high, with gracefully spreading branches and long slender droop-ing branchlets, covered after the leaves fall with thin bright cinnamon-brown bark separating into thin loose papery scales; often a shrub. **Bark** about ½′ thick, reddish brown, separating into long narrow loosely attached scales.

Fig. 82

Distribution. In the United States only on the slopes of the Chisos Mountains, in Brewster County, southern Texas; common in northeastern Mexico, growing at elevations of 6000°–8000° on the hills east of the Mexican table-lands.

Occasionally cultivated in the gardens of southern France and of Algeria.

6. Juniperus pachyphlæa Torr.   Juniper.   Checkered-bark Juniper.

Leaves appressed, acute and apiculate at apex, thickened, obscurely keeled and glandular on the back, bluish green, rather less than ⅛′ long; on vigorous shoots and young branchlets linear-lanceolate, tipped with slender elongated points, and pale blue-green like the young branchlets. **Flowers** opening in February and March: the male stout, ⅛′ long, with 10 or 12 stamens, their connectives broadly ovate, obscurely keeled on the back, short-

Fig. 83

pointed: scales of the female flower, ovate, acuminate, and spreading. **Fruit** ripening in the autumn of its second season, subglobose to short-oblong, irregularly tuberculate, ⅓′–½′ in diameter, usually marked with the short tips of the flower-scales, occasionally opening and discharging the seeds at the apex, dark red-brown, more or less covered with a glaucous bloom, especially during the first season and then occasionally bluish in color, with a thin skin closely investing the thick dry mealy flesh, and usually 4 seeds; **seeds** acute or obtusely pointed, conspicuously ridged and gibbous on the back, with a thick shell and 2 cotyledons.

A tree, often 50°–60° high, with a short trunk 3°–5° in diameter, long stout spreading branches forming a broad-based pyramidal or ultimately a compact round-topped head, and slender branchlets covered after the disappearance of the leaves with thin light red-brown usually smooth close bark occasionally broken into large thin scales. **Bark** ¾′–4′ thick, on young stems reddish brown becoming on old trunks whitish, deeply fissured and divided into nearly square plates 1′–2′ long, and separating on the surface into small thin closely appressed scales. **Wood** light, soft, not strong, brittle, close-grained, clear light red often streaked with yellow, with thin nearly white sapwood; often producing vigorous shoots from the base of the trunk or from the stumps of felled trees.

Distribution. Dry arid mountain slopes usually at elevations of 4000°–6000° above the sea, from the Eagle and Limpio mountains in southwestern Texas, westward along the desert ranges of New Mexico and Arizona, extending northward to the lower slopes of many of the high mountains of northern Arizona, and southward into Mexico.

7. Juniperus occidentalis Hook.   Juniper.

Leaves opposite or ternate, closely appressed, acute or acuminate, rounded and conspicuously glandular on the back, denticulately fringed, gray-green, about ⅛′ long. **Flowers:** male stout, obtuse, with 12–18 stamens, their connectives broadly ovoid, rounded,

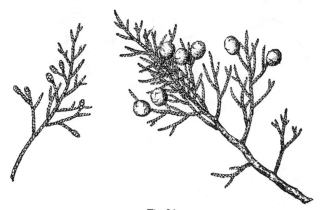

Fig. 84

acute or apiculate and scarious or slightly ciliate on the margins: scales of the female flower ovate, acute, spreading, mostly obliterated from the fruit. **Fruit** subglobose or short-oblong, ¼′–⅓′ in diameter, with a thick firm blue-black skin coated with a glaucous bloom, thin dry flesh filled with large resin-glands, and 2 or 3 seeds; **seeds** ovoid, acute, rounded and deeply grooved or pitted on the back, flattened on the inner surface, about ⅛′ long, with a thick bony shell, a thin brown inner seed-coat, and 2 cotyledons.

A tree, occasionally 60° high, with a tall straight trunk 2°–3° in diameter, more often not more than 20° in height, with a short trunk sometimes 10° in diameter, enormous branches, spreading at nearly right angles and forming a broad low head, and stout branchlets covered after the leaves fall with thin bright red-brown bark broken into loose papery scales; frequently when growing on dry rocky slopes and toward the northern limits of its range a shrub, with many short erect or semi-prostrate stems. **Bark** about

½′ thick, bright cinnamon-red, divided by broad shallow fissures into wide flat irregularly connected ridges separating on the surface into thin lustrous scales. **Wood** light, soft, very close-grained, exceedingly durable, light red or brown, with thick nearly white sapwood; used for fencing and fuel. The fruit is gathered and eaten by the California Indians.

Distribution. Mountain slopes and high prairies of western Idaho and of eastern Washington to the eastern slopes of the Cascade Mountains; eastern and southern Oregon up to altitudes of 4500°; along the summits and upper slopes of the Sierra Nevada of California, and southward to the San Bernardino Mountains, here abundant in Bear and Holcomb valleys; attaining its greatest trunk diameter on the wind-swept peaks of the California sierras, usually at altitudes between 6000° and 10,000° above the sea.

8. Juniperus monosperma Sarg. Juniper.

Leaves opposite or ternate, often slightly spreading at apex, acute or occasionally acuminate, much thickened and rounded on the back, usually glandular, denticulately fringed, gray-green, rather less than ⅛′ long, turning bright red-brown before falling; on vigorous shoots and young plants ovate, acute, tipped with long rigid points, thin, con-

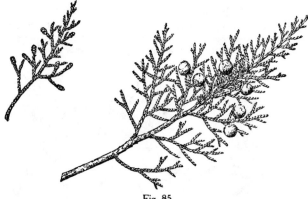

Fig. 85

spicuously glandular on the back, often ½′ long. **Flowers:** male with 8–10 stamens, their broadly ovate, rounded or pointed connectives slightly erose on the margins: female with spreading pointed scales. **Fruit** subglobose or short-oblong, ⅛′–¼′ long, dark blue or perhaps occasionally light chestnut-brown with a thick firm skin covered with a thin glaucous bloom, thin flesh, and 1 or rarely 2 seeds; **seeds** often protruding from the top of the fruit, ovoid, often 4-angled, somewhat obtuse at apex, with a small hilum, and 2 cotyledons.

A tree, occasionally 40°–50° high, with a stout much-lobed and buttressed trunk sometimes 3° in diameter, short stout branches forming an open very irregular head, and slender branchlets covered after the falling of the leaves with light red-brown bark spreading freely into thin loose scales; more often a much branched shrub sometimes only a few feet high. **Bark** ashy gray, divided into irregularly connected ridges, separating into long narrow persistent shreddy scales. **Wood** heavy, slightly fragrant, light reddish brown, with nearly white sapwood and eccentric layers of annual growth; largely used for fencing and fuel. The fruit is ground into flour and baked by the Indians, who use the thin strips of fibrous bark in making saddles, breechcloths, and sleeping-mats.

Distribution. Along the eastern base of the Rocky Mountains from the valley of the Platte River, Wyoming (near Alcova, Natrona County) and the divide between the

Platte and Arkansas rivers in Colorado; western Oklahoma (near Kenton, Cimarron County, common) and western Texas; on the Colorado plateau, northern Arizona; over the mountain ranges of southwestern Wyoming, Nevada, southern New Mexico and Arizona, and southward into northern Mexico; often covering, with the Nut Pine, in southern Colorado and Utah, and in northern and central New Mexico and Arizona, great areas of rolling hills 6000°–7000° above the sea-level; reaching its largest size in northern Arizona.

9. Juniperus mexicana Spreng. Cedar. Rock Cedar.

Juniperus sabinoides Nees.

Leaves usually opposite or ternate, thickened and keeled on the back, obtuse or acute at apex, mostly without glands, denticulately fringed, rather more than $\frac{1}{16}'$ long, dark blue-green, on vigorous young shoots and seedling plants lanceolate, long-pointed, rigid,

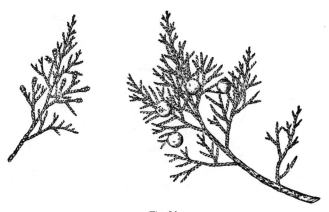

Fig. 86

$\frac{1}{4}'-\frac{1}{2}'$ long. **Flowers:** male with 12–18 stamens, their connectives ovoid, obtuse, or slightly cuspidate: scales of the female flower ovate, acute, and spreading, very conspicuous when the fruit is half grown, becoming obliterated at its maturity. **Fruit** short-oblong to subglobose, $\frac{1}{4}'-\frac{1}{2}'$ in diameter, dark blue, with a thin skin covered with a glaucous bloom, sweet resinous flesh, and 1 or 2 seeds; **seeds** ovoid, acute, slightly ridged, rarely tuberculate, dark chestnut-brown, with a small hilum, a thin outer seed-coat, a membranaceous dark brown inner coat, and 2 cotyledons.

A tree, occasionally 100° but generally not more than 20°–30° high, with a short or elongated slightly lobed trunk seldom exceeding a foot in diameter, small spreading branches forming a wide round-topped open and irregular or a narrow pyramidal head, slender sharply 4-angled branchlets becoming terete after the falling of the leaves, light reddish brown or ashy gray, with smooth or slightly scaly bark; often a shrub, with numerous spreading stems. **Bark** on old trees $\frac{1}{4}'-\frac{1}{2}'$ thick, brown tinged with red, and divided into long narrow slightly attached scales persistent for many years and clothing the trunk with a loose thatch-like covering. **Wood** light, hard, not strong, slightly fragrant, brown streaked with red; largely used for fencing, fuel, telegraph-poles, and railway-ties.

Distribution. From Brazos County over the low limestone hills of western and southern Texas, and southward into Mexico; forming great thickets and growing to its largest size on the San Bernardo River; much smaller farther westward, and usually shrubby at the limits of vegetation on the high mountains of central Mexico.

10. Juniperus virginiana L.   Red Cedar.   Savin.

Leaves usually opposite, acute or acuminate or occasionally obtuse, rounded and glandular or eglandular on the back, about $\frac{1}{16}'$ long, dark blue-green or glaucous (var. *glauca* Carr.), at the north turning russet or yellow-brown during the winter, beginning in their third season to grow hard and woody, and remaining two or three years longer on the branches, on young plants and vigorous branchlets linear-lanceolate, long-pointed, light yellow-green, without glands, $\frac{1}{2}'-\frac{3}{4}'$ long.   **Flowers:** diœcious or very rarely monœcious: male with 10 or 12 stamens, their connectives rounded and entire, with 4 or occasionally 5 or 6 pollen-sacs; scales of the female flower violet color, acute and spreading, becoming obliterated from the fruit.   **Fruit** subglobose, $\frac{1}{4}'-\frac{1}{3}'$ in diameter, pale green when fully grown, dark blue and covered with a glaucous bloom at maturity, with a firm skin, thin

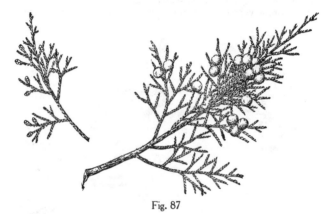

Fig. 87

sweetish resinous flesh, and 1 or 2 or rarely 3 or 4 seeds; **seeds** acute and occasionally apiculate at apex, $\frac{1}{8}'-\frac{1}{6}'$ long, with a comparatively small 2-lobed hilum, and 2 cotyledons.

A tree, occasionally 100° high, with a trunk 3°–4° in diameter, often lobed and eccentric, and frequently buttressed toward the base, generally not more than 40°–50° tall, with short slender branches horizontal on the lower part of the tree, erect above, forming a narrow compact pyramidal head, in old age usually becoming broad and round-topped or irregular, and slender branchlets terete after the disappearance of the leaves and covered with close dark brown bark tinged with red or gray; on exposed cliffs on the coast of Maine, sometimes only a few inches high with long branches forming broad dense mats.   **Bark** $\frac{1}{8}'-\frac{1}{4}'$ thick, light brown tinged with red, and separated into long narrow scales fringed on the margins, and persistent for many years.   **Wood** light, close-grained, brittle, not strong, dull red, with thin nearly white sapwood, very fragrant, easily worked; largely used for posts, the sills of buildings, the interior finish of houses, the lining of closets and chests for the preservation of woolens against the attacks of moths, and largely for pails and other small articles of woodenware, and now for lead pencils.   A decoction of the fruit and leaves is used in medicine, and oil of red cedar distilled from the leaves and wood as a perfume.

Distribution.   Dry gravelly slopes and rocky ridges, often immediately on the seacoast, from southern Nova Scotia and New Brunswick to the coast of Georgia, the interior of southern Alabama and Mississippi, and westward to the valley of the lower Ottawa River, southern Michigan, eastern North and South Dakota, Nebraska and Kansas, and eastern Texas, not ascending the mountains of New England and New York nor the high southern Alleghanies; in middle Kentucky and Tennessee, and northern Alabama and Mississippi, covering great areas of low rolling limestone hills with nearly pure forests of small bushy trees.

Often cultivated, in several forms, in the northern and eastern states as an ornamental tree and occasionally in the gardens of western and central Europe.

11. Juniperus lucayana Britt. Red Cedar.

Juniperus barbadensis Sarg. not L.

Leaves usually opposite, narrow, acute, or gradually narrowed above the middle and acuminate, marked on the back by conspicuous oblong glands. **Flowers** opening in early March: male elongated, $\frac{1}{8}'$ to nearly $\frac{1}{4}'$ long, with 10 or 12 stamens, their connectives rounded, entire, and bearing usually 3 pollen-sacs: female with scales gradually narrowed above the middle, acute at apex, and obliterated from the ripe fruit. **Fruit** subglobose to short-oblong, dark blue, covered when ripe with a glaucous bloom, about $\frac{1}{24}'$ in diameter, with a thin skin, sweet resinous flesh, and 1 or 2 seeds; **seeds** acute, prominently ridged.

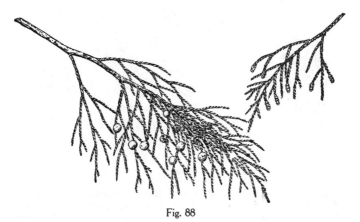

Fig. 88

A tree, sometimes 50° high, with a trunk occasionally 2° in diameter, small branches erect when the tree is crowded in the forest, spreading when it has grown in open ground and forming a broad flat-topped head often 30° or 40° in diameter, long thin secondary branches erect at the top of the tree and pendulous below, and pendulous branchlets about $\frac{1}{24}'$ in diameter, becoming light red-brown or ashy gray at the end of four or five years after the disappearance of the leaves. **Bark** thin, light red-brown, separating into long thin scales. **Wood** light, close, straight-grained, fragrant, dull red; formerly exclusively used in the manufacture of the best lead pencils.

Distribution. Inundated river swamps from southern Georgia, southward to the shores of the Indian River, Florida, and on the west coast of Florida from the northern shores of Charlotte Harbor to the valley of the Apalachicola River, often forming great thickets under the shade of larger trees; along streams and creeks in low woods near Houston, Harris County, and Milano, Milam County, Texas (*E. J. Palmer*); common in the Bahamas, San Domingo, eastern Cuba, and on the mountains of Jamaica and Antigua.

Often planted for the decoration of squares and cemeteries in the cities and towns in the neighborhood of the coast from Florida to western Louisiana, and now often naturalized beyond the limits of its natural range on the Gulf coast; occasionally cultivated in the temperate countries of Europe, and in cultivation the most beautiful of the Junipers

12. Juniperus scopulorum Sarg.   Red Cedar.

Leaves usually opposite, closely appressed, acute or acuminate, generally marked on the back by obscure elongated glands, dark green, or often pale and very glaucous. **Flowers:** male with about 6 stamens, their connectives rounded and entire, bearing 4 or 5 anthersacs: scales of the female flower spreading, acute or acuminate, and obliterated from the mature fruit. **Fruit** ripening at the end of the second season, nearly globose, $\frac{1}{4}'-\frac{1}{3}'$ in diameter, bright blue, with a thin skin covered with a glaucous bloom, sweet resinous flesh, and 1 or usually 2 seeds; **seeds** acute, prominently grooved and angled, about $\frac{3}{16}'$ long, with a thick bony outer coat and a small 2-lobed hilum.

A tree, 30°–40° high, with a short stout trunk sometimes 3° in diameter, often divided near the ground into a number of stout spreading stems, thick spreading and ascending

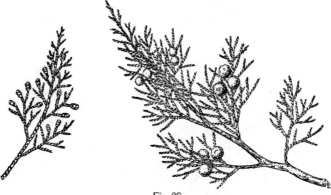

Fig. 89

branches covered with scaly bark, forming an irregular round-topped head, and slender 4-angled branchlets becoming at the end of three or four years terete and clothed with smooth pale bark separating later into thin scales. **Bark** dark reddish brown or gray tinged with red, divided by shallow fissures into narrow flat connected ridges broken on the surface into persistent shredded scales.

Distribution. Scattered often singly over dry rocky ridges, usually at altitudes of 5000° or 6000° but occasionally ascending in Colorado to 9000° above the sea, from the eastern foothill region of the Rocky Mountains from Alberta to the Black Hills of South Dakota, the valley of the Niobrara River, Sheridan County, northwestern Nebraska (*J. M. Bates*) and to western Texas and eastern and northern New Mexico, and westward to eastern Oregon, Nevada, and northern Arizona; descending to the sea level in Washington on the shores of the northern part of Puget Sound and on the islands and mainland about the Gulf of Georgia, British Columbia.

II. TAXACEÆ.

Slightly resinous trees and shrubs, producing when cut vigorous stump shoots, with fissured or scaly bark, light-colored durable close-grained wood, slender branchlets, linear-lanceolate entire rigid acuminate spirally disposed leaves, usually appearing 2-ranked by a twist in their short compressed petioles and persistent for many years, and small ovoid acute buds. Flowers opening in early spring from buds formed the previous autumn, diœcious or monœcious, axillary and solitary, surrounded by the persistent decussate scales of the buds, the male composed of numerous filaments united into a column, each filament surmounted by several more or less united pendant pollen-cells; the female of a single erect ovule, becoming at maturity a seed with a hard bony shell, raised upon or more or less surrounded by the enlarged and fleshy aril-like disk of the flower; embryo axile, in fleshy ruminate or uniform albumen; cotyledons 2, shorter than the superior radicle. Of the ten genera widely distributed over the two hemispheres, two occur in North America.

CONSPECTUS OF THE NORTH AMERICAN GENERA.

Filaments dilated into 4 pollen-sacs united into a half ring; seeds drupe-like, green or purple, ripening at the end of the second season; albumen ruminate.   1. **Torreya.**
Filaments dilated into a globose head of 4–8 connate pollen-sacs; seeds berry-like, scarlet, ripening at the end of the first season; albumen uniform.   2. **Taxus.**

1. TORREYA ARN.

Tumion Raf.

Glabrous fœtid or pungent aromatic trees, with fissured bark and verticillate or opposite spreading or drooping branches. Leaves thin, long-pointed, abruptly contracted at base, dark green, lustrous and slightly rounded above, thickened and revolute on the margins, with pale bands of stomata on each side of the midvein on the lower surface. Flowers diœcious; the male crowded in the axils of adjacent leaves, on shoots of the previous year, oval or oblong, composed of 6 or 8 close whorls each of 4 stamens, subverticillately arranged on a slender axis; filaments stout and expanded above into 4 globose yellow pollen-sacs united into a half ring, their connectives produced above the cells; the female on shoots of the year less numerous and scattered, sessile, the ovule surrounded by and finally inclosed in an ovoid urn-shaped fleshy sac, and becoming at the end of the second season an oblong-ovate yellow-brown seed, rounded and apiculate at apex, acute and marked at base by the large dark hilum; seed-coat thick and woody, its inner layer folded into the thick white albumen, surrounded and finally inclosed in the thick green or purple enlarged disk of the flower composed of thin flat easily separable fibers, splitting longitudinally when ripe into two parts and separating from the basal scales persistent on the short stout stalk of the seed.

Torreya is now confined to Florida and Georgia, western California, Japan, the island of Quelpart, and central and northern China. Four species are recognized. Of the exotic species the Japanese *Torreya nucifera* S. & Z. is occasionally cultivated in the eastern states.

The genus is named in honor of Dr. John Torrey, the distinguished American botanist.

CONSPECTUS OF THE NORTH AMERICAN SPECIES.

Leaves slightly rounded on the back, pale below; leaves, branches, and wood fœtid; branchlets gray or yellowish green.   1. **T. taxifolia** (C).
Leaves nearly flat, green below; leaves, branches and wood pungent-aromatic; branchlets reddish brown.   2. **T. californica** (G).

1. Torreya taxifolia Arn.   Stinking Cedar.   Torreya.

Tumion taxifolium Greene.

Leaves slightly falcate, $1\frac{1}{2}'$ long, about $\frac{1}{8}'$ wide, somewhat rounded, dark green and lustrous above, paler and marked below with broad bands of stomata. **Flowers** appearing in March and April; male with pale yellow anthers; female broadly ovoid, with a dark purple fleshy covering to the ovule, $\frac{1}{4}'$ long, and inclosed at the base by broad thin rounded scales. **Seed** fully grown at midsummer, slightly obovoid, dark purple, $1'-1\frac{1}{4}'$ long, $\frac{3}{4}'$ thick, with a thin leathery covering, a light red-brown seed-coat furnished on the inner surface with 2 opposite longitudinal thin ridges extending from the base toward the apex, and conspicuously ruminate albumen.

A tree, occasionally 40° high, with a short trunk 1°–2° in diameter, whorls of spreading slightly pendulous branches forming a rather open pyramidal head tapering from a broad base. **Bark** ½′ thick, brown faintly tinged with orange color, and irregularly divided by

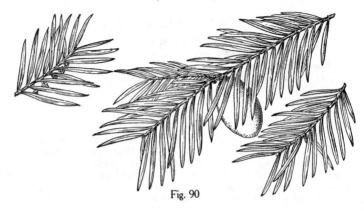

Fig. 90

broad shallow fissures into wide low ridges slightly rounded on the back and covered with thin closely appressed scales. **Wood** hard, strong, clear bright yellow, with thin lighter colored sapwood; largely used for fence-posts.

Distribution. On bluffs along the eastern bank of the Apalachicola River, Florida, from River Junction to the neighborhood of Bristol, Liberty County, and in the south-western corner of Decatur County, Georgia (*R. M. Harper*). Rare and local.

Now often planted in the public grounds and gardens of Tallahassee, Florida.

2. Torreya californica Torr. California Nutmeg.

Tumion californicum **Greene.**

Leaves slightly falcate, nearly flat, dark green and lustrous on the upper, somewhat paler and marked below with a narrow band of stomata, tipped with slender callous

Fig. 91

points, $1'-3\frac{1}{2}'$ long, $\frac{1}{16}'-\frac{1}{8}'$ wide. **Flowers** appearing in March and April; male with broadly ovate acute scales; female nearly $\frac{1}{4}'$ long, with oblong-ovate rounded scales. **Seed** ovoid or oblong-ovoid, $1'-1\frac{1}{2}'$ long, light green more or less streaked with purple.

A tree, $50°-70°$ but occasionally $100°$ high, with a trunk $1°-2°$ or rarely $4°$ in diameter, and whorls of spreading slender slightly pendulous branches forming a handsome pyramidal and in old age a round-topped head. **Bark** $\frac{1}{8}'-\frac{1}{2}'$ thick, gray-brown tinged with orange color, deeply and irregularly divided by broad fissures into narrow ridges covered with elongated loosely appressed plate-like scales. **Wood** light, soft, close-grained, clear light yellow, with thin nearly white sapwood; occasionally used for fence-posts.

Distribution. Borders of mountain streams, California, nowhere common but widely distributed from Mendocino County to the Santa Cruz Mountains in the coast region and along the western slopes of the Sierra Nevada from Eldorado to Tulare Counties at altitudes of $3000°-5000°$ above the sea; most abundant and of its largest size on the northern coast ranges.

Rarely cultivated as an ornamental tree in California and western Europe.

2. TAXUS L. Yew.

Trees or shrubs, with brown or dark purple scaly bark, and spreading usually horizontal branches. Leaves flat, often falcate, gradually narrowed at the base, dark green, smooth and keeled on the upper surface, paler, papillate, and stomatiferous on the lower surface, their margins slightly thickened and revolute. Flowers dioecious or monœcious: the male composed of a slender stipe bearing at the apex a globular head of 4–8 pale yellow stamens consisting of 4–6 conic pendant pollen-sacs peltately connate from the end of a short filament; the female sessile in the axils of the upper scale-like bracts of a short axillary branch, the ovule erect, sessile on a ring-like disk, ripening in the autumn into an ovoid-oblong seed gradually narrowed and short-pointed at apex, marked at base by the much-depressed hilum, about $\frac{1}{3}'$ long, entirely or nearly surrounded by but free from the now thickened succulent translucent sweet scarlet aril-like disk of the flower open at apex; seed-coat thick, of two layers, the outer thin and membranaceous or fleshy, the inner much thicker and somewhat woody; albumen uniform.

Taxus with six or seven species, which can be distinguished only by their leaf characters and habit, is widely distributed through the northern hemisphere, and is found in eastern North America where two species occur, in Pacific North America, Mexico, Europe, northern Africa, western and southern Asia, China, and Japan. Of the exotic species the European, African, and Asiatic *Taxus baccata* L., and its numerous varieties, is often cultivated in the United States, especially in the more temperate parts of the country, and is replaced with advantage by the hardier *Taxus cuspidata* S. & Z., of eastern Asia in the northern states, where the native shrubby *Taxus canadensis* Marsh, with *monœcious* flowers is sometimes cultivated.

Taxus, from τάξος, is the classical name of the Yew-tree.

CONSPECTUS OF THE NORTH AMERICAN ARBORESCENT SPECIES.

Leaves usually short, yellow-green.   1. T. brevifolia (G).
Leaves elongated, usually falcate, dark green.   2. T. floridana (C).

1. Taxus brevifolia Nutt. Yew.

Leaves $\frac{1}{2}'-1'$ long, about $\frac{1}{16}'$ wide, dark yellow-green above, rather paler below, with stout midribs, and slender yellow petioles $\frac{1}{12}'$ long, persistent for 5–12 years. **Flowers** and fruit as in the genus.

A tree, usually $40°-50°$ but occasionally $70°-80°$ high, with a tall straight trunk $1°-2°$ or rarely $4\frac{1}{2}°$ in diameter, frequently unsymmetrical, with one diameter much exceeding the other, and irregularly lobed, with broad rounded lobes, and long slender horizontal or slightly pendulous branches forming a broad open conical head. **Bark** about $\frac{1}{4}'$ thick and covered with small thin dark red-purple scales. **Wood** heavy, hard, strong, bright red, with thin light yellow sapwood; used for fence-posts and by the Indians of the northwest coast for paddles, spear-handles, bows, and other small articles.

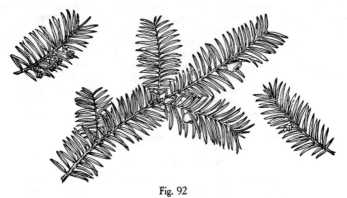

Fig. 92

Distribution. Banks of mountain streams, deep gorges, and damp ravines, growing usually under large coniferous trees; nowhere abundant, but widely distributed usually in single individuals or in small clumps from the extreme southern part of Alaska, southward along the coast ranges of British Columbia, Washington, and Oregon, where it attains its greatest size; along the coast ranges of California as far south as the Bay of Monterey, and along the western slopes of the Sierra Nevada to Tulare County at altitudes between 5000° and 8000° above the sea-level, ranging eastward in British Columbia to the Selkirk Mountains, and over the mountains of Washington and Oregon to the western slopes of the continental divide in northern Montana; in the interior much smaller than near the coast and often shrubby in habit.

Occasionally cultivated in the gardens of western Europe.

2. Taxus floridana Chapm. Yew.

Leaves usually conspicuously falcate, $\frac{3}{4}'$ to nearly 1′ long, $\frac{1}{18}'-1\frac{1}{2}'$ wide, dark green above, pale below, with obscure midribs and slender petioles about $\frac{1}{18}'$ in length. **Flowers** appearing in March. **Fruit** ripening in October.

Fig. 93

A bushy tree, rarely 25° high, with a short trunk occasionally 1° in diameter, and numerous stout spreading branches; more often shrubby in habit and 12°–15° tall. **Bark** $\frac{1}{8}'$ thick, dark purple-brown, smooth, compact, occasionally separating into large thin irregular plate-like scales. **Wood** heavy, hard, very close-grained, dark brown tinged with red, with thin nearly white sapwood.

Distribution. River bluffs and ravines on the eastern bank of the Apalachicola River, in Gadsden County, Florida, from Aspalaga to the neighborhood of Bristol.

Class 2. ANGIOSPERMÆ.

Carpels or pistils consisting of a closed cavity containing the ovules and becoming the fruit.

Division 1. Monocotyledons.

Stems with woody fibres distributed irregularly through them, but without pith or annual layers of growth. Parts of the flower in 3's; ovary superior; embryo with a single cotyledon. Leaves parallel-veined, alternate, long-persistent, without stipules.

III. PALMÆ.

Trees, growing by a single terminal bud, with stems covered with a thick rind, usually marked below by the ring-like scars of fallen leaf-stalks, and clothed above by their long-persistent sheaths; occasionally stemless. Leaves clustered at the top of the stem, plaited in the bud, fan-shaped or pinnate, their rachis sometimes reduced to a narrow border, long-stalked, with petioles dilated into clasping sheaths of tough fibres (*vaginas*); on fan-shaped leaves, furnished at the apex on the upper side with a thickened concave body (*ligule*). Flowers minute, perfect or unisexual, in the axils of small thin mostly deciduous bracts, in large compound clusters (*spadix*) surrounded by boat-shaped bracts (*spathes*); sepals and petals free or more or less united; stamens usually 6; anthers 2-celled, introrse, opening longitudinally; ovary 3-celled, with a single ovule in each cell; styles 1–3. Fruit a drupe or berry; embryo cylindric in a cavity of the hard albumen near the circumference of the seed. Of the 130 genera now usually recognized and chiefly inhabitants of the tropics, seven have arborescent representatives in the United States.

CONSPECTUS OF THE NORTH AMERICAN ARBORESCENT GENERA.

Leaves fan-shaped.
  Leaf-stalks unarmed.
    Calyx and corolla united into a short 6-lobed perianth.
      Fruit white, drupaceous; albumen even.   1. **Thrinax.**
      Fruit black, baccate; albumen channeled.   2. **Coccothrinax.**
    Calyx and corolla distinct ; fruit baccate.   3. **Sabal.**
  Leaf-stalks armed with marginal spines.
    Filaments slender, free; fruit baccate.   4. **Washingtonia.**
    Filaments triangular, united into a cup adnate to the base of the corolla; fruit
      drupaceous.   5. **Acœlorraphe.**
Leaves pinnate.
  Flower-clusters produced on the stem below the leaves; fruit violet-blue.
                                         6. **Roystonea.**
  Flower-clusters produced from among the leaves; fruit bright orange-scarlet.
                                        7. **Pseudophœnix.**

1. THRINAX Sw.

Small unarmed trees, with stems covered with pale gray rind. Leaves orbicular, or truncate at the base, thick and firm, usually silvery white on the lower surface, divided to below the middle into narrow acuminate parted segments with thickened margins and midribs; rachis a narrow border, with thin usually undulate margins; ligule thick, concave, pointed, lined while young with hoary tomentum; petioles compressed, rounded above and below, thin and smooth on the margins, with large clasping bright mahogany-red sheaths of slender matted fibres covered with thick hoary tomentum. Spadix interfoliar, stalked, its primary branches short, alternate, flattened, incurved, with numerous slender rounded flower-bearing branchlets; spathes numerous, tubular, coriaceous, cleft and more or less tomentose at the apex. Flowers opening in May and June, and occasionally irregularly in the autumn, solitary, perfect; perianth 6-lobed; stamens inserted on the base of the perianth, with subulate filaments thickened and only slightly united at the base, or nearly triangular and united into a cup adnate to the perianth, and oblong anthers; ovary 1-celled, gradually narrowed into a stout columnar style crowned by a large funnel-formed flat or oblique stigma; ovule basilar, erect. Fruit a globose drupe with juicy bitter ivory-white flesh easily separable from the thin-shelled tawny brown nut. Seed free, erect, slightly flattened at the ends, with an oblong pale conspicuous subbasilar hilum, a short-branched raphe, a thin coat, and uniform albumen more or less deeply penetrated by a broad basal cavity; embryo lateral.

Thrinax is confined to the tropics of the New World and is distributed from southern Florida through the West Indies to the shores of Central America. Seven or eight species are now generally recognized.

The wood of the Florida species is light and soft, with numerous small fibro-vascular bundles, the exterior of the stem being much harder than the spongy interior. The stems are used for the piles of small wharves and turtle-crawls, and the leaves for thatch, and in making hats, baskets, and small ropes.

Thrinax, from θρῖναξ, is in allusion to the shape of the leaves.

CONSPECTUS OF THE NORTH AMERICAN SPECIES.

Flowers on elongated pedicels; perianth obscurely lobed; stamens much exserted, their filaments subulate, barely united at base; stigma oblique; cavity of the seed extending to the apex.
    Perianth obscurely lobed; style abruptly enlarged into a large oblique stigma; leaves silvery white on the lower surface.   1. T. floridana (D).
    Perianth deeply lobed; style narrowed gradually into a small oblique stigma; leaves green on both surfaces.   2. T. Wendlandiana (D).
Flowers on short pedicels; lobes of the perianth ovate, acuminate; filaments nearly triangular, united below into a cup; stigma flat; cavity of the seed extending only to the middle.
    Seeds pale chestnut-brown; spadix about 6° long; leaves 3°–4° in diameter.
       3. T. keyensis (D).
    Seeds dark chestnut-brown; spadix less than 3° long; leaves not over 2° in diameter.
       4. T. microcarpa (D).

1. Thrinax floridana Sarg. Thatch.

Leaves 2½°–3° in diameter, rather longer than broad, yellow-green and lustrous on the upper surface, silvery white on the lower surface, with a long-pointed, bright orange-colored ligule ¾′ long and broad; petioles 4°–4½° long, pale yellow-green or orange color toward the apex, coated at first with hoary deciduous tomentum, much thickened and tomentose toward the base. **Flowers:** spadix 3°–3½° long, the primary branches 6′–8′ long and ivory-white, flower-bearing branches 1½′–2′ in length; flowers on slender pedicels nearly ⅛′ long, ivory-white, very fragrant, with an obscurely-lobed perianth, much exserted stamens barely united at the base, and a large stigma. **Fruit** ⅜′ in diameter, somewhat depressed at the ends; **seed** from ⅛′ to nearly ¼′ in diameter, dark chestnut-brown.

A tree, with a slightly tapering stem 20°–30° high and 4'–6' in diameter, clothed to the middle and occasionally almost to the ground with the sheaths of dead leaf-stalks.

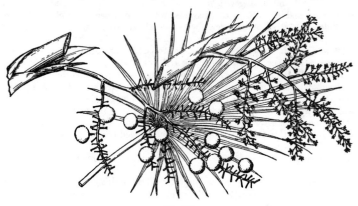

Fig. 94

Distribution. Florida, dry coral ridges and sandy shores of keys from Long Key to Torch Key, and on the mainland from Cape Romano to Cape Sable.

2. Thrinax Wendlandiana Becc. Thatch.

Leaves 2½°–3° in diameter, orbicular, pale yellow-green, lustrous above, with a thick concave ligule, acuminate or rarely rounded at apex; petioles 2°–4° long, much thick-

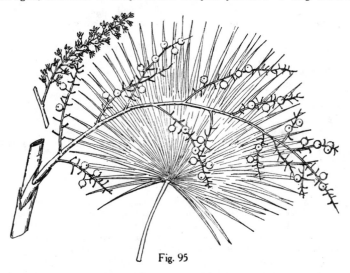

Fig. 95

ened and tomentose toward the base. **Flowers:** spadix stalked, 2°–4° long, its primary branches short, flattened, incurved, with numerous terete flower-bearing branchlets; flowers on slender pedicels $\frac{1}{10}'–\frac{1}{8}'$ long, with a deeply lobed perianth, the lobes nearly triangular, acuminate, and a small stigma. **Fruit** $\frac{1}{4}'$–$\frac{3}{8}'$ in diameter, globose; **seed** from $\frac{1}{8}'$–$\frac{1}{4}'$ in diameter, dark chestnut-brown.

A tree, in Florida, with a smooth pale trunk 20°–25° high and 3'–4' in diameter.

Distribution. Florida: Dade County, Madeira Hammock, Pumpkin Key, Flamingo, and northwest of Cape Sable; also in Cuba and on Mugueres Island, Gulf of Honduras.

3. Thrinax keyensis Sarg. Thatch.

Leaves rather longer than broad, 3°–4° long, the lowest segments parallel with the petiole or spreading from it nearly at right angles, light yellow-green and lustrous on the upper surface, with bright orange-colored margins, below coated while young with deciduous hoary tomentum and pale blue-green and more or less covered with silvery white pubescence at maturity, with a thick pointed ligule 1' long and wide, lined at first with hoary tomentum; petioles flattened above, obscurely ridged on the lower surface, tomentose while young, pale blue-green, 3°–4° long. **Flowers:** spadix usually about 6° long, spreading and gracefully incurved, with spathes more or less coated with hoary tomentum, large compressed primary branches, and short bright orange-colored flower-bearing branches;

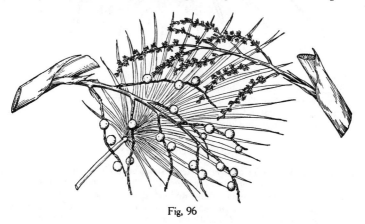

Fig, 96

flowers on short thick disk-like pedicels, about $\frac{1}{8}'$ long, white, slightly fragrant, with a tubular perianth, the lobes broadly ovate and acute, stamens with nearly triangular filaments united at the base, and a flat stigma. **Fruit** $\frac{1}{16}'$ to nearly $\frac{1}{4}'$ in diameter; **seed** brown, $\frac{3}{16}'$ in diameter.

A tree, with a stem often 25° high and 10'–14' in diameter, raised on a base of thick matted roots 2°–3° high and 18'–20' in diameter, and a broad head of leaves, the upper erect, the lower pendulous and closely pressed against the stem.

Distribution. Dry, sandy soil close to the beach on the north side of the largest of the Marquesas Keys, and on Crab Key, a small island to the westward of Torch Key, one of the Bahia Honda group, Florida; on the Bahamas.

4. Thrinax microcarpa Sarg. Silvertop Palmetto. Brittle Thatch.

Leaves 2°–3° across, pale green above, silvery white below, more or less thickly coated while young with hoary tomentum, especially on the lower surface, divided near the base almost to the rachis, with an orbicular thick concave ligule lined with a thick coat of white tomentum; petioles thin and flexuose. **Flowers:** spadix elongated, with short, compressed erect branches slightly spreading below, numerous slender pendulous flower-bearing branches, and long acute spathes deeply parted at the apex, coriaceous and coated above the middle with thick hoary tomentum; flowers on short thick disk-like pedicels, with a cupular perianth, the lobes broadly ovate and acute, stamens with thin nearly triangular exserted filaments slightly united at base and oblong anthers becoming reversed and extrorse at maturity, and a deep orange-colored ovary narrowed above into a short thick

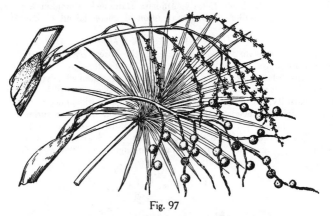

Fig. 97

style dilated into a large funnel-formed stigma. **Fruit** globose, ⅛′ in diameter; **seed** subglobose, bright to dark chestnut-brown, depressed.

A tree, rarely more than 30° high, with a trunk 8′–10′ in diameter.

Distribution. Dry coral soil, on the shores of Sugar Loaf Sound, and on No Name and Bahia Honda keys, Florida; in Cuba.

2. COCCOTHRINAX Sarg.

Small unarmed trees, with simple or clustered stems or rarely stemless. Leaves orbicular, or truncate at base, pale or silvery white on the lower surface, divided into narrow obliquely folded segments acuminate and divided at apex; rachis narrow; ligules thin, free, erect, concave, pointed at the apex; petioles compressed, slightly rounded and ridged above and below, thin and smooth on the margins, gradually enlarged below into elongated sheaths of coarse fibres forming an open network covered while young by thick hoary tomentum. Spadix interfoliar, paniculate, shorter than the leaf-stalks, its primary branches furnished with numerous short slender pendulous flower-bearing secondary branches; spathes numerous, papery, cleft at the apex. Flowers solitary, perfect, jointed on elongated slender pedicels; perianth cup-shaped, obscurely lobed; stamens 9, inserted on the base of the perianth, with subulate filaments enlarged and barely united at the base, and oblong anthers; ovary 1-celled, narrowed into a slender style crowned by a funnel-formed oblique stigma; ovule basilar, erect. Fruit a subglobose berry raised on the thickened torus of the flower, with thick juicy black flesh. Seed free, erect, depressed-globose, with a thick hard vertically grooved shell deeply infolded in the bony albumen; hilum subbasilar, minute; raphe hidden in the folds of the seed-coat; embryo lateral.

Coccothrinax is confined to the tropics of the New World. Two species, of which one is often stemless northward, inhabit southern Florida, and at least two other species are scattered over several of the West Indian islands.

Coccothrinax, from κόκκος and *Thrinax*, is in allusion to the berry-like fruit.

1. Coccothrinax jucunda Sarg. Brittle Thatch.

Leaves nearly orbicular, the lower segments usually parallel with the petiole, thin and brittle, 18′–24′ in diameter, divided below the middle of the leaf or toward its base nearly to the ligule, with much-thickened bright orange-colored midribs and margins, pale yellow-green and lustrous on the upper surface, bright silvery white and coated at first on the lower surface with hoary deciduous pubescence, with a thin undulate obtusely short-pointed dark orange-colored rachis, and a thin concave crescent-shaped often oblique slightly undulate short-pointed and light or dark orange-colored ligule ¾′ wide, ⅓′ deep; petioles slender, pale yellow-green, 2½°–3° long. **Flowers:** spadix 18′–24′ long, with flattened stalks, slender much-flattened primary branches 8′–10′ long, light orange-colored slender terete flower-bearing branches 1½′–3′ long, and pale reddish brown spathes coated toward the ends with pale pubescence; flowers opening in June and irregularly also in the autumn on ridged spreading pedicels ⅛′ long, with an orange-colored ovary surmounted by an elongated style dilated into a rose-colored stigma. **Fruit** ripening at the end of six

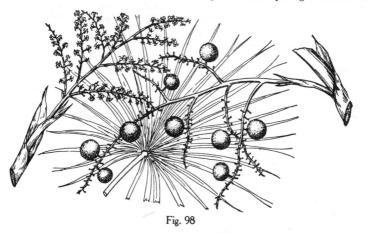

Fig. 98

months, from ½′–¾′ in diameter, bright green at first when fully grown, becoming deep violet color, with succulent very juicy flesh, ultimately black and lustrous; seed light tawny brown.

A tree, with a stem slightly enlarged from the ground upward, 15°–25° high, 4′–6′ thick, covered with pale blue rind, and surmounted by a broad head of leaves at first erect, then spreading and ultimately pendulous. **Wood** used for the piles of small wharves and turtle-crawls. The soft tough young leaves are made into hats and baskets.

Distribution. Dry coral ridges and sandy flats from the shores of Bay Biscayne along many of the southern keys to the Marquesas group (var. *marquesensis* Becc.) Florida; and on the Bahamas (var. *macrosperma* Becc.).

3. SABAL Adans. Palmetto.

Unarmed trees, with stout columnar stems covered with red-brown rind. Leaves flabellate, tough and coriaceous, divided into many narrow long-pointed parted segments plicately folded at base, often separating on the margins into narrow threads; rachis extending nearly to the middle of the leaves, rounded and broadly winged toward the base on the lower side, thin and acute on the upper side; ligule adnate to the rachis, acute, concave, with thin incurved entire margins; petioles rounded and concave on the lower side, conspicuously ridged on the upper side, acute and entire on the margins, with elongated chestnut-brown shining sheaths of stout fibres. Spadix interfoliar, stalked, decompound, with a flattened stem, short branches, slender densely flowered ultimate branches, and numerous acuminate spathes, the outer persistent and becoming broad and woody. Flowers solitary, perfect; calyx tabular, unequally lobed, the lobes slightly imbricated in the bud; corolla deeply lobed, with narrow ovate-oblong concave acute lobes valvate at the apex in the bud; stamens 6, those opposite the corolla lobes rather longer than the others, with subulate filaments united below into a shallow cup adnate to the tube of the corolla, and ovoid anthers, their cells free and spreading at the base; ovary of 3 carpels, 3-lobed, 3-celled, gradually narrowed into an elongated 3-lobed style truncate and stigmatic at the apex; ovule basilar, erect. Fruit a small black 1 or 2 or 3-lobed short-stemmed berry with thin sweet dry flesh. Seed depressed-globose, marked on the side by the prominent micropyle, with a shallow pit near the minute basal hilum, a thin seed-coat, and a ventral raphe; embryo minute, dorsal, in horny uniform albumen penetrated by a hard shallow basal cavity filled by the thickening of the seed-coat.

Sabal belongs to the New World, and is distributed from the Bermuda Islands and the South Atlantic and Gulf states of North America through the West Indies to Venezuela and Mexico.

Of the eight species now recognized four inhabit the United States; of these two are small stemless plants.

The generic name is of uncertain origin.

CONSPECTUS OF THE NORTH AMERICAN ARBORESCENT SPECIES.

Spadix short; fruit subglobose, 1-celled; seed-coat light chestnut color. 1. S. Palmetto (C).
Spadix elongated; fruit often 2 or 3-lobed, with 2 or 3 seeds; seed-coat dark chestnut-brown.
2. S. texana (E).

1. Sabal Palmetto R. & S. Cabbage Tree. Cabbage Palmetto.

Leaves 5°–6° long and 7°–8° broad, dark green and lustrous, deeply divided into narrow parted recurved segments, with ligules 4′ long and more or less unsymmetrical at apex; petioles 6°–7° long and 1½′ wide at apex. Flowers: spadix 2°–2½° long, with slender incurved

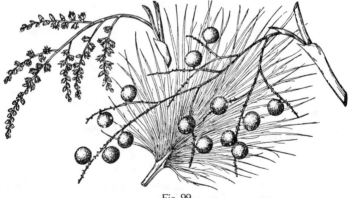

Fig. 99

branches, slender ultimate divisions, and thin secondary spathes flushed with red at apex and conspicuously marked by pale slender longitudinal veins; flowers in the axils of minute deciduous bracts much shorter than the perianth, opening in June. Fruit ripening late in the autumn, subglobose or slightly obovoid, gradually narrowed at base, 1-seeded, about ⅓′ in diameter; seed light bright chestnut-colored, ¼′ broad.

A tree, often 40°–50° and occasionally 80°–90° high, with a tall clear trunk often 2° in diameter, sometimes branched by the destruction of the terminal bud, divided by shallow irregular interrupted fissures into broad ridges, with a short pointed knob-like underground stem surrounded by a dense mass of contorted roots often 4° or 5° in diameter and 5° or 6° deep, from which tough light orange-colored roots often nearly ½′ in diameter penetrate the soil for a distance of 15° or 20°, and a broad crown of leaves at first upright, then spreading nearly at right angles with the stem, and finally pendulous. Wood light, soft, pale brown, or occasionally nearly black, with numerous hard fibro-vascular bundles, the outer rim about 2′ thick and much lighter and softer than the interior. In the southern states the trunks are used for wharf-piles, and polished cross sections of the stem sometimes serve for the tops of small tables; the wood is largely manufactured into canes. From the sheaths of young leaves the bristles of scrubbing-brushes are made. The large succulent leaf-buds are cooked and eaten as a vegetable, and coarse hats, mats, and baskets are made from the leaves. Pieces of the spongy bark of the stem are used as a substitute for scrubbing-brushes.

Distribution. Sandy soil in the immediate neighborhood of the coast from the neighborhood of Cape Hatteras and Smith Island at the mouth of Cape Fear River, North Carolina, southward near the coast to northern Florida; in Florida extending across the peninsula and south to Upper Matecumbe Key, and along the west coast to Saint Andrews Bay. Most abundant and of its largest size on the west coast of the Florida peninsula.

Often planted as a street tree in the cities of the southern states.

2. Sabal texana Becc. Palmetto.

Sabal mexicana S. Wats., not Mart.

Leaves dark yellow-green and lustrous, 5°–6° long, often 7° wide, divided nearly to the middle into narrow divided segments, with thickened pale margins separating into long

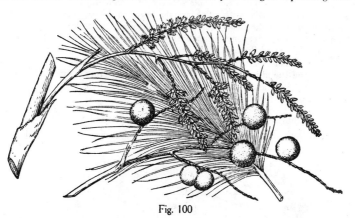

Fig. 100

thin fibres, with ligules about 6′ long; petioles 7°–8° long, 1½′ wide at the apex. **Flowers:** spadix 7°–8° long, with stout ultimate divisions; flowers in Texas appearing in March or April in the axils of persistent bracts half as long as the perianth. **Fruit** ripening early in the summer, globose, often 2 or 3-lobed; **seeds** nearly ½′ broad and ¼′ wide, dark chestnut-brown, with a broad shallow basal cavity, and a conspicuous orange-colored hilum.

A tree, with a trunk 30°–50° high, often 2½° in diameter, and a broad head of erect ultimately pendulous leaves. **Wood** light, soft, pale brown tinged with red, with thick light-colored rather inconspicuous fibro-vascular bundles, the outer rim 1′ thick, soft, and light colored. On the Gulf coast the trunks are used for wharf-piles, and on the lower Rio Grande the leaves for the thatch of houses.

Distribution. Rich soil of the bottom-lands on the Bernado River, Cameron County, and near the mouth of the Rio Grande, Texas, and southward in Mexico in the neighborhood of the coast.

Frequently planted as a street tree in the towns in the lower Rio Grande valley.

4. WASHINGTONIA H. Wendl.

Trees, with stout columnar stems and broad crowns of erect and spreading finally pendulous leaves. Leaves flabellate, divided nearly to the middle into many narrow deeply parted recurved segments separating on the margins into numerous slender pale fibres; rachis short, slightly rounded on the back, gradually narrowed from a broad base, with concave margins furnished below with narrow erect wings, and slender and acute above; ligule elongated, oblong, thin and laciniate on the margins; petioles elongated, broad and thin, flattened or slightly concave on the upper side, rounded on the lower, armed irregularly with broad thin large and small straight or hooked spines confluent into a thin bright orange-colored cartilaginous margin, gradually enlarged at base into thick broad concave bright chestnut-brown sheaths composed of a network of thin strong fibres. Spadix interfoliar, stalked, elongated, paniculate, with pendulous flower-bearing ultimate divisions and numerous long spathes. Flowers perfect, jointed on thick disk-like pedicels; calyx tubular, scarious, thickened at base, gradually enlarged and slightly lobed at apex, the lobes imbricated in the bud; corolla funnel-formed, with a fleshy tube inclosed in the calyx and about half as long as the lanceolate lobes thickened and glandular on the inner surface at the base, imbricated in the bud; stamens inserted on the tube of the corolla, with free filaments thickened near the middle and linear-oblong anthers; ovary 3-lobed, 3-celled, with slender elongated flexuose styles stigmatic at apex; ovules lateral, erect. Fruit a small ellipsoidal short-stalked black berry with thin dry flesh. Seed free, erect, oblong-ovoid, concave above, with a flat base depressed in the centre, a minute sublateral hilum, a broad conspicuous rachis, a minute lateral micropyle, and a thin pale chestnut-brown inner coat closely investing the simple horny albumen; embryo minute, lateral, with the radicle turned toward the base of the fruit.

Three species of Washingtonia are known: one inhabits the interior dry region of southern California and the adjacent parts of Lower California, and the others the mountain cañons of western Sonora and southern Lower California.

The genus is named for George Washington.

1. Washingtonia filamentosa O. Kuntze. Desert Palm. Fan Palm.

Leaves 5°–6° long and 4°–5° wide, light green, slightly tomentose on the folds; petioles

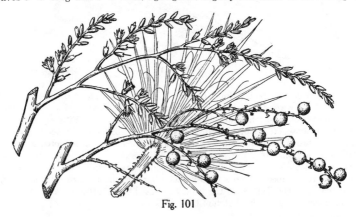

Fig. 101

4°–6° long and about 2′ broad at apex, with sheaths 16′–18′ long and 12′–14′ wide, and ligules 4′ long and cut irregularly into long narrow lobes. **Flowers:** spadix 10°–12° long, 3 or 4 being produced each year from the axils of upper leaves, the outer spathe inclosing the bud, narrow, elongated, and glabrous, those of the secondary branches coriaceous, yellow tinged with brown, and laciniate at apex; flowers slightly fragrant, opening late in May or early in June. **Fruit** produced in great profusion, ripening in September, ½′ long; **seed** ¼′ long, ⅛′ thick.

A tree, occasionally 75° high, with a trunk sometimes 50°–60° tall and 2°–3° in diameter, covered with a thick light red-brown scaly rind and clothed with a thick thatch of dead pendant leaves descending in a regular cone from the broad crown of living leaves sometimes nearly to the ground. **Wood** light and soft, with numerous conspicuous dark orange-colored fibro-vascular bundles. The fruit is gathered and used as food by the Indians.

Distribution. Often forming extensive groves or small isolated clumps in wet usually alkali soil in depressions along the northern and northwestern margins of the Colorado Desert in southern California, sometimes extending for several miles up the cañons of the San Bernardino and San Jacinto mountains; and in Lower California.

Now largely cultivated in southern California, New Orleans, southern Europe, and other temperate regions.

5. ACŒLORRAPHE H. Wendl.

Paurotia Cooke.

Trees, with tall slender often clustered stems clothed for many years with the sheathing bases of the petioles of fallen leaves. **Leaves** suborbicular, divided into numerous two-parted segments plicately folded at the base; rachis short, acute; ligule thin, concave, furnished with a broad membranaceous dark red-brown deciduous border; petioles slender, flat or slightly concave on the upper side, rounded and ridged on the lower side, with a broad high rounded ridge, thickened and cartilaginous on the margins, more or less furnished with stout or slender flattened teeth; vagina thin and firm, bright mahogany red, lustrous, closely infolding the stem, its fibres thin and tough. Spadix paniculate, interpetiolar, its rachis slender, compressed, ultimate branches, numerous, slender, elongated, gracefully drooping, hoary-tomentose, the primary branches flattened, the secondary terete in the axils of ovate acute chestnut-brown bracts; spathes flattened, thick and firm, deeply two-cleft and furnished at apex with a red-brown membranaceous border, inclosing the rachis of the panicle, each primary branch with its spathe and the node of the rachis below it inclosed in a separate spathe, the whole surrounded by the larger spathe of the node next below. **Flowers** perfect, minute, sessile on the ultimate branches of the spadix, in the axils of ovate acute chestnut-brown caducous bracts, solitary toward the end of the branches and in two- or three-flowered clusters near their base; calyx truncate at base, divided into three broadly ovate sepals dentate on the margins, valvate in æstivation, enlarged and persistent under the fruit; corolla three-parted nearly to the base, its divisions valvate in æstivation, oblong-ovate, thick, concave and thickened at apex, deciduous; stamens six, included; filaments nearly triangular, united below into a cup adnate to the short tube of the corolla; anthers short-oblong, attached on the back below the middle, introrse, two-celled, the cells opening longitudinally; ovary obovoid, of three carpels, each with two deep depressions on their outer face, united into a slender style; stigma minute, terminal, persistent on the fruit; ovule solitary, erect from the bottom of the cell, anatropous. **Fruit** drupaceous, subglobose, one-seeded, black and lustrous; exocarp thin and fleshy; endocarp thin, crustaceous; seed erect, free, subglobose, light chestnut-brown; testa thin and hard; hilum small, suborbicular; raphe ventral, oblong, elongated, black, slightly prominent, without ramifications; embryo lateral; albumen homogeneous.

Two species of Acœlorraphe have been distinguished; they inhabit southern Florida, and one species occurs also in Cuba and on the Bahama Islands.

The generic name, from ἀ priv., Κοῖλος and ῥαφή, refers to the character of the seed.

CONSPECTUS OF THE NORTH AMERICAN SPECIES.

Petioles furnished with stout marginal teeth throughout their entire length; leaves green on both surfaces, their primary divisions extending to the middle, secondary divisions only from 3½'–9' long; stems forming large thickets.   1. A. Wrightii (D).

Petioles furnished with thinner teeth, usually unarmed toward the apex; leaves green or glaucescent on the lower surface, their primary divisions extending nearly to the base, secondary divisions often 10' long or more; stems often prostrate. 2. A. arborescens (D).

1. Accœlorraphe Wrightii Becc.

Paurotia Wrightii Britt.

Leaves 30'–36' in diameter, thin, light green, divided only to the middle, the divisions of the primary lobes 3½'–9' long; petioles thin, gradually tapering from the base, 40'–60'

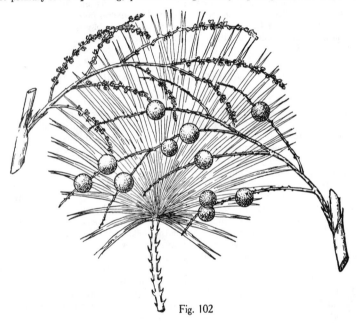

Fig. 102

in length, armed throughout with stout straight or incurved teeth. **Flowers:** spadix 4°–6° long; flowers ⅛'–⅙' long, with a light chestnut-brown calyx and a pale yellow-green corolla. Fruit ¼' in diameter.

A tree with numerous stems, in Florida sometimes 10 metres high, forming great thickets.

Distribution. Dade County, Florida, from the rear of Madeira Hummock to Cape Sable, in swamps of fresh or brackish water at some distance from the coast; also in Cuba and on the Bahamas.

2. Accœlorraphe arborescens Becc.

Serenoa arborescens Sarg.

Leaves about 2° in diameter, light yellow-green on the upper surface, blue-green or glaucescent on the lower surface, divided nearly to the base into numerous lobes slightly thickened at the pale yellow midribs and margins; petioles 18'–24' long, armed, except toward the apex, with stout flattened curved orange-colored teeth. **Flowers:** spadix

$3°-4°$ long, with a slender much-flattened stalk, panicled lower branches $18'-20'$ in length, and 6-8 thick firm pale green conspicuously ribbed spathes dilated at apex into a narrow border; flowers with a light chestnut-brown calyx and a pale yellow-green corolla. Fruit globose, $\frac{1}{3}'$ in diameter; seed somewhat flattened below, with a pale vertical mark on the lower side, and a hilum joined to the micropyle by a pale band.

A tree, from $30°-40°$ high, with 1 or several clustered erect inclining or occasionally semi-prostrate stems $3'-4'$ in diameter, covered almost to the ground by the closely clasping bases of the leaf-stalks and below with a thick pale rind.

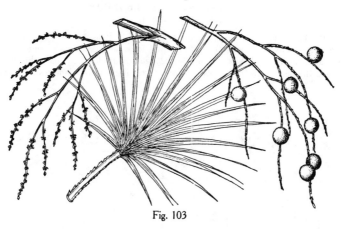

Fig. 103

Distribution. Low undrained soil covered for many months of every year in water from $1'-18'$ deep, occasionally occupying almost exclusively areas of several acres in extent or more often scattered among Cypress-trees or Royal Palms, in the swamps and along the hummocks adjacent to the Chokoloskee River and its tributaries and at the head of East River, Whitewater Bay, in southwestern Florida.

6. ROYSTONEA Cook. Royal Palm.

Unarmed trees, with massive stems enlarged near the middle, and terminating in long slender bright green cylinders formed by the closely appressed sheath of the lowest leaf Leaves equally pinnate, with linear-lanceolate long-pointed unequally cleft plicately-folded pinnæ inserted obliquely on the upper side of the rachis, folded together at the base, with thin midribs and margins; rachis convex on the back, broad toward the base of the leaf and acute toward its apex; petioles semicylindric, gradually enlarged into thick elongated green sheaths. Spadix large, decompound, produced near the base of the green part of the stem, with long pendulous branches and 2 spathes, the outer semicylindric and as long as the spadix, the inner splitting ventrally and inclosing the branches of the spadix. Flowers monœcious, in a loose spiral, toward the base of the branch in 3-flowered clusters, with a central staminate and smaller lateral pistillate flowers, higher on the branch the staminate in 2-flowered clusters; calyx of the staminate flower of minute broadly ovate obtuse scarious sepals imbricated in the bud, much shorter than the corolla; petals nearly equal, valvate in the bud, ovate or obovate, acute, slightly united at the base, coriaceous; stamens 6, 9, or 12, with subulate filaments united below and adnate to the base of the corolla, and large ovate-sagittate anthers, the cells free below; ovary rudimentary, subglobose or 3-lobed; pistillate flowers much smaller, ovoid-conic; sepals obtuse; corolla erect, divided to the middle into acute erect lobes incurved at apex; staminodia 6, scale-like, united into a cup adnate to the corolla; ovary subglobose, obscurely 2 or 3-lobed,

2 or 3-celled, gibbous, the cells crowned with a 3-lobed stigma becoming subbasilar on the fruit; ovule ascending. Fruit a short-stalked drupe with thin crustaceous flesh.   Seed oblong-reniform, marked by the conspicuous fibrous reticulate branches of the raphe radiating from the narrow basal hilum, and covered with a thin crustaceous coat; embryo minute, cylindric, lateral, in uniform albumen.

Roystonea is confined to the tropics of the New World, where two or three species occur. The genus as here limited was named for General Roy Stone of the United States army.

1. Roystonea regia Cook.   Royal Palm.

Oreodoxa regia H. B. K.

Leaves 10°–12° long, closely pinnate, the pinnæ, 2½°–3° long, 1½′ wide near the base of the leaf, and gradually decreasing in size toward its apex, deep green with slender conspicuous veins, and covered below with minute pale glandular dots; petioles almost terete, concave near the base, with thin edges separating irregularly into pale fibres, and enlarged

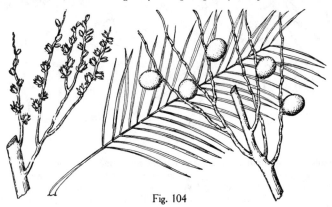

Fig. 104

into bright green cylindrical clasping bases 8° or 9° long and more or less covered with dark chaffy scales.   **Flowers:** spadix about 2° long, with a nearly terete stem and slightly ridged primary and secondary branches compressed above, abruptly enlarged at the base, and simple slender flexuose long-pointed flower-bearing branchlets 3′–6′ long, pendant and closely pressed against the secondary branches; flowers opening in Florida in January and February, the staminate nearly ¼′ long and rather more than twice as long as the pistillate.   **Fruit** oblong-obovoid, full and rounded at apex, narrowed at base, violet-blue, about ½′ long, with a thin outer coat and a light red-brown inner coat, loose and fibrous on the outer surface, and closely investing the thin light brown seed.

A tree, 80°–100° high, with a trunk rising from an abruptly enlarged base, gradually tapering from the middle to the ends and often 2° in diameter, covered with light gray rind tinged with orange color, marked with dark blotches and irregularly broken into minute plates, the green upper portion 8°–10° long, and a broad head of gracefully drooping leaves. **Wood** of the interior of the stem spongy, pale brown, much lighter than the hard exterior rim, containing numerous dark conspicuous fibro-vascular bundles.   The outer portion of the stem is made into canes, and the trunks are sometimes used for wharf-piles and in construction.

Distribution.   Florida, hummocks on Rogue River twenty miles east of Caximbas Bay, on some of the Everglades Keys, Long's Key, and formerly on the shores of Bay Biscayne near the mouth of Little River; common in the West Indies and Central America.

Largely cultivated as an ornamental tree in tropical countries, and often planted to form avenues, for which its tall pale columnar stems and noble heads of graceful foliage make it valuable.

7. PSEUDOPHŒNIX H. Wendl.

A tree, with a slender stem abruptly enlarged at the base or tapering from the middle to the ends, covered with thin pale blue or nearly white rind, and conspicuously marked by the dark scars of fallen leaf-stalks. Leaves erect, abruptly pinnate, with crowded linear-lanceolate acuminate leaflets increasing in length and width from the ends to the middle of the leaf, thick and firm in texture, dark yellow-green above, pale and glaucous below; rachis convex on the lower side, concave on the upper side near the base of the leaf, with thin margins, becoming toward the apex of the leaf flat and narrowed below and acute above, marked on the sides at the base with dark gland-like excrescences; petioles short, concave above, with thin entire margins separating into slender fibres, gradually enlarged into broad thick sheaths of short brittle fibres. Spadix interfoliar, compound, pendulous, stalked, much shorter than the leaves, with spreading primary branches, stout and much flattened toward the base, slender and rounded above the middle, furnished at the base with a thickened ear-like body, slender secondary branches, short thin rigid densely flowered ultimate divisions, and compressed light green double spathes erose on their thin dark brown margins. Flowers on slender pedicels articulate by an expanded base, widely scattered on the ultimate branches of the spadix, staminate and bisexual in the same inflorescence; calyx reduced to the saucer-like rim of the thickened receptacle, undulate on the margin, the rounded angles alternating with the petals; petals 3, valvate in the bud, oblong, rounded at apex, thick conspicuously longitudinally veined, persistent; stamens 6, with short flattened nearly triangular filaments slightly united at the base into a narrow fleshy disk, and triangular cordate anthers attached at the base in a cavity on their outer face, 2-celled, the cells opening by lateral slits; styles of the perfect flower 3-lobed at the apex with obtuse appressed lobes, that of the sterile flower as long or longer than that of the perfect flower, more slender and tapering into a narrow 3-pointed apex. Fruit a stalked globose 2 or 3-lobed orange-scarlet thin-fleshed drupe marked by the lateral style and surrounded below by the withered remnants of the flower; pedicel abruptly enlarged at base, articulate from a persistent cushion-like body furnished in the centre with a minute point penetrating a cavity in the base of the pedicel. Seed subglobose, free, erect, with a basal hilum and a thin light red-brown coat marked by the pale conspicuous ascending 2 or 3-branched raphe; embryo minute, basal, in uniform horny albumen.

Pseudophœnix with a single species inhabits the keys of southern Florida, and the Bahamas.

The generic name is in allusion to a fancied resemblance to *Phœnix*, a genus of Palms.

1. Pseudophœnix vinifera Becc.

Leaves 5°–6° long, with pinnæ often 18′ long and 1′ wide near the middle of the leaf,

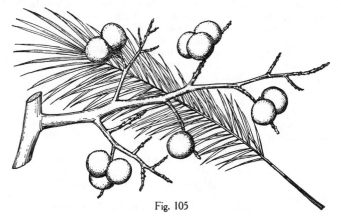

Fig. 105

becoming at its extremities not more than half as long and wide; petioles 6′–8′ in length. **Flowers:** spadix 3° long and 2½° wide. Fruit ripening in May and June, ½′–¾′ in diameter on a peduncle ¼′ long; seed ¼′ in diameter.

Distribution. Florida, east end of Elliot's Key, and east end of Key Largo near the southern shore, here forming a grove of 200 or 300 plants; more common on the Bahamas.

Occasionally cultivated in the gardens of southern Florida.

IV. LILIACEÆ.

YUCCÆ.

Leaves, alternate, linear-lanceolate. Flowers in terminal panicles; sepals and petals nearly similar, subequal, withering-persistent; ovary with more or less deeply introduced dorsal partitions; ovules numerous, 2-ranked in each cell; embryo subulate, obliquely placed across the seed; cotyledon arched in germination.

Yuccæ as here limited consists of two American genera, Hesperaloe, with two species, low plants of Texas and Mexico, and Yucca.

1. YUCCA L.

Trees with simple or branched stems prolonged by axillary naked buds, dark thick corky bark, light fibrous wood in concentric layers, and large stout horizontal roots; or often stemless. Leaves involute in the bud, at first erect, usually becoming reflexed, abruptly narrowed above the broad thickened clasping base, usually widest near the middle, concave on the upper surface, involute toward the horny usually sharp-pointed apex, convex and often slightly keeled toward the base on the lower surface, the margins serrulate or filamentose, light or dull green. Flowers fertilized by insects and opening for a single night, on slender pedicels in 2 or 3-flowered clusters or singly at the base of the large compound panicle furnished with conspicuous leathery white or slightly colored bracts, those at the base of the pedicels thin and scarious; perianth cup-shaped, with thick ovate-lanceolate creamy white segments more or less united at base, usually furnished with small tufts of white hairs at the apex, those of the outer rank narrower, shorter, and more colored than the more delicate petal-like segments of the inner rank; stamens 6, in 2 series, free, shorter than the ovary (*as long in* 1), white, with club-shaped fleshy filaments, obtuse and slightly 3-lobed at the apex, and cordate emarginate anthers attached on the back, the cells opening longitudinally, curling backward and expelling the large globose powdery pollen-grains; ovary oblong, 6-sided, sessile or stalked, with nectar-glands within the partitions, dull greenish white, 3-celled, gradually narrowed into a short or elongated 3-lobed ivory-white style forming a triangular stigmatic tube. Fruit oblong or oval, more or less distinctly 6-angled, 6-celled, usually beaked at the apex, baccate and indehiscent or capsular and 3-valved, the valves finally separating at the apex; pericarp of 2 coats, the outer at maturity thick, succulent and juicy, thin, dry and leathery, or thin and woody. Seeds compressed, triangular, obovoid, or obliquely ovoid or orbicular, thick, with a narrow 2-edged rim, or thin, with a wide or narrow brittle margin; seed-coat thin, black, slightly rugose or smooth; embryo in plain or rarely ruminate hard farinaceous oily albumen; cotyledon much longer than the short radicle turned toward the small oblong white hilum.

Yucca is confined to the New World and is distributed from Bermuda and the eastern Antilles, through the south Atlantic and Gulf states to Oklahoma and Arkansas, and through New Mexico and northward along the eastern base of the Rocky Mountains to South Dakota, westward, to middle California, and southward through Arizona, Mexico, and Lower California to Central America. About thirty species with many varieties and probable hybrids are recognized. Of the species which inhabit the territory of the United States nine assume the habit and attain the size of small trees. The root-stalks of Yucca are used as a substitute for soap, and ropes, baskets, and mats are made from the tough fibres of the leaves. Many of the species are cultivated, especially in countries of scanty rainfall, for their great clusters of beautiful flowers, or in hedges to protect gardens from cattle.

The generic name is from the Carib name of the root of the Cassava.

CONSPECTUS OF THE ABORESCENT SPECIES OF THE UNITED STATES.

Flower-clusters usually sessile, or short-stalked.
　Fruit pendulous, with thick succulent flesh; seeds thick; albumen ruminate.
　　Segments of the perianth slightly united at the base.
　　　Panicle glabrous or puberulous.
　　　　Ovary stipitate; leaves sharply toothed on their horny margins, smooth, dark
　　　　　green, slightly concave.   **1. Y. aloifolia** (C).
　　　　Ovary sessile.
　　　　　Leaves concave, blue-green, rough on the lower surface. **2. Y. Treculeana** (E).
　　　　　Leaves concave above the middle, light yellow-green, smooth.
　　　　　　Style elongated.   **3. Y. macrocarpa** (E, H).
　　　　　　Style short.   **4. Y. mohavensis** (G, H).
　　　Panicle coated with hoary tomentum; leaves concave, smooth, light yellow-green.
　　　　　　　　　　　　　　　　　　　　　　　　　　　　　　　　　5. Y. Schottii (H).
　　Segments of the perianth united below into a narrow tube; leaves flat, smooth, dark
　　　green.   **6. Y. Faxoniana** (E).
　Fruit erect or spreading, the flesh becoming thin and dry at maturity; seeds thin; albu-
　　men entire.
　　　Leaves rigid, concave above the middle, blue-green, sharply serrate.
　　　　　　　　　　　　　　　　　　　　　　　　　　　　　　7. Y. brevifolia (F, G).
　　　Leaves thin, flat or concave toward the apex, nearly entire, rough on the lower
　　　　surface, dull or glaucous green.   **8. Y. gloriosa** (C).
Flower-clusters long-stalked; fruit capsular, erect, finally splitting between the carpels
　and through their backs at the apex; seeds thin; albumen entire; leaves thin, flat,
　filamentose on the margins, smooth, pale yellow-green.   **9. Y. elata** (E, H).

1. Yucca aloifolia L.　Spanish Bayonet.

Leaves 18′–32′ long, 1¼′–2½′ wide, erect, rigid, conspicuously narrowed above the light
green base, widest above the middle, slightly concave on the upper surface, smooth, dark

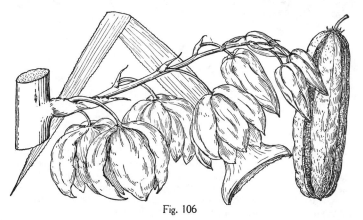

Fig. 106

rich green, with a stiff dark red-brown tip, and horny finely and irregularly serrate margins; long-persistent. **Flowers** from June until August on stout pedicels, in nearly sessile
glabrous or slightly pubescent panicles 18′–24′ long; perianth 1′–1½′ in length and 3′ or 4′
across when fully expanded, the segments ovate, thick and tumid toward the base, those
of the outer rank rounded and often marked with purple at apex, the inner acuminate

and short-pointed; stamens as long or sometimes a little longer than the light green ovary raised on a short stout stipe. **Fruit** ripening from August to October, elongated, ellipsoidal, hexagonal, 3'-4' long, 1¼'-1½' thick, light green when fully grown, and in ripening turning dark purple, the outer and inner coats forming a thick succulent mass of bitter-sweet juicy flesh, finally becoming black and drying on its stalk; **seeds** ¼'-⅓' wide, about ¹⁄₁₆' thick, with a thin narrow ring-like border to the rim.

A tree, occasionally 25° high, usually much smaller, with an erect or more or less inclining simple or branched trunk slightly swollen at base, and rarely more than 6' in diameter; sometimes with numerous clustered stems. **Bark** near the base of the trunk thick, rough, dark brown, marked above by scars left by falling leaves.

Distribution. Sand dunes of the coast from North Carolina to eastern Louisiana; west of the Apalachicola River attaining its largest size and sometimes ranging inland through Pine-forests for thirty or forty miles; and in Yucatan (var. **yucatana** Trel.).

A common garden plant in all countries with a temperate climate, and long naturalized in the southern states far beyond the limits of its natural range, in some of the West Indian islands and on the Gulf coast of Mexico. Forms with leaves variously striped with white, yellow, and red or with recurving leaves are frequent in cultivation.

2. Yucca Treculeana Carr. Spanish Bayonet. Spanish Dagger.

Leaves 2½°-4° long, 2'-3¼' wide, slightly or not at all contracted above the dark red lustrous base, concave, stiff, rigid, dark blue-green, rough on the lower surface, nearly smooth on the upper, with a short stout dark red-brown tip, and dark brown margins roughened by minute deciduous teeth and ultimately separating into slender dark fibres;

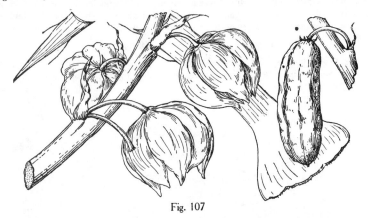

Fig. 107

persistent for many years, the dead leaves hanging closely appressed against the trunk below the terminal crown of closely imbricated living leaves. **Flowers** in March and April on slender pedicels, in dense many-flowered glabrous or puberulous panicles 2°-4° long and raised on short stout stalks; perianth 1'-2' long, 2'-4' in diameter when fully expanded, with narrow elongated ovate-lanceolate to ovate segments, ¼' wide, acute, thin and delicate, furnished at apex with a conspicuous tuft of short pale hairs; filaments slightly papillose, about as long as the prismatic ovary gradually narrowed above and crowned by the deeply divided stigmatic lobes. **Fruit** ripening in the summer, 3'-4' long, about 1' thick, dark reddish brown or ultimately black, with thin succulent sweetish flesh; **seeds** about ⅛' wide, nearly ¹⁄₁₆' thick, with a narrow border to the rim.

A tree, occasionally 25°-30° high, with a trunk sometimes 2° in diameter and numerous stout wide-spreading branches; usually smaller and often forming broad low thickets 4°-

5° tall. **Bark** on old trunks $\frac{1}{4}$–$\frac{1}{2}$' thick, dark red-brown and broken into thin oblong plates covered by small irregular closely appressed scales. **Wood** light brown, fibrous, spongy, heavy, difficult to cut and work.

Distribution. Shores of Matagorda Bay, southward through western Texas into Nuovo Leon, and through the valley of the Rio Grande to the eastern base of the mountains of western Texas; forming open stunted forests on the coast dunes at the mouth of the Rio Grande; farther from the coast often spreading into great impenetrable thickets.

Cultivated as an ornamental plant in the gardens of central and western Texas and in other southern States, and occasionally in those of southern Europe.

3. Yucca macrocarpa Coville. Spanish Dagger.

Leaves $1\frac{1}{2}$°–2° long, 1'–2' wide, gradually narrowed from the dark red lustrous base to above the middle, rigid, concave, yellow-green, rough on the lower surface and frequently also on the upper surface, with a stout elongated dark tip, and thickened margins sep-

Fig. 108

arated into stout gray filaments. **Flowers** in March and April in densely flowered sessile or short-stalked glabrous or occasionally pubescent panicles; perianth usually about 2' long, with acuminate segments, those of the outer and inner rows nearly of the same size; stamens shorter than the elongated style. **Fruit** 3'–4' long, about $1\frac{1}{2}$' thick, abruptly contracted at apex into a stout point, nearly black when fully ripe, with sweet succulent flesh; **seeds** about $\frac{1}{3}$' wide, $\frac{1}{8}$' thick, with a narrow border to the rim.

A tree, rarely exceeding 15° in height, with a usually simple stem 6'–8' in diameter, and often clothed to the ground with living leaves. **Bark** dark brown and scaly.

Distribution. Arid plains from western Texas to eastern Arizona and southward in Chihuahua.

4. Yucca mohavensis Sarg. Spanish Dagger.

Leaves 18'–20' long, about $1\frac{1}{2}$' wide, abruptly contracted above the dark red lustrous base, gradually narrowed upward to above the middle, thin and concave except toward the slightly thickened base of the blade, dark green, smooth on both surfaces, with a stout rigid sharp-pointed tip, and entire bright red-brown margins soon separating into numerous pale filaments. **Flowers** from March to May on slender erect ultimately drooping pedicels 1'–$1\frac{1}{2}$' long, in densely flowered sessile or short-stemmed panicles 12'–18' in length; perianth 1'–2' long, the segments united at the base into a short tube, thickened and hood-shaped at the apex, those of the outer rank often deeply flushed with purple, but little longer than the less prominently ribbed usually wider and thinner segments of the inner rank; stamens with more or less pilose filaments nearly as long as the short style. **Fruit** ripening in August and September, 3′–4′ long, about 1½′ thick, usually much constricted near the middle,

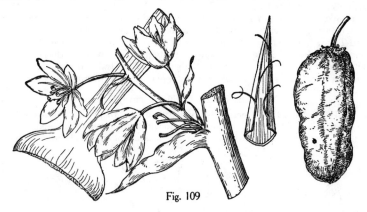

Fig. 109

abruptly contracted at apex into a short stout point, dark dull brown or nearly black, with flesh often nearly ½′ thick; **seeds** ⅓′ wide, rather less than ⅛′ thick, with a narrow border to the rim.

A tree, rarely exceeding 15° in height, with a trunk usually simple or occasionally furnished with short spreading branches, and 6′–8′ in diameter, usually surrounded by a cluster of shorter more or less spreading stems and often clothed to the ground with living leaves. **Bark** dark brown and scaly. **Wood** soft, spongy, light brown.

Distribution. Southern Nevada and northwestern Arizona across the Mohave Desert to the California coast, extending northward to the neighborhood of Monterey, California, and southward into northern Lower California; common and attaining its largest size on the Mohave Desert, and sometimes ascending arid mountain slopes to altitudes of 4000° above the sea.

5. Yucca Schottii Engelm. Spanish Dagger.

Leaves 2½°–3° long, about 1½′ wide, gradually narrowed upward from the comparatively thin lustrous red base to above the middle, flat except toward the apex, smooth, light

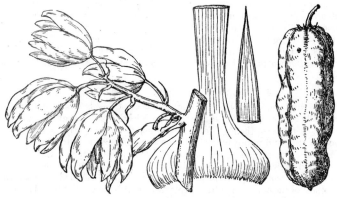

Fig. 110

yellow-green, with a long rigid sharp light red tip, and thick entire red-brown margins finally separating into short thin brittle threads. **Flowers** from July to September in erect stalked tomentose panicles; perianth 1′–1¾′ long, the broad oval or oblong-obovate thin segments pubescent on the outer surface toward the base and furnished at the apex with conspicuous clusters of white tomentum; stamens about two thirds as long as the ovary, with filaments pilose at the base, and only slightly enlarged at the apex. **Fruit** ripening in October and November, obscurely angled, 3½′–4′ long, about 1¼′ thick, often narrowed above the middle, with a stout thick point, and thin succulent flesh; **seeds** ¼′ wide, about ⅛′ thick, with a thin conspicuous marginal rim.

A tree, in Arizona rarely 18°–20° high, with a trunk often crooked or slightly inclining and simple or furnished with 2 or 3 short erect branches, covered below with dark brown scaly bark, roughened for many years by persistent scars of fallen leaves, and clothed above by the pendant dead leaves of many seasons.

Distribution. Dry slopes of the mountain ranges of Arizona near the Mexican boundary usually at altitudes between 5000° and 6000°, and southward into Sonora.

6. Yucca Faxoniana Sarg. Spanish Dagger.

Leaves 2½°–4° long, 2½′–3′ wide, abruptly contracted above the conspicuously thickened lustrous base, widest above the middle, flat on the upper surface, thickened and rounded on the lower surface toward the base, rigid, smooth and clear dark green, with a short stout

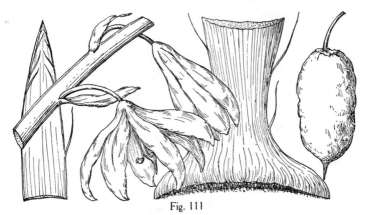

Fig. 111

dark tip, and brown entire margins breaking into numerous stout gray or brown fibres short and spreading near the apex of the leaf, longer, more remote, and forming a thick cobweb-like mass at their base. **Flowers** appearing in April on thin drooping pedicels, in dense many-flowered glabrous panicles 3°–4° long, with elongated pendulous branches; perianth 2½′ long, the segments thin, concave, widest above the middle, narrowed at the ends, united at base into a short tube, those of the outer rank being about half as wide as those of the inner rank and two thirds as long; stamens much shorter than the ovary, with slender filaments pilose above the middle and abruptly dilated at apex; ovary conspicuously ridged, light yellow marked with large pale raised lenticels, and gradually narrowed into an elongated slender style. **Fruit** ripening in early summer, slightly or not at all angled, abruptly contracted at apex into a long or short hooked beak, 3′–4′ long, 1′–1½′ thick, light orange-colored and lustrous when first ripe, becoming nearly black, with thick succulent bitter-sweet flesh; **seeds** ¼′ long, about ⅛′ thick, with a narrow nearly obsolete margin to the rim.

A tree, often 40° high, with a trunk sometimes 2° in diameter above the broad abruptly enlarged base, unbranched or divided into several short branches, and covered above by a thick thatch of the pendant dead leaves of many seasons; frequently smaller and until ten or twelve years old clothed from the ground with erect living leaves. **Bark** near the base of old trees dark reddish brown, $\frac{1}{3}'-\frac{1}{2}'$ thick, broken on the surface into small thin loose scales.

Distribution. Common on the high desert plateau of southwestern Texas.

7. Yucca brevifolia Engelm. Joshua Tree.

Yucca arborescens Trel.

Leaves 5'-8' or on young plants rarely 10'-12' long, $\frac{1}{4}'-\frac{1}{2}'$ wide, rigid, crowded in dense clusters, lanceolate, gradually tapering from the bright red-brown lustrous base, bluish green and glaucous, smooth or slightly roughened, concave above the middle, with a sharp dark brown tip, and thin yellow margins armed with sharp minute teeth; persistent

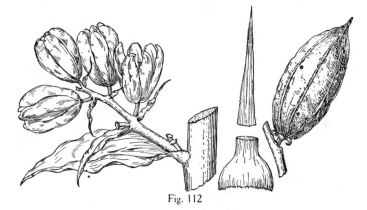

Fig. 112

for many years. **Flowers** appearing from March until the beginning of May, the creamy white closely imbricated bracts of the nearly sessile pubescent panicle forming before its appearance a conspicuous cone-like bud 8' or 10' long; perianth globose to oblong, 1'-2' long, greenish white, waxy, dull or lustrous, its segments slightly united at the base, keeled on the back, thin below the middle, gradually thickened upward into the concave incurved rounded tip, those of the outer rank rather broader, thicker, and more prominently keeled than those of the inner rank, glabrous or pubescent; stamens about half as long as the ovary, with filaments villose-papillate from the base; ovary conic, 3-lobed above the middle, bright green, with narrow slightly developed septal nectar-glands, and a sessile nearly equally 6-lobed stigma. **Fruit** ripening in May or June, spreading or more or less pendant at maturity, oblong-ovoid, acute, slightly 3-angled, 2'-4' long, 1½'-2' thick, light red or yellow-brown, the outer coat becoming dry and spongy at maturity; **seeds** nearly ½' long, rather less than $\frac{1}{16}'$ thick, with a broad well-developed margin to the rim, and a large conspicuous hilum.

A tree, 70°-60° high, with a trunk 2°-3° in diameter, rising abruptly from a broad thick basal disk, thick tough roots descending deeply into the soil, and stout branches spreading into a broad, often symmetrical head formed by the continued forking of the branches at the base of the terminal flower-clusters; the stem until 8°-10° high simple and clothed to the ground with leaves erect until after the appearance of the first flowers, then spreading at right angles and finally becoming reflexed. **Bark** 1'-1½' thick, deeply divided into oblong plates frequently 2° long. **Wood** light, soft, spongy, difficult to work, light brown or nearly white; sometimes cut into thin layers and used as wrapping material or manufactured into boxes and other small articles. The seeds are gathered and eaten by Indians

Distribution. Southwestern Utah to the western and northern rim of the Mohave Desert in California; most abundant and of its largest size on the foothills on the desert slope of the Tehachapi Mountains, California.

8. Yucca gloriosa L. Spanish Dagger.

Leaves 2°–2½° long, gradually narrowed above the broad base and then gradually broadened to above the middle, thin, flat or slightly concave toward the apex, frequently longitudinally folded, dull often glaucous green, roughened on the under surface especially above the middle, with a stout dark red tip, and pale margins serrulate toward the base of the leaf, with minute early deciduous teeth, or occasionally separating into thin fibres. **Flowers** in October, in pubescent or glabrate panicles, 2°–4° long, on stout stalks sometimes

Fig. 113

3°–4° in length, their large creamy white bracts forming before the panicle emerges a conspicuous egg-shaped bud 4′–6′ long; perianth when fully expanded 3½′–4′ across, its segments thin, ovate, acute, or lance-ovate, often tinged with green or purple, slightly united at the base, pubescent at apex; stamens about as long as the ovary, with hispid or slightly papillose filaments and deeply emarginate anthers; ovary slightly lobed, 6-sided, light green, gradually narrowed into the elongated spreading stigmatic lobes. **Fruit** very rarely produced, prominently 6-ridged, pendulous, 3′ long, 1′ in diameter, cuspidate, raised on a short stout stipe, with a thin leathery almost black outer coat; seeds ¼′ wide and about $\frac{1}{30}$′ thick, with a smooth coat and a narrow marginal rim.

A tree, with a trunk occasionally 6°–8° high and 4′–6′ in diameter, simple or rarely furnished with a few short branches and usually clothed to the base with pendant dead leaves; in cultivation often becoming much larger, with a stout trunk covered with smooth light gray bark, and erect or in one form (var. *recurvifolia* Engelm.) pendulous leaves.

Distribution. Sand dunes and the borders of beaches of the seacoast from North Carolina to northern Florida.

Often cultivated with many forms in the gardens and pleasure-grounds of all temperate countries.

9. Yucca elata Engelm. Spanish Dagger.

1. *Yucca radiosa* Trel.

Leaves 20′–30′ long, ¼′–½′ wide, rigid, gradually narrowed from the thin base, tapering toward the apex, or sometimes somewhat broadest at the middle, thin, flat on the upper surface, slightly thickened and rounded on the lower surface toward the base, smooth, pale yellow-green, with a slender stiff red-brown tip, and thickened entire pale margins soon splitting into long slender filaments. **Flowers** in May and June on slender spreading more or less recurved pedicels, in glabrous much-branched panicles 4°–6° long, raised on stout naked stem 3°–7° in length; perianth ovoid and acute in the bud, when fully expanded $3\frac{1}{2}'$–4' across, its segments united at the base into a short slender distinct tube, ovate or slightly obovate, those of the outer rank usually acute, not more than half as broad as those of the inner rank; stamens as long or a little longer than the ovary, with slender nearly terete filaments; ovary sessile, almost terete, pale green, abruptly contracted into the stout elongated style. **Fruit** an erect oblong capsule rounded and obtuse at the ends, tipped by a short stout mucro, conspicuously 3-ribbed, with rounded ridges on the back of the carpels, $1\frac{1}{2}'$–2' long, 1'–$1\frac{1}{2}'$ wide, with a thin firm light brown ligneous outer coat closely ad-

Fig. 114

herent to the lustrous light yellow inner coat, in ripening splitting from the top to the bottom between the carpels, and through their backs at the apex; **seeds** $\frac{1}{3}'$ wide and about $\frac{1}{32}'$ thick, with a smooth coat and a thin brittle wide margin to the rim.

A tree, with a rough much-branched underground stem penetrating deep into the soil and a trunk often 15°–20° high and 7'–8' in diameter, covered above with a thick thatch of the pendant dead leaves of many years, simple, or branched at the top with a few short stout branches densely covered with leaves at first erect, then spreading nearly at right angles, and finally pendulous. **Bark** dark brown, irregularly fissured, broken into thin plates, about $\frac{1}{4}'$ thick. **Wood** light, soft, spongy, pale brown or yellow.

Distribution. High desert plateaus from southwestern Texas to southern Arizona; southward into northern Mexico; most abundant and of its largest size on the eastern slope of the continental divide in southern New Mexico and along the northern rim of the Tucson Desert in Arizona.

DIVISION II. DICOTYLEDONES.

Stems formed of bark, wood, and pith, and increasing by the addition of an annual layer of wood inside the bark. Parts of the flower mostly in 4's and 5's; embryo with a pair of opposite cotyledons. Leaves netted-veined.

Subdivision 1. Apetalæ. Flowers without a corolla and sometimes without a calyx (with a corolla in *Olacaceæ*).

Section 1. Flowers in unisexual aments (*female flowers of Juglans and Quercus solitary or in spikes*); ovary inferior (*superior in Leitneriaceæ*) when calyx is present.

V. SALICACEÆ.

Trees or shrubs, with watery juice, alternate simple stalked deciduous leaves with stipules, soft light usually pale wood, astringent bark, scaly buds, and often stoloniferous roots. Flowers appearing in early spring usually before the leaves, solitary in the axils of the scales of unisexual aments from buds in the axils of leaves of the previous year, the male and female on different plants; perianth 0; stamens 1, 2 or many, their anthers introrse, 2-celled, the cells opening longitudinally; styles usually short or none; stigmas 2–4, often 2-lobed. Fruit a 1-celled 2–4-valved capsule, with 2–4 placentas bearing below their middle numerous ascending anatropous seeds without albumen and surrounded by tufts of long white silky hairs attached to the short stalks of the seeds and deciduous with them; embryo straight, filling the cavity of the seed; cotyledons flattened, much longer than the short radicle turned toward the minute hilum.

The two genera of this family are widely scattered but most abundant in the northern hemisphere, with many species, and are often conspicuous features of vegetation.

CONSPECTUS OF THE GENERA.

Scales of the aments laciniate; flowers surrounded by a cup-shaped often oblique disk; stamens numerous; buds with numerous scales.   1. **Populus.**
Scales of the aments entire; disk a minute gland-like body; stamens 1, 2 or many; buds with a single scale.   2. **Salix**

1. POPULUS L. Poplar.

Large fast-growing trees, with pale furrowed bark, terete or angled branchlets, resinous winter-buds covered by several thin scales, those of the first pair small and opposite, the others imbricated, increasing in size from below upward, accrescent and marking the base of the branchlet with persistent ring-like scars, and thick roots. Leaves involute in the bud, usually ovate or ovate-lanceolate, entire, dentate with usually glandular teeth, or lobed, penniveined, turning yellow in the autumn; petioles long, often laterally compressed, sometimes furnished at the apex on the upper side with 2 nectariferous glands, leaving in falling oblong often obcordate, elliptic, arcuate, or shield-shaped leaf-scars displaying the ends of 3 nearly equidistant fibro-vascular bundles; stipules caducous, those of the first leaves resembling the bud-scales, smaller higher on the branch, and linear-lanceolate and scarious on the last leaves. Flowers in pendulous stalked aments, the pistillate lengthening and rarely becoming erect before maturity; scales obovate, gradually narrowed into slender stipes, dilated and lobed, palmately cleft or fimbriate at apex, membranaceous, glabrous or villose, more crowded on the staminate than on the pistillate ament, usually caducous; disk of the flower broadly cup-shaped, often oblique, entire, dentate or irregularly lobed, fleshy or membranaceous, stipitate, usually persistent under the fruit; stamens 4–12 or 12–60 or more, inserted on the disk, their filaments free, short, light yellow; anthers ovoid or oblong, purple or red; ovary sessile in the bottom of the disk, oblong-conical, sub-globose or ovoid-oblong, cylindric or slightly lobed, with 2 or 3 or rarely 4 placentas; styles usually short; stigmas as many as the placentas, divided into filiform lobes or broad, dilated, 2-parted or lobed. Fruit ripening before the full growth of the leaves, greenish, reddish brown, or buff color, oblong-conic, subglobose or ovoid-oblong, separating at maturity into 2–4 recurved valves. Seeds broadly obovoid or ovoid, rounded or acute at the apex, light chestnut-brown; cotyledons elliptic.

Populus in the extreme north often forms great forests, and is common on the alluvial bottom-lands of streams and on high mountain slopes, ranging from the Arctic Circle to northern Mexico and Lower California and from the Atlantic to the Pacific in the New World, and to northern Africa, the southern slopes of the Himalayas, central China, and

Japan in the Old World. Of the thirty-four species now generally recognized fifteen are found in North America. The wood of many of the American species is employed in large quantities for paper-making, and several species furnish wood used in construction and in the manufacture of small articles of woodenware. The bark contains tannic acid and is used in tanning leather and occasionally as a tonic, and the fragrant balsam contained in the buds of some species is occasionally used in medicine. The rapidity of their growth, their hardiness and the ease with which they can be propagated by cuttings, make many of the species useful as ornamental trees or in wind-breaks, although planted trees often suffer severely from the attacks of insects boring into the trunks and branches. Of the exotic species, the Abele, or White Poplar, *Populus alba* L., of Europe and western Asia, and its fastigiate form, and the so-called Lombardy Poplar, a tree of pyramidal habit and a form of the European and Asiatic *Populus nigra* L., and one of its hybrids, have been largely planted in the United States.

Populus, of obscure derivation, is the classical name of the Poplar.

CONSPECTUS OF THE NORTH AMERICAN SPECIES.

Stigmas 2, 2-lobed, their lobes filiform; leaf stalks elongated, laterally compressed; buds slightly resinous.

Leaves finely serrate; winter-buds glabrous. **1. P. tremuloides** (A, B, F, G).

Leaves coarsely serrate; winter-buds tomentose or pubescent. **2. P. grandidentata.**

Stigmas 2–4, 2-lobed and dilated, their lobes variously divided; buds resinous.

Leaf-stalks round.

Leaves tomentose below early in the season, broadly ovate, acute or rounded at apex. **3. P. heterophylla** (A, C).

Leaves glabrous or pilose below.

Leaves dark green above, pale, rarely pilose below.

Ovary and capsule glabrous. **4. P. tacamahacca** (A, B, F).

Ovary and capsule tomentose or pubescent. **5. P. trichocarpa** (B, F).

Leaves light green on both surfaces, glabrous.

Leaves lanceolate to ovate-lanceolate. **6. P. angustifolia** (F).

Leaves rhombic-lanceolate to ovate. **7. P. acuminata** (F).

Leaf-stalks laterally compressed.

Leaves without glands at apex of the petiole, coarsely serrate, thick.

Pedicels shorter than the fruit.

Disk cup-shaped.

Branchlets stout; capsule $\frac{1}{3}'-\frac{1}{2}'$ long. **8. P. Fremontii** (G, H).

Branchlets slender; capsule not more than $\frac{1}{4}'$ long. **9. P. arizonica** (F, H).

Disk minute.

Branchlets glabrous; leaves broad-ovate to deltoid, long-pointed and acuminate at apex. **10. P. texana** (C).

Branchlets pubescent; leaves broad-ovate, abruptly short-pointed or acute at apex. **11. P. McDougallii** (G, H).

Pedicels 2 or 3 times longer than the fruit; leaves broadly deltoid, abruptly short-pointed. **12. P. Wislizenii** (E, F).

Leaves furnished with glands at apex of the petiole.

Branchlets stout; leaves thick.

Winter-buds puberulous; leaves coarsely serrate; branchlets light yellow. **13. P. Sargentii** (F).

Winter-buds glabrous; leaves less coarsely serrate; branchlets gray or reddish brown. **14. P. balsamifera** (A, C).

Branchlets slender; leaves thin, ovate, cuneate or rounded at base, finely serrate. **15. P. Palmeri** (E).

1. Populus tremuloides Michx. Aspen. Quaking Asp.

Leaves ovate to broad-ovate or rarely reniform (var. *reniformis* Tidestrom) abruptly short-pointed or acuminate at apex rounded or rarely cuneate at the wide base, closely crenately serrate with glandular teeth, thin, green and lustrous above, dull green or rarely pale below, up to $4\frac{1}{2}'$ long and broad with a prominent midrib, slender primary veins and conspicuous reticulate veinlets; petioles slender, compressed laterally, $1\frac{1}{2}'–3'$ long. **Flowers:** aments $1\frac{1}{2}'–2\frac{1}{2}'$ long, the pistillate becoming $4'$ in length at maturity; scales deeply divided into 3–5 linear acute lobes fringed with long soft gray hairs; disk oblique, the staminate entire, the pistillate slightly crenate; stamens 6–12; ovary conic, with a short thick style and erect stigmas thickened and club-shaped below and divided into linear diverging lobes. **Fruit** maturing in May and June, oblong-conic, light green, thin-walled, nearly $\frac{1}{4}'$ long; **seeds** obovoid, light brown, about $\frac{1}{32}'$ in length.

A tree, $20°–40°$ high, with a trunk $18'–20'$ in diameter, slender remote and often contorted branches somewhat pendulous toward the ends, forming a narrow symmetrical

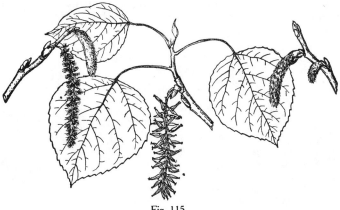

Fig. 115

round-topped head, and slender branchlets covered with scattered oblong orange-colored lenticels, bright red-brown and very lustrous during their first season, gradually turning light gray tinged with red, ultimately dark gray, and much roughened for two or three years by the elevated leaf-scars. **Winter-buds** slightly resinous, conic, acute, often incurved, about $\frac{1}{4}'$ long, narrower than the more obtuse flower-buds, with 6 or 7 lustrous glabrous red-brown scales scarious on the margins. **Bark** thin, pale yellow-brown or orange-green, often roughened by horizontal bands of circular wart-like excrescences, frequently marked below the branches by large rows of lunate dark scars. **Wood** light brown, with nearly white sapwood of 25–30 layers of annual growth.

Distribution. Southern Labrador to the southern shores of Hudson's Bay and northwesterly to the mouth of the Mackenzie River, through the northern states to the mountains of Pennsylvania, northern Ohio, Indiana and Illinois, eastern and central Iowa and northeastern Missouri; common and generally distributed usually on moist sandy soil and gravelly hillsides; most valuable in the power of its seeds to germinate quickly in soil made fertile by fire and of its seedlings to grow rapidly in exposed situations; westward passing into the var. *aurea* Daniels, with thicker rhombic to semiorbicular or broad-ovate generally smaller leaves, usually pale on the lower surface, rounded or acute and minutely short-pointed at apex, rounded or cuneate at base, often entire with slightly thickened margins, or occasionally coarsely crenately serrate, with inconspicuous reticulate veinlets, turning bright golden yellow in the autumn before falling.

A tree occasionally 100° high with a trunk up to 3° in diameter, with pale often white bark, becoming near the base of old stems 2′ thick, nearly black, and deeply divided into broad flat ridges broken on the surface into small appressed plate-like scales.

Distribution. Valley of the Yukon River to Saskatchewan, and southward through the mountain ranges of the Rocky Mountain region to southern New Mexico, the San Francisco Mountains of Arizona, and westward to the valley of the Skeena River, British Columbia, western Washington and Oregon, the western slopes of the Sierra Nevada and the high mountains of southern California, and eastward to North and South Dakota and western Nebraska; on the mountains of Chihuahua, and on the Sierra de Laguna, Lower California.

Populus tremuloides var. vancouveriana Sarg.

Populus vancouveriana Trel.

Leaves broadly ovate to semiorbicular, abruptly short-pointed or rounded at apex, rounded or slightly cordate at the broad base, coarsely crenately serrate and sometimes obscurely crispate on the margins, when they unfold covered below and on the petioles with

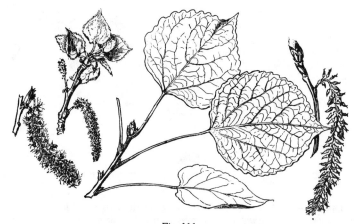

Fig. 116

a thick coat of long matted pale hairs, and slightly villose, glabrous or nearly glabrous above, soon glabrous, and at maturity thick dark green, lustrous and scabrate on the upper surface, paler on the lower surface, 3′–4½′ long and broad, with a prominent midrib and primary veins; petioles slender, compressed, becoming glabrous, 2′–3′ in length. **Flowers:** staminate aments slightly villose; pedicels pubescent; disk of the flower puberulous toward the base; flowers as in the species; pistillate aments 2′–2¼′ long, becoming 3–3½′ in length at maturity; the rachis, pedicels and slightly lobed disk of the flower densely villose-pubescent; ovary conic, pubescent, with a short style and stigma divided into narrow divergent lobes. **Fruit** on pedicel not more than $\frac{1}{24}′$ in length, oblong-conic, pubescent or glabrous, ¼′ long.

A tree 30°–36° high, with a trunk 12′–16′ in diameter, stout spreading branches forming a round-topped head, stout, reddish brown pubescent or puberulous branchlets often becoming glabrous during their first summer. **Winter-buds** acute, tomentose, pubescent or glabrous.

Coast of Vancouver Island, British Columbia and shores of Puget Sound; Tualitin, Washington County, and valley of the Willamette River at Corvallis, Benton County, Oregon.

2. Populus grandidentata Michx. Poplar.

Leaves semiorbicular to broad-ovate, short-pointed at apex, rounded, abruptly cuneate or rarely truncate at the broad entire base, coarsely repand-dentate above with few stout incurved teeth, covered like the petioles early in the season with white tomentum, soon glabrous, thin and firm in texture, dark green above, paler on the lower surface, 2′–3′ long, 2′–2½′ wide, with a prominent yellow midrib, conspicuously forked veins, and reticulate veinlets; petioles slender, laterally compressed, 1½′–2½′ long. **Flowers:** aments pubescent, 1½′–2½′ long, the pistillate becoming 4′–5′ long at maturity; scales pale and scarious below, divided above into 5 or 6 small irregular acute lobes covered with soft pale hairs; disk shallow, oblique, the staminate entire, the pistillate slightly crenate; stamens 6–12, with short slender filaments and light red anthers; ovary oblong-conic, bright green, puberulous, with

Fig. 117

a short style, and spreading stigmas divided nearly to the base into elongated filiform lobes. **Fruit** ripening before the leaves are fully grown, often more or less curved above the middle, light green and puberulous, thin-walled, 2-valved, about ⅛′ long; pedicel slender, pubescent, about 1/12′ in length; seeds minute dark brown.

A tree, often 60°–70° high, with a trunk occasionally 2° in diameter, slender rather rigid branches forming a narrow round-topped head, and stout branchlets marked by scattered oblong orange-colored lenticels, coated when they first appear with thick hoary deciduous tomentum, becoming during their first year dark red-brown or dark orange-colored, glabrous, lustrous, or covered with a delicate gray pubescence, and in their second year dark gray sometimes slightly tinged with green and much roughened by the elevated 3-lobed leaf-scars; generally smaller, and usually not more than 30°–40° tall. **Winter-buds** terete, broadly ovoid, acute, with light bright chestnut-brown scales, pubescent during the winter especially on their thin scarious margins, about ⅛′ long and not more than half the size of the flower-buds. **Bark** thin, smooth, light gray tinged with green, becoming near the base of old trunks ¾′–1′ thick, dark brown tinged with red, irregularly fissured and divided into broad flat ridges roughened on the surface by small thick closely appressed scales. **Wood** light brown, with thin nearly white sapwood of 20–30 layers of annual growth.

Distribution. Rich moist sandy soil near the borders of swamps and streams; Nova Scotia, through New Brunswick, southern Quebec and Ontario to northern Minnesota, southward through the northern states to Pennsylvania, northern Ohio, and eastern (Muscatine County) and central Iowa, and westward to central Kentucky and Tennessee; passing into the var. *meridionalis* Tidestrom with broad-ovate acuminate leaves with more numerous teeth, often 4'–5' long and 3' wide; the common form in Maryland, northern Delaware, the piedmont region of Virginia and North Carolina, southern Ohio, and southern Indiana and Illinois; rare northward to northern New England.

3. Populus heterophylla L.   Swamp Cottonwood.   Black Cottonwood.

Leaves broadly ovate, gradually narrowed and acute, short-pointed or rounded at apex, slightly cordate or truncate or rounded at the wide base, usually furnished with a narrow deep sinus, finely or coarsely crenately serrate with incurved glandular teeth, covered as they unfold with thick hoary deciduous tomentum, becoming thin and firm in texture, dark deep green above, pale and glabrous below, with a stout yellow midrib, forked veins and conspicuous reticulate veinlets, 4'–7' long, 3'–6' wide; petioles slender terete tomentose or nearly glabrous $2\frac{1}{2}'$–$3\frac{1}{2}$ in length. **Flowers:** staminate aments broad, densely flowered, 1' long, erect when the flowers first open, becoming pendulous and 2'–$2\frac{1}{2}'$ long; scales narrowly oblong-obovate, brown, scarious and glabrous below, divided into numerous elon-

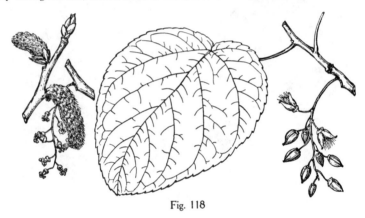

Fig. 118

gated filiform light red-brown lobes; disk oblique, slightly concave; stamens 12–20, with slender filaments about as long as the large dark red anthers; pistillate aments slender, pendulous, few-flowered, 1'–2' long, becoming erect and 4'–6' long before maturing, their scales concave and infolding the flowers, linear-obovate, brown and scarious, laterally lobed, fimbriate above the middle, caducous; disk thin, irregularly divided in numerous triangular acute teeth, long-stalked; ovary ovoid, terete or obtusely 3-angled, with a short stout elongated style and 2 or 3 much-thickened dilated 2 or 3-lobed stigmas. **Fruit on** elongated pedicels, ripening when the leaves are about one third grown, ovoid, acute, dark red-brown, rather thick-walled, 2 or 3-valved, about $\frac{1}{2}'$ long; **seeds** obovoid, minute, dark red-brown.

A tree, 80°–90° high, with a tall trunk 2°–3° in diameter, short rather slender branches forming a comparatively narrow round-topped head, and stout branchlets, marked by small elongated pale lenticels, coated at first with hoary caducous tomentum, becoming dark brown and rather lustrous or ashy gray, or rarely pale orange color and glabrous or slightly puberulous, or covered with a glaucous bloom in their first winter, growing darker in their second year and much roughened by the large thickened leaf-scars; usually much smaller and at the north rarely more than 40° tall. **Winter-buds** slightly resinous, broadly ovoid, acute, with bright red-brown scales, about $\frac{1}{4}'$ long and about one half the size of the flower-buds. **Bark** on young trunks divided by shallow fissures into broad flat ridges separating on the surface into thick plate-like scales, becoming on old trunks $\frac{3}{4}'-1'$ thick, light brown tinged with red, and broken into long narrow plates attached only at the middle and sometimes persistent for many years. **Wood** dull brown, with thin lighter brown sapwood of 12–15 layers of annual growth; now often manufactured into lumber in the valley of the Mississippi River and in the Gulf states, and as black poplar used in the interior finish of buildings.

Distribution. Southington, Connecticut, and Northport, Long Island, southward near the coast to southern Georgia, and the valley of the lower Apalachicola River, Florida, through the Gulf states to western Louisiana, and through eastern Arkansas to southeastern Missouri, western Kentucky and Tennessee, southern Illinois, northern Indiana (Laporte and Wells Counties), and in central and northern Ohio (Williams, Ottawa and Lake Counties); in the north Atlantic states in low wet swamps, rare and local; more common south and west on the borders of river swamps; very abundant and of its largest size in the valley of the lower Ohio and in southeastern Missouri, eastern Arkansas, and western Mississippi.

4. Populus tacamahaca Mill. Balsam. Tacamahac.

Populus balsamifera Du Roi, not L.

Leaves ovate-lanceolate, gradually narrowed and acuminate at apex, cordate or rounded at base, or narrow-elliptic and acute or acuminate at the ends, finely crenately serrate, with slightly thickened revolute margins, coated when they unfold with the gummy secretions

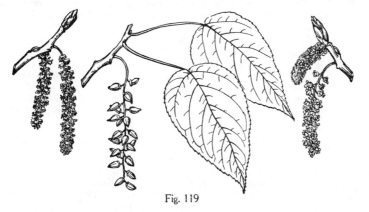

Fig. 119

of the bud, glabrous, or puberulous on the under side of the midrib, becoming thin and firm in texture, deep dark green and lustrous above, pale green or glaucous and more or less rusty and conspicuously reticulate-venulose below, $3'-5'$ long, $1\frac{1}{2}'-3'$ wide, with thin veins running obliquely almost to the margins; petioles slender, terete, $1\frac{1}{2}'$ long, glabrous or rarely puberulous. **Flowers:** aments long-stalked, the pistillate becoming $4'-5'$ long before the fruit ripens, glabrous or pubescent; scales broadly obovate, light brown and scarious, often irregularly 3-parted at apex, cut into short thread-like brown lobes; disk of the staminate flower oblique, short-stalked; stamens 20–30, with short filaments and large light red anthers; disk of the pistillate flower cup-shaped; ovary ovoid, slightly 2-lobed, with two nearly sessile large oblique dilated crenulate stigmas. **Fruit** ovoid-oblong, acute and often curved at apex, 2-valved, light brown, about $\frac{1}{4}'-\frac{1}{3}'$ long, nearly sessile or short-stalked, $\frac{1}{2}'-\frac{1}{8}'$ in length; seeds oblong-obovoid, pointed at apex, narrowed and truncate at base, light brown. about $\frac{1}{12}'$ long.

A tree, often 100° high, with a tall trunk 6°–7° in diameter, stout erect branches usually more or less contorted near the ends, forming a comparatively narrow open head, and glabrous or occasionally pubescent branchlets marked by oblong bright orange-colored lenticels, much roughened by the thickened leaf-scars, at first red-brown and glabrous or pubescent, becoming bright and lustrous in their first winter, dark orange-colored in their second year, and finally gray tinged with yellow-green; usually much smaller toward the southern limits of its range. **Winter-buds** saturated with a yellow balsamic sticky exudation, ovoid, terete, long-pointed; terminal 1′ long, $\frac{1}{3}$′ broad; axillary about $\frac{3}{4}$′ long, $\frac{1}{16}$′ broad, with 5 oblong pointed concave closely imbricated thick chestnut-brown lustrous scales. **Bark** light brown tinged with red, smooth or roughened by dark excrescences, becoming on old trunks $\frac{3}{4}$′–1′ thick, gray tinged with red, and divided into broad rounded ridges covered by small closely appressed scales. **Wood** light brown, with thick nearly white sapwood.

Distribution. Low often inundated river-bottom lands and swamp borders; Labrador to latitude 65° north in the valley of the Mackenzie River, and to the Alaskan coast, south to northern New England and New York, central Michigan, Minnesota (except in southern and southwestern counties), Turtle Mountains, Rolette County, North Dakota, the Black Hills of South Dakota, northwestern Nebraska (basin of Hat Creek), and in Colorado; the characteristic tree on the streams of the prairie region of British America, attaining its greatest size on the islands and banks of the Peace, Athabasca, and other tributaries of the Mackenzie; common in all the region near the northern boundary of the United States from Maine to the western limits of the Atlantic forests; the largest of the sub-Arctic American trees, and in the far north the most conspicuous feature of vegetation; passing into the variety *Michauxii* Farwell, with more cordate leaves, slightly pilose on the under side of the midrib and veins; common from Aroostook County, Maine, to the Province of Quebec, Newfoundland, and the shores of Hudson Bay.

Often planted at the north for shelter or ornament.

Populus candicans Ait., the Balm of Gilead of which only the pistillate tree is known, has often been considered a variety of the North American Balsam Poplar. This tree has been long cultivated in the northeastern part of the country and has sometimes escaped from cultivation and formed groves of considerable extent, as on the banks of Cullasagee Creek on the western slope of the Blue Ridge in Macon County, North Carolina. The fact that only one sex is known suggests hybrid origin but of obscure and possibly partly of foreign origin.

5. Populus trichocarpa Hook.   Black Cottonwood.   Balsam Cottonwood.

Leaves broad-ovate, acute or acuminate at apex, rounded or abruptly cuneate at base, finely crenately serrate, glabrous, dark green above, pale and rusty or silvery white and conspicuously reticulate-venulose below, 3′–4′ long, 2′–2$\frac{1}{2}$′ wide; petioles slender, pubescent, puberulous, pilose or rarely glabrous, 1$\frac{1}{2}$′–2′ in length. **Flowers:** aments stalked, villose-pubescent, the staminate densely flowered, 1$\frac{1}{2}$′–2′ long, $\frac{1}{3}$′ thick, the pistillate loosely flowered, 2$\frac{1}{2}$′–3′ long, becoming 4′–5′ long before the fruit ripens; scales dilated at the apex, irregularly cut into numerous filiform lobes, glabrous or slightly puberulous on the outer surface; disk of the staminate flower broad, slightly oblique; stamens 40–60, with slender elongated filaments longer than the large light purple anthers; disk of the pistillate flower deep cup-shaped, with irregularly crenate or nearly entire revolute margins; ovary subglobose, coated with thick hoary tomentum, with 3 nearly sessile broadly dilated deeply lobed stigmas. **Fruit** subglobose, nearly sessile, pubescent, thick-walled, 3-valved; **seeds** obovoid, apiculate at the gradually narrowed apex, light brown, puberulous toward the ends, $\frac{1}{12}$′ long.

A tree, 30°–100° high, with a trunk 1°–3° in diameter, erect branches forming an open head, and slender branchlets terete or slightly angled while young, marked by many orange-colored lenticels, glabrous or when they first appear coated with deciduous rufous or pale pubescence, reddish brown during their first year, gradually becoming dark gray, and roughened by the greatly enlarged and thickened elevated leaf-scars. **Winter-buds** resinous, fragrant, ovoid, long-pointed, frequently curved above the middle, $\frac{3}{4}'$ long and $\frac{1}{4}'$ thick, with 6 or 7 light orange-brown slightly puberulous scales scarious on the margins. Bark $\frac{1}{2}'-2\frac{1}{2}'$ thick, ashy gray, deeply divided into broad rounded ridges broken on the surface into thick closely appressed scales. Wood light, dull brown, with thin nearly white sapwood.

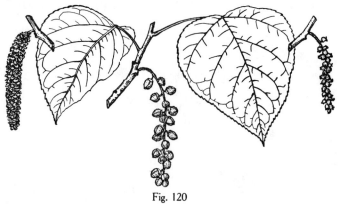

Fig. 120

Distribution. In California in small groves with widely scattered individuals on the coast ranges, the western slope of the Sierra Nevada up to elevations of 6000°–8000°, and on the southern mountains to Mt. Palomar in San Diego County; on the California islands, and on the western slopes of the San Pedro Mártir Mountains, Lower California.

On the high Sierra Nevada and in northern California passing into the var. *hastata* A. Henry, differing in its thicker leaves, usually longer in proportion to their width, often long-acuminate, rounded or cordate at base, frequently 5' or 6' long and 3' or 4' wide, with glabrous petioles and larger sometimes nearly glabrous capsules on glabrous or pubescent aments, sometimes 10'–12' in length, and in its glabrous young branchlets.

A tree sometimes 200° high, with a trunk 7°–8° in diameter, and the largest deciduous-leaved tree of northwestern North America. The wood is largely used in Oregon and Washington for the staves of sugar barrels and in the manufacture of woodenware.

Distribution. In open groves on rich bottom lands of streams from Siskiyou County, California, to southern Alaska; eastward in the United States through Oregon and Washington to western and southern Idaho; and to the mountains of western Nevada; in British Columbia to the valley of the Columbia River; on the banks of the east fork of the Kaweah River, Tulare County, California, at 10,000° above the sea.

6. Populus angustifolia James. Narrow-leaved Cottonwood.

Populus fortissima A. Nels & Macbr.

Leaves lanceolate, ovate-lanceolate, elliptic or rarely obovate, narrowed to the tapering acute or rounded apex, gradually narrowed and cuneate or rounded at base, finely or on vigorous shoots coarsely serrate, thin and firm, bright yellow-green above, glabrous or rarely puberulous and paler below, 2'–3' long, $\frac{1}{2}'-1'$ wide, or on vigorous shoots occasionally 6'–7' long, and $1\frac{1}{2}'$ wide, with a stout yellow midrib and numerous slender-oblique primary veins arcuate and often united near the slightly thickened revolute margins; petioles slender, somewhat flattened on the upper side, and in falling leaving small nearly oval obcordate scars. **Flowers:** aments densely flowered, glabrous, short-stalked, $\frac{1}{2}'-2\frac{1}{2}'$ long, the pistillate becoming $2\frac{1}{2}'-4'$ long before the fruit ripens; scales broadly obovate, glabrous, thin, scarious, light brown, deeply and irregularly cut into numerous dark red-brown filiform lobes; disk of the staminate flower cup-shaped, slightly oblique, short-stalked; stamens 12–20, with short filaments and large light red anthers; disk of the pistillate flower shallow, cup-shaped, slightly and irregularly lobed, short-stalked; ovary ovoid, more or less 2-lobed, with a short or elongated style and 2 oblique dilated irregularly lobed stigmas. **Fruit** broadly ovoid, often rather abruptly contracted above the middle, short-pointed, thin-walled, 2-valved; pedicels often $\frac{1}{4}'$ long; **seeds** ovoid or obovoid, rather obtuse, light brown, nearly $\frac{1}{8}'$ long.

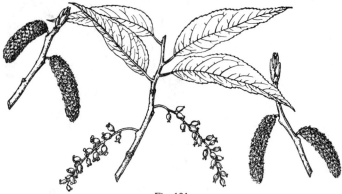

Fig. 121

A tree, 50°–60° high, with a trunk rarely more than 18' in diameter, slender erect branches forming a narrow and usually pyramidal head, and slender glabrous or rarely puberulous branchlets marked by pale lenticels, at first light yellow-green, becoming bright or dark orange color in their first season, pale yellow in their second winter, and ultimately ashy gray. **Winter-buds** very resinous, ovoid, long-pointed, covered by usually 5 thin concave chestnut-brown scales; terminal $\frac{1}{4}'$–$\frac{1}{2}'$ long and nearly twice as large as the axillary buds. **Bark** $\frac{3}{4}'$–1' thick, light yellow-green, divided near the base of old trees by shallow fissures into broad flat ridges, smooth and much thinner above. **Wood** light brown, with thin nearly white sapwood of 10–30 layers of annual growth.

Distribution. Banks of streams usually at altitudes of 5000°–10,000° above the sea; southern Alberta to the Black Hills of South Dakota and northwestern Nebraska (basin of Hat Creek) westward through Wyoming, Montana and Idaho to Yakima County, Washington, and southward to central Nevada, southwestern New Mexico (Silver City, Grant County) and northern Arizona; the common Cottonwood of northern Colorado, Utah, Wyoming, southern Montana, and eastern Idaho; on the mountains of Chihuahua.

7. Populus acuminata Rydb.   Cottonwood.

Leaves rhombic-lanceolate to ovate, abruptly acuminate, gradually or abruptly narrowed and cuneate or concave-cuneate, or rarely broad and rounded at the mostly entire base, coarsely crenately serrate except near the apex, dark green and lustrous above, dull green below, 2'–4' long, $\frac{3}{4}'$–2' wide, with a slender yellow midrib, thin remote primary veins and obscure reticulate veinlets; petioles slender, nearly terete, 1'–3' long. **Flowers:** aments slender, short-stalked, 2'–3' long, the pistillate becoming 4' or 5' long before the fruit ripens; scales scarious, light brown, glabrous, dilated and irregularly divided into filiform lobes; disk of the staminate flower wide, oblique, and membranaceous; stamens numerous, with short filaments and dark red anthers; disk of the pistillate flower deep cup-shaped; ovary broad-ovoid, gradually narrowed above, with large laciniately lobed nearly sessile stigmas. **Fruit** pedicellate, oblong-ovoid, acute, thin-walled, slightly pitted, about $\frac{1}{3}'$ long, 3 or rarely 2-valved; **seeds** oblong-obovoid, rounded at the apex, light brown, about $\frac{1}{12}'$ in length.

A tree, usually about 40° high, with a trunk 12′-18′ in diameter, stout spreading and ascending branches forming a compact round-topped head, and slender terete or slightly 4-angled pale yellow-brown branchlets roughened for two or three years by the elevated oval horizontal leaf-scars. **Winter-buds** acuminate, resinous, about $\frac{1}{3}'$ long, with 6 or 7 light chestnut-brown lustrous scales. **Bark** on young stems and large branches smooth, nearly white, becoming on old trunks pale gray-brown, about $\frac{1}{2}'$ thick, deeply divided into broad flat ridges.

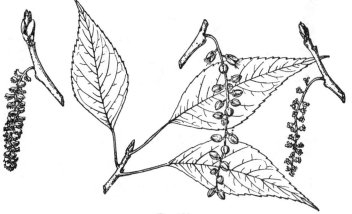

Fig. 122

Distribution. Banks of streams in the arid eastern foothill region of the Rocky Mountains; Assiniboia to the Black Hills of South Dakota, northwestern Nebraska, eastern Wyoming, southern Colorado, and southwestern New Mexico (Fort Bayard, Grant County); in Colorado crossing the Continental Divide to southeastern Utah; passing into the var. *Rehderi* Sarg. differing in the larger leaves on longer petioles, and in the pubescent branchlets and winter-buds. Borders of streams southeastern New Mexico.

Sometimes planted as a shade-tree in the streets of cities in the Rocky Mountain region.

× *Populus Andrewsii* Sarg. intermediate in its character between *P. acuminata* and *P. Sargentii* and believed to be a natural hybrid of these species has been found growing naturally near Boulder and Walsenburg, Colorado, and as a street tree in Montrose, Colorado.

8. Populus Fremontii S. Wats. Cottonwood.

Leaves deltoid or reniform, generally contracted into broad short entire points, or rarely rounded or emarginate at apex, truncate, slightly cordate or abruptly cuneate at the entire base, coarsely and irregularly serrate, with few or many incurved gland-tipped teeth, coated like the petioles when they unfold with short spreading caducous pubescence, at maturity thick and firm, glabrous bright green and lustrous, 2′-2$\frac{1}{2}'$ long, 2$\frac{1}{2}'$-3′ wide, with a thin yellow midrib and 4 or 5 pairs of slender veins; petioles flattened, yellow, 1$\frac{1}{2}'$-3′ long. **Flowers:** staminate aments densely flowered, 1$\frac{1}{2}'$-2′ long, nearly $\frac{1}{2}'$ thick, with slender glabrous stems, the pistillate sparsely flowered, with stout glabrous or puberulous stems, becoming before the fruit ripens 4′ or 5′ long; scales light brown, thin and scarious, dilated and irregularly cut at apex into filiform lobes; disk of the staminate flower broad, oblique, slightly thickened on the entire revolute margin; stamens 60 or more, with large dark red anthers; disk of the pistillate flower cup-shaped; ovary ovoid or ovoid-oblong, with 3 or rarely 4 broad irregularly crenately lobed stigmas. **Fruit** ovoid, acute or obtuse, slightly

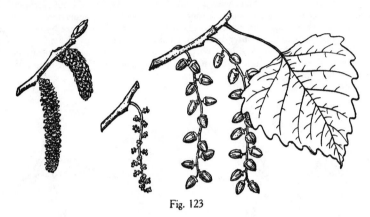

Fig. 123

pitted, thick-walled, 3 or rarely 4-valved, $\frac{1}{3}'-\frac{1}{2}'$ long; pedicel stout, from $\frac{1}{20}'-\frac{1}{8}'$ long; **seeds** ovoid, acute, light brown, nearly $\frac{1}{8}'$ in length.

A tree, occasionally 100° high, with a short trunk 5°–6° in diameter, stout spreading branches pendulous at the ends and forming a broad rather open graceful head, and slender terete branchlets light green and glabrous, becoming light yellow before winter, dark or

Fig. 124

light gray more or less tinged with yellow in their second year, and only slightly roughened by the small 3-lobed leaf-scars. **Winter-buds** ovoid, acute, with light green lustrous scales, the terminal usually about $\frac{1}{3}'$ long and usually two or three times as large as the lateral buds. **Bark** on young stems light gray-brown, thin, smooth or slightly fissured, becoming on old trees $1\frac{1}{2}'-2'$ thick, dark brown slightly tinged with red, and deeply and irregularly divided into broad connected rounded ridges covered with small closely appressed scales. **Wood** light brown, with thin nearly white sapwood.

Distribution. Banks of streams; valley of the upper Sacramento River southward through western California to the San Pedro Mártir Mountains, Lower California; most abundant in the San Joaquin Valley, and ascending the western slopes of the southern Sierra Nevada to altitudes of 3000°.

Often planted in southern California as a shade-tree, and for the fuel produced quickly and abundantly from pollarded trees.

In San Bernardino and San Diego Counties, California, generally replaced by the var. *pubescens* Sarg., differing in its pubescent branchlets and ranging eastward to southwestern Nevada and southern Utah. In southern Arizona and near Silver City, Grant County, New Mexico, represented by the var. *Thornberii* Sarg., differing from the typical *P. Fremontii* in the more numerous serratures of the leaves, in the ellipsoidal not ovoid capsules with smaller disk and shorter pedicels, and by the var. *Toumeyi* Sarg., differing from the type in the shallow cordate base of the leaves, gradually narrowed and cuneate to the insertion of the petiole, and in the larger disk of the fruit (Fig. 124). The var. *macrodisca* Sarg. with a broad disc nearly inclosing the ellipsoidal fruit is known only in the neighborhood of Silver City.

× *Populus Parryi* Sarg., a probable hybrid of *P. Fremontii* and *P. trichocarpa*, with characters intermediate between those of its supposed parents, grows naturally along Cottonwood Creek on the west side of Owens Lake, Inyo County, and in the neighborhood of Fort Tejon, Kern County, and as a street tree is not rare in San Bernardino, California.

9. Populus arizonica Sarg. Cottonwood.

Populus mexicana Sarg. not Wesm.

Leaves deltoid or reniform, gradually or abruptly long-pointed at the acuminate entire apex, truncate or broad-cuneate at the wide base, finely serrate with numerous teeth, as

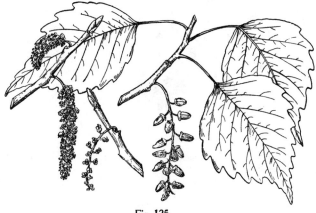

Fig. 125

they unfold dark red covered below with pale pubescence, pubescent above, ciliate on the margins, thin, glandular with bright red caducous glands, soon becoming glabrous, at maturity subcoriaceous, bright yellow-green, very lustrous, $1\frac{1}{2}'-2'$ long and broad, with a slender yellow midrib and obscure primary veins; petioles laterally compressed, sparingly villose when they first appear, soon glabrous, $1\frac{1}{2}'-2'$ long; leaves on vigorous leading shoots often rounded at apex, cuneate at base, and often $2'$ long and $3'$ wide, with petioles often $3'$ in length.   **Flowers:** staminate aments dense, cylindric, $1'-1\frac{1}{2}'$ long, the pistillate slender, many-flowered, $1\frac{1}{2}'-2'$ long, becoming $3'-4'$ long before the fruit ripens; disk of the staminate flower broad-oblong; stamens numerous; disk of the pistillate flower deep cup-shaped, nearly entire; ovary ovoid, rounded at apex, slightly 3 or 4-angled, short-stalked, nearly inclosed in the cup-shaped membranaceous disk.   **Fruit** on short stout pedicels, round-ovoid, buff color, slightly 3 or 4-lobed, deeply pitted, thin-walled, about $\frac{1}{4}'$ long.

A tree, $50°-70°$ high, with a trunk occasionally $3°$ in diameter, gracefully spreading and ascending branches forming a broad open head of wide-spreading branches, and slender often pendulous branchlets, pale green and glabrous or puberulous when they first appear, soon becoming glabrous, and light yellow during their first season.   **Winter-buds** narrow, acute, light orange-brown, puberulous toward the base of the outer scales, the terminal about $\frac{1}{4}'$ long, and two or three times as large as the much-compressed oblong lateral buds.   **Bark** pale gray or rarely white, and deeply divided into broad flat ridges.

Distribution.   Banks of mountain streams; southwestern California (Mill Creek, above Forest Home, San Bernardino Mountains) and southern and central Arizona; widely distributed through northern Mexico (*var. Jonesii* Sarg.); well distinguished from the other Cottonwoods of the United States by its small fruit.

Often planted as a street tree in the towns of southern Arizona.

10. **Populus texana Sarg.**

Leaves thin, glabrous, broadly ovate, gradually narrowed, long-pointed and acuminate at apex, truncate at base, coarsely crenately serrate below the middle, entire above, $3'-3\frac{1}{4}'$

Fig. 126

lo ig and $2\frac{1}{4}'-2\frac{1}{2}'$ wide; petioles slender, compressed, $1\frac{1}{2}'-2\frac{1}{2}'$ in length.   **Flowers** not seen. **Fruit:** aments slender, glabrous, $2\frac{1}{2}'-3'$ long; fruit oblong-ovoid, acute, deeply pitted, glabrous, thin-walled, 3-valved, $\frac{1}{3}'$ in length; disk slightly lobed; pedicel slender, $\frac{1}{16}'-\frac{1}{8}'$ in length; **seeds** ovoid, acuminate, $\frac{1}{16}'$ long.

A tree up to $60°$ high, with a trunk sometimes $3°$ in diameter, stout more or less pendulous branches and stout glabrous pale yellow-brown branchlets.   **Winter-buds** acuminate, glabrous.

In cañons and along the streams of northwestern Texas, where it appears to be the only Cottonwood.

11. Populus MacDougalii Rose.

Leaves broadly ovate, abruptly short-pointed or acute at apex, broadly or acutely cuneate or truncate, or on vigorous shoots rarely slightly cordate at base, finely or often coarsely crenately serrate, bluish green, thin, pubescent on the under sides of the midrib and primary veins early in the season, otherwise glabrous, $1\frac{1}{2}'$–$3'$ long and broad, with slender midribs and veins; petioles slender, slightly compressed, pubescent early in the season, becoming glabrous, $1\frac{1}{2}'$–$2'$ in length. **Flowers** not seen. **Fruit:** aments glabrous, short-stalked, $2'$–$2\frac{1}{2}'$ long; fruit ovoid and acute at apex to ellipsoidal and acute or acuminate at ends, glabrous, slightly pitted, thin-walled, 3-valved, $\frac{5}{12}'$–$\frac{1}{2}'$ long; disk not more than $\frac{1}{8}'$ in diameter; pedicels glabrous, $\frac{1}{8}'$–$\frac{1}{5}'$ in length; **seeds** oblong-ovoid, acuminate, $\frac{1}{8}'$ long.

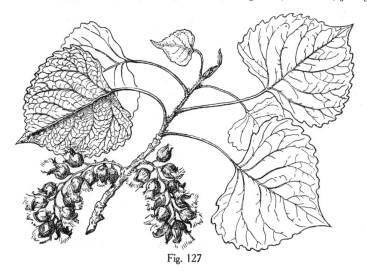

Fig. 127

A tree rarely 90°–110° high, usually much smaller, with erect branches and slender branchlets pubescent or puberulous when they first appear, sometimes becoming glabrous during their first season, and sometimes pubescent during two years.

Distribution. Banks of streams and springs, San Bernardino County, California (Cottonwood Springs, Meca, etc.), and eastward to the bottoms of the Colorado River from Clark County, Nevada, to Yuma, Arizona, and probably the only Cottonwood in this arid region.

Often planted as a street tree in the towns of southwestern California and of adjacent Nevada and Arizona.

12. Populus Wislizenii Sarg. Cottonwood.

Leaves broadly deltoid, abruptly short- or long-pointed at apex, truncate or sometimes cordate at the broad entire base, coarsely and irregularly crenately serrate except toward the entire apex, coriaceous, glabrous, yellow-green and lustrous, $2'$–$2\frac{1}{2}'$ long, usually about $3'$ wide, with a slender yellow midrib, thin remote primary veins and conspicuous reticulate veinlets; petioles slender, glabrous, $1\frac{1}{2}'$–$2'$ long; on vigorous shoots often $3\frac{1}{2}'$–$4'$ long and wide with petioles $3\frac{1}{2}'$–$4'$ in length. **Flowers:** aments $2'$–$4'$ long, the pistillate becoming $4'$–$5'$ long before the fruit ripens; scales scarious, light red, divided at the apex into elongated filiform lobes; disk of the staminate flower broad and oblique; stamens numerous, with large oblong anthers and short filaments; disk of the pistillate flower cup-shaped, irregularly dentate, inclosing to the middle the long stalked ovary full and rounded at apex, with 3 broad crenulate lobed stigmas raised on the short branches of the style. **Fruit** oblong-ovoid, thick-walled, acute, 3 or 4-valved, slightly ridged, buff color, $\frac{1}{4}'$ long; pedicels slender, $\frac{1}{2}'-\frac{3}{4}'$ in length and placed rather remotely on the slender glabrous rachis of the ament.

A large tree, with wide-spreading branches, and stout light orange-colored glabrous branch-

Fig. 128

lets. **Winter-buds** acute lustrous, puberulous. **Bark** pale gray-brown, deeply divided into broad flat ridges. **Wood** used as fuel, for fence-posts and the rafters of Mexican houses.

Distribution. Western Texas through New Mexico to the valley of Grand River, western Colorado (Grand Junction, Mesa County); common in the valley of the Rio Grande in western Texas and New Mexico, and the adjacent parts of Mexico.

Often planted as a shade tree in New Mexico.

13. Populus Sargentii Dode.

Populus deltoides var. *occidentalis* Rydb.

Leaves ovate, usually longer than broad, abruptly narrowed into a long slender entire acuminate point or rarely rounded at apex, truncate or slightly cordate at base, and coarsely crenately serrate, as they unfold slightly villose above and tomentose on the margins, soon glabrous, light green and very lustrous, $3'-3\frac{1}{2}'$ long, $3\frac{1}{2}'-4'$ wide, with a thin midrib slender primary veins and reticulate veinlets occasionally furnished on the upper side at the insertion of the petiole with one or two small glands; petioles slender, compressed laterally, $2\frac{1}{2}'-3\frac{1}{2}'$ long. **Flowers:** aments short-stalked, glabrous, the staminate $2'-2\frac{1}{2}'$ in length, the pistillate becoming $4'-8'$ long before the fruit ripens; scales fimbriately divided at apex, scarious, light brown; disk of the staminate flower broad, oblique, slightly thickened on the margins; stamens 20 or more, with short filaments and yellow anthers; disk of the pistillate flower cup-shaped, slightly lobed on the margin; ovary subglobose, with 3 or 4 sessile dilated or laciniately lobed stigmas. **Fruit** oblong-ovoid, gradually or abruptly narrowed to the blunt apex, thin-walled, about $\frac{2}{8}'$ long and three or four times longer than the pedicel; **seeds** oblong-obovoid, rounded at apex, about $\frac{1}{16}'$ in length.

A tree $60°-90°$ tall with a trunk often $6°$ or $7°$ in diameter, erect and spreading branches forming a broad open head, and stout glabrous light yellow often angular branchlets conspicuously roughened by the elevated scars of fallen leaf-stalks. **Winter-buds** ovoid, acute, with light orange-brown puberulous scales. Bark pale, thick, divided by deep fissures into broad rounded ridges broken into closely appressed scales.

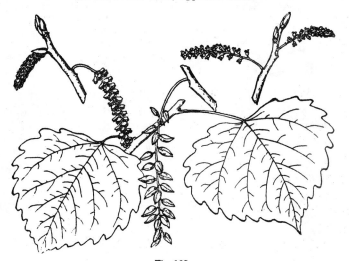

Fig. 129

Distribution. The common Cottonwood along the streams in the eastern foothill region of the Rocky Mountains from Saskatchewan to New Mexico, and ranging east to the Dakotas, western Nebraska, Kansas, Oklahoma and Texas.

Often planted as a shade and street tree in the Rocky Mountain states; hardy in Massachusetts.

14. Populus balsamifera L. Cottonwood.

Populus angulata Michx. f.

Leaves ovate, longer than broad, abruptly acuminate and often long-pointed at apex, subcordate or rarely truncate at the wide base, finely crenately serrate with glandular teeth, furnished on the upper surface at the insertion of the petiole with two glands, thick, glabrous, green and lustrous on the upper surface, paler below, $5'$–$7'$ long and $4'$–$5'$ wide, with stout midribs and conspicuous primary veins sometimes sparingly pilose below early in the season; petioles much compressed laterally, often more or less tinged with red, $3'$–$4'$ in length. **Flowers:** aments glabrous, short-stalked, the staminate densely flowered, $1\frac{1}{2}'$–$2'$ long, $\frac{1}{2}'$–$\frac{3}{4}'$ in diameter, the pistillate slender, sparsely flowered, $3'$–$3\frac{1}{2}'$ in length; scales scarious, light brown, glabrous, dilated and irregularly divided at apex into filiform lobes; disk of the staminate flower broad, oblique, slightly thickened and revolute on the margins; stamens 60 or more, with short filaments and large dark red anthers; disk of the pistillate flower broad, slightly crenate, inclosing about $\frac{1}{3}'$ of the ovoid obtusely pointed ovary, with 3 or 4 sessile dilated lacinately lobed stigmas. **Fruit** on aments $8'$–$12'$ in length, ellipsoidal, pointed, thin-walled, 3 or 4-valved, $\frac{1}{3}'$ long, the disk little enlarged; pedicels $\frac{1}{6}'$–$\frac{1}{4}'$ in length; **seeds** oblong-obovoid, rounded at apex, light brown, about $\frac{1}{12}'$ long.

A large tree with massive spreading branches and stout yellow-brown often angular branchlets. **Winter-buds** resinous, acute, $\frac{1}{2}'$ long with light chestnut brown lustrous scales.

Distribution. Shores of Lake Champlain (Shelburne Point, Chittenden County), Vermont; western New York; Island of the Delaware River above Easton, Northampton County, Pennsylvania; Baltimore County, and Bare Hills, Maryland; northern banks of

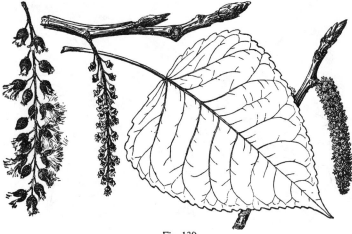

Fig. 130

the Potomac River opposite Plummer's Island near Washington, D.C.; Artesia, Lowndes County, and Starkville, Oktibbeha County, Mississippi; rare and local.

Populus balsamifera var. virginiana Sarg. Cottonwood.

Populus deltoidea Marsh. at least in part.

Populus nigra β virginiana Castiglioni.

Leaves deltoid to ovate-deltoid, acuminate with entire points, truncate, slightly cordate or occasionally abruptly cuneate at the entire base, crenately serrate above, with incurved glandular teeth, fragrant with a balsamic odor, glabrous, thick and firm, light bright green and lustrous, paler on the lower than on the upper surface, 3′–5′ long and broad, with a stout yellow midrib often tinged with red toward the base, raised and rounded on the upper side, and conspicuous primary veins; petioles slender, pilose at first, soon glabrous, compressed laterally, yellow often more or less tinged with red, $2\frac{1}{2}′$–$3\frac{1}{2}′$ long. **Flowers** and **Fruit:** as on the type.

A tree, sometimes 100° high, with a trunk occasionally 7°–8° in diameter, divided often 20°–30° above the ground into several massive limbs spreading gradually and becoming pendulous toward the ends, and forming a graceful rather open head frequently 100° across, or on young trees nearly erect above and spreading below almost at right angles with the stem, and forming a symmetrical pyramidal head, and stout branchlets marked with long pale lenticels, terete, or, especially on vigorous trees, becoming angled in their second year, with thin more or less prominent wings extending downward from the two sides and from the base of the large 3-lobed leaf-scars. **Winter-buds** very resinous, ovoid, acute, the lateral much flattened, $\frac{1}{2}′$ long, with 6 or 7 light chestnut-brown lustrous scales. **Bark** thin, smooth, light yellow tinged with green on young stems and branches, becoming on old trunks $1\frac{1}{2}′$–2′ thick, ashy gray, and deeply divided into broad rounded ridges broken into closely appressed scales. **Wood** dark brown, with thick nearly white sapwood, warping badly in drying and difficult to season.

Distribution. Banks of streams, often forming extensive open groves, and toward the western limits of its range occasionally in upland ravines and on bluffs; Province of Quebec and the shores of Lake Champlain, through western New England, western New York, Pennsylvania west of the Alleghany Mountains, and westward to southern Minnesota, North and South Dakota, eastern Nebraska, eastern Kansas, Oklahoma and Texas, and southward through the Atlantic states from Delaware to western Florida (valley of the Apalachicola River), and through the Gulf states to western Texas (Brown County). In the south Atlantic states and the valley of the Lower Ohio River and southward sometimes replaced by a variety with leaves covered above when they unfold with soft white hairs and below with close pubescence more or less persistent during the season especially on the midribs and veins (f. *pilosa* Sarg.).

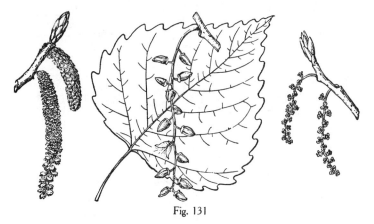

Fig. 131

Often planted for shelter and ornament on the treeless plains and prairies between the Mississippi River and the Rocky Mountains, and as an ornamental tree in the eastern United States and largely in western and northern Europe.

× *Populus canadensis* Moench, believed to be a hybrid between the northern glabrous form of *P. balsamifera* and the European *P. nigra* L., with several varieties, is cultivated in Europe and occasionally in the United States. The best known of these varieties, × *P. canadensis* var. *Eugenie* Schelle, the Carolina Poplar of American nurseries, believed to be a hybrid of the northern Cottonwood with the Lombardy Poplar, has been planted in the United States in immense numbers.

× *Populus Jackii* Sarg., believed to be a hybrid of the northern Cottonwood with *P. tacamahacca*, with characters intermediate between those of its supposed parents, grows spontaneously near the mouth of the Chateaugay River and at Beauharnois, Province of Quebec, and at South Haven, Michigan, and is now occasionally cultivated.

15. Populus Palmeri Sarg.

Leaves thin, ovate, gradually or abruptly contracted at apex into a narrow acuminate entire point, cuneate or rounded at the broad base, finely serrate with incurved teeth, ciliate on the margins when they unfold, otherwise glabrous, $2\frac{1}{2}'$–$5'$ long and $1\frac{1}{2}'$–$2\frac{1}{4}'$ wide; petioles slender, glabrous, $1\frac{1}{2}'$–$2\frac{1}{2}'$ in length. **Flowers** not seen. **Fruit:** aments glabrous, 12–15cm. long; fruit ovoid, obtuse, slightly pitted, puberulous, thin-walled, 4-valved, $\frac{1}{4}'$–$\frac{1}{3}'$ long, the disk deeply lobed; pedicel slender, $\frac{1}{4}'$–$\frac{1}{3}'$ in length.

A tree 60° tall, with a straight trunk 3° in diameter, erect smooth pale branches forming an open pyramidal head, the lower branches smaller, horizontal or pendulous, and slender glabrous branchlets light reddish brown early in the season, becoming pale grayish brown in their second year. **Bark** pale, 3'-4' thick, deeply divided by wide fissures into narrow ridges.

Distribution. In moist fertile soil near springs, at the base of high chalky bluffs of

Fig. 132

Nueces Cañon of the upper Nueces River, Uvalde County, growing with *Salix nigra* var. *Lindheimeri, Carya pecan, Morus rubra* and *Ulmus crassifolia*, and at Strawn, Palo Pinto County, Texas.

2. SALIX L. Willow.

Trees or shrubs, with watery juice, scaly bark, soft wood, slender terete tough branchlets often easily separated at the joints, and winter-buds covered by a single scale of 2 coats, the inner membranaceous, stipular, rarely separable from the outer, inclosing at its base 2 minute opposite lateral buds alternate with 2 small scale-like caducous leaves coated with long pale or rufous hairs. Leaves variously folded in the bud, alternate, simple, lanceolate, obovate, rotund or linear, penniveined ; petioles sometimes glandular at the apex, and more or less covering the bud, in falling leaving U-shaped or arcuate elevated leaf-scars displaying the ends of 3 small equidistant fibro-vascular bundles; stipules oblique, serrate, small and deciduous, or foliaceous and often persistent, generally large and conspicuous on vigorous young branches, leaving in falling minute persistent scars. Flowers in sessile or stalked aments, terminal and axillary on leafy branchlets; scales of the ament lanceolate, concave, rotund or obovate, entire or glandular-dentate, of uniform color or dark-colored toward the apex, more or less hairy, deciduous or persistent; disk of the flower nectariferous, composed of an anterior and posterior or of a single posterior gland-like body; stamens 3-12 or 1 or 2, inserted on the base of the scale, with slender filaments free or rarely united and usually light yellow, glabrous, or hairy toward the base, and small ovoid or oblong anthers generally rose-colored before anthesis, becoming orange or purple; ovary sessile or stipitate, conic, obtuse to subulate-rostrate, glandular at the base, glabrous, tomentose or villose, with an abbreviated style divided into 2 short recurved retuse or 2-parted stigmas; ovules 4-8 on each of the 2 placentas. Fruit an acuminate 1-celled capsule separating at maturity into 2 recurved valves. Seeds minute, narrowed at the ends, dark chestnut-brown or nearly black; cotyledons oblong.

Salix inhabits the banks of streams and low moist ground, the alpine summits of mountains, and the Arctic and sub-Arctic regions of the northern hemisphere, ranging south in the New World, with a few species, through the West Indies and Central America to Brazil, and the Andes of Chili, and in the Old World to Madagascar, southern Africa, the Himalayas, Burmah, the Malay peninsula, Java, and Sumatra. Of the 160 or 170 species which are now recognized about seventy are found in North America. Of these twenty-four attain the size and habit of trees, the others being small and sometimes prostrate shrubs. Of exotic species, *Salix alba*, L., and *Salix fragilis* L., important European timber-trees, are now generally naturalized in the northeastern states. The flexible tough branches of several species are used in making baskets; the bark is rich in tannic acid and is used in tanning leather and yields salicin, a bitter principle valuable as a tonic. Many of the species are cultivated as ornamental trees.

Salix is the classical name of the Willow-tree.

CONSPECTUS OF THE NORTH AMERICAN ARBORESCENT SPECIES

Scales of the flowers deciduous, pale straw color.
  Stamens 3 or more.
    Leaves green on both surfaces; petioles without glands at the base of the leaves;
      branchlets easily separable.
      Branchlets reddish or grayish purple; leaves mostly narrow-lanceolate; capsule
        glabrous.   1. **S. nigra** (A, C, E).
      Branchlets yellowish-gray; leaves lanceolate to elliptic-lanceolate; capsule often
        more or less pubescent.   2. **S. Gooddingii** (F, G, H).
    Leaves (at least when fully grown) pale or glaucous below.
      Petioles without glands.
        Branchlets easily separable.
          Leaves narrow-lanceolate to lanceolate; petioles less than $\frac{1}{2}'$ long.
                    3. **S. Harbisonii** (C).
        Leaves lanceolate to ovate-lanceolate, caudate; petioles $\frac{1}{2}'-\frac{3}{4}'$ long.
                    4. **S. amygdaloides** (A, B).
      Branchlets not easily separable.
        Capsules short-stalked (pedicels hardly more than $\frac{1}{24}'$ long), ovoid-conic, up
          to $\frac{1}{5}'$ in length; leaves more or less narrow-lanceolate, petioles glabrous or
          nearly so.   5. **S. Bonplandiana** (H).
        Capsules long-stalked (pedicels $\frac{1}{12}'-\frac{1}{6}'$ long), more or less acuminate.
          Petioles puberulous; leaves lanceolate to ovate-lanceolate; stipules without
            glands on their inner surface; capsules hardly more than $\frac{1}{4}'$ long.
                    6. **S. lævigata** (G, F).
          Petioles hairy-tomentose; leaves lanceolate; stipules glandular on their inner
            surface; capsules $\frac{1}{4}'-\frac{3}{4}'$ long.   7. **S. longipes** (C, D.)
      Petioles glandular; leaves lanceolate to broadly ovate, caudate; branchlets easily
        separable.
        Leaves distinctly pale or glaucous below, lanceolate to ovate-lanceolate.
                    8. **S. lasiandra** (B, G).
        Leaves pale green below, ovate to elliptic-lanceolate, abruptly caudate-acu-
          minate.   9. **S. lucida** (A).
  Stamens 2.
    Stigmas linear, 4 or 5 times longer than broad.
      Leaves linear, hardly more than $\frac{1}{2}'$ long; anthers very small, globose; aments small,
        in fruit hardly up to $\frac{4}{5}'$ in length.   10. **S. taxifolia** (H).
      Leaves linear-lanceolate to elliptic-lanceolate; up to $2'$ in length; anthers ellipsoid;
        aments longer   11. **S. sessilifolia** (B, G).
    Stigmas short, hardly 2 or 3 times longer than broad.

Mature leaves covered below with appressed white silky hairs, those of flowering branchlets entire or barely denticulate.   12. S. exigua (B, F, G).

Mature leaves glabrous below, those of flowering branchlets more or less distinctly denticulate.   13. S. longifolia (A, F).

Scales of the flowers persistent, dark brown or fuscous, at least toward the apex (in *S. Bebbiana* more or less straw-colored or tawny).

Stamens 2.

Ovaries glabrous.

Leaves more or less denticulate or serrate; styles short.

Base of leaf cuneate or rounded.

Leaves acute, oblanceolate to narrowly lanceolate; filaments mostly united below.   14. S. lasiolepis (G).

Leaves mostly acuminate; filaments free.

Branchlets glabrous, lustrous; leaves oblanceolate to narrowly obovate, up to 2′ in length; pedicels ⅛′–⅙′ long; stipules small.
          15. S. Mackenzieana (A, G).

Branchlets pubescent; leaves narrowly lanceolate to ovate-lanceolate, 4′–6′ long; pedicels 1.5–2.5 mm. long.   16. S. missouriensis (A).

Base of leaf mostly more or less cordate; leaves glabrous; filaments free; pedicels long.   17. S. pyrifolia (A).

Leaves entire, oval to broad-obovate; branchlets villose-pubescent during their first season.   18. S. amplifolia.

Ovaries pubescent (glabrous often in No. 23).

Leaves covered with a soft dense felt-like tomentum, oblong-lanceolate to elliptic-lanceolate.   19. S. alaxensis (B).

Leaves glabrous or more or less villose-pubescent below.

Bracts of the flowers pale or tawny, often reddish at the tip; pedicels up to ⅕′ in length; leaves elliptic-lanceolate to obovate, reticulate beneath in age, pubescent or glabrate.   20. S. Bebbiana.

Bracts of the flowers brown or fuscous.

Stipules more or less distinctly developed; pedicels several times longer than the short styles.

Leaves elliptic-lanceolate to oblong-elliptic; mostly glabrous in age.
          21. S. discolor (A, B, F).

Leaves oblanceolate to cuneate-obovate, covered beneath with short hairs or at maturity with a gray villose-pubescence.
          22. S. Scouleriana (A, B).

Stipules usually wanting; pedicels hardly longer than the distinct styles; leaves broad-elliptic to obovate-oblong, more or less grayish villose beneath.   23. S. Hookeriana (B, G).

Stamens usually 1; leaves obovate-oblong, densely covered below with lustrous silvery white silky tomentum.   24. S. sitchensis (B, G).

1. Salix nigra Marsh. Black Willow.

Leaves lanceolate, long-acuminate, often falcate, gradually cuneate or rounded at base, finely serrate, thin bright light green, rather lustrous, with obscure reticulate veins, glabrous or often pubescent on the under side of the midribs and veins and on the short slender petioles, 3′–6′ long, ¼′–¾′ wide; at the north turning light yellow before falling in the autumn; stipules semicordate, acuminate, foliaceous, persistent, or ovoid, minute, and deciduous. **Flowers:** aments terminal on leafy pubescent branches, narrowly cylindric, 1′–3′ long; scales yellow, elliptic to obovate, rounded at apex and coated on the inner surface with pale hairs; stamens 3–5, with filaments hairy toward the base; ovary ovoid, short-stalked, glabrous, gradually narrowed above the middle to the apex, with nearly sessile slightly divided stigmatic lobes. **Fruit** ovoid-conic, short-stalked, glabrous, about ⅛′ long, light reddish brown.

A tree, usually 30°–40° high, with usually several clustered stout stems, thick spreading upright branches forming a broad somewhat irregular open head, and reddish brown or gray-brown branchlets pubescent when they first appear, soon glabrous, and easily separated at the joints. **Winter-buds** acute, about $\frac{1}{8}'$ long. **Bark** $1'$–$1\frac{1}{4}'$ thick, dark brown or nearly black and deeply divided into broad flat connected ridges separating freely into

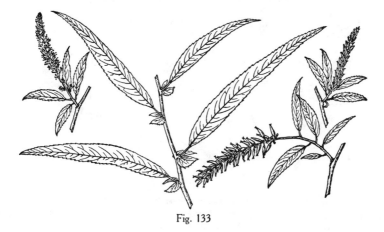

Fig. 133

thick plate-like scales and becoming shaggy on old trunks. **Wood** light, soft, weak, light reddish brown, with thin nearly white sapwood ; now sawed into lumber in the valley of the lower Mississippi River and largely used for packing cases, cellar and barn floors, in furniture, and in the manufacture of toys and other purposes where strength is not important as it does not warp, check or splinter.

Distribution. Low moist alluvial banks of streams and lakes; southern New Brunswick through southern Quebec and Ontario to the region north of Lake Superior, southward to northern and western North Carolina, through the Piedmont region of South Carolina and Georgia to eastern and central Alabama, and westward to southeastern North Dakota, eastern South Dakota, Nebraska, Kansas, the valley of Wichita River, Oklahoma, and central and western Texas to Valverde County.

In southern Arkansas, in Louisiana and in eastern Texas *Salix nigra* is often replaced by var. *altissima* Sarg., differing from the type in the more pubescent young branchlets, leaves and petioles, in the more acute base of the leaves and longer petioles, and in its later flowering. A tree sometimes 120 feet high and the tallest of American Willows.

Salix nigra var. Lindheimeri Schn.

Salix Wrightii Sarg. not Anders.

Leaves lanceolate, often slightly falcate, long-pointed and acuminate at apex, cuneate at base, finely glandular-serrate, glabrous, light green on the upper surface, paler below, $4'$–$5'$ long, $\frac{1}{3}'$–$\frac{1}{2}'$ wide; petioles pubescent early in the season, becoming glabrous, $\frac{1}{2}'$–$\frac{3}{4}'$ in length. **Flowers:** aments slender, densely villose, $2'$–$3'$ long; scales ovate, acute or rarely rounded at apex, covered with matted white hairs, more abundant on the inner surface; stamens 4 or 5; filaments villose below the middle; ovary ovoid, gradually narrowed to the apex, the 2-lobed stigmas nearly sessile. **Fruit** ovoid-conic; pedicels about $\frac{1}{4}'$ long.

A tree, 50°–70°, high with a trunk often 3° in diameter, large erect spreading branches forming an open irregular head, and slender branchlets light green and slightly pubescent when they first appear, becoming light orange or yellow-brown and lustrous. **Bark** thick, pale yellow-brown, deeply furrowed, the surface sometimes separating into long plate-like scales.

Fig. 134

Distribution. River banks, central and western Texas from Grayson and Dallas Counties and the lower valley of the Brazos River to the valleys of the San Antonio and upper Guadalupe Rivers; in Coahuila, Nuevo Leon and Tamaulipas.

2. Salix Gooddingii Ball.

Salix vallicola Britt.

Leaves lanceolate to narrow elliptic-lanceolate, acute or acuminate, acutely cuneate at base, finely glandular-serrate, often slightly falcate, silky pubescent when they unfold especially below, glabrous and dull green at maturity, $1\frac{1}{2}'-3'$ long, $\frac{1}{4}'-\frac{1}{2}'$ wide, or on vigorous shoots $5'$ or $6'$ long and $\frac{3}{4}'$ wide; petioles pubescent, usually becoming glabrous, $\frac{1}{8}'-\frac{1}{4}'$ in

Fig. 135

length; stipules orbicular-cordate, coarsely glandular-serrate, pubescent. **Flowers:** aments pubescent terminal on leafy pubescent branchlets, narrow-cylindric, 1′–2′ long; scales linear-oblanceolate, acute, yellow, hoary tomentose; stamens 3–5; filaments villose toward the base; ovary ovoid-conic, gradually narrowed to the acuminate apex, pubescent or glabrous; style distinct, 2-lobed. **Fruit** ovoid, acute, light reddish brown, glabrous or pubescent, $\frac{1}{4}$′ long; pedicels glabrous or rarely pubescent, $\frac{1}{16}$′–$\frac{1}{8}$′ in length.

A tree, 25°–50° high, with slender light orange-colored or grayish glabrous or pubescent easily separable branchlets. **Bark** rough, thick, deeply furrowed, sometimes nearly black.

Distribution. River banks; Reed Creek, Shasta County, and Red Bluff, Tehama County, California, southward in the interior valleys and on the western foothills of the Sierra Nevada to the mountain valleys in the southern part of the state, and to northern Lower California; eastward through central and southern Arizona; in southeastern Nevada; through southern New Mexico to western Texas (El Paso, El Paso County, and Fort Davis, Jeff Davis County); and southward into northern Mexico.

3. Salix Harbisonii Schn.

Leaves linear-lanceolate, narrow-elliptic or rarely obovate-lanceolate, acute or short-acuminate, obtusely or acutely cuneate at the base, and finely glandular dentate; when the flowers open more or less pubescent especially below or glabrous, and at maturity green on

Fig. 136

the upper surface, pale on the lower surface, glabrous, 4′ or 5′ long, $\frac{3}{4}$′ broad; petioles villose early in the season, becoming glabrous, $\frac{1}{4}$′ in length, minutely glandular at apex; stipules wanting or minute, semicordate, acute, pubescent on vigorous leading branches and sometimes $\frac{1}{4}$′ long. **Flowers:** aments terminal on leafy branchlets, 2$\frac{1}{2}$′–3′ in length, their rachis villose-pubescent; scales ovate or ovate-oblong, obtuse or acute; stamens usually 5–7, rarely 3–9; filaments densely villose; ovary ovoid, long-acuminate, glabrous, long-stalked; style short, distinct, 2-lobed. **Fruit** acuminate and long-pointed, acute at base, $\frac{1}{4}$′ long and about as long as its pedicel.

A tree, 30°–50° high, with a trunk 10′ or 12′ in diameter, with often pendulous branches, and slender branchlets more or less densely pubescent or tomentose or nearly glabrous when they first appear, becoming glabrous and dark reddish purple in their second season, and easily separable at the joints; often only a large shrub. **Bark** thick, deeply furrowed, dark red-brown, separating on the surface into small appressed scales.

Distribution. River banks and the borders of swamps; Dismal Swamp, Norfolk County, Virginia; near Goldsboro, Wayne County, North Carolina; common in the coast region of South Carolina and Georgia, extending up the Savannah River at least as far as Augusta, Richmond County, and through southern Georgia to the valley of the Flint River; swamps near Jacksonville, Duval County, and in the neighborhood of Apalachicola, Florida.

4. Salix amygdaloides Anders. Peach Willow. Almond Willow.

Leaves lanceolate to ovate-lanceolate, frequently falcate, gradually or abruptly narrowed into a long slender point, cuneate or gradually rounded and often unequal at base, finely serrate, slightly puberulous when they unfold, becoming at maturity thin and firm in texture, light green and lustrous above, pale and glaucous below, $2\frac{1}{2}'-4'$ long, $\frac{3}{4}'-1\frac{1}{4}'$ wide, with a stout yellow or orange-colored midrib, prominent veins and reticulate veinlets; petioles slender, nearly terete $\frac{1}{2}'-\frac{3}{4}'$ in length; stipules reniform, serrate, often $\frac{1}{2}'$ broad on vigorous shoots, usually caducous. **Flowers:** aments on leafy branchlets, elongated, cylindric, slender, arcuate, stalked, pubescent or tomentose, $2'-3'$ long; scales yellow, sparingly villose on the outer, densely villose on the inner face, the staminate broadly ovate, rounded

Fig. 137

at the apex, the pistillate oblong-obovate, narrower, caducous; stamens 5-9, with free filaments slightly hairy at the base; ovary oblong-conic, long-stalked, glabrous, with a short style and emarginate stigmas. **Fruit** globose-conic, light reddish yellow, about $\frac{1}{4}'$ in length.

A tree, sometimes 60°-70° high, with a single straight or slightly inclining trunk rarely more than 2° in diameter, straight ascending branches, and slender glabrous or rarely pilose (f. *pilosiuscula* Schn.) branchlets marked with scattered pale lenticels, dark orange color or red-brown and lustrous, becoming in their first winter light orange-brown. **Winter-buds** broadly ovoid, gibbous, dark chestnut-brown, very lustrous above the middle, light orange-brown below, $\frac{1}{8}'$ long. **Bark** $\frac{1}{2}'-\frac{3}{4}'$ thick, brown somewhat tinged with red, and divided by irregular fissures into flat connected ridges separating on the surface into thick plate-like scales. **Wood** light, soft, close-grained, light brown, with thick nearly white sapwood.

Distribution. Banks of streams; Province of Quebec from the neighborhood of Montreal to Winnipeg, and along the fiftieth degree of north latitude to southeastern British Columbia, and to central New York, along the southern shores of Lake Erie, and through northern Ohio to northern Indiana, southwestern Illinois, northern and central Missouri, and to

Kansas, northwestern Oklahoma and northwestern Texas; in Colorado, Utah and Nevada to central Oregon and southeastern Washington.

Salix amygdaloides var. Wrightii Schn.

Salix Wrightii Anders.

Leaves lanceolate, gradually acuminate and long-pointed at apex, cuneate at base, finely serrate, occasionally slightly falcate, glabrous, yellow-green on the upper surface, pale on the lower surface, $1\frac{1}{2}'-2'$ long, $\frac{1}{4}'-\frac{1}{3}'$ wide, and on vigorous summer shoots sometimes $4'$ or $5'$ long and $\frac{1}{2}'$ wide; petioles slender, glabrous, $\frac{1}{4}'-\frac{1}{3}'$ in length. **Flowers** and **Fruit** as in the species.

Fig. 138

A small or large tree best distinguished from *S. amygdaloides* by the distinctly yellow or yellowish brown glabrous branchlets.

Distribution. Barstow, Ward County, common along the Rio Grande near El Paso and at Belon, El Paso County, and on Amarillo Creek, Potter County, western Texas; through southern New Mexico to the Sacramento Mountains, Otero County.

5. Salix Bonplandiana var. Toumeyi Schn.

Salix Toumeyi. Britt.

Leaves $4'-6'$ long, $\frac{1}{2}'-\frac{3}{4}'$ wide, linear-lanceolate to oblong-lanceolate, acuminate with a long slender point at apex, gradually narrowed and often unequal at the cuneate base, obscurely serrate with glandular teeth, or entire with revolute margins, thick and firm, reticulate-venulose, yellow-green and lustrous above, silvery white below, with a broad yellow midrib; falling irregularly during the winter; petioles stout, grooved, reddish; stipules ovate, rounded, slightly undulate, thin and scarious, $\frac{1}{8}'-\frac{1}{4}'$ broad, often persistent during the summer. **Flowers:** aments on leafy branchlets, cylindric, erect, slender, short-stalked, the staminate $1'-1\frac{1}{2}'$ long and somewhat longer than the pistillate; scales broadly obovate, rounded at the apex, light yellow, villose on the outer surface and glabrous or slightly hairy above the middle on the inner surface; stamens usually 3, with free filaments slightly hairy at the base; ovary slender, oblong-conic, short-stalked, glabrous, with nearly sessile much-thickened club-shaped stigmas, sometimes nearly encircled below by the large broad ventral gland. **Fruit** ovoid-conic, rounded at base, light reddish yellow.

A tree, rarely more than $30°$ high, with a trunk $12'-15'$ in diameter, slender erect and spreading branches often pendulous at the ends, forming a broad round-topped head, and slender glabrous branchlets marked with occasional pale lenticels, light yellow, becoming light or dark red-brown and lustrous, and paler orange-brown in their second year.   **Winter-buds** narrowly ovoid, long-pointed, more or less falcate, bright red-brown, lustrous, ¼′ long.   **Bark** ½′–¾′ thick, dark brown or nearly black, and deeply divided by narrow fissures into broad flat ridges separating on the surface into closely appressed scales.

Fig. 139

Distribution.   Banks of streams in the cañons of the mountains of central and southern Arizona (Sycamore Cañon near Flagstaff and Sabino Cañon, Santa Catalina Mountains); and southwestern New Mexico (cañon, Saint Louis Mountains, Grant County); in Chihuahua, Sonora and Lower California.

The typical *S. Bonplandiana* H. B. K. with broader and more coarsely serrate leaves, and flower-aments appearing from July to January from the axils of mature leaves is widely distributed in Mexico and ranges to Guatemala.

6. Salix lævigata Bebb.   Red Willow.

Leaves obovate, narrowed and rounded or acute and mucronate at apex, cuneate at base, with slightly revolute obscurely serrate margins, on sterile branches lanceolate or oblong-

Fig. 140

lanceolate, acute or acuminate, when they unfold light blue-green and coated on the lower surface with long pale or tawny deciduous hairs, at maturity glabrous, dark blue-green and lustrous above, paler and glaucous below, 3'–7' long, $\frac{3}{4}$'–1$\frac{1}{2}$' wide, with a broad flat yellow midrib; petioles broad, grooved, puberulous, rarely $\frac{1}{2}$' long; stipules ovate, acute, finely serrate, usually small and caducous. **Flowers:** aments cylindric, slender, lax, elongated, 2'–4' long, on leafy branchlets; scales peltate, dentate at apex, covered with long pale hairs, the staminate obovate, rounded, the pistillate narrower and more or less truncate; stamens usually 5 or 6, with free filaments hairy at the base; ovary conic, acute, rounded below, short-stalked, glabrous, with broad spreading emarginate stigmatic lobes. **Fruit** elongated, conic, long-stalked, nearly $\frac{1}{4}$' in length.

A tree, 40°–50° high, with a straight trunk 2° in diameter, slender spreading branches, and slender light or dark orange-colored or bright red-brown glabrous, or in one form tomentose or villose (f. *araquipa* Jeps.) branchlets; often much smaller, with an average height of 20°–30°. **Winter-buds** ovoid, somewhat obtuse, pale chestnut-brown, $\frac{1}{8}$'–$\frac{1}{4}$' long. **Bark** $\frac{3}{4}$'–1' thick, dark brown slightly tinged with red and deeply divided into irregular connected flat ridges broken on the surface into thick closely appressed scales. **Wood** light, soft, light brown tinged with red, with thick nearly white sapwood.

Distribution. Banks of streams; western California from the Oregon boundary to the southern borders of the state, ascending to altitudes of 4500° on the western slopes of the southern Sierra Nevada, and eastward to Mohave and Yavapai Counties, Arizona, southeastern Nevada and southwestern Utah.

7. Salix longipes Shuttl.

Salix amphibia Small.

Leaves lanceolate, acuminate or on fertile branches occasionally rounded at the apex, rounded or cuneate at the base, finely serrate, hoary-tomentose early in the season, becoming glabrous above, and pale and glabrous or pubescent below, 2'–4' long, $\frac{1}{2}$'–$\frac{3}{4}$' wide; peti-

Fig. 141

oles hoary-tomentose, $\frac{1}{4}$'–$\frac{1}{2}$' long; stipules minute, ovate, acute, hoary-tomentose, caducous, on vigorous shoots foliaceous, reniform, serrate above the middle, often $\frac{3}{4}$' in diameter. **Flowers:** aments terminal on leafy tomentose or glabrous branchlets, narrow-cylindric, 3' or 4' long; scales ovate, rounded at the apex, yellow, densely villose-pubescent; stamens 3–7, usually 5 or 6, the filaments hairy toward the base; ovary ovoid-conic, acute, cuneate at the base with a short 2-lobed style, and pedicels up to $\frac{1}{4}$' in length. **Fruit** ovoid, often rather abruptly contracted above the middle, $\frac{1}{4}$' in length.

A tree, 20°–30°, high with a trunk occasionally 12′–18′ in diameter, spreading branches, and glabrous or pubescent red-brown or gray-brown branchlets; or more often a shrub. **Bark** dark, sometimes nearly black, deeply divided into broad ridges covered by small closely appressed scales.

Distribution. Borders of swamps and streams; coast of North Carolina southward to the Everglade Keys of Florida, ranging westward in Florida to the valley of the Saint Marks River, Wakulla County; in Cuba.

A variety with narrower summer leaves and longer petioles is var. *venulosa* Schn.

Distribution. Newbern, Craven County, North Carolina, southward near the coast to northern and western Florida, ranging inland in Georgia to the banks of the Savannah River near Augusta, Richmond County, and to Traders Hill, Charlton County; in the neighborhood of New Orleans, Louisiana (*Drummond*); in southwestern Oklahoma and in western Texas (Blanco, Kendall, Kerr, Bandera and Uvalde Counties).

A variety with obtuse stipules, usually glabrous branchlets and lanceolate or narrow elliptic-lanceolate leaves is distinguished as var. *Wardii* Schn.

A shrub or small tree.

Distribution. Banks of the Potomac River, District of Columbia, and Alleghany County, Maryland to Natural, Rockbridge, Fairfax and Elizabeth Counties, Virginia; northern Kentucky; northern Tennessee; northeastern Mississippi (near Iuka, Tishomingo County); St. Clair and Madison Counties, Illinois; more abundant in Missouri from Pike County southward to southwestern Kansas, western Arkansas and eastern Oklahoma.

8. Salix lasiandra Benth.   Yellow Willow.

Leaves lanceolate to ovate-lanceolate, acuminate and long-pointed at apex, cuneate or rounded at base, often slightly falcate, finely serrate, glabrous, dark green and lustrous above, pale or glaucous below, 1½′–3′ long, about ½′ wide, on vigorous summer shoots often

Fig. 142

6′ or 7′ long and 1½′ wide; petioles slender, glabrous, glandular at apex, ¼′ in length, or on summer shoots stout and 1′–1½′ long; stipules reniform, caducous. **Flowers:** aments terminal on leafy puberulous branchlets, narrow-cylindric, 2½′–3′ in length; scales pale pubescent, those of the staminate ament lanceolate-acuminate to obovate and rounded at apex and entire, those of the pistillate ament obovate and usually dentate near the apex; stamens 5–9; filaments hairy below the middle; ovary rather abruptly narrowed above the middle and acuminate, long-stalked; style short with slightly emarginate lobes. **Fruit** light red-brown, ¼′ long; pedicels about $\frac{1}{16}$′ in length.

A tree often 60° in height with a trunk 2°–3° in diameter, or sometimes shrubby, and with straight ascending branches and rather stout branchlets, at first dark purple, reddish brown, or yellow, pilose with scattered hairs or pubescent or tomentose, and often covered by glaucous bloom, becoming dark purple, bright reddish brown or bright orange color. Winter-buds broadly ovate, acute, light chestnut brown and lustrous above the middle, pale at base, and nearly $\frac{1}{4}'$ in length. Bark $\frac{1}{2}'-\frac{3}{4}'$ thick, dark brown, slightly tinged with red, and divided by shallow fissures in broad flat scaly ridges broken by cross fissures into oblong plates.

Distribution. Valley of the Yukon River near Dawson, Yukon, Vancouver Island, and southward near the coast of Washington and Oregon, and on the western slope of the Sierra Nevada and on the coast ranges to southern California, ranging from the sea-level to altitudes of 8500° on the southern Sierra Nevada; in New Mexico (Glenwood, Soccoro County, and Santa Fé, Santa Fé County); in Colorado (Buena Vista, Chaffee County, *Alice Eastwood*). Passing into var. *caudata* Sudw., distinguished by its caudate-acuminate leaves green on both surfaces, and by its bright yellow or orange-yellow branchlets, and ranging from northeastern Oregon and eastern Washington through Idaho, and from northern Wyoming to southern Colorado, Utah and Nevada.

A variety (var. *lancifolia* Bebb), differing from the typical *S. lasiandra* in the gray or rusty villose pubescence covering the branchlets during their first and sometimes their second season and the lower surface of the young leaves, is distributed from Dawson in the valley of the Yukon River southward to the valley of the upper Nesqually River, Washington, to the valley of the Willamette River (Salem, Oregon), to Santa Cruz, Santa Cruz County, and to the San Bernardino Mountains, California.

9. Salix lucida Muehl. Shining Willow.

Leaves ovate-lanceolate, or narrow lanceolate (f. *angustifolia* Anders.), acuminate and long-pointed at apex, cuneate or rounded at base, finely serrate, 3'–5' long, 1'–1½' wide, covered when they unfold with scattered pale caducous hairs, at maturity coriaceous, smooth and lustrous, dark green above, paler below, with a broad yellow midrib, and slender

Fig. 143

primary veins arcuate and united near the margins; petioles stout, yellow, puberulous, glandular at the apex, with several dark or yellow conspicuous glands, $\frac{1}{4}'-\frac{1}{2}'$ long; stipules nearly semicircular, glandular-serrate, membranaceous, $\frac{1}{8}'-\frac{1}{4}'$ wide, often persistent during the summer. **Flowers:** aments erect, tomentose, on stout puberulous peduncles terminal on short leafy branchlets, the staminate oblong-cylindric, densely flowered, about $1\frac{1}{2}'$ in length, the pistillate slender, elongated, $1\frac{1}{2}'$–$2'$ long, often persistent until late in the season; scales oblong or obovate, rounded, entire, erose or dentate at apex, light yellow, nearly glabrous or coated on the outer surface with pale hairs, often ciliate on the margins; stamens usually 5, with elongated free filaments slightly hairy at base; ovary narrowly cylindric, long-stalked, elongated, glabrous, with nearly sessile emarginate stigmas. **Fruit**: cylindric, lustrous, about $\frac{1}{3}'$ long.

A tree, occasionally $25°$ high, with a short trunk $6'$–$8'$ in diameter, erect branches forming a broad round-topped symmetrical head, and stout glabrous branchlets dark orange color and lustrous in their first season, becoming darker and more or less tinged with red the following year; usually smaller and shrubby in habit. **Winter-buds** narrowly ovoid, acute, light orange-brown, lustrous, about $\frac{1}{4}'$ long. **Bark** thin, smooth, dark brown slightly tinged with red.

Distribution. Banks of streams and swamps; Newfoundland to the shores of Hudson's Bay and northwestward to the valley of the Mackenzie River and the eastern base of the Rocky Mountains, southward to southern Pennsylvania, northeastern Iowa, the Turtle Mountains, North Dakota, and eastern Nebraska; very abundant at the north, rare southward; a variety from extreme northeastern New England and adjacent New Brunswick and Quebec (var. *intonsa* Fernald) is distinguished by its often linear leaves rufous pubescent during the season on the under side of the veins and by its pubescent branchlets; a shrub or tree up to $25°$.

10. Salix taxifolia H. B. K.

Leaves linear-lanceolate, narrowed at the ends, acute, slightly falcate, mucronate at the apex, entire or rarely obscurely dentate above the middle, coated as they unfold with long

Fig. 144

soft white hairs, at maturity pale gray-green, slightly puberulous, $\frac{1}{3}'$–$1\frac{1}{3}'$ long, $\frac{1}{12}'$–$\frac{1}{8}'$ wide, with a slender midrib, thin arcuate veins, and thickened slightly revolute margins; petioles stout, puberulous, rarely $\frac{1}{12}'$ long; stipules ovate, acute, scarious, minute, caducous. **Flowers**: aments densely flowered, oblong-cylindric or subglobose, $\frac{1}{4}'$–$\frac{1}{2}'$ long, terminal, or terminal and axillary on the staminate plant, on short leafy branchlets; scales oblong or obovate, rounded or acute and sometimes apiculate at apex, coated on the outer surface with hoary tomentum and pubescent or glabrous on the inner; stamens 2, with free filaments hairy below the middle; ovary ovoid-conic, short-stalked or subsessile, villose, with nearly sessile deeply emarginate stigmas. **Fruit** cylindric, long-pointed, bright red-brown, more or less villose, short-stalked, about ¼′ long.

A tree, often 40°–50° high, with a trunk 18′ in diameter, erect and drooping branches forming a broad open head, and slender branchlets covered during their first season with hoary tomentum, becoming light reddish or purplish brown and much roughened by the elevated persistent leaf-scars. **Winter-buds** ovoid, acute, dark chestnut-brown, puberulous, about ₁₆′ long and nearly as broad as long. **Bark** of the trunk ¾–1′ thick, light gray-brown, and divided by deep fissures into broad flat ridges covered by minute closely appressed scales.

Distribution. Near El Paso, Texas; southwestern New Mexico, and along mountain streams in southern Arizona; southward through Mexico to Guatemala, and on the Sierra de la Victoria, Lower California.

11. Salix sessilifolia Nutt.

Leaves linear-lanceolate to elliptic-lanceolate, acute or acuminate at apex, cuneate at base, entire or furnished above the middle with a few remote apiculate glandular teeth, bluish green and thickly covered with silky white hairs most abundant on the lower side of the midrib, 1′–2′ long, ½′–¾′ wide, or on vigorous summer shoots often 4′ long and 1¼′ wide; petioles densely villose-pubescent, ₁₆′–⅛′ in length; stipules ovate to lanceolate, acute, entire or denticulate. **Flowers:** aments appearing after the leaves, terminal on leafy branchlets, densely hoary-tomentose, 1½′–2½′ long; scales broadly elliptic, acute or rounded

Fig. 145

at apex, cuneate at base, densely villose-tomentose; stamens 2; filaments villose below the middle; ovary sessile, villose, the stigmas sessile, deeply 2-lobed. **Fruit** ovoid-acuminate, densely villose, pubescent.

A shrub or small tree occasionally 20° high, with short hairy tomentose branchlets.

Distribution. River banks, southwestern British Columbia; Whitcomb County, Washington, and on the Umpqua and Willamette Rivers, western Oregon. Southward passing into

Var. *Hindsiana* Anders., a large shrub with numerous stems often 20° high, differing in its more linear or narrow lanceolate usually entire leaves on longer petioles, smaller aments and pubescent, not tomentose, branchlets; and distributed from the valleys of central California to southwestern Oregon. A shrubby form of *S. sessilifolia* (var. *leucodendroides* Schn.) with longer and broader leaves is common on the banks of streams in southern California.

12. Salix exigua Nutt.

Leaves lanceolate to oblanceolate, acuminate at the ends, often slightly falcate, minutely glandular-serrate above the middle, bluish green and glabrous above, covered below with appressed silky white hairs, $1\frac{1}{2}'$–$3'$ long, $\frac{1}{8}'$–$\frac{1}{4}'$ wide, or on summer shoots sometimes $4\frac{1}{2}'$ long and $1\frac{1}{2}'$ wide; petioles glabrous, $\frac{1}{16}'$ long or less; stipules minute or wanting.　**Flowers:** aments terminal and solitary or terminal and axillary, on leafy glabrous branchlets, $1'$–$2'$ in length; scales hoary pubescent, lanceolate and acute on staminate aments, often wider, obovate and rounded at the apex on pistillate aments; stamens, 2, filaments hairy below the middle; ovary sessile, villose, the stigmatic lobes sessile.　**Fruit** ovoid, acuminate, glabrous.

A shrub with stems 10° or 12° tall, or rarely a tree 25° high, with a trunk 5' or 6' in diameter, thin spreading branches forming a round-topped head, and slender glabrous red-brown branchlets.　**Bark** of the trunk thin, longitudinally fissured, grayish brown.

Fig. 146

Distribution.　Southern Alberta and valley of the Fraser River (Clinton), British Columbia, southward through western Washington and Oregon to San Diego County, California, and southeastern Nevada, and eastward to southern Idaho, central Nevada and western Wyoming (Yellowstone National Park).

Apparently only truly a tree on the banks of the Palouse and other streams of eastern Washington.

Several shrubby forms of *S. exigua* found in Nevada, Arizona, Colorado, western Nebraska and in Lower California are distinguished.

13. Salix longifolia Muehl.　Sand Bar Willow.

Salix fluviatalis Sarg. not Nutt.

Leaves linear-lanceolate, often somewhat falcate, gradually narrowed at the ends, long-pointed, dentate with small remote spreading callous glandular teeth, $2'$–$6'$ long, $\frac{1}{8}'$–$\frac{1}{3}'$ wide, when they unfold coated below with soft lustrous silky hairs, at maturity thin, glabrous, light yellow-green, darker on the upper than on the lower surface, with a yellow midrib, slender arcuate primary veins, and slender reticulate veinlets; petioles grooved, $\frac{1}{8}'$–$\frac{1}{4}'$ long; stipules ovate-lanceolate, foliaceous, about $\frac{1}{4}'$ long, deciduous.　**Flowers:** aments cylindric on leafy branchlets, pubescent, the staminate about $1'$ long, $\frac{1}{3}'$ broad, terminal and axillary, the pistillate elongated, $2'$ or $3'$ long, about $\frac{1}{4}'$ broad; scales obovate-oblong, entire, erose or dentate above the middle, light yellow-green, densely villose on the outer surface, slightly hairy on the inner; stamens 2, with free filaments slightly hairy at the base; ovary oblong-cylindric, acute, short-stalked, glabrous or pubescent, with large sessile deeply lobed stigmas. **Fruit** light brown, glabrous or villose, about ¼′ long.

A tree, usually about 20° high, with a trunk only a few inches in diameter, spreading by stoloniferous roots into broad thickets, short slender erect branches, and slender glabrous light or dark orange-colored or purplish red branchlets, growing darker after their first season; occasionally 60°–70° high, with a trunk 2° in diameter; often a shrub not more than 5°–6° tall. **Winter-buds** narrowly ovoid, acute, chestnut-brown, about ⅛′ long. **Bark** ⅛′–¼′ thick, smooth, dark brown slightly tinged with red and covered with small closely appressed irregularly shaped scales. **Wood** light, soft, light brown tinged with red, with thin light brown sapwood.

Distribution. River banks, sand bars and alluvial flats; shores of Lake St. John, Quebec to Manitoba, and southward through western New England to northeastern Virginia, southern Ohio, Indiana and Illinois, western Kentucky, south Tennessee, to the mouth of the Mississippi River, and westward to southwestern South Dakota, southwestern Wyoming, northeastern Colorado, western Kansas and Oklahoma, and northern Texas.

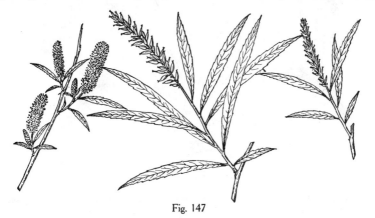

Fig. 147

From central and northwestern Texas to northeastern Mexico and southern New Mexico represented by var. *angustissima* Anders., differing in the absence of a dorsal gland in the male flowers and in the silky pubescence of the young ovary.

In the northern Rocky Mountains region replaced by var. *pedunculata* Anders., differing from the type in its narrower linear leaves, glabrous ovaries and longer pedicels of the fruit, and ranging from western South Dakota and northwestern Wyoming, through eastern Montana, Saskatchewan, and Alberta, to the valley of the Yukon River in the neighborhood of Dawson.

A shrubby form with leaves densely covered with silky pubescence (var. *Wheeleri* Schn.) is distributed from New Brunswick to North Dakota, Nebraska and Beckham County, Oklahoma.

14. Salix lasiolepis Benth. Arroyo Willow.

Leaves oblanceolate to lanceolate-oblong, often inequilateral and occasionally falcate, acute or acuminate or rarely rounded at apex, gradually or abruptly cuneate or rounded at base, entire or remotely serrate, pilose above and coated below with thick hoary tomentum when they unfold, at maturity thick and subcoriaceous, conspicuously reticulate-venulose, dark green and glabrous above, pale or glaucous and pubescent or puberulous below, 3′–6′ long, ½′–1′ wide, with a broad yellow midrib and slender arcuate veins forked and united within the slightly thickened and revolute margins; petioles slender, $\frac{1}{8}'-\frac{1}{2}'$ long; stipules ovate, acute, coated with hoary tomentum, minute and caducous, or sometimes folia-ceous, semilunar, acute or acuminate, entire or denticulate, dark green above, pale below, persistent. **Flowers**: aments erect, cylindric, slightly flexuose, densely flowered, nearly sessile on short tomentose branchlets, $1\frac{1}{2}'$ long, the staminate $\frac{1}{2}'$ thick, and nearly twice as thick as the pistillate; scales oblong-obovate, rounded or acute at the apex, dark-colored, clothed with long crisp white hairs, persistent under the fruit; stamens 2, with elon-gated glabrous filaments more or less united below the middle; ovary narrow, cylindric acute and long-pointed, dark green, glabrous, with a short style and broad nearly sessile stigmas. **Fruit** oblong-cylindric, light reddish brown, about $\frac{1}{4}'$ long.

A tree, 20°–35° high, with a trunk 3′–7′ in diameter, slender erect branches forming a loose open head, and stout branchlets coated at first with hoary tomentum, bright yellow or dark reddish brown and puberulous or pubescent during their first year, becoming darker

Fig. 148

and glabrous in their second season; or often at the north and at high altitudes a low shrub. **Winter-buds** ovoid, acute, compressed, contracted laterally into thin wing-like margins, light brownish yellow, glabrous or puberulous. **Bark** on young stems and on the branches thin, smooth, light gray-brown, becoming on old trunks dark, about $\frac{1}{3}'$ thick, roughened by small lenticels and broken into broad flat irregularly connected ridges. **Wood** light, soft, close-grained, light brown, with thick nearly white sapwood; in southern California often used as fuel.

Distribution. Banks of streams in low moist ground; valley of the Klamath River, California, southward along the foothills of the Sierra Nevada, the central valley, and on the Coast Ranges to southern California; on Santa Catalina Island and on the mountains of southern Arizona; on the Sierra de Laguna, Lower California; occasionally ascending to altitudes of 4000° above the sea.

15. Salix Mackenzieana Barr.

Leaves lanceolate to oblanceolate, or elliptic, long-pointed at apex, cuneate or rounded at base, finely crenately serrate, reddish and pilose with caducous pale hairs when they un-fold, at maturity thin and firm in texture, light green above, pale below, $1\frac{1}{2}'-2'$ long, about $\frac{1}{2}'-\frac{3}{4}'$ wide, on summer shoots, often 4′ long and $1\frac{1}{2}'$ wide, with a slender yellow midrib, arcuate veins, and obscure reticulate veinlets; petioles thin, yellow, about $\frac{1}{3}'$ long; stipules reniform, conspicuously veined, about $\frac{1}{16}'$ broad. **Flowers**: aments densely flowered, gla-brous, erect, often more or less curved, about $1\frac{1}{2}'$ long, terminal on short leafy branchlets; scales oblanceolate, acute, dark-colored; stamens 2, with elongated free glabrous filaments;

ovary cylindric, long-stalked, elongated, gradually narrowed into a short style, with spreading emarginate stigmas. **Fruit** ovoid, acuminate, light brown, about $\frac{1}{3}'$ long; pedicels about $\frac{1}{8}'$ in length.

A small tree, with a slender trunk, upright branches forming a narrow shapely head, and slender branchlets marked with scattered lenticels, glabrous or slightly puberulous and often tinged with red when they first appear, soon becoming yellow and lustrous, growing lighter colored in their second year. **Winter-buds** ovoid, rounded on the back, compressed and acute at the apex, bright orange color, about $\frac{1}{8}'$ long.

Distribution. Borders of streams and swamps; shores of Great Slave Lake southward through the region at the eastern base of the Rocky Mountains to Saskatchewan, northern

Fig. 149

Idaho, and northwestern Wyoming, and to western Nevada (Lake County; *M. S. Bebb*), and on the high Sierra Nevada in Calaveras and Mariposa Counties, California (*W. L. Jepson*).

16. Salix missouriensis Bebb.

Leaves lanceolate or oblanceolate, acuminate and long-pointed at apex, gradually narrowed from above the middle to the cuneate or rounded base, finely glandular-serrate,

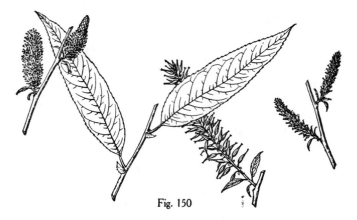

Fig. 150

coated with pale hairs on the lower surface and pilose on the upper surface when they unfold, soon becoming nearly glabrous, at maturity thin and firm, dark green above, pale and often silvery white below, 4'–6' long, 1'–1½' wide, with slender veins often united near the margins and connected by coarse reticulate veinlets; petioles stout, pubescent or tomentose, ½'–¾' long; stipules foliaceous, semicordate, pointed or rarely reniform and obtuse, serrate with incurved teeth, dark green and glabrous on the upper side, coated on the lower with hoary tomentum, reticulate-venulose, often ½' long, deciduous or persistent during the season. **Flowers:** aments oblong-cylindric, densely flowered, appearing early in February on short leafy branchlets, the staminate 1½' long and nearly ½' wide and rather longer than the more slender pistillate aments becoming at maturity lax and 3'–4' long; scales oblong-obovate, light green, and covered on the outer surface with long straight white hairs; stamens 2, with elongated free glabrous filaments; ovary cylindric, short-stalked, beaked, glabrous, with a short style and spreading entire or slightly emarginate stigmas. **Fruit** narrow, long-pointed light reddish brown, ⅓' in length; pedicels about half the length of the scales.

A tree, 40°–50° high, with a tall straight trunk 10'–12' or rarely 18' in diameter, rather slender upright slightly spreading branches forming a narrow open symmetrical head, and slender branchlets marked by small scattered orange-colored lenticels, light green and coated during their first year with thick pale pubescence, becoming reddish brown and glabrous or puberulous in their second winter. **Winter-buds** ovoid, round, or flattened, acute at the apex, reddish brown, hoary-tomentose, nearly 1' long. **Bark** thin, smooth, light gray, slightly tinged with red, and covered with minute closely appressed plate-like scales. **Wood** dark red-brown, with thin pale sapwood; durable, used for fence-posts.

Distribution. Deep sandy alluvial bottom-lands of the Missouri River in southwestern Nebraska to western Missouri; through northeastern Kansas and eastern Oklahoma to Cache Creek, Comanche County (*G. W. Stevens*); and from the neighborhood of St. Louis to southeastern and western Iowa; and to the neighborhood of Olney, Richland County, Illinois (*R. Ridgway*).

17. Salix pyrifolia Anders.

Salix balsamifera Barr.

Leaves ovate to oblong-lanceolate, acute at apex, broad and rounded and usually subcordate at base, finely glandular serrulate, balsamic particularly while young, when they unfold thin, pellucid, red and coated below with long slender caducous hairs, at maturity thin and firm, dark green above, pale and glaucous below, 2'–4' long, 1'–1½' wide,

Fig. 151

with a yellow midrib and conspicuous reticulate veinlets; petioles reddish or yellow, $\frac{1}{3}'-\frac{1}{2}'$ long; stipules often wanting or on vigorous shoots foliaceous, broadly ovate and acute. **Flowers:** aments cylindric, $1'-1\frac{1}{2}'$ long, on short leafy branchlets, the staminate $1'-1\frac{1}{4}'$ long and $\frac{3}{4}'$ in diameter and shorter and broader than the pistillate ament; scales obovate, rose-colored, coated with long white hairs; stamens 2, with free filaments and reddish ultimately yellow anthers; ovary narrow-ovoid, long-stalked, gradually contracted above the middle, with a short style and emarginate stigmas. **Fruit** ovoid-conic, $\frac{1}{4}'$ long, dark orange color; pedicels $\frac{1}{6}'$ in length.

Usually a shrub, often making clumps of crowded slender erect stems generally destitute of branches except near the top, rarely arborescent, with a height of 25°, a trunk $12'-14'$ in diameter, erect branches, and comparatively stout reddish brown branchlets becoming olive-green in their second year and marked with narrow slightly raised leaf-scars. **Winter-buds** acute, much-compressed, bright scarlet, very lustrous, about $\frac{1}{4}'$ long. **Bark** thin, smooth, dull gray.

Distribution. Cold wet bogs; Newfoundland and the coast of Labrador to the valley of the Saskatchewan and the Mackenzie, and British Columbia, and to northern Maine, New Hampshire, Vermont, New York, Michigan, and northeastern South Dakota; reported to become arborescent only near Fort Kent on the St. John River, Aroostook, Maine.

18. Salix amplifolia Cov.

Leaves oval to broadly obovate, rounded or broadly pointed at apex, gradually or abruptly narrowed at the cuneate base, dentate-serrulate or entire, densely villose when they unfold, with long matted white hairs, at maturity nearly glabrous, pale yellow-green above, slightly glaucous below, $2'-2\frac{1}{2}'$ long, $1'-1\frac{1}{2}'$ wide, with a midrib broad and hoary-tomentose toward the base of the leaf and thin and glabrous above the middle; petioles

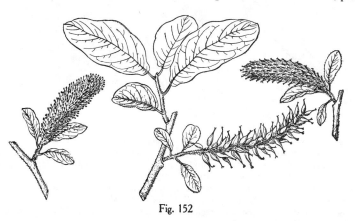

Fig. 152

slender, tomentose. **Flowers:** aments appearing about the middle of June, stout, pedunculate, tomentose, on leafy branchlets, the staminate $1\frac{1}{2}'-2'$ long and shorter than the pistillate; scales oblanceolate or lanceolate, dark brown or nearly black, covered with long pale hairs; stamens 2, with slender elongated glabrous filaments; ovary ovoid-lanceolate, short-stalked, glabrous or slightly pubescent, gradually narrowed into the elongated slender style crowned with a 2-lobed slender stigma. **Fruit** ovoid-lanceolate, glabrous, short-stalked, $\frac{1}{4}'$ long.

A tree, occasionally 25° high, with a trunk a foot in diameter, and stout branchlets conspicuously roughened by the large elevated U-shaped leaf-scars, and marked by occasional pale lenticels, coated at first with thick villose pubescence, becoming during their second and third years dark dull reddish purple.

Distribution. Sand dunes on the shores of Yakutat Bay and Disenchantment Bay, Alaska.

19. Salix alaxensis Cov. Feltleaf Willow.

Leaves elliptic-lanceolate to obovate, acute, acuminate or occasionally rounded at apex, gradually narrowed into a short thick petiole, coated above as they unfold with thin pale deciduous tomentum and covered below with a thick mass of snowy white lustrous hairs persistent on the mature leaves, entire, often somewhat wrinkled, dull yellow-green above, 2′–4′ long, 1′–1½′ wide, with a broad yellow midrib; stipules linear-lanceolate to filiform, entire, ½′–¾′ long, usually persistent until midsummer. **Flowers:** aments appearing in June when the leaves are nearly fully grown, stout, erect, tomentose, stalked, on leafy branchlets, the staminate 1′–1½′ long, much shorter than the pistillate; scales oblong-ovate, rounded at apex, dark-colored, and coated with long silvery white soft hairs; stamens 2, with slender elongated filaments; ovary acuminate, short-stalked, covered with soft pale hairs, gradually narrowed into the elongated slender style, with 2-lobed stigmas. **Fruit** nearly sessile, ovoid, acuminate covered with close dense pale tomentum, ¼′ long.

A tree, sometimes 30° high, with a trunk 4′–6′ in diameter, and stout branchlets thickly

Fig. 153

coated at first with matted white hairs, becoming in their second year glabrous, dark purple, lustrous, marked by large elevated pale scattered lenticels and much roughened by large U-shaped leaf-scars; often shrubby, and in the most exposed situations frequently only a foot or two high, with semiprostrate stems.

Distribution. Coast of Alaska from the Alexander Archipelago to Cape Lisbourne, and eastward to the valley of the Mackenzie River and to the shores of Coronation Gulf; the only arborescent Willow in the coast region west and north of Kadiak Island; attaining its largest size from the Shumagin Islands eastward.

20. Salix Bebbiana Sarg.

Leaves oblong-obovate to oblong-elliptic or lanceolate, acuminate and short-pointed or acute at apex, gradually narrowed and cuneate or rounded at base, remotely and irregularly serrate usually only above the middle, or rarely entire, when they unfold pale gray-green, glabrous or villose, and often tinged with red on the upper surface and coated on the lower with pale tomentum or pubescence, at maturity thick and firm, dull green and glabrous or puberulous above, blue or silvery white and covered with pale rufous pubescence below, especially along the midrib, veins, and conspicuous reticulate veinlets, 1′–3′ long, ½′–1′ wide; petioles slender, often pubescent, reddish, ¼′–½′ long; stipules foliaceous, semicordate, glandular-dentate, sometimes nearly ½′ long on vigorous shoots, deciduous. **Flowers:**

aments terminal on short leafy branchlets; scales ovate or oblong, rounded at apex, broader on the staminate than on the pistillate plant, yellow below, rose color at apex, villose with long pale silky hairs, persistent under the fruit; staminate aments cylindric, obovoid, narrowed at base, densely flowered, $\frac{3}{4}$'–1' long, $\frac{1}{2}$'–1' thick; pistillate aments oblong-cylindric, loosely flowered, 1'–1$\frac{1}{4}$' long, $\frac{1}{2}$' thick; stamens 2, with free glabrous filaments; ovary cylindric, villose; with long silky white hairs, gradually narrowed at apex, with broad sessile entire or emarginate spreading yellow stigmas; pedicel villose, about $\frac{1}{4}$' in length, and about as long as the scale. **Fruit** elongated-cylindric, gradually narrowed into a long thin beak, and raised on a slender stalk sometimes $\frac{1}{8}$' long.

A bushy tree, occasionally 25° high, with a short trunk 6'–8' in diameter, stout ascending branches forming a broad round head, and slender branchlets coated at first with hoary deciduous tomentum, varying during their first winter from reddish purple to dark orange-brown, marked by scattered raised lenticels and roughened by conspicuous elevated leaf-scars, growing lighter-colored and reddish brown in their second year; usually much smaller and often shrubby in habit. **Bark** thin, reddish or olive-green or gray tinged with red, and

Fig. 154

slightly divided by shallow fissures into appressed plate-like scales. **Winter-buds** oblong, gradually narrowed and rounded at apex, full and rounded on the back, bright light chestnut-brown, nearly $\frac{1}{4}$' long.

Distribution. Borders of streams, swamps, and lakes, hillsides, open woods and forest margins, usually in moist rich soil; valley of the St. Lawrence River to the shores of Hudson's Bay, the valley of the Mackenzie River within the Arctic Circle, Cook Inlet, Alaska, and the coast ranges of British Columbia, forming in the region west of Hudson's Bay almost impenetrable thickets, with twisted and often inclining stems; common in all the northern states, ranging southward to Pennsylvania and westward to Minnesota and through the Rocky Mountain region from western Idaho and northern Montana to northern North Dakota, eastern South Dakota, northeastern and central Iowa, and western Nebraska, and southward through Colorado to northern Arizona; ascending as a low shrub in Colorado to an altitude of 10,000°.

21. Salix discolor Muehl. Glaucous Willow.

Leaves lanceolate to elliptic, gradually narrowed at the ends, remotely crenulate-serrate, as they unfold thin, light green often tinged with red, pubescent above and coated with a pale tomentum below, at maturity thick and firm, glabrous, conspicuously reticulate-venulose, bright green above, glaucous or silvery white below, 3'–5' long, $\frac{3}{4}$'–1$\frac{1}{2}$' wide, with a broad yellow midrib and slender arcuate primary veins; petioles slender, $\frac{1}{2}'$–$1'$ long; stipules foliaceous, semilunar, acute, glandular-dentate, about $\frac{1}{4}'$ long, deciduous. **Flowers:** aments appearing late in winter or in very early spring, erect, terminal on short scale-bearing branchlets coated with thick white tomentum, oblong-cylindric, about $1'$ long and $\frac{2}{3}'$ thick, the staminate soft and silky before the flowers open and densely flowered; scales oblong-obovate, dark reddish brown toward the apex, covered on the back with long silky silvery white hairs; stamens 2, with elongated glabrous filaments; ovary oblong-cylindric, narrowed above the middle, villose, with a short distinct style and broad spreading entire stigmas; pedicel glabrous, about twice the length of the scale. **Fruit** cylindric, more or less contracted above the middle, long-pointed, light brown, coated with pale pubescence.

A tree, rarely more than $25°$ high, with a trunk about $1°$ in diameter, stout ascending

Fig. 155

branches forming an open round-topped head, and stout branchlets marked by occasional orange-colored lenticels, dark reddish purple and coated at first with pale deciduous pubescence; more often shrubby, with numerous tall straggling stems. **Winter-buds** semiterete, flattened and acute at the apex, about $\frac{3}{8}'$ long, dark reddish purple and lustrous. **Bark** $\frac{1}{4}'$ thick, light brown tinged with red, and divided by shallow fissures into thin plate-like oblong scales. **Wood** light, soft, close-grained, brown streaked with red, with lighter brown sapwood.

Distribution. Moist meadows and the banks of streams and lakes; Nova Scotia to Manitoba, and southward to Delaware, southern Indiana and Illinois, eastern and southwestern Iowa, the Black Hills of South Dakota, and northeastern Missouri; common.

A form of *Salix discolor* with more densely flowered and more silvery pubescent aments is described as var. *eriocephala* Schn. and a form with loosely flowered aments with less tomentose fruits with longer styles and with narrower leaves as var. *prinoides* Schn.

22. Salix Scouleriana Barr.   Black Willow.

Salix Nuttallii Sarg.

Leaves oblong-obovate to elliptic, acute or abruptly acuminate with a short or long-pointed apex, gradually narrowed and cuneate at the often unsymmetrical base, entire or remotely and irregularly crenately serrate, thin and firm, dark yellow-green and lustrous above, pale or glaucous and glabrous or pilose below, $1\frac{1}{4}'$–$4'$ long, $\frac{1}{2}'$–$1\frac{1}{2}'$ wide, with a broad yellow pubescent midrib and slender veins forked and arcuate within the slightly thickened and revolute margins and connected by conspicuous reticulate veinlets; petioles slender, puberulous, $\frac{1}{4}$–$\frac{1}{2}'$ in length; stipules foliaceous, semilunar, glandular-serrate, $\frac{1}{8}$–$\frac{1}{4}'$ long, caducous. **Flowers**: aments appearing before the leaves, oblong-cylindric, erect, nearly sessile on short tomentose scale-bearing branchlets, the staminate about 1′ long and rather more than $\frac{1}{2}'$ thick, the pistillate $1\frac{1}{2}'$ long, about $\frac{5}{12}'$ thick; scales oblong, narrowed at the ends, dark-colored, covered with long white hairs, persistent under the fruit; stamens 2, with free glabrous filaments; ovary cylindric, short-stalked, with a distinct style and broad emarginate stigmas; pedicels less than half the length of the scale, villose. **Fruit** oblong-ovoid, acuminate, light reddish brown, pale pubescent, about $\frac{1}{3}'$ long.

A tree, occasionally 30° high, with a short trunk rarely exceeding 1° in diameter, slender pendulous branches forming a rather compact round-topped shapely head, and stout branchlets marked by scattered yellow lenticels, coated when they first appear with pale early deciduous pubescence, becoming bright yellow or dark orange color, and in their second year dark red-brown and much roughened by the conspicuous leaf-scars; or more often a shrub. **Winter-buds** ovoid, acute, nearly terete or slightly flattened, with narrow lateral wing-like margins, light or dark orange color, glabrous or pilose at the base, about

Fig. 156

$\frac{1}{4}'$ long. **Bark** thin, dark brown slightly tinged with red, and divided into broad flat ridges. **Wood** light, soft, close-grained, light brown tinged with red, with thick nearly white sapwood.

Distribution. Cook's Inlet, coast of Alaska, and valley of the Yukon River near Dawson southward through western British Columbia to northern California, ranging eastward through Washington and northwestern Oregon to northern Idaho and Montana.

From central California to San Bernardino County represented by the variety *crassijulis* Andr. (S. *brachystachys* Benth.) with shorter and broader obovate leaves rounded at apex, pubescent and tomentose branchlets and larger pubescent winter-buds. A tree sometimes 70° high with a trunk often $2\frac{1}{2}°$ in diameter.

On the high Sierra Nevada eastward to the eastern ranges of the Rocky Mountains of Colorado and to northern New Mexico, northern Wyoming and the Black Hills of South Dakota represented by the var. *flavescens* Schn. A shrub or rarely a small tree with obovate rounded yellowish leaves and branchlets.

23. Salix Hookeriana Barr.

Leaves oblong to oblong-obovate, acute or abruptly acuminate, or rarely rounded and frequently apiculate at apex, gradually narrowed and cuneate or rounded at base, coarsely crenately serrate, especially those on vigorous shoots, or entire, when they unfold villose with pale hairs, or tomentose above and clothed below with silvery white tomentum, at maturity thin and firm, bright yellow-green and lustrous, nearly glabrous or tomentose on the upper surface, pale and glaucous and tomentose or pubescent on the lower surface, especially along the midrib and slender arcuate primary veins and conspicuous reticulate veinlets, 2'–6' long, 1'–1½' wide; petioles stout, tomentose, ¼'–⅓' long. **Flowers:** aments oblong-cylindric, erect, rather lax, often more or less curved, about 1½' long, on short tomentose scale-bearing branchlets, the staminate ⅔' thick and rather thicker than the pistillate; scales oblong-obovate, yellow, coated with long pale hairs, the staminate rounded above and rather shorter than the more acute scales of the pistillate ament persistent under the fruit; stamens 2, with free elongated glabrous filaments; ovary conic, glabrous, stalked, with a slender stalk about one third as long as the scale, gradually narrowed above, with a slender elongated bright red style and broad spreading entire stigmas. **Fruit** oblong-cylindric, narrowed above, about ¼' long.

Fig. 157

A tree, occasionally 30° high, with a trunk about 1° in diameter, and stout branchlets marked by large scattered orange-colored lenticels, covered during their first season with hoary tomentum and rather bright or dark red-brown and pubescent in their second summer; more often shrubby, with numerous stems 4'–8' thick and 15°–20° high; frequently a low bush, with straggling almost prostrate stems. **Winter-buds** ovoid, acute, nearly terete, dark red, coated with pale pubescence, about ¼' long. **Bark** nearly ¼' thick, light red-brown, slightly fissured and divided into closely appressed plate-like scales. **Wood** light, soft, close-grained, light brown tinged with red, with thin nearly white sapwood.

Distribution. Borders of salt marshes and ponds and sandy coast dunes; Vancouver Island southward along the shores of Puget Sound and the Pacific Ocean to southern Oregon.

24. Salix sitchensis Sanson.

Leaves oblong-obovate to oblanceolate, entire or minutely glandular dentate, acute or acuminate, or rounded and short-pointed, or rounded at apex, gradually narrowed and cuneate at base, when they unfold pubescent or tomentose on the upper surface, and coated on the lower with lustrous white silky pubescence or tomentum persistent during the season or sometimes deciduous from the leaves of vigorous young shoots, at maturity thin and firm, dark green, lustrous and glabrous above, with the exception of the pubescent midrib, 2'–5' long, ¾'–1½' wide, with conspicuous slender veins arcuate and united within the margins and prominent reticulate veinlets; petioles stout, pubescent, rarely ½' long; stipules rarely produced, foliaceous, semilunar, acute or rounded at apex, glandular-dentate, coated below with hoary tomentum, often ½' long, caducous. **Flowers:** aments

cylindric, densely flowered, erect on short tomentose leafy branchlets, the staminate
1½′–2′ long and ½′ thick, the pistillate 2½′–3′ long, and ¼′ thick; scales yellow or tawny, the
staminate oblong-obovate, rounded at the apex, covered with long white hairs, much longer
than the more acute pubescent scales of the pistillate ament; stamen 1, with an elongated
glabrous filament, or very rarely 2, with filaments united below the middle or nearly to the
apex; ovary short-stalked, ovoid, conic, acute, pubescent and gradually narrowed into
the elongated style, with entire or slightly emarginate short stigmas. Fruit ovoid, narrowed above, light red-brown, pubescent about ¼′ long.

Fig. 158

A much-branched tree, occasionally 25°–30° high, with a short contorted often inclining
trunk sometimes 1° in diameter, and slender brittle branchlets coated at first with hoary
tomentum, pubescent and tomentose and dark red-brown or orange color during their first
winter, becoming darker, pubescent or glabrous, and sometimes covered with a glaucous
bloom in their second season; more often shrubby and 6°–15° tall. Winter-buds acute,
nearly terete, light red-brown, pubescent or puberulous, about ¼′ long. Bark about ⅛′
thick and broken into irregular closely appressed dark brown scales tinged with red. Wood
light, soft, close-grained, pale red, with thick nearly white sapwood.

Distribution. Banks of streams and in low moist ground; Cook Inlet and Kadiak Island,
Alaska, southward in the neighborhood of the coast to Santa Barbara, California; on the
Marble Creek of the Kaweah River at 6900° altitude (f. *Ralphiana* Jeps.)

VI. MYRICACEÆ.

Aromatic resinous trees and shrubs, with watery juice, terete branches, and small scaly
buds. Leaves alternate, revolute in the bud, serrate, resinous-punctate, persistent in our
species, in falling leaving elevated semiorbicular leaf-scars showing the ends of three nearly
equidistant fibro-vascular bundles. Flowers unisexual, diœcious or monœcious, usually
subtended by minute bractlets, in the axils of the deciduous scales of unisexual or androgynous simple oblong aments from buds in the axils of the leaves of the year, opening in early
spring, the staminate below the pistillate in androgynous aments; staminate, perianth 0;
stamens 4 or many, inserted on the thickened base of the scales of the ament; filaments
slender, united at the base into a short stipe; anthers ovoid, erect, 2-celled, introrse, opening longitudinally; ovary rudimentary or 0; pistillate flowers single or in pairs; ovary sessile, 1-celled; styles short, divided into 2 elongated filiform stigmas stigmatic on the inner
face; ovule solitary, erect from the base of the cell, orthotropous, the micropyle superior.
Fruit a globose or ovoid dry drupe usually covered with wax; nut hard, thick-walled. Seed

erect, with a thin coat, without albumen; embryo straight; cotyledons plano-convex, fleshy; radicle short, superior, turned away from the minute basal hilum.

The family consists of the genus *Myrica* L., of about thirty or forty species of small trees and shrubs, widely distributed through the temperate and warmer parts of both hemispheres. Of the seven North American species three are trees. Wax is obtained from the exudations of the fruit of several species. The bark is astringent, and sometimes used in medicine, in tanning, and as an aniline dye. *Myrica rubra* Sieb and Zucc., of southern Japan and China, is cultivated for its succulent aromatic red fruit.

The generic name is probably from the ancient name of some shrub, possibly the Tamarisk.

CONSPECTUS OF THE NORTH AMERICAN SPECIES.

Flowers diœcious.
    Leaves oblanceolate, usually acute or rarely rounded at apex, mostly coarsely serrate above the middle, yellow-green, coated below with conspicuous orange-colored glands.   **1. M. cerifera** (A, C).
    Leaves usually broadly oblong-obovate, rounded or rarely acute at apex, entire, dark green and lustrous.   **2. M. inodora** (C).
Flowers monœcious; leaves oblanceolate or oblong-lanceolate, sharply serrate, dark green and lustrous.   **3. M. californica** (G).

1. Myrica cerifera L. Wax Myrtle.

Leaves oblanceolate or rarely oblong-lanceolate, acute or rarely gradually narrowed and rounded at apex, cuneate at base, decurrent on short stout petioles, coarsely serrate above the middle or entire, yellow-green, covered above by minute dark glands and below

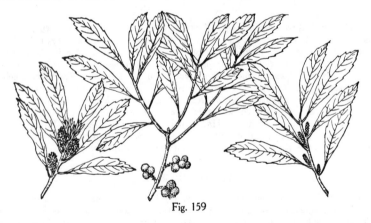

Fig. 159

by bright orange-colored glands, $1\frac{1}{2}'$–$4'$ long and $\frac{1}{4}'$–$\frac{1}{2}'$ wide, with a slender pale midrib often puberulous below, and few obscure arcuate veins, fragrant with a balsamic resinous odor; gradually deciduous at the end of their first year. **Flowers** in small oblong aments, with ovate acute ciliate scales, those of the staminate plant $\frac{1}{2}'$–$\frac{3}{4}'$ long, about twice as long as those of the pistillate plant; stamens few, with oblong slightly obcordate anthers at first tinged with red, becoming yellow; ovary gradually narrowed into 2 slender spreading stigmas longer than its scale. **Fruit** in short spikes, ripening in September and October and persistent on the branches during the winter, irregularly deciduous in the spring and early summer, globose, about $\frac{1}{8}'$ in diameter, slightly papillose, light green, coated with thick pale blue wax; seed pale, minute.

A tree, occasionally 40° high, with a tall trunk 8′–10′ in diameter, or more often a large or small shrub, with slender upright or slightly spreading branches forming a narrow round-topped head, and slender branchlets marked by small pale lenticels, coated at first with loose rufous tomentum and caducous orange-colored glands, bright red-brown or dark brown tinged with gray, usually lustrous and nearly glabrous during their first winter, finally becoming dark brown; generally smaller, frequently shrubby. **Winter-buds** oblong, acute, $\frac{1}{16}′$–$\frac{1}{8}′$ long, with numerous ovate acute imbricated scales, the inner scales becoming nearly $\frac{1}{2}′$ long, and often persistent until the young branch has completed its growth. **Bark** of the trunk $\frac{1}{4}′$ thick, compact, smooth, light gray. **Wood** light, soft and brittle, dark brown, with thin lighter-colored sapwood.

Distribution. In the neighborhood of the coast; Cape May, New Jersey, southern Delaware and Maryland to the keys of southern Florida, and through the Gulf states to the shores of Aranzas Pass, San Patricio County, Texas, ranging inland over the coastal plain of Georgia to the neighborhood of Natchez, Adams County, Mississippi, the valley of the Red River (Natchitoches, Louisiana and Fulton, Arkansas), and to Cherokee County, Texas, and northward to the valley of the Ouachita River, Arkansas; on the Bermuda and Bahama Islands and on several of the Antilles; most abundant and of its largest size on the south Atlantic and Gulf coasts in sandy swamps and pond holes; the most common woody plant and forming great thickets on the Everglades east of Lake Okeechobee, Florida; in the sandy soil of Pine-barrens and on dry arid hills of the interior, often only a few inches in height, var. *pumila* Michx.

2. Myrica inodora W. Bartr. Wax Myrtle.

Leaves broadly oblong-obovate or rarely ovate, rounded or sometimes pointed and occasionally apiculate at apex, narrowed at base, decurrent on short stout petioles, entire or

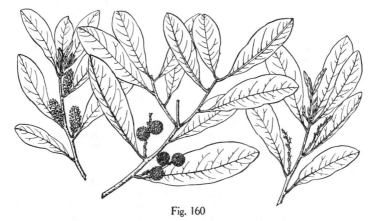

Fig. 160

rarely obscurely toothed toward the apex, thick and coriaceous, glandular-punctate, dark green and very lustrous above, bright green below, 2′–4′ long, $\frac{3}{4}′$–1$\frac{1}{2}′$ wide, with a broad conspicuously glandular midrib slightly pubescent on the lower side, and few remote slender obscure primary veins forked and arcuate near the much-thickened and revolute margins; gradually deciduous from May until midsummer. **Flowers** in aments $\frac{3}{4}′$–1′ long, with ovate acute glandular scales; stamens numerous, with oblong slightly emarginate yellow anthers; pistillate flowers usually in pairs, with an ovate glabrous ovary and slender bright red styles. **Fruit** produced sparingly in elongated spikes, oblong, $\frac{1}{3}′$–$\frac{1}{2}′$ long, papillose, black, and covered with a thin coat of white wax: seed oblong-oval, acute at apex, rounded at base, $\frac{1}{8}′$ long, bright orange-brown, with a pale yellow hilum.

Usually a shrub, with numerous slender stems, occasionally arborescent and 18°–20°

high, with a straight trunk 6°–8° tall and 2′–3′ in diameter, and stout branchlets roughened by small scattered lenticels, coated at first with dense pale tomentum, soon becoming bright red-brown, scurfy, and glabrous or pubescent. **Winter-buds** ovoid, acute, nearly ⅛′ long, with numerous loosely imbricated lanceolate acute red-brown scurfy-pubescent scales. **Bark** thin, smooth, nearly white.

Distribution. Small non-alluvial swamps mostly within fifty miles of the coast, Round Lake, Jackson County, and Apalachicola, and Saint Andrews Bay, Florida; near Mobile and Stockton, Alabama; near Poplarville, Pearl County, Mississippi, and Bogalusa, Washington Parish, Louisiana.

3. Myrica californica Cham. Wax Myrtle.

Leaves oblanceolate to oblong-lanceolate, acute at apex, remotely serrate except at the gradually narrowed base with small incurved teeth, decurrent on a short stout petiole, thin and firm, dark green and lustrous above, yellow-green, glabrous or puberulous and

Fig. 161

marked by minute black glandular dots below, 2′–4′ long, ½′–¾′ wide, with a narrow yellow midrib and numerous obscure primary veins arcuate near the thickened and revolute margins, slightly fragrant, gradually deciduous after the end of their first year. **Flowers** subtended by conspicuous bractlets, those of the two sexes on the same plant; staminate in oblong simple aments often 1′ long, pistillate in shorter aments in the axils of upper leaves, and androgynous aments occurring between the two with staminate flowers at their base and pistillate flowers above, or with staminate flowers also mixed with the pistillate at their apex; scales of the aments ovate, acute, coated with pale tomentum; stamens numerous, with oblong slightly emarginate dark red-purple anthers soon becoming yellow; ovary ovoid, with bright red exserted styles. **Fruit** in short crowded spikes ripening in the early autumn and usually falling during the winter, globose, papillose, dark purple, covered with a thin coat of grayish white wax; **seed** pale reddish brown, minute.

A tree, occasionally 40° high, with a trunk 14′–15′ in diameter, short slender branches forming a narrow compact round-topped head, and stout branchlets coated at first with loose tomentum, dark green or light or dark red-brown, glabrous or pubescent during their first season, becoming in their second year much roughened by the elevated leaf-scars, darker and ultimately ashy gray; usually smaller at the north and toward the northern and southern limits of its range reduced to a low shrub often only 3°–4° tall. **Winter-buds** ovoid, acute, about ¼′ thick, with loosely imbricated ovate acute dark red-brown tomentose scales nearly ½′ long when fully grown and long-persistent on the branch. **Bark** smooth, compact, 1/16′–⅛′ thick, dark gray or light brown on the surface and dark red-brown internally. **Wood** heavy, very hard and strong, brittle, close-grained, light rose color, with thick lighter colored sapwood.

Distribution. Ocean sand-dunes and moist hillsides in the vicinity of the coast from the shores of Puget Sound to the neighborhood of Santa Monica, Los Angeles County, California; of its largest size on the shores of the Bay of San Francisco.

Occasionally used in California as a garden plant.

VII. LEITNERIACEÆ.

A tree or shrub, with pale slightly fissured bark, scaly buds, stout terete pithy branchlets marked by pale conspicuous nearly circular lenticels and by elevated crescent-shaped angled or obscurely 3-lobed leaf-scars, very light soft wood, and thick fleshy stoloniferous yellow roots. **Leaves** involute in the bud, lanceolate to elliptic-lanceolate, acuminate or acute and short-pointed at apex, gradually narrowed at base, entire, with slightly revolute undulate margins, penniveined with remote primary veins arcuate and united near the margins, and conspicuous reticulate veinlets, petiolate, at first coated on the lower surface and on the petioles with thick pale tomentum and puberulous on the upper surface, thick and firm at maturity, bright green and lustrous above, pale and villose-pubescent below, deciduous. **Flowers** in unisexual aments, with ovate acute concave tomentose scales, the male and female on different plants, opening in early spring from buds formed the previous autumn and covered with acute chestnut-brown hairy scales; the staminate clustered near the end of the branches, their scales bearing on the thickened stipe a ring of 3–12 stamens, with slender incurved filaments and oblong light yellow introrse 2-celled anthers opening longitudinally; perianth 0; pistillate aments scattered, shorter and more slender than the staminate, their scales bearing in their axils a short-stalked pistil surrounded by a rudimentary perianth of small gland-fringed scales, the 2 larger lateral, the others next the axis of the inflorescence; ovary superior, pubescent, 1-celled, with an elongated flattened style inserted obliquely, curving inward above the middle in anthesis, grooved and stigmatic on the inner face; ovule solitary, attached laterally, ascending, semianatropous; micropyle directed upward. **Fruit** an oblong compressed dry drupe thick and rounded on the ventral, narrowed on the dorsal edge, rounded at base, thin and pointed at apex, chestnut-brown, rugose, with a thick dry exocarp closely investing the thin-walled light brown crustaceous rugose nutlet. **Seed** flattened, rounded at the ends, light brown, marked on the thick edge with the oblong nearly black hilum; embryo erect, surrounded by thin fleshy albumen; cotyledons oblong, flattened; radicle superior, conical, short, and fleshy.

The family consists of a single genus, *Leitneria* Chapm., with one species of the southern United States, named for a German naturalist killed in Florida during the Seminole War.

1. Leitneria floridana Chapm. Cork Wood.

Leaves 4′–6′ long, 1½′–2½′ wide, with petioles 1′–2′ in length. **Flowers** opening at the end of February or early in March; staminate aments 1′–1¼′ long, ¼′ thick, and twice as long as the pistillate. **Fruit** solitary or in clusters of 2–4, ripening when the leaves are about half grown, ¾′ long, ¼′ wide.

A shrub or small tree, occasionally 20° high, with a slender straight trunk 4′–5′ in diameter above the swollen gradually tapering base, spreading branches forming a loose open head, and branchlets at first light reddish brown and thickly coated with gradually deciduous hairs, becoming in their first winter glabrous or puberulous, especially toward the ends, and dark red-brown. **Winter-buds:** terminal broad, conic, ⅛′ long, covered by 10 or 12 oblong nearly triangular closely imbricated scales coated with pale tomentum and long-persistent at the base of the branch; lateral scattered, ovoid, flattened. **Bark** about 1/16′ thick, dark gray faintly tinged with brown, divided by shallow fissures into narrow rounded ridges. **Wood** soft, exceedingly light, close-grained, the layers of annual growth hardly distinguishable, pale yellow, without trace of heartwood; occasionally used for the floats of fishing-nets.

Distribution. Borders of swamps of the lower Altamaha River, Georgia (*C. L. Boynton*);

muddy saline shores on the coast of the Gulf of Mexico near Apalachicola, Florida; swampy prairies, Velasco (*E. J. Palmer*), and swamps of the Brazos River near Columbia, Brazoria County, Texas; Varner, Lincoln County (*B. F. Bush*), and Moark, Clay County

Fig. 162

(*E. J. Palmer*) Arkansas; and in Butler and Dunklin Counties, southeastern Missouri, here sometimes occupying muddy sloughs of considerable extent to the exclusion of other woody plants.

VIII. JUGLANDACEÆ.

Aromatic trees, with watery juice, terete branchlets, scaly buds, the lateral buds often superposed, 2–3 together, and alternate unequally pinnate deciduous leaves with elongated grooved petioles and without stipules, the leaflets increasing in size from the lowest upward, penniveined, sessile, short-stalked or the terminal usually long-stalked. Flowers monœcious, opening after the unfolding of the leaves, the staminate in lateral aments and composed of a 3–6-lobed calyx in the axil of and adnate to an ovate acute bract, and numerous stamens inserted on the inner and lower face of the calyx in 2 or several rows, with short distinct filaments and oblong anthers opening longitudinally; the pistillate in a spike terminal on a branch of the year and composed ot a 1–3-celled ovary subtended by an involucre fre : toward the apex and formed by the union of an anterior bract and 2 lateral bractlets, a 1 or 4-lobed calyx inserted on the ovary, a short style with 2 plumose stigmas stigmatic on the inner face, and a solitary erect orthotropous ovule. Fruit drupaceous. the exocarp (husk) indehiscent or 4-valved, inclosing a thick- or thin-shelled nut divided by partitions extending inward from the shell, and like the shell more or less penetrated by internal longitudinal cavities often filled with dry powder. Seed solitary, 2-lobed from the apex nearly to the middle, light brown, its coat thin, of 2 layers, without albumen; cotyledons fleshy and oily, sinuose or corrugated, 2-lobed; radicle short, superior, filling the apex of the nut. Of the six genera of the Walnut family two occur in North America.

CONSPECTUS OF THE NORTH AMERICAN GENERA.

Aments of staminate flowers simple; husk of the fruit indehiscent; nut sculptured; pith in plates.   1. **Juglans**.

Aments of staminate flowers branched; husk of the fruit 4-valved; nut not sculptured; pith solid.   **2. Carya**

1. JUGLANS L. Walnut.

Trees, with furrowed scaly bark, durable dark-colored wood, stout branchlets, laminate pith, terminal buds with 2 pairs of opposite more or less open scales often obscurely pinnate at apex, those of the inner pair more or less leaf-like, and obtuse slightly flattened axillary buds formed before midsummer and covered with 4 ovate rounded scales, closed or open during winter. Leaves with numerous leaflets, and terete petioles leaving in falling large conspicuous elevated obcordate 3-lobed leaf-scars displaying 3 equidistant U-shaped clusters of dark fibro-vascular bundle-scars; leaflets conduplicate in the bud, ovate, acute or acuminate, mostly unequal at base, with veins arcuate and united near the margins. Aments of the staminate flowers many-flowered, elongated, solitary or in pairs from lower axillary buds of upper nodes, appearing from between persistent bud-scales in the autumn and remaining during the winter as short cones covered by the closely imbricated bracts of the flowers; calyx 3–6-lobed, its bract free only at the apex; stamens 8–40, in 2 or several ranks, their anthers surmounted by a conspicuous dilated truncate or lobed connective; pistillate flowers in few-flowered spikes, their involucre villose, free only at the apex and variously cut into a laciniate border shorter than the erect calyx-lobes; ovary rarely of 3 carpels; stigmas club-shaped, elongated, fimbriately plumose. Fruit ovoid, globose or pyriform, round or obscurely 4-angled, with a fleshy indehiscent glabrate or hirsute husk; nut ovoid or globose, more or less flattened, hard, thick-walled, longitudinally and irregularly rugose, the valves alternate with the cotyledons, and more or less ribbed along the dorsal sutures and in some species also on the marginal sutures. Seed more or less compressed, gradually narrowed or broad and deeply lobed at base, with conspicuous dark veins radiating from the apex and from the minute basal hilum.

Juglans is confined to temperate North America, the West Indies, South America from Venezuela to Peru, western and northern China, Korea, Manchuria, Japan, and Formosa. Eleven species are known. Of exotic species *Juglans regia* L., an inhabitant probably originally of China, is cultivated in the middle Atlantic and southern states and largely in California for its edible nuts, which are an important article of commerce. The wood of several species is valued for the interior finish of houses and for furniture.

Juglans, from Jupiter and glands, is the classical name of the Walnut-tree.

CONSPECTUS OF THE NORTH AMERICAN SPECIES.

Fruit racemose; nut 4-ribbed at the sutures with smaller intermediate ribs, 2-celled at the base; heartwood light brown; leaflets 11–17, oblong-lanceolate.　　1. **J. cinerea** (A, C).
Fruit usually solitary or in pairs; nut without sutural ribs, 4-celled at the base; heartwood dark brown.
　　Nuts prominently and irregularly ridged with often interrupted ridges; leaflets 15–23, ovate-lanceolate.　　　　　　　　　　　　　　　2. **J. nigra** (A, C)
　　Nuts more or less deeply longitudinally grooved.
　　　Nuts up to 1½′ in diameter; leaflets 9–13, rarely 19, oblong-lanceolate to ovate, acuminate, coarsely serrate.　　　　　　　　　　　3. **J. major** (F, H).
　　　Nuts not more than ¾′ in diameter.
　　　　Leaflets 17–23, narrow-lanceolate, long-pointed.　　　4. **J. rupestris** (C).
　　　　Leaflets 11–15 or rarely 19, oblong-lanceolate, acute or acuminate, the lower often rounded at the apex.　　　　　　　　　　5. **J. californica** (G).
　　Nuts obscurely or not at all grooved, up to 2′ in diameter; leaflets 15–19, ovate-lanceolate to lanceolate, long-pointed.　　　　　　　6. **J. Hindsii** (G).

1. Juglans cinerea L. Butternut.

Leaves 15′–30′ long, with stout pubescent petioles, and 11–17 oblong-lanceolate acute or acuminate leaflets 2′–3′ long, 1½′–2′ wide, finely serrate except at the unequal rounded base, glandular and sticky as they unfold, at maturity thin, yellow-green and rugose above, pale and soft-pubescent below; turning yellow or brown and falling early in the autumn. **Flowers:** staminate in thick aments $3'$–$5'$ long; calyx usually 6-lobed, light yellow-green, puberulous on the outer surface, $\frac{1}{4}'$ long, its bract rusty-pubescent, acute at apex; stamens 8–12, with nearly sessile dark brown anthers and slightly lobed connectives; pistillate in 6–8-flowered spikes, constricted above the middle, about $\frac{1}{8}'$ long, its bract and bractlets coated with sticky white or pink glandular hairs and rather shorter than the linear-lanceolate calyx-lobes; stigmas bright red, $\frac{1}{2}'$ long. **Fruit** in 3–5 fruited drooping clusters, obscurely 2 or rarely 4-ridged, ovoid-oblong, coated with rusty clammy matted hairs, $1\frac{1}{2}'$–$2\frac{1}{2}'$ long with a thick husk; **nut** ovoid, abruptly contracted and acuminate at apex, with 4 prominent and 4 narrow less conspicuous ribs, light brown, deeply sculptured between the ribs into thin broad irregular longitudinal plates, 2-celled at the base and 1-celled above the middle; **seed** sweet, very oily, soon becoming rancid.

A tree, occasionally 100° high, with a tall straight trunk 2°–3° in diameter, and sometimes free of branches for half its height; more frequently divided 20° or 30° above the ground into many stout limbs spreading horizontally and forming a broad low symmetrical

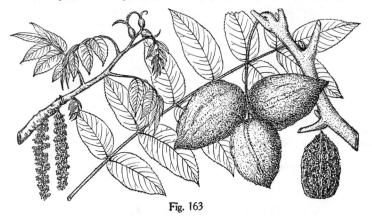

Fig. 163

round-topped head, and dark orange-brown or bright green rather lustrous branchlets coated at first with rufous pubescence, covered more or less thickly with pale lenticels, gradually becoming puberulous, brown tinged with red or orange in their second year and marked by light gray leaf-scars with large black fibro-vascular bundle-scars and elevated bands of pale tomentum separating them from the lowest axillary bud. **Winter-buds:** terminal $\frac{1}{2}'$–$\frac{2}{3}'$ long, $\frac{1}{4}'$ wide, flattened and obliquely truncate at apex, their outer scales coated with short pale pubescence; axillary buds ovoid, flattened, rounded at apex, $\frac{1}{8}'$ long, covered with rusty brown or pale pubescence. **Bark** of young stems and of the branches smooth and light gray, becoming on old trees $\frac{3}{4}'$–$1'$ thick, light brown, deeply divided into broad ridges separating on the surface into small appressed plate-like scales. **Wood** light, soft, not strong, coarse-grained, light brown, turning darker with exposure, with thin light-colored sapwood composed of 5 or 6 layers of annual growth; largely employed in the interior finish of houses, and for furniture. The inner bark possesses mild cathartic properties. Sugar is made from the sap, and the green husks of the fruit are used to dye cloth yellow or orange color.

Distribution. Rich moist soil near the banks of streams and on low rocky hills, southern New Brunswick to the valley of the St. Lawrence River in Ontario, the northern peninsular of Michigan, southern Minnesota, eastern South Dakota, eastern Iowa, southeastern Nebraska, and southward to central Kansas, northern Arkansas, Delaware, eastern

Virginia, and on the Appalachian Mountains and their foothills to northern Georgia; in northern Alabama, southern Illinois and western Tennessee; most abundant northward. Occasionally cultivated.

× *Juglans quadrangulata* A. Rehd., a natural hybrid of *J. cinerea* and the so-called English Walnut (*J. regia*) is not uncommon in eastern Massachusetts, and a hybrid of *J. cinerea* with the Japanese *J. Sieboldiana* Maxm. has appeared in the United States.

2. Juglans nigra L. Black Walnut.

Leaves 1°–2° long, with pubescent petioles, and 15–23 ovate-lanceolate leaflets 3′–3½′ long, 1′–1¼′ wide, long-pointed, sharply serrate except at the more or less rounded often unequal base, thin, bright yellow-green, lustrous and glabrous above, soft-pubescent below, especially along the slender midrib and primary veins; turning bright clear yellow in the autumn before falling. **Flowers:** staminate in stout puberulous aments 3′–5′ long, calyx rotund, 6-lobed, with nearly orbicular lobes concave and pubescent on the outer surface, its bract ¼′ long, nearly triangular, coated with rusty brown or pale tomentum; stamens 20–30, arranged in many series, with nearly sessile purple and truncate connectives; pistillate in 2–5 flowered spikes, ovoid, gradually narrowed at the apex, ¼′ long, their bract and bractlets coated below with pale glandular hairs and green and

Fig. 164

puberulous above, sometimes irregularly cut into a laciniate border, or reduced to an obscure ring just below the apex of the ovary; calyx-lobes ovate, acute, light green, puberulous on the outer, glabrous or pilose on the inner surface; stigmas yellow-green tinged on the margins with red, ½′–¾′ long. **Fruit** solitary or in pairs, globose, oblong and pointed at apex, or slightly pyriform, light yellow-green, roughened by clusters of short pale articulate hairs, 1½′–2′ in diameter, with a thick husk; **nut** oval or oblong, slightly flattened, 1⅛′–1½′ in diameter, dark brown tinged with red, deeply divided on the outer surface into thin or thick often interrupted irregular ridges, 4-celled at base and slightly 2-celled at the apex; **seed** sweet, soon becoming rancid.

A tree, frequently 100° and occasionally 150° high, with a straight trunk often clear of branches for 50°–60° and 4°–6° in diameter, thick limbs spreading gradually and forming a comparatively narrow shapely round-topped head of mostly upright rigid branches, and stout branchlets covered at first with pale or rusty matted hairs, dull orange-brown and pilose or puberulous during their first winter, marked by raised conspicuous orange-colored lenticels and elevated pale leaf-scars, gradually growing darker and ultimately light brown. **Winter-buds:** terminal ovoid, slightly flattened, obliquely rounded at apex, coated with pale silky tomentum, ⅓′ long, with usually 4 obscurely pinnate scales; axillary

¹⁄₈' long, tomentose, their outer scales opening at the apex during the winter. **Bark of** young stems and branches light brown and covered with thin scales, becoming on old trees 2'-3' thick, dark brown slightly tinged with red, and deeply divided into broad rounded ridges broken on the surface into thick appressed scales. **Wood** heavy, hard, strong, rather coarse-grained, very durable, rich dark brown, with thin lighter colored sapwood of 10–20 layers of annual growth; largely used in cabinet-making, the interior finish of houses, gun-stocks, air-planes, and in boat and shipbuilding.

Distribution. Rich bottom-lands and fertile hillsides, western Massachusetts to southern Ontario, southern Michigan, southeastern Minnesota, central and northern Nebraska, central Kansas, eastern Oklahoma, and southward to western Florida, central Alabama and Mississippi, Louisiana, and the valley of the San Antonio River, Texas; most abundant in the region west of the Alleghany Mountains, and of its largest size on the western slopes of the high mountains of North Carolina and Tennessee, and on the fertile river bottom-lands of southern Illinois and Indiana, southwestern Arkansas, and Oklahoma; largely destroyed for its valuable timber, and now rare.

Occasionally cultivated as an ornamental tree in the eastern United States, and in western and central Europe. × *Juglans intermedia* Carr., a natural hybrid, of *J. nigra* with the so-called English Walnut (*J. regia*) has appeared in the United States and Europe, and on the banks of the James River in Virginia has grown to a larger size than any other recorded Walnut-tree. In California a hybrid, known as " Royal," between *J. nigra* and *J. Hindsii* has been artificially produced.

3. Juglans major Hell. Nogal.

Juglans rupestris var. *major* Torr.

Juglans rupestris Sarg., in part, not Engelm.

Leaves 8'-12' long, with slender pubescent petioles and rachis, and 9–13 rarely 19 oblong-lanceolate to ovate acuminate often slightly falcate coarsely serrate leaflets cuneate or rounded at base, coated when they first appear with scurfy pubescence, soon becoming

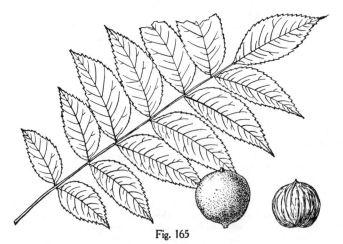

Fig. 165

glabrous, or at maturity slightly pubescent on the midrib below, 3'-4', or those of the lower pairs 1½'-2' long, and 1'-1½' wide, thin, yellow-green, with a thin conspicuous yellow midrib and primary veins. **Flowers:** staminate in slender puberulous or pubescent aments 8'-10' long; calyx nearly orbicular, long-stalked, pale yellow-green, 5 or 6-lobed, the lobes ovate, acute, hoary pubescent on the outer surface, their bract acute, coated with thick pale tomentum; stamens 30–40, with nearly sessile yellow anthers, and slightly divided connectives; pistillate not seen. **Fruit** subglobose to slightly ovoid or oblong, abruptly contracted at apex into a short point (*J. elæopyren Dode*), densely tomentose when half grown, $1'-1\frac{1}{2}'$ in diameter, with a thin husk covered with close rufous pubescence; **nut** dark brown or black, slightly compressed, usually rather broader than high, or ovoid, rounded or bluntly acute at apex, rounded and sometimes depressed at base, longitudinally grooved with broad deep grooves, thick shelled; **seed** small and sweet.

A tree sometimes 50° high, with a straight trunk occasionally 3°–4° in diameter, or divided at the ground into several large stems, stout branches forming a narrow head, and slender branchlets thickly coated when they first appear with rufous pubescence, becoming red-brown, pubescent or puberulous and marked by many small pale lenticels at the end of their first season and ashy gray the following year.

Distribution. Near Fort Worth, Tarrant Country, Texas (*E. J. Palmer*); and banks of streams in the cañons of central and southern New Mexico and Arizona, and on Oak Creek near Flagstaff, Arizona on the Colorado plateau (*P. Lowell*).

4. Juglans rupestris Engelm. Walnut.

Leaves 9′–12′ long, with slender pubescent or puberulous petioles and rachis, and 13–23 narrow lanceolate long-pointed usually falcate finely serrate leaflets entire or nearly entire on their incurved margins, cuneate or rounded at base, thin, light green, glabrous or pubes-

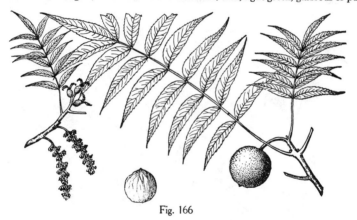

Fig. 166

cent on the midrib below, 2′–3′ long and $\frac{1}{3}-\frac{2}{3}'$ wide. **Flowers:** staminate in slender aments, 3′–4′ long, pubescent when they first appear, becoming glabrous; calyx short-stalked, nearly orbicular, light yellow-green, puberulous on the outer surface, 3–5-lobed with rounded lobes, their bracts ovate-lanceolate, coated with hoary tomentum; stamens about 20, with nearly sessile yellow anthers and slightly lobed connectives; pistillate flowers oblong, narrowed at the ends, thickly coated with rufous pubescence; bract and bractlets irregularly divided into a laciniate border rather shorter than the ovate acute calyx-lobes; stigmas green tinged with red, $\frac{1}{3}'$ long. **Fruit** globose or subglobose, tipped with the persistent remnants of the calyx, pubescent or puberulous with rusty hairs, $\frac{1}{2}'-\frac{3}{4}'$ in diameter, with a thin husk; **nut** subglobose to slightly ovoid, sometimes obscurely 4-ridged from the apex nearly to the middle (*J. subrupestris* Dode), deeply grooved with longitudinal simple or forked grooves, 4-celled at base, 2-celled at apex, thick shelled; **seed** small and sweet.

A shrubby round-headed tree occasionally 20°–30° high, with a short generally leaning trunk 18'-30' in diameter, usually branching from near the ground, and slender branchlets coated with pale scurfy pubescence often persistent for two or three years, orange-red and marked by pale lenticels in their first winter and ultimately ashy gray; often a shrub with clustered stems only a few feet high. **Winter-buds:** terminal, $\frac{1}{4}$'-$\frac{1}{2}$' long, compressed, narrowed and often oblique at apex, covered with pale tomentum; axillary $\frac{1}{8}$' long, compressed, coated with pale pubescence. **Wood** heavy, hard, not strong, rich dark brown with thick white sapwood. The beauty of the veneers obtained from the stumps of the large trees is fast causing their destruction.

Distribution. Limestone banks of the streams of southern, central and western Texas from the Rio Grande to the mountains in the western part of the state; western Oklahoma (Kiowa, Greer, Beckham, Rogel, Mills and Ellis Counties); southeastern New Mexico.

Occasionally cultivated in the eastern United States and in Europe, and hardy as far north as eastern Massachusetts; interesting as producing the smallest nuts of any of the known Walnut-trees.

5. Juglans californica S. Wats.

Leaves 6'-9' long, with glandular pubescent petioles and rachis, and 11-15, rarely 19, oblong-lanceolate acute or acuminate glabrous finely serrate leaflets cuneate or rounded at base, 1'-2$\frac{1}{2}$' long and $\frac{1}{3}$'-$\frac{3}{4}$' wide, the lower often rounded at apex. **Flowers:** staminate in slender glabrous or puberulous aments 2'-3' long; calyx puberulous on the outer surface with acute or rarely rounded lobes, its bract, puberulous; stamens 30–40, with yellow anthers and short connectives bifid at apex; the pistillate subglobose, puberulous; stigmas

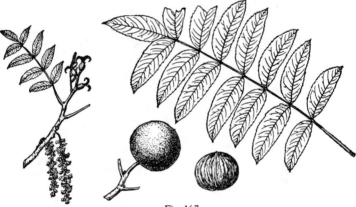

Fig. 167

yellow, $\frac{1}{2}$' long. **Fruit** globose, $\frac{1}{3}$'-$\frac{3}{4}$' in diameter, with a thin dark-colored puberulous husk; **nut** nearly globose, deeply grooved with longitudinal grooves, thick shelled, 4-celled at base, imperfectly 2-celled at apex; **seed** small and sweet.

A shrubby round-headed tree or shrub generally 12°-20°, rarely 40°-50° high, usually branching from the ground or with a short trunk 1° or rarely 2°-3° in diameter, and slender branchlets coated with scurfy rufous pubescence when they first appear, glabrous, reddish brown and marked by pale lenticels at the end of their first season and gray the following year. **Winter-buds** coated with rufous tomentum.

Distribution. Banks of streams and bottom-lands in the southern California coast region from Santa Barbara and the Ojai valley to San Fernando and the Sierra Santa Monica, and along the foothills of the Sierra Madre to the San Bernardino Mountains and southward to the Sierra Santa Anna.

A curious seminal variety (var. *quercina* Babcock) with compound leaves composed of 3 oval leaflets, the terminal long-stalked and 2 or 3 times larger than the lateral leaflets, is occasionally cultivated in California.

6. Juglans Hindsii Rehd.

Juglans californica S. Wats., in part.

Juglans californica var. *Hindsii* Jep.

Leaves 9′–12′ long, with slender villose pubescent petioles and rachis, and 15–19, usually 19, ovate-lanceolate to lanceolate long-pointed often slightly falcate leaflets, serrate with remote teeth except toward the usually rounded cuneate or rarely cordate base, thin, puberulous above while young, becoming bright green, lustrous and glabrous on the upper

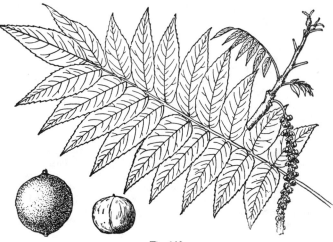

Fig. 168

surface, below furnished with conspicuous tufts of pale hairs, and villose-pubescent along the midrib and primary veins, 2½′–4′ long and ¾′–1′ wide. **Flowers:** staminate in slender glabrous or sparingly villose aments 3′–5′ long; calyx elongated, coated like its bract with scurfy pubescence, divided into 5 or 6 acute lobes; stamens 30–40, with short connectives bifid at apex; ovary of the pistillate flower oblong-ovoid, thickly covered with villose pubescence, ⅛′ long, the border of the thin bract and bractlets much shorter than the calyx-lobes; stigma yellow. **Fruit** globose, 1¼′–2′ in diameter, with a thin dark-colored husk covered with short soft pubescence; **nut** nearly globose, somewhat flattened at the ends, faintly grooved with remote longitudinal depressions, thick shelled; **seed** small and sweet.

A tree usually 30°–40°, occasionally 75° high, with a tall trunk 1°–2° in diameter, stout pendulous branches forming a narrow round-topped head, and comparatively slender branchlets thickly coated when they first appear with villose pubescence, reddish brown and puberulous, and marked by pale lenticels and small elevated obscurely 3-lobed leaf scars during their first winter, becoming darker and nearly glabrous in their second year. **Winter-buds** coated with hoary tomentum; terminal acute, compressed, more or less enlarged at apex, ¼′–⅓′ long; axillary usually solitary, nearly globose, about 1/10′ in diameter. **Bark** gray-brown, smoothish, longitudinally fissured into narrow plates. **Wood** heavy, hard, rather coarse-grained, dark brown often mottled, with thick pale sapwood of from 8 to 10 layers of annual growth.

Distribution. Coast region of central California; banks of the lower Sacramento River; along streams near the western base of Mt. Diablo, and on eastern slope of the Napa Range near Atlas Peak east of Napa Valley; near Loyalton in the Sierra Valley.

Often cultivated in California as a shade tree and as stock on which to graft varieties of *Juglans regia* L., and rarely in the eastern states and in Europe. In California, a hybrid known as "Paradox" between *J. Hindsii* and *J. regia* has been artificially produced.

2. CARYA NUTT. Hickory.

Hicoria Rafn.

Trees, with smooth gray bark becoming on old trunks rough or scaly, strong hard tough brown heartwood, pale sapwood and tough terete flexible branchlets, solid pith, buds covered with few valvate or with numerous imbricated scales, the axillary buds much smaller than the terminal. Leaves often glandular-dotted, their petioles sometimes persistent on the branches during the winter, and in falling leaving large elevated oblong or semiorbicular more or less 3-lobed emarginate leaf-scars displaying small marginal clusters and central radiating lines of dark fibro-vascular bundle-scars; leaflets involute in the bud, ovate or obovate, usually acuminate, thick and firm, serrate, mostly unequal at base, with veins forked and running to the margins; turning clear bright yellow in the autumn. Aments of the staminate flowers ternate, slender, solitary or fascicled in the axils of leaves of the previous or rarely of the current year, or at the base of branches of the year from the inner scales of the terminal bud, the lateral branches in the axils of lanceolate acute persistent bracts; calyx usually 2 rarely 3-lobed, its bract free nearly to the base and usually much longer than the ovate rounded or acuminate calyx-lobes; stamens 3–10, in 2 or 3 series, their anthers ovate-oblong, emarginate or divided at apex, yellow or red, pilose or hirsute, as long or longer than their slender connectives; pistillate flowers sessile, in 2–10-flowered spikes, with a perianth-like involucre, slightly 4-ridged, unequally 4-lobed at apex, villose and covered on the outer surface with yellow scales more or less persistent on the fruit, the bract much longer than the bractlets and the single calyx-lobe; stigmas short, papillose-stigmatic. Fruit ovoid, globose or pyriform, with a thin or thick husk becoming hard and woody at maturity, 4-valved, the sutures alternate with those of the nut, sometimes more or less broadly winged, splitting to the base or to the middle; nut oblong, obovoid or subglobose, acute, acuminate, or rounded at apex, tipped by the hardened remnants of the style, narrowed and usually rounded at base, cylindric, or compressed contrary to the valves, the shell thin and brittle or thick, hard, and bony, smooth or variously rugose or ridged on the outer surface, 4-celled at base, 2-celled at apex. Seed compressed, variously grooved on the back of the flat or concave lobes, sweet or bitter.

Carya is confined to the temperate region of eastern North America from the valley of the St. Lawrence River to the highlands of Mexico, and to southern China where one species occurs. Of the seventeen species, fifteen inhabit the territory of the United States.

The generic name is from Καρύα an ancient name of the Walnut.

CONSPECTUS OF THE SPECIES OF THE UNITED STATES.

Bud-scales valvate, the inner strap-shaped and only occasionally slightly accrescent; fruit more or less broadly winged at the sutures; the thin partitions of the nut containing cavities filled with dark astringent powder (absent in 3 and 5).

Shell of the nut thin and brittle; leaflets more or less falcate.

　　Aments of staminate flowers nearly sessile, usually on branches of the previous year: lobes of the seed entire or slightly notched at apex.

　　　　Leaflets 9–17; nut ovoid-oblong, cylindric; seed sweet.　　　1. C. pecan (A, C).

　　　　Leaflets 7–13; nut oblong, compressed; seed bitter.　　　2. C. texana (C).

　　Aments of staminate flowers pedunculate, on branches of the year or of the previous year; lobes of the bitter seed deeply 2-lobed.

Leaflets 7–9; nut cylindric or slightly compressed.   3. **C. cordiformis** (A, C).

Leaflets 7–13; nut compressed, usually conspicuously wrinkled. 4. **C. aquatica** (C).

Shell of the ellipsoidal cylindric nut thick and hard; lobes of the sweet seed deeply 2-lobed; leaflets 7–9, occasionally 5, rarely slightly falcate; aments of staminate flowers long-pedunculate at the base of branches of the year.   5. **C. myristicæformis** (C).

Bud-scales imbricated, the inner becoming much enlarged and often highly colored; aments of staminate flowers on peduncles from the base of branches of the year, rarely from the axils of leaves; fruit usually without wings; partitions of the nut thick without cavities filled with astringent powder; seed sweet, its lobes deeply 2-lobed.

Branchlets usually stout (slender in 7); involucre $\frac{1}{4}$'–$\frac{1}{2}$' in thickness, opening freely to the base.

Bark on old trunks separating into long, broad, loosely attached plates; nuts pale.

Branchlets light red-brown; shell of the nut thin.

Leaflets 5 or rarely 7, obovate to ovate, acute or acuminate; nut much compressed, often long-pointed at apex; branchlets glabrous or pubescent. 6. **C. ovata** (A, C).

Leaflets 5, lanceolate, acuminate; nut little compressed, acute at apex; branchlets slender, glabrous.   7. **C. carolinæ-septentrionalis** (C).

Branchlets pale orange color, pubescent; leaflets usually 7–9; shell of the nut thick. 8. **C. laciniosa** (A, C).

Bark not scaly, on old trunks dark, deeply ridged; leaflets 7–9, often subcoriaceous, pubescent below; nut reddish brown, often long-pointed, thick shelled; branchlets pubescent.   9. **C. alba** (A, C).

Branchlets slender; leaves 5–7-foliolate; involucre of the fruit tardily dehiscent to the middle, indehiscent or opening freely to the base; shell of the nut thick, bark close, (sometimes scaly in 13).

Branchlets and leaves not covered when they first appear with rusty brown pubescence.

Involucre of the fruit 3–5.5 mm. in thickness, opening freely to the base, leaves usually 7-foliolate; winter-buds pubescent.

Leaflets hoary tomentose below in early spring, slightly pubescent at maturity; petioles and rachis glabrous; fruit broad-obovoid; branchlets glabrous. 10. **C. leiodermis** (C).

Leaflets covered in early spring with silvery scales, pale and pubescent below during the season; petioles and rachis more or less thickly covered with fascicled hairs; fruit ellipsoidal to obovoid or globose; branchlets glabrous or slightly pubescent.   11. **C. pallida** (A, C).

Involucre of the fruit 1–3 mm. in thickness; winter-buds glabrous or puberulous.

Leaves 5, rarely 7-foliolate, glabrous or rarely slightly pubescent; fruit obovoid, often narrowed below into a stipitate base, the involucre indehiscent or tardily dehiscent.   12. **C. glabra** (A, C).

Leaves generally 7-foliolate, glabrous or rarely pubescent; fruit ellipsoidal, subglobose or obovoid, the involucre opening freely to the base; bark often more or less scaly.   13. **C. ovalis** (A, C).

Branchlets and leaves densely covered when they first appear with rusty brown pubescence; leaflets usually 5–7; winter-buds rusty pubescent.

Fruit obovoid; the involucre 2–3 mm. in thickness; peduncles of the aments of staminate flowers often from the axils of leaves; branchlets soon becoming glabrous.   14. **C. floridana** (C).

Fruit subglobose to broadly obovoid, ellipsoidal or pyriform, the involucre on the different varieties 2–13 mm. in thickness; branchlets pubescent through their first season.   15. **C. Buckleyi** (A, C).

1. Carya pecan Engl. & Graebn.   Pecan.

Leaves 12'–20' long, with slender glabrous or pubescent petioles, and 9–17 lanceolate to oblong-lanceolate more or less falcate long-pointed coarsely often doubly serrate leaflets rounded or cuneate at the unequal base, sessile, except the terminal leaflet, or short-stalked, dark yellow-green and glabrous or pilose above, and pale and glabrous or pubescent below, 4'–8' long, 1'–3' wide, with a narrow yellow midrib and conspicuous veins. **Flowers:** staminate in slender puberulous clustered aments 3'–5' long, from buds formed in the axils of leaves of the previous year or occasionally on shoots of the year, sessile or short-stalked, light yellow-green and hirsute on the outer surface, with broadly ovate acute lobes rather shorter than the oblong or obovate bract; stamens 5' or 6'; anthers yellow, slightly villose; pistillate in few or many flowered spikes, oblong, narrowed at the ends, slightly 4-angled and coated with yellow scurfy pubescence. **Fruit** in clusters of 3–11, pointed at apex, rounded at the narrowed base, 4-winged and angled, 1'–2½' long, ½'–1' broad, dark brown and more or less thickly covered with yellow scales, with a thin, brittle husk splitting at maturity nearly to the base and often persistent on the branch during the winter after the discharge of the nut; **nut** ovoid to ellipsoidal, nearly cylindric or slightly 4-angled toward the pointed apex, rounded and usually apiculate at base, bright reddish brown, with irreg-

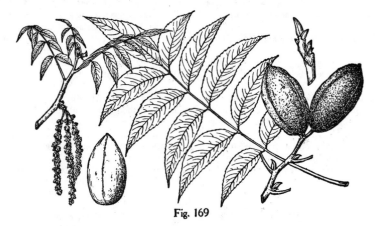

Fig. 169

ular black markings with a thin shell and papery partitions; **seed** sweet, red-brown, its nearly flat lobes grooved from near the base to the apex by 2 deep longitudinal grooves.

A tree, 100°–180° high, with a tall massive trunk occasionally 6° or 7° in diameter above its enlarged and buttressed base, stout slightly spreading branches forming in the forest a narrow symmetrical and inversely pyramidal head, or with abundant room a broad round-topped crown, and branchlets at first slightly tinged with red and coated with loose pale tomentum, becoming glabrous or puberulous in their first winter, and marked by numerous oblong orange-colored lenticels and by large oblong concave leaf-scars with a broad thin membranaceous border surrounding the lower axillary bud. **Winter-buds** acute, compressed, covered with clusters of bright yellow articulate hairs and pale tomentum; terminal ½' long; axillary ovoid, often stalked, especially the large upper bud. **Bark** 1'–1½' thick, light brown tinged with red, and deeply and irregularly divided into narrow forked ridges broken on the surface into thick appressed scales. **Wood** heavy, hard, not strong, brittle, coarse-grained, light brown tinged with red, with thin light brown sapwood; less valuable than that of most Hickories, and used chiefly for fuel, and occasionally in the manufacture of wagons and agricultural implements. The nuts, which vary in size and shape and in the thickness of their shells and in the quality of the kernels, are an important article of commerce.

Distribution. Low rich ground in the neighborhood of streams; in the valley of the Mississippi River, Iowa (Clinton and Muscatine Counties), southern Illinois, southwestern

Indiana (Sullivan and Spencer Counties), western Kentucky and Tennessee, western Mississippi and Louisiana, extreme western and southwestern Missouri (Jackson County southward, common only on the Marais de Cygne River), eastern Kansas to Kickapoo Island in the Missouri River near Fort Leavenworth, Oklahoma to the valley of the Salt Fork of the Arkansas River (near Alva, Woods County) and to creek valleys near Cache, Comanche County (*G. W. Stevens*), through Arkansas; and in Texas to the valley of the Devil's River and to that of Warder's Creek, Hardiman County; reappearing on the mountains of Mexico; most abundant and of its largest size in southern Arkansas and eastern Texas.

Largely cultivated in the Southern States, in many selected varieties, for its valuable nuts.

2. Carya texana Schn. Bitter Pecan.

Leaves 10′–12′ long, with slender petioles, and 7–13 lanceolate acuminate finely serrate leaflets, hoary-tomentose when they unfold, and more or less villose in the autumn, thin and firm, dark yellow-green and nearly glabrous above, pale yellow-green and puberulous below, 3′–5′ long, about 1½′ wide, the terminal leaflet gradually narrowed to the acute base and short-stalked, the lateral often falcate, unsymmetrical at the base, subsessile or short-

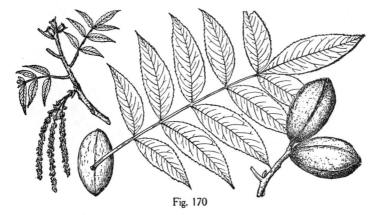

Fig. 170

stalked. **Flowers:** staminate in villose aments 2′–3′ long, light yellow-green and villose on the outer surface, with oblong-ovate rounded lobes; pistillate in few fruited spikes, oblong, slightly 4-angled, villose. **Fruit** oblong or oblong-obovoid, apiculate at apex, slightly 4-winged at base, dark brown, more or less covered with yellow scales, 1½′–2′ long, with a thin husk; **nut** oblong-ovoid or oblong-obovoid, compressed, acute at the ends, short-pointed at apex, apiculate at base, obscurely 4-angled, bright red-brown, rough and pitted, with a thin brittle shell, thin papery walls, and a low basal ventral partition; **seed** very bitter, bright red-brown, flattened, its lobes rounded and slightly divided at apex, longitudinally grooved and deeply penetrated on the outer face by the prominent reticulated folds of the inner surface of the shell of the nut.

A tree, sometimes 100° high on the bottoms of the Brazos River, with a tall straight trunk 3° in diameter, and ascending branches, or on the borders of prairies in low wet woods usually 15°–25° tall, with a short trunk 8′–10′ in diameter, small spreading branches forming a narrow round-topped head, and slender branchlets coated at first with thick hoary tomentum sometimes persistent until the autumn, bright red-brown and marked by occasional large pale lenticels during their first winter and by the large concave obcordate leaf-scars nearly surrounding the lowest axillary bud, becoming darker in their second season and dark or light gray-brown in their third year. **Winter-buds** covered with light yellow articulate hairs; the terminal oblong, acute, or acuminate, somewhat compressed, about $\frac{1}{4}'$ long, and rather longer than the upper lateral bud. **Bark** $\frac{1}{2}'-\frac{3}{4}'$ thick, light reddish brown, and roughened by closely appressed variously shaped plate-like scales. **Wood** close-grained, tough and strong, light red-brown, with pale brown sapwood.

Distribution. Bottom-lands and low wet woods; valley of the lower Brazos River, Texas; near Lake Charles, Calcasieu Parish, and Laurel Hill, West Feliciana Parish, Louisiana; near Natchez, Adams County, Mississippi; valley of the Arkansas River (Arkansas Post, Arkansas County, and Van Buren, Crawford County), Arkansas.

3. Carya cordiformis K. Koch. Pignut. Bitternut.

Leaves 6'–10' long, with slender pubescent or hirsute petioles, and 7–9 lanceolate to ovate-lanceolate or obovate long-pointed sessile leaflets coarsely serrate except at the equally or unequally cuneate or subcordate base, thin and firm, dark yellow-green and glabrous above, lighter and pubescent below, especially along the midrib, 4'–6' long, $\frac{3}{4}'-1\frac{1}{4}'$ wide, or occasionally 2'–4' wide (var. *latifolia* Sarg.). **Flowers:** staminate in slightly

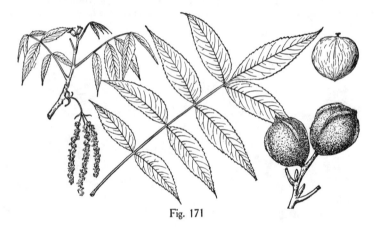

Fig. 171

pubescent aments, 3'–4' long, coated with rufous hairs like its ovate acute bract; stamens 4, with yellow anthers deeply emarginate and villose at apex; pistillate in 1 or 2-flowered spikes, slightly 4-angled, covered with yellow scurfy tomentum. **Fruit** cylindric or slightly compressed, $\frac{3}{4}'-1\frac{1}{2}'$ long, obovoid to subglobose, or oblong and acute at apex (var. *elongata* Ashe), 4-winged from the apex to about the middle, with a thin puberulous husk, more or less thickly coated with small yellow scales; **nut** ovoid or oblong, often broader than long, compressed and marked at base with dark lines along the sutures and alternate with them, depressed or obcordate, and abruptly contracted into a long or short point at apex, gray tinged with red or light reddish brown, with a thin brittle shell; **seed** bright reddish brown, very bitter, much compressed, deeply rugose, with irregular cross-folds.

A tree, often 100° high, with a tall straight trunk 2°–3° in diameter, stout spreading branches forming a broad handsome head, and slender branchlets marked by oblong pale lenticels, bright green and covered more or less thickly with rusty hairs when they first appear, reddish brown and glabrous or puberulous during their first summer, reddish brown and lustrous during the winter and ultimately light gray, with small elevated obscurely 3-lobed obcordate leaf-scars. **Winter-buds** compressed, scurfy pubescent, bright yellow; terminal $\frac{1}{3}'-\frac{3}{4}'$ long, oblique at apex, with 2 pairs of scales; lateral 2-angled, often stalked, $\frac{1}{8}'-\frac{1}{4}'$ long, with ovate pointed slightly accrescent scales keeled on the back. **Bark** $\frac{1}{3}'-\frac{3}{4}'$ thick, light brown tinged with red, and broken into thin plate-like scales separating on the surface into small thin flakes. **Wood** heavy, very hard, strong, tough, close-grained, dark brown, with thick light brown or often nearly white sapwood; largely used for hoops and ox-yokes, and for fuel.

Distribution. Low wet woods near the borders of streams and swamps or on high rolling uplands often remote from streams, southern Maine to Quebec and Ontario, the northern shores of the Lower Peninsula of Michigan, northern Minnesota, southeastern Nebraska, eastern Kansas, eastern Oklahoma, and southward to northwestern Florida, Dallas County, Alabama, West Feliciana Parish, Louisiana, and eastern Texas; generally distributed, but not very abundant in all the central states east and west of the Appalachian Mountains; ranging farther north than the other species, and growing to its largest size on the bottomlands of the lower Ohio basin; the common Hickory of Iowa, Nebraska, and Kansas. Very common in West Feliciana Parish, and up to 170 feet in height (*R. S. Cocks*).

A natural hybrid, × *C. Brownii* Sarg. of *C. cordiformis* with *C. pecan*, with characters intermediate between those of its supposed parents, occurs on bottom-land of the Arkansas River near Van Buren, Crawford County, Arkansas; Missouri (Richards, Vernon County) and Kansas (Arkansas City, Cowley County). Probably of the same parentage is the so-called Galloway Nut found in Hamilton County, Ohio. Another hybrid, × *C. Brownii* var. *varians* Sarg., probably of the same parentage also, occurs near Van Buren, Arkansas, and near Natchez, Mississippi, × *C. Laneyi* Sarg., a natural hybrid evidently of *C. cordiformis* with *C. ovata*, has been found in Rochester, New York, and trees considered varieties of the same hybrid, var. *chateaugayensis* Sarg., occur near the mouth of the Chateaugay River, Province of Quebec, and at Summertown, Ontario.

4. Carya aquatica Nutt. Water Hickory.

Leaves 9′–15′ long, with slender dark red puberulous or tomentose petioles, and 7–13 ovate-lanceolate long-pointed falcate leaflets symmetrical and rounded or cuneate and unsymmetrical and oblique at base, finely or coarsely serrate, sessile or stalked, 3′–5′ long,

Fig. 172

$\frac{1}{2}′$–$1\frac{1}{2}′$ wide, covered with yellow glandular dots, thin, dark green above, brown and lustrous or tomentose on the lower surface, especially on the slender midrib and primary veins, the terminal leaflet more or less decurrent by its wedge-shaped base on a slender stalk or rarely nearly sessile. **Flowers:** staminate in solitary or fascicled hirsute aments $2\frac{1}{2}′$–3′ long, covered like their bract with yellow glandular pubescence; stamens 6, with yellow puberulous antlers; pistillate in several flowered spikes, oblong, slightly flattened, 4-angled, glandular-pubescent. **Fruit** often in 3 or 4-fruited clusters, much compressed, usually broadest above the middle, rounded at the slightly narrowed base, rounded or abruptly narrowed at apex, conspicuously 4-winged, dark brown or nearly black, covered more or less thickly with bright yellow scales, $1\frac{1}{2}'$ long, $1'-1\frac{1}{4}'$ wide, with a thin brittle husk splitting tardily and usually only to the middle; **nut** flattened, slightly obovoid, nearly as broad as long, rounded and abruptly short-pointed at apex, rounded at the narrow base, 4-angled and ridged, dark reddish brown, and longitudinally and very irregularly wrinkled, with a thin shell; **seed** oblong, compressed, dark brown, irregularly and usually longitudinally furrowed, very bitter.

A tree, occasionally 80°–100° high, with a trunk rarely exceeding 2° in diameter, slender upright branches forming a narrow head, and slender dark reddish brown or ashy gray lustrous branchlets marked by numerous pale lenticels, at first slightly glandular and coated with loose pale tomentum, glabrous or puberulous during the summer, and marked during the winter by small nearly oval or obscurely 3-lobed slightly elevated leaf-scars, growing dark red-brown and ultimately gray. **Winter-buds** slightly flattened, acute, dark reddish brown, covered with caducous yellow scales; terminal $\frac{1}{8}'-\frac{1}{4}'$ long, often villose; axillary much smaller, frequently nearly sessile, often solitary. **Bark** $\frac{1}{2}'-\frac{2}{3}'$ thick, separating freely into long loose plate-like light brown scales tinged with red. **Wood** heavy, strong, close-grained, rather brittle, dark brown, with thick light-colored or often nearly white sapwood; occasionally used for fencing and fuel.

Distribution. River swamps often inundated during a considerable part of the year from southeastern Virginia southward through the coast regions to the shores of Indian River and the valley of the Suwanee River, Florida, through the maritime portions of the Gulf states to the valley of the Brazos River, Texas, and northward through western Louisiana to southeastern Missouri, and to northeastern Louisiana, western Mississippi, and southern Illinois; passing into the var. *australis* Sarg. with narrower leaflets, smaller ellipsoidal fruit, pale red-brown nuts without longitudinal wrinkles, and with close not scaly bark of the trunk. A large tree in dry sandy soil; high banks of the St. John's River, near San Mateo, Putnam County, near Jupiter, Palm Beach County, banks of the Caloosahatchee River at Alva and La Belle, Lee County, and Old Town, Dixie County, Florida; near Marshall, Harrison County, Texas.

5. Carya myristicæformis Nutt.   Nutmeg Hickory.

Leaves $7'-14'$ long, with slender terete scurfy-pubescent petioles, and 7–9, occasionally 5, ovate-lanceolate to broadly obovate acute leaflets usually equally or sometimes unequally cuneate or rounded at the narrow base, coarsely serrate, short-stalked or nearly

Fig. 173

sessile, thin and firm, dark green above, more or less pubescent or nearly glabrous and sil-very white and very lustrous below, 4′–5′ long, 1′–1½′ wide, with a pale scurfy pubescent midrib; changing late in the season to bright golden-bronze color and then very conspicu-ous. **Flowers:** staminate in aments 3′–4′ long and coated like the ovate-oblong acute bract and calyx of the flower with dark brown scurfy pubescence; stamens 6, with yellow anthers; pistillate oblong, narrowed at the ends, slightly 4-angled, covered with thick brown scurfy pubescence. **Fruit** usually solitary, ellipsoidal or slightly obovoid, 4-ridged to the base, with broad thick ridges, 1½′ long, coated with yellow-brown scurfy pubescence, the husk not more than $\frac{1}{32}$′ thick, splitting nearly to the base; **nut** ellipsoidal or some-times slightly obovoid, 1′ long, ¾′ broad, rounded and apiculate at the ends, smooth, dark reddish brown, and marked by longitudinal broken bands of small gray spots covering the entire surface at the ends with a thick hard and bony shell, a thick partition, and a low thin dorsal division; **seed** sweet, small, dark brown; the lobes deeply 2-lobed at apex.

A tree, 80°–100° high, with a tall straight trunk often 2° in diameter, stout slightly spreading branches forming a comparatively narrow rather open head, and slender branch-lets coated with lustrous golden or brown scales often persistent until the second year, light brown or ashy gray during their first winter, ultimately dark reddish brown, and marked by small scattered pale lenticels and small oval emarginate elevated leaf-scars. **Winter-buds** covered with thick brown scurvy pubescence; terminal ⅛′–¼′ long, ovoid, rather obtuse; axillary much smaller, acute, slightly flattened, sessile or short-stalked, often solitary. **Bark** ½′–¾′ thick, dark brown tinged with red, and broken irregularly into small thin appressed scales. **Wood** hard, very strong, tough, close-grained, light brown, with thick lighter colored sapwood of 80–90 layers of annual growth.

Distribution. Banks of rivers and swamps in rich moist soil or rarely on higher ground; eastern South Carolina, central Alabama, eastern, and northwestern (bluffs of the Yazoo River at Yazoo City) Mississippi, southern and central Arkansas northward to Faulkner County, western Louisiana, southeastern Oklahoma to Clear Boggy Creek, western Choc-taw County, and in Beaumont County, Texas; on the mountains of northeastern Mexico; rare and local; abundant only near Selma, Alabama, and in southern Arkansas.

6. Carya ovata K. Koch. Shellbark Hickory. Shagbark Hickory.

Leaves 8′–14′ long, with stout glabrous or pubescent petioles, and 5 or rarely 7 ovate to ovate-lanceolate or obovate leaflets, acuminate or rarely rounded at apex, more or less

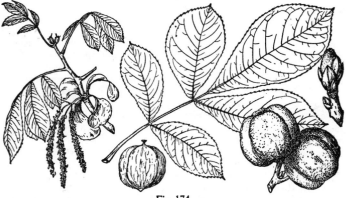

Fig. 174

thickly ciliate on the margins, finely serrate except toward the usually cuneate base, dark yellow-green and glabrous above, paler, glabrous and lustrous or puberulous below, the terminal leaflet decurrent on a slender stalk, 5′–7′ long, 2′–3′ wide, rather larger than the sessile or short-stalked upper leaflets, and two or three times as large as those of the lowest pair. **Flowers:** staminate opening after the leaves have grown nearly to their full size, in slender light green glandular-hirsute aments $4'-5'$ long, glandular-hirsute, their elongated ovate-lanceolate acute bract two or three times as long as the ovate concave rounded or acute calyx-lobes; stamens 4, with yellow or red anthers hirsute above the middle; pistillate in 2–5-flowered spikes, $\frac{1}{3}'$ long, clothed with rusty tomentum. **Fruit** solitary or in pairs, subglobose, rather longer than broad or slightly obovoid, depressed at apex, dark reddish brown or nearly black at maturity, roughened by small pale lenticels, glabrous or pilose, $1'-2\frac{1}{2}'$ long, the husk, $\frac{1}{8}'-\frac{1}{2}'$ thick, splitting freely to the base; **nut** oblong, nearly twice as long as broad, or obovoid and broader than long, compressed, prominently or obscurely 4-ridged and angled, acute and gradually or abruptly narrowed or rounded or nearly truncate at apex, gradually narrowed and rounded at base, pale or nearly white, with a usually thin shell; **seed** light brown, lustrous, sweet, with an aromatic flavor.

A tree, $70°–90°$ and occasionally $120°$ high, with a tall straight trunk $3°–4°$ in diameter, in the forest often free of branches for $50°–60°$ above the ground and then divided into a few small limbs forming a narrow head, or with more space sometimes dividing near the ground or at half the height of the tree into stout slightly spreading limbs, forming a narrow inversely conic round-topped head of more or less pendulous branches, and stout branchlets marked with oblong pale lenticels, covered at first with caducous brown scurf and coated with pale glandular pubescence, soon bright reddish brown, and lustrous, glabrous or pubescent, growing dark gray in their second year and ultimately light gray, and marked by pale and slightly elevated ovate semiorbicular or obscurely 3-lobed leaf-scars. **Winter-buds:** terminal broadly ovoid, rather obtuse, $\frac{1}{2}'-\frac{3}{4}'$ long, $\frac{1}{3}'-\frac{1}{2}'$ broad, the 3 or 4 outer scales nearly triangular, acute, dark brown, pubescent and hirsute on the outer surface, the exterior scales often abruptly narrowed into long rigid points and deciduous before the unfolding of the leaves, the inner scales lustrous, covered with resinous glands, yellow-green often tinged with red, oblong-obovate, pointed, becoming $2\frac{1}{2}'-3'$ long and $\frac{1}{2}'$ broad, usually persistent until after the fall of the staminate aments; axillary buds coated at first with thick white tomentum, becoming $\frac{1}{3}'-\frac{1}{2}'$ long when fully grown. **Bark** light gray, $\frac{3}{4}'-1'$ thick, separating in thick plates often a foot or more long and $6'-8'$ wide, and more or less closely attached to the trunk by the middle, giving it the shaggy appearance to which this tree owes its common name. **Wood** heavy, very hard and strong, tough, close-grained, flexible, light brown, with thin nearly white sapwood; largely used in the manufacture of agricultural implements, carriages, wagons, and for axe-handles, baskets, and fuel. The nut is the common Hickory nut of commerce.

Distribution. Low hills and the neighborhood of streams and swamps in rich deep moderately moist soil; southern Maine to the valley of the St. Lawrence River near Montreal, along the northern shores of Lakes Erie and Ontario to central Michigan, central Wisconsin, southeastern Minnesota, eastern Iowa and southeastern Nebraska, and southward to western Florida, northern Alabama and Mississippi, and to eastern Kansas, eastern Oklahoma, and eastern Texas; ranging further north than other Hickories with the exception of *C. cordiformis;* and in the Carolinas ascending to $3000°$ above the sea in valleys on the western slope of the Blue Ridge. Variable in the size and shape of the nut and in the character and amount of pubescence on the leaves and branchlets. These varieties are distinguished: var. *Nuttallii* Sarg., with nuts rounded, obcordate or rarely pointed at apex, rounded or abruptly pointed at base, much compressed, and only about $\frac{3}{5}'$ long and $\frac{2}{5}'-\frac{1}{2}'$ broad; not rare and widely distributed northward. Var. *complanata* Sarg., with oblong-obovoid fruit and broadly obovoid much compressed slightly angled nuts cuneate at base and rounded, truncate or slightly obcordate at apex; a single tree on the Drushel Farm near Mt. Hope, Holmes County, Ohio. Var. *ellipsoidalis* Sarg., with ellipsoidal much compressed nuts abruptly long-pointed at apex, and slender reddish branchlets; near Hannibal, Marion County, and Oakwood, Rolles County, northeastern Missouri, and Indian River, Lewis County, and near Rochester, Monroe County, New York. Var. *pubescens* Sarg., differing in the dense pubescence of pale fascicled hairs on the young branchlets, and on the petioles, rachis and under surface of the leaflets; bottoms of the

Savannah River, Calhoun Falls, Abbeville County, South Carolina, bottoms of Little River, Walker County, Georgia, Chattanooga Creek, Hamilton County, Tennessee, Valley Head, DeKalb County, Alabama, and Columbus, Lowndes County, Starkville, Oktibbeha County, and Brookville, Noxubee County, Mississippi. More distinct is

Carya ovata var. fraxinifolia Sarg.

Leaves 7'–9' long, with slender glabrous or puberulous petioles and 5 lanceolate to slightly oblanceolate acuminate finely serrate leaflets glabrous except on the under side of the midrib, the terminal leaflet 4'–7' long and $1\frac{1}{2}$'–1' wide, the lateral sessile, unsymmetri-

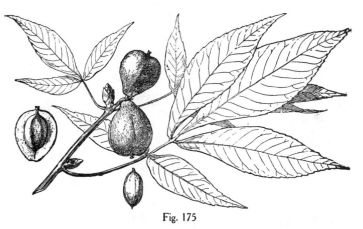

Fig. 175

cal at base, those of the upper pair often larger than the terminal leaflet, those of the lower pair 2'–$2\frac{1}{2}$' long and 1'–$1\frac{1}{4}$' wide. **Flowers** as in the species. **Fruit** obovoid, usually rounded at apex, compressed, about $1\frac{1}{4}$' long, the husk splitting freely to the base, $\frac{1}{6}$'–$\frac{1}{5}$' in thickness; **nut** much compressed, rounded at the ends, prominently angled.

A large tree with bark separating in long loose plates, and slender reddish glabrous or puberulous branchlets.

Distribution. Near Rochester, Monroe County, New York; common; near Kingston, Ontario, and westward through Ohio and Indiana; at Keosauqua, Van Buren County, Iowa, and near Myers, Osage County, Oklahoma.

7. Carya carolinæ-septentrionalis Engl. & Graebn. Shagbark Hickory.

Leaves 4'–8' long, with slender glabrous petioles, and usually 5 but occasionally 3 lanceolate long-pointed leaflets gradually narrowed at the acuminate symmetrical or unsymmetrical base, coarsely serrate, ciliate with long white hairs as the leaves unfold, thin, dark green above, pale yellow-green and lustrous below, the upper leaflets 3'–4' long, 1'–$1\frac{1}{2}$' wide, and about twice as large as those of the lower pair, turning dull brown or yellow-brown some time before falling. **Flowers:** staminate in slightly villose aments, glandular-hirsute on the outer surface, with linear elongated acuminate villose bracts; stamens 4; anthers puberulous; pistillate usually in 2-flowered spikes, oblong and covered with clustered golden hairs, their bract linear and ciliate on the margins. **Fruit** broader than high, or short-oblong, slightly depressed at apex, $\frac{3}{4}$'–$1\frac{1}{2}$' wide, dark red-brown, roughened by small pale lenticels, the husk $\frac{1}{6}$'–$\frac{3}{8}$' thick, splitting freely almost to the base; **nut** ovoid, compressed, prominently 4-angled, acute at ends, nearly white or pale brown, with a thin shell; **seed** light brown, sweet.

A tree, on moist bottom-lands sometimes 80° tall, with a trunk 2°–3° in diameter, and short small branches forming a narrow oblong head, or on dry hillsides usually not more than 20°–30° tall, with a trunk generally not exceeding a foot in diameter, and slender red-brown branchlets marked by numerous small pale lenticels and by the small low truncate or slightly obcordate leaf-scars, becoming ultimately dull gray-brown. **Winter-buds:** terminal ovoid, gradually narrowed to the obtuse apex, about $\frac{1}{4}'$ long, with glabrous bright red-brown and lustrous acute and apiculate strongly keeled spreading outer scales, the inner scales becoming when fully grown bright yellow, long-pointed, and sometimes 2'

Fig. 176

long; axillary buds oblong, obtuse, not more than $\frac{1}{16}'$ long. **Bark** light gray, $\frac{1}{4}'-\frac{3}{4}'$ thick, separating freely into thick plates often a foot or more long, 3' or 4' wide, and long-persistent, giving to the trunk the shaggy appearance of the northern Shagbark Hickory. **Wood** hard, strong, very tough, light reddish brown, with thin nearly white sapwood.

Distribution. Dry limestone hills, river-bottoms and low flat often inundated woods, frequently in clay soil; central North Carolina to northern Georgia, and through western North Carolina to eastern Tennessee, eastern Mississippi, and in Cullman and Dallas Counties, Alabama.

8. Carya laciniosa Loud. Big Shellbark. King Nut.

Leaves 15'–22' long, with stout glabrous or pubescent petioles often persistent on the branches during the winter, and 5–9, usually 7, ovate to oblong-lanceolate or broadly obovate leaflets, the upper 5'–9' long and 3'–5' wide and generally two or three times as large as those of the lowest pair, usually equilateral and acuminate at apex, equally or unequally cuneate or rounded at the often oblique base, finely serrate, sessile or short-stalked, dark green and lustrous above, pale yellow-green or bronzy brown and covered with soft pubescence below. **Flowers:** staminate in aments 5'–8' long, glabrous or covered with rufous scurfy tomentum, with linear-lanceolate acute bracts two or three times as long as the broad rounded calyx-lobes; anthers hirsute, yellow, more or less deeply emarginate; pistillate in 2–5-flowered spikes, oblong-ovoid, about twice as long as broad, slightly angled, clothed with pale tomentum, their linear bracts acute much longer than the nearly triangular bractlets and calyx-lobe. **Fruit** solitary or in pairs, ellipsoidal, ovoid or subglobose, depressed at apex, roughened with minute orange-colored lenticels, downy or glabrous, light orange-colored or dark chestnut-brown at maturity, $1\frac{3}{4}'-2\frac{1}{2}'$ long and $1\frac{1}{4}'-2'$ broad, with a hard woody husk pale and marked on the inside with dark delicate veins, and $\frac{1}{4}'-\frac{1}{3}'$ thick; **nut** ellipsoidal or slightly obovoid, longer than broad or sometimes broader than long, flattened and rounded at the ends, or gradually narrowed and rounded at base and occasionally acuminate at apex, more or less compressed, prominently 4-ridged and angled or often 6-ridged, furnished at base with a stout long point, light yellow to reddish brown, $1\frac{1}{4}'-2\frac{1}{2}'$ long and $1\frac{1}{2}'-1\frac{3}{4}'$ wide, with a hard bony shell sometimes $\frac{1}{4}'$ thick; **seed** light chestnut-brown, very sweet.

A tree, occasionally 120° high, with a straight slender trunk often free of branches for more than half its height and rarely exceeding 3° in diameter, comparatively small spreading branches forming a narrow oblong head, and stout dark or light orange-colored branchlets at first pilose or covered with pale or rufous pubescence or tomentum, roughened by scattered elevated long pale lenticels, orange-brown and glabrous or puberulous during their first winter, and marked by oblong 3-lobed emarginate leaf-scars. **Winter-buds:** terminal ovoid, rather obtuse, sometimes 1' long and $\frac{2}{3}'$ wide, and three or four times as large as the axillary buds, usually covered by 11 or 12 scales, the outer dark brown, puberulous, generally keeled, with a long point at apex, the inner scales obovate, pointed or rounded at apex, light green tinged with red, or bright red or yellow, covered with silky pubescence on the outer face, slightly resinous, becoming 2'–3' long and 1' wide. **Bark** 1'–2' thick, light gray, separating into broad thick plates frequently 3°–4° long, sometimes

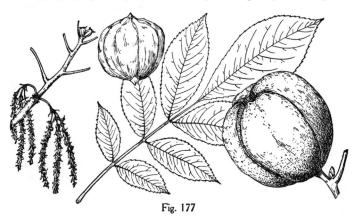

Fig. 177

remaining for many years hanging on the trunk. **Wood** heavy, very hard, strong and tough, close-grained, very flexible, dark brown, with comparatively thin nearly white sapwood. The large nuts are often sold in the markets of western cities and commercially are not often distinguished from those of the Shellbark Hickory.

Distribution. Rich bottom-lands usually inundated during several weeks of every year; central and western New York and southeastern Ontario, and westward through southern Ohio, southern Michigan, Indiana and Illinois to southeastern Iowa and southeastern Nebraska, through Missouri and Arkansas to southeastern Kansas and northeastern Oklahoma, and southward through eastern Pennsylvania to western West Virginia; in southeastern Tennessee; banks of the Alabama River, Dallas County, Alabama, and in West Feliciana Parish, Louisiana.

✕ *Carya Nussbaumerii* Sarg. with leaves like those of *C. laciniosa*, slender branchlets, and large fruit of the shape of that of the Pecan but without sutural wings and white or nearly white nuts, believed to be a hybrid of these species, has been found near Fayetteville, St. Clair County, Illinois, at Mt. Vernon, Posey County, Indiana, near Burlington, Des Moines County, Iowa, and from the neighborhood of Rockville, Bates County, Missouri.

Trees intermediate in character between *C. laciniosa* and *C. ovata* growing on the bottoms of the Genessee River at Golah, Monroe County, New York, and believed to be hybrids of these species, are ✕ *C. Dunbarii* Sarg.

9. Carya alba K. Koch. Hickory.

Leaves glandular, resinous, fragrant, 8′–12′ long, with petioles covered like the rachis and the under surface of the leaflets with fascicled hairs, and 5 or 7 oblong-lanceolate to ob-ovate-lanceolate leaflets gradually or abruptly acuminate, mostly equilateral, equally or unequally rounded or cuneate at base, minutely or coarsely serrate, sessile or short-stalked, dark yellow-green and rather lustrous above, lustrous, paler or light orange-colored or brown on the lower surface, the upper leaflets 5′–8′ long and 3′–5′ wide, and two or three times as large as those of the lowest pair. **Flowers:** staminate in aments 4′–5′ long, with slender light green stems coated with fascicled hairs, pale yellow-green, scurfy-pubescent, with elongated ovate-lanceolate bracts ending in tufts of long pale hairs, and three or four times as long as the calyx-lobes; stamens 4, with oblong bright red hirsute anthers; pistillate in crowded 2–5-flowered spikes, slightly contracted above the middle, coated with pale tomentum, the bract ovate, acute, sometimes ¼′ long, about twice as long as the broadly ovate nearly triangular bractlets and calyx-lobes; stigmas dark red. **Fruit** ellipsoidal or obovoid, gradually narrowed at the ends, acute at apex, abruptly contracted toward the base, rarely obovoid with a stipe-like base

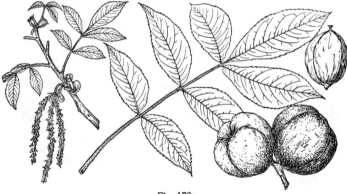

Fig. 178

(var. *ficoides* Sarg.), or ovoid with a long acuminate apex (var. *ovoidea* Sarg.), pilose or nearly glabrous, dark red-brown, 1½′–2′ long, with a husk about ⅛′ thick splitting to the middle or nearly to the base; **nut** nearly globose, ellipsoidal, obovoid-oblong or ovoid, narrowed at ends, rounded at base, acute, and sometimes attenuated and long-pointed at apex, much or only slightly compressed, obscurely or prominently 4-ridged, light reddish brown, becoming darker and sometimes red with age, with a very thick hard shell and partitions; in drying often cracking transversely; **seed** small, sweet, dark brown, and lustrous.

A tree, rarely 100° high, usually much smaller, with a tall trunk occasionally 3° in diameter, comparatively small spreading branches forming a narrow or often a broad round-topped head of upright rigid or of gracefully pendulous branches, and stout branchlets clothed at first with pale fascicled hairs, rather bright brown, nearly glabrous or more or less pubescent, and marked by conspicuous pale lenticels during their first season, becoming light or dark gray, with pale emarginate leaf-scars almost equally lobed, or elongated with the lowest lobe two or three times as long as the others. **Winter-buds:** terminal broadly ovoid, acute or obtuse, ½′–¾′ long, two or three times as large as the axillary buds, the three or four outer bud-scales ovate, acute, often keeled and apiculate, thick and firm, dark reddish brown and pilose, usually deciduous late in the autumn, the inner scales ovate, rounded or acute and short-pointed at apex, light green covered with soft silky pubescence on the outer, and often bright red and pilose on the inner surface, becoming $1'-1\frac{1}{2}'$ long and $\frac{1}{2}'$ broad. **Bark** $\frac{1}{2}'-\frac{3}{4}'$ thick, close, slightly ridged by shallow irregular interrupted fissures and covered by dark gray closely appressed scales. **Wood** very heavy, hard, tough, strong, close-grained, flexible, rich dark brown, with thick nearly white sapwood; used for the same purposes as that of the Shellbark Hickory.

Distribution. Eastern Massachusetts southward to Lake County, Florida, and eastern Texas, and through Ohio, southwestern Ontario, southern Michigan, Illinois and Indiana to southeastern Iowa, and through Missouri to eastern Oklahoma; comparatively rare at the north, growing on dry slopes and ridges and less commonly on alluvial bottomlands; absent from eastern Canada, northern and western New England, and New York except in the neighborhood of the coast; the most abundant and generally distributed Hickory-tree of the southern states, growing to its largest size in the basin of the lower Ohio River and in Missouri and Arkansas; commonly in southern Arkansas and eastern Texas, and occasionally in other southern states represented by var. *subcoriacea* Sarg., differing in its larger, thicker, more pubescent leaflets, more prominently angled fruit with a thicker husk, larger nuts, and in its longer winter-buds often $\frac{4}{5}'$ long and $\frac{3}{4}'$ in diameter.

× *Carya Schneckii* Sarg., believed to be a hybrid of *C. alba* and *C. pecan*, has been found at Lawrenceville, Lawrence County, Illinois, and near Muscatine, Muscatine County, Iowa.

10. Carya leiodermis Sarg.

Leaves $12'-14'$ long, with slender petioles and rachis slightly or densely pubescent with fascicled hairs, becoming glabrous or nearly glabrous, and 7 or rarely 5 thin finely serrate leaflets, long-pointed at apex, and gradually narrowed, cuneate and unsymmetrical at base,

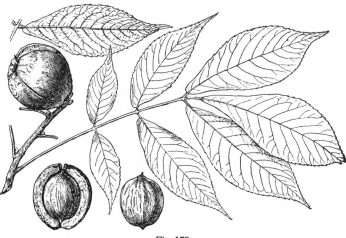

Fig. 179

at first hoary tomentose below and pubescent above, becoming dark green and lustrous on the upper surface and pale and slightly pubescent on the lower surface, especially on the stout midrib, the terminal oblong-obovate with a stalk $\frac{1}{3}'-\frac{3}{5}'$ in length, or nearly sessile, of the same shape and often smaller than the nearly sessile upper leaflets, $4'-5'$ long and $2'-2\frac{1}{2}'$ wide, and much larger than the lanceolate lower leaflets. **Flowers:** staminate opening after the leaves have grown nearly to their full size, in slender puberulous aments

4'–4½' long; bract of the flower ovate, lanceolate, ciliate on the margins with long white hairs mixed with stipitate glands, a third longer than the ciliate calyx-lobes; stamens 4, anthers red, covered with long rigid white hairs; pistillate in short spikes, their involucre and bracts densely clothed with white hairs. **Fruit** broadly obovoid, smooth, glabrous or puberulous, covered with scattered white scales, 1½'–1¾' long, about 1¼' in diameter, the husk ⅕' to nearly ¼' thick, opening freely to the base usually only by two sutures; **nut** ellipsoidal or slightly obovoid, little compressed, rounded at the ends, tinged with red, with a shell ⅙'–⅕' thick; **seed** small and sweet.

A tree 60°–75° tall with a trunk occasionally 3° in diameter, stout often pendulous branches forming a narrow round-topped head, and slender reddish brown lustrous branchlets puberulous or pubescent when they first appear, becoming glabrous or nearly glabrous by the end of their first season. **Winter-buds:** terminal acute, about ½' long, the outer scales pubescent, the inner covered with appressed pale hairs and ciliate on the margins; axillary buds ovoid and rounded at apex or subglobose. **Bark** close, pale, only slightly ridged.

Distribution.   Low wet woods; Louisiana to southern Arkansas, and in northwestern Mississippi (bluffs, Yazoo County); most abundant in western Louisiana from the neighborhood of the coast to the valley of Red River, and in Tangipahoa Parish east of the Mississippi River.

Passing into var. *callicoma* Sarg., differing in the thinner husk of the fruit and in the bright red color of the unfolding leaves.

Distribution.   Low wet woods; valley of the Calcasieu River (near Lake Charles), western Louisiana to that of the Neches River (near Beaumont), Texas; in western and southern Mississippi (Warren, Adams, Hinds, Lafayette, Copiah, Lowndes and Oktibbeha Counties).

11. Carya pallida Engl. & Graebn.

Leaves 7'–15' long, with slender petioles and rachis covered, like the under side of the midrib, with prominent persistent clusters of fascicled hairs mixed with silvery scales, and

Fig. 180

usually 7, rarely 9, lanceolate or oblanceolate leaflets, the terminal rarely obovate, finely serrate, resinous, fragrant, acuminate and long-pointed at apex, cuneate or rounded and often unsymmetrical at base, covered in spring with small silvery peltate scales, and at maturity light green and lustrous above, pale and pubescent or puberulous below, the terminal short-stalked or nearly sessile, 4'–6' long and 1'–2' wide, and as large or slightly larger than the upper lateral leaflets, those of the lower pairs usually not more than 2' long and

$\frac{1}{2}'$ wide. **Flowers:** staminate in aments covered with fascicled hairs and silvery scales, $2\frac{1}{2}'$–5′ long, puberulous and glandular on the outer surface, with linear acuminate bracts; stamens 4, anthers hirsute; pistillate usually solitary, oblong, covered with yellow scales, their bract ovate-lanceolate, ciliate on the margin. **Fruit** pubescent and covered with yellow scales, ellipsoidal to obovoid, broad-obovoid, subglobose to depressed-globose, and from $\frac{1}{2}'$–$1\frac{1}{2}'$ in length, with a husk from $\frac{1}{8}'$–$\frac{1}{6}'$ in thickness, splitting tardily to the base by 2 or 3 of the sutures, or occasionally remaining unopened until midwinter; **nut** white, rounded at the ends, or obcordate or obtusely pointed at apex, compressed, more or less prominently ridged nearly to the base, with a shell $\frac{1}{8}'$–$\frac{1}{12}'$ thick; **seed** small and sweet.

A tree occasionally 90°–110° high, with a tall trunk $2\frac{1}{2}°$–3° in diameter, usually not more than 30°–40° tall, with a trunk 12′–18′ in diameter, stout branches, the upper erect, the lower often pendulous, and slender red-brown glabrous or pubescent branchlets. **Winter-buds** acute or obtuse, reddish brown, puberulous and covered with silvery scales, the terminal $\frac{1}{4}'$ long with 6–9 scales and rather larger than the lateral buds usually covered with fewer scales. **Bark** of large trees grown in good soil pale and slightly ridged, that of trees on dry ridges, rough, deeply furrowed, dark gray and southward often nearly black. **Wood** brown with nearly white sapwood; probably little used except as fuel.

Distribution. Sandy soil in the neighborhood of Cape May, New Jersey, in southern Delaware, and in the southern part of the Maryland peninsula; common in rich soil in Gloucester and James City Counties, Virginia, growing here to its largest size, and southward from southeast Virginia through the Piedmont region of North and South Carolina, ascending to altitudes of 2200° in the mountain valleys of these states; common in northern and central Georgia and southeastern Tennessee, occasionally reaching the Georgia coast and the southwestern part of that state; in western Florida, through northern and central Alabama to Dallas County, and through southern Mississippi to northeastern Louisiana (near Kentwood, Tangipahoa Parish); in Mississippi extending northward to the valley of the Yazoo River in Yazoo County; in southern Tennessee (Lexington, Henderson County); in Alabama the common Hickory on the dry gravelly and poor soils of the upland table-lands and ridges of the central part of the state.

12. Carya glabra Sweet. Pignut.

Carya porcina Nutt.

Leaves 8′–12′ long, with slender glabrous petioles and rachis, and 5 or rarely 7 lanceolate or oblanceolate finely serrate leaflets acuminate at the ends, yellow-green and glabrous above, glabrous, or pubescent on the midrib below, the terminal leaflet sometimes obovate, 4′–4$\frac{1}{2}'$ long and 5′ or 6′ wide, and raised on a glabrous or sparingly pubescent stalk, $\frac{1}{4}'$–$\frac{1}{2}'$ in length, the lateral leaflets sessile, those of the upper pair about the size of the terminal leaflet, and two or three times larger than those of the lower pair. **Flowers:** staminate in short-stalked pubescent aments 2′–2$\frac{1}{2}'$ long, yellow-green, the bract villose, much longer than the calyx-lobes; stamens 4, anthers yellow, villose toward the apex; pistillate in few-flowered spikes, oblong, coated with hoary tomentum like the lanceolate acuminate bract. **Fruit** obovoid, compressed, rounded at apex, gradually narrowed below and often abruptly contracted into a stipe-like base, about 1′ long and $\frac{3}{4}'$ wide, with a husk from $\frac{1}{12}'$–$\frac{1}{8}'$ in thickness, opening late by one or two sutures or often remaining closed; **nut** obovoid, compressed, without ridges, rounded or slightly obcordate at apex, gradually narrowed and rounded below, with a hard thick shell; **seed** small and sweet.

A tree 60°–90° high, with a trunk 2°–2$\frac{1}{2}°$ in diameter, with small spreading often drooping branches forming a tall narrow head, and slender glabrous reddish branchlets marked by pale lenticels. **Winter-buds** ovoid, acute, light brown, glabrous, $\frac{1}{3}'$–$\frac{1}{2}'$ long and $\frac{1}{5}'$–$\frac{1}{4}'$ in diameter, the inner scales covered with close pubescence. **Bark** close, ridged, light gray. **Wood** heavy, hard, strong and tough, flexible, light or dark brown, with thick lighter-colored sapwood; used for the handles of tools and in the manufacture of wagons and agricultural implements, and largely for fuel.

Distribution. Hillsides and dry ridges; southwestern Vermont to western New York, southeastern Ontario, southern Indiana and southwestern Illinois, and southward to Dela-

Fig. 181

ware, the District of Columbia and eastern Virginia, and along the Appalachian Mountains to North Carolina; in northern, central and eastern Georgia, northern Alabama and eastern Mississippi.

The name " Pignut " usually applied to this tree and to the forms of *C. ovalis* Sarg., especially in the north, properly belongs to *C. cordiformis* Schn.

Passing into

Carya glabra var. megacarpa Sarg.

Carya megacarpa Sarg.

Leaves 12′–14′ long, with slender glabrous petioles and 5–7 lanceolate to oblanceolate leaflets long-pointed and acuminate at apex, gradually narrowed and unsymmetrical at base, finely serrate, glabrous or very rarely pubescent, often furnished below with small clusters of axillary hairs, the three upper 8′–10′ long and $1\frac{1}{2}′–2\frac{1}{2}′$ wide and about twice as large as those of the lowest pair. **Flowers:** staminate in slightly villose aments $2\frac{1}{2}′–3′$ in length, villose, their bract long-pointed, acuminate, villose, twice longer than the calyx-lobes, stamens 4–6, anthers yellow, villose above the middle; pistillate in short-stalked spikes, their involucre only slightly angled, covered with pale yellow hairs, the bract acuminate, twice longer than the bractlets and calyx-lobes. **Fruit** oblong-obovoid with a stipe-like base to short-obovate and rounded or abruptly cuneate at base, rarely depressed at apex, slightly flattened, often covered with bright yellow scales, 1′–2′ long, 1′–$1\frac{1}{2}′$ in diameter, with a husk $\frac{1}{8}′–\frac{1}{5}′$ in thickness, opening tardily to the middle usually by one or by two sutures, or often remaining closed; **nut** broadest toward the rounded apex or oblong and occasionally acute at apex, gradually narrowed and acute at base, often compressed, slightly or rarely prominently angled (f. *angulata* Sarg.), with a shell $\frac{1}{8}′–\frac{1}{6}′$ in thickness; **seed** small and sweet.

A tree 50°–70° high, with a trunk up to 2° in diameter, stout spreading and drooping branches, and stout or rarely slender glabrous branchlets, reddish brown at the end of their first season, becoming dark gray-brown. **Winter-buds** ovoid, acute, glabrous, up to $\frac{1}{2}'$ in length, the inner scales puberulous. **Bark** close, only slightly ridged, light or dark gray.

Distribution. Rochester, Monroe County, New York, through southern Ohio and Indiana to southern Illinois (Tunnel Hill, Johnson County); coast of New Jersey; District

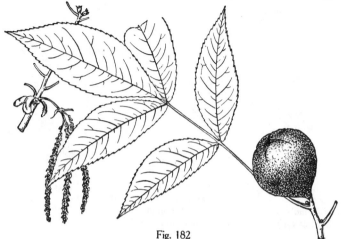

Fig. 182

of Columbia and southward to the shores of Indian River and the valley of the Caloosahatchee River, Florida, and through southern Alabama to western Louisiana; one of the commonest Hickories in the coast region of the south Atlantic and east Gulf states, occasionally ranging inland to central and northern Georgia and western Mississippi.

13. Carya ovalis Sarg.

Leaves 6′–10′ long, with slender petioles often scurfy-pubescent early in the season, soon glabrous, and 7 or rarely 5 lanceolate to oblanceolate, or occasionally obovate finely serrate leaflets, long-pointed and acuminate or rarely rounded at apex, cuneate and unsymmetrical at base, early in the season often scurfy-pubescent and furnished below with small axillary tufts of pale hairs, soon glabrous, the upper 3′ or 7′ long and $1\frac{1}{2}'$–$2'$ wide, and raised on a stalk $\frac{1}{4}'$–$\frac{1}{2}'$ in length, the lateral sessile, those of the upper pairs as large or slightly smaller than the terminal leaflet. **Flowers:** staminate in puberulous aments 6′–7′ long, pubescent, their bracts twice longer than the ovate acute calyx-lobes; stamens 4, anthers yellow, thickly covered with pale hairs; pistillate in 1 or 2-flowered spikes, obovoid, more or less thickly covered with yellow scales. **Fruit** ellipsoidal, acute or rounded at apex, rounded at base, puberulous, 1′–$1\frac{1}{4}'$ long, about $\frac{3}{4}'$ in diameter, with a husk $\frac{1}{12}'$–$\frac{1}{10}'$ in thickness, splitting freely to the base; **nut** pale, oblong, slightly flattened, rounded at base, acute or acuminate and 4-angled at apex, the ridges extending for one-third or rarely for one-half of its length, with a shell rarely more than $\frac{1}{5}'$ in thickness; **seed** small and sweet.

A tree sometimes 100° high, with a tall trunk occasionally 3° in diameter, small spreading branches forming a narrow often pyramidal head, and slender lustrous red-brown branchlets marked by pale lenticels, often slightly pubescent when they first appear, soon glabrous. **Winter-buds** ovoid, obtuse, acute or acuminate; the terminal often $\frac{1}{2}'$ long and twice as large as the lateral, the outer scales red-brown, lustrous and glabrous, the inner covered with close pale tomentum. **Bark** slightly ridged, pale gray, usually separating freely into small plate-like scales, or occasionally close. **Wood** heavy, hard and tough, flexible, light or dark brown, with thick lighter-colored sapwood; used for the handles of tools, in the manufacture of wagons and agricultural implements, and largely for fuel.

Distribution. Hillsides and rich woods; western New York, eastern Pennsylvania **and** the District of Columbia to southern Illinois and central Iowa (Ames, Story County), and

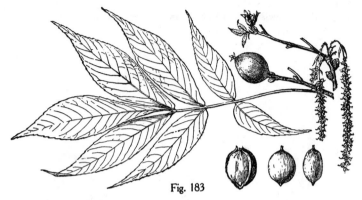

Fig. 183

southward to the mountains of North Carolina and Tennessee, and to central Georgia and Alabama; usually rare and local; most abundant and generally distributed in Indiana. With its varieties usually but incorrectly called " Pignut."

The following varieties differing in the shape of their fruit are distinguished:

Carya ovalis var. obcordata Sarg.

Carya microcarpa Darling. in part.
Hicoria microcarpa Britt. in part.

Fruit subglobose to short-oblong or slightly obovoid, $1'-1\frac{1}{4}'$ in diameter, with a husk $\frac{1}{12}'-\frac{1}{8}'$ in thickness, splitting freely to the base or nearly to the base by often narrow-winged

Fig. 184

sutures; **nut** much compressed, slightly angled and often broadest above the middle, rounded and usually more or less obcordate at apex, narrowed and rounded at base.

Distribution. Southern New England to southern Wisconsin, southwestern Missouri, western North Carolina, central and eastern Georgia, eastern Mississippi and central Alabama; the common and most widely distributed northern variety of *Carya ovalis;* common in the mountain districts of central Alabama and West Feliciana Parish, Louisiana; varying to the f. *vestita* Sarg. with stouter branchlets covered during their first year with rusty tomentum and more or less pubescent in their second and third seasons, leaflets slightly pubescent below, and with more compressed nuts and puberulous winter-buds. A single tree near Davis Pond, Knox County, Indiana.

Carya ovalis var. odorata Sarg.

Carya microcarpa Darling. in part.
Hicoria microcarpa Britt. in part.
Hicoria glabra var. *odorata* Sarg. in part.

Fruit subglobose or slightly longer than broad, much flattened, $\frac{1}{2}'-\frac{3}{5}'$ in diameter, with a husk not more than $\frac{1}{24}'$ in thickness, splitting freely to the base by sutures sometimes fur-

Fig. 185

nished with narrow wings; **nut** compressed, rounded at apex, rounded or acute at base, slightly or not at all ridged, pale or nearly white, with a shell $\frac{1}{12}'$ or less in thickness.

Distribution. Southern New England, eastern Pennsylvania and the District of Columbia to western New York, and southeastern Ontario, and through Ohio and Indiana to southern Illinois, southeastern Missouri and Heber Springs, Arkansas; near Atlanta, Georgia, and Starkville, Oktibbeha County, Mississippi; less variable in the size and shape of the fruit than the other varieties of *C. ovalis.*

Carya ovalis var. obovalis Sarg.

Hicoria glabra Sarg. in part.

Fruit more or less obovoid, about $1'$ long and $\frac{4}{5}'$ in diameter, with a husk $\frac{1}{12}'-\frac{1}{8}'$ thick, splitting freely to the base. (Fig. 186.)

Distribution. Southern New England to Missouri and northern Arkansas; on the mountains of North Carolina, on the coast of Georgia and in north central Alabama, and West Feliciana Parish, Louisiana. The common "Pignut" in the middle western states, varying to f. *acuta* Sarg. with nuts pointed at the ends and closer bark; only near Rochester, Monroe County, New York.

Other forms of *C. ovalis* are var. *hirsuta* Sarg. (*Hicoria glabra hirsuta* Ashe) with obovoid compressed fruit narrowed into a stipitate base, with a husk $\frac{1}{2}'-\frac{1}{4}'$ in thickness, scaly bark, pubescent winter-buds, leaves with pubescent petioles and leaflets pubescent on the lower surface; a common tree on the mountains of North Carolina up to altitudes of 2000° above the sea; and var. *borealis* Sarg. (*Hicoria borealis* Ashe) with pubescent branch-

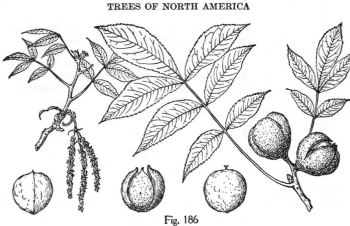

Fig. 186

lets and winter-buds, leaves pubescent early in the season, ellipsoidal or ovoid flattened fruit with a husk $\frac{1}{8}'-\frac{1}{5}'$ in thickness, an ovoid nut ridged to the base, and scaly bark; only in southeastern Michigan.

14. Carya floridana Sarg.

Leaves 6′–8′ long, with slender petioles rusty pubescent when they first appear, soon glabrous, with 5 or rarely 7 lanceolate to oblanceolate leaflets long-pointed and acuminate at apex, unsymmetrical and rounded or cuneate at base, serrate with remote cartilaginous teeth, sessile or the terminal leaflet short-stalked, covered when they unfold with rufous

Fig. 187

pubescence, soon glabrous, at maturity thin, conspicuously reticulate-venulose, yellow-green above, often brownish below, the upper three $3\frac{1}{2}'-4'$ long, 1′–2′ wide, and about twice larger than those of the lowest pair. **Flowers:** staminate in long-stalked scurfy pubescent aments 1′–1$\frac{1}{2}'$ in length, produced at the base of branchlets of the year from the axils of bud-scales, and often of leaves, scurfy pubescent, their bract ovate, acuminate, a third longer than the calyx-lobes; stamens 4 or 5, anthers yellow, slightly villose near the apex; pistillate in 1 or 2-flowered spikes, obovoid, thickly covered, like their bracts, with yellow scales. Fruit obovoid, gradually narrowed, rounded and sometimes slightly depressed at apex, narrowed below into a short stipe-like base, occasionally slightly winged at the sutures, often roughened by prominent reticulate ridges, puberulous and covered with small yellow scales, $\frac{4}{5}'-1\frac{1}{2}'$ long, $\frac{3}{4}'-1'$ in diameter with a husk $\frac{1}{12}'-\frac{1}{8}'$ thick, splitting freely to the base by 2 or 3 sutures; nut pale or reddish, subglobose, not more than $\frac{3}{5}'$ in diameter, or ovoid or rarely oblong, acute at base, narrowed and rounded at apex, slightly compressed, with a shell $\frac{1}{12}'-\frac{1}{8}'$ in thickness.

A tree 50°–70° high with a trunk up to 20' in diameter, slender spreading branches forming a broad head, and slender branchlets at first coated with rufous pubescence, soon puberulous or glabrous, bright red-brown and marked by pale lenticels during their first winter; or in dry sand often a shrub producing abundant fruit on stems 3° or 4° high. **Winterbuds** ovoid, acute or obtuse, the outer scales covered with thick rusty pubescence and more or less thickly with yellow or rarely silvery scales, the inner coated with pale pubescence; the terminal $\frac{1}{5}'-\frac{1}{3}'$ in length and twice as large as the axillary buds. **Bark** slightly ridged, close dark gray-brown. **Wood** dark brown, with pale sapwood; probably used only for fuel.

Distribution. Dry sandy ridges and low hills, Florida; east coast, Volusia County to Jupiter Island, Palm Beach County; in the interior of the peninsula as a shrub, from Orange to De Soto Counties, and on the shores of Pensacola Bay.

15. Carya Buckleyi Durand.

Carya texana Buckl., not *Le Conte*

Leaves 8'–12' long, with slender petioles rusty pubescent and sparingly villose early in the season, and 5–7, usually 7, lanceolate to oblanceolate acuminate bluntly serrate sessile

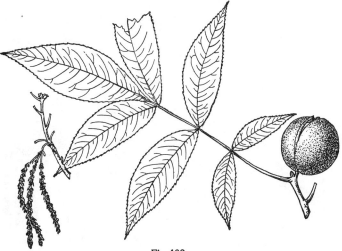

Fig. 188

leaflets, the terminal occasionally broadly obovate and abruptly pointed, and sometimes raised on a winged stalk $\frac{1}{4}'-\frac{1}{2}'$ in length, when they unfold thickly covered with rusty pubescence mixed with small white scales and villose on the lower side of the midrib and veins, and at maturity dark green, lustrous, glabrous or puberulous along the midrib above, paler, glabrous or sparingly villose and furnished with small tufts of axillary hairs below, the upper three leaflets 4′–6′ long and 2′–2¼′ wide, and twice the size of those of the lowest pair. **Flowers:** staminate in rusty pubescent aments 2′–3′ long, their bract slender, long acuminate, 3 or 4 times longer than the acuminate calyx-lobes; stamens 4 or 5, anthers yellow, slightly villose toward the apex; pistillate in 1 or 2-flowered short-stalked spikes, slightly angled, thickly coated with rufous hairs like the bract and bractlets. **Fruit** sub-globose, puberulous, 1¼′–1¾′ in diameter, with a husk $\frac{1}{12}′–\frac{1}{8}′$ thick, splitting freely to the base by slightly winged sutures; **nut** slightly compressed, rounded at base, abruptly narrowed and acute at apex, 4-angled above the middle or nearly to the base, dark reddish brown, conspicuously reticulate-venulose with pale veins, with a shell about ⅛′ thick; in drying often cracking longitudinally between the angles; **seed** small and sweet.

A tree, usually 30°–45° or rarely 60° high, with a trunk 12′–24′ in diameter, large spreading often drooping more or less contorted branches forming a narrow head, and slender light red-brown branchlets marked by pale lenticels, more or less densely rusty pubescent during their first season and dark gray-brown and glabrous or nearly glabrous the following year. **Winter-buds** ovoid, covered with rusty pubescence mixed with silvery scales, furnished at apex with long pale hairs; the terminal bud abruptly contracted and long-pointed at apex, ⅖′–½′ in length and ¼′–⅓′ in diameter, and 2 or 3 times larger than the flattened acute lateral buds. **Bark** thick, deeply furrowed, rough, dark often nearly black. **Wood** hard, brittle, little used except for fuel.

Distribution.　Dry sandy uplands with Post and Black Jack Oaks; northern and eastern Texas (Grayson, Cherokee, San Augustine and Atascosa Counties), and in central Oklahoma (dry sand hills, Muskogee County).

Carya Buckleyi var. arkansana Sarg.

Carya arkansana Sarg.

Differing from *Carya Buckleyi* in the shape of the fruit and sometimes in the bark of the trunk. **Fruit** obovoid, rounded at apex, rounded or gradually narrowed or abruptly con-

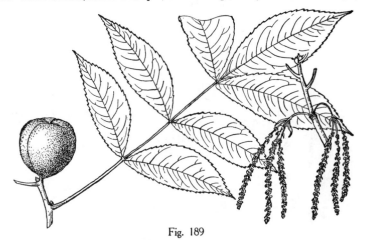

Fig. 189

tracted into a more or less developed stipe at base, or ellipsoidal, or ovoid and rounded at the ends, ⅘′–1½′ in length and in diameter, with a husk $\frac{1}{12}′–\frac{1}{6}′$ thick, splitting to the middle or nearly to the base by slightly winged sutures; **nut** oblong to slightly obovoid, rounded at the ends, compressed, slightly 4-angled occasionally to the middle, pale brown, with a shell $\frac{1}{5}'-\frac{1}{6}'$ in thickness; seed small and sweet.

A tree from 60°–75° high, with a trunk 2° in diameter; southward usually much smaller. Bark on some trees dark gray, irregularly fissured, separating into thin scales, and on others close, nearly black and deeply divided into rough ridges.

Distribution. Dry hillsides, rocky ridges, or southward on sandy upland; southwestern Indiana (Knox County), southern Illinois, northeastern Missouri and southward through Missouri and Arkansas to eastern Oklahoma, western Louisiana and northern and eastern Texas to the valley of the Atascosa River, Atascosa County; the common Hickory of the Ozark Mountain region, Arkansas, and here abundant on dry rocky ridges at altitudes of 1200°–1800°; in Texas the common Hickory from the coast to the base of the Edwards Plateau; trees with the smallest fruit northward; those with the largest fruit with thickest husks in Louisiana, and in southern Arkansas (f. *pachylemma* Sarg.), a tree with slender nearly glabrous branchlets, deeply fissured pale gray bark, rusty pubescent winter-buds and fruit $2\frac{1}{2}'$ long and 2' in diameter, with a husk $\frac{1}{2}'$ in thickness.

Carya Buckleyi var. villosa Sarg.

Hicoria glabra var. *villosa* Sarg.
Hicoria villosa Ashe.
Carya villosa Schn.
Carya glabra var. *villosa* Robins.

Leaves 6'–10' long, with slender petioles and rachis pubescent with fascicled hairs early in the season, generally becoming glabrous, and 5–7, usually 7, lanceolate to oblanceolate finely serrate leaflets long-pointed and acuminate at apex, cuneate or rounded and often unsymmetrical at base, sessile or the terminal leaflet sometimes short-stalked, dark green and gla-

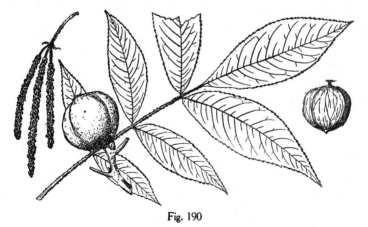

Fig. 190

brous above, pale and pubescent below, the lower side of the midrib often covered with fascicled hairs, the upper leaflets 3'–4' long and 1'–1½' wide, and twice as long as those of the lowest pair. **Flowers:** staminate in aments pubescent with fascicled hairs, 4'–8' long, pubescent, their bract acuminate, not much longer than the rounded calyx-lobes; pistillate in 1 or 2-flowered spikes, rusty pubescent, slightly angled. **Fruit** obovoid to ellipsoidal, rounded at apex, cuneate and often abruptly narrowed into a stipitate base, rusty pubescent and covered with scattered yellow scales, about 1' long and $\frac{3}{4}'$ in diameter, with a husk $\frac{1}{12}'$ in thickness, splitting tardily to the base by 1 or 2 sutures or indehiscent; **nut** ovoid, rounded at base, pointed at apex, only slightly angled, faintly tinged with red, with a shell rarely more than $\frac{1}{12}'$ in thickness; seed small and sweet.

A tree 30°–40° high, with a trunk 12′–18′ in diameter, stout often contorted branches and slender branchlets covered at first with rusty pubescence mixed with fascicled hairs and pubescent or glabrous during their first winter. **Winter-buds** ovoid, acute, covered with rusty pubescence mixed with yellow scales, often furnished near the apex with tufts of white hairs, the terminal $\frac{1}{4}'$ long and about twice as large as the compressed axillary buds.

Distribution. Dry rocky hills, Allenton, Saint Louis County, Missouri, to southern Illinois, northern Arkansas, and northeastern Oklahoma. Distinct from other forms of *Carya Buckleyi* in the often indehiscent fruit and more numerous and longer fascicled hairs, and possibly better considered a species.

IX. BETULACEÆ.

Trees, with sweet watery juice, without terminal buds, their slender terete branchlets marked by numerous pale lenticels and lengthening by one of the upper axillary buds formed in early summer, and alternate simple penniveined usually doubly serrate deciduous stalked leaves, obliquely plicately folded along the primary veins, their petioles in falling leaving small semioval slightly oblique scars showing three equidistant fibro-vascular bundle-scars; stipules inclosing the leaf in the bud, fugacious. Flowers vernal, appearing with or before the unfolding of the leaves, or rarely autumnal, monœcious, the staminate 1–3 together in the axils of the scales of an elongated pendulous lateral ament and composed of a 2–4-parted membranaceous calyx and 2–20 stamens inserted on a receptacle, with distinct filaments and 2-celled erect extrorse anthers opening longitudinally, or without a calyx, the pistillate in short lateral or capitate aments, with or without a calyx, a 2-celled ovary, narrowed into a short style divided into two elongated branches longer than the scales of the ament and stigmatic on the inner face or at the apex, and a single anatropous pendulous ovule in each cell of the ovary. Fruit a small mostly 1-celled 1-seeded nut, the outer layer of the shell light brown, thin and membranaceous, the inner thick, hard, and bony. Seed solitary by abortion, filling the cavity of the nut, suspended, without albumen, its coat membranaceous, light chestnut-brown; cotyledons thick and fleshy, much longer than the short superior radicle turned toward the minute hilum.

Of the six genera, all confined to the northern hemisphere, five are found in North America; of these only Corylus is shrubby.

CONSPECTUS OF THE NORTH AMERICAN ARBORESCENT GENERA.

Scales of the pistillate ament deciduous; nut wingless, more or less inclosed in an involucre formed by the enlargement of the bract and bractlets of the flower; staminate flowers solitary in the axils of the scales of the ament; caylx 0; pistillate flowers with a calyx.

    Staminate aments covered during the winter: involucre of the fruit flat, 3-cleft, foliaceous.   **1. Carpinus.**

    Staminate aments naked during the winter: involucre of the fruit bladder-like, closed.   **2. Ostrya.**

Scales of the pistillate ament persistent and forming a woody strobile; nut without an involucre, more or less broadly winged; staminate flowers 3–6 together in the axils of the scales of the ament; calyx present; pistillate flowers without a calyx.

    Pistillate aments solitary, their scales 3-lobed, becoming thin, brown, and woody, deciduous; stamens 2; filaments 2-branched, each division bearing a half-anther; winter-buds covered by imbricated scales.   **3. Betula.**

    Pistillate aments racemose, their scales erose or 5-toothed, becoming thick, woody, and dark-colored, persistent; stamens 1–3 or 4; filaments simple; wings of the nut often reduced to a narrow border; winter-buds without scales.   **4. Alnus.**

1. CARPINUS L. Hornbeam.

Trees, with smooth close bark, hard strong close-grained wood, elongated conic buds covered by numerous imbricated scales, the inner lengthening after the opening of the buds. Leaves open and concave in the bud, ovate, acute, often cordate; stipules strap-shaped to oblong-obovate. Flowers: staminate in aments emerging in very early spring from buds produced the previous season near the ends of short lateral branchlets of the year and inclosed during the winter, composed of 3–20 stamens crowded on a pilose receptacle adnate to the base of a nearly sessile ovate acute coriaceous scale longer than the stamens; filaments short, slender, 2-branched, each branch bearing a 1-celled oblong yellow half-anther hairy at the apex; pistillate in lax semi-erect aments terminal on leafy branches of the year, in pairs at the base of an ovate acute leafy deciduous scale, each flower subtended by a small acute bract with two minute bractlets at its base; calyx adnate to the ovary and dentate on the free narrow border. Nut ovoid, acute, compressed, conspicuously longitudinally ribbed, bearing at the apex the remnants of the calyx, marked on the broad base by a large pale scar and separating at maturity in the autumn from the leaf-like 3-lobed conspicuously serrate green involucre formed by the enlargement of the bract and bractlets of the flower and inclosing only the base of the nut, fully grown at mid-summer and loosely imbricated into a long-stalked open cluster. (*Eucarpinus.*)

Carpinus is confined to the northern hemisphere, and is distributed from the Province of Quebec through the eastern United States to the highlands of Central America in the New World, and from Sweden to southern Europe, Asia Minor, the temperate Himalayas, Korea, southern China, Japan and Formosa in the Old World. Fifteen or sixteen species are recognized. Of the exotic species, the European and west Asian *Carpinus Betulus* L. is frequently planted as an ornamental tree in the northeastern United States, where some of the species of eastern Asia promise to become valuable.

Carpinus is the classical name of the Hornbeam.

1. Carpinus caroliniana Walt. Hornbeam. Blue Beech.

Leaves often somewhat falcate, long-pointed, sharply doubly serrate with stout spreading glandular teeth, except at the rounded or wedge-shaped often unequal base, pale

Fig. 191

bronze-green, and covered with long white hairs when they unfold, at maturity thin and firm, pale dull blue-green above, light yellow-green and glabrous or puberulous below, with small tufts of white hairs in the axils of the veins, 2′–4′ long, 1′–1¾′ wide, with a slender yellow midrib, numerous slender veins deeply impressed and conspicuous above, and prominent cross veinlets; turning deep scarlet and orange color late in the autumn;

petioles slender, terete, hairy, about ⅓' long, bright red while young; stipules ovate-lanceolate, acute, pubescent, hairy on the margins, bright red below, light yellow-green at the apex, ⅓' long.   **Flowers:** staminate aments 1½' long when fully grown, with broadly ovate acute boat-shaped scales green below the middle, bright red above; pistillate aments ½'–¾' long, with ovate acute hairy green scales; styles scarlet.   **Fruit:** nut ⅓' long, its involucre short-stalked, with one of the lateral lobes often wanting, coarsely serrate, but usually on one margin only of the middle lobe, 1'–1½' long, nearly 1' wide, crowded on slender terete pubescent red-brown stems 5'–6' in length.

A bushy tree, rarely 40° high, with a short fluted trunk occasionally 2° in diameter, long slightly zigzag slender tough spreading branches pendulous toward the ends, and furnished with numerous short thin lateral branches growing at acute angles, and branchlets at first pale green coated with long white silky hairs, orange-brown and sometimes slightly pilose during the summer, becoming dark red and lustrous during their first winter and ultimately dull gray tinged with red.   **Winter-buds** ovoid, acute, about ⅛' long, with ovate acute chestnut-brown scales white and scarious on the margins.   **Bark** light gray-brown, sometimes marked with broad dark brown horizontal bands, 1/16'–⅛' thick.   **Wood** light brown, with thick nearly white sapwood; sometimes used for levers, the handles of tools, and other small articles.

Distribution.   Borders of streams and swamps, generally in deep rich moist soil; Nova Scotia and southern and western Quebec to the northern shores of Georgian Bay, southward nearly to the shores of Indian River and those of Tampa Bay, Florida, and westward to central Minnesota, eastern Iowa, eastern Nebraska (reported), eastern and southern Missouri, eastern Oklahoma, and eastern Texas; reappearing on the mountains of southern Mexico and Central America; common in the eastern and central states; most abundant and of its largest size on the western slopes of the southern Alleghany Mountains and in southern Arkansas and eastern Texas.

2. OSTRYA Scop. Hop Hornbeam.

Trees, with scaly bark, heavy hard strong close-grained wood, and acute elongated winter-buds formed in early summer and covered by numerous imbricated scales, the inner lengthening after the opening of the bud.   Leaves open and concave in the bud; petioles slender, nearly terete, hairy; stipules strap-shaped to oblong-obovate.   Flowers: staminate in long clustered sessile or short-stalked aments developed in early summer from lateral buds near the ends of short lateral branchlets of the year and coated while young with hoary tomentum, naked and conspicuous during the winter, and composed of 3–14 stamens crowded on a pilose receptacle adnate to the base of an ovate concave scale rounded and abruptly short-pointed at the apex, ciliate on the margins, longer than the stamens; filaments short, 2-branched, each branch bearing a 1-celled half-anther hairy at the apex; pistillate in erect lax aments terminal on short leafy branches of the year, in pairs at the base of an elongated ovate acute leaf-like ciliate scale persistent until midsummer, each flower inclosed in a hairy sack-like involucre formed by the union of a bract and 2 bractlets; calyx adnate to the ovary, denticulate on the free narrow border.   Nut ovoid, acute, flattened, obscurely longitudinally ribbed, crowned with the remnants of the calyx, marked at the narrow base by a small circular pale scar, inclosed in the much enlarged pale membranaceous conspicuously longitudinally veined reticulate-venulose involucres of the flower, short, pointed and hairy at the apex, hirsute at the base, with sharp rigid stinging hairs, imbricated into a short strobile fully grown at midsummer, and suspended on a slender hairy stem.

Ostrya is widely distributed in the northern hemisphere from Nova Scotia to Texas, northern Arizona, and to the highlands of southern Mexico and Guatemala in the New World, and through southern Europe and southwestern Asia, and in northern Japan and on the Island of Quelpart in the Old World.   Of the four species now recognized two are North American.

Ostrya is the classical name of the Hop Hornbeam.

CONSPECTUS OF THE NORTH AMERICAN SPECIES.

Leaves oblong-lanceolate, acuminate or acute at apex. 1. O. virginiana (A, C).
Leaves elliptic or obovate, acute or rounded at apex. 2. O. Knowltonii (F).

1. Ostrya virginiana K. Koch. Hop Hornbeam. Ironwood.

Leaves oblong-lanceolate, gradually narrowed into a long slender point or acute at apex, narrowed and rounded, cordate, or wedge-shaped at the often unequal base, sharply serrate, with slender incurved callous teeth terminating at first in tufts of caducous hairs, when they unfold light bronze-green, glabrous above and coated below on the midrib and primary veins with long pale hairs, at maturity thin and extremely tough, dark dull yellow-green above, light yellow-green and furnished with conspicuous tufts of pale hairs in the axils of the veins below, 3'–5' long, 1½'–2' wide, with a slender midrib impressed and puberulous above, light yellow and pubescent below, and numerous slender veins forked near the margins; turning clear yellow before falling in the autumn; petioles hairy about ¼' long; stipules rounded and often short-pointed at apex, ciliate on the margins with long pale hairs, hairy on the back, about ½' long and ⅛' wide. **Flowers:** staminate aments about ½' long during their first season, with light red-brown rather loosely imbricated scales nar-

Fig. 192

rowed into a long slender point, becoming when the flowers open 2' long, with broadly obovate scales rounded and abruptly contracted at apex into a short point, ciliate on the margins, green tinged with red above the middle, light brown toward the base; pistillate aments slender, about ¼' long, on thin hairy stems, their scales lanceolate, acute, light green, often flushed with red above the middle, hirsute at the apex, decreasing in size from the lowest. **Fruit:** nuts ⅓' long, about ¼' wide, rather abruptly narrowed below the apex, their involucres in clusters 1½'–2' long and ⅔'–1' wide, on slender hairy stems about 1' in length.

A tree, occasionally 50°–60° high, with a short trunk 2° in diameter, usually not more than 20°–30° tall, with a trunk 18'–20' thick, long slender branches drooping at the ends and forming a round-topped or open head frequently 50° across, and slender, very tough branchlets, light green, coated with pale appressed hairs when they first appear, becoming light orange color and very lustrous by midsummer, glabrous, dark red-brown and lustrous during their first winter, and then growing gradually darker brown and losing their lustre; or covered like the petioles and peduncles with short erect glandular hairs (var. *glandulosa* Sarg.).

Winter-buds ovoid, light chestnut-brown, slightly puberulous, $\frac{1}{4}'$ long. Bark about $\frac{1}{4}'$ thick, broken into thick narrow oblong closely appressed plate-like light brown scales slightly tinged with red on the surface. Wood strong, hard, tough, durable, light brown tinged with red or often nearly white, with thick pale sapwood of 40–50 layers of annual growth; used for fence-posts, handles of tools, mallets, and other small articles.

Distribution. Dry gravelly slopes and ridges often in the shade of oaks and other large trees; Island of Cape Breton and the shores of the Bay of Chaleur, through the valley of the St. Lawrence River, and along the northern shores of Lake Huron to western Ontario, Manitoba, Minnesota, eastern North Dakota, the foothills of the Black Hills of South Dakota, eastern, northern and northwestern Nebraska, eastern Kansas and Oklahoma, and southward to central Florida and eastern Texas; most abundant and of its largest size in southern Arkansas and in Texas. From Quebec and Ontario to western New England, western New York, Ohio and in Central Michigan, the glandular form prevails: the two forms occur in New Jersey, Pennsylvania, Indiana, northern Illinois, southwestern Missouri, Oklahoma, and southward on the high Appalachian Mountains.

2. Ostrya Knowltonii Cov. Ironwood.

Leaves elliptic to obovate, acute or round at apex, gradually narrowed and often unequal at the rounded cuneate rarely cordate base, sharply serrate with small triangular callous teeth, covered with loose pale tomentum when they unfold, at maturity dark yellow-green and pilose above, pale and soft-pubescent below, $1'-2'$ long, $1'-1\frac{1}{2}'$ wide, with a slender yellow midrib slightly raised on the upper side, and slender primary veins connected by obscure reticulate veinlets; turning dull yellow in the autumn before falling; petioles $\frac{1}{8}'-\frac{1}{4}'$ long; stipules pale yellow-green, often tinged with red toward the apex, $\frac{1}{2}'$ long, about $\frac{1}{2}'$ wide. Flowers: staminate aments on stout stalks covered with rufous tomentum and sometimes $\frac{1}{2}'$ long, rarely sessile, about $\frac{1}{2}'$ long during their first season, with

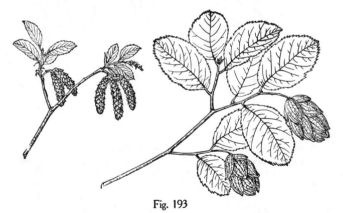

Fig. 193

dark brown puberulous scales gradually contracted into a long slender subulate point, becoming when the flowers open $1'-1\frac{1}{4}'$ long, with broadly ovate concave scales abruptly narrowed into a nearly triangular point, yellow-green near the base, bright red above the middle; pistillate aments about $\frac{1}{4}'$ long, with ovate-lanceolate light yellow-green puberulous scales ciliate on the margins. Fruit: nuts $\frac{1}{4}'$ long, gradually narrowed at the apex, their involucres $1'$ long, nearly glabrous at the apex, sometimes slightly stained with red toward the base, in clusters $1'-1\frac{1}{2}'$ long and about $\frac{3}{4}'$ broad, on stems $\frac{1}{2}'$ in length.

A tree 20°-30° high, with a trunk 12'-18' in diameter, usually divided 1° or 2° above the ground into 3 or 4 stout upright stems 4'-5' thick, slender pendulous often much contorted branches forming a narrow round-topped symmetrical head, and slender branchlets dark green and coated with hoary tomentum when they first appear, dark red-brown and pubescent during their first summer, becoming light cinnamon-brown, glabrous, and lustrous in the winter, and ultimately ashy gray. **Winter-buds** ovoid, dark brownish red, about $\frac{1}{8}'$ long. **Bark** internally bright orange color, $\frac{1}{8}'$ thick, separating into loose hanging plate-like scales light gray slightly tinged with red, and 1'-2' long and wide. **Wood** light reddish brown, with thin sapwood.

Distribution. On the southern slope of the cañon of the Colorado River in Coconino County, Arizona, at altitudes of 6000°-7000° above the sea (Hance trail, seventy miles north of Flagstaff); in the cañon of Oak Creek, south of Flagstaff (*P. Lowell*); and on Grand River, Utah (Moab, Grant County, *M. E. Jones*).

3. BETULA L. Birch.

Trees, with smooth resinous bark marked by long longitudinal lenticels, often separating freely into thin papery plates, becoming thick, deeply furrowed, and scaly at the base of old trunks, short slender branches more or less erect and forming on young trees a narrow symmetrical pyramidal head, becoming horizontal and often pendulous on older trees, tough branchlets, short stout spur-like 2-leaved lateral branchlets much roughened by the crowded leaf-scars of many years, and elongated winter-buds covered by numerous ovate acute scales, and fully grown and bright green at midsummer. Leaves open and convex in the bud, often incisely lobed; stipules ovate and acute or oblong-obovate, scarious. Flowers in 3-flowered cymes, the lateral flowers of the cyme subtended by bractlets adnate to the base of the scale of the ament; staminate aments long, pendulous, solitary or clustered, appearing in summer or autumn in the axils of the last leaves of a branchlet or near the ends of short lateral branchlets, erect and naked during the winter, their scales in the spring broadly ovate, rounded, short-stalked, yellow or orange-color below the middle and dark chestnut-brown and lustrous above it; staminate flowers composed of a membranaceous 4-lobed calyx often 2-lobed by suppression, the anterior lobe obovate, rounded at apex, as long as the stamens, much longer than the minute posterior lobe, and of 2 stamens inserted on the base of the calyx, with short 2-branched filaments, each branch bearing an erect half-anther; pistillate aments oblong or cylindric, terminal on the short spur-like lateral branchlets, their scales closely imbricated, oblong-ovate, 3-lobed, light yellow, often tinged with red above the middle, accrescent, becoming brown and woody at maturity, and forming sessile or stalked erect or pendulous short or elongated strobiles usually ripening in the autumn, deciduous with the nuts from the slender rachis; calyx of the pistillate flower 0; ovary sessile, compressed, with styles stigmatic at apex. Nut minute, oval or obovoid, compressed, bearing at the apex the persistent stigmas, marked at the base by a small pale scar, the outer coat of the shell produced into a marginal wing interrupted at the apex.

Betula is widely distributed from the Arctic circle to Texas in the New World, and to southern Europe, the Himalayas, China, and Japan in the Old World, some species forming great forests at the north, or covering high mountain slopes. Of the twenty-eight or thirty species now recognized twelve are found in North America; of these nine are trees. Of exotic species the European and Asiatic *Betula pendula* Roth. in a number of forms is a common ornamental tree in the northern states, where several of the Birch-trees of eastern Asia also flourish. Many of the species produce wood valued by the cabinet-maker, or used in the manufacture of spools, shoe-lasts, and other small articles. The thin layers of the bark are impervious to water and are used to cover buildings, and for shoes, canoes, and boxes. The sweet sap provides an agreeable beverage.

Betula is the classical name of the Birch-tree.

CONSPECTUS OF THE NORTH AMERICAN ARBORESCENT SPECIES.

Strobiles oblong-ovoid, nearly sessile, erect, the lateral lobes of their scales broad and slightly divergent; wing not broader than the nut; leaves with 9–11 pairs of veins; bark of young branches aromatic.

　　Leaves heart-shaped or rounded at base; scales of the strobiles glabrous; bark dark brown, not separating into thin layers.　　　　　　　**1. B. lenta** (A, C).

　　Leaves cuneate or slightly heart-shaped at base; scales of the strobiles pubescent; bark yellow, or silvery white, rarely dull yellowish brown; separating into thin layers.
　　　　　　　　　　　　　　　　　　　　　　　　　　　　　　2. B. lutea (A).

Strobiles oblong or cylindric, erect, spreading or pendant, on slender peduncles; wing broader than the nut; leaves with 5–9 pairs of veins.

　　Strobiles oblong, erect, ripening in May or June, their scales pubescent, deeply lobed, the lateral lobes erect; leaves rhombic-ovate, glaucescent and more or less silky-pubescent beneath; bark light reddish-brown, separating freely into thin persistent scales.
　　　　　　　　　　　　　　　　　　　　　　　　　　　　　　3. B. nigra (A, C).

Strobiles cylindric, pendant or spreading.

　　Scales of the strobiles pubescent, with recurved lateral lobes, the middle lobe triangular, nearly as broad as long; leaves long-pointed; petioles slender, elongated.

　　　　Leaves triangular to rhombic, bright green and lustrous; bark chalky white, not separable into thin layers.　　　　　　　**4. B. populifolia** (A).

　　　　Leaves ovate, cuneate to truncate or rounded at base, dull blue-green; bark white tinged with pink, lustrous, not easily separable into thin layers.
　　　　　　　　　　　　　　　　　　　　　　　　　　　　　　5. B. cœrulea (A).

　　Scales of the strobiles with ascending or spreading lateral lobes, the middle lobe usually acuminate, longer than broad; leaves acute or acuminate.

　　　　Bark separating freely into thin layers; scales of the strobiles glabrous.

　　　　　　Bark creamy white, or in some forms orange-brown; leaves ovate.
　　　　　　　　　　　　　　　　　　　　　　　　6. B. papyrifera (A, B, C, F).

　　　　　　Bark dull reddish brown or nearly white; leaves rhombic to deltoid-ovate.
　　　　　　　　　　　　　　　　　　　　　　　　　7. B. alaskana (A, B).

　　　　Bark not separable into thin layers, dark brown; scales of the strobiles glabrous or puberulous; branchlets glandular.

　　　　　　Leaves ovate, acute or acuminate, truncate or rounded at the broad base.
　　　　　　　　　　　　　　　　　　　　　　　　　8. B. fontinalis (B, F, G).

　　　　　　Leaves broad-ovate to elliptic, acute, rounded or abruptly short-pointed, cuneate at base.　　　　　　　　　　　　　**9. B. Eastwoodæ** (F).

1. Betula lenta L.　Cherry Birch.　Black Birch.

Betula alleghaniensis Britt.

Leaves ovate to oblong-ovate, acute or acuminate, gradually narrowed and often unequal at the cordate or rounded base, sharply serrate with slender incurved teeth, or very rarely laciniately lobed (f. *laciniata* Rehdr.), when they unfold light green, coated on the lower surface with long white silky hairs, and slightly hairy on the upper surface, at maturity thin and membranaceous, dark dull green above, light yellow-green below, with small tufts of white hairs in the axils of the veins, $2\frac{1}{2}'$–6′ long, $1\frac{1}{2}'$–3′ wide, with a yellow midrib and primary veins prominent and hairy on the lower surface, and obscure reticulate cross veinlets; turning bright clear yellow late in the autumn; petioles stout, hairy, deeply grooved on the upper side, $\frac{3}{4}'$–1′ long; stipules ovate, acute, light green or nearly white, scarious and ciliate above the middle.　**Flowers:** staminate aments during the winter about $\frac{3}{4}'$ long, nearly $\frac{1}{4}'$ thick, with ovate acute apiculate scales bright red-brown above the middle and light brown below it, becoming 3′–4′ long; pistillate aments $\frac{1}{2}'$–$\frac{3}{4}'$ long, about $\frac{1}{8}'$ thick, with ovate pale green scales rounded at the apex; styles light pink.　**Fruit:** strobiles oblong-ovoid, sessile, erect, glabrous, 1′–$1\frac{1}{2}'$ long, about $\frac{1}{2}'$ thick; nut obovoid, pointed at base, rounded at apex, about as broad as its wing.

A tree, with aromatic bark and leaves, 70°–80° high, with a trunk 2°–5° in diameter, slender branches spreading almost at right angles, becoming pendulous toward the ends and gradually forming a narrow round-topped open graceful head, and branchlets light green, slightly viscid and pilose when they first appear, soon turning dark orange-brown, lustrous during the summer, bright red-brown in their first winter, becoming darker and finally dark dull brown slightly tinged with red. **Winter-buds** ovoid, acute, about $\frac{1}{4}'$ long, with ovate acute light chestnut-brown loosely imbricated scales, those of the inner ranks becoming $\frac{1}{2}'$–$\frac{3}{4}'$ long. **Bark** on young stems and branches close, smooth, lustrous, dark brown tinged with red, and marked by elongated horizontal pale lenticels, becoming on old trunks $\frac{1}{2}'$–$\frac{3}{4}'$ thick, dull, deeply furrowed and broken into large thick irregular plates

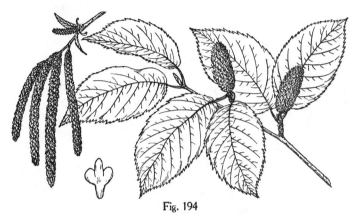

Fig. 194

covered with closely appressed scales. **Wood** heavy, very strong and hard, close-grained, dark brown tinged with red, with thin light brown or yellow sapwood of 70–80 layers of annual growth; largely used for floors, in the manufacture of furniture and for fuel, and occasionally in ship and boatbuilding. Sweet birch-oil distilled from the wood and bark is used for medicinal purposes and for flavoring as a substitute for oil of wintergreen, and beer is obtained by fermenting the sugary sap.

Distribution. Rich uplands from southern Maine to northwestern Vermont, and eastern Ohio and southward to northern Delaware and along the Appalachian Mountains up to altitudes of 4000° to northern Georgia; in Alabama, and in eastern Kentucky and Tennessee; a common forest tree at the north, and of its largest size on the western slopes of the southern Alleghany Mountains.

× *Betula Jackii* Schn., a natural hybrid of *B. lenta* with *B. pumila* Michx., has appeared in the Arnold Arboretum.

2. Betula lutea Michx. Yellow Birch. Gray Birch.

Leaves ovate to oblong-ovate, acuminate or acute at apex, gradually narrowed to the rounded cuneate or rarely heart-shaped usually oblique base, sharply doubly serrate, when they unfold bronze-green or red, and pilose with long pale hairs above and on the under side of the midrib and veins, at maturity dull dark green above, yellow-green below, $3'$–$4\frac{1}{2}'$ long, $1\frac{1}{2}'$–$2'$ wide, with a stout midrib and primary veins covered below near the base of the leaf with short pale or rufous hairs; turning clear bright yellow in the autumn; petioles slender, pale yellow, hairy, $\frac{3}{4}'$–$1'$ long; stipules ovate, acute, light green tinged with pink above the middle, about $\frac{1}{2}'$ long. **Flowers:** staminate aments during the winter $\frac{3}{4}'$–$1'$ long, about $\frac{1}{8}'$ thick, with ovate rounded scales light chestnut-brown and lustrous above the middle, ciliate on the margins, becoming $3'$–$3\frac{1}{2}'$ long and $\frac{1}{3}'$ thick; pistillate aments about $\frac{2}{3}'$ long, with acute scales, pale green below, light red and tipped with clusters of long white hair at apex, and pilose on the back. **Fruit:** strobiles erect, sessile, short-stalked, pubescent, $1'-1\frac{1}{2}'$ long, about $\frac{3}{4}'$ thick; nut ellipsoidal to obovoid, about $\frac{1}{8}'$ long, rather broader than its wing.

A tree, with slightly aromatic bark and leaves, occasionally 100° high, with a trunk 3°–4° in diameter, spreading and more or less pendulous branches forming a broad round-topped head, and branchlets at first green and covered with long pale hairs, light orange-brown and pilose during their first summer, becoming glabrous and light brown slightly tinged with orange, and ultimately dull and darker. **Winter-buds** about $\frac{1}{4}'$ long, somewhat viscid and covered with loose pale hairs during the summer, becoming light chestnut-brown, acute, and slightly puberulous in winter. **Bark** of young stems and of the branches bright silvery gray or light orange color, very lustrous, separating into thin loose persistent scales more or less rolled on the margins, becoming on old trees $\frac{1}{3}'$ thick. reddish

Fig. 195

brown, and divided by narrow irregular fissures into large thin plates covered with minute closely appressed scales, or sometimes dull yellowish brown (*B. alleghaniensis* Britt.). **Wood** heavy, very strong, hard, close-grained, light brown tinged with red, with thin nearly white sapwood; largely used for floors, in the manufacture of furniture, button and tassel moulds, boxes, the hubs of wheels, and for fuel.

Distribution. Moist uplands, and southward often in swamps; one of the largest deciduous-leaved trees of northeastern America; Newfoundland and along the northern shores of the Gulf of St. Lawrence to the valley of Rainy River, and southward to Long Island (Cold Spring Harbor) and western New York, Pennsylvania, northern Delaware, southeastern Ohio, northern Indiana, southwestern Wisconsin, northern, northeastern and central Iowa, and from the mountains of Virginia and West Virginia to the highest peaks of North Carolina and Tennessee at altitudes between 3000° and 5000°; very abundant and of its largest size in the eastern provinces of Canada and in northern New York and New England; small and rare in southern New England and southward.

$\times$ *Betula Purpusii* Schn. believed to be a natural hybrid of *B. lutea* with *B. pumila* var. *glandulifera* Regel has been found in Michigan and in Tamarack Swamps in Hennepin, Pine and Anoka Counties, Minnesota.

3. Betula nigra L.   Red Birch.   River Birch.

Leaves rhombic-ovate, acute, abruptly or gradually narrowed and cuneate at base, doubly serrate, and on vigorous young branches often more or less laciniately cut into acute doubly serrate lobes, when they unfold light yellow-green and pilose above and coated below, especially on the midrib and petioles, with thick white tomentum, at maturity thin and tough, $1\frac{1}{2}'-3'$ long, $1'-2'$ wide, deep green and lustrous above, glabrescent, pubescent or ultimately glabrous below, except on the stout midrib and remote primary veins; turning dull yellow in the autumn; petioles slender, slightly flattened, tomentose, about $\frac{1}{2}'$ long; stipules ovate, rounded or acute at apex, pale green, covered below with white hairs. **Flowers:** staminate aments clustered, during the winter about $\frac{7}{8}'$ long and $\frac{1}{16}'$ thick, with ovate rounded dull chestnut-brown lustrous scales, becoming $2'-3'$ long and $\frac{1}{4}'$ thick; pistillate aments about $\frac{1}{3}'$ long, with bright green ovate scales pubescent on the back, rounded or acute at apex, and ciliate with long white hairs. **Fruit** ripening in May and June; strobiles cylindric, pubescent, $1'-1\frac{1}{2}'$ long, $\frac{1}{2}'$ thick, erect on stout tomen-

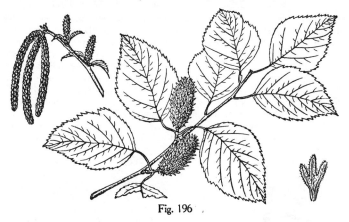

Fig. 196

tose peduncles $\frac{1}{2}'$ long; nut ovoid to ellipsoidal, $\frac{1}{8}'$ in length, pubescent or puberulous at apex, about as broad as its thin puberulous wing, ciliate on the margin.

A tree, $80°-90°$ high, with a trunk often divided $15°-20°$ above the ground into 2 or 3 slightly diverging limbs, and sometimes $5°$ in diameter, slender branches forming in old age a narrow irregular picturesque crown, and branchlets coated at first with thick pale or slightly rufous tomentum gradually disappearing before winter, becoming dark red and lustrous, dull red-brown in their second year, and then gradually growing slightly darker until the bark separates into the thin flakes of the older branches; or often sending up from the ground a clump of several small spreading stems forming a low bushy tree. **Winter-buds** ovoid, acute, about $\frac{1}{4}'$ long, covered in summer with thick pale tomentum, glabrous or slightly puberulous, lustrous and bright chestnut-brown in winter, the inner scales strap-shaped, light brown tinged with red, and coated with pale hairs. **Bark** on young stems and large branches thin, lustrous, light reddish brown or silvery gray, marked by narrow slightly darker longitudinal lenticels, separating freely into large thin papery scales persistent for several years, and turning back and showing the light pink-brown tints of the freshly exposed inner layers, becoming at the base of old trunks from $\frac{3}{4}'-1'$ thick, dark red-brown, deeply furrowed and broken on the surface into thick closely appressed scales. **Wood** light, rather hard, strong, close-grained, light brown, with pale sapwood of 40–50 layers of annual growth; used in the manufacture of furniture, woodenware, wooden shoes, and in turnery.

Distribution. Banks of streams, ponds, and swamps, in deep rich soil often inundated for several weeks at a time; near Manchester, Hillsboro County, New Hampshire, northeastern Massachusetts, Long Island, New York, southward to northern Florida through the region east of the Alleghany Mountains except in the immediate neighborhood of the coast, through the Gulf states to the valley of the Navasota River, Brazos County, Texas, and through Arkansas, eastern Oklahoma, southeastern Kansas, and Missouri to Tennessee and Kentucky, southern and eastern Iowa, southern Minnesota, the valley of the Eau Claire River, Eau Claire County, Wisconsin, southern Illinois, the valley of the Kankakee River, Indiana, and southern Ohio; the only semiaquatic species and the only species ripening its seeds in the spring or early summer; attaining its largest size in the damp semitropical lowlands of Florida, Louisiana, and Texas; the only Birch-tree of such warm regions.

Often cultivated in the northeastern states as an ornamental tree, growing rapidly in cultivation.

4. Betula populifolia Marsh. Gray Birch. White Birch.

Leaves nearly triangular to rhombic, long-pointed, coarsely doubly serrate with stout spreading glandular teeth except at the broad truncate or slightly cordate or cuneate base, thin and firm, dark green and lustrous and somewhat roughened on the upper surface early in the season by small pale glands in the axils of the conspicuous reticulate veinlets, $2\frac{1}{2}'$–$3'$ long, $1\frac{1}{2}'$–$2\frac{1}{2}'$ wide, with a stout yellow midrib covered with minute glands, and raised and rounded on the upper side, and obscure yellow primary veins; turning pale yellow in the autumn; petioles slender, terete, covered with black glands, often stained with red on the upper side, $\frac{3}{4}'$–$1'$ long; stipules broadly ovate, acute, membranaceous, light green slightly tinged with red. Flowers: staminate aments usually solitary or rarely in pairs, $1\frac{1}{4}'$–$1\frac{1}{2}'$ long, about $\frac{1}{8}'$ thick during the winter, becoming $2\frac{1}{2}'$–$4'$ long, with ovate acute apiculate scales; pistillate aments slender, as long as their glandular peduncles about $\frac{1}{2}'$ in length,

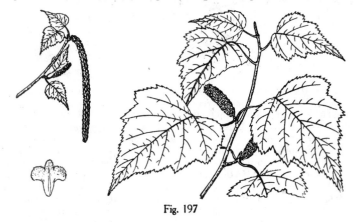

Fig. 197

with ovate acute pale green glandular scales. Fruit: strobiles cylindric, pubescent, obtuse at apex, about $\frac{3}{4}'$ long and $\frac{1}{4}'$ thick, pendant or spreading on slender stems; nut ellipsoidal to obovoid, acute or rounded at base, a little narrower than its obovate wing.

A short-lived tree, $20°$–$30°$ or exceptionally $40°$ high, with a trunk rarely $18'$ in diameter, short slender often pendulous more or less contorted branches usually clothing the stem to the ground and forming a narrow pyramidal head, and branchlets roughened by small raised lenticels, resinous-glandular when they first appear, gradually growing darker, bright yellow and lustrous before autumn like the young stems, bright reddish brown during their first winter, and ultimately white near the trunk; often growing in clusters of spreading stems springing from the stumps of old trees. Winter-buds ovoid, acute, pale chestnut-brown, glabrous, about $\frac{1}{4}'$ long. Bark about $\frac{1}{3}'$ thick, dull chalky white on the outer surface, bright orange on the inner, close and firm, with dark triangular markings at the insertion of the branches, becoming at the base of old trees thicker, nearly black, and irregularly broken by shallow fissures. **Wood** light, soft, not strong, close-grained, not durable, light brown, with thick nearly white sapwood; used in the manufacture of spools, shoe-pegs and wood pulp, for the hoops of barrels, and largely for fuel.

Distribution. Dry gravelly barren soil or on the margins of swamps and ponds; Prince Edward Island, Nova Scotia, New Brunswick, and the valley of the lower St. Lawrence River southward to northeastern, central and on South Mountain, Franklin County, Pennsylvania, and northern Delaware, and westward through northern New England and New York, ascending sometimes to altitudes of 1800°, to the southern shores of Lake Ontario, and at the foot of Lake Michigan, Indiana; rare and local in the interior, very abundant in the coast region of New England and the middle states; springing up in great numbers on abandoned farm-lands or on lands stripped by fire of their original forest covering; most valuable in its ability to grow rapidly in sterile soil and to afford protection to the seedlings of more valuable and less rapid-growing trees.

A form with deeply divided leaves (var. *laciniata* Loud.) and one with purple leaves (var. *purpurea* E & B) are occasionally cultivated.

A shrub believed to be a natural hybrid of *B. populifolia* with *B. pumila* Michx. has been found near Mt. Mansfield, Vermont.

5. Betula cœrulea Blanch. Blue Birch.

Leaves ovate, long-pointed, broadly or narrowly concave-cuneate at the entire often unequal base, sharply mostly doubly serrate above with straight or incurved glandular often apiculate teeth, covered above when they unfold with pale deciduous glands, at maturity dull bluish green above, pale yellow-green below, and sparingly villose along the under side of the slender yellow midrib and primary veins, $2'-2\frac{1}{2}'$ long, $1'-1\frac{1}{2}'$ wide:

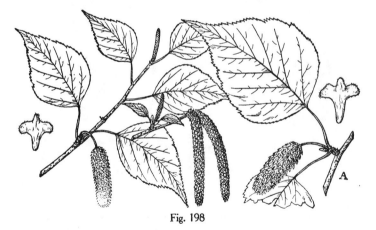

Fig. 198

petioles slender, $\frac{3}{4}'-1\frac{1}{4}'$ long, yellow more or less deeply tinged with red. **Flowers:** staminate aments usually in pairs, or singly or in 3's, $1\frac{1}{4}'-2'$ long, about $\frac{3}{16}'$ thick, with ovate rounded short-pointed scales; pistillate aments slender, about $\frac{1}{3}'$ long, with acuminate pale green much reflexed scales. **Fruit:** strobiles cylindric, pubescent, slightly narrowed at the obtuse apex, about $1'$ long and $\frac{1}{4}'$ thick, pendant on slender peduncles $\frac{1}{4}'-\frac{1}{2}'$ in length; **nut** ellipsoidal, much narrower than its broad wing.

A tree, rarely more than 30° high, with a trunk $8'-10'$ in diameter, small ascending finally spreading branches, and slender branchlets marked by numerous small raised pale lenticels, purplish and sparingly villose when they first appear, soon glabrous, becoming bright red-brown; often forming clumps of several stems. **Bark** thin, white tinged with rose, lustrous, not readily separable into layers, the inner bark light orange color.

Distribution. Moist slopes, Stratton and Windham, Windham County, Vermont, at altitudes of about 1800° (*W. H. Blanchard*), Haystack Mountain, Aroostook County, Maine (*M. L. Fernald*); the American representative of the European *Betula pendula* Roth., and probably widely distributed over the hills of northern New England and eastern Canada. Perhaps with its variety best considered a natural hybrid between *B. papyrifera* and *B. populifolia*.

Apparently passing into a form with larger leaves often rounded and truncate at the broad base, 3′–3½′ long and 2′ wide, stouter staminate aments, and strobiles frequently 1½′ long and ½′ thick (var. *Blanchardii* Sarg. fig. 198 A). This under favorable conditions is a tree 60°–70° high, with a trunk 18′ in diameter; common with *Betula cœrulea* at Windham and Stratton, Vermont (*W. H. Blanchard*), and on a hill near the coast in Washington County, Maine (*M. L. Fernald*).

6. Betula papyrifera Marsh. Canoe Birch. Paper Birch.

Leaves ovate, acute or acuminate with a short broad point, coarsely usually doubly and often very irregularly serrate except at the rounded abruptly cuneate or gradually narrowed base, bright green, glandular-resinous, pubescent and clothed below on the midrib and primary veins and on the petioles with long white hairs when they unfold, at maturity thick and firm, dull dark green and glandless or rarely glandular on the upper surface, light yellow-green and glabrous or puberulous, with small tufts of pale hairs in the axils of the primary veins and covered with many black glands on the lower surface, 2′–3′ long, 1½′–2′ wide, with a slender yellow midrib marked, like the remote primary veins, with minute

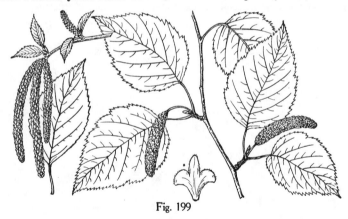

Fig. 199

black glands, turning light clear yellow in the auutmn; petioles stout, yellow, glandular, glabrous or pubescent, ½′–¾′ long; stipules ovate, acute, ciliate on the margins with pale hairs, light green. **Flowers:** staminate aments clustered during the winter, ¾′–1¼′ long, about ⅛′ thick, with ovate, acute scales light brown below the middle, dark red-brown above it, becoming 3½′–4′ long, and about ⅓′ thick; pistillate aments 1′–1¼′ long, about 1⁄16′ thick, with light green lanceolate scales long-pointed and acute or rounded at apex; styles bright red. **Fruit:** strobiles cylindric, glabrous, about 1½′ long and ⅓′ thick, hanging on slender stalks, their scales very rarely entire (var. *elobata* Sarg.); nut ellipsoidal, about 1⁄16′ long, much narrower than its thin wing.

A tree, usually 60°–70° tall, with a trunk 2°–3° in diameter, becoming in old age, or when crowded by other trees, branchless below and supporting a narrow open head of short pendulous branches, and branchlets at first light green, slightly viscid, marked by scattered orange-colored oblong lenticels and covered with long pale hairs, dark orange color and glabrous or pubescent during the summer, becoming dull red in their first winter, gradually growing dark orange-brown, lustrous for four or five years and ultimately covered with the white papery bark of older branches. **Winter-buds** obovoid, acute, about $\frac{1}{4}'$ long, pubescent below the middle and coated with resinous gum at midsummer, dark chestnut-brown, glabrous and slightly resinous during the winter, their inner scales becoming strap-shaped, rounded at apex, about $\frac{1}{2}'$ long and $\frac{1}{8}'$ wide. **Bark** on young trunks and large limbs thin, creamy white or rarely bronze color or orange-brown and lustrous on the outer surface, bright orange color on the inner, marked by long narrow slightly darker colored raised lenticels, separating into thin papery layers, pale orange color when first exposed to the light, becoming on old trunks for a few feet above the ground sometimes $\frac{1}{2}'$ thick, dull brown or nearly black, sharply and irregularly furrowed and broken on the surface into thick closely appressed scales. **Wood** light, strong, hard, tough, very close-grained, light brown tinged with red, with thick nearly white sapwood; largely used for spools, shoe-lasts, pegs, and in turnery, the manufacture of wood-pulp, and for fuel. The tough resinous durable bark impervious to water is used by all the northern Indians to cover their canoes and for baskets, bags, drinking-cups, and other small articles, and often to cover their wigwams in winter.

Distribution. Rich wooded slopes and the borders of streams, lakes, and swamps scattered through forests of other trees; Labrador to the southern shores of Hudson's Bay, and southward to Long Island, New York, northern Pennsylvania, central Michigan, northern Indiana, northern Wisconsin, northern-central Iowa, eastern Nebraska, North and South Dakota and Wyoming; common in the maritime provinces of Canada and North of the Great Lakes, and in northern New England and New York; small and comparatively rare in the coast region of southern New England and southward; on the highest mountains of New England and northward the var. *minor* S. Wats and Cov. is common as a small shrub.

Often planted in the northeastern states as an ornamental tree.

× *Betula Sandbergii* Britt. and its f. *maxima* Rosend. generally believed to be natural hybrids of *B. papyrifera* and *B. pumila* var. *glandulifera* Regl. occur in Tamarack swamps in Hennepin County, Minnesota.

Passing into the following varieties.

Betula papyrifera var. cordifolia Fern.

Leaves ovate, abruptly pointed and acuminate or acute at apex, cordate at base, coarsely doubly serrate, glabrous or pilose on the under side of the midrib and veins, often furnished

Fig. 200

below with axillary tufts of pale hairs, $1\frac{1}{2}'-3'$ long, $1'-2\frac{1}{2}'$ wide; petioles glabrous or rarely villose, $\frac{1}{2}'-\frac{3}{4}'$ in length.   **Fruit:** strobiles $\frac{3}{4}'-2'$ long and $\frac{1}{4}'-\frac{1}{2}'$ thick, on villose peduncles up to $\frac{3}{4}'$ in length; scales glabrous or pubescent.

A tree rarely more than $30°$ tall, with slender glabrous or pubescent branchlets, and at high altitudes on the New England mountains reduced to a low shrub.   Bark separating in thin layers, white or dark reddish brown.

Distribution.   Labrador and Newfoundland to northern New England, and westward to the shores of Green Bay, Wisconsin, and those of Lake Superior, Minnesota (Grand Marais, Cook County); on Mt. Mitchell, North Carolina, at an altitude of $5550°$ (*W. W. Ashe*).

Betula papyrifera var. subcordata Sarg.

Betula subcordata Rydb.

Leaves ovate, acute or acuminate at apex, slightly cordate or rounded at base, rarely slightly lobed above the middle, finely often doubly serrate with teeth pointing forward or spreading, glabrous, $2'-2\frac{1}{2}'$ long, $1'-1\frac{1}{2}'$ wide; petioles sparingly villose or glabrous, $\frac{1}{2}'-\frac{3}{4}'$ in length.   **Fruit:** strobiles drooping on slender peduncles $1'-1\frac{1}{2}'$ long, about $\frac{1}{3}'$ thick,

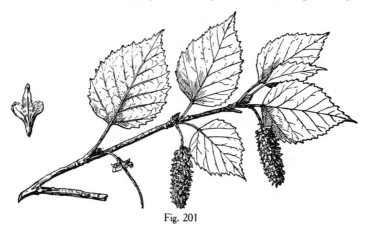

Fig. 201

their scales puberulous, ciliate on the margins, the middle lobe acute, rather longer than the broad truncate lateral lobes; nut obovoid, cuneate at base, $\frac{1}{12}'$ long, narrower than its wings.

A tree $25°-40°$ or occasionally $60°$ high, with a trunk $12'-18'$ in diameter, and slightly glandular glabrous red-brown branchlets.   Bark separating freely into thin layers, white or occasionally dark reddish brown or orange color.

Distribution.   Alberta (Crow Nest Pass, neighborhood of Jasper and Cypress Hills), through northern Montana and Idaho to western Washington, northeastern Oregon (Minum River Valley) and British Columbia.

Betula papyrifera var. montanensis Sarg.

Betula montanensis Butler.

Leaves broadly ovate, acute at apex, truncate or rounded at base to oblong-ovate or lanceolate and long-pointed and acuminate at apex, narrowed and rounded at base, coarsely doubly serrate, thick, dark green above, paler, sparingly pubescent and furnished with conspicuous tufts of axillary hairs below, 3′–5′ long, 2′–2¼′ wide; petioles puberulous, ¾′–1′ in length. **Flowers** unknown. **Fruit:** strobiles cylindric, 1¾′–2′ long, ½′ thick, pendent on puberulous peduncles ½′–¾′ in length, their scales puberulous, finely ciliate on

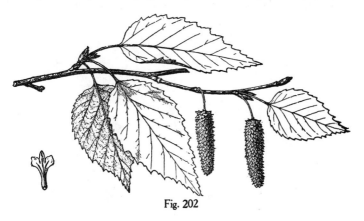

Fig. 202

the margins, the slender base of those below the middle of the ament rather more than twice as long as the expanded upper portion of the scale.

A tree 40°–50° high, with a trunk 12′–18′ in diameter, and slender branchlets red-brown, lustrous, marked by small pale lenticels and puberulous during their first season. **Winter-buds** narrow-obovoid, acuminate, dark red-brown, resinous, ⅓′ long. **Bark** white, or dark gray or brown.

Distribution. Shore of Yellow Bay, Flathead Lake, Flathead County, Montana, and at Sandpoint, Bonner County, Idaho.

Betula papyrifera var. occidentalis Sarg.

Betula occidentalis Hook.

Leaves ovate, acute, or abruptly acuminate at apex, rounded or occasionally cordate or rarely cuneate at the broad base, coarsely and generally doubly serrate with straight or incurved glandular teeth, thin and firm in texture, dull dark green above, pale yellow-green below, and puberulous on both sides of the stout yellow midrib and slender primary veins, 3′–4′ long, 1½′–2′ wide; petioles stout, glandular, at first tomentose, ultimately pubescent or puberulous, about ¾′ long; stipules oblong-obovate, rounded and acute or apisculate at apex, ciliate on the margin, puberulous, glandular-viscid. **Flowers:** staminate aments during the winter about ¾′ long and ⅛′ thick, with ovate scales rounded or abruptly narrowed and acute at apex, puberulous on the outer surface, ciliate on the margins, becoming 3′–4′ long and about ¼′ thick; pistillate aments about 1′ long and ₁⁄₁₆′ thick, with acuminate bright green scales. **Fruit:** strobiles cylindric, puberulous, spreading, 1¼′–1½′ long, ¼′–½′ thick, on stout peduncles ¾′ in length, their scales ciliate on the margins; nut oval, about ₁⁄₁₆′ in length, and nearly as wide as its wings.

A tree, 100°–120° high, with a trunk 3°–4° in diameter, comparatively small branches often pendulous on old trees, and pale orange-brown branchlets more or less glandular and coated with long pale hairs when they first appear, becoming bright orange-brown and nearly destitute of glands during their first winter, and in their second year orange-brown, glabrous, and very lustrous. **Winter-buds** acute, bright orange-brown, ⅛′–¼′ long, their light brown inner scales sometimes becoming ¾′ in length. **Bark** thin, marked by long oblong horizontal raised lenticels, dark orange-brown or white, very lustrous, separating freely into thin papery layers displaying in falling the bright orange-yellow inner bark.

Distribution.   Banks of streams and lakes; southwestern British Columbia and north-western Washington and eastward through eastern Washington and northern Idaho to

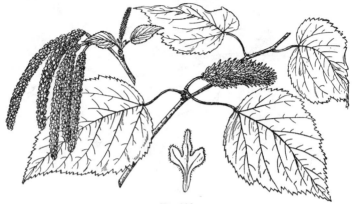

Fig. 203

northern Montana west of the continental divide; nowhere common and probably of its largest size on the alluvial banks of the lower Fraser River, and on the islands of Puget Sound.

Betula papyrifera var. kenaica A. Henry.   Red Birch.   Black Birch.

Betula kenaica Evans.

Leaves ovate, acute or acuminate, broadly cuneate or somewhat rounded at the entire base, irregularly coarsely often doubly serrate, glabrous, dark dull green above, pale yel-

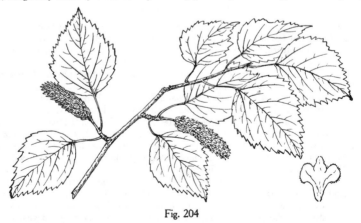

Fig. 204

low-green below, $1\frac{1}{2}'$–$2'$ long, $1'$–$1\frac{3}{4}'$ wide, with a slender yellow midrib and 5 pairs of thin primary veins; petioles slender, $\frac{3}{4}'$–$1'$ long.   **Flowers:** staminate aments clustered, $1'$ long, with ovate acute scales apiculate at apex, puberulous on the outer surface; pistillate aments, $\frac{1}{3}$–$\frac{1}{2}$' long, about $\frac{1}{16}$' thick, on slender glandular pubescent peduncles $\frac{1}{2}$–$\frac{3}{4}$' in length; scales acuminate light green strongly reflexed; styles bright red. **Fruit:** strobiles cylindric, glabrous, 1' long, their scales ciliate on the margins; nut oval, somewhat narrower than its thin wing.

A tree, 30°–40° high, with a trunk 12'–20' in diameter, wide-spreading branches, stout branchlets marked by numerous small pale lenticels, bright red-brown during 2 or 3 years, gradually becoming darker. **Bark** thin, more or less furrowed, very dark brown or nearly black near the base of the trunk, grayish white or light reddish brown and separating into thin layers higher on the stem and on the branches.

Distribution. Coast of Alaska from Cook Inlet southward to the head of the Lynn Canal.

7. Betula alaskana Sarg. White Birch.

Leaves rhombic to deltoid-ovate, long-pointed, truncate, rounded or broadly cuneate, or on leading shoots occasionally cordate at the entire base, coarsely and often doubly glandular-serrate, thin, dark green above, pale and yellow-green below, 1$\frac{1}{2}$'–3' long, 1'–1$\frac{1}{2}$' wide, with a slender midrib and primary veins pubescent or ultimately glabrous below; petioles often bright red, somewhat hairy at first, finally glabrous, about 1' long; **Flowers:** staminate aments clustered, sessile, 1' long, $\frac{1}{8}$' thick, with ovate acuminate scales

Fig. 205

puberulous on the outer surface, and bright red, with yellow margins; pistillate aments slender, cylindric, glandular, 1' long, $\frac{1}{8}$' thick, on stout peduncles nearly $\frac{1}{2}$' in length. **Fruit:** strobiles glabrous, pendulous or spreading, 1'–1$\frac{1}{4}$' long, $\frac{1}{3}$–$\frac{1}{2}$' thick, their scales ciliate on the margins; nut oval, narrower than its broad wing.

A tree, usually 30°–40°, occasionally 80°, high, with a trunk 6'–12' in diameter, slender erect and spreading or pendulous branches, and glabrous bright red-brown branchlets more or less thickly covered during their first year with resinous glands sometimes persistent until the second or third season. **Winter-buds** ovoid, obtuse at the gradually narrowed apex, about $\frac{1}{4}$' long, with light red-brown shining outer scales sometimes ciliate on the margins, and oblong rounded scarious inner scales hardly more than $\frac{1}{2}$' long when fully grown. **Bark** thin, marked by numerous elongated dark slightly raised lenticels, dull reddish brown or sometimes nearly white on the outer surface, light red on the inner surface, close and firm, finally separable into thin plate-like scales.

Distribution. Valley of the Saskatchewan northwestward to the valley of the Yukon, growing sparingly near the banks of streams in forests of coniferous trees and in large numbers on sunny slopes and hillsides; the common Birch-tree of the Yukon basin.

× *Betula commixta* Sarg., a shrub, growing on the tundra near Dawson, Yukon Territory, is believed to be a hybrid between *B. alaskana* and *B. glandulosa* Michx.

8. Betula fontinalis Sarg.   Black Birch.

Leaves ovate, acute or acuminate, sharply and often doubly serrate, except at the rounded or abruptly cuneate often unequal base, and sometimes slightly laciniately lobed, pale green, pilose above, and covered by conspicuous resinous glands when they unfold, at maturity thin and firm, dark dull green above, pale yellow-green, rather lustrous and covered by minute glandular dots below, $1'$–$2'$ long, $\frac{3}{4}'$–$1'$ wide, with a slender pale midrib, remote glandular veins, and rather conspicuous reticulate veinlets; turning dull yellow in the autumn; petioles stout, puberulous, light yellow, glandular-dotted, flattened on the upper side, often flushed with red, $\frac{1}{3}'$–$\frac{1}{2}'$ long; stipules broadly ovate, acute or rounded at apex, slightly ciliate, bright green, soon becoming pale and scarious. **Flowers:** staminate aments clustered, $\frac{1}{2}'$–$\frac{3}{4}'$ long and $\frac{1}{16}'$ thick during the winter, with ovate acute light chestnut-brown scales pale and slightly ciliate on the margins, becoming $2'$–$2\frac{1}{2}'$ long, and about $\frac{1}{8}'$ thick, with apiculate scales; pistillate aments short-stalked, about $\frac{3}{4}'$ long, with ovate acute green scales; styles bright red.   **Fruit:** strobiles cylindric, rather obtuse, puberulous or nearly glabrous, $1'$–$1\frac{1}{4}'$ long, $\frac{1}{2}'$ thick, erect or pendulous on

Fig. 206

slender glandular peduncles, $\frac{1}{4}'$ to nearly $\frac{3}{4}'$ in length; their scales ciliate, puberulous, the lateral lobes ascending, shorter than the middle lobe; nut ovoid or obovoid, puberulous at apex, nearly as wide as its wing.

A tree $20°$–$25°$ high with a short trunk, rarely more than $12'$ or $14'$ in diameter, ascending spreading and somewhat pendulous branches forming a broad open head, and slender branchlets, when they first appear light green glabrous or puberulous and covered with lustrous resinous glands persistent during their second season, and dark red-brown in their first winter; more commonly shrubby, with many thin spreading stems forming open clusters, $15°$–$20°$ high; often much lower, and frequently crowded in almost impenetrable thickets.   **Winter-buds** ovoid, acute, very resinous, chestnut-brown, $\frac{1}{4}'$ long.   **Bark** about $\frac{1}{4}'$ thick, dark bronze color, very lustrous, marked by pale brown longitudinal lenticels becoming on old trunks often $6'$–$8'$ long and $\frac{1}{4}'$ wide.   **Wood** soft and strong, light brown, with thick lighter-colored sapwood; sometimes used for fuel and fencing.

Distribution.   Moist soil near the banks of streams usually in mountain cañons; generally distributed, although nowhere very common: valley of the Saskatchewan (Saskatoon), Saskatchewan, westward to the basin of the upper Fraser and Pease Rivers, British Columbia, southward along the Rocky Mountains to eastern Utah, northern New Mexico and Arizona, the valleys of the Shasta region and the eastern slope of the Sierra Nevada, northern California, and eastward in the United States to the eastern foothills of the Rocky Mountains of Colorado, the Black Hills of South Dakota, and northwestern Nebraska. Passing into

Betula fontinalis var. Piperi Sarg.

Betula Piperi Britt.

A tree occasionally 50°–60° high with a tall trunk 12′–18′ in diameter, short spreading branches, and usually longer and often narrower strobiles.

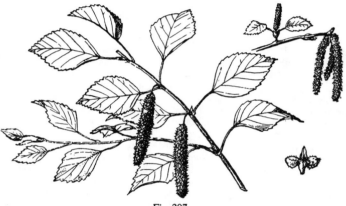

Fig. 207

Distribution. Spokane, Spokane County, Almota and Pullman, Whitman County, eastern Washington.

9. Betula Eastwoodæ Sarg.

Leaves broad-ovate to elliptic, acute, rounded or abruptly short-pointed at apex, coarsely serrate except at the cuneate base, thick, glabrous, dark green above, pale below, reticulate-

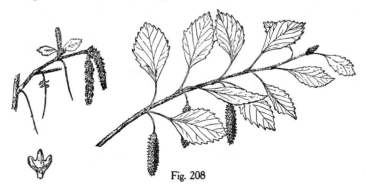

Fig. 208

venulose, the veinlets more conspicuous on the lower surface, $1'$–$1\frac{1}{2}'$ long, $\frac{3}{4}'$–$1\frac{1}{2}'$ wide; petioles slender, glabrous $\frac{1}{5}'$–$\frac{1}{3}'$ in length; stipules scarious, ovate-oblong, rounded at apex. **Flowers:** staminate aments usually solitary or in pairs, sessile, $1'$–$1\frac{1}{4}'$ long, $\frac{1}{5}'$ thick, with broadly ovate pubescent dark red scales acute and apiculate at apex; pistillate aments $\frac{1}{2}'$ long, about $\frac{1}{12}'$ thick, with acute light green scales. **Fruit:** strobiles pendulous on peduncles $\frac{1}{4}'$–$\frac{1}{2}'$ long, cylindric, $\frac{3}{4}'$ in length, about $\frac{1}{5}'$ thick, their scales glabrous longer than broad, the lobes narrowed at the rounded apex, ciliate, the lateral slightly spreading, one third shorter than the terminal lobe.

A tree 18°–20° high, with a trunk rarely more than 6′ in diameter, and slender red glabrous branchlets thickly covered with circular white glands. **Bark** close, chestnut-brown, marked by conspicuous horizontal white lenticels, about $\frac{1}{5}'$ thick.

Distribution. Swamps near Dawson, Yukon Territory, forming jungles with *Betula glandulosa* Michx., *B. alaskana* Sarg., and various Willows; as a large shrub in Jasper Park near Jasper, Alberta.

4. ALNUS L. Alder.

Trees and shrubs, with astringent scaly bark, soft straight-grained wood, naked stipitate winter-buds formed in summer and nearly inclosed by the united stipules of the first leaf, becoming thick, resinous, and dark red. Leaves open and convex in the bud, falling without change of color; stipules of all but the first leaf ovate, acute, and scarious. Flowers vernal, or rarely opening in the autumn from aments of the year, in 1–3-flowered cymes in the axils of the peltate short-stalked scales of stalked aments formed in summer or autumn in the axils of the last leaves of the year or of those of minute leafy bracts; staminate aments elongated, pendulous, paniculate, naked and erect during the winter, each staminate flower subtended by 3–5 minute bractlets adnate to the scales of the ament, and composed of a 4-parted calyx, and 1–3 or usually 4 stamens inserted on the base of the calyx opposite its lobes, with short simple filaments; pistillate aments ovoid or oblong, erect, stalked, produced in summer in the axils of the leaves of a branch developed from the axils of an upper leaf of the year, and below the staminate inflorescence, inclosed at first in the stipules of the first leaf, emerging in the autumn and naked during the winter, or remaining covered until early spring; pistillate flowers in pairs, each flower subtended by 2–4 minute bractlets adnate to the fleshy scale of the ament becoming at maturity thick and woody, obovate, 3–5-lobed or truncate at the thickened apex, forming an ovoid or subglobose strobile persistent after the opening of its closely imbricated scales; calyx 0; ovary compressed; nut minute. bright chestnut-brown, ovoid to oblong, flat, bearing at the apex the remnants of the style, marked at the base by a pale scar, the outer coat of the shell produced into lateral wings often reduced to a narrow membranaceous border.

Alnus inhabits swamps, river bottom-lands, and high mountains, and is widely and generally distributed through the northern hemisphere, often forming the most conspicuous feature of vegetation on mountain slopes, ranging at high altitudes southward in the New World through Central America to Colombia, Peru, and Bolivia, and to upper Assam and Japan in the Old World. Of the eighteen or twenty species now recognized nine are North American; of these, six attain the size and habit of trees. Of the exotic species, *Alnus vulgaris* Hill., a common European, north African, and Asiatic timber-tree, was introduced many years ago into the northeastern states, where it has become locally naturalized. The wood of Alnus is very durable in water, and the astringent bark and strobiles are used in tanning leather and in medicine.

Alnus is the classical name of the Alder.

CONSPECTUS OF THE NORTH AMERICAN ARBORESCENT SPECIES.

Flowers opening in spring with or after the leaves; stamens 4; pistillate aments inclosed during the winter; wing of the nut broad; leaves ovate, sinuately lobed, lustrous on the lower surface.   **1. A. sinuata** (B, F, G).

Flowers opening in winter or early spring before the unfolding of the leaves; pistillate aments usually naked during the winter.

Wing of the nut broad; leaves ovate or elliptic, rusty-pubescent on the lower surface; pistillate aments often inclosed during the winter; stamens 4.   **2. A. rubra** (B, G).

Wing of the nut reduced to a narrow border.

Stamens 4; leaves oblong-ovate, glabrous or puberulous on the lower surface.
                                                      3. A. tenuifolia (B, F, G).

Stamens usually 2, or 3.

Leaves ovate or oval.   **4. A. rhombifolia** (B, F, G).

Leaves oblong-lanceolate, acute.   **5. A. oblongifolia** (H).

Flowers opening in autumn from aments of the year; stamens 4; wing of the nut reduced to a narrow border; leaves oblong-ovate or obovate, dark green and lustrous above, pale yellow-green below.   **6. A. maritima** (A).

1. Alnus sinuata Rydb.   Alder.

Alnus sitchensis Sarg.

Leaves ovate, acute, full and rounded and often unsymmetrical and somewhat oblique or abruptly narrowed and cuneate at base, divided into numerous short acute lateral lobes, sharply and doubly serrate with straight glandular teeth, glandular-viscid as they unfold, at maturity membranaceous, yellow-green on the upper surface, pale and very lustrous on

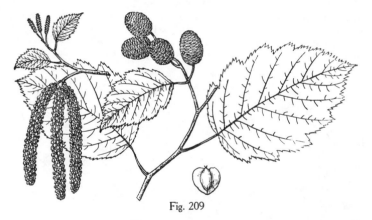

Fig. 209

the lower surface, glabrous, or villose along the under side of the stout midrib with short brown hairs also forming tufts in the axils of the numerous slender primary veins, $3'-6'$ long, $1\frac{1}{2}'-4'$ wide; petioles stout, grooved, abruptly enlarged at the base, $\frac{1}{2}'-\frac{3}{4}'$ in length; stipules oblong to spatulate, rounded and apiculate at apex, puberulous, about $\frac{1}{4}'$ long. **Flowers:** staminate aments sessile, in pairs in the axils of the upper leaves sometimes reduced to small bracts, and single in the axil of the leaf next below, during the winter about $\frac{1}{2}'$ long and $\frac{1}{8}'$ thick, with dark red-brown shining puberulous apiculate scales, becoming when the flowers open from spring to midsummer $4'$ or $5'$ long, with a puberulous light red rachis and ovate acute apiculate 3-flowered scales; calyx-lobes rounded, shorter than the 4 stamens; pistillate aments in elongated panicles, inclosed during winter in buds formed the previous summer in the axils of the leaves of short lateral branchlets, long-pedunculate, $\frac{1}{4}'$ long, $\frac{1}{8}'$ thick. **Fruit:** strobiles on slender peduncles in elongated sometimes leafy panicles $4'-6'$ in length, oblong, $\frac{1}{2}'-\frac{5}{8}'$ long, about $\frac{1}{3}'$ thick, their truncate scales thickened at the apex; nut oval, about as wide as its wings.

A tree, sometimes 40° high, with a trunk 7'–8' in diameter, short small nearly horizontal branches forming a narrow crown, and slender slightly zigzag branchlets puberulous and very glandular when they first appear, bright orange-brown and lustrous and marked by numerous large pale lenticels during their first season, much roughened during their second year by the elevated crowded leaf-scars, becoming light gray. **Winter-buds** acuminate, dark purple, covered especially toward the apex with close fine pubescence, about $\frac{1}{2}'$ long. **Bark** thin bluish gray, with bright red inner bark; often a shrub only a few feet tall spreading into broad thickets.

Distribution. Northwest coast from the borders of the Arctic Circle to the high mountains of northern California; common in the valley of the Yukon and eastward through British Columbia to Alberta, and through Washington and Oregon to the western slopes of the Rocky Mountains in Montana; at the north with dwarf Willows, forming great thickets; in southeastern Alaska often a tall tree on rich moist bottom-lands near the mouths of mountain streams, and at the upper limits of tree growth a low shrub; very abundant in the valley of the Yukon on the wet banks of streams and often arborescent in habit; in British Columbia and the United States generally smaller and a shrub, growing usually only at altitudes of more than 3000° above the sea, and often forming thickets on the banks of streams and lakes.

2. Alnus rubra Bong.   Alder.

Alnus oregona Nutt.

Leaves ovate to elliptic, acute, abruptly or gradually narrowed and cuneate at base, crenately lobed, dentate with minute gland-tipped teeth, and slightly revolute on the margins, covered when they unfold with pale tomentum, at maturity thick dark green and glabrous or pilose with scattered white hairs above, clothed below with short rusty pubes-

Fig. 210

cence, 3'–5' long, $1\frac{3}{4}'$–3' wide, or on vigorous branchlets sometimes 8'–10' long, with a broad midrib and primary veins green on the upper side and orange-colored on the lower, the primary veins running obliquely to the points of the lobes and connected by conspicuous slightly reticulate cross veinlets; petioles orange-colored, nearly terete, slightly grooved, $\frac{1}{4}'$–$\frac{3}{4}'$ in length; stipules ovate, acute, pale green flushed with red, tomentose, $\frac{3}{8}'$–$\frac{1}{4}'$ long. **Flowers:** staminate aments in red-stemmed clusters, during the winter $1\frac{1}{4}'$ long, $\frac{1}{8}'$ thick, with dark red-brown lustrous closely appressed scales, becoming 4'–6' long and $\frac{1}{4}'$ thick, with ovate acute orange-colored glabrous scales; calyx yellow, with ovate rounded lobes rather shorter than the 4 stamens; pistillate aments in short racemes usually inclosed during the winter in buds formed during the early summer and opening in the early spring, $\frac{1}{3}-\frac{1}{2}'$ long, about $\frac{1}{16}'$ thick, with dark red acute scales; styles bright red. **Fruit:** strobiles raised on stout orange-colored peduncles sometimes $\frac{1}{2}'$ in length, ovoid or oblong, $\frac{1}{2}-1'$ long, $\frac{1}{3}-\frac{1}{2}'$ thick, with truncate scales much thickened toward the apex; nut orbicular to obovoid, surrounded by a membranaceous wing.

A tree, usually 40°–50°, occasionally 90° high, with a trunk sometimes 3° in diameter, slender somewhat pendulous branches forming a narrow pyramidal head, and slender branchlets marked by minute scattered pale lenticels, light green and coated at first with hoary tomentum sometimes persistent until their second year, becoming during the first winter bright red and lustrous and ultimately ashy gray. **Winter-buds** about $\frac{1}{3}'$ long, dark red, covered with pale scurfy pubescence. **Bark** rarely more than $\frac{3}{4}'$ thick, close, roughened by minute wart-like excrescences, pale gray or nearly white, with a thin outer layer, and bright red-brown inner bark. **Wood** light, soft, brittle, not strong, close-grained, light brown tinged with red, with thick nearly white sapwood; in Washington and Oregon largely used in the manufacture of furniture and for smoking salmon; by the Indians of Alaska the trunks are hollowed into canoes.

Distribution. Shores of Yakutat Bay, southeastern Alaska, southward near the coast to the cañons of the Santa Inez Mountains, Santa Barbara County, California; common along the banks of streams, and of its largest size near the shores of Puget Sound; in California most abundant in Mendocino, Humbolt and Marin Counties, forming groves on bottom-lands near the coast; often ranging inland for 20 or 30 miles, and occasionally ascending to altitudes of 2000° above the sea.

3. Alnus tenuifolia Nutt. Alder.

Leaves ovate-oblong, acute or acuminate, broad and rounded or cordate or occasionally abruptly narrowed and cuneate at base, usually acutely laciniately lobed and doubly ser-

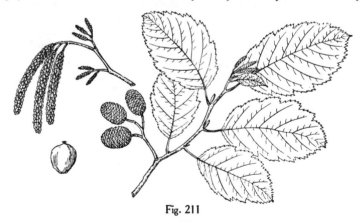

Fig. 211

rate, when they unfold light green often tinged with red, pilose on the upper surface and coated on the lower with pale tomentum, at maturity thin and firm, dark green and glabrous above, pale yellow-green and glabrous or puberulous below, $2'-4'$ long, $1\frac{1}{2}'-2\frac{1}{2}'$ wide, with a stout orange-colored midrib impressed on the upper side, and slender primary veins running to the points of the lobes; petioles stout, slightly grooved, orange-colored, $\frac{1}{2}'-1'$ in length; stipules ovate, acute, thin, and scarious, $\frac{1}{2}'$ long, about $\frac{1}{8}'$ wide, covered with pale pubescence. **Flowers:** staminate aments 3 or 4 in number in slender-stemmed racemes, nearly sessile or raised on stout peduncles often $\frac{1}{2}'$ long, during the winter light purple, $\frac{3}{4}'-1'$ long and $\frac{1}{4}'$ thick, becoming $1\frac{1}{2}'-2'$ in length; calyx-lobes rounded, shorter than the 4 stamens; pistillate aments naked during the winter, dark red-brown, nearly $\frac{1}{4}'$ long, with acute apiculate loosely imbricated scales, only slightly enlarged when the flowers open. **Fruit:** strobiles obovoid-oblong, $\frac{3}{8}'-\frac{1}{2}'$ long, their scales much thickened, truncate and 3-lobed at apex; nut nearly circular to slightly obovoid, surrounded by a thin membranaceous border.

A tree, occasionally 30° tall, with a trunk 6'-8' in diameter, small spreading slightly pendulous branches forming a narrow round-topped head, and slender branchlets marked at first by a few large orange-colored lenticels and coated with fine pale or rusty caducous pubescence, becoming light brown or ashy gray more or less deeply flushed with red in their first winter and ultimately paler; more often shrubby, with several spreading stems, and at the north and at high altitudes frequently only 4°-5° tall. **Winter-buds** $\frac{1}{4}'-\frac{1}{3}'$ long, bright red, and puberulous. **Bark** rarely more than $\frac{1}{4}'$ thick, bright red-brown and broken on the surface into small closely appressed scales.

Distribution. Banks of streams and mountain cañons from Francis Lake in latitude 61° north to the valley of the lower Fraser River, British Columbia, eastward along the Saskatchewan to Prince Albert, and southward through the Rocky Mountains to northern New Mexico; on the Sierra Nevada of southern California, and in Lower California; the common Alder of mountain streams in the northern interior region of the continent; very abundant on the eastern slopes of the Cascade Mountains, and on the southern California Sierras; forming great thickets at 6000°-7000° above the sea along the head-waters of the rivers of southern California flowing to the Pacific Ocean; the common Alder of eastern Washington and Oregon, and of Idaho and Montana; very abundant and of its largest size in Colorado and northern New Mexico.

4. Alnus rhombifolia Nutt. White Alder. Alder.

Leaves ovate or oval or sometimes nearly orbicular, rounded or acute at apex, especially on vigorous shoots, gradually or abruptly narrowed and cuneate at base, finely or sometimes coarsely and occasionally doubly serrate, slightly thickened and reflexed on the some-

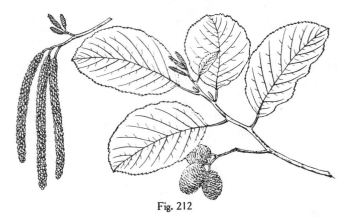

Fig. 212

what undulate margins, when they unfold pale green and covered with deciduous matted white hairs, at maturity dark green and lustrous on the upper surface, frequently marked, especially on the midrib, with minute glandular dots, light yellow-green and slightly puberulous below, 2'-3' long, $1\frac{1}{2}'-2'$ wide, with a stout yellow midrib and primary veins; petioles slender, yellow, hairy, flattened and grooved on the upper side, $\frac{1}{2}'-\frac{3}{4}'$ long; stipules ovate, acute, scarious, puberulous, about $\frac{1}{4}'$ in length. **Flowers:** staminate aments in slender-stemmed pubescent clusters, usually short-stalked, during the summer dark olive-brown and lustrous, $\frac{3}{4}$–1' long and about $\frac{1}{16}$' thick, beginning to lengthen late in the autumn before the leaves fall, fully grown and 4'–6' long and $\frac{1}{4}$' thick in January, with dark orange-brown scales, and deciduous in February before the appearance of the new leaves; calyx yellow, 4-lobed, rather shorter than the 2 or occasionally 3 or rarely single stamen; pistillate aments in short pubescent racemes emerging from the bud in December, their scales broadly ovate and rounded. **Fruit:** strobiles oblong, $\frac{1}{3}$–$\frac{1}{2}$' long, with thin scales slightly thickened and lobed at apex, fully grown at midsummer, remaining closed until the trees flower the following year; nut broadly ovoid, with a thin margin.

A tree, frequently 70°–80° high, with a tall straight trunk 2°–3° in diameter, long slender branches pendulous at the ends, forming a wide round-topped open head, and slender branchlets marked by small scattered lenticels, at first light green and coated with pale caducous pubescence, soon becoming dark orange-red and glabrous, and darker during the winter and following summer. **Winter-buds** nearly $\frac{1}{2}$' long, very slender, dark red, and covered with pale scurfy pubescence. **Bark** on old trunks 1' thick, dark brown, irregularly divided into flat often connected ridges broken into oblong plates covered with small closely appressed scales. **Wood** light, soft, not strong, brittle, close-grained, light brown, with thick lighter colored often nearly white sapwood.

Distribution. Banks of streams from northern Idaho to the eastern slope of the Cascade Mountains of Washington and southeastern Oregon, and southward from the valley of the Willamette River, Oregon (near Salem, Marion County, *J. C. Nelson*) over the coast ranges and along the western slopes of the Sierra Nevada to the mountains of southern California (San Bernardino, San Jacinto, and Cuyamaca Ranges); the common Alder of the valleys of central California, occasionally ascending on the southern Sierra Nevada to altitudes of 8000°, and the only species at low altitudes in the southern part of the state.

5. Alnus oblongifolia Torr. Alder.

Alnus acuminata Sarg., not H. B. K.

Leaves oblong-lanceolate, acute; or rarely obovate and rounded at apex, gradually narrowed and cuneate at base, sharply and usually doubly serrate, more or less thickly covered, especially early in the season, with black glands, dark yellow-green and glabrous or slightly

Fig. 213

puberulous above, pale and glabrous or puberulous below, especially along the slender yellow midrib and veins, with small tufts of rusty hairs in the axils of the primary veins, 2'–3' long, about 1$\frac{1}{2}$' wide; petioles slender, grooved, pubescent, $\frac{3}{4}$' long; stipules ovate-lanceolate, brown and scarious, about $\frac{1}{4}'$ in length. **Flowers:** staminate aments in short stout-stemmed racemes, during the winter light yellow, $\frac{1}{2}'-\frac{3}{4}'$ long and about $\frac{1}{16}'$ thick, becoming when the flowers open at the end of February before the appearance of the leaves $2'-2\frac{1}{2}'$ in length, with ovate pointed dark orange-brown scales; calyx 4-lobed; stamens 3 or occasionally 2, with pale red anthers soon becoming light yellow; pistillate aments naked during the winter, $\frac{1}{8}'$ to nearly $\frac{1}{4}'$ long, with light brown ovate rounded scales; stigmas bright red.   **Fruit:** strobiles $\frac{1}{2}'-1'$ long, with thin scales slightly thickened and nearly truncate at apex; nut broadly ovoid, with a narrow membranaceous border.

A tree, in the United States rarely more than $20°-30°$ high, with a trunk sometimes $8'$ in diameter, long slender spreading branches forming an open round-topped head, and slender branchlets slightly puberulous when they first appear, light orange-red and lustrous during their first winter, and marked by small conspicuous pale lenticels, becoming in their second year dark red-brown or gray tinged with red and much roughened by the elevated leaf-scars. **Winter-buds** acute, red, lustrous, glabrous, $\frac{1}{2}'$ long. **Bark** thin, smooth, light brown tinged with red.

Distribution. Banks of streams in cañons of the mountains of southern New Mexico and Arizona at altitudes of $4000°-6000°$ above the sea; in Oak Creek Cañon near Flagstaff, northern Arizona (tree $100° \times 3°$, *P. Lowell*); and on the mountains of northern Mexico.

6. Alnus maritima Nutt. Alder.

Leaves oblong-ovate, or obovate, acute, acuminate or rounded at apex, gradually narrowed and cuneate at base, remotely serrate with minute incurved glandular teeth, and somewhat thickened on the slightly undulate margins, when they unfold, light green tinged with red, hairy on the midrib, veins, and petioles, and coated above with pale scurfy

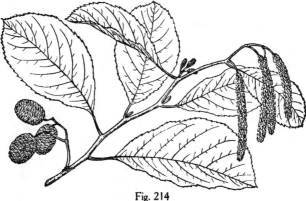

Fig. 214

pubescence, at maturity dark green, very lustrous, and covered below by minute pale glandular dots, $3'-4'$ long, $1\frac{1}{2}'-2'$ wide, with a stout yellow midrib and primary veins prominent and glandular on the upper side and slightly puberulous below; petioles stout, yellow, glandular, flattened and grooved on the upper side, $\frac{1}{2}'-\frac{3}{4}'$ in length; stipules oblong, acute, about $\frac{1}{8}'$ long, dark reddish brown, caducous. **Flowers** opening in the autumn: aments appearing in July on branches of the year and fully grown in August or early in September; staminate in short scurfy-pubescent glandular-pitted racemes on slender peduncles sometimes $1'$ in length from the axils of upper leaves, covered at first with ovate acute dark green very lustrous scales slightly ciliate on the margins and furnished at apex with minute red points, at maturity $1\frac{1}{2}'-2\frac{1}{2}'$ long, $\frac{1}{4}'$ to nearly $\frac{1}{2}'$ thick, with dark orange-brown scales raised on slender stalks, and 4 bright orange-colored stamens; pistillate usually solitary from the axils of the lower leaves on stout pubescent peduncles, bright red at apex and light green below before opening, with ovate acute scales slightly ciliate on the margins, about ⅛′ long when the styles protrude from between the scales, beginning to enlarge the following spring. **Fruit** attaining full size at midsummer and then raised on a stout peduncle, broadly ovoid, rounded and depressed at base, gradually narrowed to the rather obtuse apex, about ⅝′ long and ½′ broad, with thin lustrous scales slightly thickened and crenately lobed at apex, turning dark reddish brown or nearly black and opening late in the autumn and remaining on the branches until after the flowers open the following year; nut oblong-obovoid, gradually narrowed and apiculate at apex, with a thin membranaceous border.

A tree, occasionally 30° high, with a tall straight trunk 4′–5′ in diameter, small spreading branches forming a narrow round-topped head, slender slightly zigzag branchlets, light green and hairy at first, pale yellow-green, very lustrous, slightly puberulous, marked with occasional small orange-colored lenticels, and glandular with minute dark glandular dots during their first summer, becoming dull light orange or reddish brown in the winter, and ashy gray often slightly tinged with red the following season; more often shrubby, with numerous slender spreading stems 15°–20° tall. **Winter-buds** acute, dark red, coated with pale lustrous scurfy pubescence, about ¼′ long. **Bark** ⅛′ thick, smooth, light brown or brown tinged with gray. **Wood** light, soft, close-grained, light brown, with thick hardly distinguishable sapwood.

Distribution. Banks of streams and ponds in southern Delaware and Maryland, and in south central Oklahoma (Johnson and Bryan Counties).

Occasionally cultivated as an ornamental tree in the eastern states and hardy as far north as Massachusetts.

X. FAGACEÆ.

Trees, with watery juice, slender terete branchlets marked by numerous usually pale lenticels, alternate stalked penniveined leaves, and narrow mostly deciduous stipules. Flowers monœcious, the staminate in unisexual heads or aments, composed of a 4–8-lobed calyx, and 4 or 8 stamens, with free simple filaments and introrse 2-celled anthers, the cells parallel and contiguous, opening longitudinally; the pistillate solitary or clustered, in terminal unisexual or bisexual spikes or heads, subtended by an involucre of imbricated bracts becoming woody and partly or entirely inclosing the fruit, and composed of a 4–8-lobed calyx adnate to the 3–7-celled ovary with as many styles as its cells and 1 or 2 pendulous anatropous or semi-anatropous ovules in each cell. Fruit a nut 1-seeded by abortion, the outer coat cartilaginous, the inner membranaceous or bony. Seed filling the cavity of the nut, without albumen; seed-coat membranaceous; cotyledons fleshy, including the minute superior radicle; hilum, basal, minute.

The six genera of this widely distributed family occur in North America with the exception of Nothofagus, separated from Fagus to receive the Beech-trees of the southern hemisphere.

CONSPECTUS OF THE NORTH AMERICAN GENERA.

Staminate flowers fascicled in globose-stalked heads; the pistillate in 2–4-flowered clusters.
1. **Fagus.**
Staminate flowers in slender aments.
Pistillate flowers in 2–5-flowered clusters below the staminate, in bisexual aments.
Nut inclosed in a prickly burr.
Leaves deciduous; ovary 6-celled; nut maturing in one season; branchlets lengthening by an upper axillary bud; bud-scales 4. 2. **Castanea.**
Leaves persistent; ovary 3-celled; nut maturing at the end of the second season; branchlets lengthening by a terminal bud; bud-scales numerous. 3. **Castanopsis.**

Nut inclosed only partly in a shallow cup covered by slender recurved scales united only at the base, free above.   **4. Lithocarpus.**

Pistillate flowers solitary, in few-flowered unisexual spikes; nut more or less inclosed in a cup covered by thin or thickened scales, closely appressed or often free toward its rim.   **5. Quercus.**

1. FAGUS L. Beech.

Trees, with smooth pale bark, hard close-grained wood, and elongated acute bright chestnut-brown buds, their inner scales accrescent and marking the base of the branchlets with persistent ring-like scars. Leaves convex and plicate along the veins in the bud, thick and firm, deciduous; petioles short, nearly terete, in falling leaving small elevated semioval leaf-scars, with marginal rows of minute fibro-vascular bundle-scars; stipules linear-lanceolate, infolding the leaf in the bud. Flowers vernal after the unfolding of the leaves; staminate short-pedicellate, in globose many-flowered heads on long drooping bibracteolate stems at base of shoots of the year or from the axils of their lowest leaves, and composed of a subcampanulate 4–8-lobed calyx, the lobes imbricated in æstivation, ovate and rounded, and 8–16 stamens inserted on the base of and longer than the calyx, with slender filaments and oblong green anthers; pistillate in 2–4-flowered stalked clusters in the axils of upper leaves of the year, surrounded by numerous awl-shaped hairy bracts, the outer bright red, longer than the flowers, deciduous, the inner shorter and united below into a 4-lobed involucre becoming at maturity woody, ovoid, thick-walled, and covered by stout recurved prickles, inclosing or partly inclosing the usually 3 nuts, and ultimately separating into 4 valves; calyx urn-shaped, villose, divided into 4 or 5 linear-lanceolate acute lobes, its 3-angled tube adnate to the 3-celled ovary surmounted by 3 slender recurved pilose styles green and stigmatic toward the apex and longer than the involucre; ovules 2 in each cell. Nut ovoid, unequally 3-angled, acute or winged at the angles, concave and longitudinally ridged on the sides, chestnut-brown and lustrous, tipped with the remnants of the styles, marked at the base by a small triangular scar, with a thin shell covered on the inner surface with rufous tomentum. Seed dark chestnut-brown, suspended with the abortive ovules from the tip of the hairy dissepiment of the ovary pushed by the growth of the seed into one of the angles of the nut; cotyledons sweet, oily, plano-convex.

Fagus as here limited is confined to the northern hemisphere, with a single American species and seven Old World species; of these one is widely distributed through Europe, another is found in the Caucasus, and the others are confined to eastern temperate Asia. Of exotic species, the European *Fagus sylvatica* L., an important timber-tree, is frequently planted for ornament in the eastern states in several of its forms, especially those with purple leaves, and with pendulous branches. The wood of Fagus is hard and close-grained. The sweet seeds are a favorite food of swine, and yield a valuable oil.

Fagus is the classical name of the Beech-tree.

1. Fagus grandifolia Ehrh. Beech.

Fagus americana Sweet.

Leaves remote at the ends of the branches and clustered on short lateral branchlets, oblong-ovate, acuminate with a long slender point, coarsely serrate with spreading or incurved triangular teeth except at the gradually narrowed generally cuneate base, when they unfold pale green and clothed on the lower surface and margins with long pale lustrous silky hairs, at maturity dull dark bluish green above, light yellow-green, very lustrous, and glabrous or rarely pilose below (f. *pubescens* Fern. & Rehd.) with tufts of long pale hairs in the axils of the veins, 2½′–5′ long, 1′–3′ wide, with a slender yellow midrib covered above with short pale hairs, and slender primary veins running obliquely to the points of the teeth; turning bright clear yellow in the autumn; very rarely deeply laciniate; petioles hairy, ¼′–½′ in length; stipules ovate-lanceolate on the lower leaves, strapshaped to linear-lanceolate on the upper, brown or often red below the middle, membranaceous, lustrous, $1'-1\frac{1}{2}'$ long. **Flowers** opening when the leaves are about one third grown; staminate in globose heads $1'$ in diameter, on slender hairy peduncles about $2'$ long; pistillate in usually 2-flowered clusters, on short clavate hoary peduncles $\frac{1}{2}'-\frac{3}{4}'$ long. **Fruit**: involucres $\frac{1}{2}'-\frac{3}{4}'$ in length often shorter than the nuts, on stout hairy club-shaped peduncles $\frac{1}{4}'-\frac{3}{4}'$ long, fully grown at midsummer, and then puberulous, dark orange-green, and covered by long slender recurved prickles red above the middle, becoming at maturity in the autumn light brown and tomentose, with crowded much recurved pubescent prickles, persistent on the branch after opening late into the winter; nut about $\frac{3}{4}'$ long.

A tree, usually $70°-80°$ but exceptionally $120°$ high, sending up from the roots numerous small stems sometimes extending into broad thickets round the parent tree, in the forest with a long comparatively slender stem free of branches for more than half its length, and short branches forming a narrow head, in open situations short-stemmed, with a trunk often $3°-4°$ in diameter, and numerous limbs spreading gradually and forming a broad com-

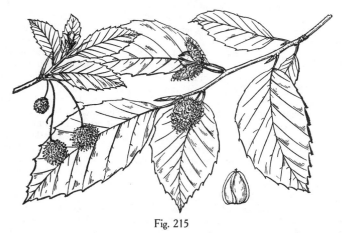

Fig. 215

pact round-topped head of slender slightly drooping branches clothed with short leafy laterals, and branchlets pale green and coated with long soft caducous hairs when they first appear, olive-green or orange-colored during their first summer, and conspicuously marked by oblong bright orange lenticels, gradually growing red, bright reddish brown during their first winter, darker brown in their second season and ultimately ashy gray. **Winter-buds** puberulous, especially toward the apex, $\frac{3}{4}'$ to nearly $1'$ long, about $\frac{1}{8}'$ broad, the inner scales hirsute on the inner surface and along the margins and when fully grown often $1'$ long, lustrous, brown above the middle, and reddish below. **Bark** $\frac{1}{4}'-\frac{1}{2}'$ thick, with a smooth light steel-gray surface. **Wood** hard, strong, tough, very close-grained, not durable, difficult to season, dark or often light red, with thin nearly white sapwood of 20–30 layers of annual growth; largely used in the manufacture of chairs, shoe-lasts, plane-stocks, the handles of tools, and for fuel. The sweet nuts are gathered and sold in the markets of Canada and of some of the western and middle states.

Distribution. Rich uplands and mountain slopes, often forming nearly pure forests, and southward on the bottom-lands of streams and the margins of swamps; Nova Scotia, valley of the Restigouche River, New Brunswick, to the northern shores of Lake Huron and the southern shores of Lake Superior, and southward to Virginia, Ohio, Michigan, the ravines of Rock River near Oregon, Ogle County, Illinois, and Minnesota; southward passing into the var. *caroliniana* Fern. & Rehd., differing in its ovate to short-ovate thicker leaves, usually rounded or subcordate at base, and often less coarsely serrate or undulate on the margins, glabrous or rarely densely soft pubescent below (f. *mollis* Fern. & Rehd.), in the often shorter involucre of the fruit with shorter and less crowded prickles; usually on the bottom-lands of streams and the borders of swamps, New Jersey, and southern Ohio and southeastern Missouri to western Florida, Alabama, Mississippi, Louisiana, eastern Texas, and northeastern Oklahoma; ascending on the southern Appalachian Mountains to altitudes of 4000° or over; probably growing to its largest size in eastern Louisiana.

The northern form is occasionally planted in the northern states as a shade and park tree.

2. CASTANEA Adans. Chestnut.

Trees or shrubs, with furrowed bark, porous brittle wood, durable in the ground, terete branchlets without terminal buds, axillary buds covered by 2 pairs of slightly imbricated scales, the outer lateral, the others accrescent, becoming oblong-ovate and acute and marking the base of the branch with narrow ring-like scars, and stout perpendicular tap-roots; producing when cut numerous stout shoots from the stump. Leaves convolute in the bud, ovate, acute, coarsely serrate, except at the base, with thin veins running to the points of the slender glandular teeth, deciduous; petioles leaving in falling small elevated semioval leaf-scars marked by an irregular marginal row of minute fibro-vascular bundle-scars; stipules ovate to linear-lanceolate, acute, scarious, infolding the leaf in the bud, caducous. Flowers opening in early summer, unisexual, strong-smelling; the staminate, in 3–7-flowered cymes, in the axils of minute ovate bracts, in elongated simple deciduous aments first appearing with the unfolding of the leaves from the inner scales of the terminal bud and from the axils of the lower leaves of the year, composed of a pale straw-colored slightly puberulous calyx deeply divided into 6 ovate rounded segments imbricated in the bud, and 10–20 stamens inserted on the slightly thickened torus, with filiform filaments incurved in the bud, becoming elongated and exserted, and ovoid or globose pale yellow anthers; the pistillate scattered or spicate at the base of the shorter persistent androgynous aments from the axils of later leaves, sessile, 2 or 3 together or solitary within a short-stemmed or sessile involucre of closely imbricated oblong acute bright green bracts scurfy-pubescent or tomentose below the middle, subtended by a bract and 2 lateral bractlets, each flower composed of an urn-shaped calyx, with a short limb divided into 6 obtuse lobes, minute sterile stamens shorter than the calyx-lobes, an ovary 6-celled after fecundation, with 6 linear spreading white styles hairy below the middle and tipped by minute acute stigmas, and 2 ovules in each cell, attached on its inner angle, descending, semianatropous. Fruit maturing in one season, its involucre inclosing 1–3 nuts, globose or short-oblong, pubescent or tomentose and spiny on the outer surface, with elongated ridged bright green ultimately brown branched spines fascicled between the deciduous scales, coated on the inner surface with lustrous pubescence, splitting at maturity into 2–4 valves; nut ovoid, acute, crowned by the remnants of the style, bright chestnut-brown and lustrous, tomentose or pubescent at apex, cylindrical, or when more than 1 flattened, marked at the broad base by a large conspicuous pale circular or oval thickened scar, its shell lined with rufous or hoary tomentum. Seed usually solitary by abortion, dark chestnut-brown, marked at apex by the abortive ovules, with thick and fleshy more or less undulate ruminate sweet farinaceous cotyledons.

Castanea is confined to the northern hemisphere, and is widely distributed through eastern North America, southern Europe, northern Africa, southwestern Asia, and central and northern China, Korea, and Japan. Seven species are distinguished. In the countries of the Mediterranean Basin much attention has been given to improving the fruit of the native species *Castanea sativa* Mill., which is occasionally planted in the middle United States; in Japan the seeds of *Castanea crenata* S. & Zucc. in many varieties and in China those of *Castanea mollissima* Bl. are important articles of food. Castanea produces coarse-grained wood very durable in contact with the soil, and rich in tannin. Chestnut-trees suffer in the eastern United States from the attacks of a fungus, *Endothia parasitica* Anders. which has nearly exterminated them in many parts of the country.

Castanea is the classical name of the Chestnut-tree.

CONSPECTUS OF THE NORTH AMERICAN SPECIES.

Involucre of the fruit containing 2 or 3 flattened nuts.   1. **C. dentata** (A, C).
Involucre of the fruit containing a single terete nut.
Involucre of the fruit densely covered with spines; branchlets hoary tomentose.
                                                      2. **C. pumila** (A, C).
Involucre of the fruit covered with scattered spines; branchlets glabrous or sparingly
    pilose.   3. **C. alnifolia** (C).

1. Castanea dentata Borkh. Chestnut.

Leaves oblong-lanceolate, acute and long-pointed at apex, gradually narrowed and
cuneate at base, when they unfold puberulous on the upper surface and clothed on the
lower with fine cobweb-like tomentum, at maturity thin, glabrous, dark dull yellow-green
above, pale yellow-green below, 6′–8′ long, about 2′ wide, with a pale yellow midrib and

Fig. 216

primary veins; turning bright clear yellow late in the autumn; petioles stout, slightly
angled, puberulous, ½′ long, often flushed with red; stipules ovate-lanceolate, acute, yellow-
green, puberulous, about ½′ long. **Flowers:** staminate aments about ½′ long when they
first appear, green below the middle and red above, becoming when fully grown 6′–8′ long,
with stout green puberulous stems covered from base to apex with crowded flower-clusters;
androgynous aments, slender, puberulous, 2½′–5′ long, with 2 or 3 irregularly scattered
involucres of pistillate flowers near their base. **Fruit:** involucre attaining its full size by
the middle of August, 2′–2½′ in diameter, sometimes a little longer than broad, somewhat flattened at apex, pubescent and covered on the outer surface with crowded fascicles
of long slender glabrous much-branched spines, opening with the first frost and gradually
shedding their nuts; nuts usually much compressed, ½′–1′ wide, usually rather broader than
long, coated at apex or nearly to the middle with thick pale tomentum, the interior of the
shell lined with thick rufous tomentum; **seed** very sweet.
A tree, occasionally 100° high, with a tall straight columnar trunk 3°–4° in diameter,
or often when uncrowded by other trees with a short trunk occasionally 10°–12° in diameter, and usually divided not far above the ground into 3 or 4 stout horizontal limbs forming
a broad low round-topped head of slightly pendulous branches frequently 100° across, and
branchlets at first light yellow-green sometimes tinged with red, somewhat angled, lustrous,
slightly puberulous, soon becoming glabrous and olive-green tinged with yellow or brown

tinged with green and ultimately dark brown. **Winter-buds** ovoid, acute, about $\frac{1}{4}'$ long, with thin dark chestnut-brown scales scarious on the margins. **Bark** from $1'-2'$ thick, dark brown and divided by shallow irregular often interrupted fissures into broad flat ridges separating on the surface into small thin closely appressed scales. **Wood** light, soft, not strong, liable to check and warp in drying, easily split, reddish brown, with thin lighter colored sapwood of 3 or 4 layers of annual growth; largely used in the manufacture of cheap furniture and in the interior finish of houses, for railway-ties, fence-posts, and rails. The nuts, which are superior to those of the Old World chestnuts in sweetness were formerly gathered in great quantities in the forest and sold in the markets of the eastern cities.

Distribution. Southern Maine to Woodstock, Grafton County, New Hampshire (rare) and to the valley of the Winooski River, Vermont, southern Ontario, and southern Michigan, southward to Delaware and Ohio, southern Indiana, and southwestern Illinois (Pulaski County) along the Appalachian Mountains up to altitudes of 4000° to northern Georgia, and to western Florida (Crestview, Okaloosa County), southeastern (Henry and Dale Counties) and south central (Dallas County) Alabama, northern, central and southeastern Mississippi (Pearl River County), and to central Kentucky and Tennessee; very common on the glacial drift of the northern states and, except at the north, mostly confined to the Appalachian hills; attaining its greatest size in western North Carolina and eastern Tennessee.

Formerly sometimes planted in the eastern states as an ornamental and timber tree, and for its nuts, of which several varieties have been recognized.

× *Castanea neglecta* Dode with leaves intermediate between those of *C. dentata* and *C. pumila* and an involucre containing a single large nut occurs on the Blue Ridge near Highlands, Macon County, North Carolina.

2. Castanea pumila Mill. Chinquapin.

Leaves oblong-elliptic to oblong-obovate, acute, coarsely serrate, with slender rigid spreading or incurved teeth, gradually narrowed and usually unequal and rounded or cuneate at

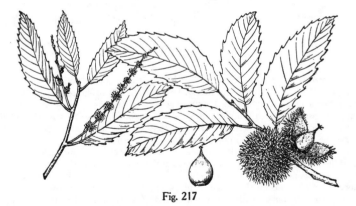

Fig. 217

base, when they unfold tinged with red and coated above with pale caducous tomentum and below with thick snowy white tomentum, at maturity rather thick and firm in texture, bright yellow-green on the upper surface, hoary or silvery pubescent on the lower, $3'-5'$ long, $1\frac{1}{2}'-2'$ wide; turning dull yellow in the autumn; petioles stout, pubescent, flattened on the upper side, $\frac{1}{4}'-\frac{1}{2}'$ long; stipules light yellow-green, pubescent, those of the 2 lowest leaves broad, ovate, acute, covered at apex by rufous tomentum, on later leaves ovate-lanceolate, often oblique and acute, becoming linear at the end of the branch. **Flowers:**

staminate aments $\frac{1}{2}'$ long when they first appear, pubescent, green below, bright red at apex, becoming when fully grown 4'-6' long, with stout hoary tomentose stems and crowded or scattered flower-clusters; androgynous aments silvery tomentose, 3'-4' long; involucres 1-flowered, scattered at the base of the ament or often spicate and covering its lower half, sessile or short-stalked. **Fruit:** involucre $1'-1\frac{1}{2}'$ in diameter, with thin walls covered with crowded fascicles of slender spines tomentose toward the base; nut ovoid, terete, rounded at the slightly narrowed base, gradually narrowed and pointed at apex, more or less coated with silvery white pubescence, dark chestnut-brown, very lustrous, $\frac{3}{4}'-1'$ long, $\frac{1}{3}'$ thick, with a thin shell lined with a coat of lustrous hoary tomentum, and a sweet seed.

A round-topped tree, rarely 50° high, with a short straight trunk 2°-3° in diameter, slender spreading branches, and branchlets coated at first with pale tomentum, becoming during their first winter pubescent or remaining tomentose at the apex, bright red-brown, glabrous, lustrous, olive-green or orange-brown during their second season and ultimately darker; east of the Mississippi River often a shrub spreading into broad thickets by prolific stolons, with numerous intricately branched stems often only 4° or 5° tall. **Winter-buds** ovoid, or oval, about $\frac{1}{8}'$ long, clothed when they first appear in summer with thick hoary tomentum, becoming red during the winter and scurfy-pubescent. **Bark** $\frac{1}{2}'-1'$ thick, light brown tinged with red, slightly furrowed and broken on the surface into loose plate-like scales. **Wood** light, hard, strong, coarse-grained, dark brown, with thin hardly distinguishable sapwood of 3 or 4 layers of annual growth; used for fence-posts, rails, and railway-ties. The sweet nuts are sold in the markets of the western and southern states.

Distribution. Dry sandy ridges, rich hillsides and the borders of swamps; southern New Jersey and Pennsylvania to central (Lake County) and western Florida and westward through the Gulf States to the valley of the Neches River, Texas; on the Appalachian Mountains ascending to altitudes of 4500°; most abundant and of its largest size in southern Arkansas and eastern Texas. In Arkansas, southern Missouri, and eastern Oklahoma replaced by *C. ozarkensis* Ashe.

3. Castanea alnifolia Nutt. Chinquapin

A low shrub spreading into broad thickets by underground stems, with leaves pale pubescent on the lower surface; and distributed in the neighborhood of the coast from the valley of the Cape Fear River, North Carolina, to southern Georgia. Passing into

Castanea alnifolia var. floridana Sarg. Chinquapin

Leaves oblong-obovate to elliptic, acute, acuminate or rounded at apex, gradually narrowed and cuneate or rounded at base, irregularly sinuate-toothed with apiculate teeth.

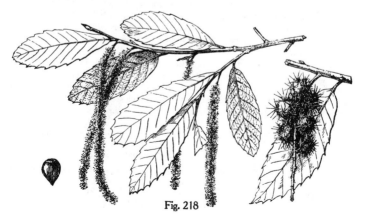

Fig. 218

hoary tomentose below when they unfold, soon glabrous with the exception of the last leaves of vigorous summer shoots, and at maturity thin, glabrous, dark green above, light green and lustrous below, 3'–4' long and 1'–1¾' wide; petioles stout, glabrous, about $\frac{1}{12}$' in length. **Flowers:** staminate aments pale pubescent, 4'–5' long; androgynous aments pubescent, as long or rather longer with ten or twelve involucres of pistillate flowers below the middle, often only the lowest being fertilized. **Fruit:** involucre 1-seeded, subglobose to short-oblong, pale tomentose, ¾' to 1¼' in diameter, covered with stout pubescent scattered spines divided at base into numerous branches; nut ovoid, terete, acute, dark chestnut-brown, lustrous, ½' to nearly ¾' in length.

A tree occasionally 40°–45° high, with a tall trunk sometimes a foot in diameter, small irregularly spreading branches forming a narrow head, and slender glabrous or rarely pilose red-brown branchlets; more often a shrub sometimes with broader obovoid leaves sometimes puberulous on the lower surface.

Dry sandy soil; coast of North Carolina, near Wrightsville, New Hanover County; Dover, near the Ogechee River, Screven County, Georgia; Jacksonville, Duval County, and Panama City on Saint Andrew's Bay, Bay County, Florida; near Selma, Dallas County, Alabama; and Covington, St. Tammany Parish, Louisiana.

A tree only on the shores of Saint Andrew's Bay.

3. CASTANOPSIS Spach.

Trees, with scaly bark, astringent wood, and winter-buds covered by numerous imbricated scales. Leaves convolute in the bud, 5-ranked, coriaceous, entire or dentate, penniveined, persistent; stipules obovate or lanceolate, scarious, mostly caducous. Flowers in 3-flowered cymes, or the pistillate rarely solitary or in pairs, in the axils of minute bracts, on slender erect aments from the axils of leaves of the year; the staminate on usually elongated and panicled aments, and composed of a campanulate 5 or 6-lobed or parted calyx, the lobes imbricated in the bud, usually 10 or 12 stamens inserted on the slightly thickened torus, with elongated exserted filiform filaments and oblong anthers, and a minute hirsute rudimentary ovary; the pistillate on shorter simple or panicled aments or scattered at the base of the staminate inflorescence, the cymes surrounded by an involucre of imbricated scales; calyx urn-shaped, the short limb divided into 6 obtuse lobes; abortive stamens inserted on the limb of the calyx and opposite its lobes; ovary sessile on the thin disk, 3-celled after fecundation, with 3 spreading styles terminating in minute stigmas, and 2 ovules in each cell attached to its interior angle. Fruit maturing at the end of the second or rarely of the first season, its involucre inclosing 1–3 nuts, ovoid or globose, sometimes more or less depressed, rarely obscurely angled, dehiscent or indehiscent, covered by stout spines, tuberculate or marked by interrupted vertical ridges; nut more or less angled by mutual pressure when more than 1, often pilose, crowned with the remnants of the style, marked at the base by a large conspicuous circular depressed scar, the thick shell tomentose on the inner surface. Seed usually solitary by abortion, bearing at apex the abortive ovules; cotyledons plano-convex, fleshy, farinaceous.

Castanopsis inhabits California with two species, and southeastern Asia where it is distributed with about twenty-five species from southern China to the Malay Archipelago and the eastern Himalayas. Of the California species one is usually arborescent and the other *Castanopsis sempervirens* Dudley is a low alpine shrub of the coast ranges and the Sierra Nevada.

Castanopsis, from κάστανα and ὄψις, in allusion to its resemblance to the Chestnut-tree.

1. Castanopsis chrysophylla A. DC.   Chinquapin.   Golden-leaved Chestnut.

Leaves lanceolate or oblong-ovate, gradually narrowed at the ends or sometimes abruptly contracted at apex into a short broad point, entire with slightly thickened revolute margins, when they unfold thin, coated below with golden yellow persistent scales and above with scattered white scales, at maturity thick and coriaceous, dark green and lustrous above, 2'–6' long, $\frac{1}{2}$ to nearly 2' wide, with a stout midrib raised and rounded on the upper side; turning yellow at maturity and falling gradually at the end of their second or in their third year; petioles $\frac{1}{4}$–$\frac{1}{3}$' in length; stipules ovate, rounded or acute at apex, brown and scarious, puberulous, $\frac{1}{4}$–$\frac{1}{3}$' long. **Flowers** appearing irregularly from June until February in the axils of broadly ovate apiculate pubescent bracts on staminate and androgynous scurfy stout-stemmed aments 2'–2$\frac{1}{2}$' long and crowded at the ends of the branches; calyx of the staminate flower coated on the outer surface with hoary tomentum, divided into broadly ovate rounded lobes much shorter than the slender stamens; calyx of the pistillate flower oblong-campanulate, free from the ovary, clothed with hoary tomentum, divided at apex into short rounded lobes, rather shorter than the minute abortive stamens; anthers red; ovary conic, hirsute, with elongated slightly spreading thick pale stigmas. **Fruit** ripening at the end of the second season, involucre globose, dehiscent, irregularly 4-valved, often slightly shorter than the nuts, sessile, solitary, or clustered, tomentose and covered on the outer surface by long stout or slender rigid spines, 1'–1$\frac{1}{2}$' in diameter, containing 1 or occasionally 2 nuts; nuts broadly ovoid, acute, obtusely 3-angled, light yellow-brown and lustrous; **seeds** dark purple-red, sweet and edible.

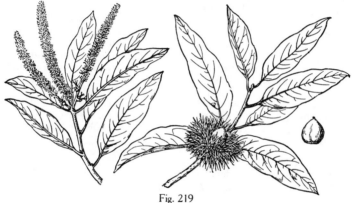

Fig. 219

A tree, 50°–100° high, with a massive trunk 3°–6° in diameter, frequently free of branches for 50°, stout spreading branches forming a broad compact round-topped or conic head, and rigid branchlets coated when they first appear with bright golden-yellow scurfy scales, dark reddish brown and slightly scurfy during their first winter, and gradually growing darker in their second season; often much smaller and sometimes reduced to a shrub, 2°–12° high (var. *minor* A. De Candolle). **Winter-buds** fully grown at mid-summer, usually crowded near the end of the branch, ovoid or subglobose, with broadly ovate apiculate thin and papery light brown scales slightly puberulous on the back, ciliate on the scarious often reflexed margins, the terminal about $\frac{1}{4}$' long and broad and rather larger than the often stipitate axillary buds. **Bark** 1'–2' thick and deeply divided into rounded ridges 2'–3' wide, broken into thick plate-like scales, dark red-brown on the surface and bright red internally. **Wood** light, soft, close-grained, not strong, light brown tinged with red, with thin lighter colored sapwood of 50–60 layers of annual growth; occasionally used in the manufacture of ploughs and other agricultural implements.

Distribution. Skamania County, Washington, valley of the lower Columbia River, Oregon, southward along the western slopes of the Cascade Mountains, and in California along the western slopes of the Sierra Nevada and through the coast ranges to the elevated valleys of the San Jacinto Mountains, sometimes ascending to altitudes of 4000° above the sea; of its largest size in the humid coast valleys of northern California.

Occasionally cultivated in the gardens of temperate Europe.

4. LITHOCARPUS Bl.

Pasania Örst.

Trees, with astringent properties, pubescence of fascicled hairs, deeply furrowed scaly bark, hard close-grained brittle wood, stout branchlets, and winter-buds covered by few erect or spreading foliaceous scales. Leaves convolute in the bud, petiolate, persistent, entire or dentate, with a stout midrib, primary veins running obliquely to the points of the teeth, or on entire leaves forked and united near the margins, and reticulate veinlets; stipules oblong-obovate to linear-lanceolate, those of the upper leaves persistent and surrounding the buds during the winter. Flowers in erect unisexual and in bisexual tomentose aments from the axils of leaves of the year, from the inner scales of the terminal bud or from separate buds in the axils of leaves of the previous year; staminate in 3-flowered clusters in the axils of ovate rounded bracts, the lateral flowers subtended by similar but smaller bracts, each flower composed of a 5-lobed tomentose calyx, with nearly triangular acute lobes, 10 stamens, with slender elongated filaments and small oblong or emarginate anthers, and an acute abortive hairy ovary; pistillate scattered at the base of the upper aments below the staminate flowers, solitary in the axils of acute bracts, furnished with minute lateral bractlets, and composed of a 6-lobed ovoid calyx, with rounded lobes, inclosed in the tomentose involucral scales, 6 stamens, with abortive anthers, an ovoid-oblong 3-celled ovary, 3 elongated spreading light green styles thickened and stigmatic at apex, and 2 anatropous ovules in each cell. Fruit an oval or ovoid nut maturing at the end of the second season, 1-seeded by abortion, surrounded at base by the accrescent woody cupular involucre of the flower, marked by a large pale circular basal scar, the thick shell tomentose on the inner surface. Seed red-brown, filling the cavity of the nut, bearing at apex the abortive ovules; cotyledons thick and fleshy, yellow and bitter.

Lithocarpus is intermediate between the Oaks and the Chestnuts, and, with the exception of one California species, is confined to southeastern Asia, where it is distributed with many species from southern Japan and southern China through the Malay Peninsula to the Indian Archipelago.

Lithocarpus from λίθος and καρπός, in allusion to the character of the fruit.

1. Lithocarpus densiflora Rehd.   Tan Bark Oak.   Chestnut Oak.

Quercus densiflora Hook. & Arn.

Pasania densiflora Örst.

Leaves oblong or oblong-obovate, rounded or acute or rarely cordate at base, acute or occasionally rounded at apex, or rarely lanceolate and acuminate (f. *lanceolata* Rehdr.) repand-dentate, with acute callous teeth, or entire with thickened revolute margins, coated when they unfold with fulvous tomentum and glandular on the margins with dark caducous glands, at maturity pale green, lustrous and glabrous or covered with scattered pubescence on the upper surface, rusty-tomentose on the lower, ultimately becoming glabrous above and glabrate and bluish white below, 3'–5' long, ¾'–3' wide, with a midrib raised and rounded on the upper side, thin or thick primary veins and fine conspicuous reticulate veinlets; persistent until the end of their third or fourth year; petioles stout, rigid, tomentose, ½'–¾' in length; stipules brown and scarious, hirsute on the outer surface. Flowers in early spring and frequently also irregularly during the autumn; aments stout-stemmed, 3'–4' long; staminate flowers crowded, hoary-tomentose in the bud, their bracts tomentose. Fruit solitary or often in pairs, on a stout tomentose peduncle ½'–1' in length; nut full and rounded at base, gradually narrowed and acute or rounded at apex, scurfy-pubescent when fully grown, becoming light yellow-brown, glabrous and lustrous at maturity, ¾'–1' long, ½'–1' thick, its cup shallow, tomentose with lustrous red-brown hairs on the inner surface, and covered by long linear rigid spreading or recurved light brown scales coated with fascicled hairs, frequently tipped, especially while young, with dark red glands and often tomentose near the base of the cup.

A tree, usually 70°–80° but sometimes 150° high, with a trunk 1°–4° in diameter, stout branches ascending in the forest and forming a narrow spire-like head, or in open positions spreading horizontally and forming a broad dense symmetrical round-topped crown, and branchlets coated at first with a thick fulvous tomentum of fascicled hairs often persistent until the second or third year, becoming dark reddish brown and frequently covered with a glaucous bloom; or sometimes reduced to a shrub, with slender stems only a few feet high (var. *montana* Rehdr.). **Winter-buds** ovoid, obtuse, $\frac{1}{4}'–\frac{1}{3}'$ long, often surrounded by the persistent stipules of the upper leaves, with tomentose loosely imbricated scales, those of the outer ranks linear-lanceolate, increasing in width toward the interior of the bud, those of the inner ranks ovate or obovate and rounded at apex. **Bark** $\frac{3}{4}'–1\frac{1}{2}'$ thick,

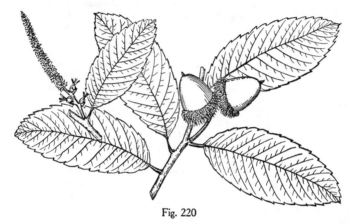

Fig. 220

deeply divided by narrow fissures into broad rounded ridges broken into nearly square plates covered by closely appressed light red-brown scales. **Wood** hard, strong, close-grained, brittle, reddish brown, with thick darker brown sapwood; largely used as fuel. The bark is exceedingly rich in tannin and is largely used for tanning leather.

Distribution. Valley of the Umpqua River, Oregon, southward through the coast ranges to the Santa Inez Mountains, California, and along the western slope of the Sierra Nevada up to elevations of 4000° above the sea to Mariposa County; very abundant in the humid coast region north of San Francisco Bay and on the Santa Cruz and Santa Lucia Mountains, and of its largest size in the Redwood forest of Napa and Mendocino Counties; southward and on the Sierras less abundant and of smaller size; the form *lanceolata* in southern Oregon and in Del Norte and Mendocino Counties, California; the var. *montana* at high altitudes on the Siskiyou Mountains, in the region of Mount Shasta and on the northern Sierra Nevada.

5. QUERCUS L. Oak.

Trees or shrubs, with astringent properties, pubescence of fascicled hairs, scaly or dark and furrowed bark, hard and close-grained or porous brittle wood, slender branchlets marked by pale lenticels and more or less prominently 5-angled. Winter-buds clustered at the ends of the branchlets, with numerous membranaceous chestnut-brown slightly accrescent caducous scales closely imbricated in 5 ranks, in falling marking the base of the branchlet with ring-like scars. Leaves 5-ranked, lobed, dentate or entire, often variable on the same branch, membranaceous or coriaceous, the primary veins prominent and extending to the margins or united within them and connected by more or less reticulate veinlets, deciduous in the autumn or persistent until spring or until their third or fourth year;

petioles in falling leaving slightly elevated semiorbicular more or less obcordate leaf-scars broader than high, marked by the ends of numerous scattered fibro-vascular bundles; stipules obovate to lanceolate, scarious, caducous, or those of upper leaves occasionally persistent through the season.   Flowers vernal with or after the unfolding of the leaves; staminate solitary in the axils of lanceolate acute caducous bracts, or without bracts, in graceful pendulous clustered aments, from separate or leaf-buds in the axils of leaves of the previous year, or from the axils of the inner scales of the terminal bud or from those of the leaves of the year; calyx campanulate, lobed or divided to the base into 4–7, usually 6, membranaceous lobes; stamens 4–6, rarely 2, or 10–12, inserted on the slightly thickened torus, with free filiform exserted filaments and ovate-oblong or subglobose glabrous or rarely hairy 2-celled usually yellow anthers; pistillate solitary, subtended by a caducous bract and 2 bractlets, in short or elongated few-flowered spikes from the axils of leaves of the year; calyx urn-shaped, with a short campanulate 6-lobed limb, the tube adnate to the incompletely 3 or rarely 4 or 5-celled ovary inclosed more or less completely by an accrescent involucre of imbricated scales, becoming the cup of the fruit; styles as many as the cells of the ovary, short or elongated, erect or incurved, dilated above, stigmatic on the inner face or at apex only, generally persistent on the fruit; ovules anatropous or semianatropous, 2 in each cell.   Fruit a nut (*acorn*) maturing in one or in two years, ovoid, subglobose, or turbinate, short-pointed at apex, 1-seeded by abortion, marked at base by a large conspicuous circular scar, with a thick shell, glabrous or coated on the inner surface with pale tomentum, more or less surrounded or inclosed in the accrescent cupular involucre of the flower (*cup*), its scales thin or thickened, loosely or closely imbricated.   Seed marked at base or at apex or rarely on the side by the abortive ovules; cotyledons thick and fleshy, usually plano-convex and entire.

Quercus inhabits the temperate regions of the northern hemisphere and high altitudes within the tropics, ranging in the New World southward to the mountains of Colombia and in the Old World to the Indian Archipelago.   Two hundred and seventy-five species have been described; of the North American species fifty-four are large or small trees. Of exotic species, the European *Quercus robur* L., and *Quercus sessiliflora* Salisb., have been frequently cultivated as ornamental trees in the eastern United States, where, however, they are usually short-lived and unsatisfactory.   Many of the species are important timber-trees; their bark is often rich in tannin and is used for tanning leather, and all produce wood valuable for fuel and in the manufacture of charcoal.

Quercus is the classical name of the Oak-tree.

CONSPECTUS OF THE NORTH AMERICAN ARBORESCENT SPECIES.

Fruit maturing at the end of the second season (except 22); shell of the nut silky tomentose on the inner surface; leaves or their lobes bristle-tipped. BLACK OAKS.
  Stamens usually 4–6; styles elongated, finally recurved; abortive ovules apical.
    Leaves deciduous in their first autumn or winter.
      Leaves pinnately lobed, convolute in the bud.
        Leaves green on both surfaces.
          Scales of the cup of the fruit closely appressed.
            Leaves usually dull on the upper surface, 7–11-lobed; cup of the fruit cup-shaped or in one variety broad and saucer-shaped, its scales thin.
                                                                        1. Q. borealis (A).

          Leaves lustrous.
            Leaves dimorphous, 5–7-lobed, axillary clusters of hairs large and prominent; cup of the fruit saucer-shaped or in one form deep cup-shaped.
                                                                2. Q. Shumardii (A, C).
          Leaves similar on upper and lower branches.
            Cup of the fruit turbinate or deep cup-shaped.
              Leaves 5-lobed, the lobes usually entire, rarely furnished with tufts of axillary hairs below.   3. Q. texana (C).

Leaves 5–7-lobed, the lobes dentate, furnished with tufts of axillary
hairs below. 4. **Q. ellipsoidalis** (A).
Cup of the fruit deep cup-shaped to turbinate; leaves 5–9-lobed, the
lobes toothed. 5. **Q. coccinea** (A, C).
Cup of the fruit saucer-shaped.
Leaves 5–9-lobed. 6. **Q. palustris** (A, C).
Leaves 3–5-lobed. 7. **Q. georgiana** (C).
Scales of the cup of the fruit more or less loosely imbricated, forming a free
margin on its rim.
Leaves usually 7-lobed.
Winter-buds tomentose. 8. **Q. velutina** (A, C).
Winter-buds pubescent only at apex. 9. **Q. Kelloggii** (G).
Leaves usually 3–5-lobed; winter-buds rusty pubescent. 10. **Q. Catesbæi** (C).
Leaves whitish or grayish tomentulose below.
Leaves mostly acutely 5-lobed, pale or silvery white below. 11. **Q. ilicifolia** (A).
Leaves often dimorphous, 3–11-lobed, the lobes often falcate.
12. **Q. rubra** (A, C).
Leaves broad-obovate, often abruptly dilated at the wide obscurely lobed apex.
Leaves rounded or cordate at base.
Lower surface of the leaves orange color or brownish, the upper scales of the cup
forming with several rows a thick rim on its inner surface, often reflexed.
13. **Q. marilandica** (A, C).
Lower surface of the leaves pale, the erect scales on the rim of the cup in a
single row. 14. **Q. arkansana** (C).
Leaves cuneate at base.
Leaves oblong-obovate. 15. **Q. nigra** (C).
Leaves rhombic. 16. **Q. obtusata** (C).
Leaves lanceolate-oblong or lanceolate-obovate, usually entire, involute in the
bud. WILLOW OAKS.
Leaves glabrous.
Leaves lanceolate to oblanceolate, deciduous in autumn. 17. **Q. Phellos** (A, C).
Leaves elliptic or rarely oblong-obovate, deciduous in the late winter.
18. **Q. laurifolia** (C).
Leaves tomentose or pubescent below, oblong-lanceolate to oblong-obovate.
Leaves pale blue-green, hoary tomentose below. 19. **Q. cinerea** (C).
Leaves dark green, pubescent below. 20. **Q. imbricaria** (A).
Leaves not deciduous in the autumn, revolute in the bud (convolute in 23).
Leaves mostly persistent until after the appearance of those of the following year.
Leaves lanceolate, oblong-lanceolate or elliptic, pale and tomentose below.
21. **Q. hypoleuca** (E, H).
Leaves oval, orbicular to oblong, green and pubescent below; fruit maturing at
the end of the first season. 22. **Q. agrifolia** (G).
Leaves persistent until their second summer or autumn.
Leaves lanceolate to oval or oblong-lanceolate, entire or serrate; cup of the fruit
turbinate or tubular. 23. **Q. Wislizenii** (G).
Leaves oval to oblong-obovate; cup of the fruit saucer-shaped or turbinate.
24. **Q. myrtifolia** (C).
Stamens usually 6–8; styles dilated; abortive ovules basal or lateral; leaves persistent
until their third or fourth season, involute in the bud.
Leaves oblong, entire, dentate, or sinuate-toothed, fulvous-tomentose and ultimately
pale on the lower surface; cup of the fruit usually thick. 25. **Q. chrysolepis** (G, H).
Leaves oblong-lanceolate, crenate-dentate or entire, pubescent or tomentose below;
cup of the fruit usually thin. 26. **Q. tomentella** (G).
Fruit maturing at the end of the first season; shell of the nut glabrous on the inner surface

(hoary-tomentose in 27); abortive ovules basal; stamens 6–8; styles dilated; lobes of the leaves not bristle-tipped. WHITE OAKS.

Leaves mostly persistent until the appearance of those of the following year, revolute in the bud (convolute in 28).

Leaves yellow-green.

Fruit sessile or short-stalked.

Leaves oblong-lanceolate, entire or repand-dentate; inner surface of the nut hoary tomentose. 27. Q. Emoryi (F, H).

Leaves oblong or obovate, entire, sinuate-toothed or lobed. 28. Q. dumosa (G).

Fruit long-stalked; leaves oblong, elliptic or obovate, pale, glabrous or in one form densely tomentose below. 29. Q. virginiana (C).

Leaves blue-green.

Fruit usually in many-fruited long-stalked clusters; leaves broad-obovate, coarsely reticulate-venulose. 30. Q. reticulata (H).

Fruit solitary or in pairs.

Cup of the fruit saucer-shaped; leaves ovate to ovate-oblong, entire.
31. Q. Toumeyi (H).

Cup of the fruit cup-shaped or hemispherical, oblong-lanceolate to broad-obovate, pubescent below. 32. Q. arizonica (H).

Cup of the fruit usually cup-shaped or turbinate.

Leaves ovate, oval or obovate, usually cordate at base; fruit rather long-stalked. 33. Q. oblongifolia (E, H).

Leaves oblong to obovate, usually cuneate or rounded or cordate at base.
34. Q. Engelmannii (G).

Leaves deciduous in their first season.

Leaves blue-green.

Arboreous; leaves oblong, lobed, spinescent-dentate or entire, pubescent below; cup of the fruit shallow cup-shaped. 35. Q. Douglasii (G).

Arborescent or shrubby.

Leaves oblong to oblong-obovate, undulate-lobed; cup of the fruit saucer-shaped to cup-shaped. 36. Q. Vaseyana (C).

Leaves oblong-obovate to elliptic or lanceolate, undulate, serrate-toothed or irregularly lobed; cup of the fruit hemispheric to cup-shaped. 37. Q. Mohriana (C).

Leaves oblong to oblong-ovate, slightly lobed or entire; cup of the fruit cup-shaped or rarely saucer-shaped. 38. Q. Laceyi (C).

Leaves yellow-green.

Leaves entire or slightly lobed.

Leaves different on upper and lower branches, oblong to oblong-obovate, slightly lobed or entire.

Cup of the fruit cup-shaped. 39. Q. annulata (C).

Cup of the fruit shallow saucer-shaped. 40. Q. Durandii (C).

Leaves similar on upper and lower branches, entire or slightly sinuate-lobed toward the apex, oblong or oblong-obovate. 41. Q. Chapmanii (C).

Leaves more or less deeply sinuate-lobed.

Leaves white-tomentulose below (sometimes green and pubescent in 43).

Leaves obovate or oblong, lyrately pinnatifid or deeply sinuate-lobed; cup of the fruit fringed by the awned scales. 42. Q. macrocarpa (A, C, F).

Leaves obovate-oblong, deeply 5–9-lobed or pinnatifid; nut often inclosed in the cup. 43. Q. lyrata (A, C).

Leaves pubescent below.

Leaves usually covered above with fascicled hairs, obovate, 3–5-lobed, their lobes truncate or rounded. 44. Q. stellata (A, C).

Leaves glabrous above at maturity.

Leaves obovate to oblong; cup of the fruit shallow cup-shaped or slightly turbinate, its scales usually thin. 45. Q. Garryana (B, G.)

Leaves oblong-obovate; cup of the fruit hemispheric, the scales often much
thickened. 46. **Q. utahensis** (F).
Leaves oblong-obovate, deeply lobed; nut conic, elongated, inclosed for one-
third its length in the cup-shaped cup. 47. **Q. lobata** (G).
Leaves glabrate or puberulous below, oblong to oblong-obovate.
48. **Q. leptophylla** (F).
Leaves glabrous below.
Leaves oblong-obovate, usually 5-lobed. 49. **Q. austrina** (C).
Leaves oblong-obovate, obliquely pinnatifid or 3–9-lobed. 50. **Q. alba** (A, C).
Leaves coarsely sinuate-toothed. Chestnut Oaks.
Fruit on peduncles much longer than the petioles; leaves obovate or oblong-
obovate, generally sinuate-dentate or lobed, pubescent, and usually hoary on
the lower surface. 51. **Q. bicolor** (C).
Fruit on peduncles about as long or shorter than the petioles.
Leaves obovate or oblong-obovate, cuneate or rounded at the broad or narrow
base, tomentose or pubescent and often silvery white below.
52. **Q. Prinus** (A, C).
Leaves obovate or oblong to lanceolate, acuminate, with rounded or acute
teeth. 53. **Q. montana** (A, C).
Fruit sessile or nearly so; leaves oblong to lanceolate, acute or acuminate or
broadly obovate, puberulous and pale, often silvery white on the lower
surface. 54. **Q. Muehlenbergii** (A, C).

1. Quercus borealis Michx. f. Red Oak.

Leaves obovate or oblong, acute or acuminate, abruptly or gradually cuneate or
rounded at the broad or narrow base, usually divided about half way to the midrib by

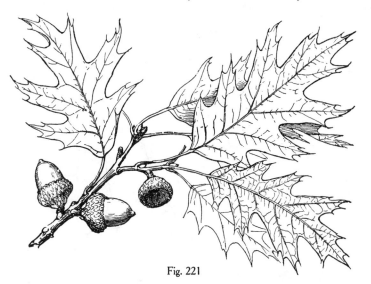

Fig. 221

wide oblique sinuses rounded at the bottom into 11 or sometimes into 7 or 9 acute oblique
ovate lobes tapering from broad bases and mostly sinuately 3-toothed at apex with elongated
bristle-pointed teeth, or sometimes oblong-obovate, gradually narrowed and cuneate
at base, and sinuately lobed with broad acute usually entire or slightly dentate lobes.
when they unfold pink, covered with soft silky pale pubescence on the upper surface and

below with thick white tomentum, soon glabrous, at maturity thin and firm, dark green, dull and glabrous above, pale yellow-green, glabrous or rarely puberulous and sometimes furnished with small tufts of rusty hairs in the axils of the veins below, 5′–9′ long, 4′–6′ wide; falling early in the autumn after turning dull or sometimes bright orange color or brown; petioles stout, yellow or red, 1′–2′ in length. **Flowers:** staminate in pubescent aments 4′–5′ long; calyx divided into 4 or 5 narrow ovate rounded lobes shorter than the stamens; pistillate on short glabrous peduncles, their involucral scales broadly ovate, dark reddish brown, shorter than the conspicuous linear acute bract of the flower and as long as the lanceolate acute calyx-lobes; stigmas bright green. **Fruit** solitary or in pairs, sessile or short-stalked, ovoid, gradually narrowed and acute at apex or cylindric and rounded at apex, pale brown, lustrous, more or less tomentose toward the ends, $\frac{1}{2}$′–1′ long; $\frac{1}{2}$′–$\frac{3}{4}$′ in diameter; cup cup-shaped, puberulous on the inner surface, covered with small closely appressed ovate acute red-brown pubescent scales slightly thickened on the back toward the base of the cup, with a thin dark-colored tip and margins.

A tree usually not more than 60°–70° high, with a trunk 2°–3° in diameter, often much smaller, stout branches forming a narrow head, and slender lustrous branchlets light green and covered with pale scurfy pubescence when they first appear, dark red during their first winter and ultimately dark brown. **Winter-buds** ovoid, gradually narrowed to the acute apex, about $\frac{1}{4}$′ long, with thin ovate acute light chestnut-brown scales. **Bark** on young stems and on the upper part of the limbs of old trees 1′–1$\frac{1}{2}$′ thick, dark brown tinged with red and divided into small thick appressed plates scaly on the surface. **Wood** heavy, hard, strong, close-grained, light reddish brown, with thin lighter-colored sapwood; used in construction, for the interior finish of houses, and in furniture.

Distribution. Nova Scotia and New Brunswick, through Quebec to southern Ontario, and southward to northern New England, western New York, northern Pennsylvania (Presque Isle, Erie County), northern Michigan, southeastern Wisconsin, central Minnesota, central Iowa (Winneshick County), and on the Appalachian Mountains of North Carolina at altitudes of about 4000°. Passing with many intermediate forms differing in the size of the nut and in the depth of the cup into

Quercus borealis var. maxima Ashe. Red Oak.

Quercus rubra Du Roi, not L.

Fruit solitary or in pairs, sessile or short-stalked; nut ovoid to slightly obovoid, gradually narrowed and rounded at apex, slightly narrowed at base, usually 1′–1$\frac{1}{4}$′ long and $\frac{1}{2}$′–$\frac{2}{3}$′ thick, occasionally not more than $\frac{2}{3}$′ long and thick, inclosed only at the base in a thick saucer-shaped cup.

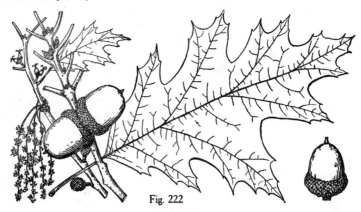

Fig. 222

A tree, usually 70°–80°, or occasionally 150° high, with a trunk 3°–4° in diameter, and stout spreading and ascending branches forming a broad head.

Distribution. Province of Quebec in the neighborhood of Montreal, and southern Ontario, westward through southern Michigan to southeastern Nebraska, and southward to northern Georgia, on the southern Appalachian Mountains up to altitudes of 4000°, southern Kentucky, eastern and central Tennessee, northeastern (Tishomingo County), northwestern (Yazoo County), and central and southern (Hinds and Union Counties) Mississippi, northern and southwestern Alabama (Dekalb, Cullman, Jefferson, and Dallas Counties), northwestern Arkansas, and eastern Kansas and Oklahoma; one of the largest and most generally distributed trees of the northern states; rare and local in the south; of its largest size in the region north of the Potomac and Ohio Rivers.

Often planted as a park and shade tree in the northeastern states and in the counties of western and northern Europe; generally more successful in Europe than other American Oaks.

× *Quercus Lowellii* Sarg., a possible hybrid of *Quercus borealis* and *Q. ilicifolia*, has been found in the neighborhood of Seabury, York County, Maine.

× *Quercus Porteri* Trel., probably a hybrid of *Quercus borealis* var. *maxima* and *Q. velutina*, has been found on Bowditch Hill, Jamaica Plain, Suffolk County, Massachusetts, on College Hill, Easton, Northampton County, Pennsylvania, and near Columbus, Franklin County, Ohio, and Dumas, Clark County, Missouri.

× *Quercus runcinata* Engelm., believed to be a hybrid of *Quercus borealis* var. *maxima* and *Q. imbricaria* first found near St. Louis, occurs also in the neighborhood of Independence, Jackson County, and at Williamsville, Wayne County, Missouri, and in Richland and Wayne Counties, Illinois.

2. Quercus Shumardii Buckl.

Quercus texana Sarg., in part, not Buckl.

Leaves obovate, seven rarely five-lobed, the lobes two or three-lobed and sometimes dentate at apex, on leaves of lower branches short and broad, and separated by narrow sinuses pointed or rounded in the bottom, on upper branches deeply divided by broad rounded sinuses into narrow acuminate lobes, when they unfold often tinged with red and covered with pale loose tomentum deciduous before they are half grown, at maturity glabrous, dark green and lustrous above, paler and furnished below with large axillary tufts

Fig. 223

of pale hairs, 6'–8' long, 4'–5' wide, with a thin midrib and slender primary veins running to the points of the lobes; petioles slender, glabrous, 2'–2½' in length. **Flowers:** staminate in slender glabrous aments 6'–7' long; calyx divided into 4 or 5 rounded slightly villose lobes shorter than the stamens; pistillate on pubescent peduncles, their involucral scales ovate, light brown, pubescent; stigmas red. **Fruit:** nut oblong-ovoid, narrowed and rounded at apex, ¾'–1¼' long, ½'–1' in diameter, inclosed at the base only in the thick saucer-shaped cup with a slightly incurved rim and covered with closely appressed ovate pale pubescent or nearly glabrous scales narrowed above the middle, abruptly long-pointed, thin or often conspicuously tuberculate.

A tree up to 120° high, with a tall trunk occasionally 5° in diameter, stout wide-spreading branches forming a broad rather open head, and gray or grayish brown glabrous branchlets. **Winter-buds** ovoid, acute or acuminate, about ¼' long, with closely imbricated gray glabrous or rarely pubescent scales. **Bark** 1'–1½' thick, ridged, broken into small appressed plates scaly on the surface. **Wood** heavy, hard, close-grained, light reddish brown, often manufactured into lumber in the Mississippi valley and considered more valuable than that of the northern Red Oak.

Distribution. Borders of streams and swamps in moist rich soil; coast region of Texas eastward from the Colorado River and ranging inland up the valley of that river to Burnet County, southeastern Oklahoma, through Arkansas, southeastern Kansas and Missouri to Fayette County, Iowa, southern Illinois and Indiana, the neighborhood of Columbus, Franklin County, Ohio, and southeastern Michigan (near Portage Lake, Jackson County); through the eastern Gulf States to western and central Florida and northward in the neighborhood of the coast to the valley of the Neuse River, North Carolina; Chesapeake Beach, Calvert County, Maryland (*W. W. Ashe*); ranging inland in the south Atlantic States to Rome, Floyd County, Georgia, Calhoun Falls, Abbeville County, and Columbia, Richland County, South Carolina, and Chapel Hill, Orange County, North Carolina. Passing into

Quercus Shumardii var. Schneckii Sarg

Quercus texana Sarg. in part, not Buckl.

Quercus Schneckii Britt.

Differing from the type in the deep cup-shaped cup of the fruit covered with thin scales, rarely much thickened and tuberculate at base (only on river banks near Vicksburg,

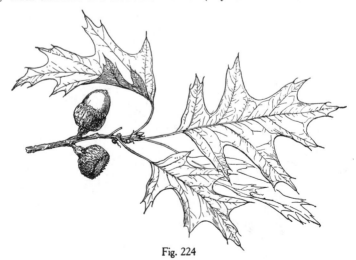

Fig. 224

Warren County, Mississippi), and connected with it by forms with the cups of the fruit differing from saucer to deep cup-shaped.

Distribution. Growing with *Quercus Shumardii;* more common in Texas and in the
Mississippi valley than the type, and ranging eastward through Louisiana and Mississippi
to central and southern Alabama, central and southeastern Tennessee (neighborhood of
Chattanooga), and central Kentucky, Illinois (Wabash and Pope Counties), Indiana (Wells,
Clark, Jennings, Galen, and Posey Counties), and Ohio (Franklin and Gallia Counties);
apparently not reaching the Atlantic States.

3. Quercus texana Buckl.

Leaves widest above the middle, broad-cuneate, concave-cuneate or nearly truncate at
base, deeply or rarely only slightly divided by broad sinuses rounded in the bottom into 5 or 7
lobes, the terminal lobe 3-lobed and acute at apex, the upper lateral lobes broad and more
or less divided at apex and much larger and more deeply lobed than those of the lowest
pair, when they unfold densely covered with fascicled hairs and often bright red, soon glabrous, thin, dark green and lustrous above, pale and lustrous and rarely furnished below

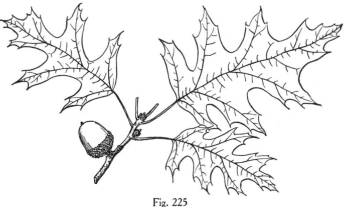

Fig. 225

with small inconspicuous axillary tufts of pale hairs, 3′–3½′ long, 2½′–3′ wide, with a thin
midrib and slender primary veins running to the points of the lobes; petioles slender, soon
glabrous, ¾′–1½′ in length. **Flowers:** staminate in slender villose aments 3′–4′ long; calyx
thin, villose on the outer surface, divided into 4 or 5 acute lobes shorter than the stamens;
pistillate on short hoary tomentose peduncles, their involucral scales brown tinged with
red; stigmas bright red. **Fruit** short-stalked, usually solitary; nut ovoid, narrowed and
rounded at apex, light red-brown, often striate, ¼′–¾′ long and broad, sometimes acute,
nearly 1′ in length and not more than ¾′ in diameter; cup turbinate, covered with thin
ovate acuminate slightly appressed glabrous scales, in the small fruit of trees on dry hills
inclosing a third or more of the nut, in the larger fruit of trees on better soil comparatively
less deep.

A tree on dry hills rarely more than 30° tall, with a trunk 8′–10′ in diameter, small spreading
or erect branches and slender red or reddish brown glabrous or rarely pubescent branchlets;
often a shrub; on better soil at the foot of hills occasionally 50° high with a trunk 12′–
18′ in diameter. **Winter-buds** ovoid, acute, ⅙′–¼′ long and covered with closely imbricated acute slightly or densely pubescent red scales. **Bark** light brown tinged with red,
¾′–1′ thick, deeply ridged and broken into plate-like scales.

Distribution. Dry limestone hills and ridges, and in the more fertile soil at their base;
central and western Texas (Dallas, Tarrant County to Travis and Bexar Counties), and
to the Edwards Plateau (San Saba, Kerr, Brown, Coke and Uvalde Counties); westward

replaced by the var. *chesosensis* Sarg. differing in the acuminate lobes of the leaves and smaller cups of the fruit; known only on the dry rocky slopes of the Chesos Mountains, Brewster County, Texas; and by the var. *stellapila* Sarg., differing in the presence of fascicled hairs on both surfaces of the mature leaves and on the branchlets of the year; above Fort Davis, Jeff Davis County, Texas.

4. Quercus ellipsoidalis E. J. Hill.   Black Oak.

Leaves elliptic to obovate-orbicular, acute or acuminate, truncate or broadly cuneate at base, deeply divided by wide sinuses rounded in the bottom into 5–7 oblong lobes repandly dentate at apex, or often, especially those of the upper pair, repandly lobulate, when they unfold slightly tinged with red and hoary-tomentose, soon becoming glabrous with the exception of small tufts of pale hairs in the axils of the principal veins, at maturity thin and firm, bright green and lustrous above, paler and sometimes entirely glabrous below, 3′–5′ long, 2½′–4′ wide, with a stout midrib and primary veins and prominent reticulate veinlets; late in the autumn turning yellow or pale brown more or less blotched

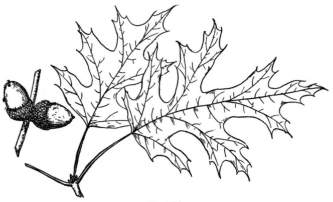

Fig. 226

with purple; petioles slender, glabrous or rarely puberulous, 1½′–2′ in length. **Flowers:** staminate in puberulous aments 1½′–2′ long; calyx campanulate, usually tinged with red, 2–5-lobed or parted into oblong-ovate or rounded segments, glabrous or slightly villose, fringed at apex with long twisted hairs, about as long as the 2–5 stamens, with short filaments and oblong anthers; pistillate on stout tomentose 1–3-flowered peduncles, red, their involucral scales broad, oblong, acute, hairy; calyx campanulate, 4–7-lobed, ciliate on the margins. **Fruit** short-stalked or nearly sessile, solitary or in pairs; nut ellipsoidal to subglobose, chestnut-brown, often striate and puberulous, inclosed for one third to one half its length in a turbinate or cup-shaped cup gradually narrowed at base, thin, light red-brown, and covered by narrow ovate obtuse or truncate brown pubescent closely appressed scales.

A tree, 60°–70° high, with a short trunk rarely 3° in diameter, much forked branches ascending above and often pendulous low on the stem, forming a narrow oblong head, and slender branchlets covered at first with matted pale hairs, bright reddish brown during their first winter, becoming dark gray-brown or reddish brown in their second season. **Winter-buds** ovoid, obtuse or acute, sometimes slightly angled, about ⅛′ long, with ovate or oval red-brown lustrous slightly puberulous outer scales ciliate on the margins. **Bark** thin, light yellow internally, close, rather smooth, divided by shallow connected fissures into thin plates, dark brown near the base of the tree, dull above, gray-brown and only slightly furrowed on the large branches.

Distribution. In the neighborhood of Chicago, Illinois, to southeastern Minnesota common; often covering large areas of sandy soil with a stunted growth and on the prairies sometimes a low shrub; eastern Iowa (Muscatine County), and the Lower Peninsular of Michigan (Montmorency, Arenac, and St. Clair Counties).

5. Quercus coccinea Muench. Scarlet Oak. Spanish Oak.

Leaves oblong-obovate or elliptic, truncate or cuneate at base, deeply divided by wide sinuses rounded in the bottom into 7 or rarely 9 lobes repand-dentate at apex, the terminal lobe, ovate, acute, and 3-toothed, the middle division the largest and furnished with 2 small lateral teeth, the lateral lobes obovate, oblique or spreading, sometimes falcate, usually broad and oblique at the coarsely toothed apex, when they unfold bright red covered with loose pale pubescence above and below with silvery white tomentum, green at the end of a few days, at maturity thin and firm, bright green, glabrous and very lustrous above, paler and less lustrous and sometimes furnished with small tufts of rusty pubescence in the axils of the veins below, 3'–6' long, 2½'–4' broad, with a yellow midrib and primary veins,

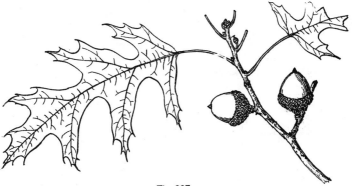

Fig. 227

late in the autumn turning brilliant scarlet; petioles slender, terete, 1½'–2½' in length. **Flowers:** staminate in slender glabrous aments 3'–4' long; calyx pubescent, bright red before opening, divided into 4 or 5 ovate acute segments shorter than the stamens; pistillate on pubescent peduncles sometimes ½' long, bright red, their involucral scales ovate, pubescent, shorter than the acute calyx-lobes. **Fruit** sessile or stalked, solitary or in pairs; nut oval, oblong-ovate or hemispheric, truncate or rounded at base, rounded at apex, ½'–1' long, ⅓'–⅔' thick, light reddish brown and occasionally striate, inclosed for one third to one half its length in a deep cup-shaped or turbinate thin cup light reddish brown on the inner surface, covered by closely imbricated oblong-ovate acute thin, or rarely much thickened (var. *tuberculata* Sarg.) light reddish brown slightly puberulous scales.

A tree, 70°–80° high, with a trunk 2°–3° in diameter, comparatively small branches spreading gradually and forming a rather narrow open head, and slender branchlets coated at first with loose scurfy pubescence, soon pale green and lustrous, light red or orange-red in their first winter and light or dark brown the following year; usually much smaller. **Winter-buds** ellipsoidal or ovoid, gradually narrowed at apex, ⅛'–¼' long, dark reddish brown, and pale-pubescent above the middle. **Bark** of young stems and branches smooth, light brown, becoming on old trunks ½'–1' thick and divided by shallow fissures into irregular ridges covered by small light brown scales slightly tinged with red. **Wood** heavy, hard, strong, coarse-grained, light or reddish brown, with thicker darker colored sapwood.

Distribution. Light dry usually sandy soil; valley of the Androscoggin River, Maine,

southern New Hampshire and Vermont to southern Ontario, southward to the District of
Columbia and along the Appalachian Mountains to eastern Kentucky and Tennessee,
and northern Georgia; in central Georgia and northeastern Mississippi (near Corinth,
Alcorn County), and westward through New York, Ohio, Indiana, Illinois and southern
Wisconsin to central Missouri (Jerome, Phelps County); in eastern Oklahoma (Arkansas
River valley near Fisher, Creek County, *G. W. Stevens*); ascending to altitudes of nearly
5000° on the southern mountains; the prevailing Oak above 2500° to the summits of the
Blue Ridge of the Carolinas; very abundant in the coast region from Massachusetts Bay
to southern New Jersey; less common in the interior, growing on dry gravelly uplands, and
on the prairies skirting the western margins of the eastern forest.   The var. *tuberculata* from
southern Massachusetts to Georgia, Alabama, Tennessee, Indiana, southern Illinois, and
Missouri.

Occasionally planted in the northeastern states and in Europe as an ornamental tree
valued chiefly for the brilliant autumn color of the foliage.

× *Quercus Robbinsii* Trel., believed to be a hybrid of *Quercus coccinea* and *Q. ilicifolia*,
occurs at North Easton, Bristol County, Massachusetts.

× *Quercus Benderi* Baenitz, a supposed hybrid of *Quercus coccinea* and *Q. borealis*
var. *maxima*, appeared several years ago in Silesia, and a similar tree has been found in
the Blue Hills Reservation near Boston.

6. Quercus palustris Muench.   Pin Oak.   Swamp Spanish Oak.

Leaves obovate, narrowed and cuneate or broad and truncate at base, divided by
wide deep sinuses rounded in the bottom into 5–7 lobes, the terminal lobe ovate, acute,

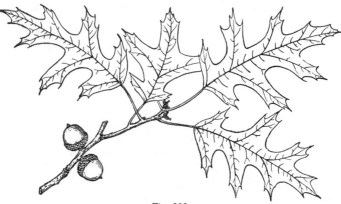

Fig. 228

3-toothed toward the apex, or entire, the lateral lobes spreading or oblique, sometimes falcate, especially those of the lowest pair, gradually tapering and acute at the dentate apex,
or obovate and broad at apex, when they unfold light bronze-green stained with red on the
margins, lustrous and puberulous above, coated below and on the petioles with pale scurfy
pubescence, at maturity thin and firm, dark green and very lustrous above, pale below,
with large tufts of pale hairs in the axils of the conspicuous primary veins; 4′–6′ long, 2′–4′
wide, with a stout midrib; late in the autumn gradually turning deep scarlet; petioles
slender, yellow, ½′–2′ in length.   **Flowers:** staminate in hairy aments 2′–3′ long; calyx
puberulous and divided into 4 or 5 oblong rounded segments more or less laciniately cut
on the margins, shorter than the stamens; pistillate on short tomentose peduncles, their
involucral scales broadly ovate, tomentose, shorter than the acuminate calyx-lobes; stigmas bright red.   **Fruit** sessile or short-stalked, solitary or clustered; nut nearly hemispheric,

about $\frac{1}{2}'$ in diameter, light brown, often striate, inclosed only at the base in a thin saucer-shaped cup dark red-brown and lustrous within, and covered by closely appressed ovate light red-brown thin puberulous scales.

A tree, usually 70°–80° high, with a trunk 2°–3° in diameter, often clothed with small tough drooping branches, or when crowded in the forest sometimes 120° high, with a trunk 60°–70° tall and 4°–5° in diameter, slender branches beset with short-ridged spur-like laterals a few inches in length, forming on young trees a broad pyramidal head, becoming on older trees open and irregular, with rigid and more pendulous branches often furnished at first with small drooping branchlets, and slender tough branchlets dark red and covered by short pale silvery tomentum, soon becoming green and glabrous, lustrous dark red-brown or orange color in their first winter, growing darker in their second year and ultimately dark gray-brown. **Winter-buds** ovoid, gradually narrowed and acute at apex, about $\frac{1}{8}'$ long, with imbricated light chestnut-brown scales puberulous toward the thin sometimes ciliate margins. **Bark** of young trunks and branches smooth, lustrous, light brown frequently tinged with red, becoming on older trunks $\frac{3}{4}'$–$1\frac{1}{4}'$ thick, light gray-brown, generally smooth and covered by small closely appressed scales. **Wood** heavy, hard, strong, coarse-grained, light brown, with thin rather darker colored sapwood; sometimes used in construction, and for shingles and clapboards.

Distribution. Borders of swamps and river-bottoms in deep rich moist soil; valley of the Connecticut River in western Massachusetts and Connecticut; on Grand Isle in the Niagara River, New York to southern Ontario and southwestern Michigan, and westward to eastern Iowa (Muscatine County), and southward to southern West Virginia (Hardy and Mercer Counties), southwestern Virginia (Wythe County), central North Carolina (on Bowling's Creek, near Chapel Hill, Orange County, and on Dutchman's Creek, Forsyth County); and to southern Kentucky, central Tennessee, southern Arkansas (Fulton, Hempstead County), and northeastern Oklahoma; rare and of small size in New England; exceedingly common in the green sand belt of New Jersey and Delaware; very abundant on the bottom-lands of the streams of the lower Ohio River.

Often cultivated as an ornamental tree in the northeastern states and occasionally in the countries of western and central Europe.

7. Quercus georgiana M. A. Curtis.

Leaves convolute in the bud, elliptic or obovate, gradually narrowed and cuneate at base, divided generally about half way to the midrib by wide or narrow oblique sinuses

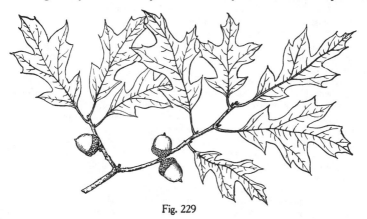

Fig. 229

rounded in the bottom into 3–7 lobes, the terminal lobe ovate, acute, or rounded and entire or frequently furnished with 1 or 2 small lateral teeth, the lateral lobes oblique or spreading, mostly triangular, acute and entire, or those of the upper and of the middle pair often broad and repand-lobulate at the oblique ends, sometimes gradually 3-lobed at the broad apex and narrowed and entire below, or equally 3-lobed, with broad or narrow spreading lateral lobes, or occasionally pinnatifid, when they unfold bright green tinged with red, ciliate on the margins and coated on the midrib, veins, and petioles with loose pale pubescence, at maturity thin, bright green and lustrous above, paler below, and glabrous or furnished with tufts of hairs in the axils of the primary veins, usually about $2\frac{1}{2}'$ long and $1\frac{1}{2}'$ wide; turning dull orange and scarlet in the autumn; petioles slender, $\frac{1}{2}'-\frac{3}{4}'$ in length. **Flowers:** staminate in slender glabrous or pubescent aments $2'-3'$ long; calyx divided into 4 or 5 broadly ovate rounded segments rather shorter than the stamens; pistillate on short glabrous slender peduncles; their involucral scales rather shorter than the acute calyx-lobes, pubescent or puberulous; stigmas bright red. **Fruit** short-stalked; nut ellipsoidal or subglobose, $\frac{1}{3}'-\frac{1}{2}'$ long, light red-brown and lustrous, inclosed for one third to nearly one half its length in a thick cup-shaped cup light red-brown and lustrous on the inner surface, and covered by thin ovate bright light red-brown truncate erose scales.

Distribution. Georgia; on Stone Mountain, and Little Stone Mountain, Dekalb County; on a few other granite or sandstone hills north and southwest of Stone Mountain (Winder, Jackson County, Rockmart, Polk County and at Warm Springs, Meriwether County).

Occasionally cultivated, and hardy in eastern Massachusetts.

× *Quercus Smallii* Trel., a possible hybrid of *Quercus georgiana* and *Q. marilandica*, occurs on the slopes and summit of Little Stone Mountain, Dekalb County, Georgia.

8. Quercus velutina Lam. Black Oak. Yellow-bark Oak.

Leaves ovate or oblong, rounded, cuneate or truncate at base, mostly 7-lobed and sometimes divided nearly to the middle by wide rounded sinuses into narrow obovate more or less repand-dentate lobes, or into elongated nearly entire mucronate lobes tapering gradually from a broad base, the terminal lobe oblong, elongated, acute, furnished with small lateral teeth, or broad, rounded, and coarsely repand-dentate, or slightly divided into broad dentate lobes or sinuate-dentate, bright crimson when they unfold, and covered above by long loose scattered white hairs and below with thick pale or silvery white tomentum, hoary-pubescent when half grown, and at maturity thick and firm or subcoriaceous, dark green and lustrous above, below yellow-green, brown or dull copper color and more or less pubescent or glabrous with the exception of tufts of rusty hairs in the axils of the principal veins, $3'-12'$ long and $2'-10'$ wide, but usually $5'-6'$ long and $3'-4'$ wide, with a stout midrib and primary veins; late in the autumn turning dull red, dark orange color, or brown, and falling gradually during the winter; petioles stout, yellow, glabrous or puberulous, $3'-6'$ in length. **Flowers:** staminate in tomentose or pubescent aments $4'-6'$ long; calyx coated with pale hairs, with ovate acute lobes; pistillate on short tomentose peduncles, their involucral scales ovate, shorter than the acute calyx-lobes; stigmas bright red. **Fruit** sessile or short-stalked, solitary or in pairs; nut ovoid-oblong, obovoid, oval or hemispheric, broad and rounded at base, full and rounded at apex, light red-brown, often striate, frequently coated with soft rufous pubescence, $\frac{1}{2}'-\frac{3}{4}'$ long and broad, or rarely $1'$ long and broad, inclosed for about half its length or rarely nearly to the apex in the thin deeply cup-shaped or turbinate cup dark red-brown on the inner surface, covered by thin light chestnut-brown acute hoary scales closely appressed at the base of the cup, loosely imbricated above the middle, with free scarious tips forming a fringe-like border to its rim.

A tree, often $70°-80°$ and occasionally $150°$ high, with a trunk $3°-4°$ in diameter, slender branches spreading gradually into a narrow open head, stout branchlets coated at first with pale or fulvous scurfy tomentum, becoming in their first winter glabrous, dull red or reddish brown, growing dark brown in their second year or brown slightly tinged with red. **Winter-buds** ovoid, strongly angled, gradually narrowed and obtuse at apex, hoary-tomentose, $\frac{1}{4}'-\frac{1}{2}'$ long. **Bark** of young stems and branches smooth, dark brown, deep orange color internally, becoming $\frac{3}{4}'$–$1\frac{1}{2}'$ thick on old trunks, and deeply divided into broad rounded ridges broken on the surface into thick dark brown or nearly black closely appressed plate-like scales   **Wood** heavy, hard, strong, coarse-grained, bright brown tinged with red, with thin lighter colored sapwood; of little value except as fuel.   The bark abounds in tannic acid and is largely used in tanning. as a yellow dye, and in medicine.

Distribution.   Dry gravelly uplands and ridges; coast of southern Maine to northern Vermont, southern and western Ontario, the southern peninsula of Michigan, northwestern, eastern and southern Iowa, and southeastern Nebraska, and southward to western Florida, southern Alabama, Mississippi, Louisiana, eastern Kansas, northeastern Oklahoma and eastern Texas to the valley of the Brazos River; one of the commonest Oaks on the gravelly drift of southern New England and the middle states; ascending on the southern Appalachian Mountains to altitudes of about 4000°, and often forming a large part of the forest growth on their foothills; abundant in all parts of the Mississippi

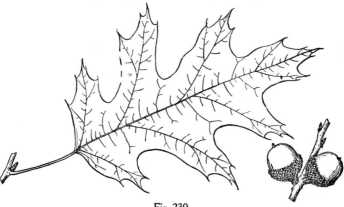

Fig. 230

basin, and of its largest size in the valley of the lower Ohio River; the common species of the Black Oak group reaching the south-Atlantic and Gulf Coast, and here generally scattered on dry ridges through the maritime Pine belt; southward often with a more crooked stem and rougher bark (*R. M. Harper*).

Quercus velutina, which is more variable in the form of its leaves than the other North American Black Oaks, is easily recognized by the bright yellow color of the inner bark, in early spring by the deep red color of the unfolding leaves, becoming pale and silvery in a few days, and by the large tomentose winter-buds.   From western Missouri to northwestern Arkansas a form occurs (var. *missouriensis* Sarg.) with the mature leaves covered above with fascicled hairs, and coated below and on the petioles and summer branchlets with rusty pubescence, and with broader more loosely imbricated hoary-tomentose cup-scales.

9. Quercus Kelloggii Newb.   Black Oak.

Quercus californica Coop.

Leaves oblong or obovate, truncate, cuneate or rounded at the narrow base, 7 or rarely 5-lobed by wide and deep or shallow and oblique sinuses rounded in the bottom, the terminal lobe ovate, 3-toothed at the acute apex, the lateral lobes tapering gradually from the base or broad and obovate, coarsely repand-dentate with acute pointed teeth, or rarely entire, when they unfold dark red or purple and pilose above and coated below and on the petioles with thick silvery white tomentum, at maturity thick and firm, lustrous, dark yellow-green and glabrous or rarely pubescent above, light yellow-green or brownish and glabrous or pubescent, or occasionally hoary-tomentose below, 3′–6′ long, 2′–4′ wide; turning yellow or brown in the autumn before falling; petioles slender, yellow, 1′–2′ in length. **Flowers:** staminate in hairy aments 4′–5′ long; calyx pubescent, divided into 4 or 5 ovate acute segments shorter than the stamens; anthers bright red; pistillate on short tomentose peduncles, their involucral scales ovate, coated like the acute calyx-lobes with pale tomentum; stigmas dark red. **Fruit** short-stalked, solitary or clustered; nut oblong, ellipsoidal or obovoid, broad and rounded at base, full and rounded or gradually narrowed and acute at the puberulous apex, 1′–1½′ long, about ¾′ broad, light chestnut-brown, often striate, inclosed for one fourth to two thirds of its length in the deep cup-shaped cup light brown on the inner surface, and covered by thin ovate-lanceolate lustrous light chestnut brown scales, sometimes rounded and thickened on the back toward the base of the cup, their tips elongated, thin and erose on the margins, often forming a narrow fringe-like border to the rim of the cup.

A tree, occasionally 100° high, with a trunk 3°–4° in diameter, stout spreading branches forming an open round-topped head, and branchlets coated at first with thick hoary ca-

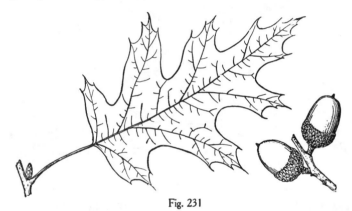

Fig. 231

ducous tomentum, bright red or brown tinged with red, and usually glabrous or pubescent or puberulous during their first winter, becoming dark red-brown in their second year; frequently much smaller and at high elevations a small shrub (f. *cibata* Jeps.). **Winter-buds** ovoid, gradually narrowed and acute at apex, about ¼′ long, with closely imbricated pale chestnut-brown scales ciliate on the thin scarious margins and pubescent toward the point of the bud. **Bark** of young stems and branches smooth, light brown, becoming on old trunks 1′–1½′ thick, dark brown slightly tinged with red or nearly black, divided into broad ridges at the base of old trees and broken above into thick irregular oblong plates covered by minute closely appressed scales. **Wood** heavy, hard, strong, very brittle, bright red, with thin lighter colored sapwood; occasionally used as fuel.

Distribution. Valleys and mountain slopes; basin of the Mackenzie River in western Oregon, southward over the California coast ranges, and along the western slopes of the Sierra Nevada up to altitudes of 6500° to the Cuyamaca Mountains near the southern boundary of California; extending across the Sierra Nevada to the foothills of Owens valley (*Jepson*) in eastern California; rare in the immediate neighborhood of the coast; the largest and most abundant Oak-tree of the valleys of southwestern Oregon and of the Sierra Nevada, sometimes forming groves of considerable extent in coniferous forests; of its largest size at altitudes of about 6000° above the sea.

10. Quercus Catesbæi Michx. Turkey Oak.

Leaves oblong or obovate or nearly triangular, gradually narrowed and cuneate at base, deeply divided by wide rounded sinuses into 3 or 5 or rarely 7 lobes, the terminal lobe ovate, elongated, acute and entire or repand-dentate, or obovate and coarsely equally or irregularly 3-toothed at apex, the lateral lobes spreading, usually falcate, entire and acute, tapering from the broad base, and broad, oblique, and repand-lobulate at apex, or 3-toothed at the broad apex and gradually narrowed to the base, coated when they unfold with rufous fascicled hairs, and when fully grown thick and rigid, bright yellow-green and lustrous above, paler, lustrous, and glabrous below, with large tufts of rusty hairs in the axils of the veins, 3′–12′ long, 1′–10′ wide, but usually about 5′ long and wide, with a broad yellow or red-brown midrib; turning bright scarlet before falling in the late autumn or early winter; petioles stout, grooved, $\frac{1}{4}′-\frac{3}{4}′$ in length. **Flowers:** staminate in slender hairy red-stemmed aments 4′–5′ long; calyx puberulous and divided into 4 or 5 ovate acute lobes; pistillate on short stout tomentose peduncles, their involucral scales bright red, pubescent, hairy at the margins; stigmas dark red. **Fruit** short-stalked, usually solitary; nut oval, full and rounded at the ends, about 1′ long and $\frac{3}{4}′$ broad, dull light brown,

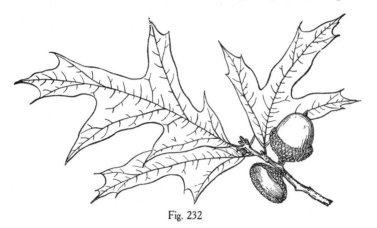

Fig. 232

covered at the apex by a thin coat of snow-white tomentum, inclosed for about one third its length in a thin turbinate cup often gradually narrowed into a stout stalk-like base, light red-brown and lustrous on the inner surface, covered by ovate-oblong rounded scales extending above the rim of the cup and down over the upper third of the inner surface, and hoary-pubescent except their thin bright red margins.

A tree, usually 20°–30°, or occasionally 50°–60° high, with a trunk rarely exceeding 2° in diameter, stout spreading more or less contorted branches forming a broad or narrow open irregular generally round-topped head, and stout branchlets coated at first with fascicled hairs, nearly glabrous and deep red when the leaves are half grown, dark red in their first winter, gradually growing dark brown; generally much smaller and sometimes shrubby. **Winter-buds** elongated, acute, $\frac{1}{2}′$ long, with light chestnut-brown scales erose on the thin margins, and coated, especially toward the point of the bud, with rusty pubescence. **Bark** $\frac{1}{2}′–1′$ thick, red internally, dark gray tinged with red on the surface, and at the base of old trunks becoming nearly black, deeply and irregularly furrowed and broken into small appressed scales. **Wood** heavy, hard, strong, rather close-grained, light brown tinged with red, with thick lighter colored sapwood; largely used for fuel.

Distribution. Dry barren sandy ridges and sandy bluffs and hummocks in the neighborhood of the coast; southeastern Virginia (near Zuni, Isle of Wight County) to the shores of Indian River and Peace River, Florida, and westward to eastern Louisiana; comparatively rare toward the western limits of its range, and most abundant and of its largest size on the high bluff-like shores of bays and estuaries in South Carolina and Georgia; the prevailing tree with *Quercus cinerea* in dry sandy uplands of the interior of the Florida peninsula as far south as the sandy ridges in the neighborhood near Fort Ogden, De Soto County; in Georgia inland over the coastal plain to the Pine Mountains, and in Alabama to Tuscaloosa County (*R. M. Harper*).

× *Quercus Mellichampii* Trel. believed to be a hybrid of *Quercus Catesbæi* and *Q. laurifolia* occurs at Bluffton on the coast of South Carolina, in the neighborhood of Orlando, Orange County and near San Mateo, Putnam County, Florida.

× *Quercus Ashei* Trel. believed to be a hybrid of *Quercus Catesbæi* with *Q. cinerea* occurs at Folkston and near Trader's Hill, Charlton County and St. Mary's, Camden County, Georgia.

× *Quercus blufftonensis* Trel., a probable hybrid of *Quercus Catesbæi* and *Q. rubra* L., has been found at Bluffton, South Carolina.

× *Quercus Walteriana* Ashe, believed to be a hybrid of *Quercus Catesbaei* and *Q. nigra*, is not rare in the immediate neighborhood of the coast of South Carolina and Georgia, and occurs on sand hills in Sampson County, North Carolina, near Jacksonville, Duval County, Florida, at Mount Vernon, Mobile County and in the neighborhood of Selma, Dallas County, Alabama.

11. Quercus ilicifolia Wang.　Bear Oak.　Scrub Oak.

Quercus nana Sarg.

Leaves obovate or rarely oblong, gradually or abruptly cuneate at base, divided by wide shallow sinuses into 3–7, usually 5, acute lobes, the terminal lobe ovate, elongated, rounded and 3-toothed or acute and dentate or entire at apex, the lateral lobes spreading,

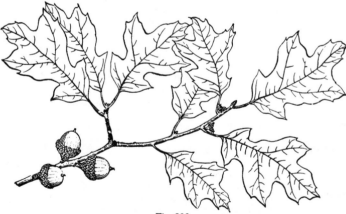

Fig. 233

mostly triangular and acute, or those of the upper pair broad, oblique and repand-lobulate or broad at apex, slightly 3-lobed and entire below, or deeply 3-lobed above and sinuate below, or occasionally oblong to oblong-obovate and entire, with undulate margins, when they unfold dull red and puberulous or pubescent on the upper surface and coated on the lower and on the petioles with thick pale tomentum, with conspicuous tufts of silvery white hairs in the axils of the veins, at maturity thick and firm, dark green and lustrous above, covered below with pale or silvery white pubescence, 2′–5′ long, 1½′–3′ wide, with a stout yellow midrib and slender primary veins; turning dull scarlet or yellow in the autumn; petioles slender, glabrous, or pubescent, $1'-1\frac{1}{2}'$ in length. **Flowers:** staminate in hairy aments $4'-5'$ long, and often persistent until midsummer; calyx red or green tinged with red and irregularly divided into 3–5 ovate rounded lobes shorter than the stamens; anthers bright red ultimately yellow; pistillate on stout tomentose peduncles, their involucral scales ovate, about as long as the acute calyx-lobes, red and tomentose; stigmas dark red. **Fruit** produced in great profusion, sessile or stalked, in pairs or rarely solitary; nut ovoid, broad, flat or rounded at base, gradually narrowed and acute or rounded at apex, about $\frac{1}{2}'$ long and broad, light brown, lustrous, usually faintly striate, inclosed for about one half its length in the cup-shaped or saucer-shaped cup often abruptly enlarged above the stalk-like base, thick, light reddish brown within, and covered by thin ovate closely imbricated red-brown puberulous scales acute or truncate at apex, the minute free tips of the upper scales forming a fringe-like border to the cup.

A tree, occasionally $18°-20°$ high, with a trunk $5'-6'$ in diameter, with slender spreading branches usually forming a round-topped head, and slender branchlets dark green more or less tinged with red and hoary-pubescent at first, during their first winter red-brown or ashy gray and pubescent or puberulous, becoming glabrous and darker in their second year and ultimately dark brown or nearly black; more frequently an intricately branched shrub, with numerous contorted stems $3°-10°$ tall. **Winter-buds** ovoid, obtuse, about $\frac{1}{8}'$ long, with dark chestnut-brown rather loosely imbricated glabrous or pilose scales. **Bark** thin, smooth, dark brown, covered by small closely appressed scales.

Distribution. Dry sandy barrens and rocky hillsides; coast of eastern Maine southward through eastern and southern New England to southern and southwestern Pennsylvania and along the Appalachian Mountains, principally on their eastern slopes, to southern Virginia; on Crowder and King Mountains, Gaston County, North Carolina; and westward to the shores of Lake George and the valley of the Hudson River; common in eastern and southern New Engnlad, in the Pine barrens of New Jersey, and in eastern Pennsylvania.

× *Quercus Brittonii* Davis, believed to be a hybrid of *Quercus ilicifolia* and *Q. marilandica*, has been found on Staten Island, New York, and at Ocean Grove, Monmouth County, New Jersey.

× *Quercus Giffordii* Trel., believed to be a hybrid of *Quercus ilicifolia* and *Q. Phellos,* has been found at May's Landing, Atlantic County, New Jersey.

× *Quercus Rehderi* Trel., believed to be a hybrid of *Quercus ilicifolia* and *Q. velutina,* is not rare in eastern Massachusetts and occurs on Martha's Vineyard (Chilmark).

12. Quercus rubra L. Red Oak. Spanish Oak.

Quercus digitata Sudw.

Leaves ovate to obovate, narrowed and rounded or cuneate at base, the terminal lobe long-acuminate, entire or slightly lobed, often falcate, usually longer than the 2 or 4 acuminate entire lateral lobes narrowed from a broad base and often falcate, or oblong-obovate and divided at the broad apex by wide or narrow sinuses broad and rounded in the bottom into 3 rounded or acute entire or dentate lobes, and entire and gradually narrowed below into an acute or rounded base (var. *triloba* Ashe), the two forms usually occurring on different but sometimes on the same tree, at maturity thin and firm, dark green and lustrous above, coated below with soft close pale or rusty pubescence, $6'-7'$ long and $4'-5'$ wide, obscurely reticulate-venulose, with a stout tomentose midrib and primary veins; turning brown or dull orange color in the autumn; petioles slender, flattened, $1'-2'$ in length. **Flowers:** staminate in tomentose aments, $3'-5'$ long; calyx thin and scarious, pubescent on the outer surface, divided into 4 or 5 ovate rounded segments; pistillate on stout tomentose peduncles, their involucral scales coated with rusty tomentum, as long or rather shorter than the acute calyx-lobes; stigmas dark red. **Fruit** sessile or short-stalked; nut subglobose to ellipsoidal, full and rounded at apex, truncate and rounded at base, about

¼' long, bright orange-brown, inclosed only at base or sometimes for one third its length in a thin saucer-shaped cup flat on the bottom or gradually narrowed from a stalk-like base, or deep and turbinate, bright red-brown on the inner surface, covered by thin ovate-oblong reddish scales acute or rounded at apex and pale-pubescent except on the margins.

A tree, usually 70°–80° high, with a trunk 2°–3° in diameter, large spreading branches forming a broad round-topped open head, and stout branchlets coated at first, like the young leaves, with thick rusty or orange-colored clammy tomentum, dark red or reddish brown and pubescent or rarely glabrous during their first winter, becoming in their second year dark red-brown or ashy gray. The var. *triloba* usually 20°–30° rarely 40°–50° high. **Winter-buds** ovoid or oval, acute, ⅛'–¼' long, with bright chestnut-brown puberulous or pilose scales ciliate with short pale hairs. **Bark** ¾'–1' thick, dark brown or pale, and divided by shallow fissures into broad ridges covered by thin closely appressed scales. **Wood**

Fig. 234

hard, strong, not durable, coarse-grained, light red, with thick lighter colored sapwood; sometimes used in construction, and largely as fuel. The bark is rich in tannin, and is used in tanning leather and occasionally in medicine.

Distribution. Southeastern and southern Pennsylvania and southern New Jersey southward to central Florida, through the Gulf states to the valley of the Brazos River, Texas, and through eastern Oklahoma, Arkansas, and southeastern Missouri to central Tennessee and Kentucky, southern Indiana and Illinois, southern Ohio (Black Fork Creek, Lawrence County), and Kanawha County, West Virginia; in the north Atlantic states only in the neighborhood of the coast and comparatively rare; very common in the south Atlantic and Gulf states on dry hills between the coast plain and the Appalachian Mountains; less abundant in the southern maritime Pine belt. The var. *triloba:* rare and local. Pleasant Grove, Lancaster County, Pennsylvania, and Jefferson County, Indiana, southward to central and western Florida, southern Alabama and Mississippi, western Arkansas and eastern Texas; on dry uplands near Milledgeville, Baldwin County, Georgia, the prevailing form.

Quercus rubra var. pagodæfolia Ashe.   Swamp Spanish Oak.   Red Oak.

Quercus pagoda Rafn.

Quercus pagodæfolia Ashe.

Leaves elliptic to oblong, acuminate, gradually narrowed and cuneate or full and rounded or rarely truncate at base, deeply divided by wide sinuses rounded in the bottom into 5–11 acuminate usually entire repand-dentate lobes often falcate and spreading at right angles to the midrib or pointed toward the apex of the leaf, when they unfold coated with pale tomentum, thickest on the lower surface, and dark red on the upper surface, at maturity dark green and very lustrous above, pale and tomentose below, 6′–8′ long and 5′–6′ wide, with a stout midrib usually puberulous on the upper side, slender primary veins arched to the points of the lobes, and conspicuous reticulate veinlets; turning bright clear yellow before falling; petioles stout, pubescent or tomentose, 1½′–2′ in length. **Flowers** and **Fruit** as in the species.

A tree, sometimes 120° high, with a trunk 4°–5° in diameter, heavy branches forming in the forest a short narrow crown, or in more open situations wide-spreading or ascending and forming a great open head, and slender branchlets hoary tomentose at first, tomentose or pubescent during their first winter, and dark reddish brown and puberulous during their second year. **Winter-buds** ovoid, acute, often prominently 4-angled, about ¼′ long, with

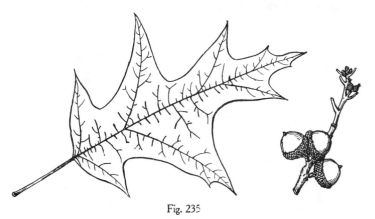

Fig. 235

light red-brown puberulous scales sometimes ciliate at the apex. **Bark** about 1′ thick and roughened by small rather closely appressed plate-like light gray, gray-brown or dark brown scales. **Wood** light reddish brown, with thin nearly white sapwood; largely manufactured into lumber in the Mississippi valley, and valued almost as highly as white oak.

Distribution. Rich bottom-lands and the alluvial banks of streams; Maryland (Queen Anne County) and coast of Virginia to northern Florida, and through the Gulf states and Arkansas to southern Missouri, western Tennessee and Kentucky, and southern Illinois and Indiana; most abundant and one of the largest and most valuable timber-trees in the river swamps of the Yazoo basin, Mississippi, and of eastern Arkansas. Differing chiefly from the type in the more numerous and more acuminate lobes of the usually more elongated leaves usually paler on the lower surface, and in the generally paler bark of the trunk; passing into *Quercus rubra* var. *leucophylla* Ashe with leaves on upper branches nearly as broad as long thickly covered below with brownish pubescence and deeply divided into 5–7 lobes, and on lower branches slightly obovate, less deeply divided, thin, dark green, sometimes pubescent becoming glabrous above and often covered below with pale or brown pubescence.

A tree sometimes 120° high; in low rich soil; coast region of southeastern Virginia, southward to western Florida and through the Gulf states to the valley of the Neches River, Texas, and northward to northern Arkansas; in southern Illinois (near Mt. Carmel, Wabash County) and southwestern Indiana (near Hovey Lake, Posey County); abundant in low woods about River Junction, Gadsden County, Florida, and in central Mississippi.

× *Quercus Willdenoviana* Zabel is believed in Europe to be a hybrid of *Quercus rubra* and *Quercus velutina*.

13. Quercus marilandica Muench. Black Jack. Jack Oak.

Leaves broadly obovate, rounded or cordate at the narrow base, usually 3 or rarely 5-lobed at the broad and often abruptly dilated apex, with short or long, broad or narrow, rounded or acute, entire or dentate lobes, or entire or dentate at apex, sometimes oblong-obovate, undulate-lobed at the broad apex and entire below, or equally 3-lobed with elongated spreading lateral lobes broad and lobulate at apex, when they unfold coated with a clammy tomentum of fascicled hairs and bright pink on the upper surface, at maturity thick and firm or subcoriaceous, dark yellow-green and very lustrous above, yellow, orange color, or brown and scurfy-pubescent below, usually 6'–7' long and broad, with a thick broad orange-colored midrib; turning brown or yellow in the autumn; petioles stout, yellow, glabrous or pubescent, $\frac{1}{2}'-\frac{3}{4}'$ in length. **Flowers:** staminate in hoary aments 2'–4' long; calyx thin and scarious, tinged with red above the middle, pale-pubescent on the outer surface, divided into 4 or 5 broad ovate rounded lobes; anthers apiculate, dark red; pistillate

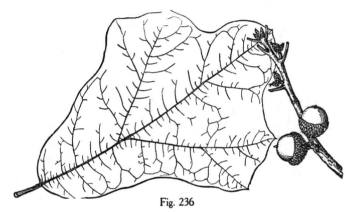

Fig. 236

on short rusty-tomentose peduncles coated like their involucral scales with thick rusty tomentum; stigmas dark red. **Fruit,** solitary or in pairs, usually pedunculate; nut oblong, full and rounded at the ends, rather broader below than above the middle, about $\frac{3}{4}'$ long, light yellow-brown and often striate, the shell lined with dense fulvous tomentum, inclosed for one third to nearly two thirds of its length in a thick turbinate light brown cup puberulous on the inner surface, and covered by large reddish brown loosely imbricated scales often ciliate and coated with loose pale or rusty tomentum, the upper scales smaller, erect, inserted on the top of the cup in several rows, and forming a thick rim round its inner surface, or occasionally reflexed and covering the upper half of the inner surface of the cup.

A tree, 20°–30°, or occasionally 40°–50° high, with a trunk rarely more than 1' in diameter, short stout spreading often contorted branches forming a narrow compact round-topped or sometimes an open irregular head, and stout branchlets coated at first with thick pale tomentum, light brown and scurfy-pubescent during their first summer, becoming reddish brown and glabrous or puberulous in the winter, and ultimatey brown or ashy gray. **Winter-buds** ovoid or oval, prominently angled, light red-brown, coated with rusty brown hairs, about $\frac{1}{4}'$ long. **Bark** 1'–1½' thick, and deeply divided into nearly square plates 1'–3' long and covered by small closely appressed dark brown or nearly black scales. **Wood** heavy, hard, strong, dark rich brown, with thick lighter colored sapwood; largely used as fuel and in the manufacture of charcoal.

Distribution. Dry sandy or clay barrens; Long Island and Staten Island, New York, eastern and southern Pennsylvania, and southern New Jersey to northern Florida, and westward through the Gulf states to western Texas (Callahan County) and to western

Oklahoma (Dewey and Kiowa Counties), Arkansas, eastern Kansas, southeastern Nebraska and through Missouri to northeastern Illinois, southwestern and southern Indiana, and northeastern Kentucky (South Portsmouth, Greenup County, *R. E. Horsey*); rare in the north, very abundant southward; west of the Mississippi River often forming on sterile soils a great part of the forest growth; of its largest size in southern Arkansas and eastern Texas.

× *Quercus Rudkinii* Britt., with characters intermediate between those of *Quercus marilandica* and *Q. Phellos*, and probably a hybrid of these species, has been found near Tottenville, Staten Island, New York, at Keyport, Monmouth County, New Jersey, and the Falls of the Yadkin River, Stanley County, North Carolina, and Fulton, Hempstead County, Arkansas.

× *Quercus sterilis* Trel., believed to be a hybrid of *Quercus marilandica* and *Q. nigra* has been found in Bladen County, North Carolina.

× *Quercus Hastingsii* Sarg., believed to be a hybrid of *Quercus marilandica* and *Q. texana*, occurs near Boerne, Kendall County, and at Brownwood, Brown County, Texas.

× *Quercus Bushii* Sarg., believed to be a hybrid of *Quercus marilandica* and *Q. velutina*, although not common, occurs in eastern Oklahoma (Sapulpa, Creek County), Arkansas (Fayetteville, Washington County, Eureka Springs, Carroll County), Missouri (Prosperity, Jasper County), Mississippi (Oxford, Lafayette County), Alabama (Dothan, Houston County, near Berlin, banks of the Alabama River near Selma, Dallas County, and Daphne, Baldwin County), Florida (Sumner, Levy County), and in Georgia (Climax, Decatur County).

14. Quercus arkansana Sarg.

Leaves broadly obovate, slightly 3-lobed or dentate at the wide apex, cuneate at base, on sterile branches often oblong-ovate, acute or rounded at apex, rounded at base, the lobes ending in long slender mucros, when they unfold tinged with red, thickly covered with pale fascicled hairs persistent until summer, the midrib and veins more thickly

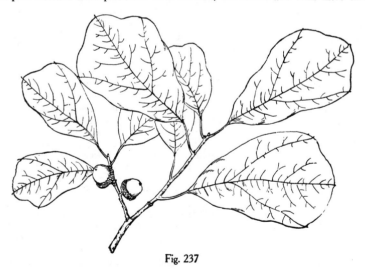

Fig. 237

clothed with long straight hairs, and at maturity glabrous, with the exception of small axillary tufts of pubescence on the lower surface, light yellow-green above, paler below $2'-2\frac{3}{4}'$ long and broad, with a slender light yellow midrib, thin primary veins and prominent veinlets; on sterile branches often $4\frac{1}{2}'-5\frac{1}{2}'$ long and $2\frac{1}{2}'-2\frac{3}{4}'$ wide; petioles slender,

coated at first with clusters of pale hairs, becoming glabrous or puberulous, $\frac{3}{5}'-\frac{4}{5}'$ in length.
Flowers: staminate in aments covered with clusters of long pale hairs, $2'-2\frac{1}{2}'$ long; calyx usually 4 rarely 3-lobed, thinly covered with long white hairs; stamens usually 4; anthers ovoid-oblong, apiculate, dark red; pistillate on stout peduncles hoary-tomentose like the scales of the involucre; stigmas dark red. **Fruit** solitary or in pairs, on short glabrous peduncles; nut broad-ovoid, rounded at apex, sparingly pubescent especially below the middle with fascicled hairs, light brown, obscurely striate, $\frac{1}{4}'-\frac{1}{3}'$ long, $\frac{1}{2}'-\frac{5}{8}'$ thick, inclosed only at base in the flat saucer-shaped cup, pubescent on the inner surface, covered with closely appressed scales obtuse at their narrow apex, red on the margins, pale pubescent, those of the upper rank smaller, erect, inserted on the top of the cup and forming a thin rim round its inner surface.

A tree when crowded in the forest often 60°–70° high, with a tall trunk, stout ascending branches forming a long narrow head, and slender branchlets thickly coated early in the season with pale fascicled hairs, pubescent or nearly glabrous in their first autumn and darker and glabrous in their second year, when not crowded by other trees rarely 40° high with a short trunk occasionally 1° in diameter. **Winter-buds** ovoid, acute, with thin light chestnut-brown slightly pubescent or nearly glabrous scales. **Bark** thick, nearly black, divided by deep fissures into long narrow ridges covered with thick closely appressed scales.

Distribution. Low woods and on rolling sand hills four miles north of Fulton, Hempstead County, and in Clark County, Arkansas; east to Pike County, Alabama. By Trelease considered a hybrid of *Q. marilandica* and *Q. nigra*. See paper on *Q. arkansana* by Palmer in Jour. Arnold Arb. vi. 195 (1925).

15. Quercus nigra L.   Water Oak.

Leaves oblong-obovate, gradually narrowed and cuneate at base and enlarged often abruptly at the broad rounded entire or occasionally 3-lobed apex, on vigorous young branchlets sometimes pinnatifid with acute, acuminate or rounded lobes or broadly oblong-obovate and rounded at apex with entire or undulate margins, on upper branches occasionally linear-lanceolate, on occasional trees narrowed below to an elongated cuneate base and gradually widened above into a more or less deeply 3-lobed apex, the lobes rounded or acute (var. *tridentifera* Sarg.), or often acute at the ends, and on upper branchlets sometimes linear-lanceolate to linear-obovate, acute or rounded at apex, divided above the middle by deep wide rounded sinuses into elongated lanceolate acute entire lobes, or pinnatifid above the middle, when they unfold thin, light green more or less tinged with red and covered by fine caducous pubescence, with conspicuous tufts of pale hairs in the axils of the veins below, at maturity thin, dull bluish green, paler below than above, glabrous or with axillary tufts of rusty hairs, usually about $2\frac{1}{2}'$ long and $1\frac{1}{2}'$ wide, or on fertile branches sometimes 6' long and $2\frac{1}{2}'$ wide; turning yellow and falling gradually during the winter; petioles stout, flattened, $\frac{1}{8}'-\frac{1}{2}'$ in length; leaves of seedling plants linear-lanceolate with entire or undulate margins, or occasionally lobed with 1 or 2 pointed lobes, often deeply 3-lobed at a wide apex, and occasionally furnished below the middle with a single acuminate lobe, all the forms often occurring on a plant less than three feet high. **Flowers:** staminate in red hairy-stemmed aments $2'-3'$ long; calyx thin and scarious, covered on the outer surface with short hairs, divided into 4 or 5 ovate rounded segments; pistillate on short tomentose peduncles, their involucral scales a little shorter than the acute calyx-lobes and coated with rusty hairs; stigmas deep red. **Fruit** usually solitary, sessile or short-stalked; nut ovoid, broad and flat at base, full and rounded at the pubescent apex, light yellow-brown, often striate, $\frac{1}{3}'-\frac{2}{3}'$ long and nearly as thick, usually inclosed only at the base in a thin saucer-shaped cup, or occasionally for one third its length in a cup-shaped cup, coated on the inner surface with pale silky tomentum and covered by ovate acute closely appressed light red-brown scales clothed with pale pubescence except on their darker colored margins.

A tree, occasionally 80° high, with a trunk $2°-3\frac{1}{2}°$ in diameter, numerous slender branches spreading gradually from the stem and forming a symmetrical round-topped head, and slender glabrous branchlets light or dull red during their first winter, becoming grayish brown in their second season. **Winter-buds** ovoid, acute, strongly angled, covered by loosely imbricated dark red-brown puberulous scales slightly ciliate on the thin margins. **Bark** $\frac{1}{2}'-\frac{3}{4}'$ thick, with a smooth light brown surface slightly tinged with red and covered by smooth closely appressed scales. **Wood** heavy, hard, strong, close-grained, light brown, with thick lighter colored sapwood; little valued except as fuel.

Fig. 238

Distribution. High sandy borders of swamps and streams and the rich bottom-lands of rivers, or northward sometimes in dry woods; southern Delaware, southward to the shores of the Indian River and Tampa Bay, Florida, ranging inland in the south Atlantic states through the Piedmont region, and westward through the Gulf states to the valley of the Colorado River, Texas, and through eastern Oklahoma and Arkansas to southeastern Missouri and to central Tennessee and Kentucky. The var. *tridentifera* Sarg. rare and local; southwest Virginia to Alabama (near Selma, Dallas County), central and western Mississippi, eastern Louisiana; valley of Navidad River, Lavaca County, Texas. A form (f. *microcarya* Sarg. — *Quercus microcarya* Small) occurs in the dry soil on slopes of Little Stone Mountain, Dekalb County, Georgia.

The Water Oak is commonly planted as a shade-tree in the streets and squares of the cities and towns of the southern states.

16. Quercus obtusata Ashe.

Quercus rhombica Sarg.

Leaves rhombic, rarely oblong-obovate to lanceolate, acute or rounded and apiculate at apex, cuneate at base, the margins entire or slightly undulate, those on vigorous shoots occasionally furnished on each side near the middle with a short lobe, when they unfold deeply tinged with red, covered with short pale caducous pubescence and furnished below with usually persistent tufts of axillary hairs, at maturity thin, dark green and lustrous above, pale below, $3\frac{1}{2}'-4'$ long, $1\frac{1}{2}'-2'$ wide, with a stout conspicuous yellow midrib and slender forked primary veins; turning yellow and falling gradually in early winter, rarely at the ends of branches, obovate and rounded, slightly 3-lobed or undulate at the broad apex (var. *obovatifolia* Sarg.); petioles yellow, $\frac{1}{5}'-\frac{1}{2}'$ in length. **Flowers** not seen. **Fruit** sessile or short-stalked; nut ovoid, rounded at apex, thickly covered with pale pubescence, $\frac{2}{5}'-1'$ long, $\frac{3}{5}'$ thick; inclosed only at the base in a saucer-shaped cup, rounded on the bottom, silky pubescent on the inner surface, and covered with slightly pubescent reddish brown loosely appressed scales rounded at apex, with free tips, those of the upper rank thin and ciliate on the margins.

A tree often 120°–150° high, with a tall trunk 3°–4½° in diameter, stout, wide-spreading smooth branches forming a broad open head, and slender glabrous branchlets red-brown during their first season and dark gray the following year. **Bark,** pale gray, slightly furrowed and covered with closely appressed scales, $\frac{1}{2}'-\frac{3}{4}'$ thick.

Distribution. Borders of swamps and low wet woods of the coast region; southeastern Virginia (Dismal Swamp) sparingly in Jackson County, west Florida, and through the Gulf states to the valley of the Neches River (Beaumont, Jefferson County), eastern Texas; in

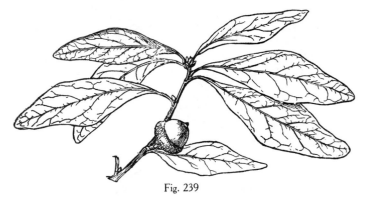

Fig. 239

Louisiana northward to the valley of the Red River; most abundant in south central Alabama and in Louisiana.

× *Quercus beaumontiana* Sarg., believed to be a hybrid of *Quercus obtusata* and *Q. rubra* has been found growing by a street in Beaumont, Jefferson County, Texas.

× *Quercus Cocksii* Sarg., probably a hybrid of *Quercus obtusata* and *Q. velutina,* has been found at Pineville, Rapides Parish, Louisiana.

17. Quercus Phellos L.　Willow Oak.

Leaves ovate-lanceolate or rarely obovate-lanceolate, often somewhat falcate, gradually narrowed and acute at the ends, and entire with slightly undulate margins, when they fold light yellow-green and lustrous on the upper surface, coated on the lower with pale

Fig. 240

caducous pubescence, at maturity glabrous, light green and rather lustrous above, dull and paler or rarely hoary-pubescent below, conspicuously reticulate-venulose, $2\frac{1}{2}'$–5′ long, $\frac{1}{4}'$–1′ wide, with a slender yellow midrib and obscure primary veins forked and united about halfway between the midrib and margins; turning pale yellow in the autumn; petioles stout, about $\frac{1}{8}'$ in length.   **Flowers:** staminate in slender-stemmed aments 2′–3′ long; calyx yellow, hirsute, with 4 or 5 acute segments; pistillate on slender glabrous peduncles, their involucral scales brown covered by pale hairs, about as long as the acute calyx-lobes; stigmas bright red.   **Fruit** short-stalked or nearly sessile, solitary or in pairs; nut hemispheric, light, yellow-brown, coated with pale pubescence, inclosed only at the very base in the thin pale reddish brown saucer-shaped cup silky-pubescent on the inner surface, and covered by thin ovate hoary-pubescent closely appressed scales rounded at apex.

A tree, often 70°–90° high, with a trunk 2° or rarely 4° in diameter, small branches spreading into a comparatively narrow open or conical round-topped head, and slender glabrous reddish brown branchlets roughened by dark lenticels, becoming in their second year dark brown tinged with red or grayish brown; usually much smaller.   **Winter-buds** ovoid, acute, about $\frac{1}{8}'$ long, with dark chestnut-brown scales pale and scarious on the margins.   **Bark** $\frac{1}{2}'$–$\frac{3}{4}'$ thick, light red-brown slightly tinged with red, generally smooth but on old trees broken by shallow narrow fissures into irregular plates covered by small closely appressed scales.   **Wood** heavy, strong, not hard, rather coarse-grained, light brown tinged with red, with thin lighter colored sapwood; occasionally used in construction, for clapboards and the fellies of wheels.

Distribution.   Low wet borders of swamps and streams and rich sandy uplands; Staten Island, New York, southern New Jersey and southeastern Pennsylvania and southward to western (Jackson County) Florida, through the Gulf states to the valley of the Navasota River, Brazos County, Texas, and through Arkansas, eastern Oklahoma and southeastern Missouri to central Tennessee and northwestern Kentucky (Ballard County), and in southwestern Illinois (Massac and Pope Counties); in the Atlantic states usually confined to the maritime plain; less common in the middle districts, rarely extending to the Appalachian foothills.

Occasionally planted as a shade-tree in the streets of southern towns, and rarely in western Europe; hardy in eastern Massachusetts.

Quercus heterophylla Michx. f.

This has usually been considered a hybrid between *Quercus Phellos* and *Quercus velutina* or *Quercus borealis* var. *maxima*; first known in the eighteenth century from an individ-

Fig. 241

ual growing in a field belonging to John Bartram on the Schuylkill River, Philadelphia. What appears to be the same form has since been discovered in a number of stations from New Jersey to Texas, and it is possible that *Quercus heterophylla* may, as many botanists have believed, best be considered a species.

× *Quercus subfalcata* Trel., believed to be a hybrid of *Quercus Phellos* and *Q. rubra* has been found at Wickliffe, Ballard County, Illinois, at Campbell, Lawrence County, Mississippi, Fulton, Hempstead County, Arkansas, and Houston, Harris County, Texas; its var. *microcarpa* Sarg., probably of the same parentage, originated in a Dutch nursery.

× *Quercus ludoviciana* Sarg., believed to be a hybrid of *Quercus Phellos* and *Q. rubra* var. *pagodæfolia* grows in low wet woods ten miles west of Opelousas, St. Landry Parish, Louisiana.

18. Quercus laurifolia Michx. Laurel Oak. Water Oak.

Leaves elliptic or rarely slightly broadest above the middle, acuminate at the ends, apiculate at apex, occasionally lanceolate or oblong-obovate and rounded at apex (var. *hybrida* Michx.) sometimes 3-lobed at apex, the terminal lobe acuminate, much larger than the others (var. *tridentata* Sarg.), frequently unequally lobed on vigorous branches of

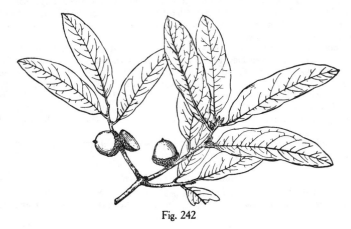

Fig. 242

young trees, with small nearly triangular lobes, when they unfold in spring yellow-green, or later in the season often pink or bright red, and slightly puberulous, at maturity thin, green, and very lustrous above, light green and less lustrous below, usually 3′–4′ long and ¾′ wide, with a conspicuous yellow midrib; many falling gradually in early spring leaving the branches partly bare during only a few weeks; petioles stout, yellow, rarely more than ¼′ in length. **Flowers:** staminate in red-stemmed hairy aments 2′–3′ long; calyx pubescent on the outer surface, divided into 4 ovate rounded lobes; pistillate on stout glabrous peduncles, their involucral scales brown and hairy, about as long as the acute calyx-lobes; stigmas dark red. **Fruit** sessile or subsessile, generally solitary; nut ovoid to hemispheric, broad and slightly rounded at base, full and rounded at the puberulous apex, dark brown, about ½′ long, inclosed for about one fourth its length in a thin saucer-shaped cup red-brown and silky-pubescent on the inner surface, and covered by thin ovate light red-brown scales rounded at apex and pale-pubescent except on their darker colored margins.

A tree, occasionally 100° high, with a tall trunk 3°–4° in diameter, and comparatively slender branches spreading gradually into a broad dense round-topped shapely head, and slender glabrous branchlets dark red when they first appear, dark red-brown during their first winter, becoming reddish brown or dark gray in their second season. **Winter-buds** broadly ovoid or oval, abruptly narrowed and acute at apex, $\frac{1}{16}'-\frac{1}{8}'$ long, with numerous thin closely imbricated bright red-brown scales ciliate on the margins. **Bark** of young trees $\frac{1}{2}'-1'$ thick, dark brown more or less tinged with red, roughened by small closely appressed scales, becoming at the base of old trees $1'-2'$ thick, nearly black, and divided by deep fissures into broad flat ridges. **Wood** heavy, very strong and hard, coarse-grained, liable to check badly in drying, dark brown tinged with red, with thick lighter colored sapwood; probably used only as fuel.

Distribution. Sandy banks of streams and swamps and rich hummocks in the neighborhood of the coast; North Carolina (near Newbern) southward to the valley of the Caloosahatchee River, Florida, and in the interior of the peninsula to the neighborhood of Lake Istokpoga, De Soto County, and westward to eastern Louisiana, ranging inland to Darlington, Darlington County, South Carolina, to the neighborhood of Augusta, Richmond County, Mayfield, Hancock County, Albany, Dougherty County, Cuthbert, Randolph County, and Bainbridge, Decatur County, Georgia, Georgiana, Butler County, and Berlin, Dallas County, Alabama, Rockport, Copiah County, Mississippi, and to the neighborhood of Bogalusa, Washington Parish, and Kisatchie, Natchitoches Parish, Louisiana (*R. S. Cocks*); nowhere abundant, but most common and of its largest size in eastern Florida.

19. Quercus cinerea Michx. Blue Jack. Upland Willow Oak.

Quercus brevifolia Sarg.

Leaves oblong-lanceolate to oblong-obovate, gradually narrowed and cuneate or sometimes rounded at base, acute or rounded and apiculate at apex, entire with slightly thickened undulate margins, or at the ends of vigorous sterile branches occasionally 3-lobed at

Fig. 243

the apex and variously lobed on the margins (β *dentato-lobata* A. De Candolle), when they unfold bright pink and pubescent on the upper surface, coated on the lower with thick silvery white tomentum, at maturity firm in texture, blue-green, lustrous, conspicuously reticulate venulose above, pale-tomentose below, $2'-5'$ long, $\frac{1}{2}'-1\frac{1}{2}'$ wide, with a stout yellow midrib and remote obscure primary veins forked and united within the margins; turning red and falling gradually late in the autumn or in early winter; petioles stout, $\frac{1}{4}'-\frac{1}{2}'$ in length. **Flowers:** staminate in hoary-tomentose aments $2'-3'$ long; calyx pubescent, bright red and furnished at apex with a thick tuft of silvery white hairs before opening, divided into 4 or 5 ovate acute lobes, becoming yellow as it opens; stamens 4 or 5; anthers apiculate, dark red in the bud, becoming yellow; pistillate on short stout tomentose peduncles, their involucral scales about as long as the acute calyx-lobes and coated with pale tomentum; stigmas dark red. **Fruit** produced in great profusion, sessile or raised on a short stalk rarely $\frac{1}{4}'$ long; nut ovoid, full and rounded at the ends or subglobose, about $\frac{1}{2}'$ long, often striate, hoary-pubescent at apex, inclosed only at the base or for one half its length in a thin saucer-shaped or cup-shaped cup bright red-brown and coated with lustrous pale pubescence on the inner surface, and covered by thin closely imbricated ovate-oblong scales hoary-tomentose except on the dark red-brown margins.

A tree on dry hills, usually 15°–20° high, with a trunk 5′–6′ in diameter, stout branches forming a narrow irregular head, and thick rigid branchlets coated at first with a dense fulvous or hoary tomentum of fascicled hairs, soon becoming glabrous or puberulous, dark brown sometimes tinged with red during their first winter and darker in their second year; or in low moist soil often 60°–75° high, with a trunk 18′–20′ in diameter, and a broad round-topped shapely head of drooping branches. **Winter-buds** ovoid, acute, with numerous rather loosely imbricated bright chestnut-brown scales ciliate on the margins, often $\frac{1}{4}'$ long on vigorous branches, frequently obtuse and occasionally much smaller. **Bark** $\frac{3}{4}'$–$1\frac{1}{2}'$ thick, and divided into thick nearly square plates 1′–2′ long, and covered by small dark brown or nearly black scales slightly tinged with red. **Wood** hard, strong, close-grained, light brown tinged with red, with thick darker colored sapwood; probably only used as fuel.

Distribution. Sandy barrens and dry upland ridges, and in the rich moist soil of the pine-covered flats of the Florida peninsula; North Carolina southward to Fort Myers, Lee County, Florida, and along the Gulf coast to the valley of the Brazos River, Texas; in the Atlantic and middle Gulf states mostly confined to a maritime belt 40°–60° wide, extending across the Florida peninsula as far south as the sand hills in the neighborhood of Lake Istokpoga, De Soto County, and west of the Mississippi River, ranging inland to the neighborhood of Dallas, Dallas County, Texas, and to southeastern Oklahoma (near Antlers, Pushmataha County).

× *Quercus dubia* Ashe, believed to be a hybrid of *Quercus cinerea* and *Q. laurifolia* occurs at Abbottsburg, Bladen County, North Carolina, on the coast of South Carolina, in southern Georgia and northern and central Florida, and at Mississippi City, Harrison County, Mississippi.

× *Quercus subintegra* Trel., a supposed hybrid of *Quercus cinerea* and *Q. rubra* occurs at Lumber City, Telfair County, Georgia, Lake City, Columbia County, Florida, and at Berlin, near Selma, Dallas County, Alabama.

× *Quercus sublaurifolia* Trel., a supposed hybrid of *Quercus cinerea* and *Q. laurifolia* occurs at Folkston, Charlton County, Georgia, and at Biloxi, Harrison County, Mississippi.

× *Quercus carolinensis* Trel., believed to be a hybrid of *Quercus cinerea* and *Q. marilandica* occurs at Newbern, Craven County, North Carolina, Lumber City, Telfair County and Climax, Decatur County, Georgia, and near Fletcher, Hardin County, Texas.

× *Quercus caduca* Trel., believed to be a hybrid of *Quercus cinerea* and *Q. nigra*, occurs at Folkston, Charlton County and Lumber City, Telfair County, Georgia, Jacksonville, Duval County, and Gainsville, Alachua County, Florida, Mississippi City, Harrison County, Mississippi, and at Milano, Milam County and Bryan, Brazos County, Texas.

× *Quercus oviedoensis* Sarg., believed to be a hybrid of *Quercus cinerea* and *Q. myrtifolia*, has been found near Oviedo, Orange County, Florida.

20. Quercus imbricaria Michx. Shingle Oak. Laurel Oak.

Leaves oblong-lanceolate to oblong-obovate, apiculate and acute or rounded at apex, gradually narrowed and cuneate or rounded at base, entire with slightly thickened, revolute often undulate margins, or sometimes more or less 3-lobed, or on sterile branches occasionally repand-lobulate, when they unfold bright red, soon becoming yellow-green, covered with scurfy rusty pubescence on the upper surface and hoary-tomentose on the lower, at maturity thin, glabrous, dark green, and very lustrous above, pale green or light brown and pubescent below, 4′–6′ long, $\frac{3}{4}'$–2′ wide, with a stout yellow midrib, numerous slender yellow veins arcuate and united at some distance from the margins, and reticulate veinlets; late in the autumn turning dark red on the upper surface; petioles stout, pubescent, rarely more than ½′ in length.   **Flowers**: staminate in hoary-tomentose aments, 2′–3′ long; calyx light yellow, pubescent, and divided into 4 acute segments; pistillate on slender tomentose peduncles, their involucral scales covered with pale pubescence and about as long as the acute calyx-lobes; stigmas greenish yellow.   **Fruit** solitary or in pairs, on stout peduncles often nearly ½′ in length; nut nearly as broad as long, full and rounded at the ends, dark chestnut-brown, often obscurely striate, ½′–⅔′ long, inclosed for one third to one half its length in a thin cup-shaped or turbinate cup bright red-brown and lustrous on the inner surface, and covered by thin ovate light red-brown scales rounded or acute at' the apex and pubescent except on their darker colored margins.

A tree, usually 50°–60° high, with a trunk rarely exceeding 3° in diameter, or rarely 100° high, with a long naked stem 3°–4° in diameter, slender tough horizontal or somewhat pendulous branches forming a narrow round-topped picturesque head, and slender branch-

Fig. 244

lets dark green, lustrous, and often suffused with red when they first appear, soon glabrous, light reddish brown or light brown during their first winter and dark brown in their second year.   **Winter-buds** ovoid, acute, about ⅛′ long, obscurely angled, and covered by closely imbricated light chestnut-brown lustrous scales erose and often ciliate on the margins.   **Bark** on young stems and branches thin, light brown, smooth, and lustrous, becoming on old trunks ¾′–1½′ thick, and slightly divided by irregular shallow fissures into broad ridges covered by close slightly appressed light brown scales somewhat tinged with red.   **Wood** heavy, hard, rather coarse-grained, light brown tinged with red, with thin lighter colored sapwood; occasionally used in construction, and for clapboards and shingles.

Distribution.   Rich hillsides and the fertile bottom-lands of streams; Lehigh County (Allenton to Dorney's Park), Bedford, Huntington, Franklin and Union Counties, Pennsylvania, westward through Ohio to southern Michigan, southern Wisconsin and southeastern and southern Iowa (Muscatine to Taylor County), and southward to the District of Columbia, along the Appalachian Mountains and their foothills, up to altitudes of 2200°, to the valley of the Little Tennessee River, North Carolina, and to northern Georgia (Wilkes County), and middle Tennessee; through Missouri to northeastern Kansas and southeastern Nebraska, and in northern and southern Arkansas (Fulton, Hempstead County); comparatively rare in the east; one of the most abundant Oaks of the lower Ohio basin; probably growing to its largest size in southern Indiana and Illinois.

Occasionally planted as an ornamental tree in the northern states, and hardy as far north as Massachusetts.

Quercus Leana, Nutt., scattered usually in solitary individuals from the District of Columbia and western North Carolina, Bowling Green, Kentucky, to southern Michigan, Illinois and Missouri, is believed to be a hybrid between this species and *Quercus velutina*.

× *Quercus tridentata* Engelm., described as a hybrid of *Quercus imbricaria* and *Q. marilandica* first found at Allenton, Saint Louis County, Missouri, occurs also near Olney, Richland County, Illinois.

× *Quercus exacta* Trel., believed to be a hybrid of *Quercus imbricaria* and *Q. palustris*, occurs near Olney, Richland County, Illinois, and at Crown Point, Lake County, Indiana.

21. Quercus hypoleuca Engelm.

Leaves lanceolate or oblong-lanceolate to elliptic, occasionally somewhat falcate, acute and often apiculate at apex, cuneate or rounded or cordate at the narrow base, entire or repandly serrate above the middle with occasionally small minute rigid spinose teeth,

Fig. 245

or on vigorous shoots serrate-lobed with oblique acute lobes, when they unfold light red, covered with close pale pubescence above and coated below with thick hoary tomentum, at maturity thick and firm, dark yellow-green and lustrous on the upper surface, covered on the lower with thick silvery white or fulvous tomentum, 2′–4′ long, ½′–1′ wide, with thickened revolute margins; turning yellow or brown and falling gradually during the spring after the appearance of the new leaves; petioles stout, flattened, pubescent or tomentose, ⅛′–¼′ in length. **Flowers:** staminate in slender aments 4′–5′ long; calyx slightly tinged with red, covered with pale hairs and divided into 4 or 5 broadly ovate rounded lobes; anthers acute, apiculate, bright red becoming yellow; pistillate mostly solitary, sessile or short-stalked, their involucral scales thin, scarious, and soft-pubescent; stigmas dark red. **Fruit** sessile or borne on a stout peduncle up to ½′ in length, usually solitary; nut ovoid, acute or rounded at the narrow hoary-pubescent apex, dark green and often striate when ripe, becoming light chestnut-brown in drying, ½′–⅔′ long, the shell lined with white tomentum, inclosed for about one third its length in a turbinate thick cup pubescent on the inner surface, and covered by thin broadly ovate light chestnut-brown scales rounded at apex and clothed, especially toward the base of the cup, with soft silvery pubescence.

A tree, usually 20°–30° or sometimes 60° high, with a tall trunk 10′–15′ in diameter, slender branches spreading into a narrow round-topped inversely conic head, and stout rigid branchlets coated at first with thick hoary tomentum disappearing during the first winter, becoming light red-brown often covered with a glaucous bloom and ultimately nearly black; frequently a shrub. **Winter-buds** ovoid, obtuse, about ⅛′ long, with thin light chestnut-brown scales. **Bark** ¾'-1' thick, nearly black, deeply divided into broad ridges broken on the surface into thick plate-like scales. **Wood** heavy, very strong, hard, close-grained, dark brown, with thick lighter colored sapwood.

Distribution. Scattered but nowhere abundant through Pine-forests on the slopes of cañons and on high ridges usually at altitudes between 6000°–7000° above the sea on the mountains of western Texas, and of southern New Mexico and Arizona; in northern Chihuahua and Sonora.

22. Quercus agrifolia Née. Live Oak. Encina.

Leaves oval, orbicular or oblong, rounded or acute and apiculate at apex, rounded or cordate at base, entire or sinuate-dentate with slender rigid spinose teeth, when they unfold tinged with red and coated with caducous hoary tomentum, at maturity subcoriaceous, convex, dark or pale green, dull and obscurely reticulate above, paler, rather lus-

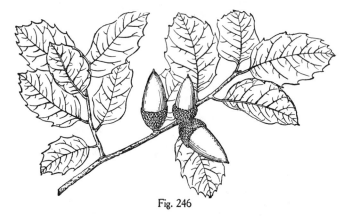

Fig. 246

trous, glabrous or pubescent below, with tufts of rusty hairs in the axils of the principal veins, or sometimes covered above with fascicled hairs and coated below with thick hoary pubescence, ¾'-4' long and ½'-3' wide, with thickened strongly revolute margins; falling gradually during the winter and early spring; petioles stout or slender, pubescent or glabrous, ½'-1' in length. **Flowers:** staminate in slender hairy aments 3'-4' long; calyx bright purple-red in the bud, sometimes furnished with a tuft of long pale hairs at the apex, glabrous or glabrate, divided nearly to the base into 5–7 ovate acute segments reddish above the middle; pistillate sessile or short-stalked, their involucral scales bright red and covered with thick hoary tomentum, or glabrous or puberulous; stigmas bright red. **Fruit** sessile or nearly so, solitary or in few-fruited clusters; nut elongated, ovate, abruptly narrowed at base, gradually narrowed to the acute puberulous apex, light chestnut-brown, ¾'-1½' long, ¼'-¾' thick, the shell lined with a thick coat of pale tomentum, inclosed for one third its length or only at the base in a thin turbinate light brown cup coated on the inner surface with soft pale silky pubescence, and covered by thin papery scales rounded at the narrow apex, and slightly puberulous, especially toward the base of the cup.

A tree, occasionally 80°–90° high, with a short trunk 3°–4° or rarely 6°–7° in diameter, dividing a few feet above the base into numerous great limbs often resting on the ground and forming a low round-topped head frequently 150° across, and slender dark gray or brown branchlets tinged with red, coated at first with hoary tomentum persistent until the second or third year; or with a trunk, rising to the height of 30° or 40°, and crowned by a narrow head of small branches; often much smaller; frequently shrubby in habit, with slender stems only a few feet high. **Winter-buds** globose and usually about $\frac{1}{16}'$ thick, or ovoid-oblong, acute, and sometimes on vigorous shoots nearly $\frac{1}{4}'$ in length, with thin broadly ovate closely imbricated light chestnut-brown glabrous or pubescent scales. **Bark** of young stems and branches thin, close, light brown or pale bluish gray, becoming on old trunks $2'-3'$ thick, dark brown slightly tinged with red, and divided into broad rounded ridges separating on the surface into small closely appressed scales. **Wood** heavy, hard, close-grained, very brittle, light brown or reddish brown, with thick darker colored sapwood; valued and largely used for fuel.

Distribution. Usually in open groves of great extent from Sonoma County, California, southward over the coast ranges and islands to the San Pedro Mártir Mountains, Lower California; less common at the north; very abundant and of its largest size in the valleys south of San Francisco Bay and their commonest and characteristic tree; frequently covering with semiprostrate and contorted stems the sand dunes on the coast in the central part cf the state; in southwestern California the largest and most generally distributed Oak-tree between the mountains and the sea, often covering low hills and ascending to altitudes of 4500° in the cañons of the San Jacinto Mountains.

Occasionally cultivated as an ornamental tree in temperate western, and in southern Europe.

23. Quercus Wislizenii A. DC. Live Oak.

Leaves narrowly lanceolate to broadly elliptic, generally oblong-lanceolate, acute or rounded and generally apiculate at apex, rounded or truncate or gradually narrowed and cuneate at base, entire, serrulate or serrate or sinuate-dentate with spreading rigid spines-

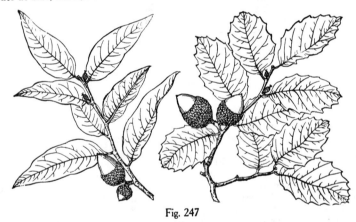

Fig. 247

cent teeth, when they unfold thin, dark red, ciliate, and covered with pale scattered fascicled hairs, at maturity thick and coriaceous, glabrous and lustrous, dark green on the upper and paler and yellow-green on the lower surface, usually $1'-1\frac{1}{2}'$ long and about $\frac{2}{3}'$ wide, with obscure primary veins and conspicuous reticulate veinlets, gradually deciduous during their second summer and autumn; petioles coated at first with hoary tomentum, usually pubescent or puberulous at maturity, $\frac{1}{8}'$ to nearly $1'$ in length. **Flowers:** staminate in hairy aments $3'-4'$ long; calyx tinged with red in the bud, divided into broadly ovate ciliate glabrous light yellow lobes shorter than the 3–6 stamens; pistillate sessile or short-stalked, their involucral scales and peduncle hoary-tomentose. **Fruit** sessile, short-stalked or occasionally spicate; nut slender, oblong, abruptly narrowed at base, pointed and pilose at the apex, $\frac{3}{4}'-1\frac{1}{2}'$ long, about $\frac{1}{3}'$ thick, light chestnut-brown, often striate, the shell lined with a scanty coat of pale tomentum, more or less inclosed in the thin turbinate sometimes tubular cup $\frac{1}{2}'$–1' deep, or rarely cup-shaped and shallow, light green and puberulous within, and covered by oblong lanceolate light brown closely imbricated thin scales, sometimes toward the base of the cup thickened and rounded on the back, usually pubescent or puberulous, especially above the middle, and frequently ciliate on the margins.

A tree, usually 70°–80° high, with a short trunk 4°–6° in diameter, stout spreading branches forming a round-topped head, and slender rigid branchlets coated at first with hoary tomentum or covered with scattered fascicled hairs, puberulous or glabrous and rather light brown during their first season, gradually growing darker in their second year; usually much smaller and sometimes reduced to an intricately branched shrub, with numerous stems only a few feet tall. **Winter-buds** ovoid or oval, acute, $\frac{1}{8}'$–$\frac{1}{4}'$ long, with closely imbricated light chestnut-brown ciliate scales. **Bark** on young trees and large branches thin, generally smooth and light-colored, becoming on old trunks 2'–3' thick, and divided into broad rounded often connected ridges separating on the surface into small thick closely appressed dark brown scales slightly tinged with red. **Wood** heavy, very hard, strong, close-grained, light brown tinged with red, with thick lighter colored sapwood; sometimes used for fuel.

Distribution. Lower slopes of Mt. Shasta southward through the coast region of California to the Santa Lucia Mountains, and to Santa Rosa and Santa Cruz Islands, and along the slopes of the Sierra Nevada to Kern County, up to altitudes of 2000° at the north and of 4500° at the south; as a shrub 4°–6° high with small thick leaves (var. *frutescens* Engelm.) on the desert slopes of the San Bernardino, San Jacinto and Cuyamaca mountains, at altitudes of 5000°–7000° above the sea, and on San Pedro Mártir in Lower California; nowhere common as a tree, but most abundant and of its largest size in the valleys of the coast region of central California at some distance from the sea, and on the foothills of the Sierra Nevada; very common as a shrub on the desert slopes of the mountains of southern California; near the coast and on the islands small and mostly shrubby.

× *Quercus morehus*, Kell., a supposed hybrid between *Quercus Wislizenii* and *Q. Kelloggii* occurs in Lake County, also in Placer, Marin, and other counties, California.

24. Quercus myrtifolia Willd.

Leaves oval to oblong-obovate, acute and apiculate or broad and rounded at apex, gradually narrowed and cuneate or broad and rounded or cordate at base, entire, with

Fig. 248

much thickened revolute sometimes undulate margins, or on vigorous shoots sinuate-dentate and lobed above the middle, when they unfold, thin, dark red, coated below and on the petioles with clammy rusty tomentum and densely pubescent above, at maturity thick and coriaceous, lustrous, dark green, glabrous and conspicuously reticulate-venulose above, paler, yellow-green, or light orange-brown, glabrous or pubescent below, with tufts of rusty hairs in the axils of the veins, $\frac{1}{2}'-2'$ long and $\frac{1}{4}'-1'$ wide; falling gradually during their second year; petioles stout, pubescent, yellow, rarely more than $\frac{1}{8}'$ in length. **Flowers:** staminate in hoary pubescent aments $1'-1\frac{1}{2}'$ long; calyx coated on the outer surface with rusty hairs and divided into 5 ovate acute segments shorter than the 2 or 3 stamens; pistillate sessile or nearly sessile, solitary or in pairs, their involucral scales tomentose and tinged with red. **Fruit** solitary or in pairs, sessile or short-stalked; nut subglobose or ovoid, acute, $\frac{1}{4}'-\frac{1}{2}'$ long, dark brown, lustrous and often striate, puberulous at apex, the shell lined with a thick coat of rusty tomentum, inclosed for one fourth to one third its length in a saucer-shaped or turbinate cup light brown and puberulous within, and covered by closely imbricated broad-ovate light brown pubescent scales ciliate on the margins and rounded at their broad apex.

A round-topped tree, rarely 40° high, with a trunk $4'-5'$ or rarely up to $15'$ in diameter, short or rarely long spreading branches and slender branchlets coated at first with a thick pale fulvous tomentum of articulate hairs usually persistent during the summer, light brown more or less tinged with red or dark gray, and pubescent or puberulous during their first winter, becoming darker and glabrous in their second season; more often an intricately branched shrub, with slender rigid stems 3°-4° or rarely 15°-20° high and $1'-3'$ in diameter. **Winter-buds** ovoid or oval, gradually narrowed to the acute apex, with closely imbricated dark chestnut-brown slightly puberulous scales. **Bark** thin and smooth, becoming near the ground dark and slightly furrowed.

Distribution. Dry sandy ridges on the coast and islands of South Carolina to Bay Biscayne, Florida, crossing the central peninsula and from the valley of the Caloosahatchee River, westward along the coast of Florida, Alabama, and Mississippi; most abundant on the islands off the coast of east Florida, and of Alabama and Mississippi; often covering large areas with low impenetrable thickets; perhaps of its largest size in Orange County, on Jupiter Island, and on the coast west of the Apalachicola River, Florida.

25. Quercus chrysolepis Liebm.   Live Oak.   Maul Oak.

Leaves oblong-ovate to elliptic, acute or cuspidate at apex, cordate, rounded or cuneate at base, mostly entire on old trees, often dentate or sinuate-dentate on young trees with

Fig. 249

1 or 2 or many spinescent teeth, the two forms often appearing together on vigorous shoots, clothed when they unfold with a thick tomentum of fulvous hairs soon deciduous from the

upper and more gradually from the lower surface, at maturity thick and coriaceous, bright yellow-green and glabrous above, more or less fulvous-tomentose below during their first year, ultimately becoming glabrate and bluish white, 1′–4′ long, ½′–2′ wide, with thickened revolute margins; deciduous during their third and fourth years; petioles slender, yellow, rarely ½′ in length. **Flowers:** staminate in slender tomentose aments 2′–4′ long; calyx light yellow, pubescent, divided usually into 5–7 broadly ovate acute ciliate lobes often tinged with red above the middle; pistillate sessile or subsessile or rarely in short few-flowered spikes, their broadly ovate involucral scales coated with fulvous tomentum; stigmas bright red. **Fruit** usually solitary, sessile or short-stalked; nut ellipsoidal or ovoid, acute or rounded at the full or narrow slightly puberulous apex, light chestnut-brown, ½′–2′ long and about as thick, the shell lined with a thin coat of loose tomentum, with abortive ovules scattered irregularly over the side of the seed, inclosed only at the base in a thin hemispheric or in a thick turbinate broad-rimmed cup pale green or dark reddish brown within, and covered by small triangular closely appressed scales with a short free tip, clothed with hoary pubescence, or often hidden in a dense coat of fulvous tomentum.

A tree, usually not more than 40°–50° high, with a short trunk 3°–5° in diameter, dividing into great horizontal limbs sometimes forming a head 150° across, and slender rigid or flexible branchlets coated at first with thick fulvous tomentum, becoming during their first winter dark brown somewhat tinged with red, tomentose, pubescent, or glabrous, and ultimately light brown or ashy gray; occasionally in sheltered cañons producing trunks 8°–9° in diameter; on exposed mountain sides forming dense thickets 15°–20° high. **Winter-buds** broadly ovoid or oval, acute, about ¼′ long, with closely imbricated light chestnut-brown usually puberulous scales. **Bark** ¾′–1½′ thick, light or dark gray-brown tinged with red, and covered by small closely appressed scales. **Wood** heavy, very strong, hard, tough, close-grained, light brown, with thick darker colored sapwood; used in the manufacture of agricultural implements and wagons.

Distribution. Southern Oregon, along the California coast ranges and the western slopes of the Sierra Nevada to the San Bernardino and San Jacinto mountains; of its largest size in the cañons of the coast ranges of central California and on the foothills of the Sierra Nevada; ascending to altitudes of 8000°–9000° above the sea; near the southern boundary of California, on the mountains of northern Lower California and Sonora and in Arizona (Santa Rita and Huachuca Mountains, on Beaver Creek and in Copper Cañon near Camp Verde, and in Sycamore Cañon south of Flagstaff), usually shrubby, with rigid branches, rigid coriaceous oblong or semiorbicular spinose-dentate leaves, subsessile or pedunculate fruit, with ovoid acute nuts 1′–1½′ long, their shells lined with thick or thin pale tomentum, and purple cotyledons (var. *Palmeri* Engelm. — *Quercus Wilcoxii* Rydb.)

26. Quercus tomentella Engelm.

Leaves oblong-lanceolate, acute, sometimes cuspidate or occasionally rounded at apex, broad and rounded or gradually narrowed and abruptly cuneate at base, remotely crenate-dentate with small remote spreading callous tipped teeth, or entire, when they unfold light green tinged with red, covered above with scattered pale fascicled hairs and below and on the petioles with thick hoary tomentum, at maturity thick and coriaceous, dark green, glabrous and lustrous on the upper surface, pale and covered with fascicled hairs on the lower surface, 2′–4′ long, 1′–2′ wide, with thickened strongly revolute margins, and a pubescent midrib; gradually deciduous during their third season; petioles stout, pubescent, about ½′ in length. **Flowers:** staminate in pubescent aments 2½′–14′ long, calyx light yellow, pubescent, divided into 5–7 ovate acute lobes; pistillate subsessile or in few-flowered spikes on short or elongated pubescent peduncles, their involucral scales like the calyx coated with fascicled hairs; stigmas red. **Fruit** subsessile or short-stalked; nut ovoid, broad at base, full and rounded at apex, about 1½′ long and ¾′ thick, inclosed only at the base in a cup-shaped shallow cup thickened below, light brown and pubescent on the inner surface, and covered by thin ovate acute scales, their free chestnut-brown tips more or less hidden in a thick coat of hoary tomentum.

A tree, 30°–40°, or occasionally 60° high, with a trunk 1°–2° in diameter, spreading branches forming a shapely round-topped head, and slender branchlets coated at first with hoary tomentum, becoming light brown tinged with red or orange color. **Winter-buds** ovoid, acute or obtuse, nearly $\frac{1}{4}'$ long, with many loosely imbricated light chestnut-brown

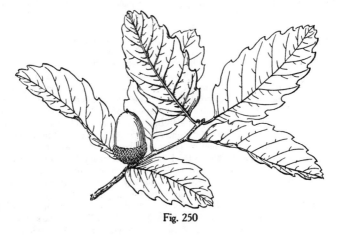

Fig. 250

scales more or less clothed with pale pubescence. **Bark** thin, reddish brown, broken into large closely appressed scales. **Wood** heavy, hard, close-grained, compact, pale yellow-brown, with lighter colored sapwood.

Distribution. Deep narrow cañons and high wind-swept slopes of Santa Rosa, Santa Cruz, and Santa Catalina islands, California; on Guadalupe Island off the coast of Lower California.

27. Quercus Emoryi Torr.   Black Oak.

Leaves oblong-lanceolate, acute and mucronate at apex, cordate or rounded at the slightly narrowed base, entire or remotely repand-serrate with 1–5 pairs of acute rigid oblique teeth, when they unfold thin, light green more or less tinged with red and covered with silvery white tomentum, at maturity thick, rigid, coriaceous, dark green, very lustrous and glabrous or coated above with minute fascicled hairs, pale and glabrous or puberulous below, usually with 2 large tufts of white hairs at the base of the slender midrib, obscurely reticulate-venulose, $1'-2\frac{1}{2}'$ long, $\frac{1}{2}'-1'$ wide; falling gradually in April with the appearance of the new leaves; petioles stout, pubescent, about $\frac{1}{4}'$ in length. **Flowers:** staminate in hoary tomentose aments; calyx light yellow, hairy on the outer surface, divided into 5–7 ovate acute lobes; pistillate sessile or short-stalked, their involucral scales covered with hoary tomentum. **Fruit** ripening irregularly from June to September, sessile or short-stalked; nut oblong, oval, or ovate, narrowed at base, rounded at the narrow pilose apex, $\frac{1}{2}'-\frac{3}{4}'$ long, about $\frac{1}{3}'$ thick, dull light green when fully grown, dark chestnut-brown or nearly black at maturity, with a thin shell lined with thick white tomentum, inclosed for from one third to one half its length in the deeply cup-shaped or nearly hemispheric cup light green and pubescent within, and covered by closely imbricated broadly ovate acute thin and scarious light brown scales clothed with short soft pale pubescence.

A tree, usually 30°–40° high, with a short trunk 2°–3° in diameter, stout rigid rather drooping branches forming a round-topped symmetrical head, and slender rigid branchlets covered at first with close hoary tomentum, bright red, pubescent or tomentose in their first winter, ultimately glabrous and dark red-brown or black; sometimes 60°–70° high, with a trunk 4°–5° in diameter, with a head occasionally 100° across; or at high altitudes or on exposed mountain slopes a low shrub. **Winter-buds** ellipsoidal, acute, about $\frac{1}{4}'$ long, pale pubescent toward the apex, with thin closely imbricated light chestnut-brown ciliate scales. **Bark** $1'-2'$ thick, dark brown or nearly black, deeply divided into large oblong thick plates separating into small thin closely appressed scales. **Wood** heavy, strong, brittle, close-grained, dark brown or almost black, with thick bright brown sapwood tinged with red. The sweet acorns are an important article of food for Mexicans and Indians, and are sold in the towns of southern Arizona and northern Mexico.

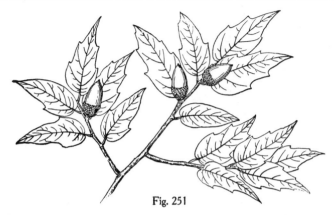

Fig. 251

Distribution. Mountain ranges of western Texas, southern New Mexico, Arizona south of the Colorado plateau, and of northern Mexico; in Texas common in the cañons and on the southern slopes of the Limpio and Chisos mountains; the most abundant Oak of southern New Mexico and Arizona, forming a large part of the forests covering the mountain slopes and extending from the upper limits of the mesa nearly to the highest ridges; attaining its largest size and beauty in the moist soil of sheltered cañons.

28. Quercus dumosa Nutt. Scrub Oak.

Leaves oblong, rounded and acute at apex, broad and abruptly cuneate or rounded at base, usually about $\frac{3}{4}'$ long and $\frac{1}{2}'$ wide, spinescent with a few minute teeth, or undulate and entire or coarsely spinescent, with an obscure midrib and primary veins, conspicuous reticulate veinlets, and stout petioles rarely $\frac{1}{8}'$ long; or sometimes oblong to oblong-obovate and divided by deep sinuses into 5–9 oblong acute rounded or emarginate bristle-tipped lobes, the terminal lobe 3-lobed, rounded or acute, $2'-4'$ long and $1'-1\frac{1}{2}'$ wide, with primary veins running to the points of the lobes, obscure reticulate veinlets, and petioles sometimes $1'$ long, thin when they unfold and clothed with scattered fascicled hairs, or rarely tomentose above and coated below and on the petioles with hoary tomentum, at maturity thick and firm, dark green and glabrous on the upper surface, paler and more or less pubescent on the lower surface; mostly deciduous during the winter. **Flowers:** staminate in pubescent aments; calyx divided into 4–7 ovate lanceolate hairy segments; pistillate sessile or stalked, in long many-flowered tomentose spikes, their involucral scales and calyx hoary-tomentose; stigmas red. **Fruit** sessile or short-stalked; nut ovoid, broad at base, broad and rounded or acute at apex, $\frac{1}{2}'-1'$ long, $\frac{1}{3}'-\frac{2}{3}'$ thick, inclosed for one half to two thirds its length in a deep cup-shaped or hemispheric cup light brown and pubescent within, covered by ovate pointed scales coated with pale or rufous tomentum, usually much thickened, united and tuberculate, those above with free acute tips forming a fringe to the rim of the cup, or frequently with basal scales but little thickened and furnished with long free tips; in var. *Alvordiana* Jeps., with a nut $1\frac{1}{2}'-1\frac{5}{8}'$ long, $\frac{1}{4}'-\frac{1}{2}'$ thick, gradually narrowed and acute at apex, inclosed only at base in a shallow cup-shaped cup.

A tree, rarely 20° high, with a trunk 12′–18′ in diameter, small branches forming a round-topped head, and slender branchlets coated at first with hoary tomentum, becoming in their first winter ashy gray or light or dark reddish brown and usually pubescent or tomentose; more often an intricately branched rigid shrub, with stout stems covered by

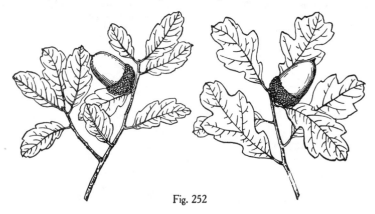

Fig. 252

pale gray bark and usually 6°–8° high, often forming dense thickets. **Winter-buds** ellipsoidal, generally acute, $\frac{1}{16}′–\frac{1}{8}′$ long, with thin pale red often pilose and ciliate scales. **Bark** of the trunk bright brown and scaly.

Distribution. California; western slopes of the central Sierra Nevada; common on the coast ranges south of San Francisco Bay and on the islands off the coast of the southern part of the state, ranging inland to the borders of the Mohave Desert and to the cañons of the desert slopes of the San Bernardino and San Jacinto mountains, and southward into Lower California; arborescent only in sheltered cañons of the islands; the var. *Alvordiana,* in the San Emidio Cañon of the coast ranges of Kern County and on the San Carlos Range, Fresno County; north of San Francisco Bay replaced by the variety *bullata* Engelm. ranging to Mendocino County and to Napa valley.

× *Quercus MacDonaldii* Greene, a shrub or small tree with characters intermediate between those of *Quercus dumosa* and *Q. Engelmannii*, is usually considered a hybrid of these species. It occurs on Santa Cruz and Santa Catalina Islands, and in Santa Barbara, and Los Angeles Counties, California.

29. Quercus virginiana Mill. Live Oak.

Leaves oblong, elliptic or obovate, rounded or acute at apex, gradually narrowed and cuneate or rarely rounded or cordate at base, usually entire with slightly revolute margins, or rarely spinose-dentate above the middle, thin, dark green and lustrous on the upper surface, pale and pubescent on the lower surface, 2′–5′ long, $\frac{1}{2}′–2\frac{1}{2}′$ wide, and inconspicuously reticulate-venulose, with a narrow yellow midrib, and few slender obscure primary veins forked and united at some distance from the margins; gradually turning yellow or brown at the end of the winter and falling with the appearance of the new leaves in the spring; petioles stout, rarely more than $\frac{1}{4}′$ in length. **Flowers:** staminate in hairy aments 2′–3′ long; calyx light yellow, hairy, divided into 5–7 ovate rounded segments; anthers hirsute; pistillate in spikes on slender pubescent peduncles 1′–3′ long, their involucral scales and ovate calyx-lobes coated with hoary pubescence; stigmas bright red. **Fruit** usually in 3–5 fruited spikes or rarely in pairs or single on stout light brown puberulous peduncles 1′–5′ long; nut ellipsoidal or slightly obovoid, narrowed at base, rounded or acute at apex, dark chestnut-brown and lustrous, about 1′ long and $\frac{1}{3}′$ thick, inclosed for about one fourth its length in a turbinate light reddish brown cup puberulous within, its scales thin, ovate, acute, slightly keeled on the back, covered by dense lustrous hoary tomentum and ending in small closely appressed reddish tips; seed sweet, with light yellow connate cotyledons.

A tree, 40°–50° high, with a trunk 3°–4° in diameter above its swollen buttressed base, usually dividing a few feet from the ground into 3 or 4 horizontal wide-spreading limbs forming a low dense round-topped head sometimes 130° across, and slender rigid branchlets coated at first with hoary tomentum, becoming ashy gray or light brown and pubescent or puberulous during their first winter and darker and glabrous the following season; occasionally 60°–70° tall, with a trunk 6°–7° in diameter; often shrubby and occasionally not more than a foot high. **Winter-buds** globose or slightly obovoid, about $\frac{1}{6}'$ long, with thin light chestnut-brown scales white and scarious on the margins. **Bark** of the trunk and large branches $\frac{1}{2}'-1'$ thick, dark brown tinged with red, slightly furrowed, separating on

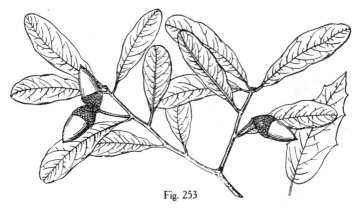

Fig. 253

the surface into small closely appressed scales. **Wood** very heavy, hard, strong, tough, close-grained, light brown or yellow, with thin nearly white sapwood; formerly largely and still occasionally used in shipbuilding.

Distribution. Shores of Mobjack Bay, Virginia, southward along the coast and islands to southern Florida, and along the shores of the Gulf of Mexico to northeastern Mexico, spreading inland through Texas to the valley of the Red River and to the mountains in the extreme western part of the state; on the mountains of Cuba, southern Mexico, and Central America; most abundant and of its largest size on the Atlantic and east Gulf coasts on rich hummocks and ridges a few feet above the level of the sea; abundant in Texas in the coast region, near the banks of streams, and westward toward the valley of the Rio Grande often forming the principal part of the shrubby growth on low moist soil; in sandy barren soil in the immediate vicinity of the seacoast or on the shores of salt water estuaries and bays often a shrub, sometimes bearing fruit on stems not more than a foot high (var. *maritima*, Sarg., and var. *dentata* Sarg.).

Occasionally planted as a shade and ornamental tree in the southern United States.

Variable in habit and in the size and thickness of the leaves the different forms of *Quercus virginiana* show little variation in their fruit. The most important of these varieties is

Quercus virginiana var. geminata Sarg.

Quercus geminata Small.

Leaves oblong-obovate to elliptic, rounded or acute at apex, cuneate or narrowed and rounded at base, occasionally slightly and irregularly dentate above the middle on vigorous shoots, conspicuously reticulate-venulose, hoary tomentose below, $1\frac{1}{2}'-3'$ long, $\frac{1}{3}'-1'$

wide, with thickened strongly revolute margins; persistent until after the leaves of the typical *Q. virginiana* in the same locality have all fallen; occasionally in Florida with oblong-elliptic to slightly obovate leaves 4½'-5' long and 1'-2' wide (f. *grandifolia* Sarg.). **Flowers** and **Fruit** as in the species.

A tree often 75° high with a trunk 3° in diameter, with the habit, branchlets, winter-buds and bark of the typical form; often much smaller and occasionally a shrub.

Distribution. Sandy soil; coast region of North Carolina south of the Cape Fear River, South Carolina and Georgia, and southward in Florida to Jupiter Island on the east coast and the valley of the Caloosahatchee River on the west coast; abundant and often the common Live Oak in the central part of the peninsula, at least as far south as Orange County, and westward through western Florida, southeastern and southern Alabama to the Gulf coast and islands of Mississippi.

Fig. 254

Other varieties of *Quercus virginiana* are var. *macrophylla* Sarg., differing from the type in its much larger ovate or slightly obovate leaves rounded or acute at base, entire or occasionally repand-dentate, pale tomentose below, 3½'-4' long and 1¼'-2½' wide. Large trees forming groves; sandy bottoms of the Atascosa River and in flat woods above them, Pleasanton, Atascosa County, Texas: var. *virescens* Sarg., differing from the type in the green glabrous or rarely puberulous lower surface of the leaves and in the glabrous branchlets. A large tree in sandy soil; Gainesville, Alachua County, Sanford, Seminole County, Sumner, Levey County, Simpson's Hummock, and near Long Key in the Everglades, Dade County, Florida: var. *eximea* Sarg., differing from the type in its narrow elliptic to narrow oblong-obovate leaves and pale bark; a tree rarely 20° high, with a trunk 8'-12' in diameter; rarely a shrub; dry sandy open woods, near Springfield, Livingston Parish and near Hammond, Tangipahoa Parish, eastern Louisiana. The following small shrubby small-leaved forms are recognized: var. *fusiformis* Sarg., with oblong-ovate leaves acute at apex, rounded or cuneate at base, entire or occasionally dentate, and pale pubescent below, and small fruit; dry limestone ridges and flat-topped hills of the Edwards Plateau (Kerr and Comal Counties), western Texas: var. *dentata* Chapm., distinct in the oblong-obovate repand-dentate lower leaves with large triangular teeth, acute at the broad apex, often 4' long and 1¼' wide at the base of the stems, and much larger than the oblong-lanceolate entire upper leaves; common in sterile pine-barrens near the coast of Florida: var. *maritima* Sarg., with oblong-obovate or rarely lanceolate leaves, acute and apiculate or rounded at apex, cuneate at base, and entire or slightly and irregularly toothed above the middle; fruit solitary or in pairs, or rarely in elongated spikes (*Quercus succu-*

lenta Small); sandy barrens near the coast, South Carolina to Miami, Dade County, Florida: var. *pygmaea* Sarg., with oblong-obovate leaves, cuneate at base, 3–5 lobed at apex with small acute lobes, or rarely elliptic and entire, and nearly sessile fruit, the nut inclosed nearly to the apex; a shrub rarely 3° high; Pine-woods in sandy soil; widely distributed in Florida.

30. Quercus reticulata H. B. K.

Leaves broadly obovate, obtuse and rounded or rarely acute at apex, usually cordate or occasionally rounded at the narrow base, repandly spinose-dentate above the middle or only toward the apex with slender teeth, and entire below, when they unfold coated with dense fulvous tomentum, at maturity thick, firm, and rigid, dark blue and covered with scattered fascicled hairs above, paler and coated with thick fulvous pubescence below, 1′–5′ long, ¾′–4′ broad, with a thick midrib, and primary veins running to the points of the

Fig. 255

teeth or arcuate and united within the slightly revolute margins, and very conspicuous reticulate veinlets; petioles stout about ¼′ in length. **Flowers:** staminate in short tomentose aments in the axils of leaves of the year; calyx light yellow, hirsute, with pale hairs, divided into 5–7 ovate acute segments; pistillate in spikes on elongated peduncles, clothed like their involucral scales with hoary tomentum; stigmas dark red. **Fruit** usually in many-fruited spikes or occasionally in pairs or rarely solitary, on slender hirsute or glabrous peduncles 2′–5′ long; nut oblong, rounded or acute at the pilose apex, broad at base, about ½′ long, inclosed for about one fourth its length in a shallow cup-shaped cup dark brown and pubescent within, hoary tomentose without and covered by small ovate acute scales, with thin free scarious tips, slightly thickened and rounded on the back at the bottom of the cup.

A tree, rarely more than 40° high, with a trunk 1° in diameter, and stout branchlets coated at first with thick fulvous tomentum, light orange color and more or less thickly clothed with pubescence during their first winter, becoming ashy gray or light brown; in the United States usually shrubby in habit and sometimes only a few feet tall; becoming on the Sierra Madre of Mexico a large tree. **Winter-buds** ovoid to oval, often surrounded by the persistent stipules of the upper leaves, about ⅛′ long, with thin loosely imbricated light red scales ciliate on the margins. **Bark** about ¼′ thick, dark or light brown, and covered by small thin closely appressed scales. **Wood** very heavy, hard, close-grained, dark brown, with thick lighter colored sapwood.

Distribution. Near the summits of the mountain ranges of southeastern New Mexico (Mogollon Mountains) and southeastern Arizona, and southward in Mexico.

31. Quercus Toumeyi Sarg.

Leaves ovate or ovate-oblong or oval, acute and apiculate at apex, rounded or cordate at base, entire with thickened slightly revolute margins, or remotely spinulose-dentate, often minutely 3-toothed at apex, thin but firm in texture, light blue-green, glabrous and lustrous above, pale and puberulous below, conspicuously reticulate-venulose; $\frac{1}{2}'-\frac{3}{4}'$ long, $\frac{1}{4}'-\frac{1}{2}'$ wide; falling early in spring with the appearance of the new leaves; petioles stout,

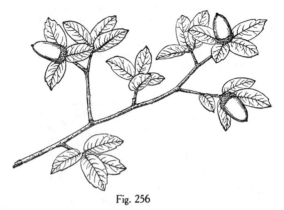

Fig. 256

tomentose, about $\frac{1}{16}'$ in length. **Flowers** unknown. **Fruit** sessile, solitary or in pairs, ripening in June; nut oval or ovoid, $\frac{1}{2}'-\frac{2}{3}'$ long, $\frac{1}{4}'$ thick, light brown and lustrous, furnished at the acute apex with a narrow ring of pale pubescence, inclosed for about one half its length in a thin shallow tomentose cup light green and pubescent within, and covered by thin ovate regularly and closely imbricated light red-brown scales ending in a short rounded tip and coated on the back with pale tomentum.

A tree, 25°–30° high, with a short trunk 6′–8′ in diameter, dividing not far from the ground into numerous stout wide-spreading branches forming a broad irregular head, and slender branchlets bright red-brown more or less thickly coated with pale tomentum at midsummer, covered during their second and third years with thin dark brown nearly black bark broken into small thin closely appressed scales. **Wood** light brown, with thick pale sapwood.

Distribution. Forming an open forest on the Mule Mountains, Cochise County, southeastern Arizona.

32. Quercus arizonica Sarg. White Oak.

Leaves oblong-lanceolate to broadly obovate, generally acute or sometimes rounded at apex, rounded or cordate at base, repandly spinose-dentate usually, except on vigorous shoots, only above the middle or toward the apex, or entire and sometimes undulate on the margins, when they unfold light red clothed with bright fulvous tomentum and furnished with dark dental glands, at maturity thick, firm and rigid, dull dark blue-green and glabrate above, duller and covered with thick fulvous or pale pubescence below, 1′–4′ long, $\frac{1}{2}'-2'$ wide, with a broad yellow midrib, slender primary veins, arcuate and united near the thickened revolute margins, and coarsely reticulate veinlets; falling in the early spring just before the appearance of the new leaves; petioles stout, tomentose, $\frac{1}{4}'-\frac{1}{2}'$ in length. **Flowers:** staminate in tomentose aments 2′–3′ long; calyx pale yellow, pubescent, and divided into 4–7 broad acute ciliate lobes; anthers red or yellow; pistillate on short stems tomentose like their involucral scales. **Fruit** sessile or on hoary-tomentose stems rarely $\frac{1}{2}'$ long, usually solitary, ripening irregularly from September to November; nut oblong, oval or slightly obovoid, obtuse and rounded at the puberulous apex, $\frac{3}{4}'$–$1'$ long, $\frac{1}{2}'$ thick, dark chestnut-brown, lustrous and often striate, soon becoming light brown, inclosed for half its length in a cup-shaped or hemispheric cup light brown and pubescent within, covered by regularly and closely imbricated scales coated with pale tomentum and ending in thin light red pointed tips, those below the middle of the cup much thickened and rounded on the back; **seed** dark purple, very astringent.

A tree, occasionally 50°–60° tall, with a trunk 3°–4° in diameter, and thick contorted branches spreading nearly at right angles and forming a handsome round-topped symmetrical head, and stout branchlets clothed at first with thick fulvous tomentum persistent during their first winter, reddish brown or light orange color and pubescent or puberulous in their second season, ultimately glabrous and darker; usually not more than 30°–40° tall; at high elevations reduced to a low shrub. **Winter-buds** subglobose, about $\frac{1}{16}'$ long, with loosely imbricated bright chestnut-brown puberulous scales ciliate on the margins. **Bark** of young stems and branches thin, pale, scaly with small appressed scales, becoming on old trunks about 1' thick and deeply divided by narrow fissures into broad ridges broken

Fig. 257

into long thick plate-like scales pale or ashy gray on the surface. **Wood** heavy, strong, hard, close-grained, dark brown or nearly black, with thick lighter colored sapwood; used only for fuel.

Distribution. The most common and generally distributed White Oak of southern New Mexico and Arizona, covering the slopes of cañons of mountain ranges at altitudes of from 5000°–10,000° above the sea, often ascending nearly to the summits of the high peaks; and in northern Mexico.

33. Quercus oblongifolia Torr. White Oak.

Leaves ovate, elliptic, or slightly obovate, rounded and occasionally emarginate or acute at apex, usually cordate or occasionally rounded at base, entire and sometimes undulate with thickened revolute margins, or remotely dentate with small callous teeth, on vigorous shoots and young plants oblong, rounded or cuneate at the narrow base, coarsely sinuate or undulate-toothed or 3-toothed at the broad apex and entire below, when they unfold bright red and coated with deciduous hoary tomentum, at maturity thin and firm, blue-green and lustrous above, paler below, 1'–2' long, $\frac{1}{2}'$–$\frac{3}{4}'$ wide, or on vigorous shoots sometimes 3'–4' long, with a prominent pale midrib, slender primary veins, and conspicuous reticulate veinlets; persistent during the winter without change of color, gradually turning yellow in the spring and falling at the appearance of the new leaves; petioles stout, nearly terete, about $\frac{1}{4}'$ in length. **Flowers:** staminate in short hoary-tomentose aments; calyx bright yellow, pilose, divided into 5 or 6 laciniately cut or entire acute segments tinged with red above the middle; pistillate usually sessile, or on peduncles tomentose like the involucral scales; stigmas bright red. **Fruit** usually solitary and sessile, rarely long-stalked; nut ovoid, ellipsoidal, or slightly obovoid, full and rounded at apex surrounded by a narrow ring of white pubescence, dark chestnut-brown, striate, and very lustrous, soon becoming light brown in drying, $\frac{1}{2}'-\frac{3}{4}'$ long, about $\frac{1}{3}'$ thick, inclosed for about one third its length in a cup-shaped or rarely turbinate thin cup yellow-green and pubescent on the inner surface and covered by ovate-oblong scales slightly thickened on the back, coated with hoary tomentum and ending in thin acute bright red tips ciliate on the margins and sometimes forming a minute fringe to the rim of the cup.

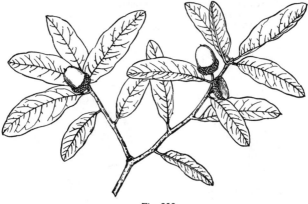

Fig. 258

A tree, rarely more than 30° high, with a short trunk 18'–20' in diameter, many stout spreading often contorted branches forming a handsome round-topped symmetrical head, and slender rigid branchlets coated at first with pale or fulvous tomentum, light red-brown, dark brown or dark orange color in their first winter, becoming ashy gray in their second or third year. **Winter-buds** subglobose, $\frac{1}{16}'-\frac{1}{8}'$ long, with thin light chestnut-brown scales. **Bark** $\frac{3}{4}'-1\frac{1}{4}'$ thick, ashy gray, and broken into small nearly square or oblong close plate-like scales. **Wood** very heavy, hard, strong, brittle, dark brown or nearly black, with thick brown sapwood; sometimes used as fuel.

Distribution. Chisos Mountains, western Texas, southeastern New Mexico, southern Arizona, and southward into northern Mexico; comparatively rare in Texas; abundant on the foothills of the mountain ranges of southern New Mexico and Arizona at altitudes of about 5000°, and dotting the upper slopes of the mesa where narrow cañons open to the plain.

34. Quercus Engelmannii Greene. Evergreen Oak.

Leaves oblong to obovate, usually obtuse and rounded or sometimes acute at apex, gradually or abruptly cuneate or rounded or cordate at base, entire, often undulate, or sinuate-toothed with occasionally rigid teeth, or at the ends of sterile branches frequently coarsely crenately serrate with incurved teeth, or rarely lobed with acute oblique rounded lobes, when they unfold bright red and coated with thick pale rufous tomentum, at maturity thick, dark blue-green and glabrous or covered with fascicled hairs above, pale, usually yellow-green and clothed with light brown pubescence, or puberulous or often glabrous below, 1'–3' long, $\frac{1}{2}'-2'$ wide; deciduous in the spring with the appearance of the new leaves; petioles slender, tomentose, becoming pubescent, $\frac{1}{4}'$–$\frac{1}{2}'$ in length. **Flowers:** staminate in slender hairy aments 2′–3′ long; calyx light yellow, pilose, with lanceolate acute segments; pistillate on slender peduncles, clothed like their involucral scales with dense pale tomentum. **Fruit** sessile or on slender pubescent peduncles sometimes $\frac{3}{4}'$ long; nut oblong, gradually narrowed and acute or broad rounded and obtuse at apex, broad or narrow at base, dark chestnut-brown more or less conspicuously marked by darker longitudinal stripes, turning light chestnut-brown in drying, $\frac{3}{4}'$–1′ long, about $\frac{1}{2}'$ thick, inclosed for about half its length in a deep saucer-shaped, cup-shaped or turbinate cup light brown and puberulous within, and covered by ovate light brown scales coated with pale tomentum, usually thickened, united and tuberculate at the base of the cup, and near its rim produced into small acute ciliate tips.

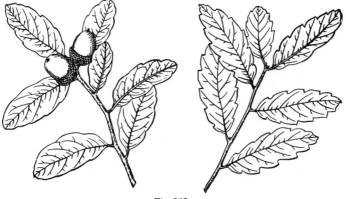

Fig. 259

A tree, 50°–60° high, with a trunk 2°–3° in diameter, thick branches spreading nearly at right angles and forming a broad rather irregular head, and stout rigid branchlets coated at first with hoary tomentum, light or dark brown tinged with red and pubescent during their first winter, becoming glabrous and light brown or gray in their second or third year. **Winter-buds** oval or ovoid, about $\frac{1}{8}'$ long, with thin light red pubescent scales. **Bark** $1\frac{1}{2}'$–2′ thick, light gray tinged with brown, deeply divided by narrow fissures and separating on the surface into small thin appressed scales. **Wood** very heavy, hard, strong, close-grained, brittle, dark brown or nearly black, with thick lighter brown sapwood; used only for fuel.

Distribution. Low hills of southwestern California west of the coast range, occupying with *Quercus agrifolia* Née, a belt about fifty miles wide, and extending to within fifteen or twenty miles of the coast, from the neighborhood of Sierra Madre and San Gabriel, Los Angeles County, to the mesa east of San Diego; in northern Lower California.

35. Quercus Douglasii Hook. & Arn. Blue Oak. Mountain White Oak.

Leaves oblong, acute or rounded at apex, gradually narrowed and cuneate or broad and rounded or subcordate at base, divided by deep or shallow, wide or narrow sinuses acute or rounded in the bottom into 4 or 5 broad or narrow acute or rounded often mucronate lobes, 2′–5′ long, 1′–1$\frac{3}{4}'$ wide, or oval, oblong or obovate, rounded or acute at apex, equally or unequally cuneate or rounded at base, regularly or irregularly sinuate-toothed with rounded acute rigid spinescent teeth, or denticulate toward the apex, 1′–2′ long, $\frac{1}{4}'$–1′ wide, when they unfold covered by soft pale pubescence, at maturity thin, firm and rather rigid, pale blue, with scattered fascicled hairs above, often yellow-green and covered by short pubescence below, with a hirsute or puberulous prominent midrib and more or less conspicuous reticulate veinlets; petioles stout, tomentose, $\frac{1}{4}'-\frac{1}{2}'$ in length. **Flowers:** staminate in hairy aments $1\frac{1}{2}'-2'$ long; calyx yellow-green, coated on the outer surface with pale hairs, deeply divided into broad acute laciniately cut segments; pistillate in short few-flowered spikes coated like the involucral scales with hoary tomentum. **Fruit** sessile or short-stalked, solitary or in pairs; nut ellipsoidal, sometimes ventricose, with a narrow base, gradually narrowed and acute at apex, $\frac{3}{4}'-1'$ long, $\frac{1}{2}'-1'$ thick, or often ovoid and acute, green and lustrous, turning dark chestnut-brown in drying, with a narrow ring of hoary pubescence at apex, inclosed only at base in a thin shallow cup-shaped cup light green and pubescent on the inner surface, covered on the outer by small acute and usually thin or sometimes, especially in the south, thicker tumid scales coated with pale pubescence or tomentum and ending in thin reddish brown tips.

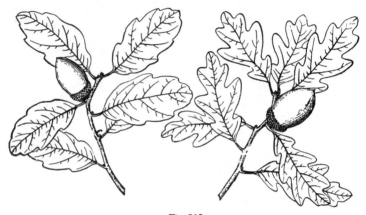

Fig. 260

A tree, usually $50°-60°$, rarely $80°-90°$ high, with a trunk $3°-4°$ in diameter, short stout branches spreading nearly at right angles and forming a dense round-topped symmetrical head, stout branchlets brittle at the joints, coated at first with short dense hoary tomentum, dark gray or reddish brown and tomentose, pubescent, or puberulous during their first winter, becoming ultimately ashy gray or dark brown; frequently not more than $20°-30°$ high, and sometimes, especially southward shrubby, in habit. **Winter-buds** ovoid, obtuse, $\frac{1}{8}'-\frac{1}{4}'$ long, with light rather bright red pubescent scales. **Bark** $\frac{1}{2}'-1'$ thick, generally pale, and covered by small scales sometimes tinged with brown or light red. **Wood** hard, heavy, strong, brittle, dark brown, becoming nearly black with exposure, with thick light brown sapwood; largely used as fuel.

Distribution. Scattered over low hills, dry mountain slopes and valleys; California, Mendocino County, and the upper valley of the Sacramento River, southward along the western slopes of the Sierra Nevada up to elevations of $4000°$, and through valleys of the coast ranges to the Tehachapi Pass, the borders of the Mohave Desert (Sierra de la Liebre) and the neighborhood of San Fernando, Los Angeles County; most abundant and of its largest size in the valleys between the coast mountains and the interior ridges of the coast ranges south of the Bay of San Francisco.

× *Quercus jolonensis* Sarg. with characters intermediate between those of *Quercus Douglasii* and *Quercus lobata* and believed to be a hybrid of those species occurs, with a number of large trees, at Jolon and between Jolon and King City, Monterey County, California.

36. Quercus Vaseyana Buckl. Shin Oak.

Quercus undulata var. *Vaseyana* Rydb.

Leaves oblong, rarely oblong-obovate, acute or rounded at apex, cuneate at base, undulately lobed with small acute lobes pointing forward, rarely nearly entire, when they unfold covered above with short fascicled hairs sometimes persistent until midsummer, and tomentose below, and at maturity thin, pale gray-green, glabrous and lustrous above, pale pubescent below, $1'-1\frac{1}{2}'$ long and $\frac{1}{2}'-\frac{3}{4}'$ wide; deciduous late in winter or in early spring; petioles covered with fascicled hairs when they first appear, becoming glabrous, $\frac{1}{4}'$ in length. **Flowers:** staminate in villose aments $1'-1\frac{1}{4}'$ long; calyx deeply divided into 4 or 5 ovate scarious lobes rounded at apex and shorter than the stamens; pistillate on short to-

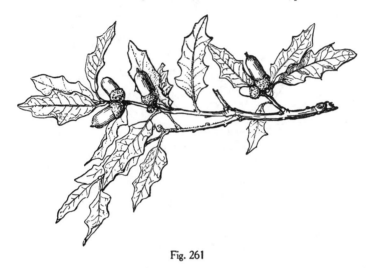

Fig. 261

mentose peduncles, their involucral scales ovate, acute, pubescent, shorter than the calyx-lobes; stigmas red. **Fruit** solitary or in pairs, sessile or short-stalked; nut ellipsoidal and only slightly narrowed at the rounded ends to oblong and slightly ovoid or obovoid, $\frac{1}{2}'-\frac{3}{4}'$ in length, $\frac{1}{4}'-\frac{1}{2}'$ in diameter, pale chestnut-brown and lustrous, the base only inclosed in the thin, saucer-shaped to cup-shaped cup, puberulous on the inner surface, covered with closely appressed ovate acute hoary tomentose scales, on some individuals abruptly contracted into short acute red-brown nearly glabrous tips.

A tree, rarely $15°-20°$ high, usually a shrub only $1°-3°$ tall, spreading into great thickets, with slender branchlets thickly covered with matted fascicled hairs during their first season, and light gray and glabrous or puberulous in their second year. **Winter-buds** ovoid or obovoid, about $\frac{1}{8}'$ long, with red-brown scales ciliate on the margins. **Bark** rough, deeply furrowed and scaly.

Distribution. Limestone slopes and ridges or in sheltered cañons; western Texas; Kimble, Real, Kendall, Kerr, Uvalda, Edwards, Menard and Valverde Counties.

37. Quercus Mohriana Rydb. Shin Oak.

Leaves oblong-obovate to elliptic or lanceolate, acute, acuminate or rounded at apex, rounded or cuneate and often unsymmetrical at base, entire, undulate, sinuately toothed with triangular apiculate teeth, or occasionally irregularly lobed above the middle with rounded lobes, thick, gray-green, lustrous and covered above with short fascicled hairs, and densely hoary tomentose below, $2°-4°$ long, $\frac{1}{2}'-1'$ wide, with a stout midrib thickly covered with fascicled hairs, sometimes becoming glabrous, slender primary veins and reticulate veinlets; petioles stout, hoary tomentose, $\frac{1}{8}'-\frac{1}{4}'$ in length. **Flowers:** staminate in short hoary tomentose aments; calyx densely villose, deeply divided into broad ovate lobes rounded at apex; anthers red; pistillate on hoary tomentose peduncles, with hairy bracts and calyx-lobes. **Fruit** solitary or in pairs, nearly sessile or raised on a pubescent peduncle $\frac{1}{2}'-\frac{3}{4}'$ in length; nut ellipsoidal or ovoid, broad and rounded at the ends, light chestnut-brown, lustrous, $\frac{1}{3}'-\frac{1}{2}'$ long, $\frac{1}{4}'-\frac{1}{3}'$ thick, inclosed for from half to two thirds its length in the hemispheric to cup-shaped cup, hoary tomentose on the inner surface, and

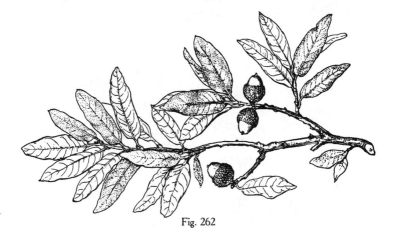

Fig. 262

covered with small closely appressed acute hoary tomentose scales much thickened below the middle of the cup, thin and much smaller toward its rim.

A tree, rarely $18°-20°$ high, with a trunk rarely $1°$ in diameter, small spreading and ascending branches forming a round-topped head, and slender branchlets thickly coated during their first season with fascicled hairs, dark gray-brown and pubescent in their second season and ultimately gray and glabrous; usually a low shrub spreading into thickets. **Winter-buds** broad-ovoid, obtuse, pale pubescent. **Bark** thin, pale, rough, deeply furrowed.

Distribution. On dry limestone hills, usually not more than $18°$ high with spreading branches; on deep sand, often not more than $3°$ high with more erect stems, often covering thousands of acres; only a tree in the protection of ledges in deep ravines and on steep hillsides; northwestern Texas (Tom Green, Coke, Nolan, Howard, Armstrong, and Wheeler Counties); central Texas (Bryan, Brazos County); southwestern Oklahoma (Beckham County).

38. Quercus Laceyi Small.

Leaves oblong to oblong-obovate, usually with two pairs of small rounded lateral lobes, occasionally 3-lobed toward the apex, rarely nearly entire, narrowed and rounded at apex, rounded, cuneate or rarely cordate at the gradually narrowed base, coated below when they unfold with loose white tomentum, soon glabrous, at maturity thin, blue-green above, yellow-green below, $2'-3'$ long, $\frac{3}{4}'-2'$ wide, with a slender midrib and primary veins, and conspicuous reticulate veinlets; deciduous late in the autumn; on vigorous shoots sometimes $6'-7'$ long and $3'-4'$ wide; petioles glabrous or sparingly villose, $\frac{1}{4}'-\frac{1}{3}'$ in length. **Flowers:** staminate in slightly villose aments $2'-2\frac{1}{2}'$ long; calyx deeply divided into 4 or 5 ovate acuminate lobes shorter than the stamens; pistillate flowers not seen. **Fruit** solitary or in pairs, sessile or raised on a stem up to $\frac{1}{2}'$ in length; nut ellipsoidal or oblong-ovoid, rounded at apex, slightly narrowed and nearly truncate at base, light chestnut-brown and lustrous, $\frac{3}{4}'-1'$ long, $\frac{1}{3}'-\frac{1}{2}'$ in diameter, the base inclosed in the thick, cup-shaped to rarely saucer-shaped cup, tomentose on the inner surface, covered with acute much thickened pale tomentose scales.

A tree, $30°-45°$ high, with a trunk $20'-30'$ in diameter, heavy erect and spreading branches and slender branchlets villose when they first appear, soon becoming glabrous and red-brown or gray during their second season; often a tall shrub with numerous stems. **Winter-buds** ovoid, acute, $\frac{1}{6}'$ long, with chestnut-brown scales ciliate on the margins. **Bark** gray, thick, deeply ridged or checkered.

Fig. 263

Distribution. Rocky banks of streams, the steep sides of cañons and on limestone bluffs; common in the southern and southwestern parts of the Edwards Plateau, western Texas (Kendall, Kerr, Bandera, Uvalde, Menard, Kemble, Real and Edwards Counties); easily distinguished in the field by the peculiar smoky or waxy appearance of the foliage.

39. Quercus annulata Buckl.

Quercus breviloba Sarg.

Leaves oblong to oblong-obovate or elliptic, rounded or acute at apex, cuneate or rounded at base, entire, undulate, slightly lobed with rounded or acute lobes, or 3-lobed, when they unfold covered above with fascicled hairs and tomentose below, and at maturity green, glabrous and lustrous above, green and pubescent below on lower branches, often pale or hoary tomentose on upper branches, $1\frac{1}{4}'-2\frac{1}{2}'$ long, $\frac{1}{2}'-1\frac{1}{4}'$ wide; petioles covered when they first appear with fascicled hairs, soon glabrous, $\frac{1}{4}'-\frac{1}{2}'$ in length; on vigorous branchlets sometimes thinner, glabrous, divided into broad rounded lateral lobes, gradually narrowed and cuneate at the long base, $4'$ long and $2\frac{1}{2}'$ wide. **Flowers:** staminate in pubescent aments $1'-2'$ long; calyx deeply divided in villose rounded lobes, shorter than the stamens; anthers red; pistillate on tomentose peduncles, their scales rounded, tomentose; stigmas red. **Fruit** solitary or in 2 or 3-fruited clusters, sessile or short-stalked, oblong-ovoid to ellipsoidal, slightly narrowed and rounded at apex, light yellow-brown and lustrous, $\frac{3}{4}'-1'$ long, $\frac{1}{3}'-\frac{1}{2}'$ in diameter; inclosed for about a quarter of its length in the cup-shaped cup, tomentose on the inner surface, covered with acute tomentose scales somewhat thickened and closely appressed below the middle of the cup, their tips chestnut-brown, free and often glabrous.

A tree, $20°-30°$ tall with a trunk rarely more than $1°$ in diameter, small spreading often slightly pendulous branches forming a round-topped head, and slender branches covered when they first appear with fascicled hairs, soon becoming glabrous and gray or grayish brown; the large stems often surrounded by a ring of smaller stems produced from its roots; more often a shrub than a tree spreading into broad thickets. **Winter-buds** ovoid

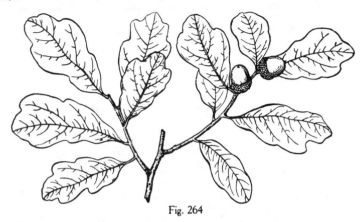

Fig. 264

to ellipsoidal, acute, $\frac{1}{8}'$–$\frac{1}{4}'$ long, with closely imbricated chestnut-brown puberulous scales ciliate on the margins. **Bark** thick, rough, deeply ridged.

Distribution. Dry limestone hills and bluffs; central and western Texas, from the neighborhood of Dallas, Dallas County, and Palo Pinto County to Kendall, Kerr, Brown, Bandera, Real and Menard Counties.

40. Quercus **Durandii** Buckl.

Quercus breviloba Sarg., in part.

Leaves thin, obovate to elliptic, entire, 3-lobed toward the rounded or acute apex or irregularly laterally lobed, the three forms appearing on different branches of the same tree, on lower branches usually lobed, dark green and lustrous above, often green and glabrous below, sometimes 6' or 7' long and 3' or $3\frac{1}{2}'$ wide, on upper branches mostly entire, white and pubescent or tomentose below, $2\frac{1}{2}'$–3' long, $\frac{1}{2}'$–$1\frac{1}{2}'$ wide; falling late in the autumn; petioles glabrous, $\frac{1}{3}'$–$\frac{1}{4}'$ in length. **Flowers:** staminate in slender villose aments 3'–4' in length; calyx deeply divided into acute villose lobes shorter than the stamens; pistillate on a short tomentose peduncle, the linear acuminate bract and involucral scales hoary-tomentose; stigmas red. **Fruit** solitary or in pairs, short-stalked or nearly sessile; nut ovoid, or slightly obovoid, rounded or rarely acute at apex, nearly truncate at base, pale chestnut-brown, lustrous, $\frac{1}{2}'$–$\frac{2}{3}'$ long, $\frac{1}{3}'$–$\frac{1}{2}'$ thick, barely inclosed at base in the thin, shallow saucer-shaped cup, pale tomentose on the inner surface, and covered with small acuminate closely appressed tomentose scales slightly thickened on the back.

A tree, often 60°–90° high with a tall trunk 2°–3° in diameter, comparatively small branches, the lower horizontal, the upper ascending, forming a dense round-topped handsome head, and slender pale gray-brown branchlets covered when they first appear with fascicled hairs, soon glabrous, or puberulous during their first season, and darker in their second season. **Winter-buds** ovoid, acute, $\frac{1}{4}'$–$\frac{1}{3}'$ long with dark chestnut-brown rounded scales ciliate on the margins. **Bark** thin, light gray or nearly white and broken into thin loosely appressed scales.

Distribution. East of the Mississippi River scattered on rich limestone prairies; westward on the well drained soil of river bottoms, and often on low hummocks; near Augusta,

Richmond County, Georgia; West Point, Clay County, Columbus, Lowndes County, Brookville, Noxubee County, and near Natchez, Adams County, Mississippi; McNab, Hempstead County, Arkansas; Natchitoches, Natchitoches Parish, western Louisiana;

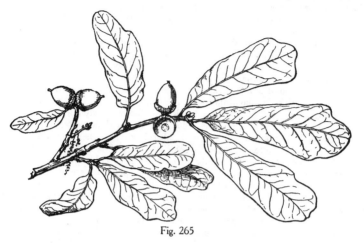

Fig. 265

coast region of eastern Texas to the bottoms of the Guadalupe River (Victoria County), ranging inland to San Saba County and to the neighborhood of Dallas, Dallas County; on the mountains near Monterey, Nuevo Leon; rare and local.

41. Quercus Chapmanii Sarg.

Leaves oblong to oblong-obovate, rounded at the narrow apex, narrowed and cuneate or rounded or broad and rounded at base, entire with slightly undulate margins, or ob-

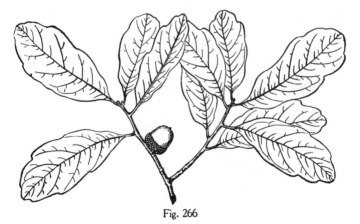

Fig. 266

scurely sinuate-lobed above the middle, when they unfold coated below with thick bright yellow pubescence and covered above with pale fascicled deciduous hairs, at maturity thick and firm or subcoriaceous, dark green, glabrous and lustrous above, light green or silvery white and glabrous below except on the slender often pubescent midrib, usually 2′–3′ long and 1′ wide, but varying from 1′–3′ in length and ¾′–1′ in width; falling gradually during the winter or sometimes persistent until the appearance of the new leaves in the spring; petioles tomentose, rarely ⅛′ in length. **Flowers:** staminate in short hirsute aments; calyx hirsute, divided into 5 acute laciniately cut segments; anthers hirsute; pistillate sessile or short-stalked, their involucral scales coated with dense pale tomentum. **Fruit** usually sessile, solitary or in pairs; nut oval, about ⅝′ long and ⅜′ thick, pubescent from the obtuse rounded apex nearly to the middle, inclosed for nearly half its length in the deep cup-shaped light brown cup slightly pubescent on the inner surface, and covered by ovate-oblong pointed scales thickened on the back, especially toward the base of the cup, and coated with pale tomentum except on their thin reddish brown margins.

Occasionally a tree, 50° high, with a trunk 1° in diameter, stout branches forming a round-topped head, and slender branchlets coated at first with dense bright yellow pubescence, becoming light or dark red-brown and puberulous during their first winter and ultimately ashy gray; more often a rigid shrub sometimes only 1°–2° tall. **Winter-buds** ovoid, acute, obtuse, about ⅛′ long, with glabrous or puberulous light chestnut-brown scales. **Bark** dark or pale, separating freely into large irregular plate-like scales.

Distribution. Sandy barrens usually in the neighborhood of the coast; Bluffton, Beaufort County, South Carolina, Colonels Islands, Liberty County, Georgia, southward along the east coast of Florida to the shores of Indian River; on the west coast from the valley of the Caloosahatchee River to the shores of Pensacola Bay, and in the interior of the peninsula from Lake County to Highlands County (neighborhood of Sebring); rare and local on the Atlantic coast; comparatively rare in the interior of the Florida peninsula; abundant in western Florida from the shores of Tampa Bay to those of Saint Andrews Bay.

42. Quercus macrocarpa Michx. Burr Oak. Mossy Cup Oak.

Leaves obovate or oblong, cuneate or occasionally narrow and rounded at base, divided by wide sinuses sometimes penetrating nearly to the midrib into 5–7 lobes, the terminal lobe large, oval or obovate, regularly crenately lobed, or smaller and 3-lobed at

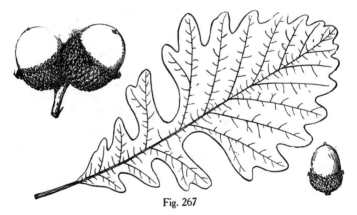

Fig. 267

the rounded or acute apex, when they unfold yellow-green and pilose above and silvery white and coated below with long pale hairs, at maturity thick and firm, dark green, lustrous and glabrous, or occasionally pilose on the upper surface, pale green or silvery white and covered on the lower surface with soft pale or rarely rufous pubescence, 6′–12′ long,

3′–6′ wide, with a stout pale midrib sometimes pilose on the upper side and pubescent on the lower, large primary veins running to the points of the lobes, and conspicuous reticulate veinlets; turning dull yellow or yellowish brown in the autumn; petioles stout, $\frac{1}{3}′$–1′ in length. **Flowers:** staminate in slender aments 4′–6′ long, their yellow-green peduncles coated with loosely matted pale hairs; calyx yellow-green, pubescent, deeply divided into 4–6 acute segments ending in tufts of long pale hairs; pistillate sessile or stalked, their involucral scales broadly ovate, often somewhat tinged with red toward the margins and coated, like the peduncles, with thick pale tomentum; stigmas bright red. **Fruit** usually solitary, sessile or long-stalked, exceedingly variable in size and shape; nut ellipsoidal or broad-ovoid, broad at the base and rounded at the obtuse or depressed apex covered by soft pale pubescence, $\frac{3}{5}′$ long and $\frac{1}{4}′$ thick at the north, sometimes 2′ long and $1\frac{1}{2}′$ thick in the south, its cup thick or thin, light brown and pubescent on the inner surface, hoary-tomentose and covered on the outer surface by large irregularly imbricated ovate pointed scales, at the base of the cup thin and free or sometimes much thickened and tuberculate, and near its rim generally developed into long slender pale awns forming on northern trees a short inconspicuous and at the south a long conspicuous matted fringe-like border, inclosing only the base or nearly the entire nut.

A tree, sometimes 170° high, with a trunk 6°–7° in diameter, clear of limbs for 70°–80° above the ground, a broad head of great spreading branches, and stout branchlets coated at first with thick soft pale deciduous pubescence, light orange color, usually glabrous or occasionally puberulous during their first winter, becoming ashy gray or light brown and ultimately dark brown, sometimes developing corky wings often 1′–$1\frac{1}{2}′$ wide; usually not more than 80° high, with a trunk 3°–4° in diameter; toward the northwestern limits of its range sometimes a low shrub. **Winter-buds** broadly ovoid, acute or obtuse, $\frac{1}{8}′$–$\frac{1}{4}′$ long, with light red-brown scales coated with soft pale pubescence. **Bark** 1′–2′ thick, deeply furrowed and broken on the surface into irregular plate-like brown scales often slightly tinged with red. **Wood** heavy, strong, hard, tough, close-grained, very durable, dark or rich light brown, with thin much lighter colored sapwood; used in ship and boatbuilding, for construction of all sorts, cabinet-making, cooperage, the manufacture of carriages, agricultural implements, baskets, railway-ties, fencing, and fuel.

Distribution. Low rich bottom-lands and intervales, or rarely in the northwest on low dry hills; Nova Scotia and New Brunswick southward to the valley of the Penobscot River, Maine, the shore of Lake Champlain, Vermont, western Massachusetts, central, southern and western Pennsylvania, northern Delaware, northern West Virginia (Hardy and Grant Counties), and middle Tennessee, and westward through the valley of the Saint Lawrence River and along the northern shores of Lake Huron to southern Manitoba, through western New York and Ohio, northern Michigan, to Minnesota (except in the northeastern counties), eastern and northwestern Nebraska, the Black Hills of South Dakota, the Turtle Mountains of North Dakota, and northeastern Wyoming, and to central Kansas, the valley of the north Fork of the Canadian River (Canton, Blaine County, and Seiling, Dewey County), Oklahoma, Caldwell Parish, Louisiana (*R. S. Cocks*), and the valley of the San Saba River (Menard County and Callahan County), Texas; attaining its largest size in southern Indiana and Illinois; the common Oak of the "oak openings" of western Minnesota, and in all the basin of the Red River of the North, ranging farther to the northwest than the other Oaks of eastern America; common and generally distributed in eastern Nebraska, and of a large size in cañons or on river bottoms in the extreme northwestern part of the state; the most generally distributed Oak in southern Wisconsin, and in Kansas growing to a large size in all the eastern part of the state.

Occasionally planted as an ornamental tree in the eastern United States and in South Africa.

× *Quercus Andrewsii* Sarg., believed to be a hybrid of *Quercus macrocarpa* and *Q. undulata* Torr., in habit and characters intermediate between those of its supposed parents with which it grows, occurs at Seiling, Dewey County, western Oklahoma.

× *Quercus guadalupensis* Sarg., with characters intermediate between those of *Quercus macrocarpa* and *Q. stellata* and evidently a hybrid of these species, occurs at Fredericksburg Junction in the valley of the Guadalupe River, Kendall County, Texas.

× *Quercus Hillii* Trel., believed to be a hybrid of *Quercus macrocarpa* and *Q. Muehlenbergii,* has been found at Roby, Lake County, Indiana, and near Independence, Jackson County, Missouri.

43. Quercus lyrata Walt.   Overcup Oak.   Swamp White Oak.

Leaves oblong-obovate, gradually narrowed and cuneate at base, divided into spreading or ascending lobes by deep or shallow sinuses rounded, straight, or oblique on the bottom, the terminal lobe oblong-ovate, usually broad, acute or acuminate at the elon-

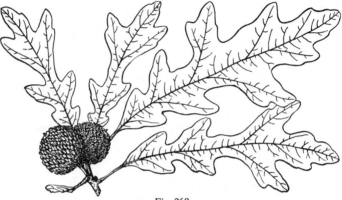

Fig. 268

gated apex, and furnished with 2 small entire nearly triangular lateral lobes, the upper lateral lobes broad, more or less emarginate, or acuminate and entire or slightly lobed and much longer than the acute or rounded lower lobes, when they unfold bronze-green and pilose above with caducous hairs, and coated below with thick pale tomentum, at maturity thin and firm, dark green and glabrous above, silvery white and thickly coated with pale pubescence, or green and often nearly glabrous below, 7′–10′ long, 1′–4′ wide; turning yellow or scarlet and orange in the autumn; petioles glabrous or pubescent, $\frac{1}{3}$′–1′ in length. **Flowers:** staminate in slender hairy aments 4′–6′ long; calyx light yellow, coated on the outer surface with pale hairs and divided into acute segments; pistillate sessile or stalked, their involucral scales covered, like the peduncles, with thick pale tomentum. **Fruit** sessile or borne on slender pubescent peduncles sometimes 1$\frac{1}{2}$′ in length; nut subglobose to ovoid or rarely to ovoid-oblong, $\frac{1}{2}$′–1′ long, usually broader at base than long, light chestnut-brown, more or less covered above the middle with short pale pubescence, entirely or for two thirds of its length inclosed in the ovoid, nearly spherical or deep cup-shaped thin cup, bright red-brown and pubescent on the inner surface, hoary-tomentose and covered on the outer by ovate united scales produced into acute tips, much thickened and contorted at its base, gradually growing thinner and forming a ragged edge to the thin often irregularly split rim of the cup.

A tree, rarely 100° high, with a trunk 2°–3° in diameter, generally divided 15°–20° above the ground into comparatively small often pendulous branches forming a handsome symmetrical round-topped head, and slender branchlets green more or less tinged with red and pilose or pubescent when they first appear, light or dark orange-color or grayish brown and usually glabrous during their first winter, ultimately becoming ashy gray or light brown. **Winter-buds** ovoid, obtuse, about $\frac{1}{8}$′ long, with light chestnut-brown scales covered, especially near their margins, with loose pale tomentum. **Bark** $\frac{3}{4}$′–1′ thick, light gray tinged with red and broken into thick plates separating on the surface into thin irregular appressed scales. **Wood** heavy, hard, strong, tough, very durable in contact with the ground, rich dark brown, with thick lighter colored sapwood; confounded commercially with the wood of *Quercus alba*, and used for the same purpose.

Distribution. River swamps and small deep depressions on rich bottom-lands, usually wet throughout the year; southern New Jersey (Riddleton, Salem County), and valley of the Patuxent River, Maryland, southward near the coast to western Florida, through the Gulf states to the valley of the Navasota River, Brazos County, Texas, and through Arkansas to the valley of the Meramec River (Allenton, St. Louis County), Missouri, and to central Tennessee and Kentucky, southern Illinois, and southwestern Indiana to Spencer County; comparatively rare in the Atlantic and east Gulf states; most common and of its largest size in the valley of the Red River, Louisiana, and the adjacent parts of Texas and Arkansas. Three individuals of this tree in the neighborhood of the town of Amana, Iowa County, Iowa, far north of its known range, are reported by Professor B. Shimek of the University of Iowa (see Bull. Torrey Bot. Club, xliv. 293, t. 16 and 17 [1922]).

Occasionally cultivated in the northeastern states and hardy in eastern Massachusetts.

× *Quercus Comptonae* Sarg., a hybrid of *Quercus lyrata* and *Q. virginiana*, with characters intermediate between those of its parents, discovered many years ago on the banks of Peyton's Creek, Matagorda County, Texas (now gone), occurs with several individuals near dwellings in Natchez, Adams County, Mississippi, near Selma, Dallas County, Alabama, and in Audubon Park and streets, New Orleans, Louisiana. A tree, sometimes 100° high and one of the handsomest of North American Oaks; also produced artificially by *Professor H. Ness* by crossing *Quercus lyrata* and *Q. virginiana*.

44. Quercus stellata Wang. Post Oak.

Quercus minor Sarg.

Leaves oblong-obovate, usually deeply 5-lobed, with broad sinuses oblique in the bottom, and short wide lobes, broad and truncate or obtusely pointed at apex, gradually narrowed and cuneate, or occasionally abruptly narrowed and cuneate or rounded at base, when

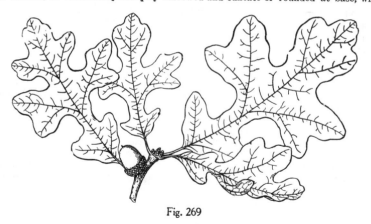

Fig. 269

they unfold dark red above and densely pubescent, at maturity thick and firm, deep dark green and roughened by scattered fascicled pale hairs above, covered below with gray, light yellow, or rarely silvery white pubescence, usually 4′–5′ long and 3′–4′ across the lateral lobes, with a broad light-colored midrib pubescent on the upper side and tomentose or pubescent on the lower, stout lateral veins arcuate and united near the margins and connected by conspicuous coarsely reticulated veinlets; turning dull yellow or brown in the autumn; petioles stout, pubescent, $\frac{1}{2}'$ to nearly 1' in length. **Flowers:** staminate in aments 3'–4' long; calyx hirsute, yellow, usually divided into 5 ovate acute laciniately cut segments; anthers covered by short scattered pale hairs; pistillate sessile or stalked, their involucral scales broadly ovate, hirsute; stigmas bright red. **Fruit** sessile or short-stalked; nut oval to ovoid or ovoid-oblong, broad at base, obtuse and naked or covered with pale persistent pubescence at apex, $\frac{1}{2}'$–1' long, $\frac{1}{4}'$–$\frac{3}{4}'$ thick, sometimes striate with dark longitudinal stripes, inclosed for one third to one half its length in the cup-shaped, turbinate, or rarely saucer-shaped cup pale and pubescent on the inner surface, hoary-tomentose on the outer surface, and covered by thin ovate scales rounded and acute at apex, reddish brown, and sometimes toward the rim of the cup ciliate on the margins with long pale hairs.

A tree, rarely 100° high, with a trunk 2°–3° in diameter, and stout spreading branches forming a broad dense round-topped head, and stout branchlets coated at first, like the young leaves and petioles, the stalks of the aments of staminate flowers and the peduncles of the pistillate flowers, with thick orange-brown tomentum, light orange color to reddish brown, and covered by short soft pubescence during their first winter, ultimately gray, dark brown, nearly black or bright brown tinged with orange color; usually not more than 50°–60° tall, with a trunk 1°–2° in diameter, and at the northeastern limits of its range generally reduced to a shrub. **Winter-buds** broadly ovoid, obtuse or rarely acute, $\frac{1}{8}'$–$\frac{1}{4}'$ long, with bright chestnut-brown pubescent scales coated toward the margins with scattered pale hairs. **Bark** $\frac{1}{2}'$–1' thick, red more or less deeply tinged with brown, and divided by deep fissures into broad ridges covered on the surface with narrow closely appressed or rarely loose scales. **Wood** very heavy, hard, close-grained, durable in contact with the soil, difficult to season, light or dark brown, with thick lighter colored sapwood; largely used for fuel, fencing, railway-ties, and sometimes in the manufacture of carriages, for cooperage, and in construction.

Distribution. Dry gravelly or sandy uplands; Cape Cod and islands of southern Massachusetts, Rhode Island, Long Island, New York, to western Florida and southern Alabama and Mississippi, and from New York westward to southern Iowa, Missouri, eastern Kansas, western (Dewey County) Oklahoma, Louisiana and Texas; most abundant and of its largest size in the Mississippi basin; ascending on the southern Appalachian Mountains to altitudes of 2500°; the common Oak of central Texas on limestone hills and sandy plains forming the Texas "Cross Timbers"; usually shrubby and rare and local in southern Massachusetts; more abundant southward from the coast of the south Atlantic and the eastern Gulf states to the lower slopes of the Appalachian Mountains; in western Louisiana rarely in the moist soil of low lands.

Showing little variation in the shape of the fruit and in the character of the cup scales *Quercus stellata* is one of the most variable of North American Oaks in habit, in the nature of the bark, and in the presence or absence of pubescence. Some of the best marked varieties are var. *araniosa* Sarg., a large tree differing from the type in the usually smooth upper surface of the leaves, in the floccose persistent tomentum on their lower surface, in the less stout usually glabrous yellow or reddish branchlets, and in its scaly bark; dry sandy soil, southern Alabama, western Louisiana, southern Arkansas, eastern Oklahoma and eastern Texas. Var. *paludosa* Sarg., a tree up to 75° in height, differing from the type in its oblong-obovate leaves 3-lobed above the middle, slightly pubescent branchlets becoming nearly glabrous, and in its scaly bark; in rich deep soil on the often inundated bottoms of Kenison Bayou, near Washington, St. Landry Parish, Louisiana. Var. *attenuata* Sarg., a large tree differing from the type in the oblong to oblong-obovate narrow leaves 3-lobed at apex and gradually narrowed to the long cuneate base; near Arkansas Post on the White River, Arkansas County, Arkansas. Var. *parviloba* Sarg., a round-topped tree 25°–30° high, differing from the type in the smaller lobes of the leaves with more prominent reticulate veinlets; dry sandstone hills near Brownwood, Brown County, Texas. Var. *anomala* Sarg., a tree 15°–18° high, differing from the type in its broadly obovate subcoriaceous leaves slightly 3-lobed and rounded at apex; dry sandstone hills near Brownwood, Brown County, Texas; possibly a hybrid. Var. *Palmeri* Sarg., a shrub 6°–15° high, forming clumps, differing from the type in its narrow oblong or slightly obovate 5–7-lobed leaves with narrow lobes, densely tomentose below, and in the thicker and more tomentose scales of the cup; sandy uplands, Elk City, Beckham County, Oklahoma. Var. *rufescens* Sarg., a shrub 12°–15° high, forming large clumps, differing from the type in the rusty brown pubescence on the lower surface of the polymorphous leaves, in the deeper cups of the fruit with thicker basal scales; sandy uplands, Big Spring, Howard County, Texas, and Elk City, Beckham County, Oklahoma. Var. *Boyntonii* Sarg, a shrub or small tree spreading into thickets, rarely more than 15° in height, differing from the type in its obovate leaves, mostly 3–5-lobed toward the apex, with small rounded lobes, and in their yellow-brown pubescence also found on the branchlets; in glades on the summit of Lookout Mountain, above Gadsden and Attala, Etowah County, Alabama.

The common and most widely distributed of the varieties of the Post Oak is

Quercus stellata var. Margaretta Sarg.

Quercus Margaretta Ashe

Leaves oblong-obovate, rounded at apex, cuneate or rounded at base, 3–5-lobed with usually narrow rounded, but often broad and truncate lobes, the two forms frequently occurring on the same branch, usually becoming glabrous on the upper surface early in the season, slightly pubescent, sometimes becoming nearly glabrous below, $2\frac{1}{2}$–5′ long and 2′–$2\frac{1}{2}$′ wide; petioles glabrous or pubescent. **Flowers** and **Fruit** as in the species.

A small tree, rarely 40° high, with slender glabrous reddish or reddish brown branchlets. **Winter-buds** ovoid, acute, $\frac{1}{4}$′ long with closely imbricated chestnut-brown scales glabrous, or ciliate on the margins. **Bark** thick, rough and furrowed, light gray.

Distribution. Usually on dry sandy slopes, hills and ridges, and southward on Pine-

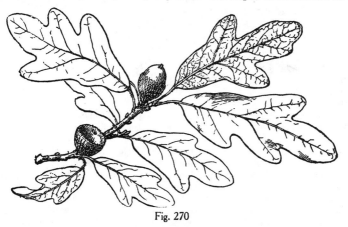

Fig. 270

barren lands; coast of Virginia (Capron, Southampton County) southward in the coast and middle districts to central (Lake and Orange Counties) and western Florida, through central and southern Alabama, and eastern and southern Mississippi: in Western Louisiana (Natchitoches and Caddo Parishes); southern Arkansas (McNab, Hempstead County), and southwestern Missouri (Prosperity, Jasper County). The common Post Oak of the south Atlantic and Gulf states; occasionally a shrub (f. *stolonifera* Sarg.) 4°–6° high, with smaller leaves, spreading into broad thickets by stoloniferous shoots; common near Selma, Dallas County, Alabama, and on the dry sand hills of central Oklahoma.

× *Quercus Harbisonii* Sarg., believed to be a hybrid of *Quercus stellata* var. *Margaretta* and *Q. virginiana* var. *geminata*, has been found in the neighborhood of Jacksonville, Duval County, Florida.

45. Quercus Garryana Hook.   White Oak.

Leaves obovate to oblong, pointed at apex, cuneate or rounded at base, coarsely pinnatifid-lobed, with slightly thickened revolute margins, coated at first with soft pale lustrous pubescence, at maturity thick and firm or subcoriaceous, dark green, lustrous and glabrous above, light green or orange-brown and pubescent or glabrate below, 4'–6' long, 2'–5' wide, with a stout yellow midrib, and conspicuous primary veins spreading at right angles, or gradually diverging from the midrib and running to the points of the lobes; sometimes turning bright scarlet in the autumn; petioles stout, pubescent, ½'–1' in length.   **Flowers:** staminate in hirsute aments; calyx glabrous, laciniately cut into ovate acute slightly ciliate or linear-lanceolate much elongated segments; pistillate sessile and coated with pale tomentum.   **Fruit** sessile or short-stalked; nut oval to slightly obovoid and obtuse, 1'–1¼' long and ½'–1' thick, inclosed at the base in a shallow cup-shaped or slightly turbinate cup puberulous and light brown on the inner surface, pubescent or tomentose

Fig. 271

on the outer, and covered by ovate acute scales with pointed and often elongated tips, thin, free, or sometimes thickened and more or less united toward the base of the cup, decreasing from below upward.

A tree, usually 60°–70° or sometimes nearly 100° high, with a trunk 2°–3° in diameter, stout ascending or spreading branches forming a broad compact head, and stout branchlets coated at first with thick pale rufous pubescence, pubescent or tomentose and light or dark orange color during their first winter, becoming glabrous and rather bright reddish brown in their second year and ultimately gray; frequently at high altitudes, or when exposed to the winds from the ocean, reduced to a low shrub.   **Winter-buds** ovoid, acute, ⅓'–½' long, densely clothed with light ferrugineous tomentum.   **Bark** ⅛'–1' thick, divided by shallow fissures into broad ridges separating on the surface into light brown or gray scales sometimes slightly tinged with orange color.   **Wood** strong, hard, close-grained, frequently exceedingly tough, light brown or yellow, with thin nearly white sapwood; in Oregon and Washington used in the manufacture of carriages and wagons, in cabinet-making, shipbuilding, and cooperage, and largely as fuel.

    Distribution.   Valleys and the dry gravelly slopes of low hills; Vancouver Island and the valley of the lower Fraser River southward through western Washington and Oregon and the California coast-valleys to Marin County; rare and local and the only Oak-tree in British Columbia; abundant and of its largest size in the valleys of western Washington and Oregon; on the islands in the northern part of Puget Sound reduced to a low shrub

(Vine Oak); ascending in its shrubby forms to considerable altitudes on the western slopes of the Cascade Mountains; abundant in northwestern California; less common and of smaller size southward.

46. Quercus utahensis Rydb.

Leaves oblong-obovate, gradually narrowed and rounded or cuneate at base, divided often nearly to the midrib by broad or narrow sinuses into four or five pairs of lateral lobes rounded or acute at apex, the upper lobes usually again lobed or undulate, the ter-

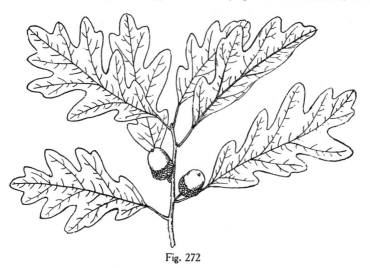

Fig. 272

minal lobe rounded at apex, entire or three-lobed, thick, dark green, glabrous or nearly glabrous above, pale and soft pubescent below, $2\frac{1}{2}'-7'$ long, $1\frac{1}{2}'-3\frac{1}{2}'$ wide, with a prominent midrib and primary veins, and conspicuous veinlets; petioles stout, hoary-tomentose early in the season, pubescent or glabrous before maturity, $\frac{2}{5}'-1'$ in length. **Flowers:** staminate in aments covered with fascicled hairs, $2'-2\frac{1}{2}'$ long; calyx scarious, divided to the middle by wide sinuses into narrow acuminate lobes; anthers yellow; pistillate usually solitary or in pairs, the scales of the involucre thickly coated with hoary tomentum. **Fruit** usually solitary, sessile or raised on a stout pubescent peduncle $\frac{1}{4}'-\frac{1}{2}'$ in length; nut ovoid, broad and rounded at the ends, $\frac{3}{5}'-\frac{3}{4}'$ long, $\frac{1}{2}'-2\frac{1}{2}'$ thick, usually inclosed for about half its length in the thick hemispheric cup covered with broad ovate pale pubescent scales much thickened on the back and closely appressed below the middle of the cup, gradually reduced in size upward, thin and less closely appressed toward its rim bordered by the free projecting tips of the upper row of scales.

A tree, occasionally 30° high, with a trunk 4'–8' in diameter, thick erect branches forming a narrow open head, and stout branchlets red-brown and covered with fascicled hairs when they first appear, becoming light orange-brown and puberulous. **Bark** dark gray-brown, rough and scaly.

Distribution. Dry foothill slopes and the sides of cañons; borders of southwestern Wyoming to the eastern base of the Rocky Mountains of Colorado, and to Utah, northern New Mexico and Arizona, passing into var. *mollis* Sarg. with thinner scales on the lower part of the cup of the fruit; with the species over its whole range, but most abundant on the Colorado Plateau of northern Arizona; here rarely 40° high, with a trunk 18'–20' in diameter.

47. Quercus lobata Née. White Oak. Valley Oak.

Leaves oblong to obovate, deeply 7–11 obliquely lobed, rounded at the narrow apex, narrow and cuneate or broad and rounded or cordate at base, the lateral lobes obovate, obtuse or retuse, or ovate and rounded, thin, $2\frac{1}{2}'$–$3'$ or rarely $4'$ long, $1'$–$2'$ wide, dark green and pubescent above, pale and pubescent below, with a stout pale midrib, and conspicuous yellow veins running to the slightly thickened and revolute margins; petioles stout, hirsute, $\frac{1}{4}'$–$\frac{1}{2}'$ in length. **Flowers:** staminate in hirsute aments $2'$–$3'$ long; calyx light yellow and divided into 6 or 8 acute pubescent ciliate lobes; pistillate solitary, sessile or rarely in elongated few-flowered spikes, their involucral scales broadly ovate, acute, coated with

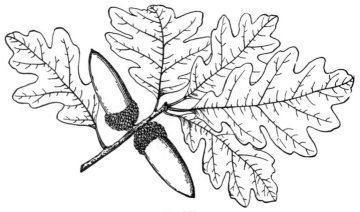

Fig. 273

dense pale tomentum, about as long as the narrow calyx-lobes. **Fruit** solitary or in pairs, nearly sessile; nut conic, elongated, rounded or pointed at apex, $1\frac{1}{4}'$–$2\frac{1}{4}'$ long, bright green and lustrous when fully grown, becoming bright chestnut-brown, usually inclosed for about one third its length in the cup-shaped cup coated with pale tomentum on the outer surface, usually irregularly tuberculate below, all but the much-thickened basal scales elongated into acute ciliate chestnut-brown free tips longest on the upper scales and forming a short fringe-like border to the rim of the cup.

A tree, often 100° feet high, with a trunk generally $3°$–$4°$, but sometimes $10°$ in diameter, divided nea' the ground or usually $20°$–$30°$ above it into great limbs spreading at wide angles and forming a broad head of slender branches hanging gracefully in long sprays and sometimes sweeping the ground; less frequently with upper limbs growing almost at right angles with the trunk and forming a narrow rigid head of variously contorted erect or pendant branches, and slender branchlets coated at first with short silky canescent pubescence, ashy gray, light reddish brown, or pale orange-brown and slightly pubescent in their first winter, becoming glabrous and lighter colored during their second year. **Winter-buds** ovoid, acute, usually about $\frac{1}{4}'$ long, with orange-brown pubescent scales scarious and frequently ciliate on the margins. **Bark** $\frac{3}{4}'$–$1\frac{1}{2}'$ thick and covered by small loosely appressed light gray scales slightly tinged with orange or brown, becoming at the base of old trees frequently $5'$–$6'$ thick and divided by longitudinal fissures into broad flat ridges broken horizontally into short plates. **Wood** hard, fine-grained, brittle, light brown, with thin lighter colored sapwood; used only for fuel.

Distribution. Valleys of western California between the Sierra Nevada and the ocean from the valley of the Trinity River to Kern and Los Angeles (rare) Counties; most abundant and forming open groves in the central valleys of the state.

48. Quercus leptophylla Rydb.

Leaves oblong to oblong-obovate, cuneate or rarely rounded at base, divided about half-way to the midrib into two to four acute or rounded lateral lobes entire or occasionally furnished on the lower side with a small nearly triangular lobe, the terminal lobe short, entire, rounded at apex or three-lobed, when they unfold thickly coated with hoary tomentum, about one-third grown when the flowers open and then covered above with fascicled hairs and tomentose below, at maturity thin, dark green, lustrous and glabrous or nearly glabrous on the upper surface, yellow-green and covered below by short white hairs most abundant on the midrib and veins, $3\frac{1}{2}'-4'$ long, $1\frac{1}{2}'-2'$ wide; petioles slender, pubescent $\frac{1}{3}'-\frac{1}{2}'$ in length. **Flowers:** staminate in slender villose aments; calyx scarious, divided into five or six narrow acute lobes; anthers dark red-brown as the flowers open; pistil-

Fig. 274

late not seen. **Fruit** solitary or racemose, sessile or raised on a stout tomentose peduncle $\frac{2}{5}'-\frac{3}{5}'$ in length; nut oblong-ovoid, abruptly narrowed and rounded at base, gradually narrowed and rounded at apex, $\frac{1}{2}'-\frac{3}{4}'$ long; inclosed for half its length in the thin, hemispheric cup, $\frac{2}{5}'-\frac{1}{2}'$ in diameter, and covered with acuminate only slightly thickened appressed scales densely covered with hoary tomentum.

A tree, 30°–45° high, with a trunk 16′–24′ in diameter, heavy spreading ashy gray branches forming a round-topped head, and stout branchlets, light red-brown or purple and covered with long fascicled hairs when they first appear, becoming light brown and glabrous before autumn. **Bark** thick, deeply furrowed, covered with small appressed pale gray scales.

Distribution. Rich bottom-lands of the Cucharas River above La Veta, Huerfano County, Colorado; on the Mogollon Mountains, Socorro County, New Mexico.

49. Quercus austrina Small.

Leaves oblong-obovate, acute or rounded at apex, gradually narrowed to the long cuneate base or rarely rounded at base, usually 5-lobed with rounded lobes, the terminal lobe often 3-lobed, the upper lateral lobes pointing forward and much larger than those of the lower pair, or occasionally 3-lobed at the broad apex, or rarely nearly entire with undulate margins, when they unfold sparsely covered below with caducous fascicled hairs, at maturity glabrous, dark green and lustrous above, paler below, $3'-8'$ long, $1'-4'$ wide, with a prominent midrib and slender primary veins; petioles slender, at first pubescent, soon glabrous, $\frac{1}{4}'-\frac{1}{3}'$ in length. **Flowers** not seen. **Fruit** solitary or in pairs, sessile or raised on a stout stalk up to $\frac{1}{2}'$ in length; nut ovoid, slightly narrowed toward the base, narrowed at the rounded pubescent apex, $\frac{1}{2}'-\frac{3}{4}'$ long, $\frac{1}{2}'$ thick, inclosed for a third to a

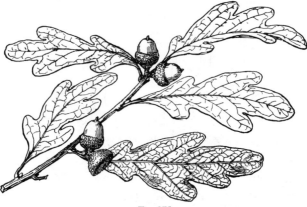

Fig. 275

half its length in the thin hemispheric or deep cup-shaped cup, pale tomentose on the inner surface and covered with thin narrow loosely appressed blunt-pointed tomentose scales.

A tree, $70°-80°$ and rarely $100°$ high, with a tall trunk $2°-3°$ in diameter, spreading and ascending branches forming a broad rather open head, and slender glabrous red-brown or gray-brown brittle-jointed branchlets. **Winter-buds** ovoid to ellipsoid, acute, $\frac{1}{8}'-\frac{1}{4}'$ long, with closely imbricated acute puberulous chestnut-brown scales ciliate on the margins. **Bark** pale, scaly, and on old trunks divided into broad ridges.

Distribution. Banks of streams and river bluffs in deep rich soil; coast of South Carolina (Bluffton, Clay County, and near Charleston); Dover, Scriven County, McIntosh County, De Soto, Sumter County, and near Bainbridge, Decatur County, Georgia, to central and western Florida (Gainsville, Alachua County, near Santos, Marion County, Lake City, Columbia County, River Junction, Gadsden County, Marianna, Jackson County); western Alabama (Gallion, Hale County, and the neighborhood of Selma [common] and Pleasant Hill, Dallas County); and southern Mississippi (Meridian, Lauderdale County, Laurel, Jones County, Byram and near Jackson, Hinds County, near Natchez, Adams County).

50. Quercus alba L. White Oak.

Leaves oblong-obovate, gradually narrowed and cuneate at base, divided often nearly to the midrib by narrow or broad sinuses usually oblique in the bottom into 7 or 9 lobes, the lateral, narrow, lanceolate or obovate, pointing forward, rounded or acute and often lobed at apex, the terminal usually obovate and 3-lobed, when they unfold bright red above, pale below and coated with soft pubescence, soon becoming silvery white and very lustrous, at maturity thin, firm, glabrous, bright green and lustrous or dull above, pale or glaucous below, 5'–9' long, 2'–4' wide, with a stout bright yellow midrib and conspicuous primary veins; turning late in the autumn deep rich vinous red, gradually withering and sometimes remaining on the branches nearly through the winter; petioles stout, glabrous, ½'–1' in length. **Flowers:** staminate in hirsute or nearly glabrous aments 2½'–3' long; calyx bright yellow and pubescent, with acute lobes; pistillate bright red, their involucral scales broadly ovate, hirsute, about as long as the ovate acute calyx-lobes. **Fruit** sessile or raised on a slender peduncle 1'–2' long, the two forms sometimes appearing on the same branch; nut ovoid to oblong, rounded at apex, lustrous, ¾' long, green when fully grown, becoming light chestnut-brown, inclosed for about one fourth its length in the cup-shaped cup coated with pale

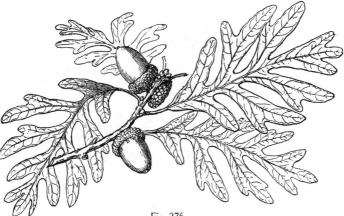

Fig. 276

or light brown tomentum, its scales at the base much thickened, united and produced into short obtuse membranaceous tips, and thinner toward the rim of the cup.

A tree, 80°–100° high, with a trunk 3°–4° in diameter, tall and naked in the forest, short in the open, and surmounted by a broad round-topped head of stout limbs spreading irregularly, small rigid branches, and slender branchlets at first bright green, often tinged with red, and coated with a loose mass of long pale or ferrugineous deciduous hairs, reddish brown during the summer, bright red and lustrous or covered with a glaucous bloom during their first winter, becoming ultimately ashy gray. **Winter-buds** broadly ovoid, rather obtuse, dark red-brown, about ⅛' long. **Bark** light gray slightly tinged with red or brown, or occasionally nearly white, broken into thin appressed scales, becoming on old trunks sometimes 2' thick and divided into broad flat ridges. **Wood** strong, very heavy, hard, tough, close-grained, durable, light brown, with thin light brown sapwood; used in shipbuilding, for construction and in cooperage, the manufacture of carriages, agricultural implements, baskets, the interior finish of houses, cabinet-making, for railway-ties and fences, and largely as fuel.

Distribution. Sandy plains and gravelly ridges, rich uplands, intervales, and moist bottom-lands, sometimes forming nearly pure forests; southern Maine to southwestern Quebec, westward through southern Ontario, the southern peninsula of Michigan, southeastern Minnesota, eastern Iowa, and southeastern Nebraska, and southward to western Florida, through the Gulf states to the valley of the Brazos River, Texas and through Arkansas to eastern Oklahoma, eastern Kansas, Missouri, Tennessee, and Kentucky; ascending the southern Appalachian Mountains as a low bush to altitudes of 4500°;

most abundant and of its largest size on the lower western slopes of the Alleghany Mountains and on the bottom-lands of the lower Ohio Basin.   Passing into

Quercus alba var. latiloba Sarg.

Leaves obovate-oblong, acute or rounded at apex, gradually narrowed and cuneate at base, divided usually less than half way to the midrib into broad rounded lobes; rarely obovate, with undulate margins, or slightly lobed, with broad rounded lobes (var. *repanda* Michx.).   **Flowers** as in the type.   **Fruit** rarely more than $1\frac{1}{2}'$ in length, with usually thinner cup scales.

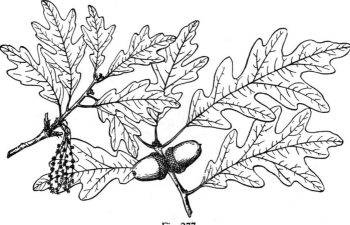

Fig. 277

Distribution.   More abundant than the species and the common northern White Oak; the var. *repanda* very common in Ponchartrain Parish, Louisiana, and in Richland County, Illinois.

× *Quercus Beadlei* Trel., believed to be a hybrid of *Quercus alba* and *Q. Prinus*, has been found in a swamp near Clarkton, Bladen County, North Carolina.

× *Quercus Bebbiana* Schn., probably a hybrid of *Quercus alba* and *Q. macrocarpa*, occurs at Charlotte, Chittenden County, Vermont, and near Kenton, Hardin County, Ohio.

× *Quercus Deamii* Trel., with characters intermediate between those of *Quercus alba* and *Q. Muehlenbergii* and evidently a hybrid of these species, is growing near Bluffton, Wells County, Indiana.

× *Quercus Faxonii* Trel., with characters intermediate between those of *Quercus alba* and *Q. prinoides* and evidently a hybrid of these species, has been found in East Walpole, Norfolk County, and Concord, Middlesex County, Massachusetts, and at Greenville, Montcalm County, Michigan.

× *Quercus Fernowii* Trel., evidently a hybrid of *Quercus alba* and *Q. stellata*, has been found near Allenton, St. Louis County, Missouri, and on Red Clay Creek, Virginia.

× *Quercus Jackiana* Schn., evidently a hybrid of *Quercus alba* and *Q. bicolor*, is growing in Franklin Park, Boston.

× *Quercus Saulei* Schn., with characters intermediate between those of *Q. alba* and *Q. montana* and evidently a hybrid of these species, occurs with widely distributed individuals in Vermont (Monkton, Addison County), eastern Massachusetts, near Providence, Rhode Island, New Jersey, Eastern Pennsylvania, and the District of Columbia, on the Appalachian Mountains near Biltmore, Buncombe County, and Highlands, Macon County, North Carolina, at Valleyhead, Gadsden County, Alabama.

51. Quercus bicolor Willd. Swamp White Oak.

Quercus platanoïdes Sudw.

Leaves obovate to oblong-obovate, rounded at the narrowed apex, acute or rounded at the gradually narrowed and cuneate entire base, coarsely sinuate-dentate, or sometimes pinnatifid, with oblique rounded or acute entire lobes, when they unfold light bronze-green and pilose above, covered below with silvery white tomentum, with conspicuous glands on the teeth, at maturity thick and firm, dark green and lustrous on the upper surface, pale or often silvery white or tawny on the lower surface, 5′–6′ long, 2′–4′ wide, with a slender yellow midrib, primary veins running to the points of the lobes, and conspicuous

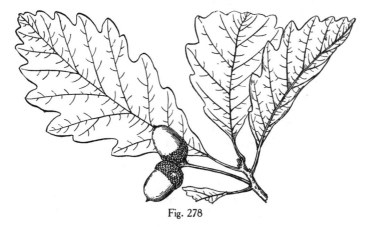

Fig. 278

reticulate veinlets; turning in the autumn dull yellow-brown or occasionally orange-color; petioles stout, pilose at first, becoming glabrous, $\frac{1}{2}′-\frac{3}{4}′$ in length. **Flowers:** staminate in hairy aments 3′–4′ long; calyx light yellow-green, hirsute with pale hairs, and deeply divided into 5–9 lanceolate acute segments rather shorter than the stamens; pistillate in few-flowered spikes on elongated peduncles covered like the involucral scales with thick white or tawny tomentum; stigmas bright red. **Fruit** usually in pairs on slender dark brown glabrous puberulous or pubescent stalks $1\frac{1}{2}′-4′$ in length; nut ovoid, with a broad base, rounded, acute and pubescent at apex, light chestnut-brown, $\frac{3}{4}′-1\frac{1}{4}′$ long, $\frac{1}{2}′-\frac{3}{4}′$ thick, inclosed for about one third its length in the thick cup-shaped light brown cup pubescent on the inner surface, hoary-tomentose, and sometimes tuberculate or roughened toward the base on the outer surface by the thickened contorted tips of the ovate acute scales, thin, free, acute and chestnut-brown higher on the cup, and often forming a short fringe-like border on its margin, or sometimes entirely covered by thin scales with free acute tips.

A tree, usually 60°–70° or exceptionally 100° high, with a trunk 2°–3° or occasionally 8°–9° in diameter, rather small branches generally pendulous below and rising above into a narrow round-topped open head and often furnished with short pendulous laterals, and stout branchlets, green, lustrous, and slightly scurfy-pubescent when they first appear, light orange color or reddish brown and glabrous or puberulous during their first winter, becoming darker and often purplish and clothed with a glaucous bloom. **Winter-buds** broadly ovoid and obtuse, or subglobose to ovoid and acute, $\frac{1}{8}′$ long, with light chestnut-brown scales usually pilose above the middle. **Bark** of young stems and small branches smooth, reddish or purplish brown, separating freely into large papery persistent scales curling back and displaying the bright green inner bark; becoming on old trunks 1′–2′

thick, and deeply and irregularly divided by continuous or interrupted fissures into broad flat ridges covered by small appressed gray-brown scales often slightly tinged with red. **Wood** heavy, hard, strong, tough, light brown, with thin hardly distinguishable sapwood; used in construction, the interior finish of houses, cabinet-making, carriage and boat-building, cooperage, and railway-ties, and for fencing and fuel.

Distribution. Borders of streams and swamps in moist fertile soil; southern Maine to northern Vermont and southwestern Quebec, through Ontario and the southern peninsula of Michigan to southeastern Minnesota, eastern and southern Iowa, southeastern Nebraska and western Missouri, and to the District of Columbia, northern Kentucky and northeastern Oklahoma, and along the Appalachian Mountains to West Virginia; widely scattered, usually in small groves but nowhere very abundant; most common and of its largest size in western New York and northern Ohio.

$\times$ *Quercus Schuettii* Trel., with characters intermediate between those of *Quercus bicolor* and *Q. macrocarpa*, and probably a hybrid of these species, occurs at Fort Howard, Brown County, Wisconsin, near Rockfield and Chateaugay, Quebec, and near Rochester and Golah, Monroe County, New York.

52. Quercus Prinus L.   Basket Oak.   Cow Oak.

Quercus Michauxii Nutt.

Leaves broadly obovate to oblong-obovate, acute or acuminate at apex with a short broad point, cuneate or rounded at the broad or narrow entire base, regularly crenately lobed with oblique rounded entire lobes sometimes furnished with glandular tips, or

Fig. 279

rarely entire with undulate margins, when they unfold bright yellow-green, lustrous and pubescent above, coated below with thick silvery white or ferrugineous tomentum, at maturity thick and firm or sometimes membranaceous, especially on young and vigorous branches, dark green, lustrous, glabrous or occasionally roughened by scattered fascicled hairs on the upper surface, more or less densely pubescent on the pale green or silvery white lower surface, 6'–8' long, 3'–5' wide; turning in the autumn dark rich crimson; petioles stout, $\frac{1}{2}'$–$1\frac{1}{2}'$ in length.   **Flowers:** staminate in slender hairy aments, 3'–4' long; calyx light yellow-green, pilose with long pale hairs, and divided into 4–7 acute lobes; pistillate in few-flowered spikes on short peduncles coated like the involucral scales with dense pale rufous tomentum; stigmas dark red.   **Fruit** solitary or in pairs, sessile or subsessile, or borne on short stout puberulous stalks rarely $\frac{1}{2}'$ in length; nut ovoid to ellipsoidal, with a broad base, and acute, rounded, or occasionally truncate at apex surrounded by a narrow ring of rusty pubescence, or sometimes pilose nearly to the middle, bright brown, rather lustrous, $1'-1\frac{1}{2}'$ long, $\frac{3}{4}'-1\frac{1}{4}'$ thick, inclosed for about one third its length in the thick cup-shaped cup often broad and flat on the bottom, reddish brown and pubescent within, hoary-tomentose and covered on the outer surface by regularly imbricated ovate acute scales rounded and much thickened on the back, their short tips sometimes forming a rigid fringe-like border to the rim of the cup; seed sweet and edible.

A tree, often 100° high, with a trunk sometimes free of branches for 40°–50°, and 3°–7° in diameter, stout branches ascending at narrow angles and forming a round-topped rather compact head, and stout branchlets at first dark green and covered by pale caducous hairs, becoming bright red-brown or light orange-brown during their first winter and ultimately ashy gray. **Winter-buds** broadly ovoid or oval, acute, $\frac{1}{4}'$ long, with thin closely and regularly imbricated dark red puberulous scales with pale margins, those of the inner ranks coated on the outer surface with loose pale tomentum. **Bark** $\frac{1}{2}'-1'$ thick, separating into thin closely appressed silvery white or ashy gray scales more or less deeply tinged with red. **Wood** heavy, hard, very strong, tough, close-grained, durable, easy to split, light-brown, with thin darker colored sapwood; largely used in all kinds of construction, for agricultural implements, wheels, in cooperage, for fences and fuel, and in baskets.

Distribution. Borders of streams, swamps, and bottom-lands often covered with water; New Jersey (Morristown, Morris County and Pittsgrove, Salem County), near Wilmington, Delaware, southward through the coast and middle districts to Putnam (San Mateo) and Citrus Counties, Florida, through the Gulf states to the valley of the Trinity River, Texas, and through Arkansas and southeastern Missouri to central Tennessee and Kentucky, the valley of the lower Wabash River, Illinois, and southern Indiana eastward to Jefferson County (*C. C. Deam*); conspicuous from the silvery white bark, the massive trunk, and the broad crown of large bright-colored foliage.

53. Quercus montana Willd. Chestnut Oak. Rock Chestnut Oak.

Quercus Prinus Engelm., not L.

Leaves obovate or oblong to lanceolate, acute or acuminate or rounded at apex, gradually or abruptly cuneate or rounded or subcordate at the narrow entire base, irregularly and coarsely crenulate-toothed with rounded, acute, or sometimes nearly triangular oblique teeth, when they unfold orange-green or bronze-red, very lustrous, and glabrous above with the exception of the slightly pilose midrib, green and coated below with soft pale pubescence, at maturity thick and firm or subcoriaceous, yellow-green and rather lustrous on the upper surface, paler and covered by fine pubescence on the lower surface, $4\frac{1}{2}'-9'$ long, $1\frac{1}{2}'-3'$ wide, with a stout yellow midrib and conspicuous primary veins, often much broader near the bottom of the tree than on fertile upper branches; turning dull orange color or rusty brown in the autumn; petioles stout or slender, $\frac{1}{2}'-1'$ in length. **Flowers:** staminate in elongated hirsute aments; calyx light yellow, pilose and deeply divided into 7–9 acute segments tipped with clusters of pale hairs; pistillate in short spikes on stout puberulous dark green peduncles, their involucral scales covered with pale hairs; stigmas dark red. **Fruit** on short stout stems singly or in pairs; nut ovoid or ellipsoidal, rounded and rather obtuse or pointed at apex, bright chestnut-brown, very lustrous, $1'-1\frac{1}{2}'$ long, $\frac{5}{8}'-1'$ thick, inclosed for about half its length or sometimes only at the base in a turbinate or cup-shaped thin cup light brown and pubescent on the inner surface, reddish brown and hoary-pubescent on the outer surface roughened or tuberculate, especially toward the base, by small scales thickened and knob-like with nearly triangular free light brown tips.

A tree, usually 60°–70° or occasionally 100° high, with a trunk 3°–4° or rarely 6°–7° in diameter, divided generally 15° or 20° above the ground into large limbs spreading into a broad open rather irregular head, and stout branchlets green tinged with purple or bronze color and glabrous or pilose when they first appear, light orange color or reddish brown during their first winter, becoming dark gray or brown; on dry exposed mountain slopes often not more than 20°–30° tall, with a trunk 8'–12' in diameter. **Winter-buds** ovoid, acute or acuminate, $\frac{1}{4}$'–$\frac{1}{2}$' long, with bright chestnut-brown scales pilose toward the apex and ciliate on the margins. **Bark** of young stems and small branches thin, smooth, purplish brown, often lustrous, becoming on old trunks and large limbs $\frac{3}{4}$'–1$\frac{1}{2}$' thick, dark reddish brown or nearly black, and divided into broad rounded ridges covered with small closely appressed scales. **Wood** heavy, hard, strong, rather tough, close-grained, durable in contact with the soil, largely used for fencing, railway-ties, and fuel. The bark, which is rich in tannin, is consumed in large quantities in tanning leather.

Distribution. Hillsides and the high rocky banks of streams in rich and deep or sometimes in sterile soil; coast of southern Maine, southern New Hampshire and eastern Massachusetts, southward to Delaware and the District of Columbia, and along the Appalachian

Fig. 280

Mountains and their foothills to northern Georgia (Wilkes County); ascending to altitudes of 4000°–4500°; in Alabama to Perry and Hale Counties; westward to the shores of Lake Champlain, western New York; southeastern and southern Ohio, and southern Indiana westward to Orange County (*C. C. Deam*) and on hills near Elberfeld, Warrick County; and to central Kentucky and Tennessee, and northeastern Mississippi (Alcorn, Prentiss and Tishomingo Counties); rare and local in New England and Ontario; abundant on the banks of the lower Hudson River and on the Appalachian hills from southern New York to Alabama; most common and of its largest size on the lower slopes of the mountains of the Carolinas and Tennessee, here often forming a large part of the forest.

× *Quercus Sargentii* Rehd. believed to be a hybrid of *Quercus montana* and the European *Q. robur* L., has been growing for nearly a hundred years at what is now Holm Lea, Brookline, Norfolk County, Massachusetts.

54. Quercus Muehlenbergii Engelm. Yellow Oak. Chestnut Oak.

Quercus acuminata Sarg.

Leaves usually crowded at the ends of the branches, oblong-lanceolate to broadly obovate, acute or acuminate with a long narrow or with a short broad point, abruptly or gradually narrowed and cuneate or slightly narrowed and rounded or cordate at base, equally serrate with acute and often incurved or broad and rounded teeth tipped with small glandular mucros, or rarely slightly undulate, when they unfold bright bronzy green and puberulous above, tinged with purple and coated below with pale tomentum, at maturity thick and firm, light yellow-green on the upper surface, pale often silvery white and covered with short fine pubescence on the lower surface, 4′–7′ long, 1′–5′ wide, with a stout yellow midrib and conspicuous primary veins running to the points of the teeth; turning in the autumn orange color and scarlet; petioles slender $\frac{3}{4}$′–1$\frac{1}{2}$′ in length. **Flowers:** staminate in pilose aments 3′–4′ long; calyx light yellow, hairy, deeply divided into 5 or 6 lanceolate ciliate segments; pistillate sessile or in short spikes coated like their involucral scales with thick white tomentum; stigmas bright red. **Fruit** sessile or raised on a short stout peduncle, solitary or often in pairs; nut broadly ovoid, narrowed and rounded at apex, $\frac{1}{2}$′ to nearly 1′ long, light chestnut-brown, inclosed for about half its length in a thin cup-shaped light brown cup pubescent on the inner, hoary-tomentose on the outer surface, and covered by small obtuse scales more or less thickened and rounded on the back toward the base of the cup, the small free red-brown tips of the upper ranks forming a minute fringe-like border to its rim; **seed** sweet and sometimes edible.

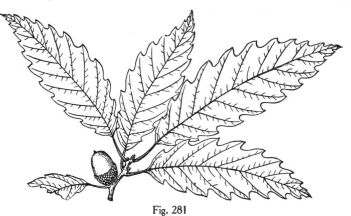

Fig. 281

A tree, 80°–100°, occasionally 160° high, with a tall straight trunk 3°–4° in diameter above the broad and often buttressed base, comparatively small branches forming a narrow shapely round-topped head, and slender branchlets, green more or less tinged with red or purple, pilose when they first appear, light orange color or reddish brown during their first winter, and ultimately gray or brown; east of the Alleghany Mountains and on dry hills often not more than 20°–30° tall. **Winter-buds** ovoid, acute, $\frac{1}{8}$′–$\frac{1}{4}$′ long, with chestnut-brown scales white and scarious on the margins. **Bark** rarely $\frac{1}{2}$′ thick, broken on the surface into thin loose silvery white scales sometimes slightly tinged with brown. **Wood** heavy, very hard, strong, close-grained, durable, with thin light-colored sapwood; largely used in cooperage, for wheels, fencing, and railway-ties.

Distribution. Gardner's Island, Lake Champlain, Vermont, western Massachusetts and Connecticut, near Newberg, Orange County, New York, westward through New York, southern Ontario and southern Michigan and western Wisconsin to northern Iowa, southeastern Nebraska, eastern Kansas, and Oklahoma to the valley of the Washita River (Garvin County) and to the Devil's Cañon near Hinton (Caddo County) and southward in the Atlantic states to the District of Columbia, eastern Virginia; sparingly on the eastern foothills of the Blue Ridge in North and South Carolina at altitudes between 1000° and 2000°; in central Tennessee and Kentucky, central and northeastern Georgia, western Florida, and through the Gulf states to the valley of the Guadalupe River, Texas; on the Guadalupe Mountains, Texas, and on the Capitan Mountains, New Mexico (Lincoln County); rare and comparatively local in the Atlantic states, usually on limestone soil; very abundant in the Mississippi basin, growing on ridges, dry flinty hills, deep rich bottom-lands and the rocky banks of streams; probably of its largest size on the lower Wabash River and its tributaries in southern Indiana and Illinois; on the Edwards Plateau (Kemble, Kerr, Uvalde, Bandera and Real Counties), Texas, a form occurs with nuts sometimes $1\frac{1}{4}'$ long with deeper cups up to $1'$ in diameter (var. *Brayi* Sarg.).

Section 2.   Flowers unisexual (*usually perfect in Ulmus*); calyx regular; stamens as many as its lobes and opposite them; ovary superior, 1-celled (*rarely 2-celled in Ulmus*); seed 1.

XI. ULMACEÆ.

Trees, with watery juice, scaly buds, terete branchlets prolonged by an upper lateral bud, and alternate simple serrate pinnately veined deciduous stalked 2-ranked leaves unequal and often oblique at base, conduplicate in the bud, their stipules usually fugaceous. Flowers perfect or monœciously polygamous, clustered, or the pistillate sometimes solitary; calyx 4–9-parted or lobed; stamens 4–6; filaments straight; anthers introrse, 2-celled, opening longitudinally; ovary usually 1-celled; ovule solitary, suspended from the apex of the cell, anatropous or amphitropous; styles 2.   Fruit a samara, nut, or drupe; albumen little or none; embryo straight or curved; cotyledons usually flat or conduplicate. Five of the thirteen genera of the Elm family occur in North America.   Of these four are represented by trees.

CONSPECTUS OF THE NORTH AMERICAN ARBORESCENT GENERA.

Fruit a dry samara, or nut-like.
   Flowers perfect; fruit a samara.   1. **Ulmus.**
   Flowers polygamo-monœcious; fruit nut-like, tuberculate.   2. **Planera.**
Fruit drupaceous.
   Pistillate flowers usually solitary.   3. **Celtis.**
   Pistillate flowers in dichotomous cymes.   4. **Trema.**

1. ULMUS L.   Elm.

Trees, or rarely shrubs, with deeply furrowed bark, branchlets often furnished with corky wings, and buds with numerous ovate rounded chestnut-brown scales closely imbricated in two ranks, increasing in size from without inward, the inner accrescent, replacing the stipules of the first leaves, deciduous, marking the base of the branchlet with persistent ring-like scars. Leaves simply or doubly serrate; stipules linear, lanceolate to obovate, entire, free or connate at base, scarious, inclosing the leaf in the bud, caducous.   Flowers from axillary buds near the ends of the branches similar to but larger than the leaf-buds, the outer scales sterile, the inner bearing flowers and rarely leaves. Flowers perfect, jointed on slender bibracteolate pedicels from the axils of linear acute scarious bracts, in pedunculate or subsessile fascicles or cymes sometimes becoming racemose, appearing in early spring before the leaves in the axils of those of the previous year, or autumnal in the axils of leaves of the year; calyx campanulate, 5–9-lobed, membranaceous, marcescent; stamens 5 or 6 inserted under the ovary; filaments filiform or slightly flattened, erect in the bud, becoming exserted; anthers oblong, emarginate, and subcordate; ovary sessile or stipitate, compressed, crowned by a simple deeply 2-lobed style, the spreading lobes papillo-stigmatic on the inner face, usually 1-celled by abortion, rarely 2-celled; ovule amphitropous; micropyle extrorse, superior. Fruit an ovoid or oblong, often oblique, sessile or stipitate samara surrounded at base by the remnants of the calyx, the seminal cavity compressed, slightly thickened on the margin, chartaceous, produced into a thin reticulate-venulose membranaceous light brown broad or rarely narrow wing naked or ciliate on the margin, tipped with the remnants of the persistent style, or more or less deeply notched at apex, and often marked by the thickened line of the union of the two carpels. Seed ovoid, compressed, without albumen, marked on the ventral edge by the thin raphe; testa membranaceous, light or dark chestnut-brown, of two coats, rarely produced into a narrow wing; embryo erect; cotyledons flat or slightly convex, much longer than the superior radicle turned toward the oblong linear pale hilum.

Ulmus, with eighteen or twenty species, is widely distributed through the boreal and temperate regions of the northern hemisphere with the exception of western North America, reaching in the New World the mountains of southern Mexico and in the Old World the Sikkim Himalaya, western China, and Japan. Of the exotic species, *Ulmus procera* Salisb., the so-called English Elm, and *Ulmus glabra*, Huds., the Scotch Elm, and several of its varieties, have been largely planted for shade and ornament in the north Atlantic states, where old and large specimens of the former can be seen, especially in the neighborhood of Boston.

Ulmus produces heavy, hard, tough, light-colored wood, often difficult to split. The tough inner bark of some of the species is made into ropes or woven into coarse cloth, and in northern China nourishing mucilaginous food is prepared from the inner bark.

Ulmus is the classical name of the Elm-tree.

CONSPECTUS OF THE NORTH AMERICAN SPECIES.

Flowers vernal, appearing before the leaves.
  Flowers on slender drooping pedicels; fruit ciliate on the margins.
    Wing of the fruit broad.
      Bud-scales and fruit glabrous; branchlets destitute of corky wings; leaves obovate-oblong to elliptic, usually smooth on the upper, soft-pubescent on the lower surface.   **1. U. americana** (A, C).
      Bud-scales puberulous; branches often furnished with corky wings; fruit hirsute; leaves obovate to oblong, smooth on the upper, soft-pubescent on the lower surface.   **2. U. racemosa** (A).
    Wing of the fruit narrow; bud-scales glabrous or slightly puberulous; branchlets usually furnished with broad corky wings; fruit hirsute, leaves ovate-oblong to oblong-lanceolate, smooth on the upper, soft-pubescent on the lower surface.
      3. U. alata (A, C).
  Flowers on short pedicels; fruit naked on the margins; bud-scales coated with rusty hairs; fruit pubescent; leaves ovate-oblong, scabrous on the upper, pubescent on the lower surface.   **4. U. fulva** (A, C).
Flowers autumnal, appearing in the axils of leaves of the year; branchlets furnished with corky wings; fruit hirsute.
    Bud-scales puberulous; flowers on short pedicels; leaves ovate, scabrous on the upper, soft-pubescent on the lower surface.   **5. U. crassifolia** (C).
    Bud-scales glabrous; flowers on long pedicels; leaves oblong to oblong-obovate, acuminate, glabrous on the upper, pale and puberulous on the lower surface.
      6. U. serotina (C).

1. Ulmus americana L. White Elm.

Ulmus floridana Chapm.

Leaves obovate-oblong to elliptic, abruptly narrowed at apex into a long point, full and rounded at base on one side and shorter and cuneate on the other, coarsely doubly serrate with slightly incurved teeth, when they unfold coated below with pale pubescence and pilose above with long scattered white hairs, at maturity 4′–6′ long, 1′–3′ wide, dark green and glabrous or scarbate above, pale and soft-pubescent or sometimes glabrous below, with a narrow pale midrib and numerous slender straight primary veins running to the points of the teeth and connected by fine cross veinlets; turning bright clear yellow in the autumn before falling; petioles stout, ¼′ in length; stipules linear-lanceolate, ½′–2′ long. **Flowers** on long slender drooping pedicels sometimes 1′ in length, in 3 or 4-flowered short-stalked fascicles; calyx irregularly divided into 7–9 rounded lobes ciliate on the margins, often somewhat oblique, puberulous on the outer surface, green tinged with red above the middle; anthers bright red; ovary light green, ciliate on the margins with long white hairs; styles light green.   **Fruit** on long pedicels in crowded clusters, ripening as the leaves unfold, ovoid to obovoid-oblong, slightly stipitate, conspicuously reticulate-venulose, ½′ long, ciliate on the margins, the sharp points of the wings incurved and inclosing the deep notch.

A tree, sometimes 100°–120° high, with a tall trunk 6°–11° in diameter, frequently enlarged at the base by great buttresses, occasionally rising with a straight undivided shaft to the height of 60°–80° and separating into short spreading branches, more commonly divided 30°–40° from the ground into numerous upright limbs gradually spreading and forming an inversely conic round-topped head of long graceful branches, often 100° or rarely 150° in diameter, and slender branchlets frequently fringing the trunk and its principal divisions, light green and coated at first with soft pale pubescence, becoming in their first winter light reddish brown, glabrous or sometimes puberulous and marked by scat-

Fig. 282

tered pale lenticels, and by large elevated semiorbicular leaf-scars showing the ends of three large equidistant fibro-vascular bundles, later becoming dark reddish brown and finally ashy gray.   **Winter-buds** ovoid, acute, slightly flattened, about ⅛′ long, with broadly ovate rounded light chestnut-brown glabrous scales, the inner bright green, ovate, acute, becoming on vigorous shoots often nearly 1′ in length.   **Bark** 1′–1½′ thick, ashy gray, divided by deep fissures into broad ridges separating on the surface into thin appressed scales. **Wood** heavy, hard, strong, tough, difficult to split, coarse-grained, light brown, with thick somewhat lighter colored sapwood; largely used for the hubs of wheels, saddle-trees, in flooring and cooperage, and in boat and shipbuilding.

Distribution.   River-bottom lands, intervales, low rich hills, and the banks of streams; southern Newfoundland to the northern shores of Lake Superior and the headwaters of the Saskatchewan, southward to the neighborhood of Lake Istokpoga, De Soto County, Florida, westward in the United States to the Turtle Mountains of North Dakota, the Black Hills of South Dakota, western Nebraska, central Kansas and Oklahoma, and the valley of the upper Colorado River (Fort Chadbourne, Coke County), Texas; very common northward, less abundant and of smaller size southward; abundant on the banks of streams flowing through the midcontinental plateau.

Largely planted as an ornamental and shade tree in the northern states, and rarely in western and northern Europe.

2. Ulmus racemosa Thomas. Rock Elm. Cork Elm.

Ulmus Thomasii Sarg.

Leaves obovate to oblong-oval, rather abruptly narrowed at apex into a short broad point, equally or somewhat unequally rounded, cuneate or subcordate at base, and coarsely doubly serrate, when they unfold pilose on the upper surface and covered on the lower with soft white hairs, at maturity $2'$–$2\frac{1}{2}'$ long, $\frac{3}{4}'$–$1'$ wide, thick and firm, smooth, dark green and lustrous above, paler and soft-pubescent below, especially on the stout midrib and the numerous straight veins running to the point of the teeth and connected by obscure cross veinlets; turning in the autumn bright clear yellow; petioles pubescent, about $\frac{1}{4}'$ in length; stipules ovate-lanceolate, conspicuously veined, light green, marked with dark red on the margins above the middle, $\frac{2}{3}'$ long, clasping the stem by their abruptly enlarged cordate base conspicuously dentate with 1–3 prominent teeth on each side, falling when the leaves are half grown. **Flowers** on elongated slender drooping pedicels often $\frac{1}{2}'$ long, in 2–4, usu-

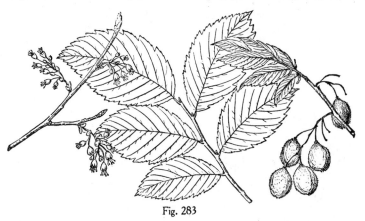

Fig. 283

ally in 3 flowered, puberulous cymes becoming more or less racemose by the lengthening of the axis of the inflorescence, and when fully grown sometimes $2'$ in length; calyx green, divided nearly to the middle into 7 or 8 rounded dark red scarious lobes; anthers dark purple; ovary coated with long pale hairs most abundant on the margins; styles light green. **Fruit** ripening when the leaves are about half grown, ovoid or obovoid-oblong, $\frac{1}{2}'$ long, with a shallow open notch at the apex, obscurely veined, pale pubescent, ciliate on the slightly thickened border of the broad wing, the margin of the seminal cavity scarcely thickened.

A tree, 80°–100° high, with a trunk occasionally 3° in diameter, and often free of branches for 60°, short stout spreading branches forming a narrow round-topped head, and slender rigid branchlets, light brown when they first appear, and coated with soft pale pubescence often persistent until their second season, becoming light reddish brown, puberulous or glabrous and lustrous in their first winter, and marked by scattered oblong lenticels and large orbicular or semiorbicular leaf-scars displaying an irregular row of 4–6 fibro-vascular bundle-scars, ultimately dark brown or ashy gray, and usually furnished with 3 or 4 thick corky irregular wings often $\frac{1}{2}'$ broad, and beginning to appear in their first or more often during their second year. **Winter-buds** ovoid, acute, $\frac{1}{4}'$ long, with broadly ovate rounded chestnut-brown scales pilose on the outer surface, ciliate on the margins, the inner scales becoming ovate-oblong to lanceolate, and $\frac{1}{2}'$ long, often dentate at the base, with 1 or 2 minute teeth on each side, bright green below the middle, marked with a red blotch above, and white and scarious at the apex. **Bark** $\frac{3}{4}'$–$1'$ thick, gray tinged with red, and deeply divided by wide irregular interrupted fissures into broad flat ridges broken on the surface into large irregularly shaped scales. **Wood** heavy, hard, very strong and tough, close-grained, light clear brown often tinged with red, with thick lighter colored sapwood; largely employed in the manufacture of many agricultural implements, for the framework of chairs, hubs of wheels, railway-ties, the sills of buildings, and other purposes demanding toughness, solidity and flexibility.

Distribution. Dry gravelly uplands, low heavy clay soils, rocky slopes and river cliffs; Province of Quebec westward through Ontario, the southern peninsula of Michigan and central Wisconsin to northeastern Nebraska, western Missouri and eastern Kansas, and southward to northern New Hampshire, southern Vermont, western New York, (valley of the Genessee River), northern New Jersey, southern Ohio (near Columbus, Franklin County), and central Indiana; rare in the east and toward the extreme western and southern limits of its range.

Occasionally planted as a shade and ornamental tree in the northern states.

3. Ulmus alata Michx. Wahoo. Winged Elm.

Leaves ovate-oblong to oblong-lanceolate, often somewhat falcate, acute or acuminate, unequally cuneate or rounded or subcordate at base, and coarsely doubly serrate with

Fig. 284

incurved teeth, when they unfold pale green often tinged with red, coated on the lower surface with soft white pubescence and glabrous or nearly so on the upper surface, at maturity thick and firm or subcoriaceous, dark green and smooth above, pale and soft-pubescent below, especially on the stout yellow midrib and numerous straight prominent veins often forked near the margins of the leaf and connected by rather conspicuous reticulate veinlets; turning yellow in the autumn; their petioles stout, pubescent, $\frac{1}{3}'$ in length; stipules linear-obovate, thin and scarious, tinged with red above the middle, often nearly 1' long. **Flowers** on drooping pedicels, in short few-flowered fascicles; calyx glabrous and divided nearly to the middle into 5 broad ovate rounded lobes as long as the hoary-tomentose ovary raised on a short slender stipe. **Fruit** ripening before or with the unfolding of the leaves, oblong, $\frac{1}{3}'$ in length, contracted at base into a long slender stalk, gradually narrowed and tipped at apex with long incurved awns, and covered with long white hairs most numerous on the thickened margin of the narrow wing; seed ovoid, pointed, $\frac{1}{8}'$ long, pale, chestnut-brown, slightly thickened into a narrow wing-like margin.

A tree, occasionally 80°–100° but usually not more than 40°–50° high, with a trunk 2°–3° in diameter, short stout straight or erect branches forming a narrow oblong rather open round-topped head, and slender branchlets glabrous or puberulous and light green tinged with red when they first appear, becoming light reddish brown or ashy gray and glabrous, or on vigorous individuals frequently pilose in their first winter, marked by occasional small orange-colored lenticels and by small elevated horizontal semiorbicular leaf-scars, sometimes naked, more often furnished with usually 2 thin corky wings beginning to grow during their first or more often during their second season, abruptly arrested at the nodes, often $\frac{1}{2}'$ wide, and persistent for many years. **Winter-buds** slender, acute, $\frac{1}{8}'$ long, dark chestnut-brown, with glabrous or puberulous scales, those of the inner ranks becoming oblong or obovate, rounded and tipped with a minute mucro, thin and scarious, light red, especially above the middle, and $\frac{1}{2}'$ long. **Bark** rarely exceeding $\frac{1}{4}'$ in thickness, light brown tinged with red, and divided by irregular shallow fissures into flat ridges covered by small closely appressed scales. **Wood** heavy, hard, not strong, close-grained, difficult to split, light brown, with thick lighter colored sapwood; sometimes employed for the hubs of wheels and the handles of tools. **Ropes** used for fastening the covers of cotton bales are sometimes made from the inner bark.

Distribution. Usually on dry gravelly uplands, less commonly in alluvial soil on the borders of swamps and the banks of streams, and occasionally in inundated swamps; southeastern Virginia, southwestern Indiana, southern Illinois (Richland and Johnson Counties) and southern Missouri, and southward to central Florida (Lake County), and the valley of the Guadalupe River, Texas; ranging westward in Oklahoma to Garfield County (near Kingfisher, *G. W. Stevens*).

Often planted as a shade-tree in the streets of towns and villages of the southern states,

4. Ulmus fulva Michx. Slippery Elm. Red Elm.

Leaves ovate-oblong, abruptly contracted into a long slender point, rounded at base on one side and short-oblique on the other, and coarsely doubly serrate with incurved

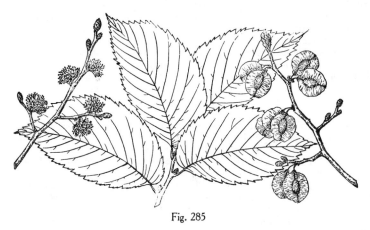

Fig. 285

callous-tipped teeth, when they unfold thin, coated below with pale pubescence, pilose above with scattered white hairs, at maturity thick and firm, dark green and rugose with crowded sharp-pointed tubercles pointing toward the apex of the leaf above, smooth, and coated below, especially on the thin midrib and in the axils of the slender straight veins with white hairs, $5'-7'$ long, $2'-3'$ wide; turning a dull yellow color in the autumn; petioles stout, pubescent, $\frac{1}{4}'$ in length; stipules obovate-oblong to oblong-lanceolate, thin and scarious, pale-pubescent, and tipped with clusters of rusty brown hairs. **Flowers** on short pedicels, in crowded fascicles; calyx green, covered with pale hairs, divided into 5-9 short rounded thin equal lobes; stamens with slender light yellow slightly flattened filaments and dark red anthers; stigmas slightly exserted, reddish purple, papillose with soft white hairs. **Fruit** ripening when the leaves are about half grown, semiorbicular, rounded and bearing the remnants of the styles or slightly emarginate at apex, rounded or cuneate at base, $\frac{1}{2}'$ broad, the seminal cavity coated with thick rusty brown tomentum, the broad thin wing obscurely reticulate-veined, naked on the thickened margin, and marked by the dark conspicuous horizontal line of union of the two carpels; seed ovoid, with a large oblique pale hilum, a light chestnut-brown coat produced into a thin border wider below than above the middle of the seed.

A tree, 60°–70° high, with a trunk occasionally 2° in diameter, spreading branches forming a broad open flat-topped head, and stout branchlets bright green, scabrate, and coated with soft pale pubescence when they first appear, becoming light brown by midsummer, often roughened by small pale lenticels, and in their first winter ashy gray, orange color or light red-brown, and marked by large elevated semiorbicular leaf-scars showing the ends of 3 conspicuous equidistant fibro-vascular bundles, ultimately dark gray or brown. **Winter-buds** ovoid, obtuse, $\frac{1}{4}'$ long, with about 12 scales, the outer broadly ovate, rounded, dark chestnut-brown, and covered by long scattered rusty hairs, the inner when fully grown $\frac{1}{2}'$ long, $\frac{1}{8}'-\frac{1}{4}'$ wide, light green, strap-shaped, rounded and tipped at the apex with tufts of rusty hairs, puberulous on the outer surface, slightly ciliate on the margins, gradually growing narrower and passing into the stipules of the upper leaves. **Bark** frequently 1′ thick, dark brown tinged with red, divided by shallow fissures and covered by large thick appressed scales. **Wood** heavy, hard, strong, very close-grained, durable, easy to split, dark brown or red, with thin lighter colored sapwood; largely used for fence-posts, railway-ties, the sills of buildings, the hubs of wheels, and in agricultural implements. The thick fragrant inner bark is mucilaginous and demulcent, and is employed in the treatment of acute febrile and inflammatory affections.

Distribution. Banks of streams and low rocky hillsides in deep rich soil; comparatively common in the valley of the St. Lawrence River, Province of Quebec, and through Ontario to northern and eastern South Dakota, northeastern and eastern Nebraska, southeastern Kansas, and Oklahoma to the valley of the Canadian River (McClain County), and southward to western Florida, central Alabama and Mississippi, western Louisiana and the valley of the upper Guadalupe (Kerr County) and Leon Rivers (Comal County), Texas; in the South Atlantic states not common and mostly confined to the middle districts, ascending to altitudes of 2000° on the southern Appalachian foothills.

5. Ulmus crassifolia Nutt. Cedar Elm.

Leaves elliptic to ovate, acute or rounded at apex, unequally rounded or cuneate and often oblique at base, coarsely and unequally doubly serrate with callous-tipped teeth, when they unfold thin, light green tinged with red, pilose above and covered below with soft pale pubescence, at maturity thick and subcoriaceous, dark green, lustrous and roughened by crowded minute sharp-pointed tubercles on the upper surface and soft pubescent on the lower surface, 1′–2′ long, $\frac{1}{2}'-1'$ wide, with a stout yellow midrib, and prominent straight veins connected by conspicuous more or less reticulate cross veinlets; usually turning bright yellow late in the autumn; petioles stout, tomentose, $\frac{1}{4}'-\frac{1}{2}'$ in length; stipules $\frac{1}{2}'$ long, linear-lanceolate, red and scarious above, clasping the stem by their green and hairy bases, deciduous when the leaves are about half grown. **Flowers** usually opening in August and sometimes also in October, on slender pedicels $\frac{1}{3}'-\frac{1}{2}'$ long and covered with white hairs, in 3–5-flowered pedunculate fascicles; calyx divided to below the middle into oblong pointed lobes hairy at base; ovary hirsute, crowned with two short slightly exserted stigmas. **Fruit** ripening in September and rarely also in November, oblong, gradually and often irregularly narrowed from the middle to the ends, short-stalked, deeply notched at apex, $\frac{1}{3}'$ to nearly $\frac{1}{2}'$ long, covered with soft white hairs, most abundant on the slightly thickened margin of the broad wing; seed oblique, pointed, and covered by a dark chestnut-brown coat.

A tree, often 80° high, with a tall straight trunk 2°–3° in diameter, sometimes free **of** branches for 30° or 40°, divided into numerous stout spreading limbs forming a broad inversely conic round-topped head of long pendulous branches, or while young or on dry uplands a compact round head of drooping branches, and slender branchlets, tinged with red and coated with soft pale pubescence when they first appear, becoming light reddish brown, puberulous and marked by scattered minute lenticels and by small elevated semiorbicular leaf-scars showing the ends of 3 small fibro-vascular bundles, and furnished with 2 corky wings covered with lustrous brown bark, about $\frac{1}{4}'$ broad and continuous except when abruptly interrupted by lateral branchlets, or often irregularly developed. **Winter-buds** broadly ovoid, acute, $\frac{1}{8}'$ long, with closely imbricated chestnut-brown scales slightly puberu-

Fig. 286

lous on the outer surface, those of the inner ranks at maturity oblong, concave, rounded at apex, thin, bright red, sometimes $\frac{3}{4}'$ long. **Bark** sometimes nearly 1' thick, light brown slightly tinged with red, and deeply divided by interrupted fissures into broad flat ridges broken on the surface into thick scales. **Wood** heavy, hard, strong, brittle, light brown tinged with red, with thick lighter colored sapwood; in central Texas used in the manufacture of the hubs of wheels, for furniture, and largely for fencing.

Distribution. Valley of the Sunflower River, Mississippi (Moorhead, Sunflower County), and western Louisiana (very common in Rayville, Natchitoches Parish (*R. S. Cocks*), through southern Arkansas, and Texas to Nuevo Leon, ranging in western Texas from the coast to the valley of the Pecos River; in Arkansas usually on river cliffs and low hillsides, and in Texas near streams in deep alluvial soil and on dry limestone hills; the common Elm-tree of Texas and of its largest size on the bottom-lands of the Guadalupe and Trinity Rivers.

Occasionally planted as a shade-tree in the streets of the cities and towns of Texas.

6. Ulmus serotina Sarg. Red Elm.

Leaves oblong to oblong-obovate, acuminate, very oblique at base, coarsely and doubly crenulate-serrate, when they unfold coated below with shining white hairs and puberulous above, at maturity thin and firm in texture, yellow-green, glabrous and lustrous on the upper surface, pale and puberulous on the midrib and principal veins below, 2'–4' long, 1'–$1\frac{3}{4}'$ wide, with a prominent yellow midrib, about 20 pairs of primary veins extending obliquely to the points of the teeth and often forked near the margins of the leaf, and numerous reticular veinlets; turning clear orange-yellow in the autumn; petioles stout, about $\frac{1}{4}'$ in length; stipules abruptly narrowed from broad clasping bases, linear-lanceolate, usually about $\frac{1}{4}'$ long, persistent until the leaves are nearly fully grown. **Flowers** opening in

September on slender conspicuously jointed pedicels often $\frac{1}{8}'$ long, in many-flowered glabrous racemes from $1'-1\frac{1}{2}'$ in length; calyx 6-parted to the base, with oblong-obovate red-
brown divisions rounded at apex; ovary sessile, narrowed below, villose. **Fruit** ripening
early in November, stipitate, oblong-elliptic, deeply divided at apex, fringed on the margins with long silvery white hairs, about $\frac{1}{2}'$ long.

A tree, $50°-60°$ high, with a trunk $2°-3°$ in diameter, comparatively small spreading
or pendulous branches often forming a broad handsome head, and slender pendulous
branchlets glabrous or occasionally puberulous when they first appear, brown, lustrous,
and marked by occasional oblong white lenticels during their first year, becoming darker

Fig. 287

the following season and ultimately dark gray-brown, and often furnished with 2 or 3
thick corky wings developed during their second or third years. **Winter-buds** ovoid,
acute, $\frac{1}{4}'$ long, their outer scales oblong-obovate, dark chestnut-brown, glabrous, the inner
often scarious on the margins, pale yellow-green, lustrous and sometimes $\frac{3}{4}'$ long when fully
grown. **Bark** $\frac{1}{4}'-\frac{3}{8}'$ thick, light brown slightly tinged with red, and divided by shallow fissures into broad flat ridges broken on the surface into large thin closely appressed scales.
Wood hard, close-grained, very strong and tough, light red-brown, with pale yellow sapwood.

Distribution. Limestone hills and river banks; rare and local; eastern (near Pikeville,
Pike County) and southern Kentucky (Bowling Green, Warren County); banks of the
Cumberland River, near Clarksville and Nashville, Tennessee; northeastern Georgia (cliffs
of the Coosa River, near Rome, Floyd County); northern Alabama (Madison, Jefferson
and Tuscaloosa Counties); valley of the Arkansas River (near Van Buren, Crawford
County, *G. M. Brown*) and northwestern Arkansas (Sulphur Springs, Benton County,
and Boston Mountains near Jasper, Newton County, *E. J. Palmer*); eastern Oklahoma (near
Muskogee, Muskogee County, *B. H. Slavin*); southwestern (Grand Tower, Jackson
County, *H. A. Gleason*) and southern Illinois (Richland County, *R. Ridgway*).

Occasionally planted as a shade-tree in the streets of cities in northern Georgia and
northern Alabama; hardy in eastern Massachusetts.

2. PLANERA Gmel.

A tree, with scaly puberulous branchlets roughened by scattered pale lenticels, and
at the end of their first season by small nearly orbicular leaf-scars marked by a row of
fibro-vascular bundle-scars, minute subglobose winter-buds covered by numerous thin

closely imbricated chestnut-brown scales, the outer more or less scarious on the margins, the inner accrescent, becoming at maturity ovate-oblong, scarious, bright red, $\frac{1}{3}'-\frac{1}{2}'$ long, marking in falling the base of the branchlet with pale ring-like scars. Leaves alternate, 2-ranked, ovate-oblong, acute or rounded at the narrowed apex, unequally cuneate or rounded at base, coarsely crenately serrate with unequal gland-tipped teeth, with numerous straight conspicuous veins forked near the margin and connected by cross reticulate veinlets more conspicuous below than above, when they unfold puberulous on the lower and pilose on the upper surface, at maturity thick or subcoriaceous and scabrate; petiolate with slender terete puberulous petioles; stipules lateral, free, ovate, scarious, bright red. Flowers polygamo-monœcious, the staminate fascicled in the axils of the outer scales of leaf-bearing buds, short-pedicellate, the pistillate or perfect on elongated puberulous pedicels in the axils of the leaves of the year in 1–3-flowered fascicles; pedicels without bracts; calyx campanulate, divided nearly to the base into 4 or 5 lobes rounded at apex, greenish yellow often tinged with red; stamens inserted under the ovary in the pistillate flower, sometimes few or 0; filaments filiform, erect, exserted; anthers broadly ovate, emarginate, cordate; ovary ovoid, stipitate, glandular-tuberculate, narrowed into a short style divided into 2 elongated reflexed stigmas papillo-stigmatic on the inner face, 0 in the staminate flower; ovule anatropous; micropyle extrorse, superior. Fruit an oblong oblique drupe, narrowed below into a short stipe, inclosed at the base by the withered calyx, crowned by the remnants of the style, its pericarp crustaceous, prominently ribbed on the anterior and posterior faces, irregularly tuberculate with elongated projections, and light chestnut-brown; seed ovoid, oblique, pointed at apex, rounded below, without albumen; testa thin, lustrous, dark brown or nearly black, of two coats; raphe inconspicuous; embryo erect; cotyledons thick, unequal, bright orange color, the apex of the larger hooded and slightly infolding the smaller, much longer than the minute radicle turned toward the linear pale hilum.

The genus is represented by a single species.

The generic name is in memory of Johann Jacob Planer, a German botanist and physician of the eighteenth century.

1. Planera aquatica Gmel. Water Elm.

Leaves $2'-2\frac{1}{2}'$ long, $\frac{3}{4}'-1'$ wide, on petioles varying from $\frac{1}{8}'-\frac{1}{4}'$ in length, dark dull green on the upper surface, paler on the lower surface, with a yellow midrib and veins. **Flowers** appearing with the leaves. **Fruit** ripening in April, $\frac{1}{3}'$ long.

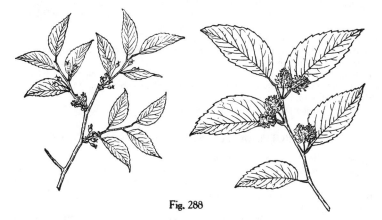

Fig. 288

A tree, 30°–40° high, with a short trunk rarely exceeding 20' in diameter, rather slender spreading branches forming a low broad head, and branchlets brown tinged with red when they first appear, dark red in their first winter, and ultimately reddish brown or ashy gray. **Bark** about $\frac{1}{4}'$ thick, light brown or gray, separating into large scales disclosing in falling the red-brown inner bark. **Wood** light, soft, not strong, close-grained, light brown, with thick nearly white sapwood of 20–30 layers of annual growth.

Distribution. Swamps covered with water during several months of the year, or low river banks; valley of the Cape Fear River, North Carolina, southward to northern Florida (Bradford County) and westward usually not far from the coast through the Gulf states to the valleys of the Navasota (Brazos County) and of the Colorado (Matagorda County) Rivers, Texas, and northward through western Louisiana, eastern Oklahoma, and Arkansas to southeastern Missouri, northeastern Mississippi (near Iuka, Tishomingo County, *T. G. Harbison*), northern Kentucky (Henderson County), and the valley of the lower Wabash River, Illinois; comparatively rare and confined to the coast plain in the Atlantic states; abundant and of its largest size in western Louisiana and southern Arkansas.

3. CELTIS L.

Trees or shrubs, with thin, smooth often more or less muricate bark, unarmed or spinose branchlets, and scaly buds. Leaves serrate or entire, 3-nerved in one species, membranaceous or subcoriaceous, deciduous; stipules lateral, free, usually scarious, inclosing their leaf in the bud, caducous. Flowers polygamo-monœcious or rarely monœcious, appearing soon after the unfolding of the leaves, minute, pedicellate, on branches of the year, the staminate cymose or fascicled at their base, the pistillate solitary or in few-flowered fascicles from the axils of upper leaves; calyx divided nearly to the base into 4 or 5 lobes, greenish yellow, deciduous; stamens inserted on the margin of the discoid torus; filaments subulate, incurved in the bud, those of the sterile flower straightening themselves abruptly and becoming erect and exserted, shorter and remaining incurved in the perfect flower; anthers ovoid, attached on the back just above the emarginate base; ovary ovoid, sessile, green and lustrous, crowned with a short sessile style divided into diverging elongated reflexed acuminate entire lobes papillo-stigmatic on the inner face and mature before the anthers of the sterile flower, deciduous; minute and rudimentary in the staminate flower; ovule anatropous. Fruit an ovoid or globose drupe tipped with the remnants of the style, with thin flesh covered by a thick firm skin, and a thick-walled bony nutlet, reticulate-pitted in the American species. Seed filling the seminal cavity; albumen scanty, gelatinous, nearly inclosed between the folds of the cotyledons, or 0; testa membranaceous, of 2 confluent coats; chalaza colored, close to the minute hilum; embryo curved; cotyledons broad, foliaceous, conduplicate or rarely flat, variously folded, corrugate, incumbent, or inclosing the short superior ascending radicle.

Celtis is widely distributed through the temperate and tropical regions of the world, fifty or sixty species being distinguished.

Trees of the American species are often disfigured by gall-making insects which distort the buds and cause the production of dark broom-like clusters of short slender branchlets at the end of the branches.

Celtis was the classical name of a species of Lotus.

CONSPECTUS OF THE NORTH AMERICAN SPECIES.

Fruit on pedicels much longer than the petioles.
    Leaves not covered below with conspicuous reticulate veinlets, green on both surfaces, smooth or rough above; fruit dark purple.   **1. C. occidentalis.**
    Leaves covered below with a network of prominent veinlets, usually rough above.
        Leaves pale on the lower surface.
            Leaves broadly ovate, obliquely rounded at base, coarsely serrate, glabrous or slightly pilose below along the midrib and veins; fruit light orange-brown, the pedicels often 3 or 4 times longer than the petioles.   **2. C. Douglasii.**

Leaves oblong-ovate, mostly cordate or occasionally rounded at base, entire or slightly serrate toward the apex, covered below with pilose pubescence; fruit dark reddish brown, the pedicels usually not more than twice as long as the petioles.   3. **C. Lindheimeri.**

Leaves green on the lower surface, broadly ovate, obliquely rounded at base, entire, pubescent along the midrib and veins below, rarely smooth on the upper surface; fruit dark orange-red, the pedicels usually not more than twice as long as the petioles.   4. **C. reticulata.**

Fruit on pedicels shorter or only slightly longer than the petioles.

Leaves oblong-lanceolate, long-acuminate, unsymmetrically cuneate at base, often falcate, entire or more or less serrate, smooth or rarely roughened on the upper surface; fruit orange color or yellow, the pedicels shorter or somewhat longer than the petioles.   5. **C. laevigata.**

Leaves ovate-lanceolate, acute or acuminate, obliquely rounded at base, coarsely serrate or nearly entire, smooth or in var. *georgiana* roughened on the upper surface; fruit dark orange red, the pedicels usually shorter than the petioles.   6. **C. pumila.**

1. Celtis occidentalis L. Hackberry. Sugarberry.

Leaves ovate, short-acuminate or acute at apex, obliquely rounded at base, sharply serrate often only above the middle, thin, slightly pubescent below on the slender midrib and veins early in the season, becoming glabrous or nearly glabrous, $2\frac{1}{2}'-3\frac{1}{2}'$ long, $1\frac{1}{2}'-2'$

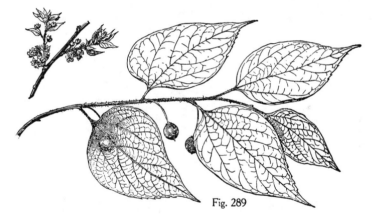

Fig. 289

wide; turning yellow late in the autumn; petioles slender, glabrous, $\frac{1}{4}'-\frac{1}{2}'$ in length. **Flowers** on drooping pedicels; calyx divided usually into 5 linear acute thin and scarious lobes rounded on the back, more or less laciniately cut, and often furnished with a tuft of pale hairs at apex; torus hoary-tomentose. **Fruit** on stems $\frac{1}{2}'-\frac{3}{4}'$ long, ripening in September and October and often remaining on the branches during the winter, subglobose, ovoid or obovoid, dark purple, $\frac{1}{3}'$ in diameter, with a thick tough skin, dark orange-colored flesh and a thick-walled oblong pointed light brown slightly rugose nutlet; **seed** pale brown.

A tree, rarely more than 40°–50° high with a trunk usually not more than 2° in diameter, spreading often pendulous branches forming a round-topped head, and slender ridged light brown glabrous branchlets marked by oblong pale lenticels, and by horizontal semioval or oblong leaf-scars showing the ends of three fibre-vascular bundles, becoming darker and in their second or third year often dark red-brown. **Winter-buds** ovoid, pointed, flattened, about $\frac{1}{4}'$ long, with three pairs of chestnut-brown ovate acute pubescent caducous scales closely imbricated in two ranks, increasing in size from without inward. **Bark** $1'-1\frac{1}{2}'$

thick, smooth, dark brown, and more or less thickly covered and roughened by irregular wart-like excrescences or by long ridges also found on the large branches. Wood heavy, rather soft, not strong, coarse-grained, clear light yellow, with thick lighter-colored sapwood; used for fencing and in the manufacture of cheap furniture.

Distribution. Rocky hills and ridges; New England (rare) to Virginia and westward to Iowa, eastern North Dakota, southwestern Missouri and northwestern Kansas.

Often planted in some of its forms as a shade and ornamental tree in the towns of the Mississippi valley and occasionally in the eastern states and in Europe.

Well distinguished by its large dark fruit, *Celtis occidentalis* is so variable in the shape of its leaves that two principal varieties are described as follows:

Celtis occidentalis var. canina Sarg. Hackberry.

Celtis canina Raf.

Leaves oblong-ovate, gradually narrowed into a long acuminate point, obliquely rounded or unsymmetrically cuneate at base, finely serrate, glabrous or rarely pilose along the midrib and veins below, $2\frac{1}{2}'$–6′ long and $\frac{3}{4}'$–$2\frac{1}{2}'$ wide; petioles slender, glabrous or rarely pubescent, $\frac{1}{2}'$–$\frac{3}{4}'$ long.

Fig. 290

A tree, often 80°–100° high; more common than the other forms of *Celtis occidentalis*.

Distribution. Rich wooded slopes and bottoms, or eastward on rocky ridges; Province of Quebec to eastern Nebraska, and southward to the coast of Massachusetts, western New York, southern Ohio, southern Indiana and Illinois, southwestern Missouri, southwestern Oklahoma (Snyder, Kiowa County), and in northwestern Georgia.

Celtis occidentalis var. crassifolia A. Gray. Hackberry.

Celtis crassifolia Lam.

Leaves thicker, long-acuminate, obliquely rounded at base, usually more coarsely serrate, rarely nearly entire, rough on the upper surface, pilose below along the prominent midrib and veins, $3\frac{1}{2}'$–5′ long, $2'$–$2\frac{1}{2}'$ wide, much smaller in the Rocky Mountain region; petioles villose-pubescent, rarely glabrous, $\frac{1}{4}'$–$\frac{1}{2}'$ in length, much shorter than the pubescent pedicels of the fruit.

A tree, 100°–120° high; with pubescent or glabrous branchlets; rarely shrubby. The most widely distributed form of *Celtis occidentalis*.

Distribution. Wooded slopes and rich bottoms; Virginia and along the Appalachian Mountains to North Carolina and westward to southern Minnesota, Missouri, central

Kansas, eastern and northwestern Oklahoma, central Nebraska, North and South Dakota, cañons of the Big Horn Mountains, Wyoming, and northwestern Idaho, and southward to Dallas County, Alabama, and eastern Texas.

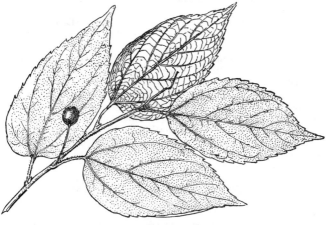

Fig. 291

Often cultivated in towns of the Mississippi Valley and in western Europe, and occasionally in the eastern states.

2. Celtis Douglasii Plan. Hackberry.

Celtis rugulosa Rydb.

Leaves broadly ovate to oblong-ovate, acuminate, obliquely rounded or unsymmetrically subcordate at base, coarsely serrate, rough on the upper surface, pale and covered below

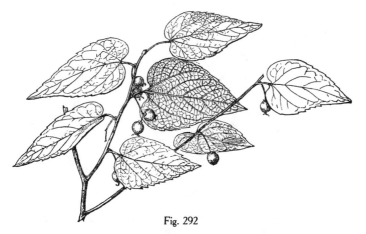

Fig. 292

with a network of reticulate veinlets inconspicuous early in the season, later becoming prominent, glabrous or sparingly pilose along the under side of the stout midrib and primary veins, $2'$–$2\frac{1}{2}'$ long, $1'$–$2'$ wide; petioles stout, slightly pubescent, $\frac{1}{4}'$–$\frac{1}{2}'$ in length. **Flowers** on slender pubescent pedicels; calyx divided into five linear acute scarious lobes laciniately cut at apex; torus hoary-tomentose. **Fruit** on slender drooping slightly pubescent or glabrous pedicels, $\frac{1}{3}'$–$\frac{1}{2}'$ in length, subglobose to ellipsoid, light orange-brown, lustrous, $\frac{1}{3}'$ in diameter.

A small tree or shrub rarely more than $20'$ high, with slender slightly pubescent or glabrous red-brown branchlets marked by small pale lenticels, becoming ashy gray in their second or third year. **Bark** rough, red-brown or gray.

Distribution. Dry hillsides and rocky river banks; eastern Oregon from the valley of the Deschutes and Columbia Rivers to the cañon of Snake River, Whitman County, Washington, and to Big Willow Creek, Cañon County, western Idaho; on the western foothills of the Wasatch Mountains, in the cañon of Grand River, and in Diamond Valley, Utah; southern California, near Independence, Inyo County, Hackberry Cañon, Kern County, and Things Valley at base of Laguna Mountain, near Campo, southern San Diego County; on Cedros Island, and in northern Lower California; rim of the Grand Cañon, Arizona, and on the eastern foothills of the Rocky Mountains of Colorado.

Occasionally planted in the towns of western Washington, and when cultivated said to grow in good soil into a larger and more shapely tree with thinner leaves.

3. Celtis Lindheimeri K. Koch. Palo Blanco.

Celtis Helleri Small.

Leaves oblong-ovate, acuminate or acute, cordate or obliquely cordate or rounded at base, entire, or crenately serrate on vigorous shoots, rough above, pale and clothed below with white hairs, becoming by midsummer thick and covered below with a conspicuous network of reticulate veinlets, $1\frac{1}{2}'$–$3'$ long, $\frac{3}{4}'$–$2'$ wide; petioles densely villose-pubescent,

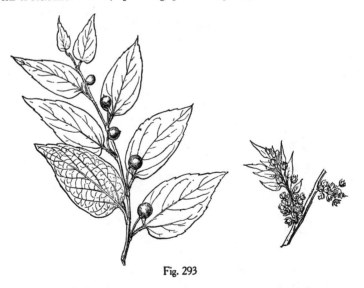

Fig. 293

$\frac{1}{4}'$–$\frac{1}{2}'$ in length. **Flowers** opening toward the end of March on pubescent pedicels; calyx divided into five oblong scarious lobes narrowed and rounded at apex; torus tomentose. **Fruit** on slender tomentose stems $\frac{1}{4}'$–$\frac{2}{3}'$ long, ripening in September and persistent on the branches until spring, subglobose to ellipsoid, dark reddish brown, lustrous, $\frac{1}{4}'$ in diameter.

A tree, occasionally 30° high, with a trunk rarely more than 12′–18′ in diameter, stout spreading branches forming a broad open irregular head, and slender pubescent branchlets roughened by numerous small lenticels, becoming darker and glabrous in their second season. **Bark** of the trunk and large branches dark and covered with high thick wart-like excrescences and ridges. **Wood** not strong nor durable, of little value even for fuel.

Distribution. Rich bottom-lands and on low adjacent hills of streams flowing southward from the Edward's Plateau (Goliad, San Antonio, New Braunfels, San Marcos) and near Austin, Travis County, Texas.

4. Celtis reticulata Torr.   Hackberry.

Leaves broadly ovate, acute or acuminate, obliquely rounded at base, entire, thick, dark green and rough or rarely smooth on the upper surface, yellow-green and conspicuously reticulate-venulose and sparingly pilose along the prominent midrib and veins on

Fig. 294

the lower surface, $1\frac{1}{4}′$–$3′$ long, $\frac{3}{4}′$–$1\frac{1}{2}′$ wide; petioles stout, $\frac{1}{8}′$–$\frac{1}{4}′$ in length, more or less densely pubescent. **Flowers** not seen. **Fruit** on pubescent pedicels $\frac{1}{3}′$–$\frac{1}{2}′$ in length, ripening in September, subglobose to ellipsoid, orange-red or yellow, lustrous, $\frac{1}{4}′$ in diameter.

A tree, rarely 30° high with stout ascending branches forming an open irregular head, and slender red-brown branchlets tomentose or pubescent early in their first season and pubescent or glabrous in their second year; or often a shrub. **Bark** thick and rough.

Distribution. Dry limestone hillsides, rocky ridges and cañon slopes, western Texas, from the valley of the upper Rio Frio, Uvalde County, to Oklahoma (Ozark region, near Page, Le Flore County to the southwestern borders of the state); in mountain ravines through southern New Mexico, and in southern central and northeastern Arizona.

A variety with more pubescent serrate leaves, those on vigorous shoots mostly cordate at base and covered above with short white hairs, is distinguished as var. *vestita* Sarg. A small tree with slender pubescent branchlets and a trunk 12′–15′ in diameter. In low ground, along the North Fork of the Canadian River, near Canton, Blaine County, Oklahoma.

5. Celtis laevigata Willd.   Sugarberry.   Hackberry.
Celtis mississippiensis Spach.

Leaves oblong-lanceolate, long-pointed and acuminate at apex, unsymmetrically rounded or cuneate or obliquely cuneate at base, often falcate, entire or furnished with a few teeth near the apex or serrate (var. *Smallii* Sarg.), thin, smooth, glabrous or rarely rough above, light green on both surfaces, $2\frac{1}{2}′$–$5′$ long and $\frac{3}{4}′$–$1\frac{1}{2}′$ wide, with a narrow yellow midrib, slender veins arcuate and united near the margins, and inconspicuous reticulate veinlets; petioles slender, glabrous, $\frac{1}{4}'-\frac{1}{2}'$ in length.   **Flowers** on slender glabrous pedicels; calyx divided into five ovate-lanceolate glabrous or puberulous scarious lobes furnished at apex with tufts of long white hairs.   **Fruit** on glabrous pedicels shorter or slightly longer than the petioles, ripening in September, short-oblong to ellipsoid or obovoid, orange-red or yellow, $\frac{1}{4}'$ in diameter; nutlet slightly rugose.

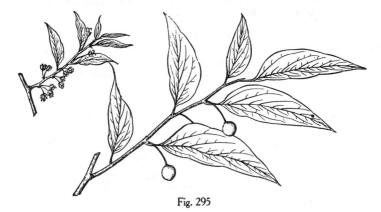

Fig. 295

A tree, 60°–80° high, with a trunk 2°–3° in diameter, spreading or pendulous branches forming a broad head, and slender branchlets light green, glabrous or pubescent when they first appear, and during their first winter bright reddish brown, rather lustrous and marked by oblong pale lenticels and narrow elevated horizontal leaf-scars showing the ends of three fibro-vascular bundles; often much smaller.   **Winter-buds** ovoid, pointed, $\frac{1}{16}'-\frac{1}{8}'$ long, with chestnut-brown puberulous scales.   **Bark** $\frac{1}{2}'-\frac{2}{3}'$ thick, pale gray and covered with prominent excrescences.   **Wood** soft, not strong, close-grained, light yellow, with thick lighter-colored sapwood; commercially confounded with the wood of *Celtis occidentalis* and its varieties, and used for the same purposes.

Distribution.   Coast of Virginia to the Everglades Keys of southern Florida, through the Gulf states to the valley of the lower Rio Grande in Nuevo Leon, and through eastern Texas, Arkansas and Missouri to eastern Oklahoma to the valley of the Washita River (Zarvin County) and to Kiowa County, eastern Kansas, central Tennessee and Kentucky, and to southern Illinois and Indiana; in Bermuda.

Often planted as a shade and street tree in the valley of the Mississippi River and in Texas.

An arborescent form from the rocky banks of the Nueces River, western Texas, with shorter and thicker leaves is distinguished as var. *brachyphylla* Sarg.; and a small shrubby form with oblong-ovate cordate leaves and dark purplish fruit covered with a glaucous bloom, growing in deep sand in Callihan County, Texas, has been described as var. *anomala* Sarg.   An Arizona form is

Celtis laevigata var. brevipes Sarg.

Celtis brevipes S. Wats.

Leaves ovate, acuminate, unsymmetrically rounded or cuneate at base, entire or rarely furnished with occasional teeth, glabrous, dark green and smooth on the upper surface, yellow-green on the lower surface, with small clusters of pale hairs in the axils of the slender veins, and inconspicuous reticulate veinlets, $1\frac{1}{2}'-2'$ long, $\frac{3}{4}'-1'$ wide; petioles slender, puberulous, $\frac{1}{4}'-\frac{1}{3}'$ in length. **Fruit** on glabrous pedicels shorter or slightly longer than the petioles, short-oblong, canary yellow, about $\frac{1}{4}'$ long.

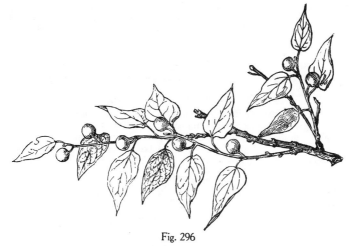

Fig. 296

A small tree with slender glabrous red-brown branchlets.
Distribution. Central and southern Arizona.
More distinct is the common Celtis of western Texas which has been described as

Celtis laevigata var. texana Sarg.

Leaves ovate to lanceolate, acuminate, unsymmetrically rounded or cordate at base, entire or sparingly and irregularly serrate, often subcoriaceous, dark green, smooth and granulate or rarely rough above, green below, with a slender midrib and primary veins glabrous or sparingly villose-pubescent and furnished with small tufts of axillary hairs, and only slightly raised reticulate veinlets, $1\frac{1}{2}'-3'$ long and $\frac{3}{4}'-1\frac{1}{2}'$ wide; petioles slender,

Fig. 297

pale pubescent, $\frac{1}{5}'-\frac{1}{4}'$ in length. **Fruit** on glabrous or puberulous pedicels slightly longer than the petioles, subglobose but rather longer than broad, dark orange-red, about $\frac{1}{4}'$ long.

An arborescent shrub or small tree rarely more than $25°$ high, with slender reddish glabrous or gray-brown pubescent branchlets; often growing in clusters. **Bark** rough, pale or grayish and not often covered with wart-like excrescences.

Distribution. Rocky bluffs near Dallas to New Braunfels, Texas, and westward to western Oklahoma, and southern New Mexico; in southwestern Missouri; in Tamaulipas and Coahuila, Mexico.   The common Celtis of the Texas Panhandle.

A shrubby form from Nolan County, Texas, with red-brown branchlets densely pubescent in their first season, becoming puberulous during their second year, and smaller leaves with more prominent reticulate veinlets, on densely pubescent petioles, is distinguished as forma *microphylla* Sarg.

6. Celtis pumila Pursh.

This shrub of the eastern states is sometimes a small tree in its southern variety,

Celtis pumila var. georgiana Sarg.

Leaves ovate, acute or acuminate, obliquely rounded at base, entire or sharply serrate, especially on vigorous leading shoots, thin, dark green and rough on the upper surface, pale and more or less pubescent or nearly glabrous along the midrib and veins below, $1\frac{1}{2}'-2\frac{1}{2}'$ long and $\frac{3}{4}'-1\frac{1}{2}'$ wide; petioles slender, pubescent, $\frac{1}{8}'-\frac{1}{4}'$ in length.   Flowers on pubescent pedicels; calyx divided into usually five lanceolate acuminate lobes; the disk

Fig. 298

pubescent.   Fruit on pubescent pedicels as long or slightly longer than the petioles, subglobose, reddish purple, often covered with a glaucous bloom, $\frac{1}{3}'$ in diameter; nutlet covered with conspicuous reticulate ridges.

A shrub or small tree occasionally 30° high, with slender dark red-brown pubescent branchlets, light red-brown and sometimes bright red-brown before the end of their first year.

Distribution.   Piedmont region of North and South Carolina, central Georgia to western Florida; and Dallas County, Alabama; in southern Missouri, and southern Illinois.

4. TREMA Lour.

Unarmed trees and shrubs with watery juices and terete branchlets.   Leaves alternate, often two-ranked, serrate, penniveined, three-nerved from the base, short-petiolate, persistent; stipules lateral, free, usually small, caducous.   Flowers apetalous, small, monœcious, diœcious or rarely perfect, in axillary cymes; calyx five or rarely four-parted, the lobes induplicate, valvate or slightly imbricated in the bud, or in perfect flowers more or less concave and induplicate; stamens five or rarely four, opposite the calyx-lobes and inserted on their base, occasionally present in the pistillate flower; filaments short, erect; anthers oblong, attached on the back near the base, introrse, two-celled, the cells opening longitudinally; ovary sessile, rudimentary or wanting in the staminate flower; style central, slightly or entirely divided into two linear fleshy stigmatic branches; ovule solitary, pendulous from the apex of the cell, anatropous; micropyle superior. Fruit drupaceous, short-oblong to subglobose, crowned by the persistent style; exocarp more or less fleshy; endocarp hard; seed filling the cavity of the nutlet; testa membranaceous, albumen fleshy, often scanty; embryo curved or slightly involute; cotyledons narrow; radicle incurved, ascending.

Trema, with about twenty species, is widely distributed in tropical and subtropical regions of the two hemispheres. Two species reach the coast region and the keys of southern Florida. Of these *Trema mollis* Lour. is a small tree, and *Trema Lamarckiana* Bl., which in Florida has been noticed only on Key Largo, where it grows as a small shrub, is widely distributed over the Bahamas and many of the West Indian islands.

1. Trema mollis Lour.

Trema floridana Britt.

Leaves 2-ranked, ovate, abruptly acuminate at apex, rounded, cordate and often oblique at base, finely serrate with incurved or rounded apiculate teeth, dark green and scabrate above, covered with pale tomentum below, 3'–4' long, 1'–2½' wide; petioles stout, tomen-

Fig. 299

tose, about ⅖' in length; stipules narrow, acuminate, covered with long white hairs, about one third as long as the petioles. **Flowers** in early spring, subtended by minute scarious deciduous bracts on short slender pedicels in bisexual many-flowered pedunculate villose cymes about as long as the petioles; calyx 5-lobed, the lobes oblong, acute and incurved at apex, villose on the outer surface; staminate with glabrous filaments and slightly exserted yellow anthers; pistillate with a style divided to the base. **Fruit** short-oblong, pale yellowish brown, ⅙'–⅕' in diameter.

A fast-growing short-lived tree, in Florida occasionally 25°–30° high, with a tall trunk 1½'–2½' in diameter, small crowded branches ascending at narrow angles, and stout hoary-tomentose red-brown 2-ranked branchlets. **Bark** thin, chocolate-brown, roughened by numerous small wart-like excrescences, and separating into small appressed papery scales.

Distribution. Rich hummocks; near the shores of Bay Biscayne, in the Everglades, and on the southern keys, Florida; common; noticed by R. M. Harper with many specimens in a large dense Palmetto grove a few miles north of Immokalee, Collier County; often springing up where the ground has been burned over, or otherwise cleared of its forests; on many of the West Indian islands and in Mexico.

XII. MORACEÆ.

Tree or shrubs, with milky juice, scaly or naked buds, and stalked alternate simple leaves with stipules. Flowers monœcious or diœcious, in ament-like spikes, or in heads on the outside of a receptacle or on the inside of a closed receptacle; calyx of the staminate flower 2-6-lobed or parted; stamens 1-4, inserted on the base of the calyx; calyx of the pistillate flower of 2-6 partly united sepals; ovary 1-2-celled; styles 1 or 2; ovule pendulous. Fruits drupaceous, inclosed in the thickened calyx of the flower and united into a compound fruit (*syncarp*). The Mulberry family is widely distributed with fifty-four genera confined largely to the warmer parts of the world. Three genera only, all arborescent, are indigenous in North America, although *Broussonetia papyrifera* Vent., the Paper Mulberry, a tree related to the Mulberry and a native of eastern Asia, and the Hop and the Hemp are more or less generally naturalized in the eastern and southern states.

CONSPECTUS OF THE NORTH AMERICAN GENERA.

Flowers on the outside of the receptacle; buds scaly.
    Flowers in ament-like spikes; syncarp oblong and succulent.   1. **Morus.**
    Staminate flowers racemose, the pistillate capitate; syncarp dry and globose.
                                         2. **Maclura.**
Flowers on the inside of a closed receptacle; buds naked; syncarp subglobose to ovoid,
    succulent.   3. **Ficus.**

1. MORUS L. Mulberry.

Trees or shrubs, with slender terete unarmed branches prolonged by one of the upper axillary buds, scaly bark, fibrous roots, and winter-buds covered by ovate scales closely imbricated in 2 ranks, increasing in size from without inward, the inner accrescent, marking in falling the base of the branch with ring-like scars. Leaves conduplicate in the bud, alternate, serrate, entire or 3-lobed, 3-5-nerved at base, membranaceous or subcoriaceous, deciduous; stipules inclosing their leaf in the bud, lateral, lanceolate, acute, caducous. Flowers monœcious or diœcious, the staminate and pistillate on different branches of the same plant or on different plants, minute, vernal, in pedunculate clusters from the axils of caducous bud-scales or of the lower leaves of the year; staminate in elongated cylindric spikes, calyx deeply divided into 4 equal rounded lobes; stamens 4, inserted opposite the lobes of the calyx under the minute rudimentary ovary, filaments filiform, incurved in the bud, straightening elastically and becoming exserted, anthers attached on the back below the middle, introrse, 2-celled, the cells reniform, attached laterally to the orbicular connective, opening longitudinally; pistillate sessile, in short-oblong densely flowered spikes; calyx 4-parted, the lobes ovate or obovate, thickened, often unequal, the 2 outer broader than the others, persistent; ovary ovoid, flat, sessile, included in the calyx, crowned by a central style divided nearly to the base into 2 equal spreading filiform villose white stigmatic lobes; ovule suspended from the apex of the cell, campylotropous; micropyle superior. Drupes ovoid or obovoid, crowned with the remnants of the styles, inclosed in the succulent thickened and colored perianth of the flower and more or less united into a more or less juicy compound fruit; flesh subsucculent, thin; walls of the nutlet thin or thick, crustaceous. Seed oblong, pendulous; testa, thin, membranaceous; hilum minute, apical; embryo incurved in thick fleshy albumen; cotyledons oblong, equal; radicle ascending, incumbent.

Morus with eight or nine species is confined to eastern temperate North America, the elevated regions of Mexico, Central America and western South America, southern and western Asia, Indo-China, China, Japan, the Bonin Islands and the mountains of the Indian Archipelago. Two species occur in North America. The most valuable species, *Morus alba* L., a native of China and Formosa, and largely cultivated in many countries for its leaves, which are the best food of the silkworm, has been planted in large quantities in the eastern United States; and *Morus nigra* L., probably a native of Persia, has been introduced into the southern and Pacific states for its large dark-colored juicy fruit. Morus produces straight-grained durable light brown or orange-colored valuable wood, and sweet acidulous and refreshing fruits.

Morus is the classical name of the Mulberry-tree.

CONSPECTUS OF THE NORTH AMERICAN SPECIES.

Leaves coated below with pale pubescence; lobes of the stigma long; syncarp oblong, dark purple.   1. **M. rubra** (A, C).
Leaves glabrous or pubescent below; lobes of the stigma short; syncarp subglobose or short-ovoid, nearly black.   2. **M. microphylla** (C, E, H).

1. Morus rubra L.   Red Mulberry.

Leaves ovate, oblong-ovate or semiorbicular, abruptly contracted into a long broad point or acute at apex, more or less deeply cordate or occasionally truncate at base, coarsely and occasionally doubly serrate with incurved callous-tipped teeth, often, especially on

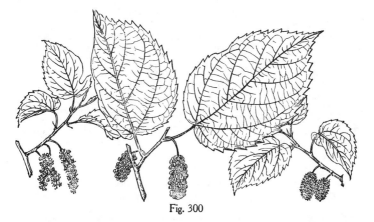

Fig. 300

vigorous young shoots, 3-lobed by broad deep oblique lateral rounded sinuses, when they unfold yellow-green, slightly pilose on the upper surface and hoary-tomentose on the lower surface, at maturity thin, dark bluish green, glabrous, smooth or scabrate above, pale and more or less pubescent below with short white hairs thickest on the orange-colored midrib, and on the primary veins arcuate and united near the margins and connected by reticulate veinlets, or sometimes hoary-tomentose below (var. *tomentosa* Bureau), 3′–5′ long, 2½′–4′ wide; turning bright yellow in the autumn; petioles stout, hoary-tomentose at first, becoming glabrous, ¾′–1¼′ in length; stipules lanceolate, acute, abruptly enlarged and thickened at base, sometimes tinged with red above the middle, coated with long white hairs, and often 1′ in length. **Flowers** appearing with the unfolding of the leaves; staminate in narrow spikes 2′–2½′ long, on stout light green peduncles covered with pale hairs; calyx divided nearly to the base into oblong concave lobes rounded at apex and hirsute on the outer surface; stamens with slightly flattened filaments narrowed from the base to the apex, and bright green anthers, their connectives orbicular, conspicuous, bright green; pistillate in oblong densely flowered spikes, 1' long, on short hairy peduncles, a few male flowers being sometimes mixed with them; calyx divided nearly to the base into 4 thick concave lobes rounded at apex, rounded or slightly keeled on the back, the 2 outer lobes twice as wide as the others, as long as and closely investing the glabrous light green ovary. **Fruit:** syncarp at first bright red when fully grown, $1'-1\frac{1}{4}'$ long, becoming dark purple or nearly black and sweet and juicy when fully ripe; drupes about $\frac{1}{32}'$ long, with a thin fleshy outer coat and a light brown nutlet; **seed** ovoid, acute, with a thin membranaceous light brown coat.

A tree, 60°–70° high, with a short trunk rarely exceeding 3°–4° in diameter, stout spreading smooth branches forming a dense broad round-topped shapely head, and slender slightly zigzag branchlets dark green often tinged with red, glabrous, more or less coated with pale pubescence, and covered with oblong straw-colored spots when they first appear, becoming in their first winter light red-brown to orange color and marked by pale lenticels and by large elevated horizontal nearly orbicular concave leaf-scars displaying a row of prominent fibro-vascular bundle-scars, and in their second and third years dark brown slightly tinged with red. **Winter-buds** ovoid, rounded or pointed at apex, $\frac{1}{4}'$ long, with 6 or 7 chestnut-brown scales, those of the outer rows broadly ovate, rounded, and slightly thickened on the back, puberulous, ciliate on the margins, and much shorter than those of the next rows, the inner scales scarious, coated with pale hairs, oblong-lanceolate, rounded or acute at apex, and $\frac{1}{2}'-\frac{2}{3}'$ long at maturity. **Bark** $\frac{1}{2}'-\frac{3}{4}'$ thick, dark brown tinged with red and divided into irregular elongated plates separating on the surface into thick appressed scales. **Wood** light, soft, not strong, rather tough, coarse-grained, very durable, light orange color, with thick lighter colored sapwood; largely used for fencing, in cooperage, and in boatbuilding.

Distribution. Intervales in rich soil and on low hills; western Massachusetts, Connecticut, and Long Island to southern Ontario, central Michigan, southeastern Minnesota, eastern Iowa, southeastern South Dakota, eastern Nebraska, central Kansas and Oklahoma, and southward to the shores of Bay Biscayne and Cape Romano, Florida, and to the cañon of the Devil's River, Valverde County, Texas; most abundant and of its largest size in the basin of the lower Ohio River and on the foothills of the southern Appalachian Mountains; ascending to altitudes of 2000°.

Occasionally planted, especially in the southern states, for its fruit valued for fattening hogs and as food for poultry. A few natural varieties, distinguished for the large size and good quality of their fruit, or for their productiveness, are occasionally propagated by pomologists.

2. Morus microphylla Buckl.   Mulberry.   Mexican Mulberry.

Morus celtidifolia Sarg. not H. B. K.

Leaves ovate, acute or acuminate, rounded or rarely truncate, or often on vigorous shoots cordate at the broad base, and 3-lobed with shallow lateral sinuses and broad coarsely serrate lobes, when they unfold coated below with pale tomentum, and puberulous above, at maturity thin and firm in texture, dark green and often roughened on the upper surface by minute pale tubercles, and paler, smooth or scabrate, and glabrous or coated with soft pubescence on the lower surface, and often hirsute with short stiff pale hairs on the broad orange-colored midrib, and on the primary veins connected by conspicuous reticulate veinlets, rarely more than $1\frac{1}{2}'$ long and $\frac{3}{4}'$ wide; turning yellow in the autumn; petioles slender, hoary-tomentose, becoming pubescent, $\frac{1}{3}'$ in length; stipules linear-lanceolate, acute, sometimes falcate, white and scarious, coated with soft pale tomentum, about $\frac{1}{2}'$ long. **Flowers** usually diœcious, staminate short-pedicellate, in short many-flowered spikes, $\frac{1}{2}'-\frac{3}{4}'$ long; calyx dark green, covered on the outer surface with soft pale hairs, deeply divided into equal rounded lobes reddish toward the apex; stamens with bright yellow anthers, their connectives conspicuous, dark green; pistillate sessile in few-flowered spikes, rarely $\frac{1}{3}'$ in length; calyx divided to the base into thick rounded lobes, the 2 outer lobes much broader than the others, dark green, covered with pale scattered hairs; ovary green and glabrous, with short stigmatic lobes. **Fruit:** syncarp $\frac{1}{2}'$ long, red becoming dark purple or nearly black, sweet and palatable; drupe $\frac{1}{6}'$ long, ovoid, rounded at the ends, with a thin fleshy outer covering and a thick-walled light brown nutlet; **seed** ovoid, pointed, pale yellow.

A tree, sometimes 15°–20° high, with a trunk occasionally 12′–14′ in diameter, and slender branchlets covered when they first appear with soft white hairs, soon becoming gla-

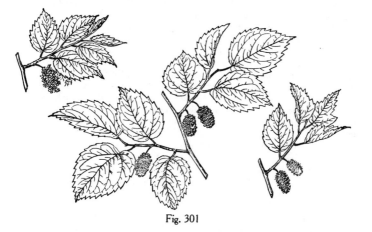

Fig. 301

brous or nearly so, and in their first winter light orange-red and marked by small lenticels and small horizontal nearly orbicular elevated concave leaf-scars displaying a ring of fibro-vascular bundle-scars; often a shrub. **Winter-buds** ovoid, acute, sharp-pointed, and covered by thin lustrous chestnut-brown ovate rounded scales scarious on the margins, those of the inner rows ovate-oblong, rounded at apex, pale-pubescent on the outer surface, and nearly 1′ long when fully grown. **Bark** smooth, sometimes nearly $\frac{1}{2}'$ thick but usually thinner, light gray slightly tinged with red, deeply furrowed and broken on the surface into slightly appressed scales. **Wood** heavy, hard, close-grained, dark orange color or sometimes dark brown, with thick light-colored sapwood.

Distribution. Dry limestone hills, or westward only in elevated mountain cañons in the neighborhood of streams; valley of the Colorado River, Texas, southward into Mexico and through the mountain regions of western Texas and southern New Mexico to the Santa Rita Mountains and the cañons of the Colorado Plateau, Arizona.

2. MACLURA Nutt.

Toxylon (Ioxylon) Rafn.

A tree, with thick milky slightly acrid juice, thick deeply furrowed dark orange-colored bark, stout tough terete pale branchlets, with thick orange-colored pith, lengthening by an upper axillary bud, marked by pale orange-colored lenticels and armed with stout straight axillary spines, short stout spur-like lateral branchlets from buds at the base of the spines, and thick fleshy roots covered by bright orange-colored bark exfoliating freely in long thin persistent papery scales. Leaves involute in the bud, ovate to oblong-lanceolate, acuminate and apiculate at apex, rounded, cuneate or subcordate at base, entire, penniveined, the veins arcuate near the margins and connected by conspicuous reticulate veinlets; petioles elongated, slender, terete, pubescent; stipules lateral, nearly triangular, minute, hoary-tomentose, caducous. Flowers diœcious, light green, minute, appearing in early summer; calyx 4-lobed, the lobes imbricated in æstivation; the staminate long-pedicellate, in short or ultimately elongated racemes borne on long slender drooping peduncles from the axils of crowded leaves on the spur-like branchlets of the previous year; calyx ovoid, gradually narrowed into the slender pubescent pedicel, coated on the outer surface with pale hairs, divided to the middle into equal acute boat-shaped lobes; stamens 4, inserted opposite the lobes of the calyx on the margins of the minute thin pulvinate disk; filaments flattened, light green, glabrous, infolded above the middle in the bud, with the anthers inverted and back to back, straightening abruptly in anthesis and becoming exserted; anthers oblong, attached on the back near the middle, introrse, 2-celled, the cells attached laterally to a minute oblong or semiorbicular connective, free and spreading above and below, opening by longitudinal lateral slits; pistillate sessile in dense globose many-flowered heads on short stout peduncles axillary on shoots of the year; calyx ovoid, divided to the base into oblong thick concave lobes, rounded, thickened, and covered with pale hairs at the apex, longer than the ovary and closely investing it, the 2 outer lobes much broader than the others, persistent and inclosing the fruit; ovary ovoid, compressed, sessile, green, and glabrous; style covered by elongated slender filiform white stigmatic hairs; ovule suspended from the apex of the cell, anatropous. Drupes oblong, compressed, rounded and often notched at apex, acute at base, with thin succulent flesh, and a thin crustaceous light brown nutlet, joined by the union of the thickened and much elongated perianths of the flowers into a globose compound fruit saturated with milky juice, mammillate on the surface by their thickened rounded summits, light yellow-green, usually of full size but seedless on isolated pistillate individuals. Seed oblong, compressed, rounded at base, oblique and marked at apex by the conspicuous oblong pale hilum, without albumen; seed-coat membranaceous, light chestnut-brown; embryo recurved; cotyledons oblong, nearly equal; radicle elongated, incumbent, ascending.

The genus is represented by a single species of eastern North America.

The generic name is in compliment to William Maclure, distinguished geologist.

1. Maclura pomifera Schn.   Osage Orange.   Bow Wood.

Toxylon (Ioxylon) pomiferum Rafn.

Leaves 3′–5′ long, 2′–3′ wide; turning bright clear yellow before falling in the autumn; petioles 1½′–2′ in length. **Flowers:** racemes of the staminate flowers 1′–1½′ long; heads

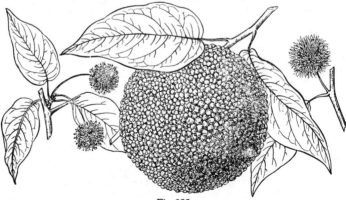

Fig. 302

of the pistillate flowers, ¾′–1′ in diameter. **Fruit** 4′–5′ in diameter, ripening in the autumn, and soon falling to the ground.

A tree, sometimes 50°–60° high, with a short trunk 2°–3° in diameter, and stout erect ultimately spreading branches forming a handsome open irregular round-topped head, and branchlets light green often tinged with red and coated with soft pale pubescence when they first appear, soon becoming glabrous, light brown slightly tinged with orange color during their first winter, and ultimately paler. **Winter-buds** depressed-globose, partly immersed in the bark, covered by few closely imbricated ovate rounded light chestnut-brown ciliate conspicuous scales. **Bark** $\frac{2}{3}'$–1′ thick, and deeply and irregularly divided into broad rounded ridges separating on the surface into thin appressed scales. **Wood** heavy, exceedingly hard, very strong, flexible, coarse-grained, very durable, bright orange color turning brown on exposure, with thin light yellow sapwood of 5–10 layers of annual growth; largely used for fence-posts, railway-ties, wheel-stock, and formerly by the Osage and other Indians west of the Mississippi River for bows and war-clubs. The bark of the roots contains moric and morintannic acid, and is used as a yellow dye. The bark of the trunk is sometimes used in tanning leather.

Distribution. Rich bottom-lands; southern Arkansas to southern Oklahoma and southward in Texas to about latitude 35° 36′; most abundant and of its largest size in the valley of the Red River in Oklahoma.

Largely planted in the prairie regions of the Mississippi basin as a hedge plant, and occasionally in the eastern states; hardy in New England; occasionally naturalized beyond the limits of its natural range.

3. FICUS L. Fig.

Trees, with milky juice, naked buds, stout branchlets, thick fleshy roots frequently produced from the branches and developing into supplementary stems. Leaves involute, entire and persistent in American species; stipules inclosing the leaf in a slender sharp-pointed bud-like cover, interpetiolar, embracing the leaf-bearing axis and inclosing the young leaves, deciduous. Flower-bearing receptacle subglobose to ovoid, sessile or stalked, solitary by abortion or in pairs in the axils of existing or fallen leaves, surrounded at base by 3 anterior bracts distinct or united into an involucral cup bearing on the interior at the apex numerous rows of minute triangular viscid bracts closing the orifice, those of the lower rows turned downward and infolding the upper flowers, those immediately above these horizontal and forming a more or less prominent umbilicus. Flowers sessile or pedicellate, the pedicels thickening and becoming succulent with the ripening of the fruit, unisexual, often separated by chaffy scales or hairs; calyx of the staminate flower usually divided into 2–6 sepals; stamen 1; filament short, erect; anther innate, ovoid, broad and subrotund, 2-celled, the cells opening longitudinally, 0 in the pistillate flower; sepals or lobes of the calyx of the pistillate flower usually narrower than those of the staminate flower; ovary sessile, erect or oblique, surmounted by the lateral elongated style crowned by a 2-lobed stigma; ovule suspended from the apex or lateral below the apex of the cell, anatropous. Fruit mostly immersed in the thickened succulent receptacle, obovoid or reniform; flesh thin, mucilaginous; nutlet with a flat crustaceous minutely tuberculate shell. Seed suspended; testa membranaceous; embryo incurved, in thin fleshy albumen, cotyledons equal or unequal, longer than the incumbent radicle.

Ficus, of which about six hundred species have been described, is largely distributed through the topics of both hemispheres, the largest number of species being found on the islands of the Indian Archipelago and the Pacific Ocean. A few species extend beyond the tropics into southern Florida, Mexico, Argentina, southern Japan and China, the countries bordering the Mediterranean, the Canary Islands, and southern Africa. Two species of the section *Urostigma* with monœcious flowers occur in tropical Florida. *Ficus Carica* L., probably a native of the Mediterranean basin, is cultivated in the southern states and in California for its large sweet succulent fruits, the figs of commerce.

CONSPECTUS OF THE NORTH AMERICAN SPECIES.

Receptacles subglobose, sessile or short-stalked; leaves oblong, usually pointed at the ends.   1. **F. aurea** (D).

Receptacles obovoid, long-stalked; leaves broadly ovate, cordate at base.   2. **F. brevifolia** (D).

1. Ficus aurea Nutt.   Wild Fig.

Leaves oblong, usually narrowed at the ends, acute or acuminate, with a short broad point at apex, cuneate or rarely broad and rounded at base, 2′–5′ long, 1½′–3′ wide, thick and coriaceous, dark yellow-green and lustrous above, paler and less lustrous below, with

Fig. 303

a broad light yellow midrib slightly grooved on the upper side, and numerous obscure primary veins arcuate and united near the margins and connected by fine closely reticulated veinlets, continuing to unfold during a large part of the year; usually falling during their second season; petioles stout, slightly grooved, ½′–1′ in length; stipules ovate-lanceolate, thick, firm, tinged with red, about 1′ long. **Flowers:** receptacles developing in succession as the branch lengthens, subglobose, sessile or short-stalked, solitary or in pairs, the orifice lateral closed and marked by a small point formed by the union of the minute bracts, becoming ⅓′ in diameter and yellow when fully grown, ultimately turning bright red; flowers reddish purple, separated by minute reddish chaff-like scales more or less laciniate at apex, sessile or long-pedicellate; calyx of the staminate flower divided to below the middle into 2 or 3 broad lobes rather shorter than the stout flattened filaments; lobes of the anther oblong, attached laterally to the broad connective; calyx of the pistillate flower divided to the middle into 4 or 5 narrow lobes, closely investing the ovate sessile ovary. **Fruit** ovoid, immersed in the thickened reddish purple walls of the receptacle; seed ovoid, rounded at the ends, with a thin light brown coat and a large lateral oblong pale hilum.

A broad round-topped epiphytal tree, 50°–60° high, germinating and growing at first on the branches and trunks of other trees and sending down to the ground stout aerial roots which gradually growing together form a trunk often 3°–4° in diameter, the growth of additional roots from the branches extending the tree over a large area, and terete pithy light orange-colored branchlets marked by pale lenticels, conspicuous stipular scars, large slightly elevated horizontal oval leaf-scars displaying a marginal ring of large pale fibro-vascular bundle-scars, and smaller elevated concave circular scars left by the receptacles in falling. **Bark** smooth, ashy gray, light brown tinged with red, $\frac{1}{2}'$ thick, and broken on the surface into minute appressed scales disclosing in falling the nearly black inner bark. **Wood** exceedingly light, soft, weak, coarse-grained, perishable in contact with the ground, light brown, with thick lighter colored sapwood.

Distribution. Hummocks on the shores and islands of southern Florida; from the Indian River on the east coast and Tampa Bay on the west coast, to the southern keys; common and now rapidly spreading over the eastern and southern borders of the Everglades; attaining its largest size in the neighborhood of Bay Biscayne; on the Bahama Islands.

2. Ficus brevifolia Nutt. Fig. Wild Fig.

Ficus populnea Sarg., not Willd.

Leaves broadly ovate or rarely obovate, contracted into a short broad point or occasionally rounded at apex, rounded, truncate or cordate at base, $2\frac{1}{2}'-5'$ long, $1\frac{1}{2}'-5'$ wide, thin and firm, dark green and lustrous on the upper surface, paler on the lower, with a light yellow midrib, and slender remote primary veins arcuate and united near the margins and connected by finely reticulate veinlets; petioles slender, sometimes $1'$ in length; stipules ovate-lanceolate, $\frac{1}{2}'$ long, tinged with red. **Flowers:** receptacles obovoid, solitary or in pairs, yellow until fully grown, ultimately turning bright red and becoming $\frac{1}{4}'-\frac{1}{2}'$ long, on stout drooping stalks $\frac{1}{4}'-1'$ in length; flowers sessile or pedicellate, separated by minute chaff-like scales more or less laciniate at apex; calyx of the staminate flower divided nearly to the base into three or four broad acute lobes; calyx of the pistillate flower with narrow lobes shorter than the ovoid pointed ovary. **Fruit** ovoid; **seed** ovoid, with a membranaceous light brown coat and an oblong lateral pale hilum.

Fig. 304

An epiphytal tree, rarely $40°-50°$ high, with a trunk $12'-18'$ in diameter, spreading branches occasionally developing aerial roots and forming an open irregular head, and terete branchlets light red and slightly puberulous when they first appear, becoming brown tinged with orange and later with red, and marked by minute pale lenticels, narrow stipular scars, large elevated horizontal oval or semiorbicular leaf-scars showing a marginal row of conspicuous fibro-vascular bundle-scars, and elevated concave receptacle scars. **Wood** light, soft, close-grained, light orange-brown or yellow, with thick hardly distinguishable sapwood.

Distribution. Usually on dry slightly elevated coral rocks; Florida from the shores of Bay Biscayne to the Everglades Keys, and on several of the southern keys to Key West; not common; on the Bahama Islands and in Cuba.

XIII. OLACACEÆ.

Trees or shrubs, with watery juices, their stems sometimes twining, and alternate usually entire persistent leaves, without stipules. Flowers perfect or polygamous, in axillary cymes or racemes, rarely solitary; calyx 4 to 6-lobed; petals 4–6, inserted on a hypogynous disk, free or united into a campanulate or tubular corolla; stamens 4–12, inserted on the tube of the corolla; filaments free, rarely united; anthers oblong, introrse, opening longitudinally; ovary superior or partly inferior, free or immersed in the disk, 1–4-celled; styles mostly united; stigmas entire or lobed; ovules 1–3 in each cell of the ovary. Fruit drupaceous, naked or nearly inclosed in the enlarged disk, 1-celled, 1-seeded; seed pendulous; embryo minute, erect, in copious fleshly albumen; radicle superior.

Olacaceæ with twenty-five genera and a large number of species is confined to the tropics, and is most abundant in those of the Old World.

CONSPECTUS OF THE NORTH AMERICAN ARBORESCENT GENERA.

Corolla-lobes short; stamens as many as its lobes; drupe almost inclosed in the enlarged disk of the flower; branches unarmed.　　　　　　　　　　　　　　　　**1. Schoepfia.**

Corolla-lobes elongated; stamens twice as many as its lobes; drupe nearly naked; branchlets armed.　　　　　　　　　　　　　　　　　　　　　　　　　　**2. Ximenia.**

1. SCHOEPFIA Schreb.

Trees or shrubs with slender unarmed branchlets. Leaves entire, subcoriaceous, petiolate. Flowers small, perfect in axillary cymes, rarely solitary; calyx disciform, obscurely 4-toothed, or nearly entire, petals 4, 5 or rarely 6, united, their tips free, valvate; stamens opposite the petals, filaments free, anthers attached by the back; ovary partly immersed in the disk, 3-celled; style elongated, stigma 3-lobed; ovules 3 in each cell, pendulous from the free apex of the axile placentas. Fruit nearly inclosed in the enlarged disk of the flower, the stone crustaceous or chartaceous.

Schoepfia with twelve or fourteen species is distributed in the New World from southern Florida and Lower California to Brazil and Peru, and in the Old World from southern Japan and southern and western China to the East Indies and the eastern Himalayas.

The generic name is in compliment to Johann David Schoepf, German physician and botanist, and traveler in North America and the West Indies.

1. Schoepfia chrysophylloides Planch.

Schoepfia Schreberi Small, not Gmel.

Leaves elliptic to oblong-ovate, often slightly falcate, acuminate at apex, cuneate and often unsymmetric at base, light green and lustrous above, paler below, $1\frac{1}{2}'$–$3'$ long, $\frac{3}{4}'$–

Fig. 305

$1\frac{1}{4}'$ wide, and on vigorous shoots sometimes $4'$ long and $1\frac{3}{4}'$ wide; petioles stout, wing-margined, $\frac{1}{4}'-\frac{1}{3}'$ in length. **Flowers** sessile, pink or red, in axillary 1–3- usually 2-flowered clusters on peduncles $\frac{1}{24}'-\frac{1}{6}'$ in length; calyx cup-shaped, the rim slightly dilated, almost filled by the fleshy disk; corolla ovate-cylindric, $\frac{1}{8}'-\frac{1}{6}'$ long, 4-lobed, the lobes ovate, acute, united, reflexed; stamens 4, adnate to the base of the lobes of the corolla; anthers sessile; ovary mostly immersed in the disk; style not more than $\frac{1}{24}'$ long; **Fruit** ovoid or ovoid-oval scarlet, $\frac{2}{5}'-\frac{1}{2}'$ in length; stone crustaceous; **seed** not seen.

A tree, sometimes $25°–30°$ high with a trunk $12'–18'$ in diameter, small erect branches and slender pale gray unarmed branchlets. **Bark** thin, grayish brown, closely and regularly reticulated.

Distribution. In sandy or rocky soil; banks of the Caloosahatchee River, Lee County, near Miami and at Cocoanut Grove, Dade County, and on the southern keys, Florida; on the Bahama Islands, and in Cuba, Jamaica, and Guatamala.

2. XIMENIA L.

Trees and shrubs, with terete armed or unarmed branchlets. Leaves entire, subcoriaceous, often fascicled, short-petiolate. Flowers perfect, white, on slender pedicels, in short axillary cymes or rarely solitary; calyx small, 4-lobed, the lobes imbricated in the bud, persistent; petals 4 or 5, hypogynous, narrow, bearded on their inner face, valvate in the bud, reflexed above the middle; stamens twice as many as the petals; filaments free, filiform; anthers linear, attached on the back near the base, 2-celled, the cells opening laterally, their connective apiculate at apex; ovary 4-celled below, only the apex 1-celled, externally 4-grooved, glandular at base, gradually narrowed into the slender style; stigma entire, subcapitate; ovules linear, solitary in each cell, pendulous from the apex of the axile placenta, anatropous; raphe dorsal; micropyle superior. Fruit ovoid or globose; exocarp thick and succulent, endocarp crustaceous or subligneous; seed filling the cavity of the endocarp, pendulous, surrounded by a thin spongy coat; testa membranaceous; cotyledons elliptic; embryo minute, erect; raphe terete.

Ximenia with four or five species is widely distributed on tropical shores of the two worlds.

Ximenia commemorates the name of Francisco Ximenes, a Dominican priest who published in Mexico in 1615 a work on the plants and animals of that country.

1. Ximenia americana L.

Leaves oblong or elliptic, rounded and often emarginate and apiculate at apex, gradually narrowed and cuneate at base, glabrous, bright green and lustrous above, pale below,

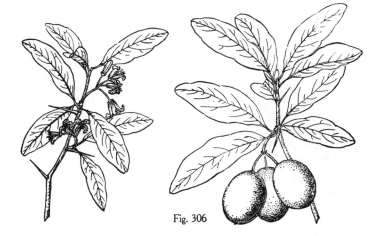

Fig. 306

$1\frac{1}{4}'-2\frac{1}{2}'$ long, $\frac{3}{5}'-1\frac{1}{4}'$ wide, with slightly thickened revolute margins, a prominent midrib and obscure primary veins; petioles slender, narrow wing-margined at apex, $\frac{1}{5}'-\frac{2}{5}'$ in length. Flowers bell-shaped, fragrant, about $\frac{1}{4}'$ long, on slender pedicels in the axils of minute acuminate caducous bractlets, in 3 or 4-flowered clusters on peduncles $\frac{1}{5}'-\frac{1}{3}'$ long; calyx-lobes acute, petals elliptic and rounded or obtusely pointed at apex, yellowish white, leathery, conspicuously bearded on the inner surface from base nearly to apex. **Fruit** broad-ovoid to subglobose, bright yellow, with thin acid flesh, $1'-1\frac{1}{4}'$ long, on slender pedicels about $\frac{1}{3}'$ in length, in usually 2 or 3-fruited drooping clusters; stone ovoid, apiculate at apex, covered with minute pits, light red; **seed** yellow, with bright orange-colored cotyledons.

A tree, occasionally 30° high, with a tall trunk $2\frac{1}{2}'-3\frac{1}{2}'$ in diameter, spreading branches armed with stout straight spines usually $\frac{3}{4}'-1'$ in length, and slender branchlets slightly angled and light reddish brown when they first appear, becoming terete and light gray or red-brown and marked by numerous lenticels; more often a shrub with long vine-like stems. **Bark** close, dark red, astringent. **Wood** very heavy, tough, hard, close-grained, compact, brown tinged with red with lighter-colored sapwood. Hydrocyanic acid has been obtained from the fruit.

Distribution. Florida, near Eustis Lake, Lake County, to the southern keys, attaining its largest size on the west coast and on Long Key in the Everglades; common on the shores of the Antilles and southward to Brazil, and on those of west tropical Africa, the Indian peninsula, the islands of the Malay Archipelago, New Guinea, Australia, and on those of many of the islands of the south Pacific Ocean.

> Section 3. Flowers perfect or unisexual; calyx 5-lobed; ovary superior, 1-celled; ovule solitary, rising from the bottom of the cell; fruit inclosed in the thickened calyx; leaves persistent.

XIV. POLYGONACEÆ.

Trees, with alternate coriaceous stalked leaves, their stipules sheathing the stem. Flowers perfect; calyx 5-lobed; stamens 8; ovary 3-celled; ovule orthotropous. Fruit a nutlet, inclosed in the thickened calyx-tube; seed erect; embryo axillary in ruminate farinaceous albumen; radicle superior, ascending, turned toward the hilum. Of this, the Buckwheat family with thirty widely distributed genera, only Coccolobis is arborescent in North America.

1. COCCOLOBIS P. Br.

Trees or shrubs. Leaves coriaceous, entire, orbicular, ovate, obovate, or lanceolate, petiolate, their stipules inclosing the branch above the node with membranaceous truncate entire brown persistent sheaths. Flowers jointed on ebracteolate pedicels, in 1 or few-flowered fascicles subtended by a minute bract and surrounded by a narrow truncate membranaceous sheath, each pedicel and those above it being surrounded by a similar sheath, the fascicles gathered in elongated terminal and axillary racemes inclosed at the base of the sheath of the nearest leaf and sometimes also in a separate sheath; calyx cup-shaped, the lobes ovate, rounded, thin, white, reflexed after anthesis, and thickening and inclosing the nutlet; stamens with filiform or subulate filaments dilated and united at base into a short discoid cup adnate to the tube of the calyx; anthers ovoid, introrse, 2-celled, the cells parallel, opening longitudinally; ovary free, sessile, 3-angled, contracted into a short stout style, divided into three short or elongated stigmatic lobes. Fruit ovoid or globose, rounded or acute and crowned at apex by the persistent lobes of the calyx, narrowed at base; flesh thin and acidulous, more or less adnate to the thin crustaceous or bony wall of the nutlet often divided on the inner surface near the base into several more or less intrusive plates. Seed subglobose, acuminate at apex, 3–6-lobed; testa membranaceous, minutely pitted, dark red-brown, and lustrous.

Coccolobis is confined to the tropics of the New World, with about one hundred and twenty species distributed from southern Florida to Mexico, Central America, Brazil, and Peru. It possesses astringent properties sometimes utilized in medicine. Many of the species produce hard dark valuable wood.

Coccolobis, from κοκκος and λοβός, is in allusion to the character of the fruit.

CONSPECTUS OF THE NORTH AMERICAN SPECIES.

Fruits crowded, in drooping racemes; leaves broadly ovate to suborbicular, cordate at base.
1. C. uvifera (D).
Fruits not crowded, in erect or spreading racemes; leaves ovate to oblong-lanceolate.
2. C. laurifolia (D).

1. Coccolobis uvifera Jacq. Sea Grape.

Leaves broadly ovate to suborbicular rounded or sometimes short-pointed at apex, deeply cordate at base, with undulate margins, thick and coriaceous, minutely reticulate-venulose, dark green and lustrous above, paler and puberulous below, 4'–5' long, 5'–6' wide, with a stout often bright red midrib frequently covered below with pale hairs, and about 5 pairs of conspicuous primary veins red on the upper side, arcuate near the margins and connected by cross veinlets; gradually turning red or scarlet and falling during their second or third

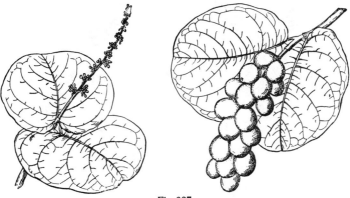

Fig. 307

years; petioles short, stout, flattened, puberulous, abruptly enlarged at base, leaving in falling large pale elevated orbicular or semiorbicular scars; stipular sheath ⅛' broad, slightly puberulous, persistent during 2 or 3 years. **Flowers** appearing almost continuously throughout the year on slender puberulous pedicels ⅛' long, in 1–6-flowered subsessile fascicles, in terminal and axillary thick-stemmed many-flowered racemes 6'–14' in length; calyx ⅛' across when expanded, the lobes puberulous on the inner surface and rather longer than the red stamens; ovary oblong, with short stigmatic lobes. **Fruit** crowded, in long hanging racemes, ovoid to obovoid, ¾' long, gradually narrowed into a stalk-like base, purple or greenish white, translucent, with thin juicy flesh, and a thin-walled light red nutlet.

A tree, in Florida rarely more than 15° high, with a short gnarled contorted trunk 3°–4° in diameter, stout branches forming a round compact head, and stout terete branchlets, with thick pith, light orange color, marked by oblong pale lenticels, gradually growing darker in their second and third years; frequently a shrub, with semiprostrate stems; in the West Indies often 50° tall. **Bark** about 1/16' thick, smooth, light brown and marked by large irregular pale blotches. **Wood** very heavy, hard, close-grained, dark brown or violet color, with thick lighter colored sapwood; sometimes used in cabinet-making.

Distribution. Saline shores and beaches; Florida, from Mosquito Inlet to the southern keys on the east coast, and from Tampa Bay to Cape Sable on the west coast; common on the Bermuda and Bahama Islands, in the Antilles, and in South America from Colombia to Brazil.

2. Coccolobis laurifolia Jacq. Pigeon Plum.

Leaves ovate, ovate-lanceolate or obovate-oblong, rounded or acute at apex, rounded or cuneate at base, with slightly undulate revolute margins, thick and firm, bright green above, paler below, 3'–4' long, 1½'–2' wide, with a conspicuous pale midrib and 3 or 4 pairs of remote primary veins connected by prominent reticulate veinlets; petioles stout, flattened, ½' in length, abruptly enlarged at base; stipular sheath glabrous, ½' wide. **Flowers** in early spring, on slender pedicels ¼' long, in few or 1-flowered fascicles on racemes terminal on short axillary branches of the previous year, and 2'–3' in length; calyx ⅛' across, the cup-shaped lobes rather shorter than the stamens, with slender yellow filaments enlarged at base, and dark orange-colored anthers; ovary oblong, with elongated stigmatic lobes.

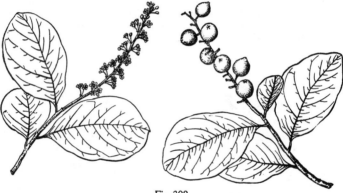

Fig. 308

Fruit in erect or spreading sparsely-fruited racemes, ripening during the winter and early spring, ovoid, narrowed at base, rounded at apex, dark red, ⅓' long, with thin acidulous flesh and a hard thin-walled light brown nutlet.

A glabrous tree, 60°–70° high, with a tall straight trunk 1°–2° in diameter, spreading branches forming a dense round-topped head, slender terete slightly zigzag branchlets usually contorted and covered with light orange-colored bark, becoming darker and tinged with red in their second or third year. **Wood** heavy, exceedingly hard, strong, brittle, close-grained, rich dark brown tinged with red, with thick lighter colored sapwood; occasionally used in cabinet-making.

Distribution. One of the largest and most abundant of the tropical trees of the seacoast of southern Florida from Cape Canaveral to the keys and on the west coast from Cape Romano to Cape Sable; common on the Bahama Islands, on many of the Antilles, and in Venezuela.

XV. NYCTAGINACEÆ.

Trees with alternate stalked persistent leaves without stipules. Flowers perfect or unisexual; calyx corolla-like, 5-lobed; stamens 5–8; ovule campylotropous. Fruit anthocarpus, crowned by the persistent teeth of the calyx. Seed erect; cotyledons unequal, folded round the soft scanty albumen; radicle short, inferior, turned toward the hilum. A family of about twenty genera widely distributed chiefly in the warmer and tropical parts of the New World, with a single arborescent representative in North America.

1. TORRUBIA Vell.

Glabrous or pubescent unarmed trees or shrubs. Leaves opposite or rarely alternate, entire, short-stalked. Flowers perfect, or rarely unisexual; calyx tubular or funnel-shaped, elongated, 5-lobed, the lobes plaited in the bud, erect or spreading; stamens inserted on the base of the calyx under the ovary, minute or rudimentary in the unisexual pistillate flower; filaments folded in the bud, filiform, unequal, free; anthers oblong, introrse, 2-celled, the cells parallel, opening longitudinally; ovary oblong-ovoid, sessile, 1-celled, gradually narrowed into a columnar style; stigmas capitate, lacerate. Fruit fleshy, cylindric, costate, smooth; utricle elongated, with a thin membranaceous wall confluent with the thin transparent coat of the erect seed.

Torrubia, with about 15 species is confined to tropical America, one species extending into southern Florida. The genus was named in honor of Joseph Torrubia, a Spanish naturalist of the 18th century.

1. Torrubia longifolia Britt. Blolly.

Pisonia longifolia Sarg.

Leaves oblong-obovate, rounded or occasionally emarginate at apex, gradually narrowed at base, $1'-1\frac{1}{2}'$ long, $\frac{1}{2}'$ wide, thick and firm, with slightly thickened undulate margins, light green and glabrous, paler on the lower than on the upper surface, with a stout midrib and

Fig. 309

obscure veins; petioles stout, channeled, $\frac{1}{2}'$ in length. **Flowers** perfect or unisexual, autumnal, greenish yellow, short-pedicellate, in terminal long-stalked few-flowered panicled cymes, with slender divergent branches, the ultimate divisions 2 or 3-flowered; bracts and bractlets minute, acute; calyx funnel-shaped, divided nearly to the middle into acute erect lobes about half as long as the stamens and as long as the style. **Fruit** ripening in the winter or early spring, prominently costate with ten rounded ribs, fleshy, smooth, bright red, $\frac{3}{4}'$ long; utricle terete, light brown.

A tree, occasionally $30°-50°$ high, with an erect or inclining trunk, $15'-20'$ in diameter, stout spreading branches forming a compact round-topped head, and slender terete branchlets light orange color when they first appear, later often producing numerous short spur-like lateral branchlets, light reddish brown or ashy gray, and marked by large elevated semi-orbicular or lunate leaf-scars; usually much smaller; often shrubby. **Bark** about $\frac{1}{16}'$ thick, light red-brown, and broken into thin appressed scales. **Wood** heavy, rather soft, weak, coarse-grained, yellow tinged with brown, with thick darker colored sapwood.

Distribution. Sea-beaches and the shores of salt water lagoons; Cape Canaveral, Florida to the southern keys, attaining its largest size in Florida on Elliott's Key and Old Rhodes Key; on the Bahama Islands and in Cuba.

Subdivision 2. Petalatæ. Flowers with both calyx and corolla (*without a corolla in Lauraceæ, in Liquidambar in Hamamelidaceæ, in Euphorbiaceæ, in some species of Acer, in Reynosia, Condalia, and Krugiodendron in Rhamnaceæ, in Fremontia in Sterculiaceæ, in Calyptranthes in Myrtaceæ, and in Conocarpus in Combretaceæ*).

Section 1. Polypetalæ. Corolla of separate petals.

A. Ovary superior (*partly inferior in Hamamelidaceæ; inferior in Malus, Sorbus, Cratægus and Amelanchier in Rosaceæ*).

XVI. MAGNOLIACEÆ.

Trees or shrubs, with watery juice, branchlets lengthening by large terminal or the flower-bearing branchlets by upper axillary buds, the other axillary buds obtuse, flattened, and rudimentary, bitter aromatic bark, and thick fleshy roots. Leaves alternate, conduplicate and inclosed in their stipules in the bud, feather-veined, petiolate. Flowers perfect, large, solitary, terminal, pedicellate, inclosed in the bud in a stipular caducous spathe; sepals and petals imbricated in the bud, inserted under the ovary, deciduous; stamens and pistils numerous, imbricated in many ranks, the stamens below the pistils on the surface of an elongated receptacle ripening into a compound fruit of 1–2-seeded follicles or samara: ovules 2, collateral, anatropous. Four of the ten genera of the Magnolia family are represented in North America; of these two are arborescent.

CONSPECTUS OF THE NORTH AMERICAN ARBORESCENT GENERA.

Anthers introrse; mature carpels, fleshy, opening on the back at maturity, persistent; seed-coat thick, pulpy, and bright scarlet; leaves entire, or auriculate at base. 1. **Magnolia.**
Anthers extrorse; mature carpels dry, indehiscent, deciduous; seed-coat dry and coriaceous; leaves lobed or truncate. 2. **Liriodendron.**

1. MAGNOLIA L. Magnolia.

Trees, with ashy gray or brown smooth or scaly bark, branchlets conspicuously marked by large horizontal or longitudinal leaf-scars and by narrow stipular rings, and large terete acuminate or often obtusely-pointed more or less gibbous winter-buds usually broadest at the middle, their scales large membranaceous stipules adnate to the base of the petioles and deciduous with the unfolding of each successive leaf, the petiole of the outer stipule rudimentary, adnate on the straight side of the bud, and marked at its apex by the scar left by the falling of the last leaf of the previous season. Leaves entire, sometimes auriculate, persistent or deciduous, often minutely punctate, their numerous primary veins arcuate and more or less united within the margins. Flowers appearing in the American species after the leaves, their stipular spathes thin and membranaceous; sepals 3, spreading or reflexed; petals 6–12 in series of 3's, concave, erect or spreading; stamens early deciduous, their filaments shorter than the 2-celled introrse anthers and terminating in apiculate fleshy connectives; ovary sessile, 1-celled; style short, recurved, stigmatic on the inner face; ovules horizontal. Fruit a scarlet or rusty brown cone formed of the coalescent 2-seeded drupaceous persistent follicles opening on the back; seeds suspended at maturity by long thin cords of unrolled spiral vessels; seed-coat thick, drupaceous, the outer portion becoming fleshy and at maturity pulpy, red or scarlet, the inner crustaceous; embryo minute at the base of the fleshy homogeneous albumen, its radicle next the hilum; cotyledons short and spreading.

Magnolia with about thirty species is confined to eastern North America, southern Mexico, and eastern and southern Asia, seven species growing naturally in the United States. All the parts are slightly bitter and aromatic, and the dried flower-buds are sometimes used in medicine. Several species from eastern Asia and their hybrids producing flowers before the appearance of the leaves are favorite garden plants in the United States.

The genus is named in honor of Pierre Magnol (1638–1715), professor of botany at Montpellier.

ˏCONSPECTUS OF NORTH AMERICAN SPECIES.

Styles deciduous from the follicles of the fruit; petals greenish or yellow; winter-buds silky tomentose.

Petals greenish; branchlets glabrous.   1. **M. acuminata** (A, C).

Petals canary yellow; branchlets pubescent.   2. **M. cordata** (C).

Styles persistent on the follicles of the fruit.

Petals white.

Leaves coriaceous, persistent; fruit and branchlets tomentose. 3. **M. grandiflora** (C).

Leaves thin, deciduous (semipersistent in 4).

Leaves cuneate at base.

Leaves scattered along the branches, pale and pubescent below; winter-buds glabrous or silky pubescent.   4. **M. virginiana** (A. C).

Leaves crowded at the ends of the flowering branches, green and glabrous below; winter-buds glabrous.   5. **M. tripetala** (A, C).

Leaves cordate at the narrow base; fruit tomentose; winter-buds hoary-tomentose.   6. **M. macrophylla** (C).

Petals pale yellow or creamy white; leaves obovate-spathulate, auriculate, crowded at the ends of the flowering branches; winter-buds glabrous.

Leaves acute; petals pale yellow; tips of the mature carpels elongated, straight or incurved.   7. **M. Fraseri** (A, C).

Leaves bluntly pointed; petals creamy white; tips of the mature carpels short, incurved.   8. **M. pyramidata** (C).

1. Magnolia acuminata L. Cucumber-tree. Mountain Magnolia.

Leaves oblong-ovate, oblong–obovate or elliptic, abruptly short-pointed at apex, rounded, cuneate or rarely slightly cordate at base, when they unfold densely villose below and slightly villose above, and at maturity thin, yellow-green and glabrous on the upper surface, paler and glabrous or villose-pubescent on the lower surface, 6′–10′ long, and 4′–6′ wide, with often undulate margins; turning dull yellow or brown in the autumn before falling; petioles slender, pubescent early in the season, becoming glabrous, 1′–1½′ in length. **Flowers** on hairy soon glabrous pedicels ½′–¾′ long, bell-shaped, green or greenish yellow covered with a glaucous bloom; sepals membranaceous, acute, 1′–1½′ long, soon reflexed; petals 6, ovate or obovate, concave, pointed, erect, 2½′–3′ long, those of the outer row rarely more than 1′ wide and much wider than those of the inner row. **Fruit** ovoid or oblong, often curved, glabrous, dark red, 2½′–3′ long, rarely more than 1′ thick; **seeds** obovoid, acute, compressed, about ½′ long.

A pyramidal tree, 60°–90° high, with a trunk 3°–4° in diameter, comparatively small branches spreading below and erect toward the top of the tree, and slender branchlets coated at first with soft pale caducous hairs, soon bright red-brown, lustrous, and marked by numerous small pale lenticels, turning gray during their third season. **Winter-buds:** terminal, oblong-ovoid, acuminate, thickly covered with long lustrous white hairs, ½′–⅜′ long, and about three times as long as the obtuse compressed lateral buds nearly surrounded by the narrow elevated leaf-scars conspicuously marked by a double row of large fibro-vascular bundle-scars. **Bark** $\frac{1}{3}'$–$\frac{1}{2}'$ thick, furrowed, dark brown, and covered by numerous thin scales. **Wood** light, soft, not strong, close-grained, durable, and light yellow-brown, with thin lighter colored often nearly white sapwood of usually 25–30 layers of annual growth; occasionally manufactured into lumber used for flooring and cabinet-making.

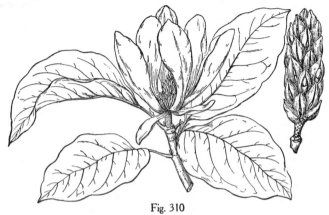

Fig. 310

Distribution. Low mountain slopes and rocky banks of streams; southern Ontario, western New York, central to western Pennsylvania, southern Ohio, Indiana and Illinois, and along the Appalachian Mountains to northern Georgia and to central Kentucky and Tennessee; banks of the Savannah River above Augusta, and in the neighborhood of Lumpkin, Stewart County, Georgia; northern Alabama, northeastern, northwestern and southcentral Mississippi; Eagle Rock, Barry County, and on bluffs of the Mississippi River, Cape Girardeau County, Missouri, and Baxter County, Arkansas; in eastern Oklahoma (Page, Le Flore County); in West Feliciana Parish, Louisiana, represented by var. *ludoviciana* Sarg. differing in its broadly obovate, oval or ovate leaves, and in its larger flowers, $3\frac{1}{2}'$–$4'$ long, the outer petals $1\frac{1}{2}'$ wide. Rare at the north; most abundant and of its largest size at the base of the high mountains of the Carolinas and Tennessee up to altitudes of 4000°.

Often planted as an ornamental tree in the eastern states and in northern and central Europe.

2. Magnolia cordata Michx.

Magnolia acuminata var. *cordata* Sarg.

Leaves oblong-obovate to elliptic, abruptly short-pointed or rounded at apex, gradually narrowed and cuneate, broad-cuneate or rarely rounded at base, when they unfold villose-pubescent more densely on the lower than on the upper surface, at maturity dark green, lustrous and glabrous above, paler and covered below with short matted pale hairs, $4'$ or $5'$ long, $2\frac{1}{2}'$–$3\frac{1}{2}'$ wide, with a slender yellow midrib and primary veins; remaining green until late in the autumn and turning brown and falling after severe frost; petioles slender, covered when they first appear with matted silky white hairs, becoming glabrous, $\frac{1}{2}'$–$\frac{3}{4}'$ in length. **Flowers** on stout pedicels, $\frac{1}{4}'$–$\frac{1}{3}'$ long and covered with long silky white hairs, cup-shaped, bright canary yellow; sepals ovate, acute, soon reflexed; petals 6, erect and spreading, $1\frac{1}{2}'$–$1\frac{3}{4}'$ long, $\frac{1}{2}'$–$\frac{3}{4}'$ wide. **Fruit** oblong, often curved, glabrous, dark red, $1'$–$1\frac{1}{2}'$ long, $\frac{1}{2}'$–$\frac{3}{4}'$ thick.

A shrub, 4°–8° high, flowering freely when not more than half that size; or in gardens a tree sometimes 20°–30° tall with a trunk $12'$–$15'$ in diameter, spreading branches forming a round-topped head, and slender dark dull red-brown branchlets thickly covered during two years with short pubescence and marked by small pale lenticels. **Winter-buds** oblong-obovate, often falcate, bluntly pointed, thickly covered with matted pale hairs, the terminal $\frac{1}{2}'$ long and $\frac{1}{4}'$ thick, the axillary $\frac{1}{6}'-\frac{1}{4}'$ in length and nearly surrounded by the narrow

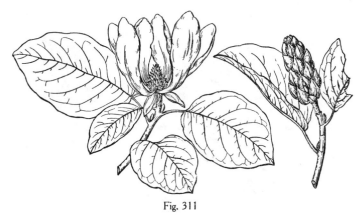

Fig. 311

leaf-scars marked by an irregular row of minute fibro-vascular bundle-scars. **Bark** dark brown, and covered with small closely appressed scales.

Distribution. Dry Oak-woods, valley of the Savannah River, Georgia; Spears Plantation six miles south and Goshen Plantation sixteen miles south of Augusta, Richmond County, near Mayfield, Hancock County, and Bath, Richmond County. Often cultivated, and preserved in gardens for more than a century; not rediscovered as a wild plant until 1913 (*L. A. Berckmans*); hardy as far north as eastern Massachusetts.

3. Magnolia grandiflora L. **Magnolia.**

Magnolia fœtida Sarg.

Leaves elliptic to oblong-obovate or ovate, acute and bluntly pointed or acuminate at apex, cuneate at base, coriaceous, bright green and shining above, more or less densely coated below with rusty tomentum, $5'-8'$ long, $2'-3'$ wide, with a prominent midrib and primary veins, deciduous in the spring at the end of their second year; petioles stout, rusty-tomentose, $1'-2'$ in length. **Flowers** on stout hoary-tomentose pedicels $\frac{1}{2}'-1'$ long, opening from April or May until July or August, fragrant, $7'-8'$ across, the petaloid sepals and 6 or sometimes 9 or 12 petals abruptly narrowed at base, oval or ovate, those of the inner ranks often somewhat acuminate, concave, and coriaceous, $3'-4'$ long and $1\frac{1}{2}'-2'$ wide; base of the receptacle and lower part of the filaments bright purple. **Fruit** ovoid or oval, rusty brown, covered while young with thick lustrous white tomentum, at maturity rusty-tomentose, $3'-4'$ long, $1\frac{1}{2}'-2\frac{1}{2}'$ thick; **seeds** obovoid or triangular-obovoid, more or less flattened, $\frac{1}{2}'$ long.

A tree, of pyramidal habit, $60°-100°$ or rarely $120°-135°$ high, with a tall straight trunk $2°-3°$ or occasionally $4°-4\frac{1}{2}°$ in diameter, rather small spreading branches, and branchlets hoary-tomentose at first, slightly tomentose in their second year, and much roughened by the elevated leaf-scars displaying a marginal row of conspicuous fibro-vascular bundle-scars. **Winter-buds** pale or rusty-tomentose, the terminal $1'-1\frac{1}{2}'$ in length. **Bark** $\frac{1}{2}'-\frac{3}{4}'$ thick, gray or light brown, and covered with thin appressed scales rarely more than $1'$ long. **Wood** hard, heavy, creamy white, soon turning brown with exposure, hardly distinguishable from the sapwood of 60–80 layers of annual growth; largely used in basket and crate making.

Distribution. Rich moist soil on the borders of river swamps and Pine-barren ponds, or rarely on high rolling hills; coast of North Carolina southward to De Soto County, Florida, extending across the peninsula, and in the neighborhood of the coast through the other Gulf states to the valley of the Brazos River, Texas, ranging inland to central Missis-

¼ NAT. SIZE

Fig. 312

sippi and to southern Arkansas, and northward on the bluffs of the lower Mississippi River to the mouth of the Yazoo River, Mississippi; best developed and most abundant on the bluff formation of the lower Mississippi River, and of its largest size in West Feliciana Parish, Louisiana.

Largely cultivated as an ornamental tree in all countries of temperate climate; in the eastern United States precariously hardy as far north as Trenton, New Jersey. Numerous varieties, differing in the form of the leaf and in the duration of the flowering period, have appeared in European nurseries; of these, the most distinct is the variety *exoniensis* Loud., with a rather fastigiate habit and broadly elliptic leaves densely clothed with rusty tomentum on the lower surface; this variety begins to flower when only a few feet high.

4. Magnolia virginiana L. Sweet Bay. Swamp Bay.

Magnolia glauca L.

Leaves oblong or elliptic and obtuse or oblong-lanceolate, covered when they unfold with long white silky deciduous hairs, at maturity bright green, lustrous and glabrous on the upper surface, finely pubescent and pale or nearly white on the lower surface, 4′–6′ long, 1½′–3′ wide, with a conspicuous midrib and primary veins; falling in the north late in November and in early winter, at the south remaining on the branches with little change of color until the appearance of the new leaves in the spring; petioles slender, ½′–¾′ in length. **Flowers** on slender glabrous pedicels ½′–¾′ long, creamy white, fragrant, globular, 2′–3′ across, continuing to open during several weeks in spring and early summer; sepals membranaceous, obtuse, concave, shorter than the 9–12, obovate often short-pointed concave petals. **Fruit** ellipsoidal, dark red, glabrous, 2′ long and ½′ thick; **seeds** obovoid, oval, or suborbicular, much flattened, ¼′ in length.

A slender tree, 20°–30° high, with a trunk rarely more than 15′–20′ in diameter, with small mostly erect ultimately spreading branches and slender bright green branchlets hoary-pubescent when they first appear, soon glabrous, marked by narrow horizontal pale lenticels, gradually turning bright red-brown in their second summer; usually a low shrub. **Winter-buds** covered with fine silky pubescence, the terminal ½′–¾′ long.

Distribution. Deep swamps; Magnolia, Essex County, Massachusetts, Long Island, New York, and southward from New Jersey generally in the neighborhood of the coast to southeastern Virginia and occasionally in North and South Carolina and Georgia; in Pennsylvania as far west as the neighborhood of Chambersburg, Franklin County. In the southern states usually replaced by the var. *australis* Sarg., differing in the thick silky white pubescence on the pedicels and branchlets. **Leaves** persistent without change of color

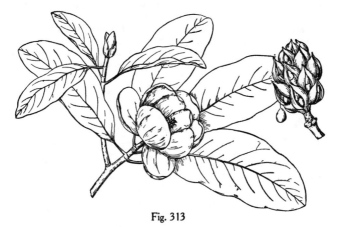

Fig. 313

until spring, elliptic to ovate, oblong-obovate or rarely lanceolate, 1′-4′ wide; petioles puberulous, pubescent or tomentose.

A tree, 60°-90° high, with a tall straight trunk occasionally 3° in diameter, small short branches forming a narrow round-topped head, and branchlets usually becoming glabrous in their second year; in southern Florida often much smaller and on the Everglade Keys shrubby, and generally not more than 10° tall. **Wood** soft, light brown tinged with red, with thick creamy white sapwood of 90–100 layers of annual growth; used in the southern states in the manufacture of broom handles and other articles of woodenware.

Distribution. Borders of Pine-barren ponds, in shallow swamps and on rich hummocks usually in the neighborhood of the coast; swamps of the lower Cape Fear River near Wilmington, New Hanover County, North Carolina, to southern Florida; common in the interior of the Florida peninsula, and westward to the valley of the Nueces River, Texas; ranging inland to Cuthbert, Randolph County, western Georgia, to Tuskegee and Selma, Alabama, Tishomingo County, northeastern Mississippi, and to Winn and Natchitoches Parishes, western Louisiana, and to the neighborhood of Malvern, Hot Spring County, Arkansas (*E. J. Palmer*); less abundant west of the Mississippi River than eastward.

The northern form is often cultivated as a garden plant in the eastern states and in Europe.

× *Magnolia major* or *Thompsoniana*, a probable hybrid between *Magnolia virginiana* and *Magnolia tripetala*, raised in an English nursery a century ago, and still a favorite garden plant, is intermediate in character between these species.

5. Magnolia tripetala L. Umbrella-tree. Elkwood.

Leaves obovate-lanceolate, narrowed at the ends, acute or bluntly pointed at apex, when they unfold nearly glabrous above, covered below with thick silky caducous tomentum, at maturity membranaceous, glabrous, 18′-20′ long, 8′-10′ wide, with a thick prominent midrib and numerous slender primary veins; falling in the autumn with little change of color; petioles stout, 1′-1½′ in length. **Flowers** on slender glabrous pedicels covered with a glaucous bloom and 2′-2½′ long, cup-shaped, white; sepals narrowly obovate, 5′-6′ long,

1½′ wide, thin, light green, becoming reflexed; petals 6 or 9, concave, coriaceous, ovate, short-pointed, erect, those of the outer row 4′–5′ long and sometimes 2′ wide, much longer and broader than those of the inner rows; filaments bright purple. **Fruit** ovoid, glabrous, 2½′–4′ long, rose color when fully ripe; **seeds** obovoid, ½′ long.

A tree, 30°–40° high, with a straight or often inclining trunk rarely more than 18′ in diameter, stout irregularly developed contorted branches wide-spreading nearly at right angles with the stem or turning up toward the ends and growing parallel with it, and stout brittle branchlets green during their first season, becoming in their first winter bright reddish brown, very lustrous, and marked by occasional minute scattered pale lenticels, and by the large oval horizontal slightly raised leaf-scars with scattered fibro-vascular bundle-scars, brown during their second and gray during their third season; generally much smaller, sometimes surrounded by several stems springing from near the base of the trunk and

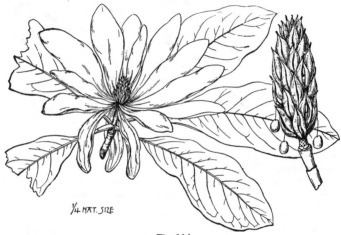

¼ NAT. SIZE

Fig. 314

growing into a large bush surmounted by the head of the central stem. **Winter-buds:** terminal, acute or bluntly pointed, purple, glabrous, covered with a glaucous bloom, usually about 1′ long; axillary globose, the color of the branch. **Bark** ½′ thick, light gray, smooth, and marked by many small bristle-like excrescences. **Wood** light, soft, close-grained, not strong, light brown, with creamy white sapwood of 35–40 layers of annual growth.

Distribution. Deep rather moist rich soil along the banks of mountain streams or the margins of swamps, and widely distributed in the Appalachian Mountain region, but nowhere very common; valley of the Susquehanna River, Pennsylvania (Lancaster and York Counties), and Jackson County, Ohio, to southern Alabama, middle Kentucky and Tennessee, and northeastern Mississippi; in central and southwestern Arkansas; and in southeastern Oklahoma (near Page, Le Flore County, *G. W. Stevens*), extending in Virginia and North Carolina nearly to the coast; of its largest size in the valleys along the western slopes of the Great Smoky Mountains in Tennessee up to altitudes of 2000°.

Often cultivated as an ornamental tree in the northern states, and in northern and central Europe.

6. Magnolia macrophylla Michx. Large-leaved Cucumber-tree.

Leaves obovate or oblong, acute or often abruptly narrowed and acute or rounded at apex, narrowed and cordate at base, bright green and glabrous on the upper surface, silvery gray and pubescent, especially along the stout midrib and primary veins on the lower surface, 20'–30' long, 9'–10' wide; falling in the autumn with little change of color; petioles stout, 3'–4' in length, at first tomentose, becoming pubescent. **Flowers** on stout hoary-tomentose pedicels 1'–1½' long, soon becoming glabrous or puberulous, cup-shaped, fragrant, 10'–12' across; sepals membranaceous, ovate or oblong, rounded at apex, much narrower than the 6 ovate concave thick creamy white petals with a rose colored blotch at base, 6'–7' long and 3'–4' wide, at maturity reflexed above the middle, those of the inner row narrower and often somewhat acuminate. **Fruit** ovoid to nearly globose, pubescent, 2½'–3' long, bright rose color when fully ripe; **seeds** obovoid, compressed, ⅔' long.

A tree, 30°–50° high, with a straight trunk 18'–20' in diameter, stout wide-spreading branches forming a broad symmetrical round-topped head, and stout brittle branchlets hoary-tomentose when they first appear, light yellow-green, pubescent, and conspicuously

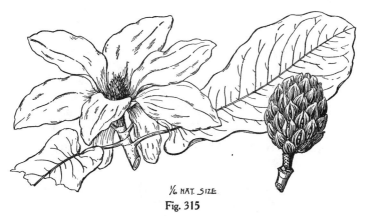

⅙ NAT. SIZE

Fig. 315

marked during their first winter by the large irregularly shaped sometimes longitudinal slightly raised leaf-scars with many scattered fibro-vascular bundle-scars, turning reddish brown during their second and gray during their third season. **Winter-buds:** terminal, bluntly pointed, covered with a thick coat of snowy white tomentum, 1¾'–2' long, ½'–¾' thick; lateral, much flattened, brownish, pubescent, ⅛'–¼' long. **Bark** generally less than ¼' thick, smooth, light gray, divided on the surface into minute scales. **Wood** hard, close-grained, light, not strong, light brown, with thick light yellow sapwood of about 40 layers of annual growth.

Distribution. Sheltered valleys in deep rich soil; nowhere common, and growing generally in isolated groups of a few individuals; Piedmont region of central North Carolina to middle and western Florida, southern Alabama, southern and northeastern Mississippi to the valley of the Green River, Kentucky; in eastern and western Louisiana; probably most abundant in south-central Mississippi.

Occasionally cultivated as an ornamental tree in the eastern states, and in the temperate countries of Europe; hardy as far north as eastern Massachusetts.

7. Magnolia Fraseri Walt. Mountain Magnolia. Long-leaved Cucumber-tree.

Leaves obovate-spatulate, acute or bluntly pointed at apex, cordate and conspicuously auriculate at base, bright green and often marked on the upper surface when young with red along the principal veins, glabrous, 10'–12' long, 6'–7' wide, or on vigorous young plants sometimes of twice that size; falling in the autumn without change of color; petioles slender, 3'–4' in length. **Flowers** on stout glabrous pedicels covered with a glaucous bloom and 1'–1½' long, pale yellow, sweet scented, 8'–10' across; sepals narrowly obovate, rounded at apex, 4′–5′ long, deciduous almost immediately after the opening of the bud, shorter than the 6 or 9 obovate acuminate membranaceous spreading petals contracted below the middle, those of the inner rows narrower and conspicuously narrowed below. **Fruit** oblong, glabrous, bright rose-red when fully ripe, 4′–5′ long, 1½′–2′ thick, the mature carpels ending in long subulate persistent tips; **seeds** obovoid, compressed, ⅝′ long.

A tree, 30°–40° high, with a straight or inclining trunk 12′–18′ in diameter, often undivided for half its length or separating at the ground into a number of stout diverging stems, regular wide-spreading or more or less contorted and erect branches, and stout brittle branchlets soon becoming bright red-brown, lustrous, marked by numerous minute pale lenticels and in their first winter by the low horizontal leaf-scars with crowded compressed fibro-vascular bundle-scars, and grayish in their second year. **Winter-buds:** ter-

¼ NAT. SIZE

Fig. 316

minal, glabrous, purple, 1½′–2′ long, ½′ thick; axillary, minute and obtuse. **Bark** rarely more than ⅓′ thick, dark brown, smooth, covered by small excrescences, or on old trees broken into minute scales. **Wood** light, soft, close-grained, not strong, light brown, with thick creamy white sapwood of 30–40 layers of annual growth.

Distribution. Valleys of the streams of the southern Appalachian Mountains from southwestern Virginia and northeastern Kentucky to northern Georgia; in northern Alabama and in West Feliciana Parish, Louisiana (Laurel Hill, *R. S. Cocks*); in South Carolina eastward to the neighborhood of Aiken, Aiken County; probably most abundant and of largest size on the upper waters of the Savannah River in South Carolina up to altitudes of 4000°.

Occasionally cultivated as an ornamental plant in the eastern states, and in the temperate countries of Europe; hardy as far north as eastern Massachusetts.

8. Magnolia pyramidata Pursh.

Leaves obovate-spatulate, the apex usually abruptly narrowed into a short blunt point, auriculate at base, with more or less spreading lobes, thin, glabrous, light yellow-green on the upper, pale and glaucous on the lower surface, particularly while young, 5½′–8½′ long, from 3½′–4½′ wide, with a slender yellow midrib, numerous slender forked primary veins and conspicuously reticulate veinlets; petioles slender, 1¼′–2½′ in length. **Flowers** creamy white, 3½′–4′ across when fully expanded; sepals oblong-obovate, abruptly narrowed to the short-pointed apex, much shorter than the oblong-acuminate petals gradually narrowed from near the middle to the base. **Fruit** oblong, 2′–2½′ long, bright rose color, the mature carpels ending in short incurved persistent tips; **seeds** ovoid, compressed.

A slender tree, 20°–30° high, with ascending branches, slender branchlets bright red-brown and marked by small pale lenticels and by the small low oval leaf-scars with many crowded fibro-vascular bundle-scars, later becoming ashy gray.

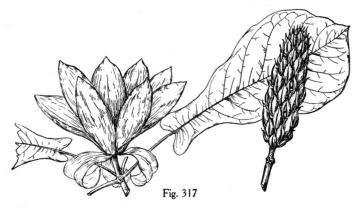

Fig. 317

Distribution. Low rich soil in the neighborhood of streams; near Cuthbert, Randolph County, Georgia; near Mariana, Jackson County, and Bristol, Liberty County, Florida; valleys of the Choctawhatchee River, Dale County, and of the Pea River, Coffee County, and near Selma, Dallas County, Alabama; rare and local.

Occasionally cultivated as an ornamental tree in western Europe.

2. LIRIODENDRON L.

Trees, with deeply furrowed brown bitter bark, and slender branchlets marked by elevated leaf-scars and narrow stipular rings, and compressed obtuse winter-buds, their scales membranaceous stipules joined at the edges, accrescent, strap-shaped, often slightly falcate, oblique at the unequal base, tardily deciduous after the unfolding of the leaf. Leaves recurved in the bud by the bending down of the petiole near the middle, bringing the apex of the blade to the base of the bud, sinuately 4-lobed, heart-shaped, truncate or slightly cuneate at base, truncate at apex by a broad shallow sinus, and minutely apiculate. Flowers appearing after the unfolding of the leaves, cup-shaped, conspicuous, inclosed in the bud in a 2-valved stipular membranaceous caducous spathe; sepals spreading or reflexed, ovate-lanceolate, concave, greenish white, early deciduous; petals erect, rounded at base, early deciduous; filaments filiform, half as long as the linear 2-celled extrorse anthers adnate to the outer face of the connective terminating in a short fleshy point; pistils imbricated on the elongated sessile receptacle into a spindle-shaped column; ovary inserted by a broad base; style narrowly acuminate, laterally flattened, appressed; stigmas short, recurved at the summit; ovules 2, suspended from near the middle of the ventral suture. Fruit a narrow light brown cone formed of the closely imbricated dry and woody indehiscent carpels consisting of a laterally compressed 4-ribbed pericarp, the lateral ribs confluent into the margins of the large wing-like lanceolate compressed style marked vertically by a thin sutural line, the carpels deciduous when ripe in the autumn from the slender elongated axis of the fruit persistent on the branch during the winter. Seeds suspended, 2 or single by abortion; testa thin, coriaceous, and marked by a narrow prominent raphe; embryo minute at the base of the fleshy albumen, its radicle next the hilum.

Liriodendron, widely distributed in North America and Europe during the cretaceous period, is now represented by two species, one in eastern North America, the other *L. chinensis* Sarg. in central China.

Liriodendron, from λίριον and δένδρον, is descriptive of the lily-like flower.

1. Liriodendron Tulipifera L.　Yellow Poplar.　Tulip-tree.

Leaves dark green and shining on the upper, paler on the lower surface, 5'–6' long and broad; turning clear yellow in the autumn before falling; petioles slender, angled, 5'–6' in length.　**Flowers** 1½'–2' deep, on slender pedicels ¾'–1' long; petals green conspicuously marked with orange at base.　**Fruit** 2½'–3' long, about ½' thick, ripening late in September and in October, the mature carpels ½'–1½' long and about ¼' wide.

A tree, sometimes nearly 200° high, with a straight trunk 8°–10° in diameter, destitute of branches for 80°–100° from the ground, short, comparatively small branches forming a

Fig. 318

narrow pyramidal, or in old age a broader spreading head, and slender branchlets light yellow-green and often covered with a glaucous bloom during their first summer, reddish brown, lustrous, and marked during their first winter by many small pale lenticels and roughened by the elevated orbicular or semiorbicular leaf-scars marked by numerous small scattered fibro-vascular bundle-scars, and dark gray during their third year.　**Winter-buds** dark red covered by a glaucous bloom, the terminal ½' long, much longer than the lateral buds.　**Bark** thin and scaly on young trees, becoming deeply furrowed, brown, and 1'–2' thick.　**Wood** light, soft, brittle, not strong, easily worked, light yellow or brown, with thin creamy white sapwood; largely manufactured into lumber used in construction, the interior finish of houses, boatbuilding, and for shingles, brooms, and woodenware.　The intensely acrid bitter inner bark, especially of the roots, is used domestically as a tonic and stimulant, and hydrochlorate of tulipiferine, an alkaloid separated from the bark, possesses the property of stimulating the heart.

Distribution.　Deep rich rather moist soil on the intervales of streams or on mountain slopes; Worcester County, Massachusetts, to southwestern Vermont (Pownal, Bennington County), and westward to southern Ontario, southern Michigan and northeastern Missouri, and southward to Orange County (Rock Spring Run), Florida, southern Alabama, Mississippi and Louisiana, southeastern Missouri and northeastern Arkansas; most abundant and of its largest size in the valleys of the lower Ohio basin, and on the slopes of the mountains of North Carolina and Tennessee up to altitudes of 5000°.

Often cultivated as an ornamental tree in the eastern states, and in western and central Europe.　A fastigiate form (var. *pyramidata* Lav.) is occasionally cultivated.

XVII. ANNONACEÆ.

Trees or shrubs, with watery juice, slender terete branchlets marked by conspicuous leaf-scars, and fleshy roots. Leaves alternate, conduplicate in the bud, entire, feather-veined, petiolate, without stipules. Flowers perfect, solitary, axillary or opposite the leaves; sepals 3, valvate in the bud; petals 6, in 2 series, imbricated or valvate in the bud; stamens numerous, inserted on the subglobose or hemispheric receptacle, with distinct filaments shorter than their fleshy connectives terminating in a broad truncate glandular appendage; anthers introrse, 2-celled, opening longitudinally; pistils inserted on the summit of the receptacle; ovary 1-celled; ovules 1 or many, anatropous. Fruit baccate or compound. Seeds inclosed in an aril; seed-coat thin, crustaceous, smooth, brown, and lustrous; albumen ruminate, deeply penetrated by the folds of the inner layer of the seed-coat; embryo minute; radicle next the hilum. Two of the forty-eight or fifty genera of the Custard-apple family, confined almost exclusively to the tropics and more numerous in the Old World than in the New, occur in North America.

CONSPECTUS OF THE NORTH AMERICAN GENERA.

Petals imbricated in the bud; ovules numerous; fruit developed from one pistil. 1. Asimina.
Petals valvate in the bud; ovule solitary; fruit developed from several confluent pistils.
2. Anona.

1. ASIMINA Adans.

Trees or shrubs, emitting a heavy disagreeable odor when bruised, with minute buds covered with cinereo-pubescent caducous scales, and branchlets marked by conspicuous leaf-scars. Leaves membranaceous, reticulate-venulose, deciduous. Flowers, solitary pedicellate, nodding; sepals ovate, smaller than the petals, green, deciduous; petals imbricated in the bud, hypogynous, sessile, ovate or obovate-oblong, reticulate-veined, accrescent, the three exterior alternate with the sepals, spreading, those of the interior row opposite the sepals, erect, and much smaller than those of the outer row; stamens linear-cuneate, densely packed on the receptacle; filaments shorter than the fleshy connective; anther-cells separated on the connective; pistils 3–15, sessile on the summit of the receptacle, projecting from the globular mass of stamens; ovary 1-celled; style oblong, slightly recurved toward the apex and stigmatic along the margin; ovules 4–20, horizontal, 2-ranked on the ventral suture, the raphe toward the suture. Fruit baccate, sessile or stipitate, oval or oblong, smooth. Seeds in 1 or 2 ranks, ovoid, apiculate, compressed, marked at the base by a large pale hilum.

Asimina is confined to eastern North America. Six species are distinguished; of these one is a small tree; the others are low shrubs of the south Atlantic and Gulf regions.

Asimina is from *Asiminier*, the old colonial name of the French in America for the Pawpaw.

1. Asimina triloba Dunal. Pawpaw.

Leaves obovate-lanceolate, sharp-pointed at apex, gradually and regularly narrowed to the base, when they unfold covered below with short rusty brown caducous tomentum and slightly pilose above, and at maturity light green on the upper surface, pale on the lower surface, 10'–12' long, 4'–6' wide, with a prominent midrib and primary veins. **Flowers** nearly 2' across when fully grown, on stout club-shaped pedicels from axils of the leaves of the previous year, 1'–1½' long and covered with long scattered rusty brown hairs; sepals ovate, acuminate, pale green, densely pubescent on the outer surface; petals green at first, covered with short appressed hairs, gradually turning brown and at maturity deep vinous red and conspicuously venulose, those of the outer row broadly ovate, rounded or pointed at apex, reflexed at maturity above the middle and 2 or 3 times longer than the sepals, those of the inner row pointed, erect, their base concave, glandular, nectariferous, marked by a broad band of a lighter color. **Fruit** attached obliquely to the enlarged torus, oblong, nearly cylindric, rounded or sometimes slightly pointed at the ends, more or less falcate, often irregular from the imperfect development of some of the seeds, $3'-5'$ long, $1'-1\frac{1}{2}'$ in diameter, greenish-yellow, becoming when fully ripe in September and October dark brown or almost black, with pale yellow or nearly white barely edible flesh on some plants and on others with orange-colored succulent flesh; **seeds** separating readily from the aril, $1'$ long, $\frac{1}{2}'$ broad, rounded at the ends.

A shrub or low tree, sometimes $35°-40°$ high, with a straight trunk rarely exceeding a foot in diameter, small spreading branches, and slender glabrous or rusty pubescent, light

Fig. 319

brown branchlets tinged with red and marked by longitudinal parallel or reticulate narrow shallow grooves. **Winter-buds** acuminate, flattened, $\frac{1}{8}'$ long, and clothed with rusty brown hairs. **Bark** rarely more than $\frac{1}{8}'$ thick, dark brown, marked by large ash-colored blotches, covered by small wart-like excrescences and divided by numerous shallow reticulate depressions. **Wood** light, soft and weak, coarse-grained, spongy, light yellow shaded with green, with thin darker colored sapwood of 12–20 layers of annual growth. The inner bark stripped from the branches in early spring is used by fishermen of western rivers for stringing fish. The sweet and luscious wholesome fruit is sold in large quantities in the cities and towns in those parts of the country where the tree grows naturally.

Distribution. Deep rich moist soil; western New Jersey and western New York (Greece, Monroe County) to the northern shores of Lake Ontario, westward to southern Michigan, southwestern Iowa, southeastern Nebraska, eastern Kansas and eastern Oklahoma, and southward to northern Florida (Clay and Taylor Counties), central Alabama, and through Mississippi and Louisiana to eastern Texas (near Marshall, Harrison County, and Dennison, Grayson County); comparatively rare in the region adjacent to the Atlantic seaboard; very common in the Mississippi valley, forming thick forest undergrowth on rich bottomlands, or thickets many acres in extent.

Occasionally cultivated in the eastern states, and hardy as far north as eastern Massachusetts; interesting as the most northern representative of the Custard-apple family and its only species extending far beyond the tropics.

2. ANNONA L.

Trees or shrubs, with glandular often reticulated bark, terete branchlets marked by conspicuous leaf-scars, and often pubescent during their first season. Leaves coriaceous, often glandular-punctate, persistent or tardily deciduous. Flowers nodding on bracted pedicels; calyx small, 3-lobed, green, deciduous; petals 6 in 2 series, valvate in the bud, hypogynous, sessile, ovate, concave, 3-angled at apex, thick and fleshy, white or yellow, the exterior alternate with the lobes of the calyx, those of the inner row often much smaller than those of the outer row; stamens club-shaped, densely packed on the receptacle; filaments shorter than the fleshy connective; anther-cells confluent; pistils sessile on the receptacle, free or united; ovary 1-celled; style sessile or slightly stipitate, oblong, stigmatic on the inner face; ovule 1, erect; raphe ventral. Fruit compound, many-celled, fleshy, ovoid or globose, many-seeded. Seeds ovoid to ellipsoidal; cotyledons appressed.

Of the fifty species of Anona widely distributed in the tropics of the two worlds, a single species reaches the coast of southern Florida. Of exotic species, *Annona muricata* L., the Soursop and *Annona reticulata* L., of the West Indies, and *Annona cherimola* Mill., of western tropical America, are now occasionally cultivated as fruit-trees in Florida.

Annona is the name given by early authors to the Soursop.

1. Annona glabra L. Pond Apple.

Annona palustris Small, not L.

Leaves elliptic or oblong, acute, tapering or rounded at base, bright green on the upper, paler on the lower surface, coriaceous, 3′–5′ long, 1½′–2′ wide, with a prominent midrib;

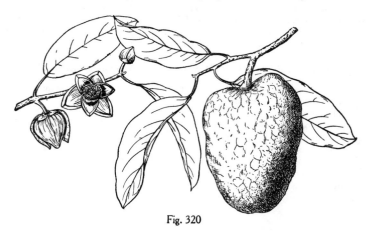

Fig. 320

deciduous late in the winter; petioles, stout ½′ in length. **Flowers** nodding on short stout pedicels thickened at the ends, opening in April from an ovoid 3-angled bud; divisions of the calyx broad-ovate, acute; petals connivent, acute, concave, pale yellow or dirty white, those of the outer row marked on the inner surface near the base by a bright red spot, and broader and somewhat longer than those of the inner row. **Fruit** ripening in November, broadly ovate, truncate or depressed at base, rounded at apex, 3′–5′ long, 2′–3½′ broad, light green when fully grown, becoming yellow and often marked by numerous dark brown blotches when fully ripe, with a thick elongate fibrous torus and light green slightly aromatic insipid flesh of no comestible value; **seeds** ½′ long, slightly obovoid, turgid, rounded at the ends, their margins contracted into a narrow wing formed by the thickening of the outer coat.

A tree, 40°–50° high, with a short trunk often 18′ in diameter above the swell of the thickened tapering base sometimes enlarged into spreading buttresses, stout wide-spreading often contorted branches, slender branchlets brown or yellow during their first season, becoming in their second year brown and marked by small scattered wart-like excrescences. Bark ⅛' thick, dark reddish brown, divided by broad shallow fissures, separating on the surface into numerous small scales. Wood light, soft, not strong, light brown streaked with yellow.

Distribution. Florida: Indian River on the east coast, and the shores of the Manatee River on the west coast to the southern Keys; in shallow fresh water ponds, on swampy hummocks, or on the borders of fresh water streams flowing from the everglades; of its largest size on the shores of Bay Biscayne near the Miami River, growing in the shade of larger trees; forming a pure forest of great extent on the swampy borders of Lake Okechobee; on the Bahama Islands and on several of the Antilles.

XVIII. LAURACEÆ.

Aromatic trees and shrubs, with slender terete or angled branchlets, naked or scaly buds, and alternate punctate leaves without stipules. Flowers small, perfect or polygamodiœcious, yellow or greenish; calyx 6-lobed, the lobes in 2 series, imbricated in the bud; corolla 0; stamens 9 or 12, inserted on the base or near the middle of the calyx in 3 or 4 series of 3's, distinct; anthers 4-celled, superposed in pairs, opening from below upward by persistent lids; ovary 1-celled; stigma discoid or capitate; ovule solitary, suspended from the apex of the cell, anatropous. Fruit a 1-seeded berry; seed without albumen; testa thin and membranaceous, of 2 coats; embryo erect; cotyledons thick and fleshy; radicle superior, turned toward the hilum, included between thick and fleshy cotyledons. The Laurel family with about forty genera, confined mostly to the tropics, is represented in North America by seven genera; of these five are arborescent.

CONSPECTUS OF THE NORTH AMERICAN ARBORESCENT GENERA.

Leaves entire, persistent; stamens 12 those of the inner row reduced to staminodes.
    Calyx-lobes persistent under the fruit, in our species.   1. **Persea.**
    Calyx-lobes deciduous.
        Flower cymose in axillary or subterminal panicles.   2. **Ocotea.**
        Flowers in axillary many-flowered umbels inclosed before anthesis in an involucre of
            deciduous scales.   3. **Umbellularia.**
Leaves entire or lobed, deciduous; stamens 9 in the American species; flowers in fewflowered drooping racemes.   4. **Sassafras.**
Leaves entire, persistent; stamens 9, those of the outer row fertile and united in a column
    inclosing the pistil; flowers in terminal or axillary cymose panicles.   5. **Misanteca.**

1. PERSEA Mill.

Trees, with naked buds. Leaves revolute in the bud, alternate, scattered, penniveined, subcoriaceous, rigid, tomentose or rarely glabrous, persistent. Flowers perfect, vernal, in short axillary or axillary and terminal panicles on slender peduncles from axils of the leaves of the year, pedicellate, their pedicels bibracteolate near the middle, the lateral flowers of the ultimate divisions of the inflorescence in the axils of small deciduous lanceolate acute bracts; calyx campanulate, divided nearly to the base into 6 lobes, those of the outer series shorter than the others, deciduous, or enlarged and persistent under the fruit; stamens about as long as the inner lobes of the calyx; filaments flattened, longer than the anthers, hirsute, those of the third series furnished near the base with 2 nearly sessile orange-colored glands rounded on the back and slightly 2-lobed on the inner face; anthers ovoid, flattened, erect, those of the outer series introrse or subintrorse, those of the third series extrorse or laterally dehiscent, the upper cells rather larger than the lower; staminodes large, sagittate, stipitate, 2-lobed on the inner face, beaded at apex; ovary sessile, subglobose, glabrous, narrowed into a slender simple style gradually enlarged at apex into a discoid obscurely 2-lobed stigma. Fruit ripening in the autumn, oblong-obovoid to sub-globose, more or less fleshy. Seed globose, pendulous, without albumen; testa thin and membranaceous, separable into 2 coats, the outer cartilaginous, grayish brown, the inner gray or nearly white, closely adherent to the thick dark red cotyledons.

About one hundred species of Persea are distinguished. They are distributed in the New World, from the coast region of the southeastern United States and Texas to Brazil and Chili, and occur in the Canary Islands and in tropical and subtropical Asia. *Persea ameri-cana* Mill., the Avocado or Alligator Pear, a native of the Antilles and cultivated for its edible fruit in all tropical countries, is now sparingly naturalized in southern Florida. Many species yield hard dark-colored handsome wood valued in cabinet-making.

Persea was the classical name of a tree of the Orient, transferred by Plumier to one of the tropical species of this genus.

CONSPECTUS OF THE NORTH AMERICAN SPECIES.

Calyx persistent under the fruit (*Tamala Raf.* Persea, sec. Eupersea Benth. *Notaphoebe* sec. *Eriodaphne* Meisn.)

    Peduncles short; leaves oblong to oblong-lanceolate, obscurely veined, glabrous; branch-lets puberulous.   **1. P. Borbonia** (C).

    Peduncles elongated; leaves elliptic to lanceolate, conspicuously veined, tomentose on the lower surface; branchlets tomentose.   **2. P. palustris Sarg.** (C).

1. Persea Borbonia Spreng.   Red Bay.

Leaves oblong to oblong-lanceolate, entire, often slightly contracted into a long point rounded at apex, gradually narrowed below, when they unfold thin, pilose, and tinged with red, and at maturity thick and coriaceous, bright green and lustrous above, pale and glaucous below, 3′–4′ long, ¾′–1½′ wide, with thickened revolute margins, a narrow orange-

Fig. 321

colored midrib, remote obscure primary veins arcuate near the margins, and thin closely reticulated veinlets; unfolding early in the spring, gradually turning yellow a year later, and falling during their second spring and summer; petioles stout, rigid, red-brown, ½′–⅔′ in length, flattened and somewhat grooved on the upper side, in falling leaving small circu-lar leaf-scars displaying the end of a single fibro-vascular bundle. **Flowers:** peduncles glabrous, ½′–1′ in length; calyx pale yellow or creamy white, about ⅛′ long, with thin lobes ciliate on the margins, the outer broadly ovate, rounded and minutely apiculate, puberulous, about half as long as the oblong-lanceolate acute lobes of the inner series covered within by long pale hairs. **Fruit** $\frac{1}{2}'$ long, dark blue or nearly black, very lustrous; flesh thin and dry, not readily separable from the ovoid slightly pointed **seed.**

A tree, 60°–70° high, with a trunk $2\frac{1}{2}'$–3′ in diameter, stout erect branches forming a dense shapely head, thick fleshy yellow roots, and branchlets many-angled, light brown, glabrous or coated with pale or rufous pubescence when they first appear, becoming in their second year terete and dark green; usually much smaller. **Winter-buds** coated with thick rufous tomentum, $\frac{1}{4}'$ long. **Bark** $\frac{1}{2}'$–$\frac{3}{4}'$ thick, dark red, deeply furrowed and irregularly divided into broad flat ridges separating on the surface into small thick appressed scales. **Wood** heavy, hard, very strong, rather brittle, close-grained, bright red, with thin lighter colored sapwood of 4 or 5 layers of annual growth; occasionally used for cabinet-making, the interior finish of houses, and formerly in ship and boatbuilding.

Distribution. Borders of streams and swamps in rich moist soil, or occasionally in dry sandy loam in forests of the Long-leaved Pine; southern Delaware (Cypress swamp near Dogsboro, Sussex County, teste *Nuttall*); coast region from Virginia to the shores of Bay Biscayne and Cape Romano, Florida, along the Gulf coast to the valley of the Brazos River, Texas, and northward through Louisiana to southern Arkansas.

2. Persea palustris Sarg.   Swamp Bay.

Persea pubescens Sarg.

Leaves elliptic or lanceolate, entire, often narrowed toward the apex into a long point, gradually narrowed at base, when they unfold dark red, thin and tomentose, at maturity pale green and lustrous above, pale and pubescent and rusty-tomentose on the midrib and

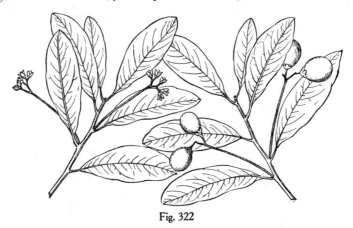

Fig. 322

primary veins below, 4′–6′ long, $\frac{3}{4}'$–$1\frac{1}{2}'$ wide, with thick conspicuous veins and slightly revolute margins; persistent until after the beginning of their second year and then turning yellow and falling gradually; petioles stout, rusty-tomentose, $\frac{1}{2}'$–$\frac{3}{4}'$ in length. **Flowers:** peduncles tomentose, 2′–3′ in length; calyx pale yellow or creamy white, often nearly $\frac{1}{4}'$ long, with thick firm lobes coated on the outer surface with rusty tomentum, those of the outer series broadly ovate, abruptly pointed at apex, pubescent on the inner surface, about half as long as the ovate lanceolate lobes of the inner series slightly thickened at the apex and hairy within. **Fruit** nearly black, $\frac{3}{4}'$ long.

A slender tree, occasionally 30°–40° high, with a trunk rarely exceeding a foot in diameter, and stout branchlets terete or slightly angled while young, coated when they first appear with rusty tomentum reduced in their second season to fine pubescence persistent until the end of their second or third year. **Bark** rarely exceeding $\frac{1}{4}'$ in thickness, dull brown, irregularly divided by shallow fissures, the surface separating into thick appressed scales. **Wood** heavy, soft, strong, close-grained, orange color streaked with brown, with thick light brown or gray sapwood of 36–40 layers of annual growth.

Distribution. Pine-barren swamps, often almost to the exclusion of other plants, usually in the neighborhood of the coast from North Carolina to the valley of the Caloosahatchee River and the Everglades Keys, Florida, Alabama and Mississippi; extending inland to the neighborhood of Wilmington, North Carolina, Aiken, South Carolina, western Georgia (Meriwether County), the interior of the Florida peninsula and to Clay, Autauga, Chilton and Tuscaloosa Counties, Alabama (*R. M. Harper*); very common in Pine barrens of eastern Louisiana (*R. S. Cocks*).

2. OCOTEA Aubl.

Leaves scattered, alternate or rarely subopposite, penniveined, coriaceous, rigid, glabrous or more or less covered with pubescence. Flowers glabrous or tomentose on slender bibracteolate pedicels from the axils of lanceolate acute minute bracts, in cymose clusters in axillary or subterminal stalked panicles; calyx-tube campanulate, the 6 lobes of the limb nearly equal, deciduous; stamens of the inner series reduced to linear staminodes, with minute abortive anthers; filaments inserted on the tube of the calyx, those of the outer series opposite its exterior lobes, shorter or sometimes rather longer than the anthers, glabrous or hirsute, furnished in the third series near the base with two conspicuous globose stalked yellow glands; anthers oblong, flattened, 4-celled, introrse in the 2 outer series, extrorse, subextrorse, or very rarely introrse in the third series, in the pistillate flower rudimentary and sterile; ovary ovoid, glabrous, more or less immersed in the tube of the calyx, gradually narrowed into a short erect style dilated at apex into a capitate obscurely lobed stigma; in the staminate flower linear-lanceolate, effete or minute, sometimes 0; raphe ventral; micropyle superior. Fruit nearly inclosed while young in the thickened tube of the calyx, exserted at maturity, surrounded at base by the cup-like truncate or slightly lobed calyx-tube; pericarp thin and fleshy. Seed ovoid, pendulous; testa thin, membranaceous.

Ocotea with nearly two hundred species is confined principally to the tropical region of the New World from southern Florida to Brazil and Peru, with Old World representatives in the Canary Islands, South Africa, and the Mascarene Islands. One species grows naturally in Florida.

Ocotea produces hard, strong, durable, beautifully colored wood often employed in cabinet-making.

The name is derived from the native name of one of the species of Guiana.

1. Ocotea Catesbyana Sarg.

Leaves oblong-lanceolate, entire, slightly contracted above into a long point rounded at apex, when they unfold thin, membranaceous, light green tinged with red, and sometimes puberulous on the lower surface, at maturity thick and coriaceous, dark green and lustrous above, pale below, 3′–6′ long, 1′–2′ wide, with thickened slightly revolute margins, a broad stout midrib, slender remote primary veins arcuate and united near the margins and connected by coarsely reticulate conspicuous veinlets; petioles broad, flat, $\frac{1}{3}'$–$\frac{1}{2}'$ in length. **Flowers** perfect, appearing in early summer in elongated panicles, their peduncles slender, glabrous, light red, solitary or 2 or 3 together from the axils of the leaves of the year or from those of the previous year, and 3′–4′ long; calyx nearly $\frac{1}{4}'$ across when expanded, puberulous on the outer surface, hoary pubescent on the inner surface and on the margins of the lobes, about twice as long as the stamens; filaments of the 2 outer series slightly hirsute at the base and shorter than their introrse anthers; filaments of the third series as long or longer than their extrorse anthers. **Fruit** ripening in the autumn, ovoid or subglobose, $\frac{2}{3}'$ long, lustrous, dark blue or nearly black, the thickened cup-like tube of the calyx truncate or obscurely lobed and bright red like the thickened pedicels; flesh thin and dry; **seed** with a thin brittle red-brown coat, the inner layer lustrous on the inner surface and marked by broad light-colored veins radiating from the small hilum; embryo $\frac{1}{3}'$ long, light red-brown.

A tree, 20°–30° high, with a trunk rarely exceeding 18' in diameter, slender spreading branches forming a narrow round-topped head, and thin terete branchlets glabrous and dark reddish brown when they first appear, soon becoming lighter colored, and in their second year light brown or gray tinged with red and often marked by minute pale lenticels, and in their second or third year by small semiorbicular leaf-scars, displaying a single central

Fig. 323

fibro-vascular bundle-scar. **Bark** about $\frac{1}{8}'$ thick, dark reddish brown, and roughened on the otherwise smooth surface by numerous small excrescences. **Wood** heavy, hard, close-grained, rich dark brown, with thick bright yellow sapwood of 20–30 layers of annual growth.

Distribution. Shores and islands of Florida south of Cape Canaveral on the east coast and of Cape Romano on the west coast; comparatively common except on some of the western keys, and most abundant and of its largest size in the rich wooded hummocks adjacent to Bay Biscayne; in the Bahamas.

3. UMBELLULARIA Nutt.

A pungent aromatic tree, with dark brown scaly bark, slender terete branchlets marked in their second and third years by small semicircular or nearly triangular elevated leaf-scars displaying a horizontal row of minute fibro-vascular bundle-scars, naked buds, and thick fleshy brown roots. Leaves alternate, involute in the bud, lanceolate or ovate-lanceolate, acute or rounded at the narrow apex, cuneate or somewhat rounded at base, entire with thickened slightly revolute margins, petiolate, coated when they appear on the lower surface with pale soft pubescence and puberulous on the upper surface, at maturity thick and coriaceous, dark green and lustrous above, dull and paler below, with a slender light yellow midrib, and remote, obscure, arcuate veins more or less united near the margins, and connected by conspicuous reticulate veinlets. Flowers perfect in axillary stalked many-flowered umbels, inclosed in the bud by an involucre of 5 or 6 imbricated broadly ovate or obovate pointed concave yellow caducous scales, the latest umbels subsessile at the base of terminal leaf-buds; pedicels slender, puberulous, without bractlets, from the axils of obovate membranaceous puberulous deciduous bracts decreasing in size from the outer to the inner; calyx divided almost to the base into 6 nearly equal broadly obovate rounded pale yellow lobes spreading and reflexed after anthesis; stamens inserted on the short slightly thickened tube of the calyx; filaments flat, glabrous, pale yellow, rather shorter than the anthers, those of the third series furnished near the base with 2 conspicuous stipitate orange-colored orbicular flattened glands; anthers oblong, flattened, light yellow, those of the first and second series introrse, those of the third series extrorse; stamens of the fourth series reduced to minute ovate acute yellow staminodes; ovary sessile, ovoid, often more or less gibbous, glabrous, abruptly contracted into a stout columnar style rather shorter than the lobes of the calyx and crowned by a simple capitate discoid stigma. Fruit ovoid, surrounded at base by the enlarged and thickened truncate or lobed tube of the calyx, yellow-green sometimes more or less tinged with purple; pericarp thin and fleshy. Seed ovoid, light brown; testa separable into 2 coats, the outer thick, hard, and woody, the inner thin and papery, closely investing the embryo, chestnut-brown and lustrous on the inner surface.

Umbellularia consists of a single species.

The generic name, a diminutive of *umbella*, relates to the character of the inflorescence.

1. Umbellularia californica Nutt. California Laurel. Spice-tree.

Leaves $2'-5'$ long, $\frac{1}{2}'-1\frac{1}{2}'$ wide, unfolding in winter or early in the spring and continuing to appear as the branches lengthen until late in the autumn; beginning to fade during the summer, turning to a beautiful yellow or orange color and falling one by one during their

Fig. 324

second season, or often remaining on the branches until the sixth year; petioles $\frac{1}{10}'-\frac{1}{5}'$ in length. **Flowers** appearing in January before the unfolding of the young leaves, the umbels on peduncles sometimes $1'$ in length. **Fruit** about $1'$ long, in clusters of 2 or 3, on elongated thickened pedicels, persistent on the branch after the fruit ripens and falls late in the autumn; seeds germinating soon after they reach the ground, the fruit remaining below the surface of the soil and attached to the young plant until midsummer.

A tree, usually $20°-75°$, occasionally $100°-175°$ high, with a trunk $3°-6°$ in diameter, sometimes tall and straight but usually divided near the ground into several large diverging stems, stout spreading or rarely pendulous (var. *pendula* Redh.) branches forming a broad round-topped head, and branchlets light green and coated with soft pale pubescence when they first appear, soon becoming glabrous and yellow-green, and in their second and third years light brown tinged with red; at high altitudes, and in southern California much smaller; often reduced to a large or small shrub, or on bluffs facing the ocean to broad mats of prostrate stems. **Bark** $\frac{3}{4}'$–1' thick, dark brown tinged with red, separating on the surface into thin appressed scales. **Wood** heavy, hard, strong, close-grained, light rich brown, with thick lighter colored sapwood of 30–40 layers of annual growth; the most valuable wood produced in the forests of Pacific North America for the interior finish of houses and for furniture. The leaves yield by distillation a pungent volatile oil, and from the fruit a fat containing umbellulic acid has been obtained.

Distribution. Valley of Coos River, Oregon, southward through the California coast ranges and along the high western slopes of the Sierra Nevada to the southern slopes of the San Bernardino Mountains up to altitudes of 2500°; usually near the banks of watercourses and sometimes on low hills; common where it can obtain an abundant supply of water; most abundant and of its largest size in the rich valleys of southwestern Oregon, forming with the Broad-leaved Maple a considerable part of the forest growth.

4. SASSAFRAS Nees. Sassafras.

Pseudosassafras H. Lec.

Aromatic trees, with thick deeply furrowed dark red-brown bark, scaly buds, slender light green lustrous brittle branchlets containing a thick white mucilaginous pith and marked by small semiorbicular elevated leaf-scars displaying a single horizontal row of minute fibro-vascular bundle-scars, and stout spongy stoloniferous roots covered by thick yellow bark. Flower-bearing buds terminal, ovoid, acute, with 9 or 10 imbricated scales increasing in size from without inward, the 3 outer scales ovate, rounded, often apiculate at apex, keeled and thickened on the back, pale yellow-green below, dull yellow-brown above the middle, loosely imbricated, slightly or not at all accrescent, deciduous at the opening of the bud, much smaller than the thin accrescent light yellow-green scales of the next rows turning dull red before falling, and obovate, rounded at apex, cuneate below, concave, coated on the outer surface with soft silky pubescence, glabrous or lustrous on the inner surface, reflexed, $\frac{3}{4}'$ long, nearly $\frac{1}{2}'$ broad, tardily deciduous, the 2 inner scales foliaceous, lanceolate, acute, light green, coated on the outer surface with delicate pale hairs, glabrous on the inner surface, infolding the leaves; sterile and axillary buds much smaller. Leaves involute in the bud, ovate or obovate, entire or often 1–3-lobed at apex, the lobes broadly ovate, acute, divided by deep broad sinuses, gradually narrowed at base into elongated slender petioles, feather-veined, with alternate veins arcuate and united or running to the points of the lobes, the lowest parallel with the margins, conspicuously reticulate-venulose, mucilaginous, deciduous. Flowers opening in early spring with the first unfolding of the leaves, the males and females usually on different individuals, in lax drooping few-flowered racemes in the axils of large obovate bud-scales, their pedicels slender, rarely forked and 2-flowered, without bracts, pilose, from the axils of linear acute scarious hairy deciduous bracts, or that of the terminal flower often without a bract; calyx pale yellow-green, divided nearly to the base into narrow obovate concave lobes spreading or reflexed after anthesis, glabrous or pubescent on the inner surface, those of the inner row a little larger than the others; stamens in the American species 9, in the Asiatic 12 with those of the inner series reduced to staminodes, inserted on the somewhat thickened margin of the shallow concave calyx-tube, those of the outer series opposite its outer lobes; filaments flattened, elongated, light yellow, those of the inner series furnished at base with 2 conspicuous orange-colored stipitate glands rounded on the back, obscurely lobed on the inner face, in the Asiatic species alternating with 3 staminodes; anthers introrse, oblong, flattened, truncate or emarginate at apex, 4-celled, 2-celled in the Formosan species, orange-colored, in the female flower reduced to flattened ovate pointed or slightly 2-lobed dark orange-colored stipitate staminodes, 6 in 2 rows in the American species and 12 similar to the stamens and staminodes of the staminate flower in the Asiatic species; or occasionally fertile and similar to or a little smaller than those of the staminate flower; ovary ovoid, light green, glabrous, nearly sessile in the short tube of the calyx, narrowed into an elongated simple style gradually enlarged above into a capitate oblique obscurely lobed stigma; in the staminate flower 0 in the American species, present, usually abortive, rarely fertile in the Asiatic species. Fruit an oblong dark blue or black lustrous berry surrounded at base by the enlarged and thickened obscurely 6-lobed or truncate scarlet or orange-red limb of the calyx, raised on a much elongated scarlet stalk thickened above the middle; pericarp thin and fleshy. Seed oblong, pointed, light brown; testa thin, membranaceous, barely separable into 2 coats, the inner coat much thinner than the outer, dark chestnut-brown, and lustrous.

Sassafras is confined to temperate eastern North America, central China and to Formosa where *Sassafras tzumu* Hemsl. and *S. randaiense* Rehd. occur.

Sassafras was first used as a popular name for this tree by the French in Florida.

11. Sassafras officinale Nees & Ebermaier.

Sassafras Sassafras Karst.

Leaves 4′–6′ long, 2′–4′ wide, densely pubescent when they first appear, pubescent or puberulous below at maturity especially on the midrib and veins; turning in the autumn delicate shades of yellow or orange more or less tinged with red; petioles $\frac{3}{4}$–$1\frac{1}{2}$′ in length. **Flowers** $\frac{1}{3}$′ long when fully expanded glabrous on the inner surface of the perianth, in

Fig. 325

racemes about 2′ in length, stamens 9. **Fruit** ripening in September and October, blue, $\frac{1}{3}$′ long, on stalks $1\frac{1}{2}$′–2′ in length, separating when ripe from the thick scarlet calyx-lobes persistent with the stalks of the fruit on the branches until the beginning of winter.

A tree, occasionally 80°–90° high, with a trunk nearly 6° in diameter, short stout more or less contorted branches spreading almost at right angles and forming a narrow usually flat-topped head, and slender branchlets light yellow-green and coated when they first appear with pale pubescence, becoming glabrous, bright green and lustrous, gradually turning reddish brown at the end of two or three years; frequently not more than 40°–50° tall; at the north and in Florida generally smaller and often shrubby. **Winter-buds** $\frac{1}{4}$′–$\frac{3}{8}$′ long. **Bark** of young stems and branches thin, reddish brown divided by shallow fissures, becoming on old trunks sometimes $1\frac{1}{2}$′ thick. dark red-brown, and deeply and irregularly divided into broad flat ridges separating on the surface into thick appressed scales. **Wood** soft, weak, brittle, coarse-grained, very durable in the soil, aromatic, dull orange-brown, with thin light yellow sapwood of 7 or 8 layers of annual growth; largely used for fence-posts and rails, in the construction of light boats, ox-yokes, and in cooperage. The roots and especially their bark are a mild aromatic stimulant, and oil of sassafras, used to perfume soap and other articles, is distilled from them. Gumbo filet, a powder prepared from the leaves by the Choctaw Indians of Louisiana, gives flavor and consistency to gumbo soup. Passing into the var. *albidum* Blake, with glabrous or nearly glabrous young leaves, glabrous often glaucous young branchlets, and lighter colored less valuable wood; uplands of western New England to the mountains of western North Carolina and eastern Tennessee.

Distribution. Usually in rich sandy well-drained soil, southern Maine and eastern Massachusetts, through southern Vermont to southern Ontario, central Michigan, and southeastern Iowa to eastern Kansas and Oklahoma, and southward to central Florida (Orange County) and the valley of the Brazos River, Texas; ascending on the southern Appalachian Mountains to altitudes of 4000°; in the south Atlantic and Gulf states often taking possession of abandoned fields.

Occasionally cultivated in the eastern states as an ornamental tree.

5. MISANTECA Cham. & Schl.

Trees with terete branchlets. Leaves coriaceous, persistent. Flowers perfect, minute, on slender pedicels, in terminal or axillary cymose panicles; peduncles and pedicels from the axils of acuminate caducous bracts and bractlets; perianth fleshy, ovoid or obovoid, 6-toothed; stamens 9, inserted near the middle of the perianth, those of the outer rank united into a fleshy column, furnished at base with three pairs of glands, inclosing the pistil and slightly longer than the perianth, those of the inner ranks, sterile, short or obsolete; anthers extrorse, 2-celled, the cells united; ovary gradually narrowed into a thick style as long as the staminal tube; stigma capitate. Fruit baccate, olive-shaped, surrounded at base by the enlarged ligneous capsular perianth of the flower much thickened on the margin; pericarp thin and fleshy; endocarp thin, crustaceous; seed filling the cavity of the fruit; testa thin, crustaceous; hilum minute, apical; cotyledons plano-convex, fleshy; radicle superior, minute.

Of the three species of the genus now known one occurs in southern Florida and Cuba, and the others in tropical Mexico.

The name of the genus is derived from the name of the tree, Palo Misanteca at Misantha, near the coast of the state of Vera Cruz where the type species was discovered.

1. Misanteca triandra Mez.

Leaves elliptic-lanceolate, ovate or broad-elliptic, entire, abruptly long-pointed and acuminate at apex, gradually narrowed and acuminate at base, deeply tinged with red and

Fig. 326

villose on the under side of the midrib when they unfold, soon glabrous, and at maturity dark green and lustrous above, pale below, 3′–4′ long and 1½′–2′ wide, with slightly undulate margins, a prominent midrib, slender primary veins, and reticulate veinlets conspicuous on the lower surface; petioles stout, narrow wing-margined at apex, pubescent when they first appear, soon glabrous, ¼′–½′ in length. **Flowers** glabrous or puberulous, purplish, about ₁₂′ long, in 3–5-flowered cymes on slender peduncles, in pubescent panicles shorter than the leaves; tube of the perianth funnel-form, the lobes equal, triangular, acute; column of stamens pilose; ovary glabrous. **Fruit** in few-fruited clusters on much elongated and thickened peduncles, ellipsoidal or slightly ovoid, acute, dark blue, ⅘′ long and ⅗′ thick; cupule light red, thickened and verrucose, acute at base, the margin reflexed, thin and entire on the inner edge, thick and crenulate on the outer edge; seed ellipsoidal, pointed at apex, rounded at base, light brown, slightly ridged when dry.

A tree in Florida 40°–50° high, with a tall trunk 15′–20′ in diameter, small spreading and pendent branches forming a broad round-topped head, and slender red branchlets pubescent when they first appear, soon becoming glabrous, and marked by numerous large pale lenticels.

Rich hummocks between Miami and Homestead, Dade County, Florida; in Cuba and Jamaica.

XIX. CAPPARIDACEÆ.

Annual or perennial herbs, trees, or shrubs, with acrid often pungent juices, alternate or rarely opposite leaves, regular or irregular usually perfect flowers in terminal cymes or racemes or solitary, numerous ovules inserted in two rows on each of the two placentas, capsular or baccate 1-celled fruit, and seeds without albumen. A family of thirty-four genera, mostly confined to the warmer parts of the world and widely distributed in the two hemispheres. Of the seven genera which occur in North America only one has an arborescent representative.

1. CAPPARIS L.

Trees, with naked buds. Leaves conduplicate in the bud, entire, feather-veined, coriaceous, persistent, without stipules. Flowers regular, in terminal cymes; sepals 4, valvate in the bud, glandular on the inner surface; petals 4, inserted on the base of the short receptacle; stamens numerous, inserted on the receptacle, their filaments free, elongated, much longer than the introrse 2-celled anthers opening longitudinally; ovary long-stalked, 2-celled, with 2 parietal placentas; stigmas sessile, orbicular; ovules campylotropous. Fruit baccate, siliquiform (in the North American species) separating into 3 or 4 valves. Seeds reniform, numerous, surrounded by pulp; seed-coat coriaceous; embryo convolute; cotyledons foliaceous, fleshy.

Capparis, with more than one hundred species, mostly tropical, is found in the two hemispheres, the largest number of species occurring in Central and South America. Two of the West Indian species reach the shores of southern Florida, the most northern station of the genus in America; of these one is arborescent.

Capparis, from κάππαρις, the classical name of *Capparis spinosa* L., is derived from the Persian *kabor*, capers, the dried flower-buds of that species.

1. Capparis jamaicensis Jacq.

Leaves oblong-lanceolate, rounded and emarginate at apex, slightly revolute, coriaceous, light yellow-green, smooth and lustrous on the upper surface, covered on the lower by minute ferrugineous scales, 2′–3′ long, 1′–1½′ wide, with a prominent midrib and inconspicuous primary veins; petioles stout covered at first with ferrugineous scales often becoming nearly glabrous, ⅓′–½′ in length. **Flowers** 1¼′ in diameter, opening in Florida in April and May from obtuse or acute, 4-angled buds; sepals ovate, acute, lepidote on the outer surface, furnished on the inner with a small ovate gland, recurved when the flower is fully expanded, and about half the size of the round white petals turning purple in fading; stamens 20–30, with purple filaments villose toward the base, $1\frac{1}{2}'-2'$ long; anthers yellow; ovary raised on a slender stipe about $1\frac{1}{2}'$ in length. **Fruit** $9'-12'$ long, terete, sometimes slightly torulose, pubescent-lepidote, the long stalk appearing jointed by the enlargement of the pedicel and torus below the insertion of the stipe; **seed** light brown, $1\frac{1}{4}'$ long.

Fig. 327

A small slender shrubby tree, 18°–20° high, with a trunk sometimes 5'–6' in diameter, and thin angled branchlets dark gray, smooth or slightly rugose, and covered with minute ferrugineous scales. **Bark** rarely more than $\frac{1}{8}'$ thick, slightly fissured, the dark red-brown surface broken into small irregularly shaped divisions. **Wood** heavy, hard, close-grained, yellow faintly tinged with red, with lighter colored sapwood of about 15 layers of annual growth.

Distribution. Coast of Florida; Cape Canaveral and Cape Sable to the southern keys; generally distributed, but nowhere abundant; common on several of the Antilles.

XX. HAMAMELIDACEÆ.

Trees or shrubs, with watery juice, slender terete branchlets, naked or scaly buds, and fibrous roots. Leaves alternate, petiolate, stipulate, deciduous. Flowers perfect or unisexual; calyx 4-parted or 0; petals 4 or 0; stamens 4–8; anthers attached at the base, introrse, 2-celled; ovary inserted in the bottom of the receptacle, 2-celled; ovules 1 or many, anatropous, suspended from an axile placenta; micropyle superior; raphe ventral. Fruit a woody capsule opening at the summit. Seed usually 1; embryo surrounded by fleshy albumen; cotyledons oblong, flat, longer than the terete radicle turned toward the hilum. The Witch Hazel family with twenty genera is confined to eastern North America, southwestern, southern, and eastern Asia, the Malay Archipelago, Madagascar, and South Africa. Of the three North American genera two are arborescent.

CONSPECTUS OF THE NORTH AMERICAN ARBORESCENT GENERA.

Flowers usually unisexual, capitate, without petals, limb of the calyx short or nearly obsolete; capsules consolidated by their base into a globose head; seed with a terminal wing; leaves palmately lobed.   1. **Liquidambar.**

Flowers usually perfect, with calyx and corolla; capsules not consolidated into a head; seed without a wing.   2. **Hamamelis.**

1. LIQUIDAMBAR L.

Trees, with balsamic juices, scaly bark, terete often winged branchlets, scaly buds, and fibrous roots. Leaves plicate in the bud, alternate, palmately lobed, glandular-serrate, long-petiolate; stipules lanceolate, acute, caducous. Flowers monœcious or rarely perfect in capitate heads surrounded by an involucre of 4 deciduous bracts, the staminate in terminal racemes, the pistillate in solitary long-stalked heads from the axils of upper leaves; staminate flowers without a calyx and corolla; stamens indefinite, interspersed with minute scales; filaments filiform, shorter than the oblong obcordate anthers opening longitudinally; pistillate flowers surrounded by long-awned scales, the whole confluent into a globular head; calyx obconic, its limb short or nearly obsolete; stamens usually 4, inserted on the summit of the calyx; anthers minute, usually rudimentary or abortive, rarely fertile; ovary partly inferior, of 2 united carpels terminating in elongated subulate recurved persistent styles stigmatic on the inner face; ovules numerous. Capsules armed with the hardened incurved elongated styles free above, septicidally dehiscent, consolidated by their base into a globose head; pericarp thick and woody; endocarp thin, corneous, lustrous on the inner surface. Seeds usually solitary or 2 by the abortion of many ovules, compressed, angulate; seed-coat opaque, crustaceous, produced into a short membranaceous obovate terminal wing rounded at the oblique apex.

Liquidambar with about four species is confined to the eastern United States, southern and central Mexico, Central America, southwestern Asia, middle and southeastern China, and Formosa. Liquid storax, an opaque grayish brown resin, is derived from *Liquidambar orientalis* Mill., a native of Asia Minor.

Liquidambar from *liquidus* and *ambar* in allusion to the fragrant juices.

1. Liquidambar Styraciflua L. Sweet Gum. Bilsted.

Leaves generally round in outline, truncate or slightly heart-shaped at base, deeply 5–7-lobed, with acutely pointed divisions finely serrate with rounded appressed teeth,

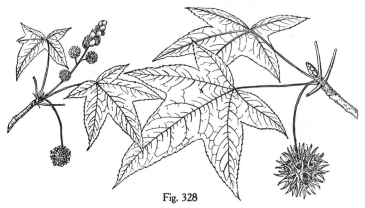

Fig. 328

when they unfold pilose on the lower surface, soon becoming glabrous with the exception of large tufts of pale rufous hairs in the axils of the principal veins, at maturity thin, bright green, smooth and lustrous, 6′–7′ across, with broad primary veins and finely reticulate veinlets; exhaling when bruised a pleasant resinous fragrance; in the autumn turning deep crimson; petioles slender, covered at first near the base with rufous caducous hairs, and 5′–6′ in length; stipules entire, glabrous, $\frac{1}{3}$′–$\frac{1}{2}$′ long. **Flowers:** staminate in terminal racemes 2′–3′ long covered with rufous hairs, in heads stalked toward the base of the raceme and nearly sessile above, $\frac{1}{4}$′ in diameter, and surrounded by ovate acute deciduous hairy bracts much larger than the lanceolate acute bracts of the female inflorescence $\frac{1}{2}$′

across and conspicuous from the broad stigmatic surfaces of the recurved and contorted styles. Fruit $1'-1\frac{1}{2}'$ in diameter, persistent during the winter, the carpels opening in the autumn; seed $\frac{1}{2}'$ long and rather longer than its wing, with a light brown coat conspicuously marked by oblong resin-ducts.

A tree, 80°–140° high, with a straight trunk 4°–5° in diameter, slender branches forming while the tree is young a pyramidal head, and in old age a comparatively small oblong crown, and slender branchlets containing a large pith, slightly many-angled, covered when they first appear with caducous rufous hairs, light orange color to reddish brown in their first winter, marked by occasional minute dark lenticels and by large arcuate leaf-scars showing the ends of 3 conspicuous fibro-vascular bundles, developing in their second season corky wings appearing on the upper side of lateral branches in 3 or 4 parallel ranks and irregularly on all sides of vertical branches, and increasing in width and thickness for many years, sometimes becoming $2'-3'$ broad and $1'$ thick. **Winter-buds** acute, $\frac{1}{4}'$ long, and covered by ovate acute minutely apiculate orange-brown scales rounded on the back, those of the inner rows accrescent, tipped with red, and about $1'$ long at maturity. **Wood** heavy, hard, straight, close-grained, not strong, bright brown tinged with red, with thin almost white sapwood of 60–70 layers of annual growth; used for the outside and inside finish of houses, in cabinet-making, for street pavement, wooden dishes, and fruit boxes.

Distribution. Fairfield County, Connecticut, and in the neighborhood of the coast to southeastern Pennsylvania, southward to Cape Canaveral and the shores of Tampa Bay, Florida, and westward through southern Ohio, Indiana and Illinois to southeastern Missouri, and through Arkansas to eastern Oklahoma and the valley of the Trinity River, Texas; reappearing on the mountains of central and southern Mexico and on the highlands of Guatemala; in the maritime region of the south Atlantic and Gulf states and in the basin of the lower Mississippi River one of the common trees of the forest, covering rich river bottom-lands usually inundated every year; in the northern and middle states on the borders of swamps and low wet swales; at the north rarely more than 60°–70° tall, with a trunk usually not more than 2° in diameter.

Unsurpassed in the brilliancy of the autumnal colors of the leaves; and often planted as an ornamental tree in the eastern states.

2. HAMAMELIS L. Witch Hazel.

Trees or shrubs, with scaly bark, terete zigzag branchlets, naked buds, and fibrous roots. Leaves involute in the bud, more or less unsymmetrical at base, crenately toothed or lobed, the primary veins conspicuous; stipules acute, infolding the bud, deciduous. Flowers perfect, autumnal or hiemal, in 3 or rarely 4-flowered terminal clusters, from buds appearing in summer, on short recurved peduncles from the axils of leaves of the year, furnished near the middle with 2 acute deciduous bractlets, covered like their acute bracts and bractlets with dark ferrugineous pubescence, each flower surrounded by 2 or 3 ovate acute bracts, the outer slightly united at base into a 3-lobed involucre; calyx 4-parted pale pubescent on the outer surface, orange-brown, yellow or red on the inner surface, persistent on the base of the ovary, the lobes reflexed; petals bright yellow, inserted on the margin of the cup-shaped receptacle, alternate with the sepals, strap-shaped, falling with the stamens when the ovules are fertilized; stamens 8, inserted in 2 rows on the margin of the receptacle, the 4 opposite the lobes of the calyx fertile, the others reduced to minute strap-shaped scales; filaments free, shorter than the calyx, prolonged into a thickened pointed connective; anthers ellipsoid, opening laterally from without by persistent valves; ovary of 2 carpels, free at apex, inserted in the bottom of the receptacle, partly superior, remaining during the winter without enlarging and surrounded and protected by the calyx; styles subulate, spreading, stigmatic at apex, persistent; ovule solitary. Fruit ripening in the autumn, usually 2 from each flower-cluster, capsular, 2-beaked at apex, surrounded for one-third or one-half its length by the enlarged persistent calyx bearing at the base the blackened remnants of the floral bracts, the thick and woody outer layer splitting from above loculicidally before the opening of the thin crustaceous inner layer. Seed oblong, acute, suspended; testa crustaceous, chestnut brown, shining; forcibly discharged when ripe by the contraction of the edges of the valves of the bony endocarp; embryo surrounded by thick fleshy albumen; cotyledons foliaceous; hilum oblong, depressed.

Hamamelis is confined to eastern North America and eastern Asia, with three American and two or three Asiatic species; of the American species two are sometimes small trees, and the third *H. vernalis* Sarg. is a shrub of southern Missouri, western Arkansas, and eastern Oklahoma.

The name is from ἅμα, at the same time with, and μηλίς an Apple-tree, and was applied by the ancients to the Medlar or some similar tree.

CONSPECTUS OF THE NORTH AMERICAN ARBORESCENT SPECIES.

Leaves smooth, conspicuously unsymmetrical at base; flowers autumnal.

                                      1. **H. virginiana** (A, C).

Leaves roughened by persistent tubercles, slightly unsymmetrical at base; flowers hiemal.

                                      2. **H. macrophylla** (C).

1. Hamamelis virginiana L.

Leaves obovate, acuminate, long-pointed or sometimes rounded at apex, very unequal at base, the lower side rounded or subcordate, the upper usually cuneate and smaller, irregularly and coarsely crenately lobed above the middle, entire or dentate below, when

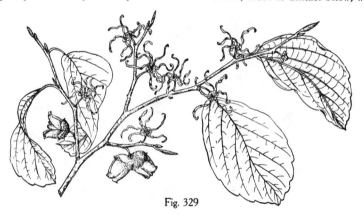

Fig. 329

they unfold coated, especially on the lower surface of the midrib and veins and on the petioles and stipules with stellate ferrugineous pubescence, at maturity membranaceous, dull dark green and glabrous or pilose above, lighter colored and lustrous below, and pubescent or puberulous on the stout midrib and 6 or 7 pairs of primary veins, 4′–6′ long, 2′–2½′ wide; turning delicate yellow in the autumn; petioles slender, pubescent early in the season, becoming glabrous ⅓′–1′ in length; stipules lanceolate, acute, coriaceous, ⅓′–½′ long. **Flowers** opening from the middle of September to the middle of November; calyx orange-brown on the inner surface; petals bright yellow; ½′–⅔′ long. **Fruit** ripening when the flowers of the season are expanding, ½′ long, pubescent, dull orange-brown and surrounded for half its length by the large persistent calyx; seed ¼′ long.

A tree, occasionally 20°–25° high, with a short trunk 12′–14′ in diameter, spreading branches forming a broad open head, and slender flexible branchlets coated at first with scurfy rusty stellate hairs, gradually disappearing during the summer, and in their first winter glabrous or slightly puberulous, light orange-brown and marked by small white dots, becoming in their second year dark or reddish brown; usually a stout shrub sending up from the ground numerous rigid diverging stems 5°–20° tall. **Winter-buds acute,** slightly falcate, light orange-brown, covered with short fine pubescence, $\frac{1}{4}'-\frac{1}{2}'$ long. **Bark $\frac{1}{8}'$** thick, light brown, generally smooth but broken into minute thin appressed scales disclosing in falling the dark reddish purple inner bark. **Wood** heavy, hard, very close-grained, light brown tinged with red, with thick nearly white sapwood of 30–40 layers of annual growth. The bark and leaves are slightly astringent and although not known to possess essential properties are largely used in the form of fluid extracts and decoctions and in homœopathic practice, Pond's Extract being made by distilling the bark in diluted alcohol.

Distribution. Nova Scotia, New Brunswick, and the valley of the St. Lawrence River to southern Ontario, southern Wisconsin, southeastern Minnesota and northeastern Iowa, and southward to central Georgia and southern Arkansas, growing usually on the borders of the forest in low rich soil or on the rocky banks of streams; of its largest size and probably only arborescent on the slopes of the high Alleghany Mountains in North and South Carolina and Tennessee.

Occasionally cultivated as an ornamental plant in the northern states, and in western and northern Europe.

2. Hamamelis macrophylla Pursh.

Leaves short-obovate or occasionally broad-elliptic, rounded, acute or rarely acuminate at apex, cuneate, rounded or cordate at the narrow slightly unsymmetrical base, crenate-lobulate above the middle with small rounded lobes, covered with short stellate hairs more

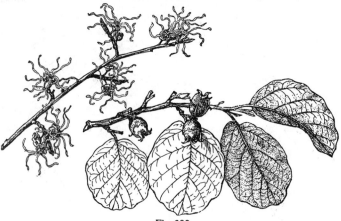

Fig. 330

abundant on the upper than on the lower surface, and at maturity dark green above, paler below, and roughened by the persistent tubercle-like bases of the stellate hairs, 3'–5' long, 2'–3' wide, with a slender midrib and five or six pairs of primary veins; petioles slender, pubescent, $\frac{1}{2}'-\frac{3}{4}'$ in length; stipules lanceolate, acuminate, scarious, hoary-pubescent, $\frac{1}{4}'-\frac{1}{2}'$ long. **Flowers** opening in December, January and February; calyx yellow on the inner surface; petals light yellow, $\frac{1}{2}'$ long and less than $\frac{1}{24}'$ wide. **Fruit** ripening in the autumn, about $\frac{1}{2}'$ in length; **seed** dark chestnut-brown or nearly black.

A tree, often 30°–45° high, producing stoloniferous shoots round the tall trunk often 1° in diameter, erect and spreading branches, and branchlets rusty or hoary-tomentose during their first year, becoming glabrous or nearly glabrous and grayish brown in their second season; often a shrub. **Winter-buds** rusty-tomentose, about $\frac{1}{3}'$ in length.

Distribution. Rich soil, by streams or along the borders of the forest; valley of the .lower Savannah River, near Savannah, Chatham County, and along the Withlacoochee River, Lowndes County, Georgia, to central and western Florida; through Alabama; in southern and central Mississippi, and through Louisiana to eastern Texas (Beaumont, Jefferson County, and Fletcher, Hardin County), and southern Arkansas; generally distributed and most abundant in Louisiana; probably of its largest size on the bluffs of the Alabama River in Dallas County, Alabama.

XXI. PLATANACEÆ.

Trees, with watery juice, thick deeply furrowed scaly bark exfoliating from the branches and young trunks in large thin plates, terete zigzag pithy branchlets prolonged by an upper axillary bud, and fibrous roots. Winter-buds axillary, conic, large, smooth, and lustrous, nearly surrounded at base by the narrow leaf-scars displaying a row of conspicuous dark fibro-vascular bundle-scars, covered by 3 deciduous scales, the 2 inner accrescent, strap-shaped, rounded at apex at maturity, marking in falling the base of the branchlet with narrow ring-like scars, the outer scale surrounding the bud and splitting longitudinally with its expansion, the second light green, covered by a gummy fragrant secretion and usually inclosing a bud in its axil, the third coated with long rufous hairs. Leaves longitudinally plicate in vernation, alternate, broadly ovate, cordate, truncate, or cuneate and decurrent on the petiole at base, more or less acutely 3–7-lobed, and occasionally furnished with a more or less enlarged basal lobe, the lobes entire, dentate with minute remote callous teeth, or coarsely sinuate-toothed, penniveined, the veins arcuate and united near the margins and connected by inconspicuous reticulate veinlets, clothed while young like the petioles, stipules, and young branchlets with caducous stellate sharp-pointed branching hairs, pale on the lower and rufous on the upper surface, long-petiolate; turning brown and withering in the autumn before falling; petioles abruptly enlarged at base and inclosing the buds; stipules membranaceous, laterally united below into a short tube surrounding the branchlet above the insertion of their leaf, acute, more or less free above, dentate or entire, thin and scarious on flowering shoots, broad and leaf-like on vigorous sterile branchlets, caducous, marking the branchlet in falling with narrow ring-like scars. Flowers minute, appearing with the unfolding of the leaves in dense unisexual pedunculate solitary or spicate heads, the staminate and pistillate heads on separate peduncles or rarely united on the same peduncle; staminate heads dark red on axillary peduncles; pistillate heads light green tinged with red, on long terminal peduncles, the lateral heads in the spicate clusters sessile and embracing at maturity the peduncle, usually persistent on the branches during the winter; calyx of the staminate flower divided into 3–6 minute scale-like sepals slightly united at base, about half as long as the 3–6 cuneiform sulcate scarious pointed petals; stamens as many as the divisions of the calyx, opposite them, with short nearly obsolete filaments, and elongated clavate 2-celled anthers, their cells opening longitudinally and crowned by a capitate pilose truncate connective; calyx of the pistillate flower divided into 3–6, usually 4, rounded sepals much shorter than the acute petals; stamens scale-like, elongated-obovoid, pilose at apex; ovaries as many as the divisions of the calyx, superior, oblong, sessile, surrounded at base by long ridged jointed pale hairs persistent round the fruit, gradually narrowed into long simple bright red styles papillose-stigmatic to below the middle along the ventral suture; ovules 1 or rarely 2, suspended laterally, orthotropous. Head of fruit composed of elongated obovoid akenes rounded and obtuse or acute at apex, surmounted by the persistent styles, 1-seeded, light yellow-brown; pericarp thin, coriaceous. Seed elongated-oblong, suspended; testa thin and firm, light chestnut-brown; embryo erect in thin fleshy albumen; cotyledons oblong, about as long as the elongated cylindric erect radicle turned toward the minute apical hilum. Wood hard and heavy not strong, light brown tinged with red, with numerous broad conspicuous medullary rays and bands of smaller ducts marking the layers of annual growth. A family of a single genus.

1. PLATANUS L.   Plane-tree.

Characters of the family.

A genus of four or five species of eastern and western North America, Mexico, Central America, and of southwestern Asia, all resembling each other except in the form of the lobes of the leaves and the amount of pubescence on their lower surface, in the pointed or obtuse apex of the akene, and in the number of heads of pistillate flowers on their peduncle.

Of the exotic species, the Old World *Platanus acerifolia* Willd., of doubtful origin, and often considered a hybrid between *P. orientalis* L. and the Plane-tree of the eastern United States, is now a common street tree in the cities of all the countries of temperate Europe, and is largely used as a street and shade tree in the eastern states and in California.

Platanus is the classical name of the Plane-tree.

CONSPECTUS OF THE NORTH AMERICAN SPECIES.

Heads of fruit usually solitary; leaves broadly ovate, slightly 3–5-lobed, the lobes broad, mostly serrulate, or entire, truncate or rarely cuneate at base.   1. **P. occidentalis** (A, C).
Heads of fruit racemose.
Leaves 3–5-lobed to below the middle, the lobes entire, remotely and obscurely dentate, or rarely sinuate-toothed, truncate or slightly cordate or cuneate at base.
                              2. **P. racemosa** (G).
Leaves deeply 5–7-lobed, the lobes elongated, slender, entire, or rarely remotely dentate, deeply cordate or rarely cuneate or truncate at base.   3. **P. Wrightii** (H).

1. Platanus occidentalis L.   Sycamore.   Buttonwood.

Leaves broadly ovate, more or less 3–5-lobed by broad shallow sinuses rounded at the bottom, the lobes broad, acuminate, sinuate-toothed with long straight or curved remote acuminate teeth, or entire with undulate margins, truncate or slightly cordate, or long-

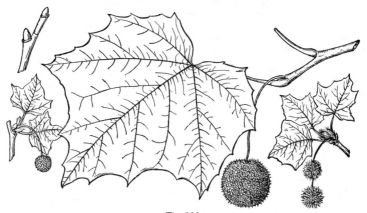

Fig. 331

cuneate and decurrent on the petiole at base (var. *attenuata* Sarg.), thin and firm, bright green on the upper surface, paler on the lower, glabrous at maturity with the exception of a slight pubescence on the under side of the thin midrib and stout yellow veins, 4′–7′ long and broad, or twice as large on vigorous shoots and then frequently furnished with dentate basal lobes; petioles stout, terete or slightly angled, becoming puberulous 3′–5′ in length; stipules 1′–1½′ long, entire or sinuate-toothed.   **Flowers:** peduncles coated with pale tomentum, bearing 1 and sometimes 2 heads of flowers.   **Fruit:** heads 1′ in diameter, on slender glabrous stems 3′–6′ in length; akene about ⅔′ long and truncate or obtusely rounded at apex.

A tree, occasionally 140°–170° high, with a trunk sometimes 10°–11° in diameter above its abruptly enlarged base, often divided near the ground into several large secondary trunks, or rising 70°–80°, with a straight column-like shaft free of branches and with little dimunition of diameter, massive spreading limbs forming a broad open irregular head sometimes 100° in diameter, their extremities usually erect or more or less pendulous, and slender branchlets coated at first like the leaves, petioles, and stipules with thick pale deciduous tomentum, during their first summer dark green and glabrous, marked by minute oblong pale lenticels, becoming dark orange-brown and rather lustrous during their first winter and light gray in their second year. **Winter-buds** $\frac{1}{4}'-\frac{3}{8}'$ long. **Bark** of young trunks and large branches rarely more than $\frac{1}{2}'$ thick, dark reddish brown, broken into small oblong thick appressed plate-like scales, smooth, light gray, and separating higher on the tree into large thin scales, in falling exposing large irregular surfaces of the pale yellow, whitish, or greenish inner bark, becoming at the base of large trunks $2'-3'$ thick, dark brown, and divided by deep furrows into broad rounded ridges covered by small thin appressed scales. **Wood** the favorite material for tobacco boxes, ox-yokes, and butcher's blocks, and now largely used for furniture and the interior finish of houses.

Distribution. Borders of streams and lakes on rich bottom-lands; southeastern Maine to northern Vermont and through southern Ontario and Michigan to central and southern Iowa, southeastern Nebraska, eastern Kansas, and eastern Oklahoma to the valley of the Arkansas River (Clay County), and southward to middle Florida (Gadsden County), central Alabama and Mississippi, and the valley of the Rio Grande (Zavalla County) western Texas; common but most abundant and of its largest size on the bottom lands of streams in the basin of the lower Ohio and Mississippi rivers; less abundant and of smaller size in the coast region of the Carolinas and in western Texas; ascending the Appalachian Mountains up to altitudes of 2500°. The most massive if not the tallest deciduous-leaved tree of eastern North America.

Sometimes planted as a street tree, especially in the cities of eastern Texas; passing into

1. Platanus occidentalis var. glabrata Sarg.

Platanus glabrata Fern.

Leaves usually broader than long, truncate, broad-cuneate or rarely cordate at base, 3-lobed by sinuses acute or rounded in the bottom, the lobes long-acuminate, entire, the lateral lobes often furnished near the base with one or rarely with two small acuminate in-

Fig. 332

curved secondary lobes occasionally found also on the terminal lobe, tcmentose below and pubescent above when the flowers open the end of March in Texas, later becoming glabrous except on the under side of the midrib and veins, usually about $2\frac{3}{4}'-5\frac{1}{2}'$ long and $3'-3\frac{1}{2}'$ wide; petioles pubescent, becoming glabrous. Peduncles bearing one or rarely two heads. **Flowers** and **Fruit** like those of the species.

Distribution. Western Texas, common; valley of the Colorado River, near Austin, Travis County, to that of the Devil's River, Valverde County; in Coahuila and Nuovo Leon; rarely northward with widely scattered individuals; the prevailing form on the Edwards Plateau and in the counties adjacent to the Rio Grande.

2. Platanus racemosa Nutt. Sycamore.

Leaves 3–5-lobed to below the middle by broad sinuses acute or rounded in the bottom, the lobes acute or acuminate, entire, dentate with remote callous tipped teeth, or occa-

Fig. 333

sionally coarsely sinuate-toothed, usually cordate or sometimes truncate, or cuneate and decurrent on the petiole at base, thick and firm, light green above, paler and more or less thickly coated below with pale pubescence most abundant along the midrib and primary veins, 6′–10′ long and broad; petioles stout, pubescent, 1′–3′ in length; stipules $1'-1\frac{1}{2}'$ long, entire or dentate, often persistent until spring. **Flowers:** peduncles hoary-pubescent, bearing usually 4 or 5 heads of staminate flowers and 2–7 heads of pistillate flowers, a head of the staminate flowers occasionally appearing on the pistillate peduncle above the heads of fertile flowers. **Fruit:** heads $\frac{3}{4}'$ in diameter, on slender zigzag glabrous or pubescent stems 6′–9′ in length; akene acute or rounded at apex, $\frac{1}{3}'$ long, tomentose while young, becoming glabrous.

A tree, 40°–90° high, with a trunk sometimes 9° in diameter above the broad tapering base, erect and free of branches for half its height, more often divided near the ground into secondary stems erect, inclining, or prostrate for 20°–30° at their base, thick heavy more or less contorted spreading branches forming an open irregular round-topped head, and branchlets coated at first with thick pale deciduous tomentum, light reddish brown, and marked by numerous small lenticels in their first winter, becoming gradually darker in their second and third years; usually smaller, with a trunk 2°–4° in diameter. **Winter-buds** nearly $\frac{1}{2}'$ long. **Bark** at the base of old trunks 3′–4′ thick, dark brown, deeply fur-rowed, with broad rounded ridges separating on the surface into thin scales; thinner, smooth, and pale, or almost white higher on the trunk and on the branches.

Distribution. Banks of the streams of western California; valley of the upper Sacramento River (Tehama County) southward through the interior valleys, along the western foothills of the Sierra Nevada and on the southern coast ranges; and on Mount San Pedro Màrtir in Lower California; exceedingly common in all the valleys of the California coast ranges from Monterey to the southern borders of the state, and ascending the southern slopes of the San Bernardino Mountains to altitudes of 3000°–4000°.

3. Platanus Wrightii S. Wats. Sycamore.

Leaves divided by narrow sinuses to below the middle and sometimes nearly to the center into 3–7 but usually into 3–5 elongated acute lobes entire, or dentate with callous-tipped teeth, or occasionally furnished with 1 or 2 lateral lobes, sometimes deeply cordate by the downward projection of the lower lobes, or often truncate or cuneate at base, thin and firm in texture, light green and glabrous above, covered below with pale pubescence, 6′–8′ long and broad, with a slender midrib, and primary veins connected by conspicuous

Fig. 334

reticulate veinlets; petioles stout, glabrous or puberulous, 1½′–3′ in length. **Flowers:** peduncles hoary-tomentose, bearing 1–4 heads of flowers. **Fruit:** heads on slender glabrous stems 6′–8′ long, about ¾′ in diameter; akenes glabrous, ¼′ long, truncate at apex.

A tree, often 60°–80° high, with a straight trunk 4°–5° in diameter, gradually tapering and free of branches for 20°–30°, or with a trunk divided at the ground into 2 or 3 large stems usually more or less reclining and often nearly prostrate for 15°–20°, thick contorted branches, the lowest growing almost at right angles to the trunk and 50°–60° long, the upper usually erect at first, finally spreading into a broad open handsome head, and slender branchlets coated when they first appear with thick pale tomentum, becoming glabrous or slightly puberulous during their first winter, marked by minute scattered lenticels, and light brown tinged with red or ashy gray, and gradually darker in their second or third year. **Winter-buds** hardly more than ¼′ long. **Bark** at the base of the trunk dark, 3′–4′ thick, deeply and irregularly divided into broad ridges, and covered on the surface with small appressed scales, thinner and separating into large scales 10°–15° above the ground, and gradually passing into the smooth much thinner creamy white bark faintly tinged with green of the upper branches.

Distribution. Banks of streams in the mountain cañons of southwestern New Mexico and southern Arizona; in northern Arizona in Oak Creek Cañon near Flagstaff (*P. Lowell*); and in Sonora; the largest and one of the most abundant of the deciduous-leaved trees on all the mountain ranges of southern Arizona, extending from the mouth of cañons up to altitudes of 5000°–6000° above the sea.

XXII. ROSACEÆ.

Trees, shrubs and herbs, with watery juices, terete branchlets, scaly buds, and alternate leaves (*opposite in Lyonothamnus*), with stipules. Flowers perfect; calyx 5-lobed; petals 5 (*0 in Cercocarpus*), imbricated in the bud, inserted with the numerous distinct stamens on the edge of a disk lining the calyx-tube; anthers introrse (*extrorse in Vauquelinia*), 2-celled, the cells opening longitudinally; ovary superior in Lyonothamnus and Heteromeles, often partly superior in Amelanchier; ovules 2 in each cell (*1 in Cowania and Cercocarpus, 4 in Lyonothamnus*), anatropous. Seeds without albumen (*albuminous in Lyonothamnus and Cowania*). A family of about ninety genera chiefly confined to the temperate parts of the world and producing many of the most valuable fruits, including the apple, pear, quince, strawberry, raspberry, and blackberry. The six tribes into which the genera of the family are grouped, have arborescent representatives in North America.

CONSPECTUS OF THE NORTH AMERICAN ARBORESCENT GENERA.

Tribe 1. SPIRÆOIDEÆ. Fruit a woody capsule.

Flowers in terminal cymose corymbs; calyx-lobes persistent; ovary 5-celled; ovules ascending; mature carpels adherent below and opening down the back; albumen 0; leaves simple. **1. Vauquelinia.**

Flowers in terminal corymbs; calyx-lobes deciduous; ovary 2-celled; ovules 4 in each cell, pendulous; mature carpels opening on the ventral and partly on the dorsal suture; albumen thin; leaves opposite, simple or pinnately divided.

2. Lyonothamnus.

Tribe 2. POMOIDEÆ. Fruit a pome composed of the thickened and succulent calyx-tube inclosing the papery or bony carpels; stipules free from the petioles.

Mature carpels papery.

Carpels as many as the styles.

Flowers in few-flowered terminal racemes on short spur-like lateral branchlets; ovary 3–5-celled; styles more or less united below; leaves simple; winter-buds small.

3. Malus.

Flowers in broad compound terminal cymes; ovary 2–4, usually 3-celled; styles distinct; fruit subglobose; leaves unequally pinnate; winter-buds large.

4. Sorbus.

Flowers in large terminal corymbose panicles; ovary nearly superior, 2-celled; styles distinct; fruit obovoid. **5. Heteromeles.**

Carpels becoming at maturity twice as many as the styles; flowers in erect or nodding racemes; ovary inferior or partly superior; styles 2–5, more or less united below; fruit subglobose or pyriform; leaves simple, deciduous. **6. Amelanchier.**

Mature carpels bony; flowers in terminal cymose corymbs; ovary 1–5-celled; styles distinct; fruit globose to pyriform; leaves simple, deciduous. **7. Cratægus.**

Tribe 3. DRYADÆ. Calyx-tube turbinate, campanulate or hemispheric; petals 5; ovary composed of 1 or several carpels; fruit an akene tipped with the elongated plumose style.

Flowers terminal on short branchlets, solitary; calyx-tube turbinate; carpels 5–12; leaves alternate, toothed or pinnatifid. **8. Cowania.**

Tribe 4. CERCOCARPÆ. Calyx-tube salver-shaped; petals 0; ovary composed of a single carpel; fruit an akene, tipped with the elongated plumose style.

Leaves alternate, simple, entire or serrate. **9. Cercocarpus.**

Tribe 5. PRUNOIDEÆ. Fruit a 1-seeded drupe; ovary 1-celled; style terminal; ovules pendulous.

Flowers in fascicled umbels, or racemes; leaves simple, deciduous or persistent.

10. Prunus.

Tribe 6. CHRYSOBALANOIDEÆ. Fruit a 1-seeded drupe; ovary 1-celled; style lateral, ovules ascending.

Flowers in axillary or terminal cymose panicles; leaves simple, persistent.

11. **Chrysobalanus.**

1. VAUQUELINIA Corr.

Trees or shrubs, with slender terete branchlets and scaly bark. Leaves alternate or rarely opposite, lanceolate, serrate, long-petiolate, reticulate-veined, coriaceous, persistent; stipules minute, acute, deciduous. Flowers on slender bibracteolate pedicels, in compound terminal leafy cymose corymbs; calyx short-turbinate, coriaceous, 5-lobed, the lobes ovate, obtuse or acute, erect, persistent; petals 5, orbicular or oblong, white, becoming reflexed, persistent; stamens 15–25, inserted in 3 or 4 series, equal or semiequal, those of the outer row opposite the petals; filaments subulate, exserted, persistent; anthers versatile, extrorse; carpels 5, opposite the sepals, inserted on the thickened base of the calyx-tube and united below into a 5-celled ovoid tomentose ovary crowned with 5 short spreading styles dilated into capitate stigmas; ovules subbasilar, ascending, prolonged at the apex into thin membranaceous wings; raphe ventral; micropyle superior. Fruit a woody ovoid 5-celled tomentose capsule inclosed at the base by the remnants of the flower, the mature carpels adherent below and at maturity splitting down the back. Seeds 2 in each cell, ascending, compressed; testa membranaceous, expanded into a long terminal membranaceous wing; embryo filling the cavity of the seed; cotyledons flat; radicle straight, erect.

Vauquelinia is confined to the New World and is distributed from New Mexico, Arizona and Lower California to southern Mexico. Three species are distinguished; of these one inhabits the mountain ranges of southern Arizona and New Mexico.

The generic name is in honor of the French chemist Louis Nicholas Vauquelin (1763–1829).

1. Vauquelinia californica Sarg.

Leaves narrowly lanceolate, acuminate or rarely rounded at apex, abruptly cuneate or slightly rounded at base, and remotely serrate with minute glandular teeth, when they unfold puberulous above and densely tomentose below, and at maturity coriaceous, bright

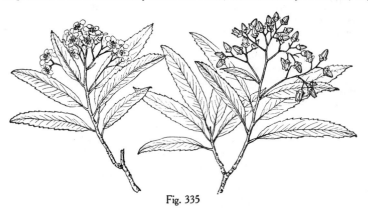

Fig. 335

yellow-green and glabrous on the upper and tomentose on the lower surface, $1\frac{1}{2}'$–$3'$ long, $\frac{1}{4}'$–$\frac{1}{2}'$ wide, with a thick conspicuous midrib grooved on the upper side, and numerous thin primary veins connected by reticulate veinlets; deciduous in spring or early summer; petioles thick, $\frac{1}{3}'$–$\frac{1}{2}'$ in length. **Flowers** appearing in June, $\frac{1}{4}'$ in diameter, in hoary-tomentose panicles $2'$–$3'$ across; petals oblong; inner surface of the disk pilose. **Fruit** fully grown by the end of August, $\frac{1}{4}'$ long, persistent on the branches after opening until the spring of the following year; conspicuous from the contrast of the bright red faded petals and the white silky pubescence of the calyx and carpels; seed $\frac{1}{12}'$ long, and one third as long as its wing.

A tree, 18°–20° high, with a slender often hollow trunk 5′–6′ in diameter, rigid upright contorted branches, and slender branchlets at first bright reddish brown and more or less thickly covered with hoary tomentum, becoming light brown or gray in their second year and marked by large elevated leaf-scars; or more often a low shrub. **Winter-buds:** axillary minute, acuminate, reddish brown, pubescent. **Bark** about $\frac{1}{16}'$ thick, dark red-brown, and broken on the surface into small square persistent plate-like scales. **Wood** very heavy, hard, close-grained, dark rich brown streaked with red, with 14 or 15 layers of annual growth.

Distribution. Bottoms and rocky sides of gulches, or on grassy slopes; mountain ranges of extreme southwestern New Mexico (Guadalupe Cañon, teste *E. A. Mearns*), southern Arizona, Sonora, and Lower California; arborescent and of its largest size in Arizona on the Santa Catalina Mountains at altitudes of about 5000° above the sea.

2. LYONOTHAMNUS A. Gray.

A tree or shrub, with scaly bark exfoliating in long strips, stout terrete pubescent ultimately glabrous branchlets, and scaly, acuminate buds. Leaves opposite, long-petiolate, lanceolate, acuminate, rounded or cuneate at base, entire, finely crenulate-serrate or serrulate lobulate below the middle, or sometimes irregularly pinnately parted into 3–8 linear-lanceolate remote lobulate segments, coriaceous, transversely many-veined, dark green above, paler and more or less pubescent below, persistent; stipules lanceolate, acute, minute, caducous. Flowers on slender pedicels, in broad compound terminal pubescent cymose corymbs, with minute acute persistent bracts and bractlets; calyx-tube hemispheric, with 1–3 bractlets, tomentose on the outer surface, the lobes nearly triangular, slightly keeled, apiculate, persistent; disk 10-lobed, with a slightly thickened margin; petals 5, orbicular, sessile, white; stamens 15, inserted in pairs opposite the petals and singly opposite the sepals; filaments subulate, incurved, as long as the petals; anthers ovate, 2-celled, the cells opening longitudinally; carpels 2, inserted in the bottom of the calyx-tube, forming a superior glandular, hairy ovary; styles 2, spreading; stigmas capitate, truncate; ovules 4 in each cell, suspended; micropyle superior; raphe ventral. Fruit of 2 woody ovoid glandular-setulose carpels, dehiscent on the ventral and partly dehiscent on the dorsal suture. Seeds ovate-oblong, pointed at the ends; seed-coat light brown, thin and membranaceous; hilum orbicular, apical; raphe broad and wing-like; cotyledons oblong, acuminate, twice as long as the straight radicle directed toward the hilum.

Lyonothamnus is represented by a single species found only on the islands off the coast of southern California.

Lyonothamnus, in honor of its discoverer, William S. Lyon.

1. Lyonothamnus floribundus A. Gray. Ironwood.

Leaves 4′–8′ long, $\frac{1}{2}'$ wide when entire, or 4′ wide when pinnately divided, when they unfold covered below with hoary deciduous tomentum, at maturity dark green and lustrous above and yellow-green, glabrous or pubescent below, with an orange-colored midrib. **Flowers** in June and July, $\frac{1}{8}'-\frac{1}{4}'$ in diameter, in clusters varying from 4′–8′ across. **Fruit** ripens in August and September, $\frac{3}{16}'$ long.

A bushy tree, rarely 30°–40° high, with a single straight trunk 8′–10′ in diameter, and slender branchlets at first pale orange color and coated with deciduous pubescence, becoming at the end of their first season bright red and lustrous; usually shrubby, with several tall stems, or in exposed situations a low bush. **Bark** $\frac{1}{4}'$ thick, dark red-brown, and composed of numerous thin papery layers, forming after exfoliating long loose strips persistent on the stem. **Wood** heavy, hard, close-grained, bright clear red faintly tinged with orange.

Distribution. Steep slopes of cañons in dry rocky soil; on the islands of Santa Catalina, Santa Cruz, San Clemente, Santa Rosa, California; most abundant and of its largest size on

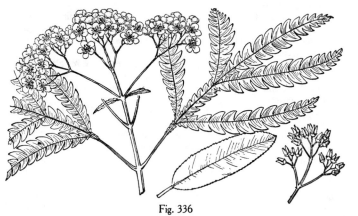

Fig. 336

the northern shores of Santa Cruz; on Santa Catalina much smaller and rarely arborescent. Now occasionally cultivated in California.

3. MALUS Miller. Apple.

Trees, with scaly bark, slender terete branchlets, small obtuse buds covered by imbricated scales, those of the inner ranks accrescent and marking the base of the branchlet with conspicuous ring-like scars, and fibrous roots.   Leaves conduplicate in the bud in the American species, simple, often incisely lobed, especially those near the end of vigorous branchlets, petiolate, deciduous, the petioles in falling leaving narrow horizontal scars marked by the ends of three equidistant fibro-vascular bundles; stipules free from the petioles, filiform, early deciduous.   Flowers in short terminal racemes, with filiform deciduous bracts and bractlets, on short lateral spur-like often spinescent branchlets; calyx-tube obconic, 5-lobed, the lobes imbricated in the bud, acuminate, becoming reflexed, persistent and erect on the fruit or deciduous; petals rounded at apex, contracted below into a stalk-like base, white, pink or rose color; stamens usually 20 in 3 series, those of the outer series opposite the petals; carpels 3–5, usually 5, alternate with the petals, united into an inferior ovary; styles united at base; ovules 2 in each cell, ascending; raphe dorsal; micropyle inferior.   Fruit a pome with homogeneous flesh, and papery carpels joined at apex, free in the middle; seeds 2, or by abortion 1 in each cell, ovoid, acute, without albumen; seed-coat cartilaginous, chestnut-brown and lustrous; embryo erect; cotyledons plano-convex, fleshy; radicle short, inferior.   Malus is confined to North America where nine species have been recognized, to western and southeastern Europe, and to central, southern, and eastern Asia.   Of exotic species, *Malus pumila* Mill. of southeastern Europe and central Asia, the Apple-tree of orchards, has become widely naturalized in northeastern North America.   Several of the species of eastern Asia and their hybrids are cultivated for their handsome flowers, or for their fruits, the Siberian Crabs of pomologists. *Malus* is the classical name of the Apple-tree.

CONSPECTUS OF THE NORTH AMERICAN SPECIES.

Calyx persistent on the green or rarely yellow fruit covered with a waxy exudation; leaves of vigorous shoots laterally lobed; anthers dark (Chloromeles).
  Leaves glabrous at maturity.

Leaves on flowering branchlets, acute or acuminate, serrate.

Leaves at the end of vigorous shoots distinctly lobed, those of flowering branchlets incisely serrate or lobed.

Leaves subcordate, with the lowest pair of veins springing directly from the base, light green on the lower surface.   1. **M. glabrata** (A).

Leaves truncate or rounded at base, the lowest pair of veins at some distance from the base.

Leaves glaucescent beneath, thickish at maturity.   2. **M. glaucescens** (A, C).

Leaves light green on the lower surface, thin.   3. **M. coronaria** (A, C).

Leaves at the end of vigorous shoots only slightly lobed, those of flowering branchlets serrate.

Leaves oval-elliptic, acute; fruit much depressed, distinctly broader than high.   4. **M. platycarpa** (A, C).

Leaves lanceolate, acuminate, thin; fruit subglobose.   5. **M. lancifolia.**

Leaves on flowering branchlets usually rounded at apex, those at the end of vigorous shoots only slightly lobed; fruit subglobose.   6. **M. angustifolia** (A, C).

Leaves tomentose or villose at maturity, at least those of vigorous shoots, strongly veined.

Calyx glabrous on the outer surface; leaves of flowering branchlets without lobes, glabrous or nearly so.   7. **M. bracteata** (A, C).

Calyx tomentose or pubescent on the outer surface; leaves usually incisely lobed, pubescent or tomentose beneath, rarely glabrous.   8. **M. ioensis** (A, C).

Calyx deciduous from the yellow or reddish fruit without a waxy exudation; leaves of vigorous shoots often 3-lobed at apex; anthers yellow (Sorbomalus).

     9. **M. fusca** (B, G).

1. Malus glabrata Rehd. Crab Apple.

Leaves triangular-ovate or ovate, acute or acuminate at apex, cordate or rarely truncate at base, lobed with 2 or 3 pairs of short-acute or short-acuminate coarsely serrate lobes,

Fig. 337

when they unfold bronze color and sparingly covered with caducous hairs, glabrous when fully expanded, and at maturity dark yellow-green and lustrous above, pale below, $2\frac{1}{2}'$–3' long and $2'$–$2\frac{1}{2}'$ wide, with 5–7 pairs of prominent primary veins, the lowest pair from the base of the leaf; petioles slender, glabrous, $\frac{4}{5}'$–$1\frac{1}{4}'$ in length; leaves at the end of vigorous shoots more deeply lobed and often 4' long and $3\frac{1}{2}'$ wide. **Flowers** about $1\frac{1}{4}'$ in diameter, on slender glabrous purple pedicels $\frac{3}{5}'$–$1\frac{1}{4}'$ long, in 4–7-flowered clusters; calyx-tube purple and glabrous, the lobes glabrous on the outer surface, slightly longer than the tube; petals suborbicular or broadly ovate, abruptly contracted below, about $\frac{2}{5}'$ wide, often erose-denticulate; stamens about one third shorter than the petals; styles 5, slightly longer than the stamens, villose below the middle. **Fruit** on slender pedicels about $\frac{4}{5}'$ in length, depressed globose, slightly angled, distinctly ribbed at the deeply impressed apex, about $1\frac{1}{4}'$ high and $1\frac{1}{2}'$ in diameter, with a deep basal cavity; **seed** obovoid-oblong, about $\frac{1}{3}'$ long.

A tree, 18°–25° high, with a short trunk rarely 1° in diameter, spreading branches often armed with stout straight spines up to $1\frac{1}{2}'$ in length, and glabrous purple branchlets, becoming purple-brown and slightly lustrous at the end of their first season, dull red-brown in their second year, and ultimately grayish brown. **Winter-buds** ovoid or oblong-ovoid, acute, glabrous, dark purple-brown up to $\frac{1}{4}'$ in length.

Distribution. A common Crab Apple in the valleys of western North Carolina at altitudes of 2000°–3500°; near Biltmore, Buncombe County, Dillsboro, Jackson County, and Highlands, Macon County.

2. Malus glaucescens Rehd. Crab Apple.

Leaves triangular-ovate or ovate, acute, short-acuminate or rounded at apex, truncate or rounded at base, those of flowering branchlets more or less lobed and coarsely serrate with abruptly acuminate teeth, their lobes triangular, broad-ovate and abruptly acumi-

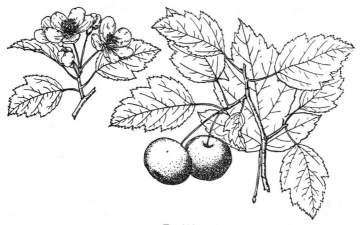

Fig. 338

nate, those of the lowest pair usually the longest, bronze color and covered with thin floccose tomentum when they unfold, soon glabrous, dull yellowish green above, glaucescent below, $1\frac{1}{2}'$–$3\frac{1}{2}'$ long and $1\frac{1}{4}'$–$3'$ wide, with 4–7 pairs of prominent primary veins; turning yellow or dark purple and falling early in the autumn; petioles slender, slightly villose at first, soon glabrous, $1\frac{1}{2}'$–$3'$ in length; stipules filiform, purple, glabrous or slightly villose, about $\frac{1}{4}'$ long; leaves at the end of vigorous shoots broad-ovate, acuminate, rounded or slightly cordate at base, often deeply lobed, $3'$–$3\frac{1}{2}'$ long, $3'$ wide, with petioles $1\frac{1}{2}'$–$2'$ in length. **Flowers** $1\frac{1}{3}'$–$1\frac{1}{2}'$ in diameter, on slender glabrous pedicels, $\frac{4}{5}'$–$1\frac{1}{4}'$ in length, in usually 5–7-flowered clusters, calyx-tube coated with floccose caducous pubescence or glabrous, slightly shorter than the long-acuminate lobes densely tomentose on the inner surface; petals oval, abruptly contracted below into a long claw, white or rose color, $\frac{1}{2}'$–$\frac{3}{5}'$ wide; stamens about one third shorter than the petals; styles 5, about as long as the stamens, densely villose below and united at base for about one fourth of their length. **Fruit** depressed globose, pale yellow when ripe, $1'-1\frac{1}{4}'$ high, $1\frac{1}{4}'-1\frac{3}{4}'$ in diameter, with a shallow only slightly corrugated cavity at apex and a shallow concave depression at base.

An arborescent shrub or small tree, rarely more than 15° high, often spreading into thickets, with a trunk 4' or 5' in diameter, spreading spinescent branches forming an open irregular head, and slender branchlets slightly pubescent at first, soon glabrous, bright red-brown in their first and second years, becoming dark gray-brown and marked by yellow lenticels. Bark dark gray, divided by shallow longitudinal fissures and finally separating into small thin scales.

Distribution.   Glades and open woods in rich soil; western New York (Ontario, Monroe, Cattaraugus and Erie Counties) to southern Ontario, western Pennsylvania (near Carnot, Allegheny County); and southeastern and northern Ohio; Tiptop, Tazewell County, Virginia; near Spruce Pine, Mitchell County, North Carolina; slopes of Lookout Mountain, above Valleyhead, DeKalb County, Alabama; apparently most generally distributed and most abundant in Ohio.

3. Malus coronaria L.   Crab Apple.   Garland Tree.

Leaves ovate to oval, rounded, acute or acuminate and often abruptly short-pointed at apex, rounded or cuneate at base, and coarsely serrate usually only above the middle, tinged with red and villose-pubescent when they unfold, soon glabrous, and at maturity

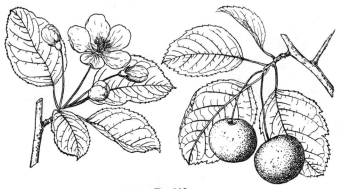

Fig. 339

yellow-green above, paler below, $2'-3'$ long and $1\frac{1}{2}'$ wide, with a prominent midrib and thin inconspicuous primary veins; turning yellow in the autumn before falling; petioles slender, at first puberulous, becoming glabrous, $\frac{1}{2}'-1'$ in length; leaves at the end of vigorous shoots broad-ovate, usually lobed with short acute lobes, more coarsely serrate, thicker, often $3'-4'$ long and $2'-3'$ wide, with a prominent midrib and primary veins, and stout petioles often tinged with red and $1\frac{1}{4}'-2'$ in length.   **Flowers** $1\frac{1}{4}'-1\frac{1}{2}'$ in diameter, on glabrous pedicels $\frac{1}{2}'-1'$ long, in 3–6-flowered clusters: calyx-tube glabrous, or rarely more or less densely villose-pubescent (var. *dasycalyx* Rehd.), the lobes long-acuminate, longer than the tube, sparingly pubescent on the outer surface, hoary-tomentose on the inner surface; petals oblong-obovate, gradually or abruptly narrowed into a long claw, about $\frac{1}{2}'$ wide; stamens shorter than the petals; styles 5, clothed for half their length with long white hairs and united at the base.   **Fruit** on slender pedicels $1\frac{1}{2}'-2'$ in length, green when fully grown, yellow-green at maturity, $\frac{3}{4}'-1'$ high and $1'-1\frac{1}{4}'$ wide.

A tree, often forming dense thickets, $25°-30°$ high, with a trunk $12'-14'$ in diameter, dividing $8°-10°$ above the ground into several stout spreading branches forming a wide open head, and branchlets hoary-tomentose when they first appear, glabrous or slightly pubescent, bright red-brown and marked by occasional small pale lenticels in their first winter, and

developing in their second year stout, spur-like, somewhat spinescent lateral branchlets.
Winter-buds obtuse, with bright red scales scarious and ciliate on the dark margins. **Bark**
⅓' thick, longitudinally fissured, the outer layer separating into long narrow persistent red-
brown scales. **Wood** heavy, close-grained, not strong, light red, with yellow sapwood of
18–20 layers of annual growth; used for levers, the handles of tools, and many small domestic
articles.

Distribution. Western New York to southern Ontario and westward through Ohio, southern Michigan, Indiana, Illinois, and southern Wisconsin to Missouri (Jackson and Butler
Counties), and southward through Pennsylvania to northern Delaware, and along the Appalachian Mountains to North Carolina, sometimes up to altitudes of 3300°; the var. *dasycalyx*
common and widely distributed in Ohio (Lorain, Clark, Franklin, Hardin and Lucas Counties, *R. E. Horsey*), and in Wells and Porter Counties, Indiana (*C. C. Deam*).

Sometimes planted in the gardens of the northern and eastern states; passing into

Malus coronaria var. elongata Rehd.

Malus elongata Ashe.

Leaves oblong-ovate, gradually narrowed and acuminate at apex, rounded or broad-
cuneate at base, incisely serrate or slightly lobed, floccose-tomentose when they unfold, soon
glabrous, dark yellow-green above, lighter below, 2'–3½' long, 1'–1¼' wide; at the end of vig-

Fig. 340

orous shoots ovate, rounded or broad and cuneate at base, acuminate, lobed with short
acuminate lobes, 3½'–4' long, 2'–2½' wide, with a prominent midrib and primary veins, and
slightly pubescent orange-colored petioles 1'–1½' in length. **Flowers** and **Fruit** as in the
species.

A shrub or small tree, sometimes forming dense almost impenetrable thickets.

Distribution. Western New York (Ontario, Cattaraugus and Erie Counties); Virginia
(on Peak Mountain, Pulaski County); West Virginia (near Elkins, Randolph County,
and White Sulphur Springs, Greenbrier County), and westward to southern Ohio (Oberlin,
Lorain County); North Carolina (near Highlands, Macon County); and northeastern
Georgia (Rabun County).

4. Malus platycarpa Rehd. Crab Apple.

Leaves ovate to elliptic, abruptly contracted at the rounded apex into a short point,
rounded at base, and sharply usually doubly serrate, when they unfold covered with long

white hairs caducous except from the midrib and at maturity glabrous; dark yellow-green, lustrous, and slightly rugulose on the upper surface, lighter on the lower surface, $2\frac{1}{2}'-3\frac{1}{4}'$ long and $1\frac{1}{2}'-2\frac{1}{2}'$ wide, with 5–7 pairs of prominent primary veins; petioles slender, villose, often becoming nearly glabrous, $1'-1\frac{1}{2}'$ in length; on vigorous shoots often broad-ovate and lobed with short triangular lobes sometimes $4'$ long and nearly as wide. **Flowers** about $1\frac{1}{2}'$ in diameter, on glabrous pedicels $1\frac{1}{2}'-2\frac{1}{2}'$ long, in 3–6-flowered clusters; calyx-tube glabrous or rarely pubescent (var. *Hoopesii* Rehd.), the lobes lanceolate, acuminate, longer than the tube, glabrous on the outer surface, densely tomentose on the inner surface; petals orbicular-obovate, usually irregularly incisely dentate and abruptly contracted at base into a short claw, slightly villose on the inner surface near the base, $\frac{1}{2}'$ to

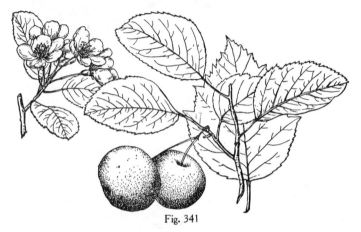

Fig. 341

nearly $1'$ wide; stamens slightly shorter than the petals; styles 5, somewhat shorter than the stamens, villose below the middle and united below for one third their length. **Fruit** on slender pedicels, $1\frac{1}{4}'-1\frac{1}{2}'$ in length, depressed globose with a deep cavity at base and apex, $1\frac{1}{2}'-1\frac{3}{4}'$ high and $2'-2\frac{1}{2}'$ wide; **seeds** oblong-obovoid, about $\frac{1}{3}'$ long.

A tree, $18°-20°$ high, with a trunk $4'$ or $5'$ in diameter, spreading unarmed branches, and branchlets clothed when they first appear with thin villose tomentum, becoming by the end of their first year glabrous, brown or purple-brown and lustrous, dull brown in their second season, and ultimately grayish brown. **Winter-buds** ovoid, acute, glabrous except on the villose margins of the purplish brown scales, about $\frac{1}{4}'$ long.

Distribution. Near Franklin, Macon County, North Carolina; Mercer Springs, Mercer County, West Virginia; near Olympia, Bath County, Kentucky; Youngstown, Mahoning County, Ohio (*R. E. Horsey*).

5. Malus lancifolia Rehd. Crab Apple.

Leaves ovate-lanceolate to oblong-lanceolate, acute or short-acuminate at apex, rounded or broad-cuneate at base, finely or coarsely doubly serrate with short or occasionally with larger teeth pointing forward, covered with thin floccose tomentum when they unfold, soon glabrous, bright yellow-green, $1\frac{1}{2}'-3'$ long, $\frac{1}{2}'-1'$ wide, with 8–10 pairs of veins; petioles slender, slightly villose at first, soon glabrous, $\frac{1}{2}'-1'$ in length; leaves on vigorous shoots ovate or oblong-ovate, slightly lobed, more densely pubescent below, $2\frac{1}{2}'-3\frac{3}{4}'$ long, $2'-2\frac{1}{2}'$ wide, with a thin midrib and 4–7 pairs of veins slightly villose through the season, and stouter petioles. **Flowers** $1\frac{1}{4}'-1\frac{1}{2}'$ in diameter, in 3–6-flowered clusters, on slender glabrous pedicels about $1\frac{1}{4}'$ in length; calyx glabrous, the lobes longer than the tube, oblong-lanceolate, glabrous on the outer surface, coated with villose tomentum on the inner surface;

petals contracted into a long narrow claw, glabrous, white or rose color, $\frac{1}{2}'$ wide; stamens shorter than the petals; styles 5, densely villose below the middle. **Fruit** on slender drooping pedicels about 1' long, subglobose, 1'–1$\frac{1}{4}'$ wide.

A tree, 20°–25° high, with a trunk 12'–15' in diameter, spreading spinescent branches forming an open pyramidal head, and slender branchlets slightly pubescent or nearly gla-

Fig. 342

brous when they first appear, becoming reddish brown at the end of their first season and ultimately gray-brown. **Bark** of the trunk brownish gray, divided by shallow longitudinal fissures and separating into thin plates.

Distribution. Northeastern Pennsylvania (Scranton, Lackawanna County) to the western and southwestern parts of the state, and southward to Randolph and Greenbrier Counties, West Virginia, Pulaski County (on Peak Mountain), Virginia, and to the mountains of North Carolina up to altitudes of 3200°, and westward to northeastern Kentucky, through southern Ohio, eastern Indiana (Delaware County) and southern Illinois (Richland, Jackson, Gallatin and Pope Counties); Missouri (Jackson and Wayne Counties).

6. Malus angustifolia Michx. Crab Apple.

Leaves elliptic to oblong-obovate, rounded or acute and apiculate at apex, gradually narrowed and cuneate at base, and crenately serrate, hoary-tomentose below and sparingly villose above when they unfold, soon glabrous, or occasionally pubescent on the midrib below, and at maturity subcoriaceous dull green on the upper and light green on the lower surface, 1'–2' long, $\frac{1}{2}'$–$\frac{3}{4}'$ wide; turning brown in drying; petioles slender, at first villose, soon glabrous, $\frac{1}{2}'$–$\frac{3}{4}'$ in length; stipules linear, rose-colored, $\frac{1}{3}'$ long; leaves at the end of vigorous shoots ovate, oblong-ovate or elliptic, usually lobed with numerous short acute lobes, or coarsely serrate, usually rounded at apex, broad-cuneate at base, at maturity glabrous, or slightly floccose-pubescent below, especially on the midrib and veins, 2'–3' long, 1$\frac{1}{2}'$–2' wide, with stout often rose-colored glabrous or pubescent petioles. **Flowers** about 1' in diameter, very fragrant, on slender glabrous or rarely puberulous pedicels, $\frac{3}{4}'$–1' long, in mostly

3–5-flowered clusters; calyx-tube short and broad, glabrous, the lobes about as long as the tube, glabrous on the outer surface, thickly covered with hoary tomentum on the inner surface; petals oblong-obovate, gradually narrowed below into a long claw, rose-colored, about $\frac{1}{4}'$ wide; stamens shorter than the petals; styles 5, united at base, villose below the middle. **Fruit** depressed-globose, pale yellow-green, $\frac{3}{4}'$–1' in diameter.

A tree, rarely 30° high, with a short trunk 8'–10' in diameter, rigid spreading or rarely slender and pendulous (var. *pendula* Rehd.) branches forming a broad open head, and young branchlets clothed at first with pale caducous pubescence, soon glabrous, in their first winter brown slightly tinged with red, and in their second year light brown and marked by occasional orange-colored lenticels. **Winter-buds** $\frac{1}{16}'$ long, chestnut-brown,

Fig. 343

slightly pubescent. **Bark** $\frac{3}{8}'$–$\frac{1}{4}'$ thick, dark reddish brown, and divided by deep longitudinal fissures into narrow ridges broken on the surface into small persistent plate-like scales. **Wood** heavy, hard, close-grained, light brown tinged with red, with thick yellow sapwood; occasionally employed for levers, the handles of tools and other small objects. The fruit is used for preserves.

Distribution. Southeastern Virginia in the neighborhood of the coast, southward to western Florida, and through southern Alabama and Mississippi to western Louisiana (near Winnfield, Winn County); in the Carolinas and Georgia, ranging inland to the Appalachian foothills and in Mississippi to the neighborhood of Iuka, Tishomingo County in the northeastern corner of the state; in southern Illinois (Pope and Johnson Counties. *E. J. Palmer*).

7. Malus bracteata Rehd.

Leaves elliptic-ovate to oblong-ovate, acute, on flowering branchlets sometimes obtusish at apex, cuneate or rounded at base, serrate or incisely serrate, sometimes slightly lobed near the base, covered below with floccose tomentum when they unfold, soon glabrous, and at maturity thin, bright yellow-green and lustrous above, light green below, $1\frac{1}{2}'$–3' long, 1'–$1\frac{1}{4}'$ wide; petioles glabrous, reddish like the under side of the midrib, $\frac{3}{4}'$–1' in length; leaves at the end of vigorous shoots ovate, acute, cuneate at base, usually lobed with 4 or 5 pairs of short acute or rounded lobes, more thickly tomentose when they unfold, at maturity thicker, glabrous above, more or less pubescent below, often 3'–$3\frac{1}{2}'$ long and 2'–$2\frac{1}{2}'$ wide, with a stout midrib and petiole. **Flowers** 1'–$1\frac{1}{4}'$ in diameter, on slender glabrous or nearly glabrous pedicels, in 3–5-flowered clusters, with subulate bractlets $\frac{1}{5}'$–$\frac{1}{3}'$ long, often persistent until after the flowers open; calyx-tube glabrous, the lobes slightly longer than the tube, villose on the inner surface; petals oval, narrowed into a slender claw, deep pink, $\frac{5}{12}'-\frac{1}{2}'$ wide; stamens about one third shorter than the petals; styles slightly shorter than the stamens, united at base and villose below for a third of their length. **Fruit** depressed-globose, with a shallow basal cavity and a shallow slightly corrugated cavity at apex. slightly viscid, $\frac{4}{5}'-1'$ high and $1'-1\frac{1}{4}'$ wide.

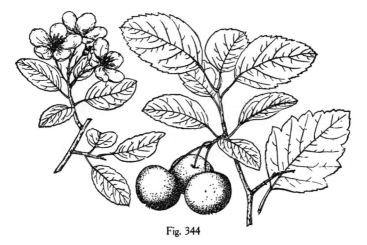

Fig. 344

A tree, 15°–30° high, with a trunk up to 6' or 7' in diameter, thick branches forming a broad often symmetrical head, and stout branchlets red and glabrous when they first appear, becoming reddish brown and lustrous at the end of their first season, and dull red-brown and armed with occasional stout spines or unarmed the following year, the vigorous shoots more or less pubescent early in the season, becoming glabrous, or often densely pubescent until autumn. **Winter-buds** red-brown, glabrous, or slightly pubescent. **Bark** dark brown and broken into thin closely appressed scales.

Distribution. Missouri (Allenton, St. Louis County, and Campbell, Dunklin County); northern Kentucky (Fordsville, Ohio County); Tennessee, without locality; North Carolina (Biltmore, Buncombe County, near Highlands, Macon County, up to altitudes of 3500°, and Abbottsburg, Bladen County); Georgia (Dillard, Rabun County, near Augusta, Richmond County); Florida (River Junction, Gadsden County).

8. Malus ioensis Britt. Crab Apple.

Leaves elliptic to ovate or oblong-obovate, acute, acuminate or rounded at apex, cuneate or rounded at the narrow base, crenately serrate, and often slightly lobed with acute or rounded lobes, hoary-tomentose below and floccose-pubescent above when they unfold, and at maturity thick and firm, dark green, lustrous and glabrous above, pale yellow-green and tomentose or nearly glabrous below, $2\frac{1}{2}'-4'$ long, $1'-1\frac{1}{2}'$ wide, with a slender midrib and primary veins; turning yellow in the autumn before falling; petioles slender, hoary-tomentose in early spring, becoming pubescent or nearly glabrous, $\frac{3}{4}'-1'$ in length; leaves at the end of vigorous shoots broad-ovate to oblong-ovate, acute, rounded at the broad or narrow base, often deeply lobed, covered below through the season with floccose easily detached tomentum, often 4' or 5' long and 3' or 4' wide, with a thick midrib and primary veins, and stout hoary-tomentose petioles $\frac{3}{4}'-1'$ in length. **Flowers** $1\frac{1}{2}'-2'$ in diameter, on villose pubescent pedicels $1'-1\frac{1}{2}'$ long, in 3–6-flowered clusters; calyx covered with hoary tomentum, the lobes narrow, rather longer than the tube; petals obovate, gradually narrowed below into a long slender claw, rose color or white, about $\frac{1}{2}'$ wide; stamens shorter than the petals; styles 5, united at base, covered below for a third of their length with long white hairs.

Fruit on stout tomentose or villose stems 1′–1½′ long, depressed globose, with shallow basal and apical depressions, green or greenish yellow, ¾′–1′ high, and 1′–1¼′ wide.

A tree, 20°–30° high, with a trunk 12′–18′ in diameter, stout spreading branches forming a wide open head, and branchlets hoary-tomentose when they first appear, glabrous or

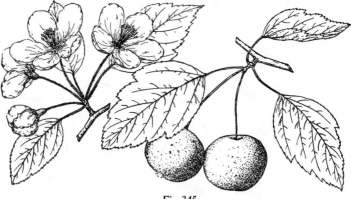

Fig. 345

slightly pubescent, bright red-brown and marked by occasional small pale lenticels in their first winter, the lateral branchlets usually spinescent. **Winter-buds** minute, obtuse, pubescent above the middle. **Bark** ⅓′ thick, covered with long narrow persistent red-brown scales.

Distribution. Southeastern Minnesota to Iowa, eastern Nebraska, and Missouri, and through southern Wisconsin and Illinois to Huntington County, Indiana. Passing into var. *Palmeri* Rehd., differing from the type in its smaller oblong more thinly pubescent leaves usually rounded at apex, those of the flowering branchlets crenately serrate and not lobed; a small tree rarely more than 15° high, with a slender stem, spiny zigzag branches and stout branchlets densely tomentose when they first appear, becoming glabrous or nearly glabrous and reddish or gray-brown at the end of their first season; the common form in Missouri, Arkansas and eastern Oklahoma. On the Edwards Plateau, in western Texas (Blanco, Kendall, and Kerr Counties) *M. ioensis* is represented by the var. *texana* Rehd., differing in its smaller and broader leaves only slightly or not at all lobed and densely villose through the season; usually an intricately branched shrub forming large dense thickets. A shrub from Campbell, Dunklin County, southeastern Missouri, with small leaves and flowers, a glabrescent calyx, and long slender flexible branches armed with numerous long straight spines is distinguished as var. *spinosa* Rehd. A variety with elliptic-ovate to oblong-ovate leaves rounded or broadly cuneate at base, nearly entire or crenately serrate, pubescent below at least on the veins, with densely villose petioles is distinguished as var. *creniserrata* Rehd.; a small tree with slender spineless branchlets villose while young; near Pineville, Rapides Parish, and Crowly, Arcadia Parish, western Louisiana. A variety with less deeply lobed glabrescent oblong-lanceolate leaves is distinguished as var. *Bushii* Rehd.; Williamsville, Wayne County, and Monteer, Shannon County, southern Missouri.

Malus ioensis var. *plena* Rehd., the Bechtel Crab, a form with large rose-colored double flowers is a favorite garden plant.

× *Malus Soulardii* Britt. with ovate, elliptic or obovate usually obtuse leaves, rugose and tomentose on the lower surface, and depressed-globose fruit 2′–2½′ in diameter, is believed to be a hybrid of *Malus ioensis* and *Malus pumila*.

9. Malus fusca Schn. Crab Apple.

Malus rivulàris Roem.

Leaves ovate to elliptic or lanceolate, acute or acuminate, cuneate or rounded at base, sharply serrate with appressed glandular teeth, and often slightly 3-lobed, when they unfold pubescent on the lower and puberulous on the upper surface, at maturity thick and firm, dark green and glabrous above, pale and pubescent or glabrous below, $1'-4'$ long, $\frac{1}{2}'-1\frac{1}{2}'$ wide, with a prominent midrib and primary veins and conspicuous reticulate veinlets; before falling in the autumn turning bright orange and scarlet; petioles stout, rigid,

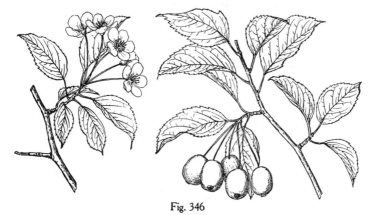

Fig. 346

pubescent, $1'-1\frac{1}{2}'$ in length; stipules narrowly lanceolate, acute, $\frac{1}{2}'-\frac{3}{4}'$ long; leaves at the end of vigorous shoots ovate to obovate, acuminate, often 3-lobed above the middle, rounded or cuneate at base, $2\frac{1}{2}'-3\frac{1}{2}'$ long and wide, with petioles often $2'$ in length. **Flowers** $\frac{3}{4}'$ in diameter on slender pubescent or glabrous pedicels, $\frac{1}{2}'-\frac{3}{4}'$ long, in short many-flowered clusters; calyx-tube deciduous from the mature fruit, glabrous, puberulous or tomentose, the lobes rather longer than the tube, minutely apiculate, glabrous or tomentose, hoary-tomentose on the inner surface; petals orbicular to obovate, erose or undulate on the margins, abruptly contracted into a short claw, $\frac{1}{4}'$ wide, white or rose color; styles 2–4, glabrous. **Fruit** obovoid-oblong, $\frac{1}{2}'-\frac{3}{4}'$ long, yellow-green, light yellow flushed with red or sometimes nearly red; flesh thin and dry.

A tree, $30°-40°$ high, with a trunk $12'-18'$ in diameter, and slender branchlets coated at first with long pale hairs soon deciduous or persistent until the autumn, becoming bright red and lustrous, and later dark brown, and marked by minute remote pale lenticels; often a shrub with numerous slender stems. **Winter-buds** $\frac{1}{16}'$ long, chestnut-brown, the inner scales at maturity lanceolate, usually bright red, and nearly $\frac{1}{2}'$ in length. **Bark** $\frac{1}{4}'$ thick, and covered by large thin loose light red-brown plate-like scales. **Wood** heavy, hard, close-grained, light brown tinged with red, with lighter colored sapwood of 20–30 layers of annual growth; used for mallets, mauls, the handles of tools, and the bearings of machinery. The fruit has a pleasant subacid flavor.

Distribution. Deep rich soil in the neighborhood of streams, often forming almost impenetrable thickets of considerable extent; Aleutian Islands southward along the coast and islands of Alaska and British Columbia to Sonoma and Plumas Counties, California; of its largest size in the valleys of western Washington and Oregon.

Occasionally cultivated as an ornamental plant in the eastern states, and in western Europe.

$\times$ *Malus Dawsoniana* Rehd., a hybrid of *Malus fusca* and a form of *M. pumila*, has been raised at the Arnold Arboretum from seeds collected in Oregon.

4. SORBUS L. Mountain Ash.

Trees or shrubs, with smooth aromatic bark, stout terete branchlets, large buds covered by imbricated scales, the inner accrescent and marking the base of the branchlet by conspicuous ring-like scars, and fibrous roots. Leaves alternate, pinnate in the American species, the pinnæ conduplicate in the bud, serrate, deciduous; stipules free from the petioles, foliaceous. Flowers in broad terminal leafy cymes; calyx-tube urn-shaped, 5-lobed, the lobes imbricated in the bud, persistent; petals rounded, abruptly narrowed below, white; stamens usually 20 in 3 series, those of the outer series opposite the petals; carpels 2–5, usually 3; styles usually 3, distinct; ovules 2 in each cell, ascending; raphe dorsal; micropyle inferior. Fruit a small subglobose red or orange-red pome with acid flesh, and papery carpels free at the apex. Seeds 2, or by abortion 1, in each cell, ovoid, acute, erect; seed-coat cartilaginous, chestnut-brown and lustrous; embryo erect; cotyledons plano-convex, flat; radicle short, inferior.

Sorbus is widely distributed through the northern and elevated regions of the northern hemisphere with three or four species in North America of which one is arborescent, and with many species in eastern Asia and in Europe. Of the exotic species, *Sorbus Aucuparia* L., the common European Mountain Ash, or Rowan-tree, with several of its varieties and hybrids, is often cultivated as an ornamental tree in Canada and the northern states and has become sparingly naturalized northward.

Sorbus is the classical name of the Pear or of the Service-tree.

1. Sorbus americana Marsh.

Leaves 6′–8′ long, with 13–17 lanceolate acute taper-pointed leaflets unequally cuneate or rounded and entire at base, sharply serrate above with acute often glandular teeth, sessile or short-stalked, or the terminal leaflet on a stalk sometimes ½′ long, when they un-

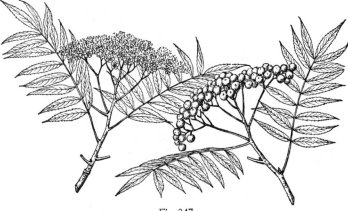

Fig. 347

fold slightly pubescent below, at maturity membranaceous, glabrous, dark yellow-green, on the upper surface, and paler or glaucescent and rarely pubescent on the lower surface, 2′–4½′ long, ¼–1′ wide, with a prominent midrib and thin veins; turning bright clear yellow before falling in the autumn; petioles grooved, dark green or red, 2′–3′ in length, the rachis often furnished with tufts of dark hairs at the base of the petiolules; stipules broad, nearly triangular, variously toothed, caducous. **Flowers** appearing after the leaves are fully grown, ⅛′ in diameter, on short stout pedicels, in flat cymes 3′–4′ across, with acute minute caducous bracts and bractlets; calyx broadly obconic and puberulous, with short, nearly triangular lobes tipped with minute glands and about half as long as the nearly orbicular creamy white petals. **Fruit** ¼′ in diameter, subglobose or slightly pyriform, bright orange-red, with thin flesh; **seeds** pale chestnut color, rounded at apex, acute at base, about ⅛′ long.

A tree, 20°–30° high, with a trunk rarely more than a foot in diameter, spreading slender branches forming a narrow round-topped head, and stout branchlets pubescent at first, soon glabrous, becoming in their first winter brown tinged with red, and marked by the large leaf-scars and by oblong pale remote lenticels, and darker in their second year, the thin papery outer layer of bark then easily separable from the bright green fragrant inner layers; more often a tall or sometimes a low shrub, with numerous stems. **Winter-buds** acute, ¼′–¾′ long, with dark vinous red acuminate scales rounded on the back, more or less pilose, covered with a gummy exudation, the inner scales hoary-tomentose in the bud. **Bark** ⅛′ thick, with a smooth light gray surface irregularly broken by small appressed plate-like scales. **Wood** close-grained, light, soft and weak, pale brown, with lighter colored sapwood of 15–20 layers of annual growth. The astringent fruit is employed domestically in infusions and decoctions, and in homœopathic remedies.

Distribution. Borders of swamps and rocky hillsides; Newfoundland to Manitoba and southward through the maritime provinces of Canada, Quebec and Ontario, the elevated portions of the northeastern United States and the region of the Great Lakes to Minnesota, and on the Appalachian Mountains from western Pennsylvania and West Virginia to North Carolina and Tennessee; in North Carolina ascending to altitudes of nearly 6000°; probably of its largest size on the northern shores of Lakes Huron and Superior; in the United States, except in New England, more often a shrub than a tree; on the Appalachian Mountains usually low, with narrower leaflets and smaller fruit than northward.

Often cultivated in Canada and the northeastern States for the beauty of its fruit and the brilliancy of its autumn foliage. Of its forms the most distinct is

Sorbus americana var. decora Sarg.

Pyrus sambucifolia A. Gray, not Cham. and Schlecht.

Pyrus americana var. *decora* Sarg.

Sorbus decora Schn.

Sorbus scopulina Britt., in part, not Greene.

Pyrus sitchensis Rob. and Fern., not Piper.

Leaves 4′–6′ long, with 7–13 oblong-oval to ovate-lanceolate leaflets blunt and rounded, abruptly short-pointed or acuminate at apex, pubescent below as they unfold, at matu-

Fig. 348

rity glabrous, dark bluish green on the upper surface and pale on the lower surface; petioles stout, usually red $1\frac{1}{2}'-2'$ in length. **Flowers** $\frac{1}{4}'$ in diameter, in rather narrower clusters, appearing eight to ten days later than those of the type. **Fruit** subglobose, bright orange-red, often $\frac{1}{2}'$ in diameter.

A tree, occasionally 30° high, with a trunk sometimes a foot in diameter, and spreading branches forming a round-topped handsome head.

Distribution. Coast of Labrador to the northern shores of Lake Superior and Minnesota, southward to the mountains of northern New Hampshire, Vermont, and New York. Distinct in its extreme forms but connected with *Sorbus americana* by intermediate forms.

This variety of *Sorbus americana*, perhaps the most beautiful of the genus when the large and brilliant fruits cover the branches in autumn and early winter, occasionally finds a place in the gardens of eastern Canada and the northern states.

5. HETEROMELES Roem.

A tree, with smooth pale aromatic bark, stout terete branchlets pubescent or puberulous while young, acute winter-buds covered by loosely imbricated red scales, and fibrous roots. Leaves oblong-lanceolate, acute at the ends, sharply and remotely serrate with rigid glandular teeth, or rarely almost entire, dark green and lustrous above, paler below, feather-veined, with a broad midrib and conspicuous reticulate veinlets; petiolate with stout petioles often furnished near the apex with 1 or 2 slender glandular teeth; stipules free from the petioles, subulate, rigid, minute, early deciduous. Flowers on short stout pedicels, in ample tomentose terminal corymbose leafy panicles, their bracts and bractlets acute, minute, usually tipped with a small gland, caducous; calyx-tube turbinate, tomentose below, glabrate above, the lobes short, nearly triangular, spreading, persistent; disk cup-shaped, obscurely sulcate; petals flabellate, erose-denticulate or emarginate at apex, contracted below into a short broad claw, thick, glabrous, pure white; stamens 10, inserted in 1 row with the petals in pairs opposite the calyx-lobes; filaments subulate, incurved, anthers oblong-ovoid, emarginate; carpels 2, adnate to the calyx-tube, and slightly united into a subglobose tomentose nearly superior ovary; styles distinct, slightly spreading, enlarged at apex into a broad truncate stigma; ovules 2 in each cell, ascending; raphe dorsal; micropyle inferior. Fruit obovoid, fleshy, the thickened calyx-tube connate to the middle only with the membranaceous carpels coated above with long white hairs filling the cavity closed by the infolding of the thickened persistent calyx-lobes, their tips erect and crowning the fruit. Seed usually solitary in each cell, ovoid, obtuse, slightly ridged on the back; seed-coat membranaceous, slightly punctate, light brown; hilum orbicular, conspicuous; embryo filling the cavity of the seed; cotyledons plano-convex; radicle short, inferior.

The genus is represented by a single species of western North America.

The generic name, from ἕτερος and μῆλον, is in reference to its difference from related genera.

1. Heteromeles arbutifolia Roem.   Tollon.   Toyon.

Leaves appearing with the flowers in early summer, $3'-4'$ long, $1'-1\frac{1}{2}'$ wide, usually persistent during at least two winters; petioles $\frac{1}{2}'-\frac{2}{3}'$ in length. **Flowers** opening from June to August in clusters $4'-6'$ across and often more or less hidden by young lateral branchlets rising above them. **Fruit** ripening in November and December, mealy, astringent and acid, scarlet or rarely yellow, $\frac{1}{3}'$ long, remaining on the branches until late in the winter.

A tree, sometimes 30° high, with a straight trunk $12'-18'$ in diameter, dividing a few feet above the ground into many erect branches forming a handsome narrow round-topped head, and slender branchlets covered at first with pale pubescence, in their first winter dark red and slightly puberulous, ultimately becoming darker and glabrous. **Winter-buds** $\frac{1}{4}'$ long. **Bark** $\frac{2}{3}'-\frac{1}{2}'$ thick, light gray, with a generally smooth surface roughened by obscure reticulate ridges. **Wood** very heavy, hard, close-grained, dark red-brown, with thin lighter colored sapwood of 7 or 8 layers of annual growth. The fruit-covered branches are gathered in large quantities and used in California in Christmas decorations.

Distribution. Usually in the neighborhood of streams or on dry hills and especially on their northern slopes, and often on steep sea-cliffs; California: coast region from Mendocino County to Lower California; most common and of its largest size on the islands off

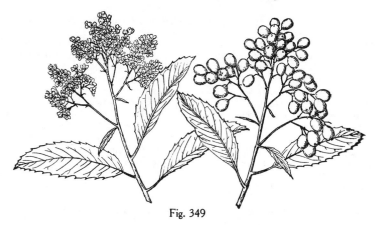

Fig. 349

the California coast; on the foothills of the Sierra Nevada and on the San Bernardino Mountains up to altitudes of 2000° above the sea and usually shrubby; very abundant and forming groves of considerable extent on the island of Santa Catalina.

Occasionally cultivated as an ornamental plant in California, and rarely in the countries of southern Europe.

6. AMELANCHIER Med.

Trees or shrubs, with scaly bark, slender terete branchlets, acute or acuminate buds, with imbricated scales, those of the inner rows accrescent and bright-colored, and fibrous roots. Leaves alternate, conduplicate in the bud, simple, entire or serrate, penniveined, petiolate, deciduous; stipules free from the petioles, linear, elongated, rose color, caducous. Flowers in erect or terminal racemes, on slender bibracteolate pedicels developed from the axils of lanceolate acuminate pink deciduous bracts; calyx-tube campanulate or urceolate, the lobes acute or acuminate, recurved, persistent on the fruit; disk green, entire or crenulate, nectariferous; petals white, obovate-oblong, spatulate or ligulate, rounded, acute or truncate at apex, gradually contracted below into a short slender claw; stamens usually 20, inserted in 3 rows, those of the outer row opposite the petals; filaments subulate, persistent on the fruit, anthers oblong; ovary inferior or superior, more or less adnate to the calyx-tube, the summit glabrous or tomentose, 5-celled, each cell incompletely divided by a false partition; styles 2–5, connate below, spreading and dilated above into a broad truncate stigma; ovules 2 in each cell, erect; micropyle inferior. Fruit subglobose or pyriform, dark blue or bluish black, often covered with a glaucous bloom, open at the summit, the cavity surrounded by the lobes of the calyx and the remnants of the filaments; flesh sweet, dry or juicy; carpels membranaceous, free or connate, glabrous, or villose at apex. Seeds 10 or often 5 by the abortion of 1 of the ovules in each cell, ovoid-ellipsoid; seed-coat coriaceous, dark chestnut-brown, mucilaginous; embryo filling the cavity of the seed; cotyledons plano-convex; radicle inferior.

Amelanchier is widely distributed with many species through the temperate, northern

and mountainous regions of eastern and western North America; it occurs with one species
in southern Europe, northern Africa and southwestern Asia, and with another in central
and western China and Japan. Only three species, all North American, attain the habit
and size of trees. The fruit of nearly all the species is more or less succulent, and several
are cultivated in gardens for the beauty of their early and conspicuous flowers, and occasionally for their fruit. The name is of doubtful origin.

CONSPECTUS OF THE NORTH AMERICAN ARBORESCENT SPECIES.

Leaves finely serrate, acute or acuminate at apex; flowers on elongated pedicels in nodding
   racemes; summit of the ovary glabrous; winter-buds lanceolate, long-acuminate.
   Leaves densely white tomentose while young; flowers appearing before or as the leaves
      unfold in silky tomentose racemes; calyx-lobes ovate, acuminate or nearly triangu-
      lar and acute; fruit dry and tasteless.   **1. A. canadensis (A).**
   Leaves slightly pubescent as they unfold, soon glabrous, dark red-brown while young;
      flowers appearing after the leaves are nearly half grown in glabrous racemes; calyx-
      lobes lanceolate or subulate, long-acuminate; fruit sweet and succulent.
                                                                  2. A. laevis (A).
Leaves coarsely serrate usually only above the middle, rounded at apex, oblong-ovate
   or oval; flowers on shorter pedicels in short erect or spreading racemes; summit of the
   ovary covered with hoary tomentum; winter-buds ovoid or ellipsoid, acute or short-
   acuminate.   **3. A. florida (F, C, G).**

1. Amelanchier canadensis Med.   Service Berry.   Shad Bush.

Amelanchier canadensis var. *tomentula* Sarg.

Leaves ovate-oval, oblong-obovate or rarely lanceolate or oblanceolate, acuminate and
often abruptly short-pointed at apex, rounded, slightly cordate or occasionally cuneate
at base, and finely serrate with acuminate teeth pointing forward; thickly coated when

Fig. 350

they unfold with silvery white tomentum, more or less densely pale pubescent below
until midsummer, later becoming glabrous or nearly glabrous, yellowish green on the
upper surface, paler on the lower surface, usually 2′–4′ long and 1′–2′ wide, southward
sometimes up to 6′ in length, with a slender midrib, and thin primary veins; petioles
slender, hoary-tomentose at first, usually becoming glabrous by midsummer, 1½′–2′ in

length. **Flowers** $\frac{1}{4}'-\frac{1}{3}'$ long, appearing in early spring before or as the leaves unfold, on pedicels $\frac{1}{4}'-\frac{1}{2}'$ in length, in short nodding silky tomentose racemes, their bracts and bractlets linear-lanceolate, villose, bright red; calyx-tube campanulate, glabrous or densely hoary-tomentose, the lobes ovate, acuminate or nearly triangular and acute, glabrous or hoary-tomentose on the outer surface, tomentose on the inner surface, reflexed after the petals fall; petals oblong-obovate, rounded or nearly truncate at apex, about $\frac{1}{6}'$ wide; summit of ovary glabrous. **Fruit** ripening in June and July, maroon-purple, dry and tasteless, about $\frac{1}{4}'$ in diameter.

A tree, occasionally 50°–70° high, with a trunk 12′–18′ in diameter, small erect and spreading branches forming a narrow round-topped head, and slender branchlets thickly covered when they first appear with long white hairs, soon glabrous, bright red-brown during their first year, becoming darker in their second season, and marked by numerous pale lenticels; usually smaller, and in the south Atlantic and Gulf states sometimes a shrub only a few feet tall. **Winter-buds** green tinged with brown, $\frac{1}{2}'-\frac{2}{3}'$ long, about $\frac{1}{12}'$ thick. **Bark** $\frac{1}{4}'-\frac{1}{2}'$ thick, dark ashy gray, divided by shallow fissures into longitudinal ridges covered by small persistent scales.

Distribution. At the north usually on dry exposed hills, on the borders of woods and in fence rows, southward often on the banks of streams and the borders of swamps; valley of the Penobscot River (Winn and Milford, Penobscot County) and Washington County (Pembroke, *M. L. Fernald*), Maine; Quebec (near Longueuil, *Bro. M. Victorin*); valley of the Connecticut River (central Vermont, southern New Hampshire, Massachusetts and Connecticut), and westward through western Massachusetts, New York, southern Ontario, southern Ohio, southern Michigan, and Indiana and Illinois; in central Iowa and southeastern Nebraska (Nemaha County, *J. M. Bates*), and southward to western Florida, southern Alabama, south central Mississippi, Louisiana westward to St. Landry Parish (near Opelousas, *R. S. Cocks*), Arkansas and northeastern Oklahoma; rare and of small size in the south Atlantic coast-region; ascending the southern Appalachian Mountains to altitudes of about 2200°, not common; abundant and probably of its largest size in western New York and southern Michigan.

Occasionally cultivated, and the first of all the cultivated species to flower in the spring.

2. Amelanchier laevis Wieg. Service Berry.

Amelanchier canadensis of many authors, in part, not L.

Leaves ovate to elliptic or rarely lanceolate, acute or acuminate and often abruptly short-pointed at apex, rounded and occasionally slightly cordate or rarely cuneate at base, and sharply and coarsely serrate with subulate callous-tipped teeth, covered when they unfold with long matted pale hairs more abundant on the lower surface than on the upper surface, soon glabrous, dark red-brown until nearly half grown, and at maturity dark green and slightly glaucous above, paler below, usually $2'-2\frac{1}{2}'$ long and $1'-1\frac{1}{2}'$ wide, rarely $3'-3\frac{1}{2}'$ long and not more than 1′ wide, with a thin midrib and primary veins, rarely deep green and lustrous above (f. *nitida* Wieg.); petioles slender, slightly villose at first, soon glabrous, $\frac{1}{2}'-1'$ in length. **Flowers** $\frac{1}{2}'-\frac{3}{4}'$ long, appearing when the leaves are nearly half grown on pedicels $\frac{1}{2}'-1'$ in length, in open few-flowered nodding racemes, becoming much lengthened before the fruit ripens, their bracts and bractlets linear-lanceolate, slightly villose, tinged with rose color; calyx-tube campanulate, glabrous, the lobes lanceolate or subulate, long-acuminate, glabrous on the outer surface, tomentose on the inner surface, usually reflexed before the petals fall; petals oblong-obovate, rounded at apex, about $\frac{1}{6}'$ wide; summit of the ovary glabrous. **Fruit** ripening in June and July, obovoid to subglobose, usually rather broader than long, about $\frac{1}{3}'$ in diameter, purple or nearly black, glaucous, sweet and succulent, on pedicels often $1\frac{1}{2}'-2'$ in length.

A tree, sometimes 30′–40′ high, often with a tall trunk 12′–18′ in diameter, small spreading branches forming a narrow round-topped head, and slender glabrous branchlets reddish brown when they first appear, rather darker during their first winter and dull grayish brown in their second season, and marked by small dark lenticels; at the north often a shrub sometimes only a few feet high. **Winter-buds** $\frac{1}{2}'$ long, about $\frac{1}{12}'$ thick, green tinged with red, the inner scales lanceolate, bright red above the middle, ciliate with silky white hairs, and sometimes 1' long when fully grown. **Bark** $\frac{1}{4}'-\frac{1}{2}'$ thick, dark reddish brown, divided by shallow fissures into narrow longitudinal ridges and covered by small persistent scales. Wood heavy, exceedingly hard, strong, close-grained, dark brown sometimes tinged with red, with thick lighter-colored sapwood of 40–50 layers of annual growth; occasionally used for the handles of tools and other small implements.

Fig. 351

Distribution. Cool ravines and hillsides; Newfoundland, through the maritime provinces of Canada, Quebec and Ontario to northern Wisconsin, and southward through New England, New York and Pennsylvania, and along the Appalachian Mountains to northern Georgia; on the North Carolina Mountains ascending to altitudes of 5500°; common and generally distributed at the north and in New England, New York and through the Appalachian forests; the forma *nitida* only in Newfoundland.

Occasionally cultivated and very beautiful in spring with its abundant pure white flowers and conspicuous red-brown leaves.

3. Amelanchier florida Lindl. Service Berry.

Amelanchier alnifolia Sarg., probably not Nutt.
Amelanchier Cusickii Fern.

Leaves oblong-ovate to oval or ovate, or at the end of vigorous shoots broad-ovate or occasionally broad-obovate, rounded or rarely acute at apex, rounded or slightly cordate at base, and coarsely serrate only above the middle with straight teeth; when they unfold often tinged with red and sometimes floccose-pubescent below, usually soon glabrous, at maturity thin, dark green on the upper surface, pale and rarely pubescent on the lower surface, $1\frac{1}{2}'-2\frac{1}{2}'$ long, and $1'-1\frac{1}{2}'$ wide, with a thin midrib and about ten pairs of primary veins; petioles slender, at first glabrous or puberulous becoming glabrous, $\frac{1}{2}'-1'$ in length. **Flowers** $\frac{1}{2}'-\frac{3}{4}'$ long, appearing when the leaves are about half grown on pedicels $\frac{1}{6}'-\frac{1}{4}'$ in length, in short crowded erect glabrous or pubescent racemes, their bracts and bractlets scarious, slightly villose; calyx-tube campanulate, glabrous or tomentose, the lobes ovate, long-acuminate, glabrous or tomentose on the outer surface, tomentose or rarely nearly glabrous on the inner surface, soon reflexed; petals oblong-obovate gradually narrowed or broad at the rounded apex, $\frac{1}{6}'-\frac{1}{4}'$ wide; summit of the ovary densely tomentose. **Fruit**

usually ripening in July, on pedicels $\frac{1}{2}'-\frac{3}{4}'$ long, in short nearly erect or spreading racemes, short-oblong or ovoid, dark blue, more or less covered with a glaucous bloom, $\frac{1}{4}'$ to nearly $\frac{1}{2}'$ in diameter, sweet and succulent.

A tree, occasionally 30°–40° high, with a tall trunk 12′–14′ in diameter, small erect and spreading branches forming an oblong open head, and slender branchlets glabrous, pubescent or puberulous when they first appear, bright red-brown and usually glabrous during their first season, rather darker in their second year, and ultimately dark gray-brown; more often a large or small shrub. **Winter-buds** ovoid to ellipsoidal, acute or acuminate,

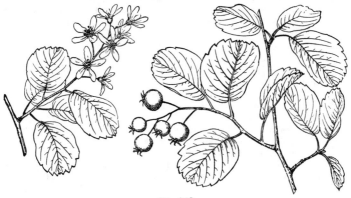

Fig. 352

dark chestnut-brown, glabrous or puberulous, $\frac{1}{6}'-\frac{1}{4}'$ long, scales of the inner ranks ovate, acute, brightly colored, coated with pale silky hairs, $\frac{1}{2}'-\frac{3}{4}'$ long. **Bark** about $\frac{1}{8}'$ thick, smooth or slightly fissured, and light brown slightly tinged with red. **Wood** heavy, hard, close-grained, light brown. The nutritious fruit was an important article of food with the Indians of northwestern America, who formerly gathered and dried it in large quantities.

Distribution. Valley of the Yukon River (near Dawson) and Wrangell, Alaska, and southward to the coast region of British Columbia, and southward in Washington and Oregon possibly to northern California, ranging east in the United States to western Idaho, and probably to the northern Rocky Mountain region; its range, like that of the other species of western North America, still very imperfectly known.

7. CRATÆGUS. Hawthorn.

Trees or shrubs, with usually dark scaly bark, rigid terete more or less zigzag branchlets marked by oblong mostly pale lenticels, and by small horizontal slightly elevated leaf-scars, light green when they first appear, becoming red or orange-brown and lustrous or gray, rarely unarmed or armed with stout or slender short or elongated axillary simple or branched spines generally similar in color to that of the branches or trunk on which they grow, often bearing while young linear elongated caducous bracts, and usually producing at their base one or rarely two buds often developing the following year into a branch, a leaf, or a cluster of flowers, or sometimes lengthening into a leafy branch. Winter-buds small, globose or subglobose, covered by numerous imbricated scales, the outer rounded and obtuse at apex, bright chestnut-brown and lustrous, the inner accrescent, green or rose color, often glandular, soon deciduous. Leaves conduplicate in the bud, simple, generally serrate, sometimes 3-nerved, often more or less lobed, especially on vigorous leading branchlets, membranaceous to coriaceous, petiolate, deciduous; stipules often glandular-serrate, linear, acuminate, frequently bright-colored, deciduous, or on vigorous branchlets often foliaceous, coarsely serrate, usually lunate and stalked and mostly persistent until autumn. Flowers pedicellate, in few or many-flowered simple or compound cymose corymbs terminal on short lateral leafy branchlets, with linear usually bright-colored often glandular caducous bracts and bractlets leaving prominent gland-like scars, the lower branches of compound corymbs usually from the axils of upper leaves; branches of the inflorescence mostly 3-flowered, the central flower opening before the others; calyx-tube usually obconic, 5-lobed, the lobes acute or acuminate and usually gland-tipped, rarely foliaceous, glandular-serrate or entire, green or reddish toward the apex, reflexed after the flowers open, persistent and often enlarged on the fruit, or deciduous; disk thin or fleshy, entire, lobed or slightly sulcate, concave or somewhat convex; petals imbricated in the bud, orbicular, entire or somewhat erose or rarely toothed at apex, white or rarely rose color, spreading, soon deciduous; stamens often variable in number in the same species by imperfect development, but normally 5 in 1 row and alternate with the petals, or 10 in 5 pairs in 1 row alternate with the petals, or 15 in 2 rows, those of the outer row in 5 pairs opposite the sepals and alternate with and rather longer than those of the inner row, or 20 in 3 rows, those of the inner row shorter and alternate with those of the 2d row, or 25 in 4 rows, those of the 4th row alternate with those of the 3d row; filaments broad at base, subulate, incurved, often persistent on the fruit; anthers pale yellow to nearly white, or pink to light or dark rose color or purple; ovary composed of 1-5 carpels inserted in the bottom of the calyx-tube and united with it; styles free, with dilated truncate stigmas, persistent on the mature carpels; ovules ascending; raphe dorsal; micropyle inferior. Fruit subglobose, ovoid or short-oblong, scarlet, orange-colored, red, yellow, blue, or black, generally open and concave at apex; flesh usually dry and mealy; nutlets 1-5; united below, more or less free and slightly spreading above the middle, thick-walled, rounded, acute, or acuminate at apex, full and rounded or narrowed at base, rounded or conspicuously ridged and grooved on the back, flattened, or nearly round when only 1, their ventral faces plane or plano-convex, in some species penetrated by longitudinal cavities or hollows, and marked by a more or less conspicuous hypostyle sometimes extending to below the middle or nearly to the base of the nutlet. Seed solitary by abortion, erect, compressed, acute, with a membranaceous light chestnut-brown coat; embryo filling the cavity of the seed; cotyledons plano-convex, radicle short, inferior.

Cratægus is most abundant in eastern North America, where it is distributed from Newfoundland to the mountains of northern Mexico, and is represented by a large number of arborescent and shrubby species. A few species occur in the Rocky Mountains and Pacific-coast regions, and in China, Japan, Siberia, central and southwestern Asia, and in Europe. The genus is still very imperfectly known in North America, and in the absence of sufficient information concerning them several arborescent species are necessarily excluded from the following enumeration. The beautiful and abundant flowers and showy fruits make many of the species desirable ornaments of parks and gardens, and several are cultivated. Of exotic species, the Old World *Cratægus Oxyacantha* L., and *C. monogyna* Jacq., early introduced into the United States as hedge plants, have now become naturalized in many places in the northeastern and middle states. Cratægus produces heavy hard tough close-grained red-brown heartwood and thick lighter colored usually pale sapwood; useful for the handles of tools, mallets, and other small articles.

The number of the stamens, although it differs on the same species within certain usually constant limits, and the color of the anthers, which appears to be specifically constant with one exception, afford the most satisfactory characters for distinguishing the species in the different groups.

Cratægus, from κράτος, is in reference to the strength of the wood of these trees.

CONSPECTUS OF THE NATURAL GROUPS OF THE NORTH AMERICAN ARBORESCENT SPECIES.

1. Nutlets without ventral cavities.
   *Veins of the leaves extending to the points of the lobes only.
   ⇁ Petioles short, usually slightly wing-margined above the middle, glandless or with occasional minute glands; leaves cuneate at base.
   Corymbs compound, generally many-flowered; flowers appearing after the unfolding of the leaves; flesh of the fruit usually green or greenish yellow, dry and mealy.
   Leaves coriaceous or subcoriaceous, rarely thin, dark green and shining above, usually serrate only above the middle, their veins thin except on vigorous shoots; fruit mostly subglobose to short-oblong; nutlets 1–5, thick, usually obtuse and rounded at the ends, prominently ridged on the back.
   I. Crus-galli (page 400).
   Leaves membranaceous or subcoriaceous, mostly acute, their veins prominent; fruit short-oblong to subglobose, often conspicuously punctate, $\frac{1}{3}'$–1' long; nutlets 2–5, prominently ridged on the back.   II. Punctatæ (page 422).
   Corymbs simple, few-flowered; flowers appearing with or before the unfolding of the leaves; fruit scarlet, lustrous; flesh yellow, juicy, subacid; nutlets rounded and slightly grooved on the back.   III. Æstivales (page 434).
   ⇁ Petioles elongated, slender, eglandular or occasionally glandular; corymbs many-flowered (*few-flowered in one species each of Dilatatæ and Intricatæ*).
   ++Leaves acute or acuminate at the ends, broad at base on one species; fruit not more than $\frac{5}{8}'$ in diameter; flesh usually thin and dry.   IV. Virides (page 437).
   ++Leaves usually broad at base.
   Fruit subglobose to short-oblong, often broader than high, red or green, often slightly 5-angled, pruinose; mature calyx raised on a short tube; flesh of the fruit dry and mealy; nutlets 5, grooved on the back.   V. Pruinosæ (page 449).
   Fruit subglobose to short-oblong, ovoid or obovoid, generally longer than broad, rarely slightly pruinose, mature calyx sessile; flesh of the fruit dry and mealy; stamens 10, anthers rose color; leaves hairy above early in the season.
   VI. Silvicolæ (page 453).
   Fruit short-oblong to obovoid, red or scarlet; flesh of the fruit usually soft and juicy; anthers rose color or pink; leaves thin, at maturity glabrous below.
   VII. Tenuifoliæ (page 456).
   Fruit subglobose, oblong or obovoid, crimson, scarlet, or rarely yellow; flesh thick, occasionally succulent, and edible; nutlets usually 5, thin, pointed at the ends, mostly obscurely grooved or ridged on the back; corymbs tomentose or pubescent; leaves membranaceous to subcoriaceous, broad, rounded or cuneate at base, at maturity usually pubescent or tomentose below.
   VIII. Molles (page 463).
   Fruit short-oblong to obovoid, scarlet; flesh usually soft and juicy; nutlets 3–5, grooved and usually ridged on the back; corymbs glabrous or tomentose; leaves thin or rarely subcoriaceous, oblong-ovate or oval, more or less acutely lobed; anthers rose or purple; rarely white in shrubby species.
   IX. Coccineæ (page 488).
   Fruit subglobose to short-oblong, crimson, or red tinged with green, its calyx enlarged and prominent; nutlets 5; stamens 20; anthers rose color; leaves thin, at the end of vigorous shoots as broad or broader than long.
   X. Dilatatæ (page 500).
   ++Leaves cuneate at base.
   Corymbs many-flowered; leaves subcoriaceous; fruit subglobose, rarely short-oblong; nutlets 2 or 3, obtuse at the ends, conspicuously ridged on the back; corymbs glabrous or tomentose; leaves dark green and lustrous above.
   XI. Rotundifoliæ (page 504).

Corymbs few-flowered (*many-flowered in one species of Bracteatæ*).

Fruit subglobose to short-oblong, greenish or yellowish; nutlets 3–5, usually rounded at the ends, conspicuously ridged on the back; leaves subcoriaceous, yellow-green.   XII. **Intricatæ** (page 508).

Fruit subglobose, red or orange-red; nutlets 3–5, slightly grooved on the back; stamens 20; anthers rose color; leaves thin, incisely lobed.

XIII. **Pulcherrimæ** (page 511).

Fruit subglobose to short-oblong, $\frac{1}{2}'-\frac{5}{8}'$ long; nutlets 3–5, narrowed at the ends, prominently ridged on the back; corymbs villose; bracts large and conspicuous; calyx-lobes foliaceous; stamens 20; anthers yellow; leaves dark green, lustrous and scabrate above, their petioles sparingly glandular through their whole length.   XIV. **Bracteatæ** (page 513).

→ Petioles long or short, leaves and corymbs glandular; corymbs usually simple, few-flowered; fruit subglobose to short-oblong or obovoid, green, orange, or red, flesh usually hard and dry; branchlets conspicuously zigzag.   XV. **Flavæ** (page 515).

**Veins of the leaves extending to the points of the lobes and to the sinuses; corymbs many-flowered; stamens usually 20.

Fruit depressed-globose to short-oblong, not more than $\frac{1}{4}'$ long, scarlet; nutlets 2–5, prominently ridged and often grooved on the back; anthers rose color or yellow.

XVI. **Microcarpæ** (page 530).

Fruit subglobose, $\frac{1}{3}'-\frac{1}{2}'$ in diameter, blue or blue-black; nutlets 3–5, obtuse at the ends, slightly ridged on the back; anthers yellow; leaves cuneate at base, dark green and lustrous.   XVII. **Brachyacanthæ** (page 533).

2. Nutlets with longitudinal cavities on their ventral faces; flowers in many flowered compound corymbs.

Fruit obovoid to subglobose or short-oblong, lustrous, orange or scarlet; nutlets 2 or 3, obtuse at the ends, prominently ridged on the back; leaves thin to subcoriaceous, mostly pubescent below.   XVIII. **Macracanthæ** (page 535).

Fruit short-oblong to subglobose, black; rarely chestnut color; nutlets 5, obtuse at the ends, obscurely ridged on the back; stamens 10–20; anthers pale rose color.

XIX. **Douglasianæ** (page 545).

Fruit subglobose, short-oblong to ovoid, scarlet; nutlets 3–5, acute at the ends, ridged on the back, ventral cavities obscure; leaves scabrate above.

XX. **Anomalæ** (page 547).

I. CRUS-GALLI.

CONSPECTUS OF THE ARBORESCENT SPECIES.

Corymbs, leaves, and young branchlets slightly hairy while young, soon becoming glabrous (*glabrous while young in* 1, 4, 6, 9, *and* 13).

Stamens 10.

Anthers rose color or purple.

Leaves glabrous, obovate-cuneiform, coriaceous, their veins within the parenchyma; fruit short-oblong to subglobose, dull red often covered with a glaucous bloom.

1. **C. Crus-galli** (A).

Leaves oblong to ovate, usually acute, coriaceous; fruit short-oblong to subglobose, dark crimson, lustrous, the flesh red and juicy.   2. **C. Canbyi** (A).

Leaves obovate, usually short-pointed at the broad apex, subcoriaceous; fruit short-oblong to obovoid, bright scarlet.   3. **C. peoriensis** (A).

Leaves oblong-obovate to oval, or broadly ovate, their petioles glandular with minute stipitate glands; fruit short-oblong to subglobose, orange-red, villose until nearly fully grown.   4. **C. fecunda** (A).

Anthers yellow.

Leaves subcoriaceous.

Leaves oval to elliptic, acute or acuminate; fruit short-oblong, green tinged with red.   5. **C. regalis** (C).

Leaves glabrous, obovate, acute, acuminate, or rounded at apex; fruit short-oblong, dull dark crimson.   6. **C. arduennæ** (A).

Leaves obovate to oblong-cuneiform, rounded or acute at apex; fruit subglobose to obovoid, dull red, or green flushed with red.   7. **C. algens** (A, C).

Leaves broadly oval to oblong, rounded or acute or short-pointed at apex; fruit subglobose, dull green tinged with red or cherry-red. 8. **C. Palmeri** (C).

Leaves thin.

Leaves ovate to obovate, acute, dull green above; fruit subglobose, flattened at the ends, dark dull crimson.   9. **C. erecta** (A).

Leaves oval to oblong-obovate, acute or acuminate, lustrous above; fruit short-oblong, rounded at the ends, bright scarlet.   10. **C. acutifolia** (A).

Stamens 20.

Anthers rose color.

Leaves broad-obovate, coarsely serrate; corymbs many-flowered; anthers large, bright rose color; fruit green tinged with dull red.   11. **C. Bushii** (C).

Leaves narrow-obovate, finely serrate; corymbs few-flowered; anthers small pale rose color; fruit crimson, lustrous.   12. **C. Cocksii** (C).

Anthers yellow.

Leaves oblong-obovate to oblanceolate; calyx-lobes slender, elongated.
                                                                13. **C. arborea** (C).

Leaves oblong-obovate; calyx-lobes short and broad.   14. **C. uniqua** (C).

Corymbs, leaves, and branchlets more or less villose or pubescent through the season.

Stamens 10.

Anthers rose color or pink.

Leaves finely crenately serrate, scabrate above; anthers rose color.
                                                            15. **C. Engelmannii** (A).

Leaves coarsely serrate with straight teeth, glabrous above; anthers pink.
                                                            16. **C. montivaga** (C).

Anthers yellow (*doubtful in* 17 *and* 18).

Leaves oval, oblong-obovate or elliptic, acute, thin to subcoriaceous; fruit globose to subglobose, orange-red.   17. **C. denaria** (C).

Leaves obovate to obovate-cuneiform, rounded or acute at apex, thin; fruit short-oblong, dark red, more or less pruinose.   18. **C. signata** (C).

Stamens 20.

Anthers rose color.

Leaves oblong-obovate, acute, scabrate; fruit short-oblong, dull green tinged with red, slightly pruinose.   19. **C. edita** (C).

Leaves oblong to obovate-cuneiform, rounded and obtuse or occasionally acute at apex, glabrous or scabrate above; fruit globose to subglobose or short-oblong, dark red.   20. **C. tersa** (C).

Anthers yellow.

Leaves oblong-obovate, rounded or gradually narrowed at apex, subcoriaceous, pale below; fruit subglobose, orange color with a red cheek. 21. **C. berberifolia** (C).

Leaves oblong or obovate-cuneiform, rounded and obtuse or rarely acute at apex, coriaceous, glabrate or slightly scabrate above; fruit subglobose, orange or yellow with a red cheek.   22. **C. edura** (C).

Leaves oblong to obovate-cuneiform, rounded or acute at apex, subcoriaceous, glabrous or glabrate above, pale below; fruit ellipsoid to short-oblong, yellow.
                                                            23. **C. crocina** (C).

Leaves oblong to obovate-cuneiform, rounded or obtuse or rarely truncate at apex, coriaceous, scabrate above; fruit globose to subglobose, bright red or scarlet.
                                                            24. **C. fera** (C).

Leaves obovate, acute, thin to subcoriaceous; fruit subglobose to short-oblong, somewhat flattened at apex, bright orange-red.   25. **C. Mohrii** (C).

1. Cratægus Crus-galli L.   Cock-spur Thorn.

Leaves glabrous, obovate, acute or rounded at apex, cuneate and gradually narrowed to the slender entire base, and sharply serrate above with minute appressed usually gland-tipped teeth, when they unfold tinged with red, membranaceous and nearly fully grown when the flowers open about the 1st of June, and at maturity thick and coriaceous, dark green and lustrous above, pale below, reticulate-venulose, 1′–4′ long, and ¼′–1′ wide, with a slender midrib, and primary veins within the parenchyma; turning bright orange and scarlet in the autumn before falling; petioles stout, ½′–¾′ in length; leaves at the end of vigorous shoots acute or acuminate, coarsely serrate, often 5′–6′ long. Flowers ⅔′ in diameter, on slender pedicels, in many-flowered glabrous corymbs; calyx-tube narrowly obconic, glabrous, the lobes linear-lanceolate, entire or minutely glandular-serrate; stamens 10; anthers rose color; styles usually 2, surrounded at base by tufts of pale hairs. Fruit

Fig. 353

ripening late in October and persistent on the branches until spring, short-oblong to subglobose, ½′ long, dull red often covered with a glaucous bloom; calyx little enlarged; nutlets usually 2, full and rounded at the ends, with a high rounded grooved ridge, ¼′ long.

A tree, sometimes 25° high, with a trunk a foot in diameter, covered with dark brown, scaly bark, stout rigid spreading branches forming a broad round-topped head, and glabrous, light brown or gray branchlets armed with stout straight or slightly curved sharp-pointed chestnut-brown or ashy gray spines 3′–4′ long and becoming on the trunk and large branches 6′–8′ in length and furnished with slender lateral spines.

Distribution. Usually on the slopes of low hills in rich soil; valley of the St. Lawrence River near Montreal, southward to Delaware and along the Appalachian foothills to North Carolina, and westward through western New York and Pennsylvania to southern Michigan, and southern Illinois.

A form, var. *pyracanthifolia* Ait., with narrower elliptic to obovate leaves acute or rounded at apex, and slightly pubescent while young on the upper side of the midrib, and with rather smaller flowers and smaller bright red fruit, is not rare in eastern Pennsylvania and northern Delaware; a form, var. *salicifolia* Ait., cultivated in European gardens, but not known in a wild state, with thinner narrower and more elongated lanceolate or oblanceolate leaves, should also probably be referred to this species. A form, var. *oblongata* Sarg., with rather brighter colored oblong fruit often 1′ long, and nutlets acute at the ends, is not rare near Wilmington, Delaware, and at Durham, Bucks County, Pennsylvania. A form, var. *capillata* Sarg., with thinner leaves, slightly villose corymbs, and 1 or rarely 2 nutlets, occurs near Wilmington, Delaware.

Often cultivated as an ornamental plant and for hedges in the eastern United States, and very frequently in the countries of eastern and northern Europe.

2. Cratægus Canbyi Sarg.

Leaves oblong-ovate to ovate, obovate or oval, acute, acuminate or rarely rounded at apex, gradually narrowed, cuneate and entire at base, and coarsely often doubly serrate above the middle, more than half grown when the flowers open about the 1st of May and then glabrous or very rarely with a few scattered hairs on the upper side of the midrib and on the corymbs, and at maturity coriaceous, glabrous, dark green and very lustrous above, pale and dull below, $2'-2\frac{1}{2}'$ long, and $1'-1\frac{1}{2}'$ wide, with a thick pale midrib, and 4 or 5 pairs of remote primary veins conspicuous on the lower surface; petioles glandular with scattered

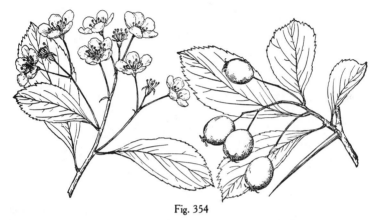

Fig. 354

dark red persistent glands, red below the middle, $\frac{1}{2}'-\frac{3}{4}'$ in length; leaves at the end of vigorous shoots often deeply and irregularly divided into broad acute lobes, and frequently $3'-4'$ long and $2'$ wide. **Flowers** $\frac{5}{8}'$ in diameter, on long slender pedicels, in broad loose many-flowered long-branched corymbs; calyx-tube narrowly obconic, the lobes entire, or serrate with minute scattered glandular teeth; stamens usually 10, occasionally 12 or 13; anthers, small, rose color; styles 3-5. **Fruit** ripening in October but persistent until after the beginning of winter, on elongated slender stems, in loose many-fruited drooping clusters, short-oblong to subglobose, rounded at the ends, with a distinct depresssion at the insertion of the stalk, lustrous, dark crimson, marked by occasional large pale dots, $\frac{1}{2}'-\frac{5}{8}'$ long; calyx-lobes reflexed, closely appressed, often deciduous before the fruit ripens; flesh thick, bright red, very juicy; nutlets 3-5, with a broad rounded ridge, bright chestnut-brown, about $\frac{1}{4}'$ long.

A bushy tree, sometimes 20° high, with a trunk $12'-18'$ in diameter, large ascending wide-spreading branches forming a broad open irregular head occasionally $30°-35°$ in diameter, and glabrous chestnut-brown branchlets armed with thick usually straight chestnut-brown spines $\frac{3}{4}'-1\frac{1}{2}'$ long.

Distribution. Hedges and thickets near Wilmington, Newcastle County, Delaware; shores of Chesapeake Bay (near Perryville, Cecil County), Maryland, and in eastern Pennsylvania.

3. Cratægus peoriensis Sarg.

Leaves obovate, short-pointed or occasionally rounded at the broad apex, gradually narrowed, cuneate and entire below, sharply and often doubly serrate usually only above the middle, and sometimes irregularly lobed with short broad terminal lobes, when they unfold villose above, especially toward the base of the midrib, and bright bronze color, becoming at maturity thick and firm, glabrous, dark green and very lustrous above, pale below, $1\frac{1}{2}'$–$2'$ long, and $\frac{3}{4}'$ wide, with 4 or 5 pairs of thin primary veins conspicuous on the under side and extending obliquely from the slender midrib to the end of the lobes; petioles usually about $\frac{1}{4}'$ in length, slightly glandular above the middle, and covered when they first appear with short pale deciduous hairs; leaves at the end of vigorous shoots deeply divided into broad acute lateral lobes, $2'$–$3'$ long, and $1\frac{1}{2}'$ wide.   **Flowers** opening in May and June, cup-shaped, about $\frac{1}{2}'$ in diameter, on slender elongated pedicels, in broad loose glabrous corymbs; calyx-tube narrowly obconic, the lobes narrow acuminate, entire or irregularly glandular-serrate, pubescent below the middle on the inner surface; stamens 10; anthers

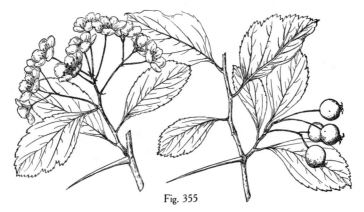

Fig. 355

small, rose color; styles 2 or 3, surrounded at base by a narrow ring of pale tomentum. **Fruit** ripening early in October, on slender elongated pedicels, in drooping many-fruited clusters, short-oblong or obovoid, rounded at the ends, slightly depressed at the insertion of the stalk, bright scarlet, marked by many small dark dots, $\frac{1}{2}'$–$\frac{3}{4}'$ long; calyx-lobes enlarged, erect, incurved and persistent; flesh thick, nearly white, firm and dry; nutlets 2 or 3, about $\frac{1}{4}'$ long.

A tree, $20°$–$25°$ high, with a trunk occasionally $1°$ in diameter, stout spreading branches forming a broad flat-topped symmetrical head, and slender orange-brown branchlets armed with straight or slightly curved thin dull chestnut-brown spines $2'$–$2\frac{1}{2}'$ long.

Distribution. Open woods, the moist borders of streams and depressions in the prairie, and on hillsides in clay soil, Short and Peoria Counties, Illinois.

4. Cratægus fecunda Sarg.

Leaves oblong-obovate to oval, or broad-ovate, acute or rarely rounded and short-pointed at apex, gradually or abruptly narrowed at base, and coarsely and usually doubly serrate except toward the base, when they unfold dark green, lustrous and roughened above by short pale appressed caducous hairs and pale yellow-green and villose on the midrib and primary veins below, about half grown when the flowers open early in May and at maturity thin and firm in texture, dark green and lustrous on the upper surface, pale yellow-green on the lower surface, $2'$–$2\frac{1}{2}'$ long, and $1\frac{1}{2}'$–$2'$ wide, with a stout midrib and remote primary veins after midsummer often bright red below; turning late in the autumn to brilliant shades of orange or scarlet or deep rich bronze color; petioles often glandular, at first coated with pale hairs, soon glabrous, dull red at maturity, $\frac{1}{4}'$–$\frac{3}{4}'$ in length; leaves at the end of vigorous shoots often slightly lobed with short broad acute lobes, convex by the hanging down of the margins, $3'$–$4'$ long, and $2'$–$3'$ wide.   **Flowers** $\frac{3}{4}'$ in diameter, on slender pedicels, in wide many-flowered slightly villose corymbs, with large glandular bracts and bractlets; calyx-tube narrowly obconic, more or less villose, the lobes elongated, acute, coarsely serrate with stipitate dark red glands, villose on the inner surface; stamens usually 10, occasionally 12–15; anthers small, dark rose color; styles 2 or 3. **Fruit** on slender pedicels often ½′ long,

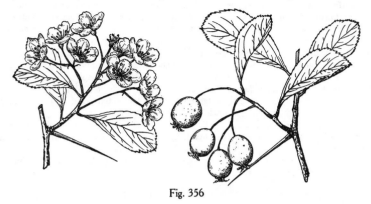

Fig. 356

in broad many-fruited drooping clusters, short-oblong to subglobose, full and rounded at the ends, covered until nearly fully grown with long soft pale hairs, and at maturity orange-red marked by many small dark dots, ⅞′–1′ long; calyx-lobes linear-lanceolate, erect and incurved, coarsely glandular-serrate above the middle, dark red on the upper side toward the base; flesh very thick, firm and hard, pale green; nutlets 2 or 3, ⅓′ long.

A tree, 20°–25° high, with a trunk 10′–12′ in diameter, covered with dark brown scaly bark, stout wide-spreading branches forming a broad symmetrical round-topped rather open head, and stout branchlets covered at first with soft matted pale hairs, soon glabrous, light orange-green, becoming ashy gray in their second season, and armed with numerous very slender straight or slightly curved chestnut-brown shining spines 2′–2½′ long.

Distribution. Rich woodlands near Allenton, St. Louis County, Missouri, and on the bottom-lands of the Mississippi River, Clair County, Illinois.

5. Cratægus regalis Beadl.

Leaves oval to elliptic, acute or acuminate at apex, gradually narrowed and concave-cuneate at the entire base, and coarsely, often doubly serrate above with acute straight or

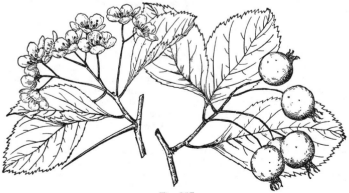

Fig. 357

incurved teeth, when they unfold tinged with red and sparingly villose above and on the midrib below, soon glabrous, nearly fully grown when the flowers open at the end of April, becoming at maturity thick and firm or subcoriaceous, bright green and lustrous on the upper surface, pale on the lower surface, $1\frac{1}{2}'-2\frac{1}{2}'$ long, and $1'-1\frac{1}{4}'$ wide, with a stout yellow midrib and primary veins; turning in the autumn yellow, orange, and brown; petioles stout, reddish brown toward the base, about $1'$ in length; leaves at the end of vigorous shoots broadly oval, coarsely serrate, mostly slightly incisely lobed, $3'-4'$ long, and $1\frac{1}{2}'-2'$ wide, with a thicker midrib and veins. **Flowers** $\frac{1}{2}'$ in diameter, on long slender pedicels, in broad many-flowered corymbs; calyx-tube narrowly obconic, the lobes linear-lanceolate, entire or remotely serrate; stamens 10; anthers yellow; styles 2 or 3. **Fruit** ripening in September or October, on slender stems, in few-fruited drooping clusters, short-oblong, $\frac{3}{8}'-\frac{1}{2}'$ long, green tinged with red; calyx-lobes slightly enlarged, reflexed and often deciduous from the ripe fruit; flesh yellow, dry and mealy; nutlets 2 or 3, about $\frac{1}{4}'$ long.

A tree, often $20°$ high, with a tall trunk $8'-12'$ in diameter, stout ascending or spreading branches forming a broad symmetrical head, and stout glabrous orange-brown branchlets armed with stout or slender nearly straight spines $1\frac{1}{2}'-2'$ long.

Distribution. Low woods, northwestern Georgia and northern Alabama; common in the flat woods near Rome, Floyd County, Georgia.

6. Cratægus arduennæ Sarg.

Leaves obovate, acute, acuminate or rounded at apex, gradually narrowed from near the middle to the entire cuneate base, and finely crenulate-serrate above with glandular teeth,

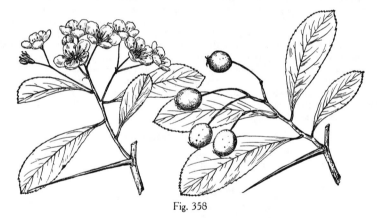

Fig. 358

glabrous and deeply tinged with red as they unfold, nearly fully grown when the flowers open at the end of May or early in June, and at maturity subcoriaceous, dark green and very lustrous above, pale below, $1\frac{1}{2}'-2\frac{1}{2}'$ long, and $\frac{1}{2}'-1'$ wide, with a slender yellow midrib, and obscure primary veins mostly within the parenchyma; petioles stout, occasionally sparingly glandular, $\frac{1}{4}'-\frac{5}{8}'$ in length; leaves at the end of vigorous shoots mostly elliptic, short-pointed, coarsely serrate, usually laterally lobed, and often $2\frac{1}{2}'-3'$ long, and $1\frac{1}{2}'-2'$ wide, with a stout midrib and prominent slender primary veins. **Flowers** $\frac{1}{2}'-\frac{5}{8}'$ in diameter, on long slender pedicels, in broad many-flowered glabrous corymbs; calyx-tube narrowly obconic, the lobes abruptly narrowed from the base, linear, acuminate, tipped with small dark red glands, entire or slightly and irregularly serrate; stamens 5-12; usually 10; anthers small, pale yellow; styles 1 or 2. **Fruit** on slender pedicels, in drooping many-fruited clusters, short-oblong, dull dark crimson, marked by large pale dots, about $\frac{1}{2}'$ long, and $\frac{3}{8}'-\frac{1}{2}'$ in diameter; calyx only slightly enlarged, the lobes reflexed and appressed; flesh thin and yellow; nutlet 1, gradually narrowed from the middle to the obtuse ends, grooved and irregularly ridged on the dorsal face, or 2 and then broad, rounded at the ends, with a high wide rounded ridge, about $\frac{5}{16}'$ long.

A tree, sometimes 20° high, with a trunk 8'–12' in diameter, covered with smooth light gray bark, spreading branches forming a round-topped head, and slender slightly zigzag branchlets light orange-green when the first appear, becoming dark purple and lustrous and ultimately grayish brown, and armed with many slender straight or slightly curved dark purple-brown shining spines 1'–2' long.

Distribution. Central and northern Missouri, northern Illinois, northeastern Indiana (Allen County), southeastern Michigan, southern Ontario, through Ohio to western New York (South Buffalo, Erie County), and in eastern Pennsylvania (Berks County).

7. Cratægus algens Beadl.

Leaves obovate to oblong or elliptic, rounded or acute at apex, gradually narrowed and concave-cuneate at the entire base, sharply serrate above, villose on the upper side of the

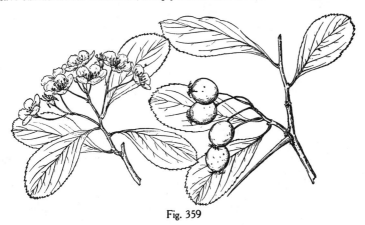

Fig. 359

midrib and nearly full grown when the flowers open at the end of May, and at maturity glabrous, subcoriaceous, dark green and lustrous above, pale below, $1\frac{1}{2}'$–2' long, and $\frac{3}{4}'$–$1\frac{1}{4}'$ wide, with a thin midrib and slender primary veins; turning in the autumn to shades of orange, yellow, and brown; petioles slender, rarely glandular with minute glands, about $\frac{1}{4}'$ in length; leaves at the end of vigorous shoots oblong-obovate, rounded or abruptly short-pointed at apex, coarsely serrate, and often 3' long and $1\frac{1}{2}'$ wide. Flowers $\frac{1}{2}'$ in diameter, on slender elongated pedicels, in broad many-flowered glabrous corymbs; calyx-tube narrowly obconic, glabrous, the lobes lanceolate, acuminate, entire or remotely serrate; stamens 10; anthers yellow; styles 1–3. Fruit ripening in September and October, on slender pedicels, in few-fruited hanging clusters, subglobose to obovoid, $\frac{3}{8}'$–$\frac{1}{2}'$ in diameter, dull red, or green flushed with red, $\frac{3}{8}'$–$\frac{1}{2}'$ long; calyx somewhat enlarged, with reflexed persistent lobes; nutlets usually 1 or 2, prominently ridged on the back, $\frac{1}{4}'$–$\frac{3}{8}'$ long.

A tree, 15°–18° high, with a short trunk occasionally 7'–8' in diameter, stout ascending wide-spreading branches forming a wide round-topped head, and stout glabrous bright chestnut-brown branchlets becoming gray in their second year, and armed with stout nearly straight spines 1'–2' long.

Distribution. Borders of woods and fields; western North Carolina to northern Georgia and central Alabama (near Selma, Dallas County, common), and to eastern Tennessee; one of the commonest species in the neighborhood of Asheville, Buncombe County, North Carolina.

8. Cratægus Palmeri Sarg.

Leaves broadly oval to oblong, rounded, acute or short-pointed at apex, gradually narrowed and cuneate at the entire base, and coarsely serrate above with straight gland-tipped teeth, nearly fully grown when the flowers open during the first week in May, and then very thin, dark green and lustrous above, pale bluish green below, and at maturity coriaceous, dark green and lustrous on the upper surface, paler on the lower surface, $1\frac{1}{2}'$–$2'$ long, and $1\frac{1}{4}'$–$1\frac{3}{4}'$ wide, with a slender yellow midrib and 4 or 5 pairs of very thin primary veins; petioles stout, rose-colored in the autumn, about $\frac{3}{8}'$ in length; leaves at the end of vigorous shoots

Fig. 360

oblong-ovate to elliptic, usually acute, coarsely serrate, occasionally laterally lobed, glandular at base, $2\frac{1}{2}'$–$3'$ long, and $1\frac{1}{2}'$–$2'$ wide. **Flowers** about $\frac{1}{2}'$ in diameter, on slender pedicels, in many-flowered corymbs; calyx-tube narrowly obconic, the lobes slender, acuminate, tipped with small dark glands, entire or slightly serrate; stamens 10; anthers pale yellow; styles 3, surrounded at base by a thin ring of pale tomentum. **Fruit** ripening in October, on slender elongated pedicels, in few-fruited drooping clusters, subglobose, dull green tinged with red or cherry-red, marked by large pale dots, about $\frac{1}{4}'$ in diameter; calyx sessile, with erect and incurved lobes mostly persistent on the ripe fruit; nutlets 3, thin, acute at the ends, slightly and irregularly ridged on the back with a low grooved ridge, $\frac{1}{4}'$–$\frac{5}{16}'$ long.

A tree, sometimes 25° high, with a trunk often a foot in diameter, covered with smooth pale bark, stout wide-spreading branches forming a broad round-topped symmetrical head, and slender nearly straight glabrous, bright chestnut-brown branchlets armed with thin straight dark red-brown shining spines $\frac{3}{4}'$–$3'$ long.

Distribution. Southwestern Missouri, usually in low rich soil; common near Carthage and Webb City, Jasper County, and near Noel, McDonald County, to southeastern Kansas and northwestern Arkansas.

9. Cratægus erecta Sarg.

Leaves oval to obovate, acute and short-pointed at apex, cuneate and entire at base, and finely glandular-serrate, when they unfold often villose with a few short caducous pale hairs on the upper side of the midrib, nearly fully grown when the flowers open early in May, and at maturity thin and firm in texture, dark dull green on the upper surface, pale on the lower surface, $1\frac{1}{2}'$–$2'$ long, and $1'$–$1\frac{1}{4}'$ wide, with a slender midrib, and thin prominent primary veins; in the autumn turning dull orange color; petioles slender, glandular with minute dark glands, usually dark red after midsummer, $\frac{1}{4}'$–$\frac{1}{2}'$ in length; leaves at the end of vigorous shoots often nearly orbicular, coarsely serrate with broad nearly straight glandular teeth, and sometimes $3'$ long and $2\frac{1}{2}'$ wide. **Flowers** $\frac{1}{2}'$–$\frac{5}{8}'$ in diameter, on slender pedicels, in broad loose many-flowered glabrous corymbs; calyx-tube narrowly obconic, the lobes narrow, elongated, acuminate, entire or occasionally obscurely and irregularly serrate; stamens usually 10, occasionally 11–13; anthers small, pale yellow; styles 3 or 4, surrounded at base by a narrow ring of short pale hairs. **Fruit** on elongated pedicels, in few-fruited drooping clusters, subglobose and usually a little longer than broad, flattened at the ends, dark dull crimson marked by occasional dark-colored dots, $\frac{1}{4}$'–$\frac{1}{3}$' long; calyx-tube short, the lobes closely appressed, gradually narrowed from a broad base and usually persistent on the ripe fruit; nutlets 3 or 4, with a broad high grooved ridge, $\frac{3}{16}$' long.

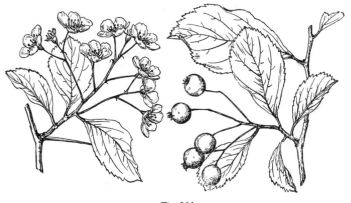

Fig. 361

A tree, 25°–40° high, with a trunk 1°–3° in diameter, thick ascending branches forming a wide open rather symmetrical head, and bright chestnut-brown or orange-brown ultimately dark brown spreading branchlets armed with thin straight chestnut-brown spines 1'–2' long.

Distribution. Rich bottom-lands of the Mississippi River, St. Clair County (East St. Louis, near Fish Lake, and Cahokia) to Richland County, and southern Illinois and southern Indiana; banks of Desperes River, south St. Louis, St. Louis County, and Osage, Cole County, Missouri, and western and southwestern Arkansas.

10. Cratægus acutifolia Sarg.

Leaves oval to oblong-obovate, acute or acuminate or rarely rounded at apex, cuneate at the usually entire base, finely crenulate-serrate often only above the middle with glandular teeth, nearly fully grown when the flowers open about the 10th of May, and then membranaceous, and lustrous above, with occasional short scattered pale caducous hairs on the upper side of the midrib, and at maturity thin and firm, dark green and lustrous above, pale yellow-green below, about 1$\frac{1}{2}$' long, and 1' wide, with a slender light yellow midrib and about 4 or 5 pairs of thin primary veins: petioles glandular when they first appear with minute dark glands, $\frac{1}{4}$'–$\frac{1}{2}$' in length; leaves at the end of vigorous shoots frequently divided at apex into 2 or 3 pairs of short acute lobes, and often 3' long and 2' wide. **Flowers** $\frac{1}{2}$' in diameter, on slender pedicels, in many-flowered compact corymbs; calyx-tube narrowly obconic, the lobes lanceolate, acuminate, entire or obscurely and irregularly glandular-serrate; stamens 10; anthers small, pale yellow; styles 2 or 3. **Fruit** ripening and falling at the end of September, on slender pedicels $\frac{1}{2}$'–$\frac{3}{4}$' long, in few-fruited drooping clusters, short-oblong, full and rounded at the ends, bright scarlet, marked by occasional dark dots, $\frac{1}{2}$' long; calyx-tube prominent, with closely appressed lobes often deciduous before the fruit ripens; nutlets 2 or 3, with a broad rounded ridge, about $\frac{3}{16}$' long.

A tree, often 30° high, with a trunk 18′ in diameter, stout wide-spreading branches forming a symmetrical round-topped rather open head, and stout bright chestnut-brown

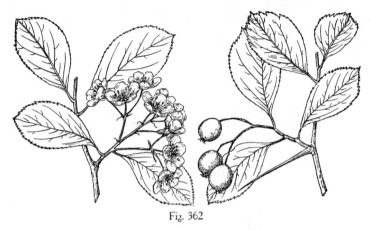

Fig. 362

branchlets dark gray-brown in their second year, and occasionally armed with scattered thin straight chestnut-brown spines 1′–2′ long.

Distribution. Open woods; banks of the Desperes River near Carondelet, St. Louis County, Missouri; in St. Clair County (north of stock yards, East St. Louis, and near Cahokia), and in Richland County, Illinois, western Tennessee and to the neighborhood of Fayetteville, Arkansas.

11. Cratægus Bushii Sarg.

Leaves obovate, broad and rounded or acute at apex, or elliptic and acute, gradually narrowed from near the middle to the cuneate entire base, and coarsely serrate above,

Fig. 363

when they unfold dark green on the upper surface, pale on the lower surface, and villose with short white hairs on both sides of the midrib and veins, nearly fully grown when the flowers open at the end of April, and at maturity coriaceous, lustrous, glabrous, 1¼′–1½′ long, and ½′–1′ wide, with a stout yellow midrib and few slender prominent primary veins; petioles villose early in the season, becoming glabrous, usually about $\frac{1}{2}'$ in length; leaves at the end of vigorous shoots usually elliptic, acute, coarsely serrate, frequently 3' long and $1\frac{1}{2}'$ wide, with stouter and more broadly winged petioles. **Flowers** $\frac{3}{4}'-1'$ in diameter, on slender pedicels, in broad many-flowered glabrous corymbs; calyx-tube broadly obconic, glabrous, the lobes elongated, linear-lanceolate, entire or occasionally slightly dentate; stamens 20; anthers large, bright rose color; styles two or three, surrounded at base by conspicuous tufts of white hairs. **Fruit** ripening late in October or in November, on slender pedicels about $\frac{1}{2}'$ long, in few-fruited drooping clusters, short-oblong, green tinged with dull red, $\frac{1}{3}'$ long, with only slightly enlarged erect and incurved calyx-lobes mostly deciduous before the fruit ripens; flesh thin, green, dry and hard; nutlets 2 or 3, with a high rounded ridge, $\frac{1}{4}'$ long.

A tree, 15°–20° high, with a trunk 8'–10' in diameter, covered with dark scaly bark, small spreading branches forming a broad open irregular head, and nearly straight dull chestnut-brown branchlets gray-brown in their second year, and unarmed or sparingly armed with stout straight chestnut-brown spines $1\frac{1}{2}'-1\frac{1}{4}'$ long.

Distribution. Rich upland woods near Fulton, Hemstead County, southern Arkansas; Chopin, Natchitoches Parish, near Winn, Winnfield Parish, and Lake Charles, Calcasieu Parish, Louisiana; in the neighborhood of Marshall, Harris County, Texas.

12. Cratægus Cocksii Sarg.

Leaves oblong-obovate, acute or rounded at apex, gradually narrowed and cuneate at base, finely serrate above the middle with straight acuminate teeth, glabrous, dark green

Fig. 364

and lustrous above, dull and paler below, 1'–1$\frac{1}{4}'$ long, and $\frac{1}{4}'-\frac{1}{2}'$ wide, with a slender midrib and primary veins mostly within the parenchyma; petioles slender, about $\frac{1}{6}'$ in length; leaves at the end of vigorous shoots broad-obovate, rounded or abruptly short-pointed at apex, thicker, more coarsely serrate, often $1\frac{1}{2}'$ long and 1' wide. **Flowers** $\frac{1}{2}'-\frac{3}{4}'$ in diameter, on slender pedicels, in compact few-flowered glabrous corymbs; calyx-tube broadly obconic, glabrous, the lobes oblong-ovate, gradually narrowed and acuminate, entire, sparingly villose on the inner surface; stamens 20, small, pale rose color; styles 2 or 3, surrounded at base by clusters of white hairs. **Fruit** ripening in October, on slender pedicels about $\frac{1}{3}'$ in length, in few-fruited clusters, short-oblong to slightly obovoid, crimson, lustrous, $\frac{1}{3}'-\frac{1}{2}'$ long, with spreading calyx-lobes mostly deciduous from the ripe fruit; nutlets 2 or 3, obovoid, acute at apex, rounded at base, prominently ridged on the back, $\frac{1}{3}'$ long.

A slender tree, 20°–25° high, with a tall trunk 4'–6' in diameter, with dark red-brown bark covered with small closely appressed scales, smooth slender drooping branches forming a broad open head, and slender bright red-brown pendulous branchlets becoming gray in their second year, and armed with straight slender dark chestnut-brown lustrous spines $1\frac{1}{4}'-1\frac{3}{4}'$ in length.

Distribution. Low rich woods at the marble quarry near Winnfield, Winn Parish, Louisiana.

Distinct in the Crus-galli Group in its head of slender pendulous branches.

13. Cratægus arborea Beadl.

Leaves obovate to oblanceolate, narrowed, acute or rounded at apex, gradually narrowed and concave-cuneate at the long tapering entire base, and finely serrate above the middle with minute straight teeth, nearly fully grown when the flowers open the middle of April and then glabrous, and at maturity subcoriaceous, bright green and lustrous above, pale below, $1\frac{1}{4}'$–$2'$ long, and about $\frac{3}{4}'$ wide; turning in the autumn orange, yellow, and brown;

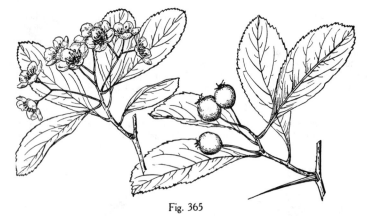

Fig. 365

petioles $\frac{1}{3}'$–$\frac{2}{3}'$ in length; leaves at the end of vigorous shoots coarsely serrate, occasionally slightly lobed, and often $3'$ long and $1\frac{1}{2}'$ wide. **Flowers** $\frac{1}{2}'$ in diameter, on slender pedicels, in broad many-flowered glabrous corymbs; calyx narrowly obconic, glabrous, the lobes slender, elongated, acuminate, slightly serrate; stamens 20; anthers pale yellow; styles usually 2. **Fruit** ripening in September and October, globose to subglobose, $\frac{1}{4}'$–$\frac{1}{3}'$ in diameter, red, the calyx enlarged, with elongated coarsely glandular-serrate reflexed lobes; nutlets usually 2, about $\frac{1}{4}'$ long.

A tree, sometimes 30° high, with a trunk $12'$–$18'$ in diameter, spreading or ascending branches forming a broad handsome head, and branchlets orange-green in their first season, becoming reddish in their first winter, and usually unarmed.

Distribution. In open woods usually in clay soil near Montgomery, Montgomery County, Alabama.

14. Cratægus uniqua Sarg.

Leaves oblong-obovate, acute or occasionally rounded at apex, gradually narrowed to the long cuneate base, and finely serrate above the middle with straight or incurved glandular teeth, more than half grown when the flowers open the middle of April, and sparingly villose on the upper side of the midrib when the flowers open the middle of April, and at maturity glabrous, dark green and lustrous above, paler below, $1'$–$1\frac{1}{2}'$ long, and $\frac{1}{2}'$–$\frac{3}{4}'$ wide, with a thin midrib, and slender primary veins mostly within the parenchyma; petioles slender, glabrous, $\frac{1}{3}'$–$\frac{1}{2}'$ in length; leaves at the end of vigorous shoots broad-obovate, rounded or acute at apex, coarsely serrate, $2'$–$2\frac{1}{2}'$ long, and $1'$–$1\frac{1}{4}'$ wide. **Flowers** $\frac{2}{3}'$–$\frac{1}{2}'$ in diameter, on slender pedicels, in mostly 5–8-flowered glabrous corymbs; calyx-tube narrowly obconic, the lobes short and broad, acuminate, entire or slightly dentate near the middle, sparingly villose on the inner surface; stamens 20; anthers small, nearly white; styles 2 or 3. **Fruit** on slender drooping pedicels, short-oblong, rounded at the ends, dull red, about $\frac{1}{2}'$ long and $\frac{1}{3}'$ thick; calyx prominent, with reflexed closely appressed persistent lobes; flesh thin, dry and hard; nutlets 2 or 3, broad and rounded at base, narrowed at apex, about $\frac{1}{4}'$ long.

A tree, 18°–20° high, with a slender stem covered with close dark slightly ridged bark, small wide-spreading branches forming a flat-topped head, and slender slightly zigzag

Fig. 366

orange or red-brown branchlets unarmed, or armed with few or many straight or slightly curved dark chestnut-brown shining spines $\frac{1}{2}'–1'$ in length.

Distribution. Woods in low sandy soil; eastern Texas (near Marshall, Harrison County, and Livingston, Polk County), to southwestern Arkansas.

15. Cratægus Engelmannii Sarg.

Leaves oblong-obovate or rarely elliptic, rounded or often short-pointed and acute at apex, gradually narrowed or entire below, finely crenulate-serrate usually only above the middle

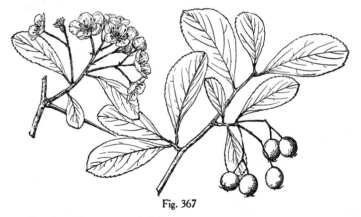

Fig. 367

and generally only at the apex, nearly fully grown and roughened on the upper surface by short rigid pale hairs when the flowers open about the middle of May, and at maturity

coriaceous, dark green, lustrous and scabrate above, pale below, and pilose on both surfaces of the slender midrib and obscure primary veins and veinlets, $1'-1\frac{1}{2}'$ long, and
$\frac{1}{2}'-1'$ wide; petioles glandular, villose when they first appear, soon glabrous, usually about
$\frac{1}{4}'$ in length.   **Flowers** $\frac{3}{4}'$ in diameter, on slender pedicels, in broad loose 8–11-flowered villose corymbs; calyx-tube narrowly obconic, villose or nearly glabrous, the lobes narrow,
acuminate, entire, glabrous on the outer surface, usually puberulous on the inner surface;
stamens 10; anthers small, rose color; styles 2 or 3.   **Fruit** ripening early in November, on
slender pedicels, in drooping many-fruited glabrous clusters, globose or short-oblong, bright
orange-red, with a yellow cheek, about $\frac{1}{3}'$ in diameter; calyx prominent, with large spreading lobes usually deciduous before the fruit ripens; nutlets 2 or 3, thick, with a broad
rounded ridge, $\frac{1}{4}'$ long.

A tree, 15°–20° high, with a trunk 5'–6' in diameter, wide-spreading usually horizontal
branches forming a low flat-topped or rounded head, and branchlets covered with long
pale hairs when they first appear, soon glabrous and bright red-brown, becoming gray or
gray tinged with red during their second year, and armed with numerous stout straight
or slightly curved spines $1\frac{1}{2}'-2\frac{1}{2}'$ long.

Distribution.   Dry limestone slopes and ridges; common near Allenton and Pacific,
St. Louis and Franklin counties, Missouri; near Eureka Springs, Carroll County, Arkansas,
southern Illinois, western Kentucky and Hot Spring and Van Buren Counties, Arkansas.

16. Cratægus montivaga Sarg.

Leaves obovate to oval, rhombic or suborbicular, rounded, acute or acuminate or abruptly short-pointed at apex, concave-cuneate at base, and sharply coarsely serrate usually

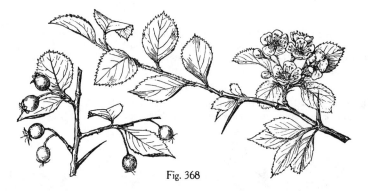

Fig. 368

to below the middle with straight acuminate glandular teeth, covered above with short
white hairs and glabrous below when they unfold, and at maturity dark green, lustrous
and scabrate above, pale yellow-green below, $1'-1\frac{1}{4}'$ long, and $\frac{3}{4}'-1'$ wide, with a slender
midrib and prominent primary veins; petioles slender, villose early in the season, becom-
ing glabrous, about $\frac{1}{4}'$ in length.   **Flowers** opening late in April, about $\frac{1}{2}'$ in diameter, on
villose pedicels $\frac{1}{4}'-\frac{1}{2}'$ long, in compact mostly 7–10-flowered villose corymbs, their bracts
and bractlets linear-obovate, conspicuously glandular-serrate; calyx-tube broadly obconic,
glabrous or with occasional hairs near the base, the lobes gradually narrowed from a wide
base, glandular-serrate, sometimes laciniate near the acuminate apex, glabrous on the
outer surface, villose on the inner surface; stamens 10–15, usually 10; anthers pink; styles
2 or 3.   **Fruit** ripening late in September or in October, on erect nearly glabrous or villose pedicels, short-oblong to ellipsoid, orange-red, about $\frac{1}{3}'$ long; the calyx enlarged and
conspicuous; flesh thin, yellow-green; nutlets 2 or 3, rounded at apex, with a low broad
rounded ridge, about $\frac{1}{4}'$ long.

A bushy tree, rarely more than 12°–15° high, with a short trunk 10'–12' in diameter, erect and spreading branches, and slender nearly straight branchlets orange-brown and covered with long scattered pale hairs when they first appear, dull red-brown and glabrous at the end of their first season, becoming gray the following year. Bark of the branches smooth and dark brown, becoming slightly scaly on the trunk.

Distribution. Rocky banks of streams; western Texas (Comal, Kendall, Bandera, Edwards, Brown and Calhoun Counties, and on the Davis Mountains, Jeff Davis County); common on the banks of the Guadalupe and other streams on the Edwards Plateau.

Interesting as the extreme southwestern representative of the Crus-galli Group, and its only species in western Texas.

17. Cratægus denaria Beadl.

Leaves oval, oblong-obovate or elliptic, acute or acuminate at apex, gradually narrowed from near the middle and cuneate and entire below, and coarsely often doubly serrate above

Fig. 369

with straight teeth, when they unfold tinged with red and slightly pilose above and glabrous below, nearly fully grown when the flowers open toward the end of May, and at maturity firm to subcoriaceous, bright green and lustrous on the upper surface, pale on the lower surface, $2\frac{1}{2}'-3'$ long, and $\frac{3}{4}'-1\frac{1}{4}'$ wide, with a slender midrib and few remote thin primary veins; turning in the autumn orange, yellow, or brown; petioles stout, conspicuously glandular, and about $\frac{1}{4}'$ in length; leaves at the end of vigorous shoots broadly oval to ovate or obovate, occasionally incisely lobed, $2\frac{1}{2}'-3'$ long, and $1\frac{1}{2}'-2'$ wide. **Flowers** $\frac{1}{2}'-\frac{2}{3}'$ in diameter, on long slender pedicels, in broad lax many-flowered sparingly villose corymbs; calyx narrowly obconic, glabrous, the lobes slender, elongated, acuminate and glandular at apex, mostly entire or slightly serrate below; stamens usually 10; styles 3-5. **Fruit** on long slender pedicels, in drooping few-fruited clusters, globose to subglobose, $\frac{1}{4}'-\frac{5}{16}'$ in diameter, orange-red, the calyx somewhat enlarged, with spreading or closely appressed lobes; nutlets 3-5, slightly ridged on the back, about $\frac{3}{16}'$ long.

A tree, 18°-20° high, with a trunk sometimes 8' in diameter, spreading branches, and branchlets sparingly villose with long matted white hairs when they first appear, soon glabrous, and unarmed or armed with occasional straight slender spines about $1\frac{1}{2}'$ long.

Distribution. Banks of streams, eastern Mississippi; common in the neighborhood of Columbus, Lowndes County.

18. Cratægus signata Beadl.

Leaves obovate to elliptic, rounded and often short-pointed or acute at apex, gradually narrowed from near the middle and cuneate at the entire base, and sharply glandular-serrate usually only above the middle, about half grown when the flowers open early in April, and then gray-green and coated above and on the lower side of the midrib and principal veins with short pale hairs, and at maturity thin and firm in texture, dark green, lustrous and slightly pilose above, paler and pubescent below on the slender midrib and 2–5 pairs of primary veins, $1\frac{1}{2}'$–$2'$ long, and $\frac{3}{4}'$–$1'$ wide; petioles slender, grooved above, glandular, usually about $\frac{1}{3}'$ in length; leaves at the end of vigorous shoots often broad-ovate to elliptic, coarsely dentate or sometimes incisely lobed, frequently $2\frac{1}{2}'$ long and $2'$ wide. **Flowers** about $\frac{3}{4}'$ in diameter, on slender pedicels, in few-flowered compact hairy corymbs; calyx-tube narrowly obconic, villose with long matted hairs, the lobes narrow, acute, entire or irregularly glandular-serrate, usually glabrous on the outer surface, villose on the inner surface; stamens 10; styles 3–5, surrounded at base by a few pale hairs. **Fruit** ripening and falling toward the end of October, in few-fruited drooping slightly villose

Fig. 370

clusters, short-oblong, rounded at the ends, dark red, more or less pruinose, marked by numerous pale dots, and about $\frac{1}{2}'$ long; calyx enlarged, with elongated closely appressed lobes usually persistent on the ripe fruit; flesh thin and yellow; nutlets 3–5, prominently ridged and grooved on the back, about $\frac{1}{4}'$ long.

A tree, usually 15°–18° high, with a tall trunk $4'$–$5'$ in diameter, covered with ashy gray bark, often nearly black near the base of old stems, and separating freely into thin plate-like scales, numerous ascending or spreading branches forming a round-topped or oval compact head, and stout chestnut-brown branchlets armed with stout, nearly straight bright chestnut-brown spines $1'$–$2'$ long.

Distribution. Open glades and dry copses of the Pine-covered coast-plain of southern Alabama.

19. Cratægus edita Sarg.

Leaves oblong-obovate or rarely elliptic, acute at the gradually narrowed apex, gradually narrowed from near the middle to the cuneate entire base, and coarsely and often doubly serrate above, when the flowers open from the 15th to the 20th of April lustrous and scabrate on the upper surface with short rigid pale hairs and puberulous on the lower surface, and at maturity coriaceous, dark green, lustrous, and slightly roughened above, pale yellow-green and scabrate below, $1\frac{1}{2}'$–$2'$ long, and $\frac{1}{2}'$–$1'$ wide; petioles stout, villose, becoming pubescent or puberulous, $\frac{1}{3}'$–$\frac{1}{2}'$ in length; leaves at the end of vigorous shoots often slightly divided into lateral lobes, more coarsely serrate and sometimes $3'$ long, and $1\frac{1}{2}'$ wide, with stout broadly winged petioles. **Flowers** $\frac{1}{2}'$–$\frac{2}{3}'$ in diameter, on slender villose pedicels, in villose few-flowered narrow corymbs; calyx-tube narrowly obconic, glabrous or slightly hairy toward the base, the lobes linear-lanceolate, usually entire or obscurely glandular-serrate, glabrous on the outer surface and puberulous on the inner surface; stamens 20; anthers small, rose color; styles 2 or 3. **Fruit** ripening early in October or in November, on stout glabrous or slightly villose pedicels usually about $\frac{1}{4}'$ long, in drooping few-fruited clusters, short-oblong, rounded at the ends, slightly pruinose, dull green tinged

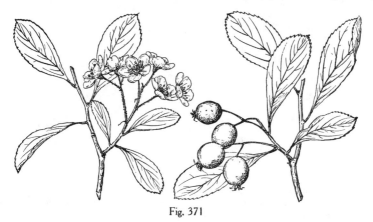

Fig. 371

with red, $\frac{1}{4}'-\frac{1}{3}'$ long, with a prominent calyx-tube and elongated spreading lobes puberulous on the inner surface and often deciduous before the ripening of the fruit; flesh very thin, green, dry and hard; nutlets 2 or 3, with a broad low rounded ridge, $\frac{1}{4}'$ long.

A tree, in low moist ground sometimes 40° high, with a trunk 1° in diameter, free of branches for 18°–20°, stout horizontal branches forming a broad round symmetrical head, and nearly straight branchlets villose when they first appear, soon glabrous, light chestnut-brown becoming dark gray-brown in their second or third year, and armed with stout or slender straight chestnut-brown spines $1'-2'$ long; or on the dry soil of low hills much smaller and generally 20°–25° high.

Distribution. Low wet woods on the borders of streams, and on dry hills in forests of Oak and Pine; near Marshall, Harris County, Texas; Natchitoches, Natchitoches Parish, and to the neighborhood of Shreveport, Louisiana.

20. Cratægus tersa Beadl.

Leaves oblong to obovate, rounded and obtuse at apex, gradually narrowed to the concave-cuneate entire base, and coarsely serrate above with acute or rounded teeth, when they unfold tinged with red, sparingly villose above and tomentulose below, nearly fully grown when the flowers open the middle of April, and at maturity coriaceous, dark green, lustrous, and glabrous or scabrate above, pale and pubescent below, $1\frac{1}{2}'-2'$ long, and $1'-1\frac{1}{4}'$ wide, with a slender midrib and thin primary veins; turning in the autumn yellow, orange, and brown; petioles stout, at first hoary-tomentose, glabrous at maturity, about $\frac{1}{2}'$ in length; leaves on the end of vigorous shoots, broad-obovate, short-pointed at the rounded apex, often 2' long and $1\frac{1}{2}'$ wide, with a prominent midrib and primary veins. **Flowers** $\frac{5}{8}'-\frac{3}{4}'$ in diameter, on short stout hairy pedicels, in usually 8–10-flowered very compact corymbs densely clothed with long matted pale hairs; calyx-tube narrowly obconic, villose, the lobes acuminate, glandular-serrate, villose on the outer and slightly pilose on the inner surface; stamens 18–20; anthers pale rose color, styles usually 2 or 3. **Fruit** ripening in October, on stout glabrous stems, in compact drooping few-fruited clusters, globose to subglobose or short-oblong, about $\frac{3}{8}'$ long, dark red; calyx prominent, with enlarged erect or spreading glandular-serrate lobes; flesh thin, yellow, dry **and** mealy; nutlets 2 or 3, mostly obtuse and rounded at the ends, about $\frac{1}{4}'$ long.ₐ

Fig. 372

A tree, sometimes 18°–20° high, with a trunk 6'–8' in diameter, spreading branches forming a broad flat-topped head, and stout chestnut-brown branchlets at first pilose, becoming glabrous before autumn, and usually unarmed.

Distribution.   Low woods west of Opelousas, St. Landry Parish, Louisiana.

21. Cratægus berberifolia T. & G.

Leaves oblong-obovate to elliptic, rounded or gradually narrowed at apex, narrowed from above the middle to the cuneate entire base, and serrate above with straight or incurved teeth, nearly fully grown when the flowers open at the end of March or early in April and then roughened above by short rigid white hairs, and whitish and pubescent below,

Fig. 373

and at maturity subcoriaceous, dark green, lustrous and nearly glabrous on the upper surface, pale and pubescent on the lower surface especially on the thin midrib and slender primary veins, $1\frac{1}{2}'$–2' long, and $\frac{3}{4}'$–1' wide; petioles comparatively slender, at first densely villose, becoming glabrous, usually about ½′ in length. **Flowers** ⅔–½′ in diameter, on slender villose pedicels, in compact mostly 4–5-flowered villose corymbs; calyx-tube narrowly obconic, thickly coated with long matted pale hairs, the lobes slender, acuminate, sparingly villose or nearly glabrous on the outer surface, villose on the inner surface, entire or slightly serrate; stamens 20; anthers yellow; styles 2 or 3, surrounded at base by a narrow ring of pale hairs. **Fruit** ripening early in October, on slender pedicels, in few-fruited drooping puberulous clusters, subglobose, orange with a red cheek, about ½′ in diameter; calyx-tube slightly enlarged, with spreading or incurved lobes; flesh thin and yellow; nutlets 2 or 3, slightly ridged on the back, about ¼′ long.

A tree, 20°–25° high, with a tall trunk 8′–10′ in diameter, covered with dark gray scaly bark, stout branches spreading into a broad flat-topped head, and slender branchlets covered at first with matted white hairs, becoming glabrous and light orange-brown at the end of their first season, and pale gray-brown the following year, and unarmed or armed with occasional slender nearly straight red-brown spines 1′–1½′ long.

Distribution. Borders of prairies and low moist soil a few miles west of Opelousas, St. Landry Parish, Louisiana.

22. Cratægus edura Beadl.

Leaves oblong-obovate, rounded and obtuse or occasionally acute at apex, gradually narrowed from above the middle to the cuneate base, and serrate only at the apex, nearly fully grown when the flowers open early in April and then thin, dark green and puberulous

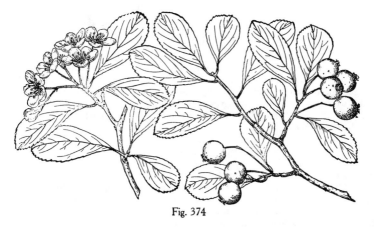

Fig. 374

above especially on the midrib, very pale and villose below, and at maturity thick and coriaceous, 1¼′–1½′ long, and 1½′–1¾′ wide, with a slender midrib, and primary veins within the parenchyma; turning in the autumn orange, yellow, or brown; petioles slender, light yellow, pilose, ⅛′–¼′ in length. **Flowers** ⅜′–½′ in diameter, on short sparingly villose pedicels, in compact hairy 5–12-flowered corymbs; calyx narrowly obconic, glabrous or with a few hairs at the base, the lobes narrow, acuminate, glabrous; stamens 16–20; anthers pale yellow or nearly white; styles 2 or 3. **Fruit** ripening and falling in September, in few-fruited drooping clusters, subglobose, orange or yellow with a red cheek, about 5⁄16′ in diameter; calyx-lobes little enlarged, closely appressed, often deciduous; nutlets 2 or 3, rather obscurely ridged on the back, about ¼′ long.

A tree, 20°–25° high, with a trunk 6′–8′ in diameter, branches spreading out into a broad flat-topped head, and branchlets pilose when they first appear, soon glabrous, becoming reddish brown, unarmed or armed with chestnut-brown or gray spines 1½′–2′ long.

Distribution. Low woods near Opelousas, St. Landry Parish, Louisiana.

23. Cratægus crocina Beadl.

Leaves oblong-obovate, rounded or acute at apex, gradually narrowed and cuneate at the slender entire base, and sharply serrate above the middle with straight or incurved glandular teeth, when they unfold more or less pubescent, and at maturity subcoriaceous, dark green, lustrous and glabrous or glabrate above, pale and covered below with short matted pale hairs most abundant on the thin midrib and obscure primary veins, $1\frac{1}{4}'-2'$

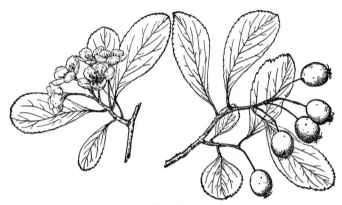

Fig. 375

long, and $\frac{1}{2}'-1'$ wide; turning in the autumn orange, yellow, or brown; petioles slender, puberulous, about $\frac{1}{4}'$ in length; leaves at the end of vigorous shoots elliptic to oblong-obovate, acuminate more coarsely serrate, often $2\frac{1}{2}'$ long and $\frac{5}{6}'$ wide. **Flowers** opening at the end of April when the leaves are fully grown, $\frac{1}{2}'-\frac{5}{8}'$ in diameter, on short villose pedicels, in compact few-flowered villose corymbs; calyx narrowly obconic, coated with matted white hairs, the lobes narrow, acute, entire or sparingly serrate, glabrous on the outer surface, slightly villose on the inner surface toward the apex; stamens 20; anthers yellow; styles usually 2 or 3. **Fruit** ripening in October, ellipsoidal or short-oblong, nearly $\frac{1}{2}'$ long, yellow, the calyx prominent, with elongated mostly recurved lobes; nutlets usually 2, narrowed and acute at the ends, ridged on the back, about $\frac{1}{4}'$ long.

A tree, $18°-20°$ high, with a short trunk $4'-6'$ in diameter, spreading branches forming a wide flat-topped head, and slender mostly unarmed branchlets covered at first with matted pale hairs, and dark orange-brown and puberulous in their first winter.

Distribution. Low woods near Opelousas, St. Landry Parish, Louisiana.

24. Cratægus fera Beadl.

Leaves oblong-obovate, rounded or rarely acute at apex, gradually narrowed and concave-cuneate at the slender entire base, and sharply serrate above the middle with straight or incurved teeth, fully grown when the flowers open the middle of April and then thin, covered above by short white hairs, and slightly villose along the midrib and veins below, and at maturity coriaceous, dark green, scabrate and lustrous on the upper surface, pale and puberulous on the lower surface on the slender midrib and obscure primary veins, $2\frac{1}{2}'-3'$ long, and about $\frac{3}{4}'$ wide; turning in the autumn orange, yellow, or brown; petioles slender, pubescent early in the season, becoming puberulous, $\frac{3}{8}'-\frac{5}{8}'$ in length; leaves at the end of vigorous shoots oblong-obovate, rounded or acute and often short-pointed at apex, coarsely serrate, often $2\frac{1}{2}'$ long, and $1\frac{1}{4}'$ wide. **Flowers:** $\frac{1}{2}'$ in diameter, on long slender villose pedicels, in broad lax compound many-flowered corymbs covered more or less thickly with white hairs; calyx-tube narrowly obconic, slightly hairy near the base, glabrous above, the lobes narrow, acuminate, entire or sparingly glandular-dentate, glabrous on the outer surface and puberulous on the inner surface; stamens 16–20; anthers light yellow; styles usually 2 or 3. **Fruit** ripening in September and October, on long slender pedicels, in few-fruited drooping clusters, globose or subglobose, bright red or scarlet, $\frac{3}{8}'$ in diameter; flesh thin and mealy; calyx enlarged, with spreading or erect persistent lobes; nutlets 2 or 3, with a high narrow ridge, $\frac{1}{4}'-\frac{5}{16}'$ long.

Fig. 376

A tree, sometimes 20° high, with a trunk 8'–9' in diameter, spreading branches forming a broad flat-topped head, and slender nearly straight branchlets, villose at first, becoming glabrous, pale reddish brown, ultimately ashy gray, and sometimes armed with slender straight spines 1'–1¼' long.

Distribution. Low open Oak and Hickory woods near Opelousas, St. Landry Parish, and Natchitoches, Natchitoches Parish, Louisiana.

25. Cratægus Mohrii Beadl.

Leaves obovate or rhombic, acute or acuminate, gradually narrowed and cuneate at the entire base, and coarsely, occasionally doubly serrate above with straight or incurved teeth,

Fig. 377

when they unfold glabrous and slightly villose along the midrib and the lower side of the principal veins, nearly fully grown when the flowers open early in May, and at maturity thin and firm or subcoriaceous, dark green and very lustrous above, pale below, 1'–1½' long, and ⅔'–1' wide, usually with 4 pairs of thin primary veins, a stout midrib sometimes puberulous on the under side and bright red in the autumn; petioles frequently red at maturity, ⅓'–½' in length; leaves at the end of vigorous shoots sometimes 3' long and 2' wide, mostly broad-elliptic, acute or acuminate, coarsely doubly serrate, and frequently divided toward the apex into short broad acute lobes; petioles, strait, glandular; petioles broadly winged, and occasionally glandular with minute dark glands. Flowers cup-shaped, about ¾' in diameter, on slender elongated pedicels, in loose thin-branched many-flowered glabrous or villose corymbs; calyx-tube narrowly obconic, glabrous or occasionally pilose toward the base, the lobes linear-lanceolate, entire or finely glandular-serrate; stamens 20; anthers small, light yellow; styles 3–5, surrounded at base by a narrow ring of pale hairs. Fruit ripening about the middle of October, gracefully drooping on elongated thin bright red pedicels, in many-fruited clusters, subglobose to short-oblong, somewhat flattened at apex, full and rounded at base, bright orange-red, about ⅓' in diameter; calyx prominent, with a short tube and usually erect lobes often deciduous before the fruit ripens; nutlets usually 3, about ¼' long.

A tree, from 20°–30° high, with a tall straight trunk 6'–8' in diameter, covered with thin ashy gray or light red-brown bark, sometimes armed with long slender or branched spines, spreading slightly pendulous branches forming a rather open broad symmetrical head, and branchlets furnished with thin nearly straight bright chestnut-brown shining spines 1'–1½' long.

Distribution. Western Georgia to central Alabama and eastern Mississippi, and northward to middle Tennessee; abundant and of its largest size in the low flat woods near Birmingham, Jefferson County, Alabama, ascending into the poorer and drier soils of the neighboring hillsides and low mountain slopes.

II. PUNCTATÆ.

CONSPECTUS OF THE ARBORESCENT SPECIES.

Fruit usually short-oblong.
  Anthers rose color or yellow; stamens 20; leaves obovate, often acutely lobed above the middle, their veins deeply impressed; fruit on stout pedicels, short-oblong to subglobose, flattened at the ends, dull red or bright yellow, marked by large pale dots.
  26. **C. punctata** (A).
  Anthers rose color; stamens 10–20; leaves oblong-obovate or oval, their veins not deeply impressed, fruit on long slender pedicels, short-oblong to obovoid, rounded at the ends, lull brick-red, marked by large pale dots.   27. **C. pausiaca** (A).
Fruit usually globose or subglobose.
  Stamens 20.
    Anthers pale yellow.
      Corymbs villose.
        Leaves obovate to oval or rarely rhombic, acute; fruit globose, or sometimes broader than high, dull red, marked by small pale dots. 28. **C. collina** (A, C).
        Leaves obovate, oval, or ovate, acute or acuminate, incisely lobed; fruit globose, dull red.   29. **C. amnicola** (C).
      Corymbs glabrous; leaves broadly oval to ovate, rounded or acute at apex, occasionally rounded at base, subcoriaceous; fruit subglobose to short-oblong, dull orange-red, marked by large pale dots.   30. **C. fastosa** (C).
    Anthers rose color.
      Leaves scabrate on the upper surface.
        Leaves ovate, oval or rarely obovate, acuminate; flowers in compact usually 6–8-flowered corymbs.   31. **C. sylvestris** (A).

Leaves obovate to rhombic, acute or rarely rounded at apex; flowers in wide
usually 9–12-flowered corymbs.   32. **C. verruculosa.**
Leaves glabrous on the upper surface.
Corymbs slightly villose.
Leaves obovate to rhombic, acute or rounded at apex; fruit globose, dark
dull red.   33. **C. sordida** (C).
Leaves oval to obovate, acute or acuminate at apex; fruit often rather longer
than broad, bright canary-yellow.   34. **C. brazoria** (C).
Corymbs densely villose; leaves obovate, acute, acuminate or rounded at apex;
fruit subglobose, dark dull red.   35. **C. dallasiana** (C).
Stamens 10.
Anthers pale yellow; leaves obovate, acute or acuminate or rounded and short-
pointed at apex; fruit subglobose, pubescent at the ends, dull orange-red.
                                                                36. **C. Lettermanii** (A).
Anthers rose color; leaves oblong-obovate, acute or rounded at apex; fruit globose,
bright scarlet, slightly pruinose.   37. **C. pratensis** (A).

26. Cratægus punctata Jacq.

Leaves obovate, pointed or rounded at apex, gradually narrowed to the cuneate entire
base, sharply and often doubly serrate above the middle with minute teeth, and sometimes
more or less incisely lobed, thickly covered below with pale hairs and pilose above when

Fig. 378

they unfold, about half grown when the flowers open from the middle of May until early in
June and then pilose on the midrib and veins below and nearly glabrous above, and at
maturity thick and firm, pale gray-green and glabrous on the upper surface, more or less
villose on the lower surface, 2′–3′ long, and $\frac{3}{4}$′–1$\frac{1}{2}$′ wide, with a broad prominent midrib, and
primary veins deeply impressed on the upper surface; turning bright orange or orange and
scarlet in the autumn; petioles stout, at first villose or tomentose, becoming pubescent or
glabrous, $\frac{1}{4}$′–$\frac{1}{2}$′ in length; leaves at the end of vigorous shoots usually incisely lobed, and
often 3′–4′ long and 1$\frac{1}{2}$′–2′ wide.   **Flowers** $\frac{1}{2}$′–$\frac{3}{4}$′ in diameter, on slender villose pedicels, in
tomentose or villose many-flowered compact corymbs; calyx-tube narrowly obconic, villose
or tomentose, the lobes narrow, acute, nearly entire or minutely glandular-serrate, villose
on the inner surface; stamens 20; anthers rose color or yellow; styles 5, surrounded at base
by conspicuous tufts of white hairs.   **Fruit** ripening and falling in October, on elongated
nearly glabrous pedicels, in drooping clusters, short-oblong to subglobose, truncate at
the ends dull red or bright yellow (var. *aurea* Ait.) and usually agreeing with the anthers
in color, marked by numerous small white dots, $\frac{1}{2}$′–1′ long; nutlets 5, about $\frac{1}{4}$′ long.

A tree, 20°–30° high, with a trunk occasionally a foot in diameter, stout branches spreading nearly at right angles and forming a round or flat-topped head, or sometimes ascending and forming a narrow open irregular head, and branchlets coated at first with pale deciduous pubescence, becoming light orange-brown or ashy gray, and armed with slender straight light orange-brown or gray spines 2′–3′ long.

Distribution. Common and generally distributed; rich hillsides; valley of the Chateaugay River, Quebec, to the valley of the Detroit River, Ontario, southward through western New England to Delaware, and along the Appalachian Mountains to northern Georgia, ascending in North Carolina and Tennessee to altitudes of nearly 6000°, and westward through New York, Ohio and Indiana to southern Michigan, Indiana, Illinois, southern Wisconsin, southeastern Minnesota, and in central Iowa. A form (var. *canescens* Britt.), densely hoary-tomentose on the under surface of the leaves, and on the petioles and corymbs, occurs in Bucks County, Pennsylvania, and near Albany, Albany County, New York; and a form (var. *microphylla* Sarg.) with smaller leaves and compact few-flowered corymbs has been found at Linesville, Crawford County, Pennsylvania.

27. Cratægus pausiaca Ashe.

Leaves oblong-obovate to oval, rounded or acute at apex, gradually narrowed from near the middle to the concave-cuneate entire base, and finely doubly serrate above with straight glandular teeth, more than half grown when the flowers open from the 20th to the end of

Fig. 379

May and then membranaceous, dark yellow-green, and slightly villose above and along the under side of the midrib and veins, and at maturity glabrous, dark yellow-green above, paler below, 2′–2½′ long, and 1¼′–1½′ wide, with a slender yellow midrib, and 5 or 6 pairs of primary veins extending very obliquely to the end of the leaf; petioles slender, wing-margined above the middle, villose only early in the season, ⅝′–1′ in length; leaves at the end of vigorous shoots elliptic to rhombic, long-pointed, slightly or deeply divided into broad lateral lobes, coarsely serrate, often 3½′–4′ long and 2′–2½′ wide. **Flowers** ½′ in diameter, on long slender hairy pedicels, in broad many-flowered thin-branched villose corymbs; calyx-tube narrowly obconic, villose below with closely appressed white hairs, glabrous above, the lobes abruptly narrowed from the base, slender, acuminate, tipped with minute dark glands, entire or occasionally obscurely toothed above the middle, glabrous on the outer surface, villose on the inner surface; stamens 10–15, rarely 20; anthers dark rose color; styles 2 or 3, surrounded at base by a broad ring of pale tomentum. **Fruit** ripening about the middle of October, on elongated slender slightly hairy pedicels, in drooping many-fruited clusters, short-oblong to obovoid, broad and rounded at the ends, dull brick-

red, marked by large pale dots, $\frac{5}{16}'-\frac{9}{16}'$ long, and about $\frac{3}{8}'$ thick; calyx small, with spreading appressed lobes mostly deciduous from the ripe fruit; flesh thin, hard, slightly juicy, green or greenish yellow; nutlets 3 or 4, thin, acute or obtuse at the ends, ridged on the back with a high broad deeply grooved ridge, about $\frac{1}{4}'$ long.

A tree, 20°–25° high, with a tall straight trunk often a foot in diameter, covered with dark brown scaly bark, stout wide-spreading branches forming a broad symmetrical round or flat-topped head, slender straight branchlets light orange-green and sparingly villose at first, becoming light orange-brown during their first season, light or dark gray-brown the following year, and armed with numerous stout slender straight orange-brown shining spines $1\frac{1}{2}'-2'$ in length, long persistent on the branches and trunk, finally ashy gray, and becoming sometimes a foot long, with long slender lateral spines.

Distribution. Dry limestone hills and low moist bottom-lands, Bucks, Berks and Delaware counties, eastern Pennsylvania; at Chapin, Ontario County, New York.

28. Cratægus collina Chapm.

Leaves obovate to oval or occasionally to rhombic, acute, gradually narrowed or broadly cuneate at the entire base, and irregularly and often doubly serrate above with glandular incurved or straight teeth, when they unfold bright red and covered with soft pale hairs

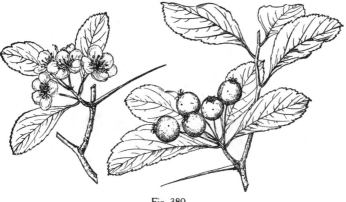

Fig. 380

most abundant on the under side of the midrib and principal veins, less than one third grown when the flowers open at the end of April, and at maturity subcoriaceous, yellow-green on the upper surface, paler on the lower surface, glabrous with the exception of a few hairs on the under side of the stout yellow midrib and 4 or 5 pairs of slender primary veins, $1\frac{1}{2}'-2'$ in length, and $1'-1\frac{1}{4}'$ wide, petioles slender, villose, soon glabrous, more or less winged toward the apex, $\frac{1}{4}'-\frac{1}{2}'$ long; leaves at the end of vigorous shoots frequently divided into short broad acute lateral lobes, more coarsely dentate and often $3'$ long and $2\frac{1}{2}'$ wide, with a stout broadly winged petiole generally light red like the lower side of the base of the midrib. **Flowers** $\frac{3}{4}'$ in diameter, on long stout pedicels, in broad many-flowered villose corymbs; calyx-tube broadly obconic, villose particularly toward the base, the lobes gradually narrowed from a broad base, acuminate, usually glabrous on the outer surface, villose on the inner surface, finely glandular-serrate with dark glands, bright red toward the apex; stamens usually 20; anthers large, pale yellow; styles 5. **Fruit** ripening in September, on stout elongated pedicels, in few-fruited erect or drooping puberulous clusters, subglobose but sometimes rather broader than long, dull red, marked by small pale dots, $\frac{1}{3}'-\frac{1}{2}'$ in diameter; calyx enlarged, the lobes closely appressed, glandular-serrate, mostly persistent;

flesh yellow; nutlets 5, broad and rounded at the ends, ridged and often grooved on the
back, about ¼' long.

A tree, usually 15°–20° but occasionally 25° high, with a tall straight trunk often buttressed at base, frequently armed with numerous large much-branched spines sometimes
6'–8' long, stout wide-spreading branches forming a handsome flat-topped symmetrical
head, and branchlets tinged with red and villose with long matted silky white hairs when
they first appear, soon puberulous, and dull reddish brown, becoming gray in their second
year, and furnished with stout lustrous spines 2'–3' long.

Distribution. Hillsides in rich soil in the foothill region of the southern Appalachian
Mountains from southwestern Virginia to central Georgia and westward to northeastern
Mississippi and middle Tennessee; in central Alabama; ascending to altitudes of 2500° above
the sea.

29. Cratægus amnicola Beadl.

Leaves obovate, oval or ovate, acute or acuminate at apex, gradually narrowed and
concave-cuneate at the entire base, coarsely sometimes doubly serrate above with straight
or incurved glandular teeth, and incisely lobed above the middle with short acute or acu-

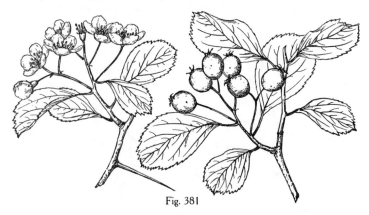

Fig. 381

minate lobes, deeply tinged with red and covered with short pale mostly caducous hairs
when they unfold, about half grown and sparingly villose on the midrib and veins when the
flowers open late in April or early in May, and at maturity subcoriaceous, bright green,
glabrous, 1¼'–1½' long, and 1'–1¼' wide; turning in the autumn yellow, orange, red, and
brown; petioles slender, sparingly villose early in the season, becoming glabrous, sometimes
slightly glandular, ¼'–⅓' in length; leaves at the end of vigorous shoots sometimes 2' long
and 1½' wide. **Flowers** about ⅝' in diameter, on elongated slender slightly villose pedicels,
in narrow many-flowered villose corymbs; calyx-tube narrowly obconic, glabrous or with a
few scattered hairs at the base, the lobes narrow, acuminate, glandular-serrate, glabrous;
stamens 20; anthers nearly white; styles 3–5. **Fruit** on slender elongated glabrous pedicels,
in drooping few-fruited clusters, subglobose, dull red, about ¼' in diameter; calyx enlarged,
with elongated coarsely serrate reflexed conspicuous lobes; flesh yellow, thin, and firm;
nutlets 3–5, rounded or slightly grooved on the back, nearly ¼' long.

A tree, occasionally 25° high, with a trunk 8'–12' in diameter, spreading or ascending
branches forming a large wide head, and branchlets villose at first with long matted white
hairs, soon glabrous, becoming orange-brown and ultimately ashy gray, and unarmed,
or armed with stout spines 1¼'–2' long.

Distribution. Low moist woods and the borders of streams, southeastern **Tennessee,**
northwestern Georgia, and northeastern Alabama; common.

30. Cratægus fastosa Sarg.

Leaves broadly oval to ovate, rounded or acute at apex, concave-cuneate or rounded at the entire base, and coarsely doubly serrate above with straight glandular teeth, when they unfold covered above with long pale hairs and provided below with large tufts of snow-white tomentum in the axils of the primary veins, when the flowers open from the 20th to the 25th of April dark yellow-green and nearly glabrous on the upper surface and still tomentose in the axils of the veins below, and at maturity subcoriaceous, glabrous, yellow-green and lustrous above, pale yellow-green below, $1\frac{1}{4}'-2'$ long, and $1'-2'$ wide, with a prominent light yellow midrib deeply impressed on the upper side, and usually 3–5 pairs of primary veins; petioles slender, at first densely villose, becoming puberulous, $\frac{1}{2}'-\frac{3}{4}'$ in length; leaves at the end of vigorous shoots occasionally lobed with broad acute lobes. **Flowers** about $\frac{3}{4}'$ in diameter, on slender pedicels, in compact many-flowered glabrous corymbs, with large conspicuous oblong-obovate and acute to lanceolate coarsely glandular-serrate bracts and bractlets usually persistent until after the petals fall; calyx broadly obconic, the lobes abruptly narrowed at base, slender, acuminate, coarsely glandular-

Fig. 382

serrate, glabrous on the outer surface, villose on the inner surface; stamens 20; anthers pale yellow; styles 5, surrounded at base by a broad ring of pale tomentum. **Fruit** ripening from the middle to the end of October, on thin reddish pedicels, in few-fruited drooping clusters. subglobose to short-oblong, dull orange-red, marked by large pale dots, $\frac{3}{8}'$ in diameter; calyx enlarged, with spreading serrate lobes villose on the upper side, mostly deciduous from the ripe fruit; flesh thin, yellow-green; nutlets 3–5, thin, narrowed at the ends, obscurely ridged on the back with a broad low often grooved ridge, about $\frac{5}{16}'$ long.

A tree, 18°–20° high, with a short trunk 8′–12′ in diameter, covered with dark brown or nearly black scaly bark, small ascending branches forming an irregular open head, and slender nearly straight branchlets, dark orange-green tinged with red when they first appear, becoming before autumn bright reddish brown and very lustrous, and dull reddish brown the following year, and armed with numerous stout nearly straight bright chestnut-brown shining spines $1\frac{1}{2}'-2'$ long.

Distribution. Low woods near Fulton, Hempstead County, Arkansas; not common.

31. Cratægus silvestris Sarg.

Leaves ovate, oval or rarely obovate, acuminate, concave-cuneate or rounded at the entire base, sharply doubly serrate above with straight glandular teeth, and slightly divided above the middle into 3 or 4 pairs of small acuminate lobes, nearly fully grown when the flowers open at the end of May and then roughened above by short white hairs, and villose below on the slender midrib and veins, and at maturity subcoriaceous, dark yellow-green lustrous and scabrate on the upper surface, paler and still villose on the lower surface, $2\frac{1}{4}'-2\frac{1}{2}'$ long, and $1\frac{3}{4}'-2'$ wide; petioles stout, slightly hairy on the upper side, occasionally glandular, and $\frac{2}{5}'-\frac{4}{5}'$ in length. **Flowers** $\frac{3}{5}'$ in diameter, on slender villose pedicels, in compact villose usually 6–8-flowered corymbs; calyx-tube narrowly obconic, glabrous, the lobes slender, acuminate, coarsely glandular-serrate, slightly villose on the inner surface; stamens 20; anthers pink; styles usually 3. **Fruit** ripening at the end of September, on slender reddish slightly hairy pedicels, in few-fruited erect or spreading clusters, subglobose to short-oblong, truncate at base, rounded at apex, dull orange-red, about $\frac{1}{2}'$ in diameter;

Fig. 383

calyx prominent with a broad deep cavity, and spreading coarsely serrate persistent lobes villose on the upper surface; flesh thick, dry and mealy; nutlets 3, gradually narrowed and rounded at the ends, ridged on the back with a high deeply grooved ridge, about $\frac{1}{3}'$ long and $\frac{1}{6}'-\frac{1}{5}'$ wide.

A tree, 30°–35° high, with a tall trunk often 1° in diameter, large ascending and spreading branches forming an open head, and stout nearly straight glabrous branchlets, light orange-green and marked by small pale lenticels when they first appear, becoming light chestnut-brown and lustrous in their first season, and dull red-brown the following year, and armed with slender straight or slightly curved dark chestnut-brown lustrous spines $1'-1\frac{1}{2}'$ long.

Distribution. Woods in low moist soil, near London, Ontario.

32. Cratægus verruculosa Sarg.

Leaves obovate to rhombic, acute or rarely rounded at apex, cuneate and entire at base, and sharply often doubly serrate above with straight or incurved glandular teeth, when they unfold dark red, covered above by short pale hairs and below by long matted white hairs most abundant on the midrib and veins, about half grown when the flowers open from the 1st to the 10th of May and then thin, dark yellow-green and scabrate on the upper surface, and paler and pubescent on the lower surface, and at maturity subcoriaceous, dark green, lustrous and nearly smooth above, pale and still pubescent below on the stout midrib and conspicuous primary veins extending very obliquely toward the end of the leaf, $1\frac{1}{2}'-2'$ long, and $1'-1\frac{1}{4}'$ wide; petioles stout, wing-margined at apex, at first villose, becoming pubescent or puberulous, $\frac{1}{4}'-\frac{1}{2}'$ in length; leaves at the end of vigorous shoots often broad-ovate to oval, sharply doubly serrate with straight teeth, sometimes slightly lobed above the middle with short acute lobes, and frequently 3' long and 2' wide. **Flowers** $\frac{3}{4}'$ in diameter, on long slender villose pedicels, in broad lax compound 6–12 usually 9-flowered villose corymbs; calyx-tube broadly obconic, thickly covered with matted pale hairs, the lobes gradually narrowed from a broad base, slender, acute, tinged with red at apex, sparingly glandular-serrate, pubescent; stamens 20; anthers pale rose color; styles 3–5 surrounded at base by a broad ring of long pale hairs. **Fruit** ripening about the 1st of October, on stout pubescent pedicels, in drooping few-fruited clusters, subglobose, somewhat flattened and pubescent at the ends, dark red; calyx prominent, with more or less deciduous lobes; nutlets 3–5, narrowed and acute at the ends, rounded and very irregularly ridged and sometimes obscurely grooved on the back, about ¼′ long.

A tree, 20°–25° high, with a tall trunk 10′–12′ in diameter, thick spreading branches forming a broad compact round-topped symmetrical head, and stout nearly straight branchlets thickly covered with matted pale hairs when they first appear, becoming reddish

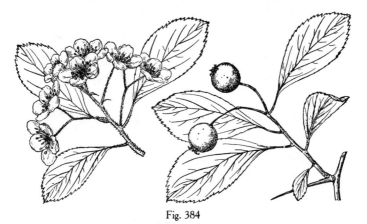

Fig. 384

or orange-brown, nearly glabrous and roughened by minute tubercles at the end of their first season, gray-brown the following year, and armed with numerous straight stout or slender dark chestnut-brown very lustrous spines ¾′–1′ long.

Distribution. Springfield, Greene County, Missouri, Hot Spring, Garland County, and Hempstead and Miller Counties, Arkansas; not rare.

33. Cratægus sordida Sarg.

Leaves rhombic, acute, or occasionally obovate and rarely rounded at apex, cuneate and entire below, serrate above with narrow straight or incurved glandular teeth, and occasionally irregularly divided above the middle into short acute lobes, about half grown when the flowers open the first week of May and then membranaceous, bright green, lustrous and glabrous with the exception of a few short caducous hairs on the upper surface, particularly on the midrib and principal veins, and at maturity subcoriaceous, dark green and lustrous above, paler below, generally about 1½′ long and 1¼′ wide; petioles stout, slightly winged toward the apex, at first villose, soon glabrous, about ½′ long, often bright red in the autumn; leaves at the end of vigorous shoots sometimes oblong or oval, coarsely dentate, usually divided above the middle into short acute lobes, 3′–4′ long, 2′–2½′ wide, and decurrent on the stout glandular petioles. **Flowers** 1′–1¼′ in diameter, on slender pedicels, in few-flowered compact slightly villose corymbs; calyx-tube narrowly obconic, the lobes narrow, acuminate, villose on the inner surface; petals dull white; stamens 20; anthers small, rose color; styles 2 or 3, surrounded at base by a narrow ring of pale hairs. **Fruit** ripening and falling the middle of September, on short pedicels, in few-fruited drooping clusters, globose, ⅓′–½′ in diameter, dark dull red; calyx prominent, with elongated coarsely serrate appressed or incurved lobes; flesh thin and yellow; nutlets 2 or 3, broad, rounded and ridged on the back with a low rounded ridge, ¼′ long.

A slender tree, 20°–25° high, with a tall trunk 5′–6′ in diameter, often armed with long-branched spines, small ascending branches forming a narrow oval head, and slender nearly straight branchlets, dark orange-green and villose with long scattered pale hairs sometimes persistent until autumn, dull chestnut-brown in their second season, and dark

Fig. 385

gray-brown the following year, and furnished with numerous thin nearly straight bright chestnut-brown shining spines 1'–2½' long, or often unarmed.

Distribution. Low woods and the gravelly banks of streams in Shannon, Carter, and Ripley Counties, southern Missouri.

34. Cratægus brazoria Sarg.

Leaves oval to obovate, acute or acuminate at apex, gradually narrowed, cuneate and entire at base, and coarsely and irregularly glandular-serrate above with straight spreading teeth, coated with hoary tomentum and often bright red when they unfold, nearly fully

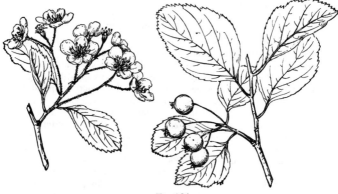

Fig. 386

grown and covered with short soft pale hairs most abundant on the under side of the thin midrib and 3 or 4 pairs of primary veins when the flowers open from the middle to the end of March, and at maturity thin and firm in texture, glabrous, dark green and lustrous above, paler below, $2'-2\frac{1}{2}'$ long, and $1\frac{1}{4}'-1\frac{1}{2}'$ wide; petioles slender, early in the season to-mentose, becoming glabrous or puberulous, $\frac{1}{2}'-\frac{3}{4}'$ in length; leaves at the end of vigorous shoots broad-ovate or oblong, rounded or broad-cuneate at base, coarsely dentate, $5'$ long, and $2\frac{1}{2}'$ wide. **Flowers** $\frac{3}{4}'$ in diameter, on long slender pedicels, in broad slightly villose 7 or 8-flowered corymbs; calyx-tube narrowly obconic, coated with long matted pale hairs, the lobes narrow, acuminate, obscurely glandular-serrate or nearly entire, villose on both surfaces; stamens 20; anthers small, dark red; styles 5, surrounded at base by a thin ring of hoary tomentum. **Fruit** ripening after the 1st of October, in spreading or drooping few-fruited clusters, subglobose and often rather longer than broad, bright canary-yellow, marked by occasional dark dots, $\frac{3}{8}'-\frac{1}{2}'$ long; calyx prominent, the lobes usually deciduous before the fruit ripens; flesh thin, light yellow, rather dry but sweet and edible; nutlets 5, rounded and grooved on the back, $\frac{1}{4}'$ long.

A tree, $20°-25°$ high, with a tall straight trunk $8'-10'$ in diameter, numerous ascending branches forming a handsome symmetrical round-topped head, and branchlets covered when they first appear with matted pale hairs, dull reddish brown and often puberulous in their second season, and reddish brown the following year, and unarmed or occasionally armed with long thin gray spines.

Distribution. Low rich woods near the banks of the Brazos River, Columbia and Bra-zoria, Brazoria County, Texas.

35. Cratægus dallasiana Sarg.

Leaves oblong, acute, acuminate or rounded at apex, gradually narrowed to the concave-cuneate entire base, coarsely doubly serrate above with straight glandular teeth, and usu-ally slightly lobed above the middle, coated below with thick hoary tomentum and villose

Fig. 387

above as they unfold, nearly fully grown and villose or tomentose below when the flowers open early in April, and at maturity thin, dark yellow-green, glabrous and lustrous on the upper surface, pale and pubescent on the lower surface on the slender midrib and 3 or 4 pairs of thin arching veins, $1\frac{3}{4}'-2\frac{1}{2}'$ long, and $1\frac{1}{4}'-1\frac{1}{2}'$ wide; petioles slender, wing-margined toward the apex, hoary-tomentose early in the season, becoming glabrous, about $\frac{1}{2}'$ in length. **Flowers** about $\frac{5}{8}'$ in diameter, on long slender hairy pedicels, in many-flowered densely villose corymbs; calyx-tube narrowly obconic, densely coated with long matted pale hairs, the lobes slender, acuminate, tipped with a minute red gland, sparingly and irregularly glandular-serrate, villose; stamens 20; anthers light rose color; styles 5. **Fruit** ripening at midsummer, on stout erect slightly hairy pedicels, in few-fruited clusters, subglobose, dull dark red, $\frac{3}{8}'-\frac{1}{2}'$ in diameter; calyx prominent, with spreading lobes bright red on the upper side at the base; nutlets 5, acute at the narrow ends, thin, rounded and grooved with a broad shallow groove or irregularly ridged on the back, $\frac{1}{4}'-\frac{5}{16}'$ long.

A tree, 20°–25° high, with a tall trunk 4′–6′ in diameter, covered with pale bark, small erect branches forming an open irregular head, and slender somewhat zigzag branchlets thickly coated at first with hoary tomentum, reddish brown and lustrous before autumn, ultimately ashy gray, and armed with straight slender gray spines $1\frac{1}{4}'-1\frac{1}{2}'$ long.

Distribution.   Forest-covered bottom-lands of the small tributaries of the Trinity River, Dallas County, Texas; not common.

36. Cratægus Lettermanii Sarg.

Leaves obovate, acute or acuminate or rounded and short-pointed at apex, gradually narrowed from near the middle and cuneate at the mostly entire base, coarsely often doubly serrate above with straight or incurved glandular teeth, and frequently slightly and

Fig. 388

irregularly divided above the middle into 3 or 4 pairs of short acute lobes, strongly plicate when they unfold and covered with a thick coat of pale tomentum, nearly half grown, roughened above by short pale hairs and pubescent below when the flowers open early in May, and at maturity thick, bright yellow-green and scabrate above, pale and pubescent below on the stout midrib and 4 or 5 pairs of primary veins, about 2′ long and $1\frac{1}{2}'$ wide; petioles stout, more or less winged above the middle, at first tomentose, becoming pubescent or nearly glabrous, usually about $\frac{3}{4}'$ in length; leaves at the end of vigorous shoots broad-oval, acute or acuminate, more coarsely serrate, $2\frac{1}{2}'-3'$ long, and $2'-2\frac{1}{2}'$ wide. **Flowers** about $\frac{3}{4}'$ in diameter, on short villose pedicels in compact, many-flowered thick-branched densely villose corymbs; calyx-tube narrowly obconic, tomentose, the lobes narrow, acuminate, finely glandular-serrate, villose; stamens 10; anthers small, pale yellow; styles 5, surrounded at base by a broad ring of hoary tomentum. **Fruit** ripening early in October, on stout pubescent pedicels, in few-fruited spreading or drooping clusters, subglobose or occasionally slightly obovoid, rounded and puberulous at the ends, dull orange-red, marked by large pale dots, about $\frac{1}{2}'$ in diameter; calyx broad, the lobes enlarged, coarsely glandular-serrate, reflexed, often deciduous before the fruit ripens; flesh thin; nutlets 5, prominently ridged on the back with a high rounded ridge, $\frac{1}{4}'$ long.

A tree, 18°–20° high, with a trunk 6′–8′ in diameter, with thin dark brown or nearly black bark separating freely into small plate-like scales, and often armed with thin much-branched spines frequently 7′–8′ long, small erect branches forming a wide open head, and branchlets coated when they first appear with hoary tomentum, dull red-brown, villose or pubescent during their first season, and furnished with stout straight bright red-brown shining spines 1½'–2' long.

Distribution. Low rich soil inundated during several weeks in winter, among Oaks and Hickories; near Allenton, St. Louis County, Missouri.

37. Cratægus pratensis Sarg.

Leaves oblong-obovate, acute or rounded at apex, gradually narrowed below from near the middle to the cuneate entire base, sharply and often doubly serrate usually only above the middle with straight or incurved teeth tipped early in the season with a minute dark red caducous gland, and often more or less deeply divided toward the apex into short broad acute lobes, when they unfold bright bronze-yellow or dark red, and covered with short pale hairs, almost smooth and nearly fully grown when the flowers open at the end of May, and at maturity glabrous, thick, dark green and lustrous above, pale below, 1½'–2' long, and 1'–1½' wide, with a thin midrib, and 4 or 5 pairs of primary veins extending obliquely toward

Fig. 389

the end of the leaf, and raised and prominent below; petioles slender, glabrous, usually about ½' in length; leaves at the end of vigorous shoots often oval or broad-ovate, frequently 3' long and 2½' wide. **Flowers** ⅔' in diameter, on long slender pedicels, in broad loose many-flowered corymbs pubescent or puberulous at first but soon glabrous; calyx-tube narrowly obconic, coated toward the base with long matted pale hairs, the lobes narrow, acuminate, coarsely glandular-serrate, glabrous on the outer surface, villose on the inner surface; stamens 10; anthers small, rose color; styles 2 or 3, surrounded at base by a narrow ring of pale tomentum. **Fruit** ripening early in October and remaining on the branches until November, on elongated pedicels, in loose drooping many-fruited clusters, globose, bright scarlet, slightly pruinose, marked by occasional large pale dots, about ⅓' in diameter; calyx prominent, with much enlarged coarsely glandular-serrate lobes often deciduous before the fruit becomes entirely ripe; flesh thin and yellow; nutlets 2 or 3, thick and broad, about ¼' long.

A tree, occasionally 20° high, with a tall trunk 3'–7' in diameter, often armed with long slender much-branched ashy gray spines, spreading branches forming a round-topped symmetrical head, and branchlets occasionally slightly villose when they first appear, soon glabrous, light orange-brown in their first season, and reddish or grayish brown the following year, and furnished with numerous thin straight or slightly curved shining chestnut-brown spines 2'–3' long.

Distribution. Open woods near the banks of small streams in the prairie region of Stark and Peoria Counties, Illinois.

GLOSSARY OF TECHNICAL TERMS

Accrescent. Increasing in size with age.

Accumbent. Lying against, as the radicle against the edges of the cotyledons.

Acuminate. Gradually tapering to the apex.

Acute. Pointed.

Adnate. Congenitally united to.

Adventitious. Said of buds produced without order from any part of a stem.

Æstivation. The arrangement of the parts of a flower in the bud.

Akene or *achene.* A small dry and hard, 1-celled, 1-seeded, indehiscent fruit.

Albumen. The deposit of nutritive material within the coats of a seed and surrounding the embryo.

Ament. A unisexual spike of flowers with scaly bracts, usually deciduous in one piece.

Amphitropous. Descriptive of an ovule with the hilum intermediate between the micropyle and chalaza.

Anatropous. Descriptive of a reversed ovule, with the micropyle close by the side of the hilum, and chalaza at the opposite end.

Androdiœcious. With perfect flowers on one individual and staminate flowers only on another.

Androgynous. Applied to an inflorescence composed of male and female flowers.

Angiospermœ. Plants with seeds borne in a pericarp.

Annular. In the form of a ring.

Anterior. The front side of a flower, that is averse from the axis of inflorescence.

Anther. The part of the stamen containing the pollen.

Anthesis. The act of opening of a flower.

Apetalous. Having no petals.

Apex. The top, as the end of the leaf opposite the petiole.

Apiculate. Ending in a short pointed tip.

Apophysis. An enlargement or swelling of the surface of an organ.

Arcuate. Moderately curved.

Areolate. Marked by areolæ or spaces marked out on a surface.

Aril. An extraneous seed-coat or covering, or an appendage growing about the hilum of a seed.

Ariloid. Furnished with an aril.

Aristate. Furnished with awns.

Articulate. Jointed or having the appearance of a joint.

Auricled or *auriculate.* Furnished with an auricle or ear-shaped appendage.

Autocarpus. A fruit consisting of pericarp alone, without adherent parts.

Axil. The angle formed on the upper side of the attachment of a leaf with a stem.

Axillary. In or from an axil.

Baccate. Berry-like.

Bark. The rind or cortical covering of a stem.

Berry. A fruit with a homogeneous fleshy pericarp.

Bipinnate. Doubly or twice pinnate.

Bract. The more or less modified leaf of a flower-cluster.

Bracteate. Furnished with bracts.

Bracteolate. Furnished with bractlets.

Bractlet. The bract of a pedicel or ultimate flower-stalk.

Branch. A secondary axis or division of a trunk.

Branchlet. An ultimate division of a branch.

Bud. The undeveloped state of a branch or flower-cluster with or without scales.

Bud-scales. Reduced leaves covering a bud.

Calyx. The flower-cup or exterior part of a perianth.

Campanulate. Bell-shaped, or elongated cup-shaped.

Campylotropous. Descriptive of an ovule or seed curved in its formation so as to bring the micropyle or apex down near the hilum.

Canescent. Hoary, with gray or whitish pubescence.

Capsule. A dry dehiscent fruit of more than one carpel.

Carpel. A simple pistil or an element of a compound pistil.

Catkin. The same as an ament.

Caudate. Furnished with a tail, or with a slender tip or appendage.

Centripetal. Developing from without toward the centre.

Chalaza. The part of an ovule where the coats and nucleus are confluent.

Chartaceous. Having the texture of paper.

Ciliate. Fringed with hairs.

Cinereous. Ashy gray.

Circinnate. Involute from the apex into a coil.

Circumscissile. Circularly and transversely dehiscent.

Clavate. Club-shaped.

Cocci. Portions into which a lobed fruit with 1-seeded cells splits up.

Cochleate. Shell-shaped, spiral like the shell of a snail.

Columella. The persistent axis of a capsule.

Commissure. The face by which 2 carpels unite.

Complanate. Flattened.

Conduplicate. Folded together lengthwise.

Cone. An inflorescence or fruit formed of imbricated scales.

Conferruminate. Stuck together by adjacent faces.

Connate. United congenitally.

Connective. The portion of a stamen which connects the two cells or lobes of an anther.

Contortuplicate. Twisted and plaited, or folded.

Convolute. Rolled up from the sides.

Cordate. Heart-shaped.

Coriaceous. Of the texture of leather.

Corymb. A flat-topped or convex open flower-cluster, the flowers opening from the outside inward.

Corymbose. Said of flowers arranged in a corymb.
Costate. Having ribs.
Cotyledons. The leaves of the embryo.
Crenate. Scalloped.
Crenulate. The diminutive of crenate.
Crispate. Curled.
Crustaceous. Of hard brittle texture.
Cucullate. Hooded or hood-shaped.
Cuneate. Wedge-shaped, or triangular with an acute angle downward.
Cyme. A flower-cluster, the flower opening from the centre outward.
Cymose. Bearing cymes or relating to a cyme.

Deciduous. Falling, said of leaves falling in the autumn, or of parts of a flower falling after anthesis.
Declinate. Bent or curved downward.
Decompound. Several times compound or divided.
Decurrent. Running down, as of the blades of leaves extending down their petioles.
Decussate. In pairs alternately crossing at right angles.
Dehiscent. The opening of an anther or capsule by slits or valves.
Deltoid. Having the shape of the Greek letter Δ.
Dentate. Toothed.
Denticulate. Minutely toothed.
Dextrorse. Turned or directed to the right.
Diadelphous Said of stamens combined by their filaments into 2 sets.
Dichotomous. Forked in pairs.
Digitate. Said of a compound leaf in which the leaflets are borne at the apex of the petiole.
Dimorphous. Said of flowers of two forms on the same plant, or on plants of the same species.
Diœcious. Unisexual, with the flowers of the 2 sexes borne by distinct individuals.
Disciferous. Bearing a disk.
Disciform. Depressed and circular like a disk
Discoid. Appertaining to a disk.
Disk. The development of the torus or receptacle of a flower within the calyx or within the corolla and stamens.
Dissepiment. A partition in an ovary or pericarp.
Distichous. Said of leaves arranged alternately in two vertical ranks upon opposite sides of an axil.
Dorsal. Relating to the back.
Dorsal suture. The line of opening of a carpel corresponding to its midrib.
Drupáceous. Resembling or relating to a drupe.
Drupe. A stone fruit.
Duct. An elongated cell or tubular vessel found especially in the woody parts of plants.

Eglandular. Without glands.
Ellipsoidal. Of the shape of an elliptical solid.
Elliptic. Of the form of an ellipse.
Emarginate. Notched at the apex.
Embryo. The rudimentary plant formed in the seed.
Endocarp. The inner layer of a pericarp.
Endogenous. Descriptive of Endogens, monocotyledonous plants with stems increasing by internal accessions.
Epicarp. The thin filmy external layer of a pericarp.
Epigynous Placed on the ovary.
Epiphytal Said of a plant growing on another plant, but not parasitic.

Erose. Descriptive of an irregularly toothed or eroded margin.
Excurrent. Running through the apex or beyond.
Exocarp. The outer layer of a pericarp.
Exogenous. Descriptive of Exogens, plants with stems increasing by the addition of a layer of wood on the outside beneath the constantly widening bark.
Extrorse. Directed outward, descriptive of an anther opening away from the axis of the flower.

Falcate. Scythe-shaped.
Fascicle. A close cluster of leaves or flowers.
Fascicled. Arranged in fascicles.
Feather-veined. Having veins extending from the sides of the midrib.
Ferrugineous. The color of iron rust.
Fibro-vascular. Consisting of woody fibres and ducts.
Filament. The stalk of an anther.
Filamentose. Composed of threads.
Fimbriate. Fringed.
Fistulose. Hollow through the whole length.
Flabellate. Fan-shaped; much dilated from a wedge-shaped base with the broader end rounded.
Floccose. Bearing flocci or tufts of woody hairs.
Foliaceous. Leaf-like in texture or appearance.
Foliolate. Having leaflets.
Foliole. A leaflet.
Follicle. A dry 1-celled seed vessel consisting of a single carpel, and opening only by the ventral suture.
Funicle. The stalk of an ovule or seed.

Gamopetalæ. Plants with a corolla of coalescent petals.
Gamopetalous. Descriptive of a corolla of coalescent petals.
Geniculate. Bent abruptly like a knee.
Gibbous. Swollen on one side.
Glabrate. Nearly glabrous or becoming glabrous.
Glabrous. Smooth, not pubescent or hairy.
Gland. A protuberance on the surface, or partly imbedded in the surface of any part of a plant, either secreting or not.
Glandular. Furnished with glands.
Glaucescent. Nearly or becoming glaucous.
Glaucous. Covered or whitened with a bloom.
Glomerate. Said of flowers gathered into a compact head.
Gymnospermæ. Plants with naked seeds, that is, not inclosed in a pericarp.
Gynophore. The stipe of a pistil.

Heartwood. The mature and dead wood of an exogenous stem.
Hermaphrodite. With staminate and pistillate organs in the same flower, equivalent to perfect.
Hilum. The scar or place of attachment of a seed.
Hirsute. Hairy, with coarse or stiff hairs.
Hispidulous. Minutely hispid.
Hypogynous. Under or free from the pistil.

Imbricate Overlapping, like the shingles on a roof.
Incumbent. Leaning or resting upon, as the radicle against the back of one of the cotyledons.
Induplicate. With edges folded in or turned inward.
Inferior. Said of an organ placed below another,

like a calyx below an ovary or an ovary below a superior calyx.

Inflorescence. Flower-cluster.

Infrapetiolar. Below the petioles.

Innate. Borne on the apex of the supporting part; in an anther the counterpart of adnate.

Interpetiolar. Between the petioles.

Introrse. Turned inward; descriptive of an anther opening toward the axis of the flower.

Inverse. Inverted.

Involucre. A circle of bracts surrounding a flower-cluster.

Involute. Rolled inward.

Laciniate. Cut into narrow incisions or lobes.

Lactescent. Yielding milky juice.

Lamellate. Composed of thin plates.

Lanceolate. Shaped like a lance; narrower than oblong and tapering to the ends, or at least to the apex.

Lanuginose. Clothed with soft reflexed hairs.

Leaf. Green expansions borne by the stem in which assimilation and the processes connected with it are carried on.

Leaflet. The separate division of a compound leaf.

Legume. The seed vessel of plants of the Pea family, composed of a solitary carpel normally dehiscent only by the ventral suture.

Lenticels. Lenticular corky growths on young bark.

Lenticellate. Having lenticels.

Lepidote. Beset with small scurfy scales.

Ligulate. Strap-shaped.

Linear. Said of a narrow leaf several times narrower than long, with parallel margins.

Lobe. The division of an organ.

Lobulate. Divided into small lobes.

Loculicidal. Dehiscent into the cavity of a pericarp by the back, that is through a dorsal suture.

Marcescent. Said of a part of a plant, withering without falling off.

Medullary rays. The rays of cellular tissue in a transverse section of an exogenous stem and extending from the pith to the bark.

Membranaceous. Thin and pliable like a membrane.

Micropyle. The spot or point in the seed at the place of the orifice of the ovule.

Midrib. The central or main rib of a leaf.

Monæcious. Unisexual, with the flowers of the two sexes borne by the same individual

Mucro. A small and abrupt tip to a leaf.

Mucronate. Furnished with a mucro.

Muricate. Rough, with short rigid excrescences.

Naked buds. Buds without scales.

Nectar. The sweet secretion of various parts of a flower.

Nectariferous. Nectar-bearing.

Node. The portion of the stem which bears a leaf or whorl of leaves.

Nucleus. The kernel of an ovule or seed.

Nut. A hard and indehiscent 1-seeded pericarp produced from a compound ovary.

Nutlet. A diminutive nut or stone.

Obclavate. Inverted club-shape.

Obcordate. Inverted heart-shaped.

Oblanceolate. Lanceolate but tapering toward the base more than toward the apex.

Oblong. Longer than broad with nearly parallel sides.

Obovate. Ovate with the broader end toward the apex.

Obovoid. Solid obovate with the broader end toward the apex.

Obpyramidal. Inversely pyramidal.

Obtuse. Blunt or rounded at the apex.

Operculate. Furnished with a lid.

Orbicular. A flat body circular in outline.

Orthotropous. Descriptive of an ovule with a straight axis much enlarged at the insertion and the orifice at the other end.

Oval. Broad-elliptic, with round ends.

Ovate. Of the shape of the longitudinal section of a hen's egg, with the broad end basal.

Ovoid. Solid ovate or solid oval.

Ovule. The part of the flower which becomes a seed.

Palmate. Lobed or divided, with the sinuses pointing to or reaching the apex of the petiole or insertion.

Panicle. A loose compound flower-cluster.

Papilionaceous. Butterfly-like.

Papilliform. The shape of papillæ.

Papillate. Bearing papillæ, minute nipple-shaped papillose projections.

Parietal placenta. A placenta borne on the wall of the ovary.

Pedicel. The stalk of a flower in a compound inflorescence.

Pedicellate. Borne on a pedicel.

Peduncle. A general flower-stalk supporting either a cluster of flowers, or a solitary flower.

Pedunculate. Borne on a peduncle.

Peltate. Descriptive of a plane body attached by its lower surface to the stalk.

Penniveined. Same as pinnately veined.

Perfect. Said of a flower with both stamens and pistil.

Perianth. The envelope of a flower consisting of calyx, corolla, or both.

Pericarp. The fructified ovary.

Persistent. Said of leaves remaining on the branches over their first winter, and of a calyx remaining under or on the fruit.

Petal. A division of the corolla.

Petiolate. Having a petiole.

Petiole. The footstalk of a leaf.

Petiolulate. Having a petiolule.

Petiolule. The footstalk of a leaflet.

Pilose. Hairy, with soft and distinct hairs.

Pinnæ. The primary divisions of a twice pinnate leaf.

Pinnate. A leaf with leaflets arranged along each side of a common petiole.

Pistil. The female organ of a flower, consisting of ovary, style, and stigma.

Pistillate. Said of a unisexual flower without fertile stamens.

Pith. The central cellular part of a stem.

Placenta. That part of the ovary which bears the ovules.

Plane. Used in describing a flat surface.

Plumule. The bud or growing part of the embryo.

Pollen. The fecundating cells contained in the anther.

Polygamodiœcious. Said of flowers sometimes perfect and sometimes unisexual, the 2 forms borne on different individuals.

Polygamomonœcious. Said, of flowers sometimes perfect and sometimes unisexual, the 2 forms borne on the same individual.

Polygamous. Said of flowers sometimes perfect and sometimes unisexual.

Pome. An inferior fruit of 2 or several carpels inclosed in thick flesh.

Posterior. The side of an axillary flower next the axis of inflorescence.

Prickle. Outgrowth of the bark.

Proliferous. Bearing offshoots.

Puberulent. Very slightly pubescent.

Puberulous. Minutely pubescent.

Pubescence. A covering of short soft hairs.

Pubescent. Clothed with soft short hairs.

Pulvinate. Cushion-shaped.

Punctate. Dotted with depressions or translucent internal glands, or with colored dots.

Punctulate. Minutely punctate.

Raceme. An indeterminate or centripetal inflorescence with an elongated axis and flowers on pedicels of equal length.

Rachis. The axis of a spike or of a compound leaf.

Radial. Belonging to a ray.

Radicle. The initial stem in an embryo.

Receptacle. The axile portion of a blossom bearing sepals, petals, stamens, and pistils; the axis or rachis of the head, spike, or other flower-cluster.

Reniform. Kidney-shaped.

Resupinate. Upside down.

Reticulate. Netted.

Retrorse. Directed backward or downward.

Retuse. With a shallow notch at a rounded apex.

Revolute. Rolled backward from the margins or apex.

Rhaphe. The adnate cord or ridge connecting the hilum with the chalaza in an anatropous ovule.

Rhombic. Having the shape of a rhomb.

Rhomboidal. Approaching a rhombic outline; quadrangular with lateral angles obtuse.

Rind. The bark of some endogenous stems, like that of Palms.

Rostrate. Narrowed into a slender tip.

Rotate. Circular, flat and horizontally spreading.

Rugose. Wrinkled.

Rugulose. Slightly wrinkled.

Ruminate. Looking as if chewed, like the albumen of the nutmeg.

Sagittate. Shaped like an arrowhead.

Samara. An indehiscent winged fruit.

Sapwood. The young living wood of an exogenous stem.

Scales. Thin scarious bodies, usually degenerate leaves.

Scarious. Thin, dry and membranaceous, not green.

Scobiform. Having the appearance of sawdust.

Scorpioid. A form of unilateral inflorescence circinately coiled in the bud.

Scurfy. Covered with small bran-like scales.

Seed. The fertilized and mature ovule, the result of sexual reproduction in a flowering plant.

Segment. One of the divisions into which a leaf, calyx, or corolla may be divided.

Semianatropous. Same as amphitropous.

Sepals. The divisions of a calyx.

Septicidal. Descriptive of a capsule splitting through the lines of junction of the carpels.

Septum. A partition.

Serrate. Beset with teeth.

Serrulate. Serrate with small fine teeth.

Sessile. Without a stalk.

Setose. Beset with bristles.

Setulose. Beset with minute bristles.

Sheath. A tubular or enrolled part or organ.

Sinistrorse. Turned or directed to the left.

Sinus. A recess between the lobes of a leaf.

Spatulate. Oblong with the lower end attenuated.

Spike. An indeterminate inflorescence with flowers sessile on an elongated common axis.

Spine. A sharp-pointed woody body, commonly a modified branch or stipule.

Spinescent. Ending in a spine.

Spinose. Furnished with spines.

Stamen. One of the male organs of a flower.

Staminate. Said of unisexual flowers without pistils.

Staminodium. A sterile or much reduced stamen.

Stigma. The part or surface of a pistil which receives the pollen for the fecundation of the ovules.

Stigmatic. Relating to the stigma.

Stipe. A stalk-like support of a pistil or of a carpel.

Stipel. An appendage to a leaflet analagous to the stipules of a leaf.

Stipellate. Having stipels.

Stipitate. Having a stipe.

Stipulate. Having stipules.

Stipules. Appendages of a leaf, placed on one side of the petiole at its insertion with the stem.

Stomata. Breathing pores or apertures in the epidermis of leaves connecting internal cavities with the external air.

Stomatiferous. Furnished with stomata.

Stone. The hard endocarp of a drupe.

Strobile. The same as cone.

Strophiolate. Said of a seed bearing a strophiole or appendage at the hilum.

Style. The attenuated portion of a pistil between the ovary and the stigma.

Subcordate. Slightly cordate.

Subulate. Awl-shaped.

Sulcate. Grooved or furrowed.

Superior. Growing or placed above; also in a lateral flower for the side next the axis.

Suture. A junction, usually a line of opening of a carpel.

Syncarp. A multiple fruit.

Taproot. The primary descending root, a direct continuation from the radicle.

Tegmen. The inner coat of a seed.

Testa. The outer seed-coat.

Thyrsoidal. Relating to a thyrsus.

Thyrsus. A mixed inflorescence with the ma n axis indeterminate and the secondary or ultimate cluster cymose.

Tomentose. Densely pubescent with matted wool or tomentum.

Tomentulose. Slightly pubescent with matted wool.

Torose. Cylindric, with contractions or bulges at intervals.

Torulose. Slightly torose.

Torus. The receptacle of a flower.

Transverse. Horizontal.

Trichotomous. Three-forked.

Trifoliate. Three-leaved.

Trifoliolate. Descriptive of leaves, with 3 leaflets.

Truncate. As if cut off at the end.

Tubercle. A small tuber or excrescence.

Tuberculate. Beset with knobby excrescences.

Turbinate. Top-shaped.

Turgid. Swollen.

Umbel. An inflorescence with numerous pedicels springing from the same point like the rays of an umbrella.

Umbilicus. The hilum of a seed

Umbo. A boss or protuberance.

Umbonate. Bearing an umbo.

Uncinate. Hooked, bent, or curved at the tip in the form of a hook.

Unequally pinnate. Pinnate, with an odd terminal leaflet.

Unguiculate. Contracted at the base into a claw or stalk.

Unisexual. Said of flowers with either the stamens or pistil 0 or abortive.

Urceolate. Hollow and contracted at or below the mouth like an urn or pitcher.

Utricle. A small bladdery pericarp.

Valvate. Said of a bud in which the parts meet without overlapping.

Valve. One of the pieces into which a capsule splits.

Veinlet. One of the ultimate or smaller ramifications of a vein.

Veins. Ramifications or threads of fibro-vascular tissue in a leaf or other flat organ.

Ventral. Belonging to the anterior or inner face of a carpel.

Ventricose. Swelling unequally or inflated on one side.

Vernation. The disposition of parts in a leaf-bud.

Verrucose. Covered with wart-like elevations.

Versatile. Said of an anther turning freely on its filament.

Verticillate. Arranged in a circle or whorl round an axis.

Villose. Hairy, with long and soft hairs.

Whorl. An arrangement of branches or leaves in a circle round an axis.

Wood. The hard part of a stem mainly composed of wood-cells, wood fibre, or tissue.

INDEX

This comprehensive index covers both volumes of the work. Volume One contains pages 1 through 433 and Volume Two contains pages 434 through 891.

A CATALOG OF SELECTED
DOVER BOOKS
IN ALL FIELDS OF INTEREST

A CATALOG OF SELECTED DOVER
BOOKS IN ALL FIELDS OF INTEREST

DRAWINGS OF REMBRANDT, edited by Seymour Slive. Updated Lippmann, Hofstede de Groot edition, with definitive scholarly apparatus. All portraits, biblical sketches, landscapes, nudes. Oriental figures, classical studies, together with selection of work by followers. 550 illustrations. Total of 630pp. 9⅛ × 12¼.
21485-0, 21486-9 Pa., Two-vol. set $25.00

GHOST AND HORROR STORIES OF AMBROSE BIERCE, Ambrose Bierce. 24 tales vividly imagined, strangely prophetic, and decades ahead of their time in technical skill: "The Damned Thing," "An Inhabitant of Carcosa," "The Eyes of the Panther," "Moxon's Master," and 20 more. 199pp. 5⅜ × 8½.   20767-6 Pa. $3.95

ETHICAL WRITINGS OF MAIMONIDES, Maimonides. Most significant ethical works of great medieval sage, newly translated for utmost precision, readability. Laws Concerning Character Traits, Eight Chapters, more. 192pp. 5⅜ × 8½.
24522-5 Pa. $4.50

THE EXPLORATION OF THE COLORADO RIVER AND ITS CANYONS, J. W. Powell. Full text of Powell's 1,000-mile expedition down the fabled Colorado in 1869. Superb account of terrain, geology, vegetation, Indians, famine, mutiny, treacherous rapids, mighty canyons, during exploration of last unknown part of continental U.S. 400pp. 5⅜ × 8½.   20094-9 Pa. $6.95

HISTORY OF PHILOSOPHY, Julián Marías. Clearest one-volume history on the market. Every major philosopher and dozens of others, to Existentialism and later. 505pp. 5⅜ × 8½.   21739-6 Pa. $8.50

ALL ABOUT LIGHTNING, Martin A. Uman. Highly readable non-technical survey of nature and causes of lightning, thunderstorms, ball lightning, St. Elmo's Fire, much more. Illustrated. 192pp. 5⅜ × 8½.   25237-X Pa. $5.95

SAILING ALONE AROUND THE WORLD, Captain Joshua Slocum. First man to sail around the world, alone, in small boat. One of great feats of seamanship told in delightful manner. 67 illustrations. 294pp. 5⅜ × 8½.   20326-3 Pa. $4.95

LETTERS AND NOTES ON THE MANNERS, CUSTOMS AND CONDITIONS OF THE NORTH AMERICAN INDIANS, George Catlin. Classic account of life among Plains Indians: ceremonies, hunt, warfare, etc. 312 plates. 572pp. of text. 6⅛ × 9¼.   22118-0, 22119-9 Pa. Two-vol. set $15.90

ALASKA: The Harriman Expedition, 1899, John Burroughs, John Muir, et al. Informative, engrossing accounts of two-month, 9,000-mile expedition. Native peoples, wildlife, forests, geography, salmon industry, glaciers, more. Profusely illustrated. 240 black-and-white line drawings. 124 black-and-white photographs. 3 maps. Index. 576pp. 5⅜ × 8½.   25109-8 Pa. $11.95

CATALOG OF DOVER BOOKS

THE BOOK OF BEASTS: Being a Translation from a Latin Bestiary of the Twelfth Century, T. H. White. Wonderful catalog real and fanciful beasts: manticore, griffin, phoenix, amphivius, jaculus, many more. White's witty erudite commentary on scientific, historical aspects. Fascinating glimpse of medieval mind. Illustrated. 296pp. 5⅜ × 8¼. (Available in U.S. only)   24609-4 Pa. $5.95

FRANK LLOYD WRIGHT: ARCHITECTURE AND NATURE With 160 Illustrations, Donald Hoffmann. Profusely illustrated study of influence of nature—especially prairie—on Wright's designs for Fallingwater, Robie House, Guggenheim Museum, other masterpieces. 96pp. 9¼ × 10¾.   25098-9 Pa. $7.95

FRANK LLOYD WRIGHT'S FALLINGWATER, Donald Hoffmann. Wright's famous waterfall house: planning and construction of organic idea. History of site, owners, Wright's personal involvement. Photographs of various stages of building. Preface by Edgar Kaufmann, Jr. 100 illustrations. 112pp. 9¼ × 10.
23671-4 Pa. $7.95

YEARS WITH FRANK LLOYD WRIGHT: Apprentice to Genius, Edgar Tafel. Insightful memoir by a former apprentice presents a revealing portrait of Wright the man, the inspired teacher, the greatest American architect. 372 black-and-white illustrations. Preface. Index. vi + 228pp. 8¼ × 11.   24801-1 Pa. $9.95

THE STORY OF KING ARTHUR AND HIS KNIGHTS, Howard Pyle. Enchanting version of King Arthur fable has delighted generations with imaginative narratives of exciting adventures and unforgettable illustrations by the author. 41 illustrations. xviii + 313pp. 6⅛ × 9¼.   21445-1 Pa. $6.50

THE GODS OF THE EGYPTIANS, E. A. Wallis Budge. Thorough coverage of numerous gods of ancient Egypt by foremost Egyptologist. Information on evolution of cults, rites and gods; the cult of Osiris; the Book of the Dead and its rites; the sacred animals and birds; Heaven and Hell; and more. 956pp. 6⅛ × 9¼.
22055-9, 22056-7 Pa., Two-vol. set $20.00

A THEOLOGICO-POLITICAL TREATISE, Benedict Spinoza. Also contains unfinished *Political Treatise*. Great classic on religious liberty, theory of government on common consent. R. Elwes translation. Total of 421pp. 5⅜ × 8½.
20249-6 Pa. $6.95

INCIDENTS OF TRAVEL IN CENTRAL AMERICA, CHIAPAS, AND YU-CATAN, John L. Stephens. Almost single-handed discovery of Maya culture; exploration of ruined cities, monuments, temples; customs of Indians. 115 drawings. 892pp. 5⅜ × 8½.   22404-X, 22405-8 Pa., Two-vol. set $15.90

LOS CAPRICHOS, Francisco Goya. 80 plates of wild, grotesque monsters and caricatures. Prado manuscript included. 183pp. 6⅛ × 9⅜.   22384-1 Pa. $4.95

AUTOBIOGRAPHY: The Story of My Experiments with Truth, Mohandas K. Gandhi. Not hagiography, but Gandhi in his own words. Boyhood, legal studies, purification, the growth of the Satyagraha (nonviolent protest) movement. Critical, inspiring work of the man who freed India. 480pp. 5⅜ × 8½. (Available in U.S. only)
24593-4 Pa. $6.95

ILLUSTRATED DICTIONARY OF HISTORIC ARCHITECTURE, edited by Cyril M. Harris. Extraordinary compendium of clear, concise definitions for over 5,000 important architectural terms complemented by over 2,000 line drawings. Covers full spectrum of architecture from ancient ruins to 20th-century Modernism. Preface. 592pp. 7½ × 9⅜. 24444-X Pa. $14.95

THE NIGHT BEFORE CHRISTMAS, Clement Moore. Full text, and woodcuts from original 1848 book. Also critical, historical material. 19 illustrations. 40pp. 4⅝ × 6. 22797-9 Pa. $2.25

THE LESSON OF JAPANESE ARCHITECTURE: 165 Photographs, Jiro Harada. Memorable gallery of 165 photographs taken in the 1930's of exquisite Japanese homes of the well-to-do and historic buildings. 13 line diagrams. 192pp. 8⅜ × 11¼. 24778-3 Pa. $8.95

THE AUTOBIOGRAPHY OF CHARLES DARWIN AND SELECTED LETTERS, edited by Francis Darwin. The fascinating life of eccentric genius composed of an intimate memoir by Darwin (intended for his children); commentary by his son, Francis; hundreds of fragments from notebooks, journals, papers; and letters to and from Lyell, Hooker, Huxley, Wallace and Henslow. xi + 365pp. 5⅜ × 8. 20479-0 Pa. $6.95

WONDERS OF THE SKY: Observing Rainbows, Comets, Eclipses, the Stars and Other Phenomena, Fred Schaaf. Charming, easy-to-read poetic guide to all manner of celestial events visible to the naked eye. Mock suns, glories, Belt of Venus, more. Illustrated. 299pp. 5¼ × 8¼. 24402-4 Pa. $7.95

BURNHAM'S CELESTIAL HANDBOOK, Robert Burnham, Jr. Thorough guide to the stars beyond our solar system. Exhaustive treatment. Alphabetical by constellation: Andromeda to Cetus in Vol. 1; Chamaeleon to Orion in Vol. 2; and Pavo to Vulpecula in Vol. 3. Hundreds of illustrations. Index in Vol. 3. 2,000pp. 6⅛ × 9¼. 23567-X, 23568-8, 23673-0 Pa., Three-vol. set $38.85

STAR NAMES: Their Lore and Meaning, Richard Hinckley Allen. Fascinating history of names various cultures have given to constellations and literary and folkloristic uses that have been made of stars. Indexes to subjects. Arabic and Greek names. Biblical references. Bibliography. 563pp. 5⅜ × 8½. 21079-0 Pa. $7.95

THIRTY YEARS THAT SHOOK PHYSICS: The Story of Quantum Theory, George Gamow. Lucid, accessible introduction to influential theory of energy and matter. Careful explanations of Dirac's anti-particles, Bohr's model of the atom, much more. 12 plates. Numerous drawings. 240pp. 5⅜ × 8½. 24895-X Pa. $4.95

CHINESE DOMESTIC FURNITURE IN PHOTOGRAPHS AND MEASURED DRAWINGS, Gustav Ecke. A rare volume, now affordably priced for antique collectors, furniture buffs and art historians. Detailed review of styles ranging from early Shang to late Ming. Unabridged republication. 161 black-and-white drawings, photos. Total of 224pp. 8⅞ × 11¼. (Available in U.S. only) 25171-3 Pa. $12.95

VINCENT VAN GOGH: A Biography, Julius Meier-Graefe. Dynamic, penetrating study of artist's life, relationship with brother, Theo, painting techniques, travels, more. Readable, engrossing. 160pp. 5⅜ × 8½. (Available in U.S. only) 25253-1 Pa. $3.95

HOW TO WRITE, Gertrude Stein. Gertrude Stein claimed anyone could understand her unconventional writing—here are clues to help. Fascinating improvisations, language experiments, explanations illuminate Stein's craft and the art of writing. Total of 414pp. 4⅝ × 6⅜.   23144-5 Pa. $5.95

ADVENTURES AT SEA IN THE GREAT AGE OF SAIL: Five Firsthand Narratives, edited by Elliot Snow. Rare true accounts of exploration, whaling, shipwreck, fierce natives, trade, shipboard life, more. 33 illustrations. Introduction. 353pp. 5⅜ × 8½.   25177-2 Pa. $7.95

THE HERBAL OR GENERAL HISTORY OF PLANTS, John Gerard. Classic descriptions of about 2,850 plants—with over 2,700 illustrations—includes Latin and English names, physical descriptions, varieties, time and place of growth, more. 2,706 illustrations. xlv + 1,678pp. 8½ × 12¼.   23147-X Cloth. $75.00

DOROTHY AND THE WIZARD IN OZ, L. Frank Baum. Dorothy and the Wizard visit the center of the Earth, where people are vegetables, glass houses grow and Oz characters reappear. Classic sequel to *Wizard of Oz.* 256pp. 5⅜ × 8.
          24714-7 Pa. $4.95

SONGS OF EXPERIENCE: Facsimile Reproduction with 26 Plates in Full Color, William Blake. This facsimile of Blake's original "Illuminated Book" reproduces 26 full-color plates from a rare 1826 edition. Includes "The Tyger," "London," "Holy Thursday," and other immortal poems. 26 color plates. Printed text of poems. 48pp. 5¼ × 7.   24636-1 Pa. $3.50

SONGS OF INNOCENCE, William Blake. The first and most popular of Blake's famous "Illuminated Books," in a facsimile edition reproducing all 31 brightly colored plates. Additional printed text of each poem. 64pp. 5¼ × 7.
          22764-2 Pa. $3.50

PRECIOUS STONES, Max Bauer. Classic, thorough study of diamonds, rubies, emeralds, garnets, etc.: physical character, occurrence, properties, use, similar topics. 20 plates, 8 in color. 94 figures. 659pp. 6⅛ × 9¼.
          21910-0, 21911-9 Pa., Two-vol. set $15.90

ENCYCLOPEDIA OF VICTORIAN NEEDLEWORK, S. F. A. Caulfeild and Blanche Saward. Full, precise descriptions of stitches, techniques for dozens of needlecrafts—most exhaustive reference of its kind. Over 800 figures. Total of 679pp. 8⅛ × 11. Two volumes.   Vol. 1 22800-2 Pa. $11.95
          Vol. 2 22801-0 Pa. $11.95

THE MARVELOUS LAND OF OZ, L. Frank Baum. Second Oz book, the Scarecrow and Tin Woodman are back with hero named Tip, Oz magic. 136 illustrations. 287pp. 5⅜ × 8½.   20692-0 Pa. $5.95

WILD FOWL DECOYS, Joel Barber. Basic book on the subject, by foremost authority and collector. Reveals history of decoy making and rigging, place in American culture, different kinds of decoys, how to make them, and how to use them. 140 plates. 156pp. 7⅞ × 10¾.   20011-6 Pa. $8.95

HISTORY OF LACE, Mrs. Bury Palliser. Definitive, profusely illustrated chronicle of lace from earliest times to late 19th century. Laces of Italy, Greece, England, France, Belgium, etc. Landmark of needlework scholarship. 266 illustrations. 672pp. 6⅛ × 9¼.   24742-2 Pa. $14.95

ILLUSTRATED GUIDE TO SHAKER FURNITURE, Robert Meader. All furniture and appurtenances, with much on unknown local styles. 235 photos. 146pp. 9 × 12. 22819-3 Pa. $7.95

WHALE SHIPS AND WHALING: A Pictorial Survey, George Francis Dow. Over 200 vintage engravings, drawings, photographs of barks, brigs, cutters, other vessels. Also harpoons, lances, whaling guns, many other artifacts. Comprehensive text by foremost authority. 207 black-and-white illustrations. 288pp. 6 × 9. 24808-9 Pa. $8.95

THE BERTRAMS, Anthony Trollope. Powerful portrayal of blind self-will and thwarted ambition includes one of Trollope's most heartrending love stories. 497pp. 5⅜ × 8½. 25119-5 Pa. $8.95

ADVENTURES WITH A HAND LENS, Richard Headstrom. Clearly written guide to observing and studying flowers and grasses, fish scales, moth and insect wings, egg cases, buds, feathers, seeds, leaf scars, moss, molds, ferns, common crystals, etc.—all with an ordinary, inexpensive magnifying glass. 209 exact line drawings aid in your discoveries. 220pp. 5⅜ × 8½. 23330-8 Pa. $3.95

RODIN ON ART AND ARTISTS, Auguste Rodin. Great sculptor's candid, wide-ranging comments on meaning of art; great artists; relation of sculpture to poetry, painting, music; philosophy of life, more. 76 superb black-and-white illustrations of Rodin's sculpture, drawings and prints. 119pp. 8⅜ × 11¼. 24487-3 Pa. $6.95

FIFTY CLASSIC FRENCH FILMS, 1912–1982: A Pictorial Record, Anthony Slide. Memorable stills from Grand Illusion, Beauty and the Beast, Hiroshima, Mon Amour, many more. Credits, plot synopses, reviews, etc. 160pp. 8¼ × 11. 25256-6 Pa. $11.95

THE PRINCIPLES OF PSYCHOLOGY, William James. Famous long course complete, unabridged. Stream of thought, time perception, memory, experimental methods; great work decades ahead of its time. 94 figures. 1,391pp. 5⅜ × 8½. 20381-6, 20382-4 Pa., Two-vol. set $19.90

BODIES IN A BOOKSHOP, R. T. Campbell. Challenging mystery of blackmail and murder with ingenious plot and superbly drawn characters. In the best tradition of British suspense fiction. 192pp. 5⅜ × 8½. 24720-1 Pa. $3.95

CALLAS: PORTRAIT OF A PRIMA DONNA, George Jellinek. Renowned commentator on the musical scene chronicles incredible career and life of the most controversial, fascinating, influential operatic personality of our time. 64 black-and-white photographs. 416pp. 5⅜ × 8¼. 25047-4 Pa. $7.95

GEOMETRY, RELATIVITY AND THE FOURTH DIMENSION, Rudolph Rucker. Exposition of fourth dimension, concepts of relativity as Flatland characters continue adventures. Popular, easily followed yet accurate, profound. 141 illustrations. 133pp. 5⅜ × 8½. 23400-2 Pa. $3.95

HOUSEHOLD STORIES BY THE BROTHERS GRIMM, with pictures by Walter Crane. 53 classic stories—Rumpelstiltskin, Rapunzel, Hansel and Gretel, the Fisherman and his Wife, Snow White, Tom Thumb, Sleeping Beauty, Cinderella, and so much more—lavishly illustrated with original 19th century drawings. 114 illustrations. x + 269pp. 5⅜ × 8½. 21080-4 Pa. $4.50

SUNDIALS, Albert Waugh. Far and away the best, most thorough coverage of ideas, mathematics concerned, types, construction, adjusting anywhere. Over 100 illustrations. 230pp. 5⅜ × 8½. 22947-5 Pa. $4.50

PICTURE HISTORY OF THE NORMANDIE: With 190 Illustrations, Frank O. Braynard. Full story of legendary French ocean liner: Art Deco interiors, design innovations, furnishings, celebrities, maiden voyage, tragic fire, much more. Extensive text. 144pp. 8⅞ × 11¾. 25257-4 Pa. $9.95

THE FIRST AMERICAN COOKBOOK: A Facsimile of "American Cookery," 1796, Amelia Simmons. Facsimile of the first American-written cookbook published in the United States contains authentic recipes for colonial favorites—pumpkin pudding, winter squash pudding, spruce beer, Indian slapjacks, and more. Introductory Essay and Glossary of colonial cooking terms. 80pp. 5⅜ × 8½. 24710-4 Pa. $3.50

101 PUZZLES IN THOUGHT AND LOGIC, C. R. Wylie, Jr. Solve murders and robberies, find out which fishermen are liars, how a blind man could possibly identify a color—purely by your own reasoning! 107pp. 5⅜ × 8½. 20367-0 Pa. $2.50

THE BOOK OF WORLD-FAMOUS MUSIC—CLASSICAL, POPULAR AND FOLK, James J. Fuld. Revised and enlarged republication of landmark work in musico-bibliography. Full information about nearly 1,000 songs and compositions including first lines of music and lyrics. New supplement. Index. 800pp. 5⅜ × 8¼. 24857-7 Pa. $14.95

ANTHROPOLOGY AND MODERN LIFE, Franz Boas. Great anthropologist's classic treatise on race and culture. Introduction by Ruth Bunzel. Only inexpensive paperback edition. 255pp. 5⅜ × 8½. 25245-0 Pa. $5.95

THE TALE OF PETER RABBIT, Beatrix Potter. The inimitable Peter's terrifying adventure in Mr. McGregor's garden, with all 27 wonderful, full-color Potter illustrations. 55pp. 4¼ × 5½. (Available in U.S. only) 22827-4 Pa. $1.75

THREE PROPHETIC SCIENCE FICTION NOVELS, H. G. Wells. *When the Sleeper Wakes, A Story of the Days to Come* and *The Time Machine* (full version). 335pp. 5⅜ × 8½. (Available in U.S. only) 20605-X Pa. $5.95

APICIUS COOKERY AND DINING IN IMPERIAL ROME, edited and translated by Joseph Dommers Vehling. Oldest known cookbook in existence offers readers a clear picture of what foods Romans ate, how they prepared them, etc. 49 illustrations. 301pp. 6⅛ × 9¼. 23563-7 Pa. $6.50

SHAKESPEARE LEXICON AND QUOTATION DICTIONARY, Alexander Schmidt. Full definitions, locations, shades of meaning of every word in plays and poems. More than 50,000 exact quotations. 1,485pp. 6½ × 9¼. 22726-X, 22727-8 Pa., Two-vol. set $27.90

THE WORLD'S GREAT SPEECHES, edited by Lewis Copeland and Lawrence W. Lamm. Vast collection of 278 speeches from Greeks to 1970. Powerful and effective models; unique look at history. 842pp. 5⅜ × 8½. 20468-5 Pa. $11.95

CATALOG OF DOVER BOOKS

THE BLUE FAIRY BOOK, Andrew Lang. The first, most famous collection, with
many familiar tales: Little Red Riding Hood, Aladdin and the Wonderful Lamp,
Puss in Boots, Sleeping Beauty, Hansel and Gretel, Rumpelstiltskin; 37 in all. 138
illustrations. 390pp. 5⅜ × 8½.   21437-0 Pa. $5.95

THE STORY OF THE CHAMPIONS OF THE ROUND TABLE, Howard Pyle.
Sir Launcelot, Sir Tristram and Sir Percival in spirited adventures of love and
triumph retold in Pyle's inimitable style. 50 drawings, 31 full-page. xviii + 329pp.
6½ × 9¼.   21883-X Pa. $6.95

AUDUBON AND HIS JOURNALS, Maria Audubon. Unmatched two-volume
portrait of the great artist, naturalist and author contains his journals, an excellent
biography by his granddaughter, expert annotations by the noted ornithologist, Dr.
Elliott Coues, and 37 superb illustrations. Total of 1,200pp. 5⅜ × 8.
                                                        Vol. I 25143-8 Pa. $8.95
                                                        Vol. II 25144-6 Pa. $8.95

GREAT DINOSAUR HUNTERS AND THEIR DISCOVERIES, Edwin H.
Colbert. Fascinating, lavishly illustrated chronicle of dinosaur research, 1820's to
1960. Achievements of Cope, Marsh, Brown, Buckland, Mantell, Huxley, many
others. 384pp. 5¼ × 8¼.   24701-5 Pa. $6.95

THE TASTEMAKERS, Russell Lynes. Informal, illustrated social history of
American taste 1850's–1950's. First popularized categories Highbrow, Lowbrow,
Middlebrow. 129 illustrations. New (1979) afterword. 384pp. 6 × 9.
                                                                 23993-4 Pa. $6.95

DOUBLE CROSS PURPOSES, Ronald A. Knox. A treasure hunt in the Scottish
Highlands, an old map, unidentified corpse, surprise discoveries keep reader
guessing in this cleverly intricate tale of financial skullduggery. 2 black-and-white
maps. 320pp. 5⅜ × 8½. (Available in U.S. only)   25032-6 Pa. $5.95

AUTHENTIC VICTORIAN DECORATION AND ORNAMENTATION IN
FULL COLOR: 46 Plates from "Studies in Design," Christopher Dresser. Superb
full-color lithographs reproduced from rare original portfolio of a major Victorian
designer. 48pp. 9¼ × 12¼.   25083-0 Pa. $7.95

PRIMITIVE ART, Franz Boas. Remains the best text ever prepared on subject,
thoroughly discussing Indian, African, Asian, Australian, and, especially, Northern American primitive art. Over 950 illustrations show ceramics, masks, totem
poles, weapons, textiles, paintings, much more. 376pp. 5⅜ × 8.   20025-6 Pa. $6.95

SIDELIGHTS ON RELATIVITY, Albert Einstein. Unabridged republication of
two lectures delivered by the great physicist in 1920–21. *Ether and Relativity* and
Geometry and Experience. Elegant ideas in non-mathematical form, accessible to
intelligent layman. vi + 56pp. 5⅜ × 8½.   24511-X Pa. $2.95

THE WIT AND HUMOR OF OSCAR WILDE, edited by Alvin Redman. More
than 1,000 ripostes, paradoxes, wisecracks: Work is the curse of the drinking classes,
I can resist everything except temptation, etc. 258pp. 5⅜ × 8½.   20602-5 Pa. $4.50

ADVENTURES WITH A MICROSCOPE, Richard Headstrom. 59 adventures
with clothing fibers, protozoa, ferns and lichens, roots and leaves, much more. 142
illustrations. 232pp. 5⅜ × 8½.   23471-1 Pa. $3.95

CATALOG OF DOVER BOOKS

PLANTS OF THE BIBLE, Harold N. Moldenke and Alma L. Moldenke. Standard reference to all 230 plants mentioned in Scriptures. Latin name, biblical reference, uses, modern identity, much more. Unsurpassed encyclopedic resource for scholars, botanists, nature lovers, students of Bible. Bibliography. Indexes. 123 black-and-white illustrations. 384pp. 6 × 9.   25069-5 Pa. $8.95

FAMOUS AMERICAN WOMEN: A Biographical Dictionary from Colonial Times to the Present, Robert McHenry, ed. From Pocahontas to Rosa Parks, 1,035 distinguished American women documented in separate biographical entries. Accurate, up-to-date data, numerous categories, spans 400 years. Indices. 493pp. 6½ × 9¼.   24523-3 Pa. $9.95

THE FABULOUS INTERIORS OF THE GREAT OCEAN LINERS IN HIS-TORIC PHOTOGRAPHS, William H. Miller, Jr. Some 200 superb photographs capture exquisite interiors of world's great "floating palaces"—1890's to 1980's: *Titanic, Ile de France, Queen Elizabeth, United States, Europa,* more. Approx. 200 black-and-white photographs. Captions. Text. Introduction. 160pp. 8⅜ × 11¼.
                                                                          24756-2 Pa. $9.95

THE GREAT LUXURY LINERS, 1927-1954: A Photographic Record, William H. Miller, Jr. Nostalgic tribute to heyday of ocean liners. 186 photos of Ile de France, Normandie, Leviathan, Queen Elizabeth, United States, many others. Interior and exterior views. Introduction. Captions. 160pp. 9 × 12.
                                                                          24056-8 Pa. $9.95

A NATURAL HISTORY OF THE DUCKS, John Charles Phillips. Great landmark of ornithology offers complete detailed coverage of nearly 200 species and subspecies of ducks: gadwall, sheldrake, merganser, pintail, many more. 74 full-color plates, 102 black-and-white. Bibliography. Total of 1,920pp. 8⅜ × 11¼.
                                                            25141-1, 25142-X Cloth. Two-vol. set $100.00

THE SEAWEED HANDBOOK: An Illustrated Guide to Seaweeds from North Carolina to Canada, Thomas F. Lee. Concise reference covers 78 species. Scientific and common names, habitat, distribution, more. Finding keys for easy identification. 224pp. 5⅜ × 8½.   25215-9 Pa. $5.95

THE TEN BOOKS OF ARCHITECTURE: The 1755 Leoni Edition, Leon Battista Alberti. Rare classic helped introduce the glories of ancient architecture to the Renaissance. 68 black-and-white plates. 336pp. 8⅜ × 11¼.   25239-6 Pa. $14.95

MISS MACKENZIE, Anthony Trollope. Minor masterpieces by Victorian master unmasks many truths about life in 19th-century England. First inexpensive edition in years. 392pp. 5⅜ × 8½.   25201-9 Pa. $7.95

THE RIME OF THE ANCIENT MARINER, Gustave Doré, Samuel Taylor Coleridge. Dramatic engravings considered by many to be his greatest work. The terrifying space of the open sea, the storms and whirlpools of an unknown ocean, the ice of Antarctica, more—all rendered in a powerful, chilling manner. Full text. 38 plates. 77pp. 9¼ × 12.   22305-1 Pa. $4.95

THE EXPEDITIONS OF ZEBULON MONTGOMERY PIKE, Zebulon Montgomery Pike. Fascinating first-hand accounts (1805-6) of exploration of Mississippi River, Indian wars, capture by Spanish dragoons, much more. 1,088pp. 5⅜ × 8½.   25254-X, 25255-8 Pa. Two-vol. set $23.90

A CONCISE HISTORY OF PHOTOGRAPHY: Third Revised Edition, Helmut Gernsheim. Best one-volume history—camera obscura, photochemistry, daguerreotypes, evolution of cameras, film, more. Also artistic aspects—landscape, portraits, fine art, etc. 281 black-and-white photographs. 26 in color. 176pp. 8⅜ × 11¼. 25128-4 Pa. $12.95

THE DORÉ BIBLE ILLUSTRATIONS, Gustave Doré. 241 detailed plates from the Bible: the Creation scenes, Adam and Eve, Flood, Babylon, battle sequences, life of Jesus, etc. Each plate is accompanied by the verses from the King James version of the Bible. 241pp. 9 × 12. 23004-X Pa. $8.95

HUGGER-MUGGER IN THE LOUVRE, Elliot Paul. Second Homer Evans mystery-comedy. Theft at the Louvre involves sleuth in hilarious, madcap caper. "A knockout."—Books. 336pp. 5⅜ × 8½. 25185-3 Pa. $5.95

FLATLAND, E. A. Abbott. Intriguing and enormously popular science-fiction classic explores the complexities of trying to survive as a two-dimensional being in a three-dimensional world. Amusingly illustrated by the author. 16 illustrations. 103pp. 5⅜ × 8½. 20001-9 Pa. $2.25

THE HISTORY OF THE LEWIS AND CLARK EXPEDITION, Meriwether Lewis and William Clark, edited by Elliott Coues. Classic edition of Lewis and Clark's day-by-day journals that later became the basis for U.S. claims to Oregon and the West. Accurate and invaluable geographical, botanical, biological, meteorological and anthropological material. Total of 1,508pp. 5⅜ × 8½.
21268-8, 21269-6, 21270-X Pa. Three-vol. set $25.50

LANGUAGE, TRUTH AND LOGIC, Alfred J. Ayer. Famous, clear introduction to Vienna, Cambridge schools of Logical Positivism. Role of philosophy, elimination of metaphysics, nature of analysis, etc. 160pp. 5⅜ × 8½. (Available in U.S. and Canada only) 20010-8 Pa. $2.95

MATHEMATICS FOR THE NONMATHEMATICIAN, Morris Kline. Detailed, college-level treatment of mathematics in cultural and historical context, with numerous exercises. For liberal arts students. Preface. Recommended Reading Lists. Tables. Index. Numerous black-and-white figures. xvi + 641pp. 5⅜ × 8½. 24823-2 Pa. $11.95

28 SCIENCE FICTION STORIES, H. G. Wells. Novels, *Star Begotten* and *Men Like Gods*, plus 26 short stories: "Empire of the Ants," "A Story of the Stone Age," "The Stolen Bacillus," "In the Abyss," etc. 915pp. 5⅜ × 8½. (Available in U.S. only) 20265-8 Cloth. $10.95

HANDBOOK OF PICTORIAL SYMBOLS, Rudolph Modley. 3,250 signs and symbols, many systems in full; official or heavy commercial use. Arranged by subject. Most in Pictorial Archive series. 143pp. 8⅛ × 11. 23357-X Pa. $5.95

INCIDENTS OF TRAVEL IN YUCATAN, John L. Stephens. Classic (1843) exploration of jungles of Yucatan, looking for evidences of Maya civilization. Travel adventures, Mexican and Indian culture, etc. Total of 669pp. 5⅜ × 8½.
20926-1, 20927-X Pa., Two-vol. set $9.90

DEGAS: An Intimate Portrait, Ambroise Vollard. Charming, anecdotal memoir by famous art dealer of one of the greatest 19th-century French painters. 14 black-and-white illustrations. Introduction by Harold L. Van Doren. 96pp. 5⅜ × 8½.
25131-4 Pa. $3.95

PERSONAL NARRATIVE OF A PILGRIMAGE TO ALMANDINAH AND MECCAH, Richard Burton. Great travel classic by remarkably colorful personality. Burton, disguised as a Moroccan, visited sacred shrines of Islam, narrowly escaping death. 47 illustrations. 959pp. 5⅜ × 8½.   21217-3, 21218-1 Pa., Two-vol. set $19.90

PHRASE AND WORD ORIGINS, A. H. Holt. Entertaining, reliable, modern study of more than 1,200 colorful words, phrases, origins and histories. Much unexpected information. 254pp. 5⅜ × 8½.   20758-7 Pa. $4.95

THE RED THUMB MARK, R. Austin Freeman. In this first Dr. Thorndyke case, the great scientific detective draws fascinating conclusions from the nature of a single fingerprint. Exciting story, authentic science. 320pp. 5⅜ × 8½. (Available in U.S. only)   25210-8 Pa. $5.95

AN EGYPTIAN HIEROGLYPHIC DICTIONARY, E. A. Wallis Budge. Monumental work containing about 25,000 words or terms that occur in texts ranging from 3000 B.C. to 600 A.D. Each entry consists of a transliteration of the word, the word in hieroglyphs, and the meaning in English. 1,314pp. 6⅜ × 10.
23615-3, 23616-1 Pa., Two-vol. set $27.90

THE COMPLEAT STRATEGYST: Being a Primer on the Theory of Games of Strategy, J. D. Williams. Highly entertaining classic describes, with many illustrated examples, how to select best strategies in conflict situations. Prefaces. Appendices. xvi + 268pp. 5⅜ × 8½.   25101-2 Pa. $5.95

THE ROAD TO OZ, L. Frank Baum. Dorothy meets the Shaggy Man, little Button-Bright and the Rainbow's beautiful daughter in this delightful trip to the magical Land of Oz. 272pp. 5⅜ × 8.   25208-6 Pa. $4.95

POINT AND LINE TO PLANE, Wassily Kandinsky. Seminal exposition of role of point, line, other elements in non-objective painting. Essential to understanding 20th-century art. 127 illustrations. 192pp. 6½ × 9¼.   23808-3 Pa. $4.50

LADY ANNA, Anthony Trollope. Moving chronicle of Countess Lovel's bitter struggle to win for herself and daughter Anna their rightful rank and fortune—perhaps at cost of sanity itself. 384pp. 5⅜ × 8½.   24669-8 Pa. $6.95

EGYPTIAN MAGIC, E. A. Wallis Budge. Sums up all that is known about magic in Ancient Egypt: the role of magic in controlling the gods, powerful amulets that warded off evil spirits, scarabs of immortality, use of wax images, formulas and spells, the secret name, much more. 253pp. 5⅜ × 8½.   22681-6 Pa. $4.00

THE DANCE OF SIVA, Ananda Coomaraswamy. Preeminent authority unfolds the vast metaphysic of India: the revelation of her art, conception of the universe, social organization, etc. 27 reproductions of art masterpieces. 192pp. 5⅜ × 8½.
24817-8 Pa. $5.95

CHRISTMAS CUSTOMS AND TRADITIONS, Clement A. Miles. Origin, evolution, significance of religious, secular practices. Caroling, gifts, yule logs, much more. Full, scholarly yet fascinating; non-sectarian. 400pp. 5⅜ × 8½.
23354-5 Pa. $6.50

THE HUMAN FIGURE IN MOTION, Eadweard Muybridge. More than 4,500 stopped-action photos, in action series, showing undraped men, women, children jumping, lying down, throwing, sitting, wrestling, carrying, etc. 390pp. 7⅞ × 10⅝.
20204-6 Cloth. $21.95

THE MAN WHO WAS THURSDAY, Gilbert Keith Chesterton. Witty, fast-paced novel about a club of anarchists in turn-of-the-century London. Brilliant social, religious, philosophical speculations. 128pp. 5⅜ × 8½. 25121-7 Pa. $3.95

A CEZANNE SKETCHBOOK: Figures, Portraits, Landscapes and Still Lifes, Paul Cezanne. Great artist experiments with tonal effects, light, mass, other qualities in over 100 drawings. A revealing view of developing master painter, precursor of Cubism. 102 black-and-white illustrations. 144pp. 8¾ × 6⅜. 24790-2 Pa. $5.95

AN ENCYCLOPEDIA OF BATTLES: Accounts of Over 1,560 Battles from 1479 B.C. to the Present, David Eggenberger. Presents essential details of every major battle in recorded history, from the first battle of Megiddo in 1479 B.C. to Grenada in 1984. List of Battle Maps. New Appendix covering the years 1967–1984. Index. 99 illustrations. 544pp. 6½ × 9¼. 24913-1 Pa. $14.95

AN ETYMOLOGICAL DICTIONARY OF MODERN ENGLISH, Ernest Weekley. Richest, fullest work, by foremost British lexicographer. Detailed word histories. Inexhaustible. Total of 856pp. 6½ × 9¼.
21873-2, 21874-0 Pa., Two-vol. set $17.00

WEBSTER'S AMERICAN MILITARY BIOGRAPHIES, edited by Robert McHenry. Over 1,000 figures who shaped 3 centuries of American military history. Detailed biographies of Nathan Hale, Douglas MacArthur, Mary Hallaren, others. Chronologies of engagements, more. Introduction. Addenda. 1,033 entries in alphabetical order. xi + 548pp. 6½ × 9¼. (Available in U.S. only)
24758-9 Pa. $11.95

LIFE IN ANCIENT EGYPT, Adolf Erman. Detailed older account, with much not in more recent books: domestic life, religion, magic, medicine, commerce, and whatever else needed for complete picture. Many illustrations. 597pp. 5⅜ × 8½.
22632-8 Pa. $8.50

HISTORIC COSTUME IN PICTURES, Braun & Schneider. Over 1,450 costumed figures shown, covering a wide variety of peoples: kings, emperors, nobles, priests, servants, soldiers, scholars, townsfolk, peasants, merchants, courtiers, cavaliers, and more. 256pp. 8⅜ × 11¼. 23150-X Pa. $7.95

THE NOTEBOOKS OF LEONARDO DA VINCI, edited by J. P. Richter. Extracts from manuscripts reveal great genius; on painting, sculpture, anatomy, sciences, geography, etc. Both Italian and English. 186 ms. pages reproduced, plus 500 additional drawings, including studies for *Last Supper, Sforza* monument, etc. 860pp. 7⅞ × 10¾. (Available in U.S. only) 22572-0, 22573-9 Pa., Two-vol. set $25.90

THE ART NOUVEAU STYLE BOOK OF ALPHONSE MUCHA: All 72 Plates from "Documents Decoratifs" in Original Color, Alphonse Mucha. Rare copyright-free design portfolio by high priest of Art Nouveau. Jewelry, wallpaper, stained glass, furniture, figure studies, plant and animal motifs, etc. Only complete one-volume edition. 80pp. 9⅜ × 12¼.   24044-4 Pa. $8.95

ANIMALS: 1,419 COPYRIGHT-FREE ILLUSTRATIONS OF MAMMALS, BIRDS, FISH, INSECTS, ETC., edited by Jim Harter. Clear wood engravings present, in extremely lifelike poses, over 1,000 species of animals. One of the most extensive pictorial sourcebooks of its kind. Captions. Index. 284pp. 9 × 12.
                                                                23766-4 Pa. $9.95

OBELISTS FLY HIGH, C. Daly King. Masterpiece of American detective fiction, long out of print, involves murder on a 1935 transcontinental flight—"a very thrilling story"—NY Times. Unabridged and unaltered republication of the edition published by William Collins Sons & Co. Ltd., London, 1935. 288pp. 5⅜ × 8½. (Available in U.S. only)   25036-9 Pa. $4.95

VICTORIAN AND EDWARDIAN FASHION: A Photographic Survey, Alison Gernsheim. First fashion history completely illustrated by contemporary photographs. Full text plus 235 photos, 1840–1914, in which many celebrities appear. 240pp. 6½ × 9¼.   24205-6 Pa. $6.00

THE ART OF THE FRENCH ILLUSTRATED BOOK, 1700–1914, Gordon N. Ray. Over 630 superb book illustrations by Fragonard, Delacroix, Daumier, Doré, Grandville, Manet, Mucha, Steinlen, Toulouse-Lautrec and many others. Preface. Introduction. 633 halftones. Indices of artists, authors & titles, binders and provenances. Appendices. Bibliography. 608pp. 8⅜ × 11¼.   25086-5 Pa. $24.95

THE WONDERFUL WIZARD OF OZ, L. Frank Baum. Facsimile in full color of America's finest children's classic. 143 illustrations by W. W. Denslow. 267pp. 5⅜ × 8½.   20691-2 Pa. $5.95

FRONTIERS OF MODERN PHYSICS: New Perspectives on Cosmology, Relativity, Black Holes and Extraterrestrial Intelligence, Tony Rothman, et al. For the intelligent layman. Subjects include: cosmological models of the universe; black holes; the neutrino; the search for extraterrestrial intelligence. Introduction. 46 black-and-white illustrations. 192pp. 5⅜ × 8½.   24587-X Pa. $6.95

THE FRIENDLY STARS, Martha Evans Martin & Donald Howard Menzel. Classic text marshalls the stars together in an engaging, non-technical survey, presenting them as sources of beauty in night sky. 23 illustrations. Foreword. 2 star charts. Index. 147pp. 5⅜ × 8½.   21099-5 Pa. $3.50

FADS AND FALLACIES IN THE NAME OF SCIENCE, Martin Gardner. Fair, witty appraisal of cranks, quacks, and quackeries of science and pseudoscience: hollow earth, Velikovsky, orgone energy, Dianetics, flying saucers, Bridey Murphy, food and medical fads, etc. Revised, expanded In the Name of Science. "A very able and even-tempered presentation."—The New Yorker. 363pp. 5⅜ × 8.
                                                                20394-8 Pa. $6.50

ANCIENT EGYPT: ITS CULTURE AND HISTORY, J. E Manchip White. From pre-dynastics through Ptolemies: society, history, political structure, religion, daily life, literature, cultural heritage. 48 plates. 217pp. 5⅜ × 8½.   22548-8 Pa. $4.95

SIR HARRY HOTSPUR OF HUMBLETHWAITE, Anthony Trollope. Incisive, unconventional psychological study of a conflict between a wealthy baronet, his idealistic daughter, and their scapegrace cousin. The 1870 novel in its first inexpensive edition in years. 250pp. 5⅜ × 8½. 24953-0 Pa. $5.95

LASERS AND HOLOGRAPHY, Winston E. Kock. Sound introduction to burgeoning field, expanded (1981) for second edition. Wave patterns, coherence, lasers, diffraction, zone plates, properties of holograms, recent advances. 84 illustrations. 160pp. 5⅜ × 8¼. (Except in United Kingdom) 24041-X Pa. $3.50

INTRODUCTION TO ARTIFICIAL INTELLIGENCE: SECOND, EN-LARGED EDITION, Philip C. Jackson, Jr. Comprehensive survey of artificial intelligence—the study of how machines (computers) can be made to act intelligently. Includes introductory and advanced material. Extensive notes updating the main text. 132 black-and-white illustrations. 512pp. 5⅜ × 8½. 24864-X Pa. $8.95

HISTORY OF INDIAN AND INDONESIAN ART, Ananda K. Coomaraswamy. Over 400 illustrations illuminate classic study of Indian art from earliest Harappa finds to early 20th century. Provides philosophical, religious and social insights. 304pp. 6⅛ × 9⅜. 25005-9 Pa. $8.95

THE GOLEM, Gustav Meyrink. Most famous supernatural novel in modern European literature, set in Ghetto of Old Prague around 1890. Compelling story of mystical experiences, strange transformations, profound terror. 13 black-and-white illustrations. 224pp. 5⅜ × 8½. (Available in U.S. only) 25025-3 Pa. $5.95

ARMADALE, Wilkie Collins. Third great mystery novel by the author of *The Woman in White* and *The Moonstone*. Original magazine version with 40 illustrations. 597pp. 5⅜ × 8½. 23429-0 Pa. $9.95

PICTORIAL ENCYCLOPEDIA OF HISTORIC ARCHITECTURAL PLANS, DETAILS AND ELEMENTS: With 1,880 Line Drawings of Arches, Domes, Doorways, Facades, Gables, Windows, etc., John Theodore Haneman. Sourcebook of inspiration for architects, designers, others. Bibliography. Captions. 141pp. 9 × 12. 24605-1 Pa. $6.95

BENCHLEY LOST AND FOUND, Robert Benchley. Finest humor from early 30's, about pet peeves, child psychologists, post office and others. Mostly unavailable elsewhere. 73 illustrations by Peter Arno and others. 183pp. 5⅜ × 8½. 22410-4 Pa. $3.95

ERTÉ GRAPHICS, Erté. Collection of striking color graphics: *Seasons, Alphabet, Numerals, Aces* and *Precious Stones*. 50 plates, including 4 on covers. 48pp. 9⅜ × 12¼. 23580-7 Pa. $6.95

THE JOURNAL OF HENRY D. THOREAU, edited by Bradford Torrey, F. H. Allen. Complete reprinting of 14 volumes, 1837–61, over two million words; the sourcebooks for *Walden*, etc. Definitive. All original sketches, plus 75 photographs. 1,804pp. 8½ × 12¼. 20312-3, 20313-1 Cloth., Two-vol. set $80.00

CASTLES: THEIR CONSTRUCTION AND HISTORY, Sidney Toy. Traces castle development from ancient roots. Nearly 200 photographs and drawings illustrate moats, keeps, baileys, many other features. Caernarvon, Dover Castles, Hadrian's Wall, Tower of London, dozens more. 256pp. 5⅜ × 8¼. 24898-4 Pa. $5.95

CATALOG OF DOVER BOOKS

AMERICAN CLIPPER SHIPS: 1833–1858, Octavius T. Howe & Frederick C. Matthews. Fully-illustrated, encyclopedic review of 352 clipper ships from the period of America's greatest maritime supremacy. Introduction. 109 halftones. 5 black-and-white line illustrations. Index. Total of 928pp. 5⅜ × 8½.

25115-2, 25116-0 Pa., Two-vol. set $17.90

TOWARDS A NEW ARCHITECTURE, Le Corbusier. Pioneering manifesto by great architect, near legendary founder of "International School." Technical and aesthetic theories, views on industry, economics, relation of form to function, "mass-production spirit," much more. Profusely illustrated. Unabridged translation of 13th French edition. Introduction by Frederick Etchells. 320pp. 6⅛ × 9¼. (Available in U.S. only) 25023-7 Pa. $8.95

THE BOOK OF KELLS, edited by Blanche Cirker. Inexpensive collection of 32 full-color, full-page plates from the greatest illuminated manuscript of the Middle Ages, painstakingly reproduced from rare facsimile edition. Publisher's Note. Captions. 32pp. 9⅜ × 12¼. 24345-1 Pa. $4.95

BEST SCIENCE FICTION STORIES OF H. G. WELLS, H. G. Wells. Full novel *The Invisible Man*, plus 17 short stories: "The Crystal Egg," "Aepyornis Island," "The Strange Orchid," etc. 303pp. 5⅜ × 8½. (Available in U.S. only)

21531-8 Pa. $4.95

AMERICAN SAILING SHIPS: Their Plans and History, Charles G. Davis. Photos, construction details of schooners, frigates, clippers, other sailcraft of 18th to early 20th centuries—plus entertaining discourse on design, rigging, nautical lore, much more. 137 black-and-white illustrations. 240pp. 6⅛ × 9¼.

24658-2 Pa. $5.95

ENTERTAINING MATHEMATICAL PUZZLES, Martin Gardner. Selection of author's favorite conundrums involving arithmetic, money, speed, etc., with lively commentary. Complete solutions. 112pp. 5⅜ × 8½. 25211-6 Pa. $2.95

THE WILL TO BELIEVE, HUMAN IMMORTALITY, William James. Two books bound together. Effect of irrational on logical, and arguments for human immortality. 402pp. 5⅜ × 8½. 20291-7 Pa. $7.50

THE HAUNTED MONASTERY and THE CHINESE MAZE MURDERS, Robert Van Gulik. 2 full novels by Van Gulik continue adventures of Judge Dee and his companions. An evil Taoist monastery, seemingly supernatural events; overgrown topiary maze that hides strange crimes. Set in 7th-century China. 27 illustrations. 328pp. 5⅜ × 8½. 23502-5 Pa. $5.95

CELEBRATED CASES OF JUDGE DEE (DEE GOONG AN), translated by Robert Van Gulik. Authentic 18th-century Chinese detective novel; Dee and associates solve three interlocked cases. Led to Van Gulik's own stories with same characters. Extensive introduction. 9 illustrations. 237pp. 5⅜ × 8½.

23337-5 Pa. $4.95

Prices subject to change without notice.

Available at your book dealer or write for free catalog to Dept. GI, Dover Publications, Inc., 31 East 2nd St., Mineola, N.Y. 11501. Dover publishes more than 175 books each year on science, elementary and advanced mathematics, biology, music, art, literary history, social sciences and other areas.